Foreigners in European Prisons

Foreigners in European Prisons

Volume 1

Edited by:

A.M. van Kalmthout,
F.B.A.M. Hofstee-van der Meulen &
F. Dünkel

Foreigners in European prisons, *A.M. van Kalmthout, F.B.A.M.Hofstee-van der Meulen & F. Dünkel (eds.).*
ISBN: 978-90-5850-275-9
Published by Wolf Legal Publishers (WLP) 2007

This study was funded by the European Commission

Published by:
Wolf Legal Publishers (WLP)
P.O. Box 31051
6503 CB Nijmegen
The Netherlands

Tel: +31 24 355 19 04
Fax: + 31 24 355 48 27

E-Mail: info@wolfpublishers.nl
Http://www.wolfpublishers.nl

Contents

Volume 1

Chapter 1 Comparative overview, Conclusions and Recommendations

Anton van Kalmthout/Femke Hofstee-van der Meulen/Frieder Dünkel

Chapter 2 Austria

Arno Pilgram/Veronika Hofinger

Chapter 3 Belgium

Sonja Snacken

Chapter 4 Cyprus

Andreas Ellinas

Chapter 5 Czech Republic

Petr Škvain

Chapter 6 Denmark

Anette Storgaard

Chapter 7 Estonia

Piret Liba

Chapter 8 Finland

Tapio Lappi-Seppälä

Chapter 9 France

Pascal Décarpes

Chapter 10 Germany

Frieder Dünkel/Andrea Gensing/Christine Morgenstern

Chapter 11 Greece

M. Akritidou/A. Antonopoulou/A. Pitsela

Chapter 12 Hungary

Tímea Szabó/Balázs Tóth/Gábor Győző/András Kádár

Chapter 13 Ireland

Mary Moore

Chapter 14 Italy

Paola Balbo

Chapter 15 Latvia

Leine Zeibote

Volume 2

Chapter 16 Lithuania

Sonata Malisauskaite – Simanaitiene

Chapter 17 Luxembourg

Stefan Braum

Chapter 18 Malta

Tonio Cachia/Mark F. Montebello

Chapter 19 Netherlands

Anton van Kalmthout/Femke Hofstee – van der Meulen

Chapter 20 Poland

Barbara Stando-Kawecka

Chapter 21 Portugal

Rui Abrunhosa Gonçalves

Chapter 22 Slovakia

Martin Skamla

Chapter 23 Slovenia

Dragan Petrovec

Chapter 24 Spain

José Luis de la Cuesta

Chapter 25 Sweden

Agneta K.Johnson

Chapter 26 United Kingdom

Nick Hammond

Chapter 27 Aire Centre

Nuala Mole

Chapter 28 Conférence Permanente Européenne de la Probation (CEP)

Leo Tigges

Chapter 29 Foreign Liaison Office of the Dutch Probation Service

Rolf Streng/Raymond Swennenhuis/Hans van Kooten

Chapter 30 International Centre for Prison Studies (ICPS)

Andrew Coyle

Chapter 31 Jesuit Refugee Service Europe (JRS-Europe)

Cornelia Bührle RSCJ

Chapter 32 Prisoners Abroad

Stephen Nash

Foreword

by Dr Silvia Casale
President of the SPT (United Nations Subcommittee on Prevention of Torture and Other Cruel, Inhuman or Degrading Treatment or Punishment) and former President of the CPT (European Committee for the Prevention of Torture and inhuman or degrading treatment or punishment).

The phenomenon of migration of people across and to Europe presents both opportunities and challenges for the states of the European Union. The cultures and skills of foreign nationals in Europe enrich the region, when states are open to experiencing diversity positively. At the same time a variety of situations arise in which foreign nationals come into contact with the legal system. In practice the responses of each country differ to foreign nationals of different legal status. The increased incidence of mobility and the co-ordinated measures to combat cross-border crimes have led to a sharp increase in the number of foreign prisoners held worldwide and this holds true for Europe also.

The studies in this compilation examine the size of the custodial population of foreign nationals in each of the states of the European Union, including over-representation in the custodial population on remand and on sentence relative to representation in the community at large, and provide insights into the treatment of and the provisions for foreign nationals under the authority of the different ministries responsible for their custody in the different jurisdictions. Both high and low numbers (in percentage and absolute terms) give rise to particular problems for foreign nationals in custody. States with a low percentage of foreign prisoners or a low number in absolute terms, often lack policies and programmes to take account of the special needs of foreign nationals, whereas states with a large population of foreign prisoners may have difficulty in coping adequately with the procedures applying to them, in particular as regards transfer or status under immigration legislation.

The detention of foreign nationals and their marginalisation within the custodial population are issues of growing concern all over Europe. Foreign prisoners may experience additional hardships above and beyond that generally faced by prison population - the inevitable distress engendered by the deprivation of liberty. All prisoners, including those of foreign nationality, retain all rights not necessarily taken away by the fact of imprisonment. It is, however, a recurring risk that foreign prisoners may not be able to exercise their rights effectively, including their fundamental human rights.

For 60 years a body of international legal instruments and mechanisms has been developing reflecting the will to create a community of states governed by the rule of law. Many of the treaties at the global and regional level affirm the fundamental prohibition of discrimination on the grounds of "race, colour, sex, language, religion, political or other opinion, national or social origin, property, birth or other status" (Universal Declaration of Human Rights, 1948). The prohibition applies to all persons, whether at liberty or in custody. A critical test of a state's commitment to the rule of law lies in the way it deals with those in custody, which, in the context of the European Union, is the state's most extreme legal measure, since the abolition of capital punishment.

The studies compiled in this report of the Social Exclusion Project on Foreign Prisoners provide an important body of information about the situation of foreign prisoners in the European Union. Although the report cannot provide exhaustive detail on all aspects of custody, it does constitute an important resource for increasing awareness and knowledge of the practical and human rights dimensions of the phenomenon. The recommendations contained in the comparative overview should inform and guide policy makers at the national and EU level. Thus it is to be hoped that the report will serve as a tool for identifying those areas in which policy and practice need to be improved in order to eliminate or reduce to a minimum the disadvantages experienced by foreign nationals in prison.

Silvia Casale,
April 2007.

Acknowledgement

In early 2005 Tilburg University was granted approval by the European Commission (DG Employment, Social Affairs and Equal Opportunities) to start a one-year project addressing the issue of social exclusion of prisoners who are detained in the EU outside their country of origin. This project was carried out together with the Liaison Office of the Dutch Probation Service, Greifswald University in Germany, Jesuit Refugee Service-Europe (JRS-Europe), the Hungarian Helsinki Committee (HHC) and the Conférence Permanente Européenne de la Probation (CEP).

This publication is the result of the studies that have been conducted by national experts from each EU country. Based on a common questionnaire these experts described and analysed the sentencing and prison system in their country, the treatment of foreign prisoners, the situation of foreigners in administrative detention and of foreign nationals detained abroad. Furthermore, this publication includes five contributions from involved organisations and a comparative overview with conclusions and recommendations.

The first results of the studies have been presented in the European Parliament in Brussels on 13 September 2006. The conference was hosted by Jules Maaten, Member of the European Parliament and Chairman of the working group *Prisoners Abroad*, and was attended by parliamentarians, representatives from European Prison Services, Consulates, Ministries of Foreign Affairs, Ministries of Justice, NGO's, academics and press.

There are many persons and organisations who have contributed to this project. We are greatly indebted to them. First of all we would like to thank our partners for their early commitment and support during the project. Secondly we thank the European Commission 'DG Employment, Social Affairs and Equal Opportunities' for acknowledging the necessity of addressing the issue of foreign prisoners and for their generous co-financing.

We are especially grateful to all national experts and other authors for their commitment and for conducting such a 'pioneering' research.

Furthermore, we are grateful to all ministries, diplomatic missions, prison services and individual penitentiary institutions for providing information and opening their 'doors'. We also want to extend our gratitude to those foreign prisoners who were interviewed for this project and gave insight into their situation.

The task of editing and revising the various contributions was not an easy one. Therefore, we are very thankful to Zarif Bahtiyar, Philip Horsfield, Carla de Jongh and Lulu van der Meer for their support and indispensable contribution.

It is our fervent hope that this volume and the continuation of this project on the topic of the detention of foreign prisoners via the website www.foreignersinprison.eu will make policy makers, prison authorities and scholars in the European Union more aware of the vulnerable position and situation of foreign prisoners and can contribute to improve their socially excluded position.

Anton van Kalmthout
Femke Hofstee-van der Meulen
Frieder Dünkel

Tilburg, Greifswald March 2007

Chapter 1

Comparative overview, Conclusions and Recommendations

1 INTRODUCTION

1 General introduction

Over the last few decades, prison populations in European countries have grown and their profiles have changed. Whereas prison populations used to be rather homogeneous, nowadays they have been transformed into more diverse populations. The portion of foreign prisoners, those without citizenship of the state in which they are detained, has increased rapidly – both in absolute and relative terms. At this moment there are more than 100.000 foreign prisoners in European countries. Their numbers vary greatly per country, but the average percentage of foreigners in the total European prison population is over 20%, which is an over-representation.

Why are foreigners over-represented in European prison populations? Who are they and on what grounds are they held in detention? Are foreign prisoners more vulnerable due to language difficulties, cultural differences and their distance from relatives? Are they being socially excluded? And how are national prison systems and other authorities addressing this issue? These are all questions to which up till now little attention has been paid to. This also explains why there has been hardly any data or information available on this issue. One could say that foreign prisoners are in general a 'forgotten group'.

In this study, the terms 'prisoners' and 'prisons' are used in a broader sense than usual. In this way, the term 'prisoners does not only include 'persons who have been remanded in custody by a judicial authority or who have been deprived of their liberty following conviction' as stated in the European Prison Rules, but also persons detained under administrative law such as: (rejected) asylum seekers or irregular migrants deprived of their liberty in preparation of their departure, expulsion or deportation. The term prison is likewise not restricted to penitentiary institutions for remand and sentenced offenders, but entails all places were people can be deprived of their liberty (such as re-trial institutions, open or closed prisons, detention centres for irregular migrants, airport reception or holding centres and police cells). With 'foreign prisoner' is meant all persons without citizenship of the state in which they are detained. It encompasses short term visitors, migrant workers, long-term residents, second generation migrants, (rejected) asylum seekers, irregular migrants and stateless people. As far as it seems to be relevant, a distinction is made between three categories of foreign prisoners: 1) those prisoners who are detained under criminal law and who after release will remain in the country of detention or 2) will be deported or expelled to their home country or a third country and 3) foreign nationals who are detained under administrative (immigration) law.

There are good grounds to adduce for the question why this study on 'foreigners in European prisons' also includes the group of foreign nationals who are administratively detained. In some countries the issue of foreign prisoners either as foreign nationals with residence in the host country or as foreigners who want to get access to stay in the host country (asylum seekers, refugees, irregular migrants etc.) increasingly have been of major concern in public and political debates. However, this does not seem to be the case in all countries. Middle and Eastern European countries are less exposed to migration and foreign immigration. On the other hand particularly the "rich" countries of Western Europe have been facing waves of legal and illegal immigration since the Second World War and particularly in the 1980's and 1990's.

If we can characterize foreign prisoners as a 'forgotten group', then this counts for certain for foreign nationals who are detained on the basis of immigration laws. The holding centres and other institutions where they are kept, awaiting their removal are officially not prisons and often not under the responsibility of the Ministry of Justice. Other Ministries, such as the Ministry of Interior, the Police Department and/or the Ministry of Defence or the Ministry for Refugees, Immigrants and Integration are responsible for administrative detention. This is why these foreigners are usually not recorded in the prison statistics and as far as they are not detained in ordinary prisons, the European Prison Rules are not applicable on them. Although administrative detainees are not allowed to be considered as criminals nor to be treated as one, the practice shows a difference. An actual look at the detention conditions of these foreigners shows quite some similarities with ordinary prisons. Certain countries apply the same penitentiary legislation on remand or sentenced prisoners, as well as on administrative detainees. In other countries, their legal position is even weaker, as they are provided with fewer safeguards. Practically, it can be said that in a substantive sense, there is no difference between criminal and administrative detainees regarding their deprivation of liberty. Furthermore, the line between the two groups is even more vague when it comes to foreigners who are detained on a criminal basis and lost their right to residence as a consequence of the committed crime, and have to leave the country after their detention, either forced or voluntarily. The regime during criminal detention has often the same restrictions which are applied on administrative detainees, as regarding to leave, conditional release and integration programmes. When a foreigner can not be immediately removed after the end of his/her detention, it is possible in a number of countries to continue the detention, whether in the same penitentiary institution or not, which then is based on the immigration laws. It is for these reasons, why administratively detained foreigners are a target group of the Council of Europe's Committee for the Prevention of Torture and Inhuman and Degrading Treatment and also a part of our research.

The following paragraphs in this chapter will summarize the main results of the European comparative project within the European Union 'Social Exclusion'-scheme which has been conducted from September 2005 until September 2006. Hereby, it is taken into account, as much as possible, the structure and order of the country reports. In the following subparagraphs of paragraph 1, an overview will be given on the sanctions and prison systems in the European countries, involvement of consulates/embassies/ probation services of home countries/NGO's, trends and the relevant national and European legislation. Paragraph 2 contains an overview regarding the treatment of foreign prisoners in the various countries with the focus on the following topics; general situation, living conditions and facilities, reception and admission, work-education-training-sports-recreation, food-religion-personal hygiene-medical care, consular help and legal aid, contact with the outside world, re-integration activities and prison leave, release and expulsion, aftercare and probation, staff and projects. In Paragraph 3 attention will be paid on the administrative detention of foreign prisoners, in which there will be dealt with the various institutions that are in use and their capacity, the responsible Ministries and legislation, length of stay, decision and appeal, data and the non-expelled foreigners, detention irregulars under criminal law and minors. Paragraph 4 will give an overview on EU foreign nationals detained abroad. The numbers and composition, countries of detention, reasons for detention and sentencing, authorities and organisations involved, release and reception home country, aftercare and the public opinion and media are the issues discussed in this part. In conclusion of this chapter, the recommendations will be presented in paragraph 5.

1.1 Overview penalties and measures

The countries involved in the foreign prisoners' project all dispose of a criminal law system as well as administrative laws by which foreigners can be dealt with.

The penal law systems differ with respect of the sanctions provided and the practice of prosecutors and courts. Foreigners in theory should not be sanctioned differently from native offenders. However, numerous examples are given in the present volume that in practice foreigners or members of ethnic minorities are discriminated insofar that they do not profit from alternative sanctions and diversion measures in the same way as non-foreigners in fact do. This is the case, for example, in the Netherlands and – although empirical evidence is not easy to acquire – also in Germany. In the Netherlands it is not Penal Law that formally discriminates foreigners, but the prosecutorial guidelines which influence the courts' sentencing practice. These guidelines provide that particular groups of foreigners like irregular migrants, foreigners who are expected to lose their residence permit because of the crime committed, etc. are excluded from alternative sanctions such as the so-called task penalty (including community service), electronic monitoring, hospital orders etc.

The average length of custodial penalties is longer in the Middle and Eastern European countries compared to continental Europe and particularly Scandinavia. This is the result of a range of custodial penalties which sometimes covers 20 or 30 years as maximum and life sentences with possibilities for conditional release only after having served 25 years (e. g. Czech Republic, Poland). In many European countries law reforms have been passed that increased minimum or maximum penalties for sexual and violent offences in the last 20 years. It is also claimed that the sentencing practice in general has become more severe. There is, however, no empirical evidence that these changes have led to a further discrimination against foreign offenders. On the other hand, at least in some countries statistical analyses show that foreigners have a higher risk of being held in pre-trial detention than national suspects (see e. g. Denmark, Malta).

Administrative detention everywhere is seen as a last resort for the execution of an expulsion order, but the practice shows a different view. It is regularly restricted to a shorter period of confinement, like for instance 40 days in Spain or six months in Germany (for more details see paragraph 3.4).

1.2 Overview of the prison system

Prison systems in nearly all European countries are administered by the Ministry of Justice. The conditions vary considerably when looking at daily life and human rights issues. Large dormitories in the Middle and Eastern European countries (with up to 70 or more persons housed in one dormitory) compared to the single cell accommodation in Scandinavia and larger parts of the prison systems in the Netherlands or Germany demonstrate that imprisonment even in the enlarged Europe of the European Union does mean very different conditions of prison life. Foreigners in all countries are accommodated in the regular prisons and not separated from national prisoners. In some prisons there are, however, departments where foreigners are overrepresented (see e.g. England and

Wales). This is more frequently the case in closed units than in open prisons. Sometimes prison authorities concentrate foreigners of the same nationality in specific departments or cells in order to make communication between prisoners easier (see e.g. Hungary). National prison law or administrative rules often provide that foreigners do not qualify for being transferred to open prisons. This is especially the case when extradition is possible or even likely to take place (see e.g. Germany).

Administrative detention of asylum seekers, refugees etc. is in most of the countries organised by the Ministry of the Interior. In some countries or regions asylum seekers who shall be expelled are held in special departments of regular prisons. According to the Council of Europe's Annual Penal Statistics SPACE I, Survey 2005, this is the case in Belgium, Hungary, Luxembourg, the Netherlands, Sweden, Switzerland and Northern Ireland.[1] According to the report on Germany in some parts of the country asylum seekers are also accommodated in prisons. Regularly – and in the vast majority of countries exclusively (30 in the SPACE survey) – administrative detention for foreigners is executed in special units of the Ministry of Interior.

1.3 Overview involvement Consulates, Embassies, Ministries Home Country, Probation Service Home Country, NGO's, etc.

Most national reports have no good data base on this issue. With the exception of the Dutch probation service that takes care of Dutch nationals incarcerated abroad, almost no systematic care from the home countries exists. On the other hand there can be found a lot of NGO's which take care of foreign prisoners in the host countries like 'Prisoners Abroad' in the United Kingdom, the *Jesuite Refugee Center* in Germany or other Christian or laic initiatives.

1.4 Overview of trends (foreign prisoners, administrative detention etc.)

The number of foreign prisoners varies considerably in the European countries. According to the SPACE I survey of 2005 the proportion is from 0,4% in Latvia up to 71.4% in Luxembourg. A very high proportion can also be seen in Belgium (41.2%), Greece (41.6%) and Cyprus (45.6%). The high rate of 40.4% in Estonia is mainly due to the fact that inmates of Russian origin are defined as foreigners as long as they have not applied for Estonian nationality, even if they have lived in Estonia for many years or were even born there. Most of the Middle and Eastern European countries quantitatively have only small minorities of foreign prisoners of regularly less than 10%, or even less than 5% of the total prison population (e.g. Hungary: 3.8%; Lithuania: 0.8%).

The following table in addition shows that large proportions of foreign prisoners are pre-trial detainees. This proves that foreigners are highly overrepresented in pre-trial detention (see e. g. Belgium, Czech Republic, Denmark, Germany, Hungary, Italy, Luxembourg, the Netherlands, Poland, Spain, and the United Kingdom). The living conditions there are often far poorer than the ones for sentenced prisoners, as can be seen in

1 See Aebi, M., Stadnic, N. (2007): SPACE I. Council of Europe Annual Penal Statistics. Survey 2005. Internet-publication www.coe.int. The statistics regarding the total numbers of prisoners are not complete as certain countries have not included the category of administrative detainees in these.

many of the reports in this volume as well as in the reports of the CPT and in the literature.[2]

Table 1: Number of foreign prisoners in Europe, 2005

Foreign prisoners	*Number of foreign prisoners (including pre-trial detainees)*	*% of foreign prisoners (including pre-trial detainees)*	*Of which: Number of foreign pre-trial detainees*	*% of foreign prisoners who are pre-trial detainees*
Austria	3,979	45.4	1,199	30.1
Belgium	3,860	41.2	1,670	43.3
Cyprus	241	45.6	57	23.7
Czech Republic	1,652	8.7	721	43.6
Denmark	754	18.2	363	48.1
Estonia[3]	1,780	40.4	466	26.2
Finland	286	7.5	114	39.9
France	11,820	20.5	No inf.	-
Germany	22,095	28.0	6,954	31.5
Greece	3990	41.6	No inf.	-
Hungary	631	3.8	No inf.	-
Ireland	3,080	9	277	
Italy	19,656	33.0	9,655	49.1
Latvia	26	0.4	No inf.	-
Lithuania	67	0.8	14	20.9
Luxembourg	495	71.4	273	55.2
Malta	91	30.5	35	38.5
Netherlands	5,818	32.9	1,666	28.6
Poland	750	0.9	408	54.4
Portugal	2,386	18.5	1,005	42.1
Slovakia	220	2.4	147	66.8
Slovenia	144	12.7	69	47.9
Spain	18,436	30.1	7,285	39.5
Sweden	1475	20.9	No inf.	-
UK: England and Wales	9,650	12.7	2,271	23.5
UK: Northern Ireland	38	2.8	15	39.5
UK: Scotland	71	1.0	15	21.1

2 See e. g. *Dünkel, J., Vagg, J.* (1994): Waiting for Trial. International Perspectives on the Use of Pre-Trial Detention and the Rights and Living Conditions of Prisoners Waiting for Trial. Vol. 1 and 2. Freiburg i. Br.: Max-Planck-Institut für ausländisches und internationals Strafrecht.

3 The numbers of "foreigners" apparently comprise Russians with no Estonian passport who, however, in most cases have been born and grown up in Estonia.

While the numbers of foreign prisoners have generally increased during the last 20 years (see e. g. Luxembourg with a more than doubled foreign prison population only between 2002 and 2006, or Spain), this trend is not uniform. In Germany and other continental European countries during the 1990's many asylum seekers and illegal immigrants arrived, creating problems of overcrowding in prisons or refugee centres. Since the mid-nineties the trend has been reversed or at least a "levelling off" of the increase of foreign prisoners' rates can be observed (e.g. Germany, Poland, and Slovakia). In Poland the number of foreigners suspected of having committed a crime as well as of foreign prisoners since 2001 dropped by more than half. In Hungary the number of convicted foreigners has increased during the last ten years, whereas the numbers of foreigners sentenced to imprisonment has been stable or lately even decreasing. Similar tendencies can be observed in countries that traditionally have been emigration instead of immigration countries like Ireland. The increase of foreigners there is not comparable to the problems with foreign prisoners in France, England, Germany, the Netherlands or Spain. Other Eastern European countries like Latvia or Lithuania do not really have a problem with foreign prisoners (the very low numbers are even decreasing), but with minorities that have no passport at all (mostly Russians refusing nationalization) or that are of Russian nationality who have been living in the country for a long time.

The foreign prison population often can be characterised by certain crimes that are overrepresented compared to the national prison population: in England and Wales, Germany or the Netherlands foreigners are overrepresented with respect to drug offences, in England also concerning fraud and forgery, whereas violent offenders are overrepresented by UK-nationals. In Germany certain groups of foreigners like Turkish and former Yugoslavian citizens are overrepresented in the field of violent crimes. Foreign drug dealers are a specific problem in the larger cities where airports with connections to Latin America etc. are situated. Therefore, foreigners are sometimes concentrated in prisons in the neighbourhoods of Amsterdam, Madrid, London Heathrow or Frankfurt/Main.

1.5 Overview of national legislation

National *penal legislation* in many countries has been amended with respect to more severe sanctions for foreign offenders (expulsion) as well as to more strict *immigration laws* that aim to prevent asylum seekers and other migrants from permanent residence in the host countries (see e.g. Germany, the Netherlands). Some countries have extended the possibilities for expulsion of foreigners under anti-terrorism legislation (see e.g. Italy). On the other hand nationalization has been made easier in some countries as well (e.g. Belgium, Finland, and Germany). Thus one has to realise that a considerable part of the "national" prison population consists of persons with a migrant background (e.g. in Germany the immigrants from states or regions of the former Soviet Union who are by definition "Germans"). A remarkable step of a legislation that wants to prevent undue discrimination is the Finish Equality Act of 2004 which among others introduced an Ombudsman for Minorities.

Prison legislation has also been changed in many countries, particularly in the Middle and Eastern European countries entering the Council of Europe and/or the European Union. Guiding principle in these countries was the adoption of human rights standards and the observation of the rule of law. Prison legislation in general does not provide specific rules or regimes for foreigners. However, foreigners can be discriminated because they are less eligible for a transfer to open prisons or relaxations of the prison regime (prison leaves etc., see e. g. Germany, Slovenia and the Netherlands).

1.6 Overview of European legislation

There are International and Regional treaties, conventions, guidelines and rules available addressing detention of foreigners. These instruments state for example procedural guarantees that have to be afforded to persons facing restrictions on their freedom of liberty, but also the conditions of detention. It is beyond the scope of this work to deal with the International legislation regarding detention in complete, as this requires an extensive study.[4] This is why the research is restricted to European legislation, in particular to the regulations of the two relevant bodies in Europe: the Council of Europe and the EU.

1.6.1 Council of Europe

The Council of Europe is the oldest political organization in Europe, founded in 1949, which groups together 46 countries. The Council was set up to, *inter alia*, defend human rights, parliamentary democracy, the rule of law and to develop continent-wide agreements to standardize member countries' social and legal practices. Among the efforts to achieve the last mentioned goal, many binding and non-binding instruments have been developed by the Council. Within the context of detention, the following can be mentioned:

- European Convention for the Protection of Human Rights and Fundamental Freedoms (ECHR).[5] According to article 1 ECHR, 'everyone' within the jurisdiction of a contracting party benefits from the rights and freedoms enumerated in the ECHR. Thus, the rights and freedoms recognized by the ECHR, are in theory at least, universally available to all individuals, including aliens, be they nationals (e.g. immigrants or refugees) or non-nationals (e.g. stateless) of a foreign state. Considerations of nationality, residence or domicile are irrelevant to a determination of a claim of a violation of the ECHR. All that needs to be shown is some physical presence in the territory of the (alleged) violator contracting party, and some exercise of control by that state over the individual and over the protection of the ECHR's rights secured within the territory of the state.[6] For the enforcement of the ECHR and its several Protocols[7], the Convention established the European Court of Human Rights (hereinafter the Court). The Court has played a crucial role in the enforcement of the rights and still is. The decisions of the Court are legally binding and since the entry

---

4 For an extensive overview of the legislation see: Undocumented Migrants Have Rights! An overview of the International Human Rights Framework, Brussels PICUM March 2007.

5 Date entry into force is 3 September 1953.

6 H. Lambert, *The position of aliens in relation to the European Convention on Human Rights*, Strasbourg: Council of Europe Publishing 2006, p. 8.

7 As of May 2006, 14 Protocols to the ECHR have been opened for signature. These can be divided into two main groups: those changing the machinery of the Convention, and those adding additional rights to those protected by the Convention. The former require unanimous ratification before coming into force, while the latter are optional Protocols which only come into force between ratifying member states.

into force of Protocol no. 11 on 1 November 1998, also individuals have gained direct access to the Court. Though, the Convention provides individuals such a high degree of protection, it may only deal with the matter after all domestic remedies have been exhausted (article 35 ECHR). A useful tool in refoulement cases in which a person is facing departure, is that the Court can take interim measures.[8] This way the State can be stopped, until the final decision is made by the Court. The supervision of the execution of judgments is done by the Committee of Ministers (article 46 ECHR).

- European Convention for the Prevention of Torture and Inhuman or Degrading Treatment or Punishment.[9] Article 1 of this Convention provided for the creation of a committee (CPT) to visit places of detention (including immigration detention centres) to ensure compliance with its provisions. The CPT has unlimited access and can organize 'ad hoc' visits as necessary. Access to persons deprived of their liberty includes free communication in private with detainees and with any person whom the CPT believes may be able to provide it with relevant information. There is also a general duty upon states to make available whatever other information the CPT requires to discharge its tasks. After completing a visit, the CPT provides information concerning its concerns confidentially to the government to begin a dialogue with the ultimate objective being improvement of the situation. Member states are expected to provide an interim report within six months of receipt of the report containing details of steps already taken and how it is intended to implement any remaining recommendations, and to furnish within twelve months a follow-up report providing a full account of action taken. According to the treaty, visits to places of detention, information received and recommendations and reports to states are confidential, but this is subject to three exceptions: according to article 11 (2) a state may request publication of the report and any comments it may have on the report; article 10 (2) states that if a state refuses to co-operate or to improve matters in light of CPT recommendations, a public statement may be issued and the committee's General reports made to the Committee of Ministers, now provide sufficient detail to provide some impressions of the care of detainees in particular states.[10] In several of its General reports, the CPT has described some of the substantive issues it addresses during its visits to places of detention. The CPT Standards[11] represent updated substantive sections of those reports providing guidance to countries on issues dealing with, *inter alia*, foreign nationals detained under aliens legislation.
- Twenty Guidelines on forced return.[12] The Guidelines constitute an international instrument in which all the stages of the procedure of forced return are covered, from the moment of the adoption of a removal order until the effective return. It is the first time that states have agreed on dealing with every aspect of this issue in a single instrument. The Guidelines on forced return serve as a practical guide to be used both

8 Rule 39 of the Rules of the European Court of Human Rights (interim measures).

9 The date of entry into force of this Convention is 1 February 1989.

10 J. Murdoch, *The treatment of prisoners. European Standards*, Strasbourg: Council of Europe Publishing 2006, p. 42-44.

11 Council of Europe, October 2001, CPT/Inf/E (2002).

12 Adopted on May 2005, on the 925th meeting of the Ministers' Deputies, the Committee of Ministers of the Council of Europe.

by government officials and by all those directly or indirectly involved in return operations in Europe.

- European Prison Rules.[13] The European Prison Rules apply only to remand or sentenced prisoners and to persons detained in prisons "for any other reason", see Rules No. 10.1 and 10.3. Foreigners in administrative detention therefore are only protected if they are held in prisons.
- Committee of Ministers, Recommendation No. R (84) 12 concerning Foreign Prisoners.[14] The principles in the Recommendation are designed to apply to foreign prisoners, that is to say to prisoners of different nationality who on account of such factors as language, customs, cultural background or religion may face specific problems. Attention is paid on, *inter alia*, treatment in prison, assistance by consular authorities, training and use of prison staff and expulsion and repatriation.
- Parliamentary Assembly Resolution 1509 (2006) on the Human Rights of Irregular Migrants.[15] With this resolution, the Parliamentary Assembly stated that: "(...) international human rights instruments are applicable to all persons regardless of their nationality or status. Irregular migrants, as they are often in a vulnerable situation, have a particular need for the protection of their human rights, including basic civil, political, economic and social rights."

1.6.2 EU

The entry into force of the 1997 Amsterdam Treaty on the EU in 1999 provided for the establishment of an 'Area of Freedom, Security and Justice' and the creation of a Directorate-General for Justice and Home Affairs. In the same year with the Treaty of Amsterdam coming into effect, the European Council held a special meeting in Tampere and placed this objective at the head of the EU's political agenda. The EU Council agreed, *inter alia*, to create a common EU policy with regard to immigration and asylum as well as setting out a political strategy and putting forward a 5 year programme. In 2004, the Brussels European Council adopted the Hague Programme which set the objectives to be implemented to 'strengthen Freedom, Security and Justice in the EU'.[16] The Programme that is drawn up for the period 2005-2010 can be seen as the successor of the Tampere programme. On EU level the following documents are relevant regarding detention:

- Charter of Fundamental Rights of the EU. As it stands, the Charter is not a treaty, constitutional, or legal document and has the ambiguous value of a 'solemn proclamation' by the European Parliament, the Council of the EU and the European Commission in December 2000. Part II of the proposed European Constitution, which was signed in October 2004 but failed to be ratified after referendum defeats in France and the Netherlands, contained a version of the Charter. The intention was to enable the EU to accede to the ECHR, thus enabling the European Court of Justice to rule on the basis of this Charter.

---

13 Recommendation Rec (2006) 2, adopted by the Committee of Ministers on 11 January 2006, on the 952nd meeting of the Ministers' Deputies.

14 Adopted on 21 June 1984.

15 Adopted on 27 June 2006.

16 Council of EU, Brussels 13 December 2004, 16054/04.

- Commission Proposal for a Directive of the European Parliament and the Council on common standards and procedures in Member States for returning illegally staying third-country nationals (Commission Proposal Returns Directive), COM (2005) 391 final.
- Proposal for a Council Framework Decision on the European supervision order in pre-trial procedures between Member States of the EU, COM (2006) 468 final.
- Proposal for a Council Framework Decision on the recognition and supervision of suspended sentences and alternative sanctions (Home Office), 5325/07 COPEN 7.

In conclusion of this part, regarding to the European legal framework, it can be said that the available European legislation is mainly soft law as they are not binding on states and thus not enforceable. This is different for the ECHR and the decisions of the Court. The case law of the Court and also the work of the CPT are important tools for the protection of detainees. It is not difficult to notice that the Council of Europe has a much more developed system than the EU does, as at EU level there is neither a common EU institution exercising responsible authority on the system nor an EU institution periodically and publicly reporting about detention centres in the EU or an EU monitoring mechanism.

Conclusions

- The portion of foreign prisoners, those without citizenship of the state in which they are detained, has been increasing rapidly – both in absolute and relative terms.
- In 2006 there were more than 100.000 foreign prisoners in European countries and although their numbers vary greatly per country the average percentage of foreigners in the total European prison population is over 20%.
- The percentage of foreign prisoners varies from less than one percent in Latvia to 75% in Luxembourg.
- Foreigners are in general an over-represented group in penitentiary institutions, in comparison with the percentage of foreign nationals residing in EU countries.
- Reasons for the over-representation of foreigners in European penitentiary institutions are the higher probability of detection and apprehension of foreigners by legal systems, the exclusion from alternatives to pre-trial detention and exclusion from non-custodial sanctions.
- Further, foreign prisoners tend not to fulfil requirements for conditional release (risk of escape, no secure home address), transfer of foreign prisoners is rarely applied, difficulties in enforcing expulsion orders and the increase of prison sentences for violation of Immigration Laws.
- European legislation regarding detention is mainly soft law.

2 TREATMENT OF FOREIGN PRISONERS

This paragraph looks into the treatment of foreign prisoners in the different EU countries. Treatment of this particular group of prisoners has hardly been studied in the past and as a result there is only very limited information, data or literature available[17]. In order to cast more light on the situation of foreign prisoners, several experts in this study have been carrying out interviews with foreign prisoners in order to get a better picture of

[17] The Prison Service of England and Wales is an exemption to this.

their actual situation. Besides individual prisoners prison staff has also been interviewed, like staff with mainly a guarding role to specialised staff like social workers, psychiatrists, psychologists, religious representatives and probation workers and also representatives from prison services and ministries of Justice. In some cases advocates, visitors and representatives of civil society organisation were also included in the research.

This paragraph will look into the situation for foreign prisoners in the following twelve topics; general treatment, living conditions and facilities, reception and admission, work/education/ training/sports and recreation, food/religion/personal hygiene and medical care, consular and legal help, contact with the outside world, reintegration activities and prison leave, release and expulsion, aftercare and probation, staff and projects.

2.1 General situation

Penal codes and regulations are in principle equally applicable to all prisoners. Prisoners should receive similar legal guarantees for just, fair and humane treatment. According to prison regulations no discrimination is allowed based on the grounds of religion or belief, race, colour, language, nationality etc. As a result all prisoners should in practice receive equal treatment. Although this concept of non-discrimination is used as a starting point in prisons in practice it is not always the case. The difficulties that foreign prisoners experience in every day life are numerous and they are often not able to exercise their formally equal rights. Very often prison authorities do not impose these disadvantages deliberately.

In order to compensate these disadvantages countries like Austria and Czech Republic have special paragraphs in their penal legislations that prescribe special treatment. It seems that the implementation of this form of 'positive discrimination' in order to meet the special needs of foreign prisoners works well but that it depends heavily on the commitment of the director and staff of individual penitentiary institutions. Even when there is attention in prisons for the special needs of foreign prisoners there are a few threats that often result in additional problems for prisoners and staff. One of them is overcrowding which can result in multiple cell sharing, lack of space and lack of attention of staff, long time behind the door, less opportunities for work, education, vocational training and reintegration activities. Another hampering fact is that most prison populations represent more than 50 different nationalities and as a result there is a large diversity of languages, religions and cultures. Racism, religious intolerance and prejudice, especially in times of fear for terrorism, are not uncommon.

The most common and significant problem faced by foreign prisoners is the lack of knowledge of the national language. As a result verbal and written communication is severely hampered and that causes feelings of social isolation, uncertainty and helplessness. The less they are in number, the more isolated they tend to become. Daily interactions between foreign prisoners and staff are crucial and it often depends on the goodwill of prison staff and fellow-prisoners and the availability of an interpreter. Linguistic barriers are often the main source of other problems that foreign prisoners are facing in penitentiary institutions.

Treatment of prisoners often depends on the kind of regime (maximum security, closed, half-open, open, conditional freedom) they are placed in. Those that are placed in (semi-) open regimes receive a more relaxed treatment with more entitlements and more opportunities to prepare for resettlement into society after release. In general, foreign prisoners are excluded from the right to be placed in (semi-) open institutions even when their sentence length is relatively short or when they have nearly finished their sentence. This is especially the case for those that will leave or will be expelled afterwards to their country of origin. The fear of escape is mainly used as argument for this discriminatory practice because many foreigners have no secure home address in the country of detention.

Prison rules in general do not contain special rules for foreign prisoners on living conditions, reception and admission, work, education, training, food, religion or any other aspect described in this book. However, the lack of special regulations sometimes generates unequal opportunities for foreign prisoners taking into account the distance from relatives, differences in culture, religion and above all communication barriers. In the following sections the differences between foreign prisoners and national prisoners are being highlighted in more detail per topic.

Conclusions

- Penal codes and regulations are in principle equally applicable to all prisoners and discrimination is not allowed on the grounds of religion or belief, race, colour, language, nationality etc. As a result all prisoners should receive equal treatment.
- Foreign prisoners experience difficulties in daily life that are connected to their foreign status and as a result they are not able to exercise the same rights as national prisoners.
- Even when there is attention for the special needs of foreign prisoners, this can be easily threatened by common struggles of daily prison life such as: overcrowding, limited number of staff, limited opportunities for work and education, large diversity of nationalities etc.
- Racism, religious intolerance and prejudice, especially in times of fear for terrorism, are not uncommon.
- The most common and significant problem faced by foreign prisoners is the lack of knowledge of the national language. Linguistic barriers are often the main source of other problems and causes feelings of social isolation, uncertainty and loneliness.
- Foreign prisoners are in general excluded from placement in (semi) open penitentiary institutions with a more relaxed regime and (more) opportunities for work, education, re-integration programmes and contact with the outside world. Main reasons for this discriminatory practice are the fear of escape and the lack of a secure home address.

2.2 Living conditions and facilities

Foreigners who are suspected of or sentenced for a criminal offence are held in the same penitentiary institutions as national prisoners in the European Union. Only foreigners under administrative detention are held in separate centres (see under paragraph 3). Foreign prisoners have access to the same living conditions and facilities as other prisoners. The kind of living conditions and facilities vary per country, per region and according to the type of prison regime (closed, semi-open and open).

2.2.1 Allocation

According to Rule 17 of the European Prison Rules prisoners should be 'allocated, as much as possible, to prisons close to their homes or places of social rehabilitation'. For foreign prisoners this is difficult. The allocation of prisoners to penitentiary institutions depends generally speaking on the decision of the court. Prisoners that have not been convicted go to pre-trial detention and convicted prisoners are allocated to prisons according to the type and length of their sentence. In principle pre-trial prisoners are not accommodated with sentenced prisoners, young offenders are separated from adults, men are separated from women, healthy prisoners from sick prisoners and smokers from non-smokers. Selection based on 'nationality' seems not to be included under the criteria that govern the allocation of prisoners.

In allocating foreign prisoners to cells many prison authorities tend to make attempts to put people of the same language/culture/religion or nationality together. Individual wishes are often taken into consideration but due to overcrowding or security risks this is not always possible. It is very important that allocation is carefully applied because it can also become the source of further segregation. In many countries, like the United Kingdom and the Netherlands this selection is done by a Selection Officer who reviews each prisoner individually before allocation is doing process for each prisoner. 'Mixing' of nationalities among prison populations can be seen as a good practice in order to prevent the creation of subcultures within prisons but on the other hand it can increase the feeling of social exclusion among foreigners. Accommodation of prisoners with the same nationality, religion or cultural background in one cell or on a particular wing can elevate this feeling of isolation but on the other hand it can also can create tensions and undesirable hierarchical or violent subcultures, for example between nationals of recently partitioned new states.

In Finish prisons, attention is given to those prisoners who felt threatened by fellow prisoners. In 2004 a specific section was established for these 'fearing' prisoners and among those 142 prisoners 25 had an ethnic background and 18 were gypsies. In the Irish 'Cloverhill' pre-trial prison in Dublin, a separate wing is used to house non-Irish nationals. In France of the total foreign prison population are accommodated in the three big Parisian prisons; 'Fleury-Mérogis', 'La Santé', and 'Fresnes'. In the pre-trial prison 'La Santé' the proportion of foreign prisoners is 55% and there is a representation of 86 different nationalities. Foreign prisoners are placed in 4 units: Unit A hosts the 'Europeans', Unit B the 'Africans', Unit C the 'North Africans' and Unit D the 'rest of the world'. The head of the prison to limit conflicts and to create more group 'affinity' is justifying this structure. In practice a Christian English prisoner can be placed in the same cell with a Muslim from African origin with a German passport. The Austrian prison service tends to send foreign prisoners, mainly from African countries, to remote prisons like 'Suben' because they are less likely to receive visitors. In Poland nationals from Eastern European countries are placed in prisons situated close to the east border to facilitate visits from families. Most foreign prisoners in Portugal are sent to 'Funchal' prison in the Island of Madeira, one of the newest prisons built (1994) and with more places available.

Although 'nationality' is not a ground for not allowing prisoners to move to a more relaxed open regime, most foreign prisoners are in reality often excluded from this entitlement. In (semi-) open institutions prisoners have more freedom to walk around on the premises, are permitted to go outside for work or training related activities in society and spend only time behind a closed door during the night.

2.2.2 Cells

Foreign prisoners, mainly from outside the EU, prefer commonly shared rooms to solitary cells. However, most European penitentiary institutions were designed for single cell accommodation. Due to overcrowding many cells have been reconstructed for multi occupancy. Penitentiary institutions from relatively new EU member states have more dormitories for 2-6 persons or even more. Foreign prisoners are accommodated in the same cells as national prisoners.

Most cells and dormitories are equipped with a bed, table, chair, wardrobe and some cells have washing facilities and a separate toilet. The size of single cells varies among countries and there is no agreed universal standard. The Council of Europe's Committee for the Prevention of Torture (CPT) recommended that cells should be not less than 4 square metres per person[18]. Material conditions and the level of hygiene differ greatly per country but overall prisoners are required to keep their cells clean and in good condition. Most cells have central heating, lighting and ventilation. In many institutions prisoners are allowed to rent a television, a refrigerator and a radio. In Dutch prisons prisoners can keep a bird in a cage or a fish in a bowl. Danish prisons are run by the principle 'normalization' which aims at creating conditions and facilities as similar as possible to normal life in society. To carry this out prisoners are requested to take care of their own needs during the day and this implies shopping, cooking, cleaning, washing clothes etc. For this reason each prison is equipped with appropriate facilities.

Overcrowding is a common phenomenon in European prisons and has a devastating effect on living conditions and facilities for prisoners and staff. Besides a lack of space prisoners are also confronted with longer hours behind a closed door because staff has to divide their time over more prisoners. In Poland this has led to remarks from the Council of Europe's Committee for the Prevention of Torture (CPT) in 2004 to redouble their efforts to combat prison overcrowding.

Conclusions

- Besides special detention centres for foreigners who are detained for administrative reasons there are no special penitentiary facilities for foreign prisoners.
- It is not uncommon that prison authorities allocate prisoners with the same nationality, language, culture or religion together in one cell or wing. Individual wishes are sometimes taken into account.

2.3 Reception and admission

2.3.1 Reception

Reception is one of the most delicate phases of imprisonment; it is the point where citizens surrender their freedom. It can be experienced as intimidating and dehumanising. It is therefore essential that prisoners have a proper understanding of what is actually hap-

---

[18] CPT Report on visit to Poland in 1996 (1998), recommendation 70, page 32.

pening. Prison authorities should acknowledge that in this situation foreign prisoners are even more vulnerable and therefore special provisions should be made. In practice many penitentiary institutions are ill prepared to receive non-national prisoners. Language barriers and lack of information about the prison, prison rules and the legal process are the main reasons for this.

2.3.2 Admission

According to Rule 15.1 of the European Prison Rules prison authorities should 'record upon admission the following details of each prisoner: identity, reasons for commitment and the authority for it, the day and hour of admission, inventory of the personal property, any visible injuries and complaints about prior ill-treatment and information about the prisoners' physical and mental well-being'. Other personal data that is normally recorded is marital status, religion, offence of which the prisoner is suspected of or convicted for, court decision and date of discharge. Further it is not uncommon that a picture is taken and a fingerprint. In case a prisoner is transferred to another penal institution the personal file will be forwarded. In most countries this information is kept in an electronic register or database but in Cyprus a register is used with numbered pages. Upon admission all prisoners are subjected to a thorough body search and search of their luggage and personal belongings. Normally a prison officer of the same sex as the prisoner performs this.

Admission procedures are in general similar for all prisoners. The main disadvantage for foreign prisoners is that staff available in reception areas does not speak normally more than one language. As a result newly arrived foreign prisoners feel even more isolated and lost.

2.3.3 Information for prisoners

Upon admission prisoners are informed about the prison regulations, prison 'house rules', aspects of daily prison life, disciplinary sanctions, visits scheme, transfer procedures, opportunities for legal assistance and above all their rights and duties inside the institution. Especially for foreign prisoners it is essential that this information is available in a language that they can understand. In practice this is often not the case and foreign prisoners have to depend on the willingness and cooperation of staff and other prisoners to be informed. As a result foreign prisoners have a very bad start and they are ill prepared for their time in prison because they are not made properly aware of prison regulations and regime.

In several countries, like Belgium and The Netherlands, prison authorities claim that information is provided in a number of languages. However in practice it seems that the availability of information in multi languages depends on individual penitentiary institutions and that in general prison authorities do not prescribe this provision. Even in Austria where there is information available in 13 languages some prisoners complained in 2004 to the Council of Europe's Committee for the Prevention of Torture (CPT) about a lack of information. As a result the Ministry of Justice is regularly reminding penal institutions about their duty to hand out these regulations. Also in the Czech Republic there is a discrepancy. Although instructions of rights and duties are translated into 25 foreign languages most interviewed foreign prisoners indicated that they were not made aware of that. In some Belgian prisons initiative has been taken to translate the house rules in other languages, usually including English and Arabic or a video is showed. However, with over 100 different nationalities, it remains difficult to cover all possible languages. In Estonia, France, Greece and Ireland prisoners are seen on the first or second day of their arrival by the director (or his/her appointee). During this meeting their rights and duties are explained. For foreign prisoners in Estonia this information is translated into Russian and English.

Spanish penitentiary institutions are obliged by law to provide informative booklets about the prison regime and system in the most 'popular' languages. In case there are no booklets in a language the prisoners can understand, an oral translation is provided by a staff member, a fellow prisoner or the help from consular services are requested. The fact that there are no interpreters is seen as a severe omission. Also in some Hungarian penitentiary institutions there are information brochures for prisoners that are developed by non-governmental organizations. Some of these brochures are translated in foreign languages. In case a foreign prisoner is unable to understand this, an interpreter will be used. Each prisoner in Hungary, including foreigners, has to sign a declaration that they have been informed properly about their rights and obligations. In the Irish Mountjoy Prison a short video message about how the prison system works and what services are available to prisoners, is shown in the reception area. It is the intention to make this video available in different languages. In another Irish prison, in Cork, information is put in strategic locations in different languages by the Education Department. Also in Latvia the extracts of the 'Regulations on the Internal Order in Prisons' are made available in Latvian and Russian on the walls in the living area of prisons.

Some local prisons in England and Wales that are close to air and seaports receive a significant proportion of foreign prisoners. Prison staffs often seek assistance of 'Foreign National Prisoner Orderlies'; these are prisoners with certain language skills that are trained in informing newcomers and to reduce their isolation. The initiative to carefully recruit and train 'Foreign National Prisoner Orderlies' came from a large local London prison called HMP Wandsworth. This practice has been praised, also in prison inspections, and adopted by other prisons.

Another good practice that can be found in England and Wales is the 'Foreign National Prisoners Information Pack' that is handed out to foreign prisoners upon admission. The Pack, available in 20 languages, contains information about the rules, prisoners' rights and duties, how to make a complaint, how to contact embassies, how to apply for repatriation etc. The Prison Service Headquarters and the Prison Reform Trust produced the first edition of the Pack in 1994. Besides a section for foreign prisoners there is also a training and education package for staff. The latest edition, which was made in co-operation with the London Probation, dates from December 2004.

2.3.4 Medical check

Rule 16 of the European Prison Rules prescribes that 'as soon as possible after admission prisoners should receive a medical examination'. In penitentiary institutions it is common that a doctor sees newly arriving prisoners for a physical examination as soon as possible but normally within two days. Besides a physical examination prisoners are also seen by the psychosocial service for a mental diagnosis. Medication is arranged if necessary. Information about the physical and mental health is recorded in their personal record.

2.3.5 Contact diplomatic mission

Prisoners are entitled to contact a representative of their diplomatic mission upon admission in a penitentiary institution. In practice prisoners are often not made aware of this right or have personal reasons not to do so. On the other hand many foreign prisoners do not want their embassy to know about their criminal situation, especially those awaiting removal or expulsion. In Hungary penitentiary institutions are obliged to immediately notify the competent embassy or consulate once a foreign prisoner is admitted. According to Article 222 of the Hungarian penitentiary regulation institutions can only refrain from this if the prisoners requests so in writing.

2.3.6 Contact with family

At reception prisoners are in principle entitled to call their families to inform them about their detention. In practice not all penitentiary institutions facilitate this or do not provide financial means to make a short phone call. In practice many prisoners, including foreign prisoners, do not have financial means to make this contact.

In France prison staff refuses conversations in any language other than French. In the Irish Cloverhill pre-trial prison special consideration is being given to foreign prisoners to contact their family at appropriate times for their families. For this reason clocks with various international time zones are placed in the main circle area of the prison. In the Netherlands prisoners are given upon admission a telephone card to make a call. In practice the amount on these cards is not sufficient to make long distance calls.

Conclusions

- Individual penitentiary institutions are in general unprepared to receive prisoners that are unable to understand the national language.
- At reception there is normally no multi-language information available about prison rules, prison procedures, disciplinary sanctions, visits scheme, transfer agreements etc.
- Prison staff in the reception area does not often speak more than one language and are not specifically trained in receiving visitors from abroad.
- In practice not all penitentiary institutions provide facilities and/or (enough) financial means for foreign prisoners to contact their family.

2.4 Work - Education - Training - Sports - Recreation

2.4.1 Work

The European Prison Rules state in Rule 26 that prison authorities should strive to provide sufficient work of a useful nature and prisoners shall receive 'equitable' remuneration for it. Work should never be a punishment and discrimination on the basis of gender is not allowed. Pre-trial prisoners are, unlike sentenced prisoners, in general not obliged to work. In principle no differentiation is made in prison regulations between nationals and foreigners regarding the allocation of work. Normally other criteria are set by prison authorities like; prisoners' skills, knowledge, experience, state of health, age, duration of the sentence, behaviour as well as preferences. But in practice most types of work require sufficient knowledge of the national language and as a result foreign prisoners are often excluded and end upon the bottom of waiting lists. Besides this, work available in penitentiary institutions tends to be limited. Shortage of labour results in long waiting lists and the phenomena that work is not seen as a legal obligation for sentenced prisoners but as a privilege. Lack of work affects both national and foreign prisoners. However, the combination of scarce work and language barriers leads to the fact that foreign prisoners are often excluded from work provisions inside European penitentiary institutions.

Being engaged in useful and paid work is essential for prisoners. Work is one of the most important activities in prison. Many prisoners and in particular foreigners depend on the small income they receive from work, especially when they have no other forms of income to buy telephone cards, rent a TV, buy additional food and items to maintain their personal hygiene or to send money back to their families. Being involved in work can mitigate the detrimental psychological effects of detention and it can teach prisoners a skill that they can use to earn a living after release. Sometimes prisoners are offered to take a vocational training in relation to the work they are doing. Further it is common that employment in prison entitles prisoners to certain privileges like more freedom of movement and more time out of cell. Prisoners are often divided into units for 'workers' and for 'non-workers', with the 'workers' having a much more relaxed regime with a good balance between work, other activities and time inside the cell. In many pre-trial prisons where no work is available prisoners spend often more than 20 hours behind closed doors. Being involved in work can also have a positive effect on the decision of a court when considering a sentence or for conditional release.

Work is generally divided into three types: maintenance work of the penitentiary institution, in-house production and work outside the prison walls. The majority of prisoners allocated to work are involved with in-house production. Normally only a limited number of prisoners are selected for maintenance work inside the institution, like cleaning the corridors, common rooms and helping in the kitchen and those who are trusted to work in the community. In general work is facilitated by the prison authorities and can be organised in collaboration or directly with external entities or firms. Prisoners working conditions should be healthy and safe and prison authorities should ensure that the conditions comply with the requirements as set by labour protection laws. Prisoners may be required to work overtime, on their day's off and on public holidays but only with the consent of the prisoners.

In Austria there is a small enterprise in Vienna's court prison where only juveniles and young adults from Africa work. Despite efforts to provide all prisoners with work it is striking that statistics of the Austrian penitentiary system show that foreigners are less often employed than nationals and as a result Austrian national prisoners earn in average twice as much as foreigners. This difference can also be explained because foreigners are more frequently in pre-trial detention where they are not obliged to work. In Portugal and Spain in some cases foreigners tend to have more access to work activities than national prisoners due to their lack of other forms of income. The most demanding and therefore well-paid prison jobs in the United Kingdom tend to have a high proportion of foreign nationals. This is due to the fact that foreign nationals often are motivated to support their dependants abroad. So-called 'Work Boards' in prison in the United Kingdom are responsible to ensure that prison jobs are distributed fairly and equitably. Maintenance work is often allocated to national prisoners because close cooperation and good communication with prison staff is required. In Hungary maintenance work is not being paid but in the Netherlands it is remunerated in the same way as other work in prison. In Austria prisoners who have worked inside the prison receive unemployment benefits after release. In Slovenia prisoners who are involved in full-time work receive all rights that arise from employment including holiday from 18 tot 30 days per year. Ordinary basic payment for prison work is in Denmark € 1. (8 Danish Kronen) per hour and for extraordinary good or demanding work it can go up to € 1.5 per hour in 2005. In The Netherlands the hourly rate is €0.64 and prisoners can earn a maximum salary of €12.80 (20 hours) per week. When there is no work or not enough work available prisoners receive 80% of their wages. Misbehaviour during work or malingering can lead to disciplinary punishment. Those Dutch open penitentiary institutions that offer work outside the institution are obliged by law to pay all prisoners, also those engaged in education, a salary of 40% of the gross minimum salary, which is approximately € 120.00 per week. In order to increase the availability of work in Estonian penitentiary institutions and to decrease the expenses of prisons a state company called 'PLC Estonian Prison Industries' (AS Eesti Vanglatööstus) was established in 2001. In case due to their fault, prisoners deliver unsatisfactory work, the prison director can reduce their remuneration by up to 60%. In Germany it is unlawful for prison authorities to reduce the remuneration for any reason.

It is remarkable to note that in many European countries foreigners are not allowed to work without a work-permit. In practice this seems to be not an obstacle for foreign prisoners to be involved in work activities inside a penitentiary institution. For example according to labour laws in the Netherlands and Slovakia the fact that condemned foreigners are working inside a penitentiary institution does not constitute a working relationship and therefore a work-permit is not obligatory.

2.4.2 Education and training

According to Rule 28 of the European Prison Rules each 'prison should seek to provide all prisoners with access to educational programmes which are as comprehensive as possible and which meet their individual needs while taking into account their aspirations. Particular attention should be paid to the education of young prisoners and those with special needs'.

Sentenced prisoners are in principle entitled to follow educational and vocational training courses. In practice the availability of educational and training courses varies a lot from country to country and from prison to prison but in general these courses are limited or hardly available. Although foreign prisoners are by law not excluded from participation in classes, in practice they are often not able to attend due to the selection criteria or tests that they cannot meet. Poor understanding of the national language is the main obstacle. Provisions for education are often not available in pre-trial detention and since many foreigners are held in remand they cannot attend educational classes. In Sweden a case was taken up by the Justice Ombudsman in 1995 when a local prison refused a foreign prisoner, who was due to be expelled, to participate in educational course. The Justice Ombudsman decided that the practice of excluding a certain sub-group of prisoners from educational activities was not in accordance with the Swedish Prison Treatment Act. Educational classes range from basic education to secondary education and in some cases prisoners are permitted to study at educational institutions or vocational training institutes located outside penitentiary institutions. In Slovenia foreigners are in practice not able to follow classes outside the prison. Since a considerable group of prisoners are illiterate or have not finished primary school the majority of educational courses are on elementary or secondary level. In Portugal, data shows that foreign prisoners from European countries and female prisoners from South American countries possess, in average, higher degrees of formal education than nationals. No information is available about the level of educational background of foreigners in other countries.

Some European penitentiary institutions offer language courses to foreigners to become more acquainted with the national language or English. These classes are in the interest of 'both sides' because it is also beneficial for staff when they can better communicate with foreign prisoners. In most institutions demand for this type of courses is greater than the supply. Besides these language courses there are in general no educational courses especially developed for foreigners. Although the CPT judged the situation in Austrian prisons as 'far from satisfactory' in 2005, prison authorities provide courses for juveniles and 'young adults' in order to obtain a compulsory school certificate and many young foreigners are participating in this. The CPT also emphasized in a report of 2002 that the Polish authorities should strive to provide young adult prisoners with a full programme of educational, recreational and other purposeful activities adapted to their specific needs. In Ireland the 'Education Service Computer Class' in Mountjoy prison accommodates juveniles of which at least half the participants are foreigners. It is remarkable to note that in various countries like Ireland and the United Kingdom, foreign prisoners tend to be in general more motivated to attend courses. The types of vocational and professional trainings offered by prison authories varies greatly but they are mainly focussed on jobs for constructions and building, painting, mechanics, electricity and computers and for women more often in the field of personal care like hairdressing. The costs related to the educational and training provisions are assumed by the prison authorities or financed from the state budget allocated for national education. Besides these costs, prison authorities are entitled to give financial remuneration to those prisoners who are participating in educational courses. According to the European Prison Rules education should have 'no less status than work within the prison regime and prisoners shall not be disadvantaged financially or otherwise by taking part in education.' In practice not all prisoners that follow educational classes or training receive a financial remuneration equal to prison work. Distance learning courses organised for foreigners by their diplomatic missions and consulates are rare.

2.4.3 Sports and recreation

Most prisoners are spending the majority of their time inside a penal institution and often behind cell doors. In these circumstances it is essential for their physical and mental health that they are given an adequate amount of time each day in the open air and are allowed participate in sports and recreational activities. Rule 27 of the European Prison Rules states that all prisoners should be able to spend 'at least one hour of exercise every day in the open air' and 'adequate exercise' and 'recreational opportunities' should form an integral part of the prison regime. Recreational activities include sport, games, cultural activities, hobbies and other leisure pursuits. Penal institutions should organise activities and provide facilities and equipment. Unlike older prisons, more recently built prisons are normally equipped with a gym hall, a fitness room and an outdoor sporting field. Specially trained prison staff supervises prisoners during sport activities like fitness, team games and contests.

In general foreign prisoners are not excluded from participating in sports or recreational activities. However, in Austria foreign prisoners are not allowed to participate in jogging-teams that make trips outside the institution because of the presumed higher risk of escape.

Foreign prisoners participate in sports and recreational activities as much as other prisoners. Although there are still communication difficulties, foreign prisoners tend to manage with non-verbal communication. Especially the recreation hours are important for foreign prisoners because they can seek assistance from other prisoners or staff for a better understanding about how the institution and its procedures function. Furthermore, foreign prisoners tend to have less visitors and for them this is a way to socialise.

The use of prison library is open to all prisoners. In most libraries in European penitentiary institutions books are also available in a limited number of foreign languages. In Belgium and Greece prison libraries often work together with local libraries in order to enlarge the selection of books. When the Greek Penitentiary Code was discussed in the Greek Parliament on 1 December 1999 it became clear that the budget for books for prisoners for the year 2000 was only □ 3.000 annually. In some countries prison libraries receive foreign national magazines and newspapers from diplomatic missions and in Austria prisons receive regularly international magazines from special foreigners 'advisors' (so called 'Ausländerreferents'). Books can often be read inside the cell.

Recreational activities and facilities can vary per country and per penitentiary institution but often prisoners can meet in a communal area on their wing where they can sit together to watch television and video movies, play table tennis, chess or darts. Sometimes art classes are offered where prisoners can watch performances like dance and drama. In some countries external welfare organisations are invited to organise cultural events. In Cyprus, prisoners can be involved in expressive art classes such as design, copper work and iconography but also in theatre. There is a team of prisoners that gives theatre performances in and outside the prison. In Austria quarterly 'instructive, artistic or amusing' events are organised like concerts, cabaret, slideshows, drum groups and even belly dancing performances. The Austrian Code of Imprisonment explicitly refers to foreign prisoners and that their special needs should be taken into account. In Greece a pay TV channel can be placed for sports events and films upon request of prisoners. The prisoners themselves cover the costs.

Conclusions

- Although foreign prisoners are in principle not excluded to participate in work they are often not able to join because it often requires a sufficient knowledge of the national language.
- Work is in general only limited available. As a result there are often long waiting lists and it is seen as a privilege.
- In practice foreign prisoners are less often engaged in work than national prisoners.
- Also educational and training programmes are limited available in European penitentiary institutions and foreign prisoners are often unable to participate due to language barriers.
- Foreign prisoners are especially over-represented in pre-trial detention and in these settings education and training programmes are often not available at all.
- Some penitentiary institutions provide national language classes for foreign prisoners. These classes are very popular and therefore there are often long waiting lists.

- Participation of foreign prisoners in sport and recreational activities seems to be no problem.

2.5 Food – Religion – Personal Hygiene – Medical Care

2.5.1 Food

Prison authorities are obliged to provide prisoners with sufficient and healthy food of reasonable variety in accordance with dietary principles and hygiene. Prison authorities are required to take into consideration religious and cultural requirements like not eating any meat, not eating particular meat (Halal), only eating food prepared under specific hygienic conditions (Kosher or according to the Cheriáa) etc. In practice this means that penitentiary institutions have to prepare several different meals on a daily basis. Although by far not all penitentiary institutions do so, especially when the number of prisoners with dietary requirements is small, often certain group preferences are being respected like serving rice for prisoners from Africa, non-pork food for Muslims etc. More common is that prison authorities respect religious holidays of religions that are well represented by groups of prisoners. In France for example Jewish prisoners receive specially prepared kosher food for Easter, New Year's Eve (Rosh-ha-Shana) and Yom Kippur. Muslim prisoners are enabled to celebrate Ramadan (Aid El Fitr) and Ail El Kebir with the appropriate food.

In Cyprus and Estonia the diet is set by the Director of the prison after consultation with the Prison's medical officer who takes into consideration age, health, work and as much as possible the religious beliefs of prisoners. Foreign prisoners in the Czech Republic can choose between nationally prepared food or non-pork food and in case they will or cannot eat that they can request 'additional' food at their own expenses. In Denmark, prisoners receive a daily sum to buy ingredients in the prison shop to prepare their own meal. A common heard complaint is that the food supply in the prison shop is too expensive, too monotonous and not fresh. Prison shops in Finland are provided also with ethnic food. French prison shops tend to have only French and European products and the prices are between 10%-50% higher than in normal supermarkets. In Latvia and Portugal no special diets are provided and therefore, especially foreign prisoners have to purchase products in the prison store. The Portuguese prison authorities accept also specially prepared food by prisoners' families. Upon admission in a Dutch penitentiary institution prisoners are being asked about their dietary requirements for medical, religious or cultural reasons. Although there is not much variation in the menu each institution prepares at least specially prepared food for Muslims, Jews and vegetarians. Due to budgetary restrictions most prisoners in Dutch prisons receive their food in a plastic box that they have to heat in a microwave. As a result the quality of the food is rather low and especially foreign prisoners regret the fact that they cannot cook their own meals. Also in the United Kingdom, where the range of food available to prisoners increased in recent years, there is criticism especially among foreign prisoners about the bland taste of the food. Penitentiary institutions in the United Kingdom provide Halal meat, kosher, vegetarian and vegan options.

2.5.2 Religion

All prisoners have the right to freedom of thought, conscience and religious belief. Prison authorities should create, as far as possible, opportunities in the prison programme to allow prisoners to observe their religion, to pray, to attend services and to read religious text. Facilities should be provided for prisoners who wish to practice their religion and qualified religious representatives should have the right to visit prisoners on a regular basis. Some religions have specific practices which have to be observed and they may include; praying at set times and under certain conditions; dietary restrictions, dress requirements and prescriptions about the length of hair. Freedom of religion also entails the right to be free from religious influence and coercion. Therefore, no prisoner can be forced to participate in any religious meeting or to receive the visit of a representative. Prisoners can choose freely if and which religion or philosophy they want to turn to and can change course during their detention. Normally upon admission prisoners can inform prison staff about their religion.

It is interesting to note that foreign prisoners in interviews for this study indicated that practicing their personal religion was an important element in their lives and in that in some cases there religious feelings became more apparent during detention. Attending religious services or private conversations with religious representatives are also seen as a way to escape daily prison routine and boredom.

Although all penitentiary institutions enable prisoners to practice their religion, not all institutions are willing or equipped to meet the religious needs of all prisoners, including foreigners. This is especially difficult for foreign prisoners because they tend not to practice the same religion as the main national religion of the country in which they are detained. As a result many foreigners are not or hardly able to practice their own religion and to observe praying, dietary and dress requirements.

European prison authorities are dealing with the rather recent development that a considerable part of their prison population consists of prisoners from various religious beliefs. As a result many prisons are struggling to meet the needs of well-represented groups of prisoners with a certain religion. In practice prisons come with creative solutions like providing a multi-faith room for the use of prisoners and for recruiting religious representatives from the community. All prisons give access to qualified religious representatives in order to organise religious services or to meet prisoners on an individual basis. These representatives are often paid by the Prison authorities or by local churches or by religious organisations. In practice it turns out to be difficult to obtain (enough) religious representatives in order to meet the needs. Further the language barrier makes it sometimes difficult for foreign prisoners to attend religious services in a language that they can understand. Contrary to the other staff members the religious staff practises professional secrecy. In many prisons religious events and holy days are respected and special food or access to religious services is provided. In some cases practicing a religion is being misused by prisoners to obtain power. In some countries prisoners who are held in isolation are not permitted to attend religious services with other prisoners. Some religious practices can cause conflicts between prisoners, especially when prisoners are sharing one cell. For example when one prisoner likes to watch television and the other one needs to pray. In many penitentiary institutions efforts are made, upon request of prisoners, to place prisoners of the same nationality and or religion together in one cell so that they can speak their own language and share their religious beliefs.

In Austria the 'Vienna-Josefstadt' prison houses a synagogue, a Catholic church, a Protestant chapel and recently also a mosque. Other prisons in Austria have fewer facilities for prisoners and most religious services are held in the refectory. In Portugal, being a Catholic country, penitentiary institutions in general only house chapels.

In Belgium religion was an important aspect of prison life until after the Second World War. Catholic chaplains were part of the prison staff and catholic nuns ran units for female prisoners until the 1980's. However, the right to freedom of religion was, together with the right of access to a lawyer, the only formally recognized prisoners' rights under the General Prison Regulation of 1965. This right has been confirmed by the new Prison Act of 12 January 2005. The following religions are officially recognized in Belgian prisons: Catholicism, Protestantism, Orthodox faith, Judaism, Islam and non-confessional moral philosophy. Representatives of these recognized religions or philosophies are attached to each prison and they can visit individual prisoners, organise meetings and receive uncensored letters from prisoners. Although the role of Imams are seen as very important for the large group of Muslim prisoners, the Belgium prison authorities could only find two Imams who have to visit 34 prisons.

The Czech Republic Prison Service has 29 prison chaplains employed from 10 state-registered churches that are active in 22 penitentiary institutions. Further there are the Prison Religious Care (PRC) associations that provide voluntary broad ecumenical services in prisons. Muslim prisoners indicated that their religious rights are not observed in Czech prisons because they are not allowed to wear their habit and to wash themselves before every prayer. The Finnish Prison Service has arrangements with the Orthodox Church to take care of the Russian prisoners and part-time orthodox clerks who hold services visit prisons. In French penitentiary institutions there were in 2003 in total 918 religious representatives working in prison of whom 323 were paid. Of this group 513 were Catholics, 267 Protestants, 69 Muslims, 64 Jewish, 3 Orthodox and 2 Buddhists. Despite the considerable number of Muslim religious representatives working for the French prison service, 'Fresnes' a big prison with 637 foreign prisoners could not find an Imam in 2004. In Greek penitentiary institutions prisoners who do not belong to the Eastern Orthodox Christian Church or Roman Catholic Church have very limited opportunities to perform their religious duties. All registered churches in Hungary, over one hundred, are allowed access to prisons and to organise religious services. In practice only relationships with the Catholic Church, Lutherans, Calvinists and the Jewish denomination have been institutionalised. In Ireland there are 20 full-time and 3 part-time chaplains working in penitentiary institutions. In 2003 the Irish chaplains came in the news when they opposed the inappropriate use of prisons as detention centres for expulsion. They recommended that this practice should stop and that a less severe but secure environment should be provided for those foreigners waiting expulsion. In Latvia the prison chaplains play an important role in organising religious services but also in social life. In case a prisoner wants to meet a religious representative, it is the prison chaplain who communicates this and sets up a meeting for the prisoner. In the United Kingdom there is a special 'Chaplain General' at the Prison Service headquarters that ensures that the religious needs of prisoners are met. In Lithuania foreign embassies sometimes help to set up religious meetings in order to meet the religious needs for foreigners. In Malta, as in several other European countries, the Imam plays an important role for Muslim foreign prisoners, especially because there is a large Arab prison community. Also in The Netherlands there are many Muslim prisoners and there is often a lack of Imams. In order to fill this gap the Minister of Justice organised a special Imam training. During Ramadan, the holiest month on the lunar Islamic calendar, Muslim prisoners are allowed to fast from sunrise to sunset and traditional Muslim food is provided between sunset and sunrise. Prisoners who are under any form of segregation or punishment can have access to services but are separated from other prisoners. Although foreign prisoners in Dutch penitentiary institutions indicated in interviews that they were satisfied with the opportunities to practice their religion, the language barriers remained. The Swedish Prison and Probation Service have a network of representatives of different nominations who visit foreign prisoners. This network, called the Council for Spiritual Welfare, consists of around 130 persons.

2.5.3 Personal hygiene

Penitentiary institutions should be properly maintained and kept clean and equipped with adequate sanitary installations. Each prisoner should receive from the prison authorities clean and adequate clothing and bedding together with products to maintain personal hygiene. The accommodation provided for prisoners should respect human dignity, and as far as possible privacy and meet the requirements of health and hygiene.

Hygienic standards may differ per person but also per culture. This can lead to tensions especially when prisoners have to share cells. In many penitentiary institutions prisoners are entitled to wear their own clothes. Newcomers that have no clean or suitable clothing are normally provided with a set of clothing by the prison authorities. Also toiletries for personal hygiene are normally given to prisoners upon admission. In some penitentiary institutions prisoners are not allowed to wear their own clothing nor footwear and for some prisoners this is problematic because it can conflict with their religious dress requirements. In other prisons people are allowed to wear their own clothes as long as they pose no security risk and are correct. In the United Kingdom prisoners are allowed to wear religious headdress such as turbans for Sikhs and headscarves for Muslim women. Normally all prisoners are able to take a shower or bath once or twice a week and upon admission. In Finland prisoners can shower as often as they wish and in Estonia they can also make use of a sauna. Further prisoners' hair can be cut on a regular basis. In case prisoners fail to take care of their own personal hygiene and when this can impose a health risk for him or herself of for other prisoners the director may impose coercion to ensure compliance with hygiene requirements. Prisoners are requested not only to observe their personal hygiene but also their clothing, beddings, cells, shower facilities and communal living facilities should be kept clean at all times.

2.5.4 Medical care

Access to healthcare is a basic right that applies to all human beings. Prison authorities are requested to provide medical care to sustain or improve the physical and mental state of health of prisoners. Medical care and treatment in penal institutions should be equal to that provided in the community and preferably there should be a close link between the public health service and the prison health service. Normally each prisoner receives a health check within 24 hours after admission. Until recently this was the case in Danish prisons but for economical reasons prisoners are now offered to have a health check.

In general foreign prisoners receive the same kind of medical treatment as national prisoners. The main obstacle is the language difficulty. Requesting interpreter assistance from non-medical staff or fellow prisoners can be practical but is not desired because of medial confidentiality and the quality of translation of medical terminology. A Danish prison report on ethnic minorities recommended that interpreters should also have a deep knowledge of the cultural background of foreign prisoners. Professional interpreters are hardly ever used. In the United Kingdom medical staff can use an interpreter-telephone service.

Two large Austrian prisons 'Wien-Josefstad't and 'Stein' have special medical departments where information sheets on medical issues are available in different languages and also medical staff has foreign language competences. In case prisoners can not be treated inside the prisons they are transferred to local hospitals or specialised prison hospitals. Statistical data from Austrian penitentiary institutions shows that foreigners are less often transferred to local hospitals compared to national prisoners. In the Netherlands if medical surgery for foreign prisoners is not strictly urgent they are normally not carried out. This decision also depends on the duration of detention and if follow-up treatment and aftercare can be given in the country of return. Prisoners in Dutch and Spanish penitentiary institutions can, at their own expenses, consult medical doctors of their own choice. With the growing number of prisoners from Central and Eastern European countries, 'new' illnesses are appearing in Belgium prisons like open TB.

Penitentiary institutions in the Czech Republic provide medical care free of charge to national prisoners but foreign prisoners without a health insurance have to pay except in emergency cases. All prisoners, including foreign prisoners, in French prisons are automatically part of the social security system. For irregular foreign nationals this affiliation is only during their time in detention and for foreigners with a legal residence it is valid up to three years after release. Health care in Malta is free for Maltese citizens but not for foreigners except when they are in prison. However, in case particular health requisites are not provided efficiently by the prison health service, foreign prisoners can purchase these on their own expenses. Drug treatment units in Danish prisons tend to have a smaller portion of foreign prisoners compared to the percentage of foreigners in the total prison population. This might have to do with communication and cultural barriers but also with the fact that treatment places are limited and expensive and that many foreigners are being expelled after release. In the United Kingdom there are special health care issues for foreign prisoners that particularly focus on mental health due to the separation from families abroad and isolation due to cultural and language differences.

Conclusions

- Many penitentiary institutions take into consideration the religious and cultural dietary requirements of foreign prisoners.
- Although prisoners are entitled to practice their religion, not all penitentiary institutions are willing and equipped to meet the religious needs of all prisoners.
- Hygienic standards may differ per person but also per culture. This may create tension.
- Foreign prisoners receive in principle similar medical care but in practice they receive less treatment (e.g. drugs) and are less often transferred to local hospitals.

2.6 Consular help and Legal aid

2.6.1 Consular help

Rule 37.1 of the European Prison Rules states that 'prisoners who are foreign nationals shall be informed, without delay, of their right to request contact and be allowed reasonable facilities to communicate with the diplomatic or consular representative of their state'. In case their country has no representation in the country they are allowed to communicate with the representative of the state that takes care of their interest. Prison authorities are requested to co-operate fully with diplomatic representatives of foreign prisoners with special needs.

In practice not all foreign prisoners are willing to contact their embassies and not all embassies and consulates are interested in their detained countrymen. The attitude of embassies varies from pro-active, helpful and caring to indifference and unwillingness to provide any assistance. As a result foreign prisoners have different opinions about the consular assistance they receive, it ranges from very positive to negative. The assistance that may be provided by consular authorities can include: personal visits, providing information on legal proceedings and advice on legal and medical assistance, sending parcels (newspapers, magazines, toiletries etc), sending money and staying in contact with relatives and state authorities in the home country. Diplomatic missions are also involved in the attainment of legal status and documentation for foreign prisoners for release or transfer. It is not uncommon that foreign prisoners are forced to stay longer in detention because their diplomatic mission does not issue travel documents on time.

In most European countries foreign prisoners are entitled upon admission to one free phone call to their diplomatic mission. In Hungary when foreign prisoners indicate that they do not want to contact their embassy they have to do this in writing. In the United Kingdom it can happen that diplomatic missions are informed of the detention of their countrymen by the prison regardless of the personal consent of the prisoner. In Belgium a delay of maximum 3 days is allowed for foreign prisoners who are on remand and who have been restricted by the investigating judge to have contact with the outside world. Article 36 of the Vienna Convention on Consular Relations (1963) requires that foreign nationals who are arrested or detained be given notice 'without delay' of their right to have their embassy or consulate notified of their arrest. In interviews with foreign prisoners in Dutch penitentiary institutions it became clear that not all foreign prisoners were made aware by prison staff about their right to contact their diplomatic mission. The reason for foreign prisoners not to inform their embassies was because they were either embarrassed or afraid of the consequences for their relatives or upon return to their home country or pessimistic about the kind of assistance they could expect from their embassies.

Correspondence with diplomatic missions is in principle confidential and cannot be controlled or censured. In Hungary foreign prisoners are entitled to keep contact with the representative of their diplomatic mission in writing or verbally (by phone or visits) without restriction and supervision but once convicted only written correspondence is exempt from supervision. In Latvia costs for correspondence with diplomatic missions are covered by the prison service and in some prisons regular consultation hours with consular representatives are organised. Also in the United Kingdom there are biannual meetings hosted by the Prison Service Headquarters and London Probation for diplomatic missions. These meetings are organised to inform consulate staff about prison regimes to enable them to provide a knowledgeable and professional service to their imprisoned nationals. These well-attended meetings have been organised since 1992. In the Netherlands the 'Foreign Liaison Office' of the Dutch Probation Service plays an important role in the care of Dutch nationals detained abroad. The 'Foreign Liaison Office' coordinates the visits of 275 volunteers who are Dutch nationals who live and work abroad and who pay social visits to Dutch nationals in detention every four to six weeks in close cooperation with diplomatic missions around the world.

2.6.2 Legal aid

According to Rule 23.1 of the European Prison Rules 'all prisoners are entitled to legal advice, and the prison authorities shall provide them with reasonable facilities for gaining access to such advice'. Prisoners may consult on any legal matter with a legal adviser of their own choice and at their own expense. Visits by lawyers are confidential and shall not be attended by prison staff or others. In case free legal aid is available, prison authorities shall bring this to the attention of all prisoners. Communication and correspondence about legal matters between prisoners and their legal advisers are in principle confidential. Prisoners are allowed to keep documents related to their legal proceedings in own possession.

In many European legal systems if accused persons cannot afford a lawyer, the court assigns at their own costs a lawyer. In case the accused person does not understand the language of the court an interpreter is being used and paid by the court. In practice some countries encountered difficulties to find suitable interpreters. Especially during the pre-trial period, information from the court is of crucial importance to prisoners. Foreign prisoners are severely disadvantaged when they are unable to understand the information and legal proceedings.

Foreign prisoners tend to be dissatisfied with the legal support they receive. Very often the lawyers do not spend any or very little time on their case, only show up (if they show up) in court, provide very little information about court proceedings and outcome of case. This is aggravated by the fact that the lawyers often do not speak the language of clients and are often not trained and familiar with legal aspects of foreign prisoners' cases.

In order to provide more insight in legal proceedings some Belgian prisons organise for lawyers 'foreign prisoners' information sessions'. Prisoners in Cyprus who cannot afford a lawyer can request free legal aid but once the person is convicted the free legal assistance stops. In the Czech Republic, the Czech Helsinki Committee provides free legal help to foreign prisoners. Also in Hungary and Malta non-governmental organisations provide assistance. In Greece if a prisoner is financially unable to pay for legal assistance a complex procedure needs to be followed. The prisoner is requested to fill out an application with supporting documents like tax return papers, statement of income by the revenue office, certificate of financial need or granting of a welfare allowance, certificate of unemployment subsidy by the Manpower Employment Organisation, records of proceedings of judicial authorities or other documents. It seems to be difficult for foreigners to provide these documents.

Legal assistance to foreign prisoners in connection with disciplinary proceedings is also unsatisfactorily organised. In Spain there is a legal procedure that states that assistance should be given by a member of the prison staff or by another prisoner. This is seen as unacceptable and therefore the assurance of permanent access to competent interpreters in order to be heard and to understand what is being said in disciplinary proceedings should be recognized as a right for foreign prisoners.

Conclusions

- Although foreign prisoners are entitled to contact their diplomatic missions in practice they do not often make use of this right. Sometimes because they are afraid or ashamed to inform them but more often because they are not made aware of this.
- The position of diplomatic missions varies from pro-active, helpful and caring to indifferent and unwilling to provide any assistance.
- Foreign prisoners are in desperate need of legal assistance since they are often unable to understand legal proceedings and as a result of that they even do not understand their own legal case.
- Very often foreign prisoners do not know if they will be expelled after release or not. This creates severe tensions and aggravates the feeling of desperation.
- Foreign prisoners tend to be dissatisfied with the (free) legal aid they receive. Lawyers do often not speak the language of their clients and are often not trained or familiar with the legal aspects of foreign prisoners' cases.

2.7 Contact with the outside world

Prisoners retain, despite being deprived of their liberty, the right to maintain contact with family, friends and the outside world. The right to interact and communicate with the outside world is of vital importance to the socialization in prison and also in the facilitation of a successful return into society after release. Foreign prisoners are hampered by the fact that they are far away from home and that maintaining contact is more difficult. The language barrier proves to be a difficult hurdle also in relation to contact with the outside world. As a result many foreign prisoners are socially isolated. According to article 24 of the European Prison Rules prison authorities are requested to provide facilities and opportunities for prisoners to maintain contact with the outside world by letter and telephone and to receive visits. Communication and visits may be subject to restrictions and monitoring when necessary for the maintenance of good order, safety and security. Contact with lawyers, diplomatic missions, Ombudsman and international organisations are in principle confidential and may not be censored by prison authorities. In many countries the rules to maintain contact with the outside world depend on the legal status of prisoners. Prisoners serving a sentence are subjected to different regulations than unconvicted prisoners in pre-trial detention. In pre-trial detention the decision over the level of contact a prisoner is allowed is also depending on the decision of the judicial authority.

The most important instruments for prisoners to maintain contact are visits, communication via telephone and letters and access to news via newspapers, magazine, television and radio.

2.7.1 Visits

Although foreign prisoners are entitled to as many visits as national visitors in practice they receive far less visitors than national prisoners and sometimes even none. Only a limited number of penitentiary institutions agreed on working with a more flexible visiting scheme in order to alleviate the social exclusion of foreign prisoners. In some special cases, like when relatives have to travel long journeys, the length of visits can be extended. In Austria, Germany, Ireland, Malta and Sweden the visiting hours are dealt with generously and foreign prisoners may receive up to a whole day of visit, or divided over some days in a row in case a visitor comes from abroad. In Hungary visits from relatives from abroad may last up to two hours but in The Netherlands no exemptions are made to the visiting rule of one hour per week.

Normally visits last about one hour and are supervised by prison staff. In some countries prisoners are also entitled to unsupervised visits. In Estonia these 'long-term' visits may last up to three days in designated rooms inside the prison without constant supervision. In Poland there are officially no conjugal (or intimate) visits but the frequency as well as conditions of visits can be modified by means of rewards granted to prisoners for good behaviour. The rewards are: the permission to receive an additional or longer visit, the permission to receive an unsupervised visit in a common room and the permission to receive an unsupervised visit in a separate room. In Spanish prisons, for those who cannot obtain permissions of leave are authorized to have a conjugal visit or family visit once a month from one to three hours.

Visiting hours granted to prisoners are often depending on their legal status. In Hungary pre-trial prisoners are, apart from the lawyer or representative of the diplomatic mission, not allowed to receive visitors without the prior authorization by the prosecutor or, in the trial stage, the court. In Austria pre-trial prisoners have in principle the right to a 15-minute visit of at least twice a week and sentenced prisoners are entitled to receive longer visits. In Belgium pre-trial prisoners are entitled to daily visits while sentenced prisoners may receive up to 3 visits. In the Czech Republic foreign prisoners are allowed to receive visits with a total time of 3 hours per month but some persons, like lawyers, representatives of diplomatic missions or NGO's may pay visits without any limitation.

In principle foreign prisoners can be visited by anyone but in most cases the visitors are direct family, partners, legal representatives, representatives from diplomatic missions, religious persons and representatives from NGO's. In some countries there are community organisations that pay social visits to prisoners, including foreigners. Sometimes family members may be unwilling to visit because of their illegal status in the country. In Belgium visitors other than direct family must request first permission from the prison director. Visitors of prisoners in French penitentiary institutions are obliged by law to speak in French but fortunately for visitors from foreign origin this rule is not strictly applied. Further, prisoners under French regime are allowed to attend family events and receive prison leave for weddings, death or in cases of illness as long as it is inside the country. Some Irish prisons have special 'Visitors Centres' that are run by prison staff for families with children that are visiting their relatives in prison. The centre provides tea and coffee facilities in a hospitable atmosphere with a child care area for children and in special cases they try to liaise on behalf of the prisoners and their families with the prison on certain issues. The number of families of foreign prisoners has been on the increase. In the Swedish Kumla Prison provisions are made for visitors from abroad to stay overnight in a local church for around □ 10 per night.

2.7.2 Telephone and correspondence

In practice written correspondence can be problematic because a considerable percentage of prisoners, including foreign prisoners, are unable to write and sometimes read. The fact that foreign prisoners write in a foreign language makes it difficult for prison authorities to censor it when there are security reasons for doing so. In German prisons the regulation that prisoners are not allowed, 'without compelling reason', to write letters in a foreign language, usually excludes letters written by foreigners. In Malta prisoners' correspondence is systematically read and therefore the CPT recommended the Maltese prison authorities in 1995 and in 2001 that 'it would be preferable to provide that, save in exceptional cases, letters may only be examined (rather than read) by prison staff.' In the United Kingdom unconvicted prisoners may send out two free letters per week and convicted prisoners one in order to maintain contact with their relatives.

International calls are expensive and penitentiary institutions often do not take into consideration the different time zones when granting prisoners permission to make a phone call. Many foreign prisoners, especially when they are not involved in work, have insufficient means to call their family abroad. Some penitentiary institutions introduced for this reason free phone cards, an international calling card or created the possibility to make 'collect calls', a system where the person who receives the call is paying. In Belgian prisons this system was recently abolished. Making a phone call is a lengthy process for prisoners in Austrian pre-trial prisons because they have to apply first for a permit to the investigating judge. Calls are only allowed during business hours and there are often not enough telephones available. In Cyprus national prisoners are allowed one telephone call per week whereas foreign prisoners are allowed telephone calls twice a week in order to compensate the fact that they receive fewer visitors. Those who are financially not able to afford a telephone card receive one from the prison authorities.

In Irish penitentiary institutions all prisoners are allowed to make a daily six-minute telephone call free of charge. In Latvia prisoners are only allowed to make 1 to 3 phone calls per month and in Lithuania in principle only 6 to 12 calls a year. In Slovakia and Spain phone calls by prisoners are made in the presence of a prison official. In Sweden listening in to any prisoner's telephone conversation may only occur with the prisoner's knowledge and calls with lawyers may never be monitored. Prisoners in Swedish closed prison settings must apply in writing for approval of each telephone number they wish to call. Before consent is being given first criminal record checks are being conducted. Those persons using a cash card where no physical person is registered are not likely to be approved. Especially for foreign prisoners with family in countries where such cash cards are used this poses a difficulty and also when security checks cannot be conducted on persons living abroad.

Prisoners in Spain cannot receive telephone calls but are allowed to make 5 calls per week of not more than five minutes per call. In Spain there are certain non-governmental organisations that provide not only financial support to foreign prisoners for stamps and telephone calls but also provide mediation between the prisoner and their families. Also in the United Kingdom there are NGO's such as the New Bridge organisation that provides support to foreign prisoners.

2.7.3 Access to news

Prisoners are allowed to keep themselves informed about public affairs by subscribing to and reading newspapers, magazines and by listening to radio and watching television.

Prisoners in Belgian penitentiary institutions are allowed to purchase all newspapers and publications that are legally available. In Cyprus, prisoners receive local newspapers daily on their wing. Foreign prisoners in Czech Republican prisons may receive by mail books, daily press and magazines without any restriction. Each penitentiary institution in Estonia has at least one daily newspaper in Estonian and one in Russian available. Also in Lithuania sentenced prisoners are in theory allowed to spend their money on buying an unlimited number of books and subscribing to newspapers and magazines as long as the publications are not propagating violence and cruelty or contain pornographic publications. In practice however most prisoners have no financial means for this and are depending on their relatives to send parcels with literature. Most Lithuanian institutions are subscribed to some foreign periodicals in Russian and Polish.

In several countries, like Belgium, Lithuania, The Netherlands, prisoners can rent a television that offers many channels, including many foreign languages. In Cyprus and in France only national channels can be watched on television. Libraries in European penitentiary institutions can provide prisoners access to news. Some prison libraries have newspapers and magazines available and sometimes embassies assist in providing foreign periodicals. Although newspapers, books and magazines in foreign languages are officially allowed inside Portuguese prisons, they are hardly available because prison directors often do not authorize them because they are in languages that are not understandable for the officers whose job is to screen them. Libraries in Swedish penitentiary institutions offer a few foreign newsmagazines and 'easy Swedish' papers for those who are learning Swedish. Further are Swedish librarians so kind to print for foreign prisoners the covers of their national newspapers.

Conclusions

- Due to language difficulties and distance from family and relatives many foreign prisoners are disconnected from the outside world and feel socially isolated.
- Prison authorities do not set up normally a more flexible visiting scheme for foreign visitors.
- In Germany prisoners are in principle not allowed to write in a foreign language and in France prisoners are not allowed to speak on the telephone in a language that prison staff can not understand. In Malta prisoners' correspondence is systematically being read by the prison authorities.
- In several penitentiary institutions, prisoners are allowed to watch television with various foreign channels.

2.8 Re-integration activities and Prison leave

Reintegration of prisoners into society is seen in the European Prison Rules as a fundamental focus of penitentiary intervention. European Prison Rule 6 states that 'detention shall be managed so as to facilitate the reintegration into free society of persons who have been deprived of their liberty'. Prison leave offers a natural way in which prisoners can gradually get used to the outside world again and start rebuilding their personal and professional lives. Reintegration activities and prison leaves are for foreign prisoners as important as for other prisoners even if they will be returning to another country.

2.8.1 Re-integration

According to Rule 33.3 of the European Prison Rules 'all prisoners should have the benefit of arrangements designed to assist them in returning to free society after release' and this should be done through a programme of positive care and assistance. In various countries prison authorities work in partnership with community organizations and authorized organizations like Probation in order to facilitate reintegration activities and facilities. In general there are no agencies or authorities specifically concerned with the foreign prisoners after they leave prison.

Educational and vocational training, especially when the training can be continued after release, can be regarded as a reintegration measure. The same applies to work, as long as it maintains or increases prisoners' ability to earn a living after release. In practice however, the lack of education and work in penitentiary institutions make these measures less effective, especially for foreign prisoners who are often not able to participate because of the language barrier. Although foreign prisoners are in principle eligible for placement in reintegration activities in practice they tend to be excluded. The main reasons for this exclusion are that reintegration activities are usually available only on a limited scale and as there are not sufficient places for all prisoners, foreign prisoners are given less priority because they might not return to society in the country of detention. Lastly as these courses tend to be given in semi-open prison settings where less foreign prisoners are allocated. Foreigner prisoners who will be expelled after release are in principle excluded from reintegration activities.

Open penitentiary institutions in Germany specialise in preparing prisoners for release by offering training programmes. In a German study (2002) it became clear that only 10% of all foreign prisoners were placed in such open institutions compared to 28% of all national prisoners. In the Czech Republic there is a similar situation. Although in principle all prisoners should be prepared for resettlement at least three months before release in practice foreign prisoners are often excluded. In Latvia a probation officer visits prisoners six month before release in order to plan and organize their return into society or stay in a halfway house. The State Probation Service started supervision of offenders in society since 2006 and assistance is granted to both national and foreign prisoners. Most probation officers also speak English. In Lithuania 46% of all prisoners participated in resocialisation programmes in 2005 against 23% of the foreign prison population. In order to stimulate the smooth transition from prison to society the Dutch prison service introduced the 'Penitentiary programme'. Motivated prisoners that have served at least five sixths of a sentence of at least 6 months are eligible to participate in this programme and are allowed to work or follow educational classes outside the institution and stay home overnight and during weekends. An additional condition for participation is that the remaining sentence amounts to a minimum of 4 weeks and a maximum of a year. Foreign prisoners are excluded from participation and there are further no reintegration programmes or facilities available.

2.8.2 Prison leave

The system of prison leave is an integral part of the overall regime for sentenced prisoners. According to European Prison Rule 24.7, 'whenever circumstances allow, the prisoner should be authorised to leave prison either under escort or alone in order to visit a sick relative, attend a funeral or for other humanitarian reasons'. Prison leave is also granted in order to facilitate re-integration by for example maintaining family ties, preparing for work or training, arranging legal matters etc.

Foreign prisoners are rarely allowed to leave prison for a certain time, especially when they will be expelled after release. The situation is slightly better for foreigners who are integrated in the country and who have a resident permit. One of the main reasons for this is that prison authorities consider a high risk of escape, especially when foreign prisoners want to avoid expulsion at the termination of their sentence.

During imprisonment prison authorities often do not know whether a prisoner will be expelled or not afterwards. In practice this means that prison authorities and individual prison directors deal with this problem differently. Some prison authorities and prison directors refuse categorically every prison leave in case of uncertainties about expulsion after custody while others let foreigners leave prison even when the immigration authority has not taken its decision yet. A precondition is that foreign prisoners have a secure home or contact address in the country. If the aim of prison leave is not re-integration and if the prisoner has no social contacts in the country, it will hardly be granted.

In Austria, prison leave exists for so-called 'Ausgang', for a maximum of 5 days to organise personal, economic, educational or legal affairs, or 'Freigang' for those prisoners working without surveillance outside the prison. Two-thirds of the national prisoners serving a sentence were granted 'Ausgang' compared to 11% of foreign prisoners. National prisoners are allowed to leave prison on average 3.4 days per 100 days compared to 0.5 days for foreign prisoners. From this group of foreign prisoners EU citizens are granted the lowest number of prison leave days, namely 0.3 per 100 days. Under 'Freigang' only 4% of the foreign prison population left prison for work compared to 31% national prisoners. On average national prisoners worked 10 per 100 days outside prison compared to 1 per 100 days for foreigners.

In Belgium, foreign prisoners who are not registered in the Foreigners' Register in the Population Register or in the EU Register are excluded from systematic prison leave. For those who are registered, the decision will depend on their administrative status. In case of expulsion, only in exceptional cases is prison leave granted but never in the case of extradition. In practice, prison leave is hardly granted to foreign prisoners since around two-thirds of them have no legal permit to stay. Swedish prisons have so-called 'Breathing space leaves' for prisoners serving sentences of two years or more, a category that often includes foreign prisoners. These leaves allow prisoners an annual leave for up to four hours to take part in an activity outside prison, like watching a football match, shopping etc. On these visits prison officials accompany prisoners.

Foreign prisoners in Cyprus, Denmark and Germany may be granted prison leave in case they will not be expelled after release. An exception is made in Germany if prison officials accompany foreign prisoners. A German research study (2002) revealed that 58% of national prisoners compared to 18% of foreign prisoners were granted prison leave. Foreign prisoners with a secure (home) address in the country of detention have a chance in Estonia, Greece, Italy, Malta and The Netherlands to obtain prison leave. The Greek

Ombudsman refers to this severe disadvantage for foreign prisoners in its annual report of 2005. Prison leave in Poland is only granted to foreign prisoners under escort by prison officials, in Lithuania no prison leave was granted to foreigners in 2005 and in Spain only in exceptional cases. Spanish NGO's like 'Horizontes Abiertos' and 'Caritas' are addressing these disadvantages for foreign prisoners by providing secure shelters and dormitories to make prison leave possible. In nearly all penitentiary institutions in Europe foreign prisoners who are awaiting expulsion are not eligible for prison leave.

Conclusions

- Foreign prisoners tend to be excluded from re-integration activities because prison authorities do not want to invest in people that might not return to their own society.
- Foreign prisoners are rarely allowed prison leave, especially when they will be expelled after release.

2.9 Release - Expulsion

Prison authorities are required by the European Prison Rules to prepare prisoners for a successful return into society and to provide them upon release with appropriate documents, financial means and adequate clothing. Prisoners that served their sentence are entitled to be released or granted conditional release (parole) when they have served a part of their sentence. Expulsion from a country can be the result of a criminal penalty or an administrative measure under the Immigration Law. Information on expulsion of foreign prisoners that are solely detained to safeguard their administrative removal can be found in chapter 3.

Foreign prisoners are in theory not exempt from conditional release provisions but in most countries parole is granted less often in comparison to national prisoners. All European countries have legal provisions to expel foreigners that have breached the (immigration) law and this provision is frequently used. The combination of complex and frequently changing criminal and administrative procedures leads to a difficult situation for foreign prisoners, full of uncertainty and anxiety.

2.9.1 (Conditional) Release

On release, the items, documents and personal clothing deposited in the prison will be returned to the prisoner. If the prisoner has no personal clothing or if the prisoner's personal clothing is not suitable for the season, the prison will provide the prisoner to be released with adequate clothing without charge. On release, the deposited savings fund accrued from the funds deposited on the personal account of the prisoner will be handed over to the prisoner. In order to prepare prisoners for release many prison authorities provide leaflets with practical information about housing, work, social insurances, social welfare allowances etc.

In Austria, all prisoners are in theory entitled to parole but in practice prisoners without Austrian citizenship are released on parole slightly less often than nationals. Nationals with a sentence of up to six months are conditionally released twice as often as foreigners whereas nationals and foreign prisoners serving a sentence six to twelve months there are no noteworthy differences. In the case of long sentences, one to three years, foreigners are more often released conditionally. In Belgium, with regards to conditional release there is officially no distinction between national and foreign prisoners but in practice there is. The system that prisoners, serving between one and three years of imprisonment, are provisionally released after serving one third of their sentence is not applicable to foreign prisoners without a legal residence permit.

In Cyprus it is not possible to apply for parole. In Denmark the decision to grant parole is based on the risk assessment of committing a new crime and conditions like appropriate housing and occupation and for example treatment for alcoholism. Foreign prisoners are not excluded from conditional release as long as they have a permanent home address. In Finland, foreign prisoners like national prisoners are granted parole after half or two-thirds of the sentence has been served. In France only 2% of the foreign prison population were granted conditional release in 1998. In Latvia, parole is granted to persons regardless of their citizenship. The application for parole is reviewed by the 'Administrative Commission' that consists of representatives from prison, probation and prosecutors office and by the judge. Although in Lithuania and in Slovakia foreigners are also eligible for parole in practice it is rarely applied. Foreign prisoners that are not subject to a removal order in Malta are treated like national prisoners and can be granted conditional release. In the Netherlands there is no parole or conditional release, it was abolished in 1986 and replaced by early release. Foreign prisoners with valid papers and a permission to stay in the Netherlands are given upon release money to travel to the location where they were arrested. In Poland, foreign prisoners, even those who are to be expelled after serving their sentences, could be released on parole according to general rules. Since the implementation of the Criminal Justice Act 2003 in England and Wales release arrangements for foreign prisoners changed considerably. It is in the majority of cases up to the prison governor to make parole decisions in respect of the 'Early Removal Scheme' (ERS). The ERS, implemented in April 2004, allows eligible foreign prisoners to be removed up to 4 ½ months before their half way release date. Foreign prisoners who appealed against expulsion or who have an outstanding asylum claim cannot be considered under the ERS.

2.9.2 Expulsion

A decision to expel or remove a foreigner after imprisonment varies per country but general criteria are based on: legal status, time spent in the country of detention before conviction, number of offences and the length of the sentence. If the person is seen as a 'danger to public interest', which is usually assumed after a 'considerable' prison sentence, the person will be expelled. Also incorrect information given to the national authorities, lack of financial means, illegal work and other (administrative) offences can lead to a ban on residence.

An expulsion order is in some countries connected to a (long) prison sentence and in some countries it can be imposed as an additional penalty to imprisonment. Foreign prisoners see the imposed expulsion order often as an additional punishment. Execution of the expulsion order has to take place after the basic penalty has been served. Foreign prisoners are entitled to appeal against the removal decision. Expulsion criteria tend to be less restrictive in case a foreigner has been living for a long time in the country of detention and when the person has strong family bonds and is well integrated. The decision of expulsion or removal is normally taken by courts and national immigration authorities and carried out in cooperation with police and border control authorities. Courts and penitentiary institutions provide information on convictions of foreigners and on the end date of the sentence. It is often up to the immigration police to determine whether the prisoner will be detained in special custody for the purpose of removal or not.

Very often expulsion cannot be enforced. Most common reasons for that are; unsafe conditions in country of return, refusal of the country of origin to take back a certain person, the expulsion decision is being legally challenged or an application is made for asylum. Legal remedies against expulsion decisions have normally a suspensive effect. In case execution of the expulsion order cannot be effectuated directly after release from prison, foreign prisoners are normally transferred to detention centres to await their removal. In some countries, like in Ireland, it is possible for foreign prisoners to apply for voluntarily return to the country of origin. The fact that the decision of expulsion or removal is often taken at the end of the detention period is very stressful for foreign prisoners. The uncertainty about what might happen after release aggravates detention.

In Belgium, foreign prisoners with a sentence of at least six months can be expelled after serving their sentence. Re-entry is prohibited for a period of ten years. The decision for expulsion is made by a 'Bureau D', the 'D' stands for detainees in the Office for Foreigners' Affairs (OFA) of the Ministry of Interior. In case foreign prisoners have requested asylum status or regularisation of their irregular status the process of reviewing is being postponed and prisoners can get 'released with a view on expulsion'. The many changes in the already complex expulsion procedures in Belgium over the last years led to dramatic situations were foreign prisoners went on hunger strikes and attempted suicides.

In the Czech Republic, the police execute the penalty of expulsion and can provide the necessary travel documents. Half of all foreign nationals that were sentenced received a penalty of expulsion in 2004. In Denmark, foreign prisoners that will be expelled have to pay for their transport themselves in case they have sufficient means. Expulsion takes place after serving 7/12 of the sentence. This '7/12' rule can be explained by the fact that foreigners who will be expelled are not given temporary prison leave and therefore receive an equivalent reduction in their sentence. In Lithuania, foreigners have to pay for the expenses of removal. In Estonia, foreign prisoners without a residence permit will be expelled upon release. If immediate expulsion from Estonia is not possible, the foreigner will be placed in an expulsion centre upon release. Before Finnish national authorities make a decision of expulsion particular attention is paid to the best interests of children and the protection of family life. Foreign prisoners that are approved asylum seekers or who have a legal residence permit are in principle protected against removal in Germany. In the majority of the German 'Länder' the expulsion is considered after the enforcement of half of the sentence and in some cases two thirds. Greek courts may order expulsion once a foreigner receives a prison sentence of at least one year. Those expelled foreigners may return to Greece three years after their expulsion once they receive permissions from the Minister of Justice. The vast majority of foreigners convicted by the criminal court in Hungary will be expelled. The expulsion order is seen, like in Latvia, as an additional penalty to imprisonment that can be with terminal effect or for a definite period between one and ten years. Besides the criminal court, the alien policing authority also has the right to order expulsion, for example when foreigners breach the provisions of immigration law. In Italy, the 'Penitentiary Police' is charged to transfer foreign prisoners who have a removal order. In Malta, a foreign prisoner that will be expelled is taken to the embassy pending the return to the home country.

Foreign prisoners in Dutch penitentiary institutions that cannot be expelled directly after release from prison are brought to the Aliens Police and put in detention centres until the Dutch Immigration and Naturalisation Service will execute the removal. There is no limit for the duration of the stay. In Slovakia, citizens from the European Economic Area (EEA) can only be expelled if they constitute a threat to the security of the country, public order, or public health. Appealing a decision of expulsion does not always suspend the execution. In Slovenia around 65% of foreign prisoners are expelled. The most common penal sentence imposed on a foreigner in Spain is expulsion. The expulsion order, that prohibits re-entry into Spain for 10 years, has to be applied without delay and within 30 days. In practice the execution of expulsion is complicated and takes much more time. Foreign prisoners that are going to be expelled in Sweden receive 10% of their own savings in cash that were held on a separate account. European Union citizens in the United Kingdom with a prison sentence of over two years, and non-EU nationals receiving a sentence of over one year are usually considered for expulsion. The changes in the parole scheme and the introduction of the ERS in England and Wales (see above) resulted in a higher proportion of foreign nationals being expelled.

Conclusions

- In practice foreign prisoners are granted less often conditional release than national prisoners.
- The decision of expulsion is normally taken by courts and national immigration authorities and carried out in cooperation with police and custom authorities. The decision is often taken at the end of the detention period which creates extra tension for foreign prisoners.
- Very often expulsion can not be enforced because of the unsafe conditions in countries of return, refusal from countries to take back people, or the expulsion decision is legally challenged or an application is made for asylum.

2.10 Aftercare - Probation

In many European countries prisoners who have been released or who will be released shortly receive aftercare support from social welfare organisations, community based organisations and non-governmental organisations. Besides aftercare services most European countries have Probation Services that provide nationwide rehabilitative assistance to (ex-) offenders. Many foreign prisoners cannot make use of this because they have to return upon release immediately to their country of origin or because probation services are not investing in foreign (ex-) offenders. Arranging good aftercare for those that return is difficult. Contacts with social welfare agencies and probation services are often difficult because of language barriers and the fact that there are, besides the 'Conférence Permanente Européenne de la Probation' (CEP), hardly any established links or networks between involved organisations.

Foreign prisoners that remain in the country of detention are in some countries entitled to make use of probation service as long as they have a residence permit and are not under a removal or expulsion order. Although these 'new clients' led to adjustments in the traditional work of some probation services, most probation services are not providing specific programmes for foreigners. Traditional activities of probation services are supervision during conditional release and providing assistance in finding a suitable house, a job training, applying for legal papers, applying for social welfare allowance, helping to re-establish family relations, mediation between victim and offender, etc. The effectiveness of aftercare and probation depends heavily on the language skills of the ex-offender.

2.10.1 Aftercare

Danish juvenile institutions have a 'mentor programme' where an adult from the outside community provides support to young foreign prisoners just before and just after release. In Estonia there are no specific aftercare facilities for foreign ex-offenders. In Finland there are special drugs and alcohol programmes developed for ex-offenders from Russia and Estonia.

In Lithuania provisions are made that foreign ex-offenders with a residence permit can apply for a single social welfare allowance from the municipality upon release. In Portugal the 'Instituto de Reinserção Social' and other social welfare services support the re-integration process of foreign ex-offenders with a residence permit. In the United Kingdom there are several non-governmental organisations, funded through charitable sources and increasingly through contracts with individual prisons that provide specific services to foreigners before and after release. These organisations are; 'Vamos Juntos', assisting Spanish, Portuguese and Latin American prisoners, 'Detention Advice Service', providing specialist immigration advice, 'New Bridge' providing general befriending support and casework and 'Hibiscus', working with Afro-Caribbean and Latin American Women.

2.10.2 Probation

In Belgium, foreign prisoners with a residence permit are entitled to the same support as national citizens but this did not led to specific programmes. The Danish Probation Service has one consultant specialised in the re-integration of ethnic minorities into society. In Estonia there are no specific probation activities for foreigners. There is no probation service for adults in Greece and the public prosecutor of the court that ordered conditional release exercises supervision. In Ireland there is no statutory aftercare for persons completing a sentence, except for prisoners who are granted temporary release with a condition of supervision by the Probation Service. The Linkage Programme, a re-integration initiative, which is supported and funded by the Probation Service has no breakdown of referrals by nationality. In Latvia ex-offenders can stay in one of the eight halfway houses financed by the Probation Service. This facility is open to foreigners but until now no foreign ex-offenders have made use of it. In the plans for the new structure of the Dutch Prison Service there are no special aftercare facilities for foreign prisoners and also the Dutch Probation Service is not able to intervene because local community authorities are responsible for providing aftercare for ex-offenders in their community. Since January 2006 the Swedish Probation Service has been given more responsibilities for providing aftercare. In the United Kingdom, an 'Offender Manager' of the local Probation Service in the area of their home address supervises foreign prisoners that have been released.

Conclusions

- Foreign prisoners that remain in the country of detention after release can make use of aftercare service if they have a residence permit and are not under an expulsion order.
- Probation services do not provide specific programmes for foreigners.

2.11 Staff

Prison authorities should recognise that dealing with prisoners in a professional, humane and personal manner requires effective management and great interpersonal and technical skills from prison staff. Prison staff carries out an important public service and they should be carefully selected, properly trained, paid as professional workers and receive a respected status in society. Prison staff should work under adequate conditions that enable them to maintain high standards in their care of prisoners. Every penal institution should have a proper management structure and sufficient range of specialist staff like psychiatrists, psychologists, doctors, nurses, social workers, pastoral workers, librarians, teachers, sport-instructors, placement officers etc. Over the last decades and especially over the last few years, the increasing presence of foreigners has changed daily prison life. In some prisons more than a quarter of the prisoners are foreigners from various countries around the world. This meant new challenges for prison staff and prison authorities have been responding to this in various ways.

Rule 81.3 of the European Prison Rules states that 'staff who are to work with specific groups of prisoners, such as foreign nationals, women, juveniles or mentally ill prisoners, etc., shall be given specific training for their specialised work. In many countries providing special training for prison staff working with foreign prisoners has not been given priority. One of the most important trainings should be language as good communication between prison staff and foreign prisoners is essential. It is therefore striking that in the recruitment process, a foreign language competence is hardly a required competence. Furthermore prison authorities should acknowledge that cultural characteristics influence persons' interactions in prison and that some staff members might have difficulties in working with persons from different cultures or are prejudiced against foreigners. It would therefore be beneficial if prison authorities provide special courses about the background of certain cultures, cultural habits, religions and also courses like 'how to handle certain situations' etc. For example how to deal with prisoners from more patriarchal cultures that refuse to accept the authority of female prison staff. Or how to assess if prisoners are justifying their behaviour by referring to their religion while infringing the rules.

2.11.1 Training

In Austria, special information about foreign cultures (16 hours) and an English course (32 hours, including technical terminology) are parts of the basic training for new prison staff since 2004. There is also a voluntary and well attended follow-up training that includes courses on migration, globalisation, foreign prisoners, 'Slav Culture' and English language. In Denmark it takes a person three years to become a trained prison official. The biggest part of the education period is practical and takes place in prison and half a year is theory and includes knowledge of society, psychology and conflict solution. The

Dutch Training Institute for prison staff offers a 42days basic training that includes one course on cultural diversity.

In Estonia and Finland there are, besides a language course, no other special trainings to deal with foreign prisoners. In Greece, Hungary, Latvia, Lithuania, Malta and Poland, there are no special language courses for prison staff. In France, Probation staffs receive a nine-hour course on 'foreign nationals' among other specific groups like women, juveniles and elderly people. The last years Portuguese prison authorities have been investing in the security side of prison and did not focus on specific programs and interventions directed to acquiring social competences and dealing with emotional problems. Although there is no legal basis for training in Slovakia, foreign languages and cultural diversity courses are included in the educational programme. In Spain special training courses, particularly for jurists and social workers, are organised by the Prison Service on an annual and voluntary basis. In order to deal with language barriers, special training in different languages is organised in connection with the Spanish Open University (UNED).

The mandatory training for prison staff in Sweden helps staff to acquire skills but also helps the Prison Service to identify individuals that demonstrate undesirable attitudes that conflict with the value system of treating all persons in a humanitarian and non-discriminatory manner. Swedish prison staffs working directly with foreign prisoners participate in a university level course on 'intercultural understanding' and training in 'Diversity and Dialogue'. Although in the United Kingdom prison staff does not receive in their initial training specific programmes for working with foreign prisoners, local or regional training events can be arranged and delivered by non-governmental organisations and others involved in this area of work.

It is remarkable to see that several prison authorities, including countries where staff has often no foreign language competence, do not provide language skills training programmes for their staff.

2.11.2 Diversity

In Belgium, prison staff of foreign origin indicated that the prison administration institutionalised racism by hiring only Belgian citizens and appointing only native Belgian citizens to important functions. Despite the positive influence on foreign prisoners, Belgian prison staff from foreign origin felt that they are not only easily accepted by their colleagues but also were seen as 'traitors' by prisoners from their country of origin. In Denmark only 1% of the prison staff has a foreign background compared to 15% of the prison population. Efforts are being made by the Danish Prison Service to recruit prison staff from various ethnic backgrounds and a pre-school for foreign aspirants was opened in 2006. In German prisons in Hamburg, with a foreign prison population of 40%, so called 'Ausländerberate' or foreigners aides are employed to assist prison staff. In Sweden a study on ethnicity in prisons in 2003 revealed that s staff speaking in a foreign language with prisoners could arouse suspicions amongst other staff since the latter are unable to be sure that the former is not being exploited or manipulated by the prisoner. In order to avoid a sense of insecurity within the work force it is crucial that prison management creates forums for open discussion to prevent that staff loses confidence in each other.

2.11.3 Treatment

In Belgium, foreign prisoners, especially the young ones, refer to the lack of respect by prison officials and that they were seldom granted positions of trust. And although a survey amongst prison directors by the 'Centre against racism and xenophobia' concluded that racism is not very prominent in Belgium prisons, prison staff indicated that there is racism based on nationality amongst prisoners.

Foreign prisoners in Czech prisons indicated that prison staff treated them similar to national prisoners and that sometimes efforts were made to speak in another language than Czech. In Ireland a 'National Action Plan Against Racism' was published in 2005 to mainstream the intercultural strategy within the prison service. The existence of Race Relations Liaison Officers (RRLO), a Race Relations Management Team and a Prisoner Diversity Representative has resulted in good practice in prisons in England and Wales. However, a prison survey in 2005 discovered that black and minority ethnic prisoners 'have worse perceptions of their treatment than white prisoners across many key areas of prison life'. In interviews held in Dutch penitentiary institutions, foreign prisoners indicated that staff in general was qualified, helpful and respectful and the fact that communication was sometimes difficult was accepted as a fact that could not be changed easily. The situation in some Dutch detention centres and detention boats for irregular migrants is less positive because staff are often hired from private security companies and are less qualified and skilled.

Conclusions

- In most European penitentiary institutions staff is not specially trained to work with foreign prisoners.
- Although prison staff is working with foreign prisoners on a daily basis and communication is an important asset of keeping order and safety in prisons, a foreign language skill is not a required competence in the recruitment process of prison staff.
- Some prison authorities, like in Denmark, are recruiting prison staff from various ethnic backgrounds.

2.12 Projects

Prison authorities have seen over the last decades a sharp increase in the number of foreign prisoners in their institutions. Besides prison authorities, individual penitentiary institutions and prison staff also universities, community based organisations, churches and non-governmental organisations have been anticipating and responding to this trend. This section will give an overview of various projects that have been developed and implemented in the various European countries in order to address the special needs of foreign prisoners.

In Austria, a special department for foreigners called the 'Ausländerreferat' was founded in 1989. The aim of this department, with one part-time staff member, is to support and advise foreign prisoners with regard to their special needs concerning language problems and cultural differences. In practice the activities are focused on managing contacts between prisons and diplomatic missions. In Austrian penitentiary institutions there are several projects implemented for foreign prisoners that are organised by individual staff members. The director of the court prison in Linz for example developed with an expert group of representatives of human rights organisations ('SOS-Menschenrechte' and 'Neustart') a '10-point-programme' to address the specific needs of foreign prisoners.

In Belgium the King Boudewijn Foundation financed a research by Professor Sonja Snacken into the situation of foreign prisoners in Belgium. Based on this research several initiatives were taken like solving the delay for foreign prisoners in receiving early release, introducing 'migration counsellors' in prisons and translating information about the new Prison Act.

In the Czech Republic the Institute of Criminology and Social Prevention in Prague carried out a study about foreign prisoners in 2002-2003.

In Danish prisons a mentor programme for young foreign prisoners was introduced in 2000. The mentor is an adult who is not part of the prison system and whose task is to support the released person just before and just after release. This programme received the 'International Community Justice Award' in 2004. In the State Prison of Ringe an evening study was introduced with an Imam and researcher for prisoners with a Muslim background. The Danish Probation Service has one consultant specialised in the re-integration of ethnic minorities into society.

In autumn 2005 the Finnish Prison Service established a working group to study whether ethnic minorities (mainly foreigners and gypsies) in prison, around 12% of the prison population, receive equal treatment.

The French prison administration announced in May 2006 that it would financially support a comprehensive 20 months research into the situation of foreign prisoners.

The University of Bielefeld in Germany recently conducted a study into the problems of foreigners and members of ethnic minorities in prisons. Researchers questioned experts of the federal state ministries and revealed the lack of appropriate programmes.

In Ireland the Irish Commission for Prisoners Overseas (ICPO) together with a commission of the Irish Bishops Conference undertook an evaluation of their family support service for families of prisoners serving sentences overseas. Financial difficulties, lack of clear information, legal support and release assistance were seen as the most significant problems faced by families of prisoners detained abroad. In 2002 the Irish Probation Service at Mountjoy Prison introduced in collaboration with the Education Unit, an inter-agency programme to address the specific needs of foreign prisoners. In 2002 an 'Evaluation of Research and Training Project for Intercultural Awareness' was conducted to determine the nature of intercultural awareness, communication and racial equality within a prison in Dublin. Further there are anti-racism trainings for both staff and prisoners on this topic and it is currently being considered for the main prison in Dublin.

The high percentage of prisoners from Arabic countries led to the appointment of an Egyptian assistant manager in the Maltese Prison Service in order to understand the needs of foreign inmates better.

In 2005 the Dutch Prison Service carried out a 'Foreign Prisoners' survey into the perception of detention by individual prisoners. Although the survey has been completed, it has not been made public yet. In 2002 Dr. Miranda Boone from the Willem Pompe Institute in Utrecht published the study 'Dutch Probation Service & Cultural Diversity'.

Based on good experiences in Wandsworth Prison in the United Kingdom, the Prison Service introduced Foreign National Orderlies to support the work of the Foreign Nationals Co-ordinator and staff in penitentiary institutions. These Orderlies are prisoners that are entrusted to provide support to foreign prisoners. They visit foreign prisoners systematically, provide them with practical information and other support, represent their

views to staff, keep a list of prisoners willing to interpret and help to identify foreign prisoners in need of particular help. Since 1992 the Prison Service hosts biannual meetings with embassies to provide them with the latest information on prison regimes and procedures.
The non- governmental organisation 'Hibiscus' is working over 20 years with female foreign prisoners in various institutions to alleviate the disadvantages they face. 'Hibiscus' has also offices in Jamaica to support the families of Jamaican prisoners and to assist with their resettlement and expulsion. In 'Morton Hall', a prison with the largest proportion of female foreign prisoners, there are two full-time Foreign National Officers and a Foreign Nationals Co-ordinator that have built an extensive international network to ensure the best resettlement provisions. The Prison Service headquarters promotes good practice by sharing initiatives amongst prisons through the provision of a quarterly Foreign Nationals Bulletin and by organising in 2004 a National Foreign National Prisoners Conference.

Besides national language courses there are no specific projects for foreign prisoners in Estonia, Finland, Greece, Hungary, Latvia, Lithuania, Poland, Portugal, Slovenia and Sweden.

Conclusions

- Over the last years, various initiatives have been taken by prison authorities, individual penitentiary institutions, universities, welfare organizations, churches and non-governmental organisations.

3 ADMINISTRATIVE DETENTION OF FOREIGN PRISONERS

Administrative detention, which can be stated as detention of non-citizens for migration related issues, is a common practice in the European countries nowadays. The detention of foreign nationals is an administrative measure and, consequently, not a measure of the penal system. Among the persons who can be subject to detention are asylum seekers regarding their asylum procedure and irregular migrants who are awaiting their removal.[19] The notion of 'irregular migrants' of the last mentioned category is in this text used in reference to the terminology of the EU and the Council of Europe. It is a comprehensive definition for foreigners who are residing in a country without a residence permit. This group includes, *inter alia*, rejected asylum seekers, 'economic refugees', tourists with expired visa dates, victims of human trafficking or - smuggling, foreigners whom residence permits are reversed or not renewed and labour migrants without a work permit. The term 'irregular migrants' is not an unambiguous one, as the terminology in use among European countries differs. While some countries also use the term 'irregular migrants', others speak about 'clandestine' or 'undeclared migrants'.[20]

Relying on only the amount of more then 650.000 removal orders that are being issued in the EU on a yearly basis makes it already presumable that the numbers of aliens

19 Some countries such as the UK do not use the legal term of forced 'removal' of irregular migrants, but instead they talk about 'deportation'. On the European continent the term deportation is often avoided because of the negative associations it brings along and a preference is given to the less emotionally charged term of removal or sometimes expulsion. In this text the term removal will be used following on the Council of Europe and the European Union.

20 For more on the terminology that is in use in Europe see S. de Tapia, *New patterns of irregular migration in Europe*, Strasbourg: Council of Europe Publishing 2003, chapter I p. 13-22.

residing temporarily or permanently in the EU without a valid residence permit are several millions. The tables 2 & 3 below show the number of removal orders that have been issued by the EU countries and also the numbers of the actual removals by the EU countries.[21]

Table 2: The number of return decisions

	2002	*2003*	*2004*	*Totals*
Austria	23.750	22.641	15.511	61.902
Belgium	53.215	52.169	50.000	155.384
Denmark	8.000	8.000	8.000	24.000
Finland	3.526	3.456	3.800	10.782
France	49.124	55.938	50.000	155.062
Germany	143.000	143.000	143.000	429.000
Greece	29.602	29.542	29.776	88.920
Ireland	2.465	2.425	2.866	7.756
Italy	94.995	70.147	70.320	235.462
Luxemburg	1.000	1.000	1.000	3.000
Netherlands	62.000	62.000	62.000	186.000
Portugal	2.000	2.000	2.000	6.000
Spain	56.130	69.773	66.419	192.322
Sweden	18.497	22.656	27.876	69.029
United Kingdom	70.000	70.000	70.000	210.000
Cyprus	1.300	1.300	1.400	4.000
Czech Republic	25.496	29.366	25.317	80.179
Estonia	1.000	1.000	1.000	3.000
Hungary	7.233	7.878	6.911	22.022
Latvia	362	709	286	1.357
Lithuania	556	823	775	1.357
Malta	1.949	970	1.319	4.238
Poland	5.796	5.531	4.275	15.062
Slovenia	6.256	3.917	3.110	13.283
Slovak Republic	1.245	1.591	2.849	5.685
EU-25	668.497.494	667.832	649.810	1.986.139

Source: Member States.

1. *Where no data were provided by the Member States, the Commission has made estimates. Some data may have been amended to take into account other statistical information (for instance the number of persons receiving a negative asylum decision).*
2. *To date no definition of a return decision exists in Community law. Data have been collected on the basis of existing information and data collections.*

21 European Commission, Common standards on return, Memo/05/288, Brussels 1 September 2005, Annexe p. 2 & 4.

Table 3: Number of removed aliens during the period 2002-2004

	Absolute number			*Indexed (2004 = 100)*		
	2002	**2003**	**2004**	**2002**	**2003**	**2004**
Belgium	10.352	9.996	9.647	107	104	100
Denmark	1.627	3.100	3.093	53	100	100
Germany	31.311	30.176	26.807	117	113	100
Greece	45.299	40.930	35.942	126	114	100
Spain	26.257	26.757	27.364	96	98	100
France	10.015	11.692	15.672	64	75	100
Ireland	:	:	:	:	:	:
Italy	33.289	31.013	27.402	121	113	100
Luxembourg	:	:	41	:	:	100
Netherlands	22.579	23.206	5.564	406	417	100
Austria	9.858	11.070	9.408	105	118	100
Portugal	1.991	2.798	3.507	57	80	100
Finland	2.223	2.773	2.775	80	100	100
Sweden	6.854	7.355	11.714	59	63	100
United Kingdom	15.100	21.380	:	:	:	:
EU15	216.755	222.246	178.936			
Czech Republic	4.873	2.602	1.528	319	170	100
Estonia	255	171	101	252	169	100
Cyprus	2.932	3.307	2.982	98	111	100
Latvia	197	375	234	84	160	100
Lithuania	487	846	306	159	276	100
Hungary	3.602	4.804	3.980	91	121	100
Malta	952	847	680	140	125	100
Poland	6.847	5.879	6.042	113	97	100
Slovenia	4.268	3.209	2.632	162	122	100
Slovakia	1.069	1.293	2.528	42	51	100
EU10	25.482	23.333	21.013			
EU25	242.237	245.579	199.949			
Bulgaria	722	814	1.271	57	64	100
Romania	333	500	650	51	77	100
Missing data for the period 2003 - 2004						
M5: Ireland, Luxembourg, The Netherlands, United Kingdom						

Traditionally the treatment of aliens has been regulated by the law of state responsibility. This is why the policies regarding administrative detention of irregular migrants vary strongly between European countries. There is currently no common legislation available in Europe, concerning the forcible return of irregular migrants. However, as more recently, the treatment of aliens has come to be measured against international standards to be found in human rights law, *all* human beings have become subjects of modern international law to the extent that human rights treaties grant rights to individuals that they may enforce directly before an international body, without a link of nationality.[22]

[22] H. Lambert, *The position of aliens in relation to the European Convention on Human Rights*, Strasbourg: Council of Europe Publishing 2006, p. 7.

This paragraph will present a comparative overview with respect to administrative detention policies in 25 EU countries.[23] The focus will be on the following topics; institutions and capacity, the responsible Ministry and legislation, length of stay, the decision procedure, appeal and review, irregular stay, data and the non-expelled foreigners, detention irregulars under criminal law and minors which will be hold to the light of relevant European legislation relating to the topic that is being discussed.

3.1 and 3.3 Institutions and capacity

Foreigners who are caught for their irregular stay are taken to places where they are detained, awaiting their removal. The most important reason for detention is 'deterrence' as it is considered to prevent people coming to European countries by irregular channels. In all of the EU countries these places are guarded institutions on which various terms are in use by European bodies. Among these terms are detention facilities, detention -, holding, - reception, - expulsion, and removal centres. Notions in national legislation are very different, too. For example, in Germany, a 'detention centre' is called *'Abschiebungshaftanstalt'*, i.e. an 'institution of 'imprisonment pending deportation'. In Italy a 'detention centre' is called *'Centro di Permanenza Temporanea e Assistenza'*, i.e. 'Centre of Temporary Permanence and Assistance. In the UK and in France they are named 'immigration removal centres' and *'centres de rétention'*.[24] Though there are countries with special detention centres for these foreigners, others accommodate them in police stations, penitentiary institutions, transit zones or in prisons. A combination of the various institutions does also occur in several countries.

EU countries with special detention centres for foreigners are, *inter alia*, Italy, Slovenia, the Czech Republic, Slovakia and Poland.

In Slovenia detained illegal residents are accommodated in so-called Illegal Residents Centres of which there are two in the country, with a total capacity of 160 places. The detention measures used for illegal residents differ by the degree of security applied and the restrictions placed on the freedom of movement. Besides the Illegal Residents Centres, they can also be placed in a social care facility or in the rigorous police supervision division within the Illegal Residents Centre. The Czech Republic has four administrative detention facilities for foreigners. With regard to Slovakia, it can be said that there are two special detention facilities for foreign administrative detainees which can accommodate up to 500 foreigners at one time in total. Poland holds administrative detainees in guarded centres for foreigners or detention centres for the purpose of expulsion. Exceptionally, if there are obstacles that make it impossible to escort or admit a foreigner to the guarded centre or to the detention centre for the purpose of expulsion, he or she may be temporarily placed in the separate facilities for detainees of the police or the border guard. In practice there is one guarded centre for foreigners which has a capacity of 131 persons (further guarded centres for foreigners are planned to be taken into operation in the near future) and over 20 expulsion-detention centres (with each a capacity between the 20 and 50 persons).

---

[23] Bulgaria and Romania, which joined the EU in January 2007, have not been part of the research.

[24] Observation and Position Document: *Detention in Europe. Administrative detention of asylum seekers and irregular migrants*, Jesuit Refugee Service Europe 2004 p. 32-35.

Luxembourg, Finland and Northern Ireland which do not face large numbers of irregular migrants, have all created one unit for administrative aliens detention. The unit in Finland has a capacity of ca. 40 detainees, as this number is 11 for Northern Ireland. Greece has only a small number of special centres for foreigners, which results in that every police station detention room – all over the country – constitutes *de facto* an institution of administrative detention for foreign nationals. Neighbouring Cyprus has detention cells in all districts, of which some are specially designated for the detention of foreigners and others hold foreigners together with penal offenders. This last mentioned practice also happens in Ireland, as it is the only country which does not have a separate location for aliens detention. Administrative detainees are placed in two prisons in Dublin where they have access to the same facilities as the prisoners.

Among the countries, which make use of the last mentioned category, which is a combination of several institutions are the Netherlands, Germany and the UK.
The Netherlands detains yearly over 20.000 irregular migrants on the basis of the Immigration Law. This is done in police stations, penitentiary institutions, detention boats and detention centres. The enforcement of the detention is similar as of criminal detention based on the Penitentiary Principles Act. The total capacity of aliens detention in 2007 will be over 3000 divided over ten institutions, five of these are boats with a capacity of 1732 in total. Germany has three different models for the accommodation of detainees pending expulsion: allocation to special establishments for the administrative detention of illegal residents; in regular penitentiary institutions ('Justizvollzugsanstalt', JVA) or in special departments of such a JVA. In Germany, roughly 2250 foreign detainees awaiting removal can be accommodated. In the UK detainees can be held in Immigration Removal Centres (of which there are ten), prisons, police stations, short term holding centres at ports, screening units and appealing hearing centres. The Detention Centre Rules 2001 provide a comprehensive set of rules and procedures covering the treatment of those held under detention. It should also be noted that in the UK it is possible for detainees to apply for bail and that the Home Office may agree to temporary release from removal, subject to a restriction order which will include the requirement to live at a specified address and report to the authorities at specified intervals.

There are two countries which also provide for accommodation in special open units for those awaiting their removal. These are Sweden and Austria. In Sweden, detainees who are not escape prone can be placed in these units, in which activities are designed to prepare foreigners for their departure from Sweden and reintegration into their home country. As it considers Austria, it can be said that the revised law of 1 January 2006 has explicitly introduced these units for the first time and that it is not a binding rule yet.

As shown in this subparagraph, all of the countries use detention as the only measure for foreigners who are awaiting their removal. There is no question of the use of alternative non-custodial measures by the countries, with the exception of a few. These alternatives are promoted by article 14 (1) of the Commission Proposal Returns Directive as well as by Guideline 6 (1) of the Twenty Guidelines on forced return (hereinafter Guidelines). According to the first mentioned article, temporary custody shall be only used when there are serious grounds to believe that there is a risk of absconding and where it would not be sufficient to apply less coercive measures such as regular reporting to the authorities, deposit of a financial guarantee, handing over documents, an obligation to stay at a designated place or other measures to prevent that risk.[25]

The types of institutions in which the foreigners are kept differ among the countries, but most of the countries have created special detention centres for foreigners who are awaiting their removal. The CPT has pointed out in its Standards what its expectations are from these centres:

> *'Obviously, such centres should provide accommodation which is adequately furnished clean and in a good state of repair, and which offers sufficient living space for the numbers involved. Further, care should be taken in the design and layout of the premises to avoid as much as possible any impression of a carceral environment. As regards regime activities, they should include outdoor exercise, access to day room and to radio/television and newspapers/magazines, as well as other appropriate means of recreation (e.g. board games, table tennis). The longer the period for which persons are detained, the more developed should be the activities which are offered to them'.*[26]

The reports of the CPT on EU countries are mainly critical about the conditions under which foreigners are detained. Points of critique are mainly on the lack of medical care, overcrowding, access to legal aid and activities. In some countries, such as the Netherlands, Malta and France, the treatment of irregular migrants who are administratively detained is worse than that of prisoners who are detained on a criminal basis. Holding detainees in police stations and prisons as done by certain countries is in contravention of the CPT Standards. These state that:

> *'Prolonged deprivation of liberty in police stations in mediocre material conditions and without activity is entirely inappropriate. Nor is it acceptable to hold immigration detainees in prisons, even when actual conditions of detention are adequate. This is a fundamentally flawed approach as a prison is by definition not a suitable place in which to detain someone who is neither convicted nor suspected of a criminal offence'.*[27]

Conclusions

- Foreigners are detained in guarded institutions on which various terms are in use by European bodies and countries.
- The majority of countries accommodate detainees in special detention centers, but police stations, prisons, penitentiary institutions and transit zones are in use as well.
- Treatment of irregular migrants who are administratively detained is often worse than that of ordinary prisoners.
- Overcrowding, lack of medical care/legal aid, unqualified staff are widespread and religious-cultural requirements are not always respected.
- Alternative non-custodial measures are not in use, except by a few countries such as the UK, Sweden and Austria.

---

[25] For the notion 'detention of illegally staying third-country nationals', the EU Commission is referring to 'temporary custody of a third-country national'.

[26] CPT Standards, Chapter IV Foreign nationals detained under aliens legislation, under point 29. Guideline 10 (2) corresponds with this point.

[27] Ibid under points 27 & 28.

3.2 The responsible Ministry and legislation

As administrative detention is not a measure of the penal system, it is in general not based on the Criminal Laws of the countries. All of the countries have specific legislation relating to the grounds, procedure and regime of the detention of foreigners.
Among the EU countries, the Ministry of Interior is often the responsible Ministry for the administrative detention of foreigners. This goes for the following EU countries:

- Hungary: Alien Policing Act, Alien Policing Detention Decree;
- Austria: Police Detention Order, Decrees on Police Detention, § 4 AnhO , Law of 1 January 2006;
- Belgium: Law of 15 December 1980 on Foreigners (which is modified and enhanced by the Laws of 6 May 1993/15 July 1996 and 29 April 1999), Royal Decree of 8 October 1981 on Foreigners and the Royal Decree of 2 August 2002 which lays down the operational rules of detention centres;
- The UK: Immigration Act 1971 schedule 2 & 3 and the Immigration and Asylum Act 1999 section 10;
- Slovakia: Foreigners Act;
- Portugal: Law 60/93 of 3 March 1993;
- Slovenia: Illegal Residents Act of 1999, amended in 2005, Regulations on the implementation of the Illegal Residents Act 1991, Regulations on special conditions for the accommodation and movement of illegal residents in the Illegal Residents Centre, and on grounds and the procedure for the use of lenient measures 2000;
- Poland: 2003 Act on Illegal Residents;
- Czech Republic: Act No. 326 of 30 November 1999 on Residence of Foreigners and Amendment to Some Acts (Aliens Act);
- Estonia: Foreigners Act, Obligation to Leave and Prohibition on Entry Act;
- Lithuania: Law on the Legal Status of Aliens;
- France: CESEDA, Book V, Title V, Decree N° 2004-1215 from 17 November 2004, Decree N° 2005-617 from May 2005;
- Germany: Immigration Law of 2005 *(Zuwanderungsgesetz)*, of which the Residence Act *(Aufenhaltsgesetz)* is a part of. It is completed by a number of further laws, which are either Federal or Regional Law *(Landesrecht)*;
- Italy: Immigration Law 1998 *(Decreto legislative n. 286/1998)* to which the 2002 Immigration and Asylum Bill *(or Bossi-Fini Law)* brought about further changes.

Regarding the three islands Ireland, Malta and Cyprus can be said that in Ireland the Ministry of Justice, Equality and Law Reform is responsible for the administrative detention of foreign prisoners and the rules are laid down in the Immigration Act 1999. Malta has a co-responsibility between the army and the police (army - Office of Prime Minister, police -Ministry of Justice and Home Affairs). To overcome this inter-ministerial responsibility, it was deemed more appropriate to have a single authority headed by an army colonel administering the closed centres. The law that covers the detention is the Immigration Act of 1970. In Cyprus the police detention cells are under the supervision of the chief of the police department which in turn is supervised by the Ministry of Justice and Public Order.

Aliens detention in the Netherlands is enforced by the Ministry of Justice (the Immigration and Naturalization Service) based on the Immigration Law. The ways for enforcement are determined by the Penitentiary Principles Act.[28] In Luxembourg detention is based on the Law on the entry and stay of foreigners, the medical control of foreigners and foreign labour.

With respect to the Scandinavian EU countries the following is the case: in Denmark the competent superior authority is the Ministry for Refugees, Immigrants and Integration, which is often simply called the Ministry of Integration. When a foreigner is confined by force he/she is under the authority of the Department of Prisons and Probation. The legal possibilities of depriving a foreigner of his liberty are mentioned in the Code on Foreigners. In Sweden, the Migration Board, subordinate to the Ministry of Foreign Affairs has the responsibility and is the detention based on the Aliens Act and Regulations of the Migration Board specific to its fields of operations. In neigbouring country Finland the Custody Unit, subordinate to the Ministry of Labour is the responsible institute. The relevant legislation is the Aliens Act (301/2004), Act on the Treatment of Aliens in Custody and on a Custody Unit (116/2002).

For the three last EU countries Greece, Spain and Latvia, the following Ministries have respectively the responsibility; the Ministry of Public Order (Foreigners Act, 3386/2005), the General Direction of Police (Foreigners Act, partly introduced by OA14/2003 - and Regulation, Royal Decree 2392/2004), since 2002 the State Border Guard and Office of Citizenship and Migration Affairs (Immigration Law 2003).

As shown above, all of the countries have separate laws regarding foreigners, which for example state the grounds for detention. The availability of the specific laws is relevant as according to article 5 (1) ECHR detention is permitted 'in accordance with a procedure prescribed by law' and for the exclusive purposes enumerated therein. With regard to administrative detention, article 5 (1)f ECHR is relevant as it permits the lawful arrest or detention of a person to prevent his effecting an unauthorized entry into the country or of a person against whom action is being taken with a view to deportation and extradition. The Court has ruled that a procedure prescribed by law implies the notion of a fair and proper procedure which means a procedure conducted by an appropriate authority and free from arbitrariness.[29] In the *Amuur*[30] judgment the Court has interpreted this requirement to mean that the domestic law authorising the deprivation of liberty "must be sufficiently accessible and precise, in order to avoid all risk of arbitrariness". It must also be of "sufficient quality ', i.e. it must offer possibilities for judicial review, provisions setting time limits and access to legal assistance, humanitarian and social assistance.[31] In 2002, the Court has recalled these principles and cited that: 'where the lawfulness of the detention is in issue, including the question whether a procedure prescribed

28 In 2002, a new function of Minister for Immigration and Integration was established. The Minister had not an own Office, but was a part of the Ministry of Justice. Under the new government that is formed in 2007, the function of Minister for Immigration and Integration is cancelled and the immigration policy placed under the responsibility of the State Secretary of Justice.

29 A.M. Gallagher, H. Ireland, N. Muchopa, *Handbook for visitors and workers in Detention Centres,* Brussels: Jesuit Refugee Service Europe 2006, p. 64. *Winterwerp v. the Netherlands*, judgment of 24 October 1979, para. 45.

30 *Amuur v. France*, judgment of 25 June 1996, para. 53.

31 H. Lambert, *The position of aliens in relation to the European Convention on Human Rights*, Strasbourg: Council of Europe Publishing 2006, p. 19.

by law has been followed, the ECHR refers essentially to the obligation to conform to the substantive and procedural rules of national law, but it requires in addition, that any deprivation of liberty should be in keeping with the purpose of article 5, namely to protect the individuals from arbitrariness'. [32]

Other legislation which state the principle of legality are the Guidelines 2 & 6 which are based on article 5 (1) ECHR and also article 14 European Prison Rules.

Conclusions

- Ministry of Interior is often the responsible one for administrative detention.
- Administrative detention is in general not based on the Criminal Laws of the countries.
- All countries have specific regulations relating to administrative detention of foreigners.
- European legislation prescribes the principle of legality of the detention of which the main purpose is to protect the individuals from arbitrariness.

3.4 Length of stay

The length of stay in administrative detention varies among EU countries, with some countries setting a low time limit and others not even having a fixed duration. The table below provides an idea of the maximum period under which migrants are held in administrative detention under the national laws of EU member states.[33]

---

32 *Conka v. Belgium*, judgment of 5 February 2002, para. 39.

33 The source for the table is A.M. Gallagher, H. Ireland, N. Muchopa, *Handbook for visitors and workers in Detention Centres*, Brussels: Jesuit Refugee Service Europe 2006, p. 30. The last two countries in the rows; Estonia and Cyprus were not mentioned in the 'Handbook' and are added according to the information from the country reports. For some countries the information from the Handbook does not correspond with what is discussed in the country reports. These deviations are placed in the third column.

Table 4

Country	*Length of stay*	*Deviations according to the country reports*
Denmark	72 hours	-
Finland	4 days (in police stations); 8 days (aliens centre)	No fixed duration of time, in practice the limit is 3 months
Sweden	10 days	Up to 2 months when an expulsion decision is taken and the person is believed to be a risk
Hungary	1 month	Depending on the type of detention, the maximum can be extended up to 12 months
France	32 days	-
Spain	40 days	-
Portugal	60 days	-
Austria	60 days	-
Italy	60 days	-
Ireland	8 weeks (for those facing removal)	
Greece	3 months	
Luxembourg	3 months	
Slovenia	6 months (migrants)	
Belgium	5 months	When necessary detention can be prolonged to the absolute maximum of 8 months
Lithuania	180 days	No fixed duration of time, average term is 63 days, but there are many cases of persons who spend 1 or 2 years in detention
Slovakia	180 days	-
Czech Republic	180 days	-
Poland	1 year	-
Germany	18 months	-
Malta	18 months	-
Latvia	20 months	-
UK	Indefinite (no maximum prescribed by law)	-
Netherlands	Indefinite (no maximum prescribed by law)	-
Estonia	-	4 months
Cyprus	-	No information available

As shown in table 4, there are quite some countries which have time limits that can lead to a long period of detention. When a foreigner can be easily send out of the country, there is no need for such a long period of detention. However, it is often the case that certain conditions are not fulfilled which lead to difficulties and makes the removal of the foreigner impossible. Among these difficulties are that the foreigner does not have a passport or another document which can be used to leave the country, is hiding his/her nationality and that there is no embassy or consulate residing of the country of origin from which documents can be obtained.[34] In these situations foreigners are detained for long periods of time, while the prospect of removal is actually unrealistic. The result of such hopeless cases is that the foreigners are eventually being released from detention. This does not mean they are safe outside, as they face the risk of being caught again for their irregular stay in the country.

The ECHR makes no specific mention of time limits for administrative detention. However, the Court developed case law regarding the just mentioned practice in countries. The Court has recalled in the *Chacal*[35] judgment that any deprivation of liberty under article 5 para. 1(f) will be justified only for as long as deportation proceedings are in progress. If such proceedings are not prosecuted with due diligence, the detention will cease to be permissible under article 5 para. 1(f). It is thus necessary to determine whether the duration of the deportation proceedings was excessive. [36] Guidelines 7 & 8 are laid down following the case law of the Court on article 5 para. 1(f). Contrary to the ECHR and the Guidelines, the Commission Proposal Returns Directive does set a time limit, as it states in article 14 (4) that 'temporary custody may be extended by judicial authorities to a maximum of six months'.

Conclusions

- Various time limits in countries, with some setting a low limit and others not even having a fixed duration.
- Uncertainty about length of stay.
- Uncertainty about the future, especially when removal can not be realized.
- The ECHR has no specific time limit, but the Court stated that has to be determined whether the duration is excessive.
- The Commission Proposal Returns Directive sets a limit of six months.

3.5 The decision procedure

As the EU countries have specific legislation relating to the grounds and procedure of administrative detention, they also differ with regard to the question on who is responsible for taking the decision on detention. On this ground, a classification in 3 categories can be made. Under the first category can be placed, the countries where the administrative authorities decide on detention, which are usually the foreigners or border police, and no judicial check takes place within a few days. The second category of countries is the one in which the administrative authorities also decide on detention, but where a con-

---

[34] There is also the principle of non-refoulement that has to be respected by countries, see above footnote 16.

[35] *Chacal v. The United Kingdom*, judgment of 15 November 1996, para. 113.

[36] See also *Shamsa v. Poland,* judgment of 27 November 2003, in which case the Polish authorities continued to try to enforce the deportation order without any legal basis even though the statutory time-limit had expired. The Court noted that there was no domestic decision or provision which laid down the conditions for such detention. Accordingly, Polish legislation did not fulfill the requirement of "foreseeability" for the purposes of Article 5 (1) ECHR.

trol within a short time does take place by the judiciary. The last category consists of countries which detain foreigners by court order.

Slovakia, Slovenia, the Netherlands, the UK, Ireland and Greece, Belgium, Malta are among the countries which belong to the first category. Under the second category there are, *inter alia*, Lithuania, Finland, Denmark and France.

In Lithuania a foreigner may be detained for a period of over 48 hours on court order on the delegation of the officer of the law enforcement institution. In Finland the police and border guards take the decision for detention after which the District Court decides on further detention. The assessment of the justification and necessity of detention is performed by the District Court at the latest within 4 days from the apprehension under section 124 of the Aliens Act. Also in Denmark the police are the responsible authority for the execution of all expulsions and at the same time the competent authority to decide whether or not a foreigner should be detained. Detention for the purpose of ensuring a person's presence for the time when an expulsion is to be executed (pursuant to article 36 of the Code on Foreigners) must be brought before a local court within 72 hours from the moment when the person is locked up. In France, administrative detention is been decided on by the préfet, who within the first 48 hours must request from the 'judge of liberties and detention' ("juge des libertés et de la détention" – JLD) the authorisation for the prolongation of detention by 15 more days. Once the 17 days have expired, the préfet may request a new extension of up to 15 days. Regarding the 'Waiting Zones' in France, it can be said that the stay is evaluated after 72 hours by a judge who will decide on its prolongation.

Portugal, Spain, Germany and Estonia belong to the last category. In these countries foreigners have to appear before a judge who may decide to place them in detention.

The States' power to detain foreigners is not unlimited. According to article 5 (1) ECHR, detention is permitted when it is 'in accordance with a procedure prescribed by law' and for the exclusive purposed enumerated therein (article 5 para. 1 (f) ECHR for administrative detention). What is meant with this article is already discussed in § 3.2 and is also relevant within the context of the decision procedure. In addition is to be mentioned the *Shamsa*[37] judgment, in which the Court pointed out that detention for several days which has not been ordered by a court or judge or any other person authorized to exercise judicial power can not be regarded as "lawful" within the meaning of article 5 (1) of the ECHR. Also article 14 (2) of the Commission Proposal Returns Directive underlines the importance of the judiciary regarding detention as it states that:

> *'Temporary custody orders shall be issued by judicial authorities and that in urgent cases they may be issued by administrative authorities, in which case the order shall be confirmed by judicial authorities within 72 hours from the beginning of the temporary custody'*

The practice in use by most of the countries, by which in general the administrative authorities issue the detention order, is not in accordance with the case law of the Court nor with article 14 (2) of the Commission Proposal Returns Directive.

Conclusions

- General practice is that administrative authorities decide on administrative detention.
- In certain countries there is no judicial check within a few days.

[37] See footnote 36.

- In Portugal, Spain, Germany, Estonia foreigners have to appear before a judge who may decide on detention.
- The case law of the Court and the Commission Proposal Returns Directive underline the importance of the judiciary regarding detention.

3.6 Appeal and review

Regarding the right of the foreigner to challenge the decision for detention, it can be said that the greater part of the EU countries provide appeal procedures through courts. That the case can be appealed does not mean in certain countries that foreigners are always enabled to make fully use of their right. This has, *inter alia*, to do with a short period of time that is given for appealing, which makes preparing the case very difficult. Examples are Poland and Cyprus, where an appeal against the decision for detention can be filed, respectively before the Regional Court and Supreme Court, within seven days of said decision. Lithuania provides ten days for appealing to the Supreme Administrative Court. In France, the appeal against the decision of the JLD to prolong the length of detention ("appel 35bis") is to be filed before the "cour d´appel - CA". To contest the legality of the removal decision, in most of the cases, it deals with a "préfectoral arrêté" against which an appeal before the administrative court (TA) ("recours 22bis") is possible within 48 hours.

In Slovenia, Denmark and Malta the administrative agencies decide upon appeal. In the first two countries the appeal does not have a suspensive effect and thus the execution of the order to remove the foreigner can be enforced immediately, which renders the right of appeal meaningless. In Slovenia it is the Ministry of Interior that takes the decision upon appeal. The illegal resident can file a lawsuit against this decision which is then decided on by the Administrative Court (Illegal Residents Act, Art. 58). In Denmark an appeal can be lodged with the Ministry of Integration. Just like Slovenia and Denmark, also in Slovakia an appeal does not have suspensive effect. Hereby, the country has no time limit for a court to decide on the appeal. The Maltese Immigration Act provides for an Immigration Appeals Board to rule on excessive length of detention. Since February 2005 the Board has been able to grant release from custody, but the Immigration Act severely restricts the cases where the Board can authorize release.

Until 2006, Sweden also belonged to the countries where appeals are made to administrative agencies. From 31 March 2006 on, three Migration Courts and a Migration Court of Appeal replaced the Aliens Appeal Board. In Finland it is not possible for the foreigner to appeal the decision of the District Court, which assesses the detention within four days from the apprehension on.

Interrelated with the right to appeal a case, is the right to have access to legal assistance. Even though foreigner can appeal a decision, this right has not much of meaning for them without access to legal aid. Detained foreigners are vulnerable and can not be expected to know how to exercise their rights. It is essential that they obtain effective legal assistance and are advised about their position. Most of the countries guarantee providing legal aid, but in practice this is not always the case. The detainees are mainly dependent on the assistance they get from international organizations and NGO's, who are active in this field.

Article 5 (4) ECHR states that:

> *Everyone who is deprived of his liberty by arrest or detention shall be entitled to take proceedings by which the lawfulness of his detention shall be decided speedily by a court and his release ordered if the detention is not lawful*[38]

This right applies to all forms of deprivation of liberty, including administrative detention. The crucial elements of the obligation in this provision are that:[39]

- The legality of the detention must be determined by a court which is independent and impartial.[40] Appeals to executive bodies do not constitute a sufficient remedy for the purposes of challenging the lawfulness of deprivations of liberty, as in the case of Slovenia, Denmark and Malta;
- The court must have the power to review both the procedural and substantive grounds for the deprivation of liberty and be empowered to make a binding order for release of the detained person in the event that his or her deprivation of liberty is unlawful;
- Every person deprived of his/her liberty is entitled to have the lawfulness of the continued detention subjected to periodic reviews for the purpose of testing whether the reasons for the deprivation of liberty remain valid. Article 14 (2) of the Commission Proposal Returns Directive is conform to this point as it states that 'temporary custody orders shall be subject to review by judicial authorities at least once a month;
- The detained person must be allowed access to legal assistance which goes beyond the preparation of a claim and entails representation in the court proceedings. [41] This right also implies that the detainee must have access to all relevant information concerning his/her case (equality of arms). The general practice is that the countries do not provide for legal assistance where the detainees are entitled to. As mentioned above, the detainees are mainly dependent on the assistance they get from international organizations and NGO's, who are active in this field. The short time of period for appealing that some countries prescribe does not allow the detainee to have a fair opportunity for preparing his/her case;
- The court must act without delay/speedily. What is considered to be 'without delay' or 'speedily' depends on the circumstances of each case.[42] A delay must not be unreasonable and a lack of resources or vacation periods are not acceptable justifications for delay. The situation in Slovakia, where there is no time limit for a court to decide on the appeal, and the practice is two or three months, is not acceptable within the context of article 5 (4) ECHR.

---

38 Guideline 9 (1) corresponds with article 5 (4) ECHR and follows from the case law of the Court relating to this article.

39 M. Macovei, *The right to liberty and security of the person. A guide to the implementation of Article 5 of the European Convention on Human Rights,* Strasbourg: Council of Europe Publishing 2002, p. 60-66. Chapter 5 Human Rights and Arrest, Pre-Trial and Administrative Detention in *Human Rights in the Administration of Justice: A Manual on Human Rights for Judges, Prosecutors and Lawyers.*

40 See Eur. Ct. *Al Nashif v. Bulgaria,* judgment of 20 June 2002.

41 Eur. Ct. *Woukam Moudefo v. France,* judgment of 11 October 1988 and Eur. Ct. *Megyeri v. Germany,* judgment of 12 may 1992.

42 See Eur. Ct. *Ilowiecki v. Poland,* judgment of 4 October 2001.

Other relevant articles within the context of judicial remedies are article 12 of the Commission Proposal Returns Directive and also Guideline 5. Both of them mention, *inter alia*, that an effective remedy should be offered to the detainee which has a suspensive effect. This is currently not the case in Slovenia and Denmark.

Conclusions

- Most of the countries provide appeal procedures through courts.
- Inadequate possibilities for judicial review by, *inter alia*, given a short period of time for appealing as is the case in Poland, Cyprus and France.
- In Slovenia, Denmark and Malta the administrative agencies decide upon appeal, which is according to the Court not a sufficient remedy for the purposes of challenging the lawfulness of the detention.
- An appeal does not have suspensive effect in Slovenia, Denmark and Slovakia.
- Legal aid is guaranteed by the states, but in practice the detainees are mainly dependent on assistance from international organizations and NGO's.

3.7 Irregular stay

With regard to the question if an irregular stay is a criminal offence, it can be said that for the greater part of the EU countries the illegal/irregular stay itself is not a crime. This means that the foreigner cannot be detained on a criminal basis for staying in the country without having the required valid documents (these countries are Portugal, Slovenia, Malta, Sweden, Hungary, Denmark, Poland, the Netherlands, Lithuania and Greece). Though an irregular stay is not a criminal offence, this does not mean that acts related to the irregular stay, such as producing false documents, illegal entry and not leaving the country while declared a 'persona non grata' (the Netherlands, 197 Penal Code) are not punishable in these countries. Also in Slovakia the illegal stay itself is not a criminal offence, but if someone has been issued with a decision on expulsion and he/she does not leave the country despite of this fact, he/she can be charged of a criminal offence for not respecting an official decision. This is different in Denmark where not leaving the country as ordered by the court is not seen as a crime and may be executed by the police.

In Germany, Finland, Ireland, France and Cyprus an irregular stay does constitute a criminal offence. Finland criminalized an illegal stay in the country as an intentional crime which makes its punishable with fines. Under the Immigration Act 2004, illegal/irregular stay in Ireland is a criminal offence on 2 grounds and the maximum penalty is 12 months imprisonment (Section 4 (2) and Section 6 (1) of the Immigration Act 2004). In addition persons can be detained on remand for immigration related reasons under the Criminal Justice Act 2001. Not having a permanent or temporary residence permit, refusal to board a plane during removal, use of false identities, refusal to give identity or nationality to oppose removal, false weddings, etc. are criminal offences in France. More than 200 immigration related offences lead to removal. An irregular migrant - illegal entry or stay - can be handed a prison sentence of up to one year. According to Cypriot law illegal residence can be punished with up to 2 years in prison. As it considers Estonia, it can be noted that § 260 of the Penal Code of the country states that a foreigner who is detected in the country at least twice within a year without having a legal basis for his/her stay shall be punished by a pecuniary punishment or up to one year of imprisonment.

Currently, there is no one who is being punished in prisons or the expulsion centre according to this paragraph.

Conclusions

- Irregular stay itself is not a criminal offence for the majority of the EU countries, though the criminalization of 'illegal immigration', particularly to create offences punishable by prison sentences, is problematic.
- In Germany, Finland, Ireland, France and Cyprus an irregular stay does constitute a criminal offence.

3.8 - 3.10 Data and the non-expelled foreigners

The number of arrivals of irregular migrants on Europe's Southern shores has increased immensely in 2006. Countries such as Spain, Italy, Malta and Greece are at the front and bear the brunt, however all European countries are facing the problems, in particular due to secondary movements of these arrivals.[43] As a consequence of the large number of arrivals also the detention of foreigners, who are awaiting their removal, is increased. This appears not only from the facilities in several EU countries which are overcrowded and unsuitable, but also from the expansion of detention capacity in some countries. Currently, there are no exact data available about the number of detainees in Europe, because of the fact that not all of the countries register them. Yet on the grounds of data, which are partially available, the number of detainees in Europe may be in the 100.000 persons per year.[44]

As there are no exact data available about the number of detainees, this also counts for the foreigners who are actually being removed after being in administrative detention. There are many countries which do not have statistics available, while others give mainly estimates on the numbers. From a comparison between the data on removals and on return decisions for the period 2002-2004 (which are given in tables 2 & 3), the European Commission concludes that only one third of the return decisions are effectively implemented and result in removal.[45] Then the question rises, what happens with the rest?

The general practice of the European countries with regard to foreigners who are not removed from the country is that they are released, either by court order or after the end of the maximum period of time for detention in the concerning country, and ordered to leave the country on their own account. This goes for; *inter alia*, Greece, Italy, Spain, the Netherlands, Germany, Slovakia, Finland and Austria. However, for many foreigners returning to the country of origin is not an option.[46] What remains is staying in the concerning country, where he/she faces the risk of being detected again by the police and subsequently detained, or travelling to other EU countries, which are among the foreign-

43 Parliamentary Assembly Council of Europe, Mass arrival of irregular migrants on Europe's Southern shores, Doc. 11053, 3 October 2006.

44 Observation and Position Document: *Detention in Europe. Administrative detention of asylum seekers and irregular migrants*, Jesuit Refugee Service Europe 2004.

45 European Commission, Common standards on return, Memo/05/288, Brussels 1 September 2005, p. 5.

46 The International Organization for Migration (IOM) has programmes for assisting migrants in voluntary return to their country of origin. For more see www.iom.int.

ers known as countries where it is easy to get documents and work, where occasionally large numbers of irregular migrants are being regularized and where illegal residence - and labour are checked to a limited extent. Within this context, countries as France, Spain, Italy and Belgium, are being mentioned.[47] Moving to another EU country, is in many occasions not a solution as again the risk of detention and removal exists. This way many foreigners move in and out of detention over again and again. The way to get out of the vicious circle where the irregular migrants find themselves in is very difficult.

Conclusions

- There are no exact data available about the number of detainees in Europe, because of the fact that not all of the countries register them.
- On the grounds of data, which are partially available, the number of administrative detainees may be in the 100.000 persons per year.
- No exact data on the actual removals after administrative detention, but the European Commission concludes that one third of the return decisions are effectively implemented and result in removal.
- Non-expelled foreigners are released and maintain their irregular stay in the concerning country or travel to another EU country, by risking detention again.

3.11 Detention irregulars under criminal law

As stated earlier, administrative detention of foreigners is not a measure of the penal system, thus the foreigners are not detained because they are convicted or suspected of a criminal offence, but solely on the ground of residing in a country without a valid residence permit. For this reason, administrative detainees should not be seen as criminals nor to be treated as one.[48] Attention has been paid in 3.1 and 3.3 on the institutions in which foreigners are kept in the EU countries. Though, the practice in Europe is that administratively detained foreigners are kept separate from criminal prisoners in special detention centres, an actual look at the detention conditions of these foreigners shows quite some similarities with ordinary prisons. In countries where administratively detainees are placed in police stations or prisons, it even occurs that they are kept together with criminal offenders. This is for example the case in Ireland where there is no difference between administrative and criminal prisoners, they are detained together in prisons. In Cyprus there are specially designated detention cells for foreigners, but also detention cells which hold foreigners together with penal offenders exist.

Portugal, France, Germany and Finland have created separate detention places for foreigners, however this does not exclude the possibility in these countries, for detaining them together with criminal prisoners. Regarding Lithuania it can be said that before the foreigners can be and are accommodated in the Foreigner's Registration Centre, they are placed together with persons who have committed criminal offences, in the police custody facilities (maximum 48 hours). If there is a possibility, the foreigners awaiting transfer to the centre are accommodated separately.

---

[47] Spain has had recent regularization programmes in 2003; 800.000 and 2005; 600.000 irregular migrants, respectively. Italy has regularized in 2003 a group of 705.000 irregular migrants.

[48] See R. Cholewinski, *Irregular migrants: access to minimum social rights*, Strasbourg: Council of Europe Publishing 2005, p.8-9.

If we take a particular look at criminal prisoners who will be removed to their country of origin (category two prisoners), it can be said that the majority of the countries have the same policy on the question; how this category relates to the one of administrative detention? Just like common criminal prisoners, they are detained in general prisons and kept separate from administrative detainees. An example is the Netherlands where category 2 foreigners first serve their term of sentence in prison, after which they are transferred to a detention centre for waiting out the time for removal. Despite the fact that in the Netherlands the detention takes place in different locations, the administrative detainees are subject to the same penitentiary rules and regulations as category 2 prisoners.

The CPT's statement on this issue is that administrative detainees have to be held separately from prisoners, whether on remand or convicted.[49] Also article 15 (2) of the Commission Proposal Returns Directive and Guideline 10 (4) call for holding foreigners, who are detained pending their removal, separate from ordinary prisoners. Countries where criminal and administrative detainees are placed together act counter to these rules.

Conclusions

- Administrative detainees are not criminals and should not be treated as one.
- The legislation calls for detention separate from criminal offenders.
- The practice is that administrative detainees are kept separate from criminal prisoners, yet there are exceptions with countries such as Portugal, France, Germany and Finland, which make it possible to detain them together.
- Criminal prisoners who will be removed to their country of origin are detained in general prisons and kept separate from administrative detainees.

3.12 Minors

Children make up a large proportion of international migration flows to Europe. This group that is in need of special care and protection includes asylum and refugee seeking children, children forced or voluntarily migrating for work, children being abandoned when their parents migrate, as well as children trafficked for various exploitative purposes. The growing number of minors who are staying in an irregular way in European countries, face similar to adults, the risk of detention awaiting their removal to their country of origin. The policies regarding detention of children in EU countries differ for unaccompanied children and children who are in the concerning country together with their family.

With the exception of a few countries, such as Ireland (which prohibits the detention of persons under the age of 18 years) and the Czech Republic (where children under the age of 15 years may not be detained), the general practice in EU countries is that they allow the detention of irregular migrant children who are accompanying their family. In this way, Belgian law does not prohibit the detention of minors and provides explicitly that families may be detained. In the Netherlands, the detention of minors younger than 16 years has to be restricted as far as possible. The removal has to take place as soon as possible, so that the detention will be restricted. The fact that the foreigner has a departure duty (article 5 Aliens Act 2000) does not change this. Greece and the UK do not

[49] CPT Standards, Chapter IV Foreign nationals detained under aliens legislation, under point 28.

have an upper or lower age for detention, which results in that minors can be detained and removed under the same conditions and regulations as adult detainees. The majority of the countries which detain minors have separate units for accompanying the minors. This goes for; *inter alia*, Slovenia, Slovakia, Austria, Lithuania, France, Spain, Germany and Portugal. However, in practice it occurs that children with parents stay together in for example detention centres, prisons, penitentiary institutions, which are not equipped for the stay of children.

In the case of unaccompanied minors in general the help of Juvenile Welfare Agencies are called in by the authorities and a guardian is appointed. In Italy and France, these minors can not be removed nor detained. In Greece, children who are not yet 13 years old and who have no relatives in Greece can not be detained and must be accommodated in special hostels or institutions while the Greek authorities attempt to locate their family. British law allows their detention only in "exceptional circumstances and then only overnight, with appropriate care, whilst alternative arrangements for their safety are made". However, the fact that this provision is not binding can raise problems. The Dutch law makes the detention of unaccompanied minors between the ages of 12 to 16 years possible, but only when the child is not later than 4 days after the deprivation of liberty, placed in a juvenile institution.[50] Poland and Hungary exclude the removal of unaccompanied minors if the unification with the family or appropriate institutional care is not guaranteed in the country of origin.

Before dealing with the relevant European legislation related to children, there is an important International instrument that deserves attention. The Convention on the Rights of the Child is the first legally binding instrument which is setting out the civil, cultural, economic, political and social rights of children.[51] The Convention is child-centric and deals with the child-specific needs and rights. It requires that states act in the best interests of the child as stated in article 3 (1) and is monitored by the Committee of the rights of the Child, which is composed of members from countries around the world.

Article 37 of the Convention regards the detention of children. Under *b.* it is prescribed that:

> *'No child shall be deprived of his or her liberty unlawfully or arbitrarily. The arrest, detention or imprisonment of a child shall be in conformity with the law and shall be used only as a measure of last resort and for the shortest appropriate period of time'*[52]

Furthermore, under *c.* it is stated that children who are deprived of their liberty have to be separated from adults unless it is considered in the child's best interest not to do so.[53]

The general practice with regard to the detention of minors in Europe is not compatible with the Convention. Detention is certainly not a measure of last resort and children are also detained together with adults. Certain countries such as Malta and the Netherlands do not even have separate accommodation places for minors. The Commissioner for Human Rights has often noted in its reports that detention or holding centres where

---

50 Part A, chapter 6 article 1.5 (c) Aliens Circular 2000.

51 Date entry into force 2 September 1990.

52 Guideline 11 (1) is inspired by article 37 b. of the Convention and is in conformity with it.

53 See also article 35.4 European Prison Rules.

minors or families are housed are absolutely unsuitable for the needs of minors: they lack of appropriate facilities, foodstuffs and supplies. A play area, for instance, is never provided for these children, who spend their whole day locked in with their parents.[54]

The Commission Proposal Returns Directive has paid attention on minors in the articles 5, 8 (2c) and 15 (3). Article 8 (2c) states that:

> *'Member States shall postpone the execution of a removal order when there is a lack of assurance that unaccompanied minors can be handed over at the point of departure or upon arrival to a family member, an equivalent representative, a guardian of the minor or a competent official of the country of return, following an assessment of the conditions to which the minor will be returned'*

Within the context of article 8 (2c), I want to mention the Kaniki Mitunga[55] case of the Court which considers the detention and removal of an unaccompanied minor from the perspective of the ECHR. A five year old child arrived at Brussels airport on her own without having the necessary documents for entering Belgium. Before her removal, she was detained for almost two months in a centre that had initially been intended for adults, even though she was unaccompanied by her parents and no one had been assigned to look after her. No measures had been taken to ensure that she received proper counselling and educational assistance from a qualified person specially assigned to her. The conditions were not adapted to the position of extreme vulnerability in which she found herself as a result of her status as an unaccompanied alien minor. When the child was removed to the Democratic Republic of Congo, she was accompanied by a social worker who placed her in the care of the police at the airport. On board the aircraft she was looked after by an air hostess who had been specifically assigned to that task by the chief executive of the airline. She travelled with three Congolese adults who were also being deported. No members of her family were waiting for her when she arrived in the Democratic Republic of Congo. The Court therefore held that on the account of the detention and the removal to the country of origin, there had been violations of articles 3 and 8 ECHR to the child and her mother and a violation of article
5 ECHR in relation to the child.

Conclusions

- Growing number of minors who are staying in an irregular way in Europe face detention, awaiting their removal.
- Children, accompanied by their parents are detained together in places which are not equipped for the stay of children.
- Unaccompanied minors are in general taken care of by Juvenile Welfare Agencies and a guardian is appointed.
- The Convention on the Rights of the Child states detention of children as a measure of last resort, but in European countries it is daily practice.

---

54 Speech by the Deputy Secretary General, Council of Europe. *European Conference on the respect of the rights of foreign minors in Europe and against their detention and forced removal*, Strasbourg, 14 March 2007.

55 Judgment of 12 October 2006.

4 NATIONALS DETAINED ABROAD

This paragraph looks into nationals from EU countries that are being detained in countries other than their country of citizenship, either within or outside Europe. Not all research experts were able to obtain up-to-date information from official bodies regarding their nationals detained abroad. One of the reasons behind it is that in some countries there is no official information or data collection on this. The countries that could not provide information are Cyprus, Czech Republic, Greece, Latvia and Luxembourg. Information on Estonian and Finish nationals detained abroad is included in this overview but official numbers are missing because they are not being recorded.

4.1 Numbers and composition

From the 18 countries[56] that provided information the majority of their nationals were detained within the European Union. Only Portugal, Slovakia, Spain, Sweden and the United Kingdom have more nationals detained outside the European Union. The total number of nationals of 18 EU countries detained abroad is nearly 23.000. This total number is based on officially recorded statistics but is likely to be considerably higher. In practice some EU citizens detained abroad do not want to inform their diplomatic mission about their detention for various reasons. It is also not uncommon that foreign nationals are not made aware by prison authorities that they are entitled to inform their diplomatic representatives about their detention. Also European citizens who are detained in another country for administrative reasons are not always included in the official prison statistics. As a result these three groups are not represented in this total number. Neither are the data of seven EU countries that could not provide information on numbers of their nationals detained abroad.

[56] Austria, Belgium, Denmark, France, Germany, Greece, Hungary, Ireland, Italy, Lithuania, Malta, Netherlands, Poland, Slovakia, Slovenia, Spain, Sweden and the United Kingdom.

Figure 1

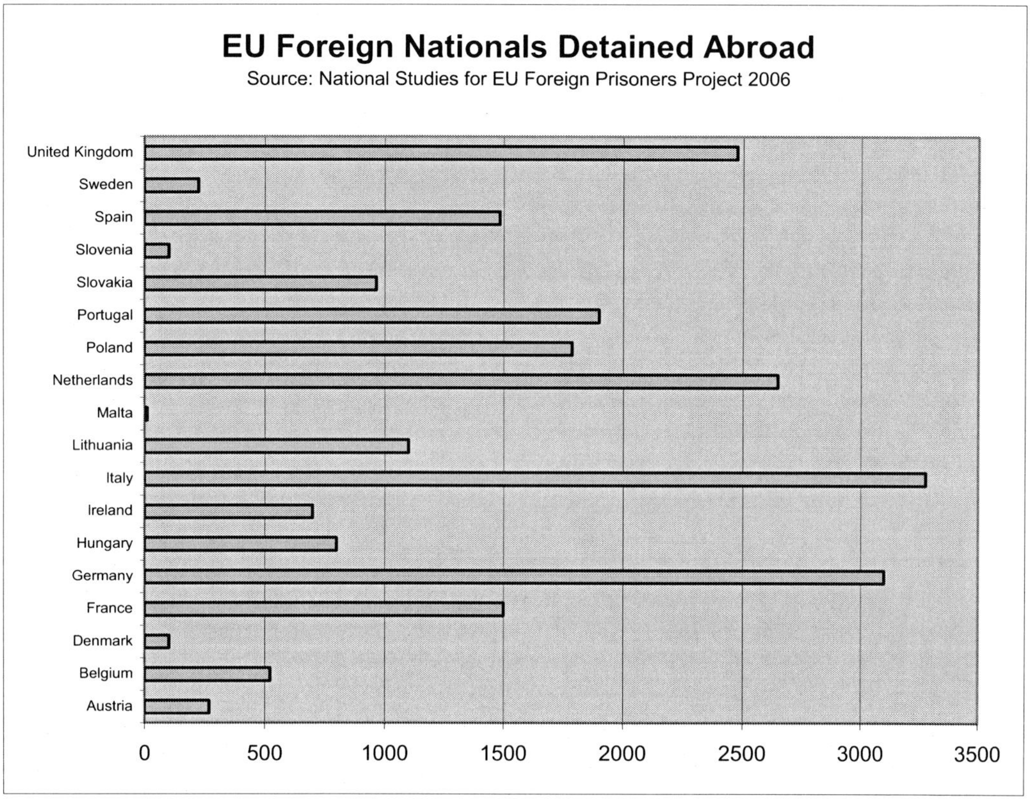

Half of the group of 23.000 are detainees with citizenship from Italy, Germany, Netherlands or the United Kingdom. The total number of Dutch nationals detained abroad, around 2.645, is remarkably high, especially in relation to the small size of the country.

Table 5: Number of Nationals Detained Abroad

Country	*Number*	*Country*	*Number*	*Country*	*Number*
Austria	270	*Greece*	-	*Poland*	1.787
Belgium	523	*Hungary*	800	*Portugal*	1.900
Cyprus	-	*Ireland*	700	*Slovakia*	965
Czech Republic	-	*Italy*	3.279	*Slovenia*	103
Denmark	103	*Latvia*	-	*Spain*	1.485
Estonia	-	*Lithuania*	1.100	*Sweden*	225[57]
Finland	-	*Luxembourg*	-	*United Kingdom*	2.476
France	1.500	*Malta*	12		
Germany	3.100	*Netherlands*	2.645	*Total*	22.973

Source: National Studies for EU Foreign Prisoners Project 2006

57 The number of nationals detained in other Nordic countries (Denmark, Finland and Norway) is not included.

Many EU countries indicate that the number of their nationals detained abroad is drastically on the rise in recent years. For example in Germany there has been an increase from 2.435 nationals in 2004 to 3.100 in 2005, an increase of 27% in only one year. There has also been a sharp increase in the Netherlands, in 1992 the number was around 1.000 and in 10 years time it has more than doubled to 2.330.

According to the Council of Europe *Convention on Mutual Assistance in Criminal Matters* (1959) each contracting party (all EU Member States) shall according to article 22 'inform others about all criminal convictions and subsequent measures in respect of nationals of the latter party. Ministries of Justice shall communicate such information to one another at least once a year'. It is therefore disappointing that even within the EU not all countries inform each other about the number of EU nationals in detention.

In Finland, for example, the Criminal Records Act reconfirms that information from the criminal records shall be delivered to a State Party of the European Convention on Mutual Assistance in criminal matters and that provisions on the delivery of data from the criminal records to another Nordic country shall be issued by Decree. However, according to the officials of the Legal Register Centre the procedure of receiving data from abroad is not realised in practise (except for data exchange between the Nordic countries). As a result there is no valid information available on the volume of the Finnish prison population detained abroad. This lack of information should be addressed.

In most countries the composition based on ethnic origin of the group EU nationals detained abroad is not being recorded. Exceptions are the United Kingdom where data is collected by Prisoners Abroad and The Netherlands where the Foreign Liaison Office of the Dutch Probation collects data. According to the Foreign Liaison Office a majority of the Dutch prisoners do not originally come from the Netherlands; many of them are born in Surinam, Netherlands Antilles/Aruba, Morocco, Turkey or the Dominican Republic. A quarter of the Dutch prisoners do not or barely speak Dutch, about 60% do not have a vocational education or diploma, and 60% do not have a job, income or allowance prior to detention. A large majority of nationals detained abroad is male; this percentage is 90% for British nationals and 84% for Dutch nationals. Information on ethnic origin is also kept by Prisoners Abroad: 76% of British citizens detained overseas are white and 17% are black or black British, 3.1% are Mixed, 2.3% are Asian or Asian British and 1.4% are Chinese or from another ethnic group. Two thirds of all Britons detained abroad are under 44 years.

4.2 Countries of detention

In nearly all EU countries a majority of nationals detained abroad are detained within the European Union and mostly in one of the neighbouring countries. In June 2006, 523 Belgian nationals were detained abroad of which 83% in Western European countries and only 1.7% in Eastern European countries. In Poland about 80% of Polish citizens arrested abroad in 2004 were detained within the EU. From the 12 Maltese citizens detained abroad 5 were held in Italy. Hungarian citizens detained abroad are mainly located in Austria, Germany and Italy. A total of 79 out of 103 Danes in prison abroad are detained in the EU. Estonians are mainly detained in Finland, Sweden, Germany, Austria and Spain.

A relatively high number of EU citizens are detained in the USA. One tenth of all German, Spanish and Swedish nationals detained abroad are locked up in the USA, for

French and Dutch nationals this is 5% and 26% for British citizens. The fact that so many British are detained in the USA, by far the country where most British nationals are detained, has a few reasons. Firstly the imprisonment rate in the USA is far higher than other countries, the USA is a popular destination for those emigrating from the UK and many of these people have not been naturalised. A majority of the Irish citizens detained abroad, around 64%, are detained in the UK (England and Wales, excluding Northern Ireland). Although Dutch prisoners are scattered around the world over 81 countries, around 60% are detained in EU member states. From this group 75% are detained in seven European countries, namely Germany (479), France (232), Spain (213), United Kingdom (155), Italy (133) and Belgium (93). Nearly half of all Slovenian foreign nationals are detained in Germany.

4.3 Reasons for detention and sentencing

In most European countries foreigners are arrested and held in detention for crimes related to smuggling, trafficking and possession of drugs. In most countries drug crimes are punished severely and offenders receive long sentences. Portuguese and Dutch nationals detained abroad are held in 80% of all cases for possession or smuggling of (mainly hard) drugs and for Spanish nationals this number is 72%. In Austria, Germany and the United Kingdom this number is 50% and in Belgium 57%. Other common reasons for arrest and detention are minor (traffic) offences, irregular stay, violence, property crimes, robbery, sex-crimes and homicide. Nearly all EU citizens that are held abroad are detained under criminal law, rather than being held under administrative or immigration law.

In France those foreign nationals that are awaiting death sentences abroad are being transferred back to France. In total there are 9 French prisoners detained abroad for political reasons. Sex tourism is a growing cause of imprisonment, but French prisoners tend to be ashamed of their crime and therefore do not contact the French authorities. Four German nationals are on death row in the USA and a further six in Kenya, Lebanon, Thailand, Taiwan and Philippines. At the moment German embassies in Tunisia, Egypt and Syria are looking into cases in which Germans were possibly tortured during their detention. In Brazil a German national is said to have died as a result of having been tortured to death. Most Hungarian nationals are detained for offences related to breaching working and staying regulations. The most frequent reason for detention for Irish citizens is homicide and for Slovak citizens property offences. Nearly half of all sentences served by Dutch nationals detained abroad are longer than one year. As a result the turnover rate is very high; in 2005 1.241 Dutch nationals were arrested abroad and 1.135 released. In 2004 a vast majority of Polish nationals were serving abroad short prison sentences imposed for misdemeanours and petty offences. In some countries, like the USA, foreign prisoners are transferred to immigration detention at the end of their criminal sentence, prior to being expelled back to their country of origin. For British nationals detained in the USA this is typically for a short period of time like a few weeks to a few months.

4.4 Authorities and organisations involved

In most countries there is more than one ministry responsible for the care of nationals detained abroad. In general these are the Ministry of Foreign Affairs and the Ministry of Justice (in some cases Ministry of Interior) that in cooperation with consulates and embassies supports national detained abroad. European citizens in need of consular help in a country without diplomatic or consular representation of their own country may turn to any consular or diplomatic mission of another EU Member State. According to Article 20 of the *Treaty establishing the European Community* and article 46 of the *Charter of Fundamental Rights of the European Union* should EU citizens 'be entitled to protection by the diplomatic or consular authorities of any Member State, on the same conditions as the nationals of that State'. The Ministry of Justice cooperates often closely with the Ministry of Foreign Affairs in transfer procedures of foreign nationals.

Consular help varies according to the individual situation in a country but in principle national authorities visit their nationals in detention, stay in contact with them and keep their relatives informed, monitor the human circumstances of detention (living conditions, food, medical care), provide magazines and newspapers, check the fairness and speed of the trial in accordance with local legislation, help to obtain a lawyer, provide information about the Council of Europe's *Convention on the Transfer of Sentenced Persons* (1983) or bi-lateral transfer agreements and help to prepare transfers. It is not unusual for EU consulates to provide small amounts of money to support nationals who do not have other sources in purchasing additional food, telephone cards and tobacco. In some cases consulates pay for the ticket back to the country of origin. Sometimes consulates facilitate money transfers from families to prisoners. Prisoners detained in developing countries may not be provided with basic essentials such as food, clothing or toiletries. British nationals can apply for grants to purchase these vital necessities, varying between □20 and □40 per prisoner per month (depending on the country). In 2005 more than □ 10.000 was provided to British prisoners for a wide variety of health issues; operations, asthma inhalers, consultations with specialists, glasses and dental treatment. In Spain nationals detained abroad can receive up to □100 per month to buy food, clothes and medicines when prison authorities provide nothing. Most common problems experienced by prisoners detained abroad are the poor living conditions, uncertainty about their situation, complex and bureaucratic legal procedures and limited contact with relatives and the outside world.

In Austria 60% of the Austrian nationals detained in the EU are supported by the Ministry of Foreign Affairs, and 80% of their nationals detained outside the EU. Some Ministries of Foreign Affairs, like in Belgium, Germany and The Netherlands, have published a booklet with information for nationals detained abroad. For example the leaflet from the Belgium department of International Judicial Cooperation of the Ministry of Foreign Affairs published a leaflet 'Help and guidance for Belgians in foreign prisons'.

In the Netherlands the 'Foreign Liaison Office' of the Dutch Probation Service plays an important role in the care of Dutch nationals detained abroad. It has been established 30 years ago and with its nine regional coordinators it coordinates the work of 275 visiting volunteers and 15 corresponding volunteers. The visiting volunteers are Dutch nationals who live and work abroad and who pay a social visit to Dutch nationals in detention every four to six weeks. These visits are carried out in close cooperation with the Consular Department of the Ministry of Foreign Affairs and the various Dutch consulates and embassies around the world. The Liaison Office receives financial assistance from both the Ministry of Foreign Affairs and the Ministry of Justice and besides friendly visits it offers study facilities through a separate foundation, the Foundation Education behind Bars.

In the United Kingdom the non-governmental organisation 'Prisoners Abroad' works with British citizens detained abroad. It is an independent organisation, formed in 1978 and funded through voluntary donations, that provides support on a voluntary basis during detention and also upon return in the UK after a period of imprisonment. Prisoners Abroad employs 16 staff, all based in their office in north London. Prisoners Abroad sends, on request, newspapers and magazines to British citizens in prison all over the world, produces a thrice-yearly newsletter, a series of leaflets and handbooks for prisoners and a pen pal scheme.

Besides authorities like ministries, consulates and embassies in some countries there are also non-governmental organisations or religious groups that provide support to nationals detained abroad. In France there was an organisation called 'FIL' (*Français incarcérés au loin / Far off imprisoned French*) but unfortunately their activities are reduced due to a lack of volunteers. The Hungarian Ministry of Foreign Affairs supports assistance from civilian organizations and volunteers that stay in contact with detained Hungarians. These visits are made on a voluntary basis and without any payment. Irish organisations involved with Irish prisoners overseas are, besides the Department of Foreign Affairs and the Department of Justice, 'Equality and Law Reform' and the 'Irish Commission for Prisoners Overseas' (ICPO).

The Epafras Foundation in the Netherlands, initiated by Reverend Joop Spoor in 1984, provides pastoral and material assistance for Dutch nationals detained abroad. Epafras is incorporated in the associated churches of the Netherlands and receives funding from the Dutch Ministry of Foreign Affairs and Ministry of Justice. Four times a year Epafras issues a special magazine 'Gezant van Nederland ('Ambassador from the Netherlands', that is send to all Dutch citizens detained abroad. In Sweden, the non-governmental organisation 'Bridges to Abroad' supports Swedish citizens imprisoned abroad. Their representatives had experienced imprisonment abroad themselves.

4.5 Release and reception home country

In principle there are no European countries that provide nationals that have been detained abroad any kind of support once they are released and return to their home country. In case things are arranged it is being done on an individual basis by the relatives or in some countries by non-governmental organisations. In Austria there is an organisation called 'Neustart' that provides probation and help on release. In Ireland the Probation Service provides a voluntary advice and referral service to prisoners returning to Ireland and the 'Irish Commission for Prisoners Overseas' (ICPO) can send a booklet 'What Now?' with information on social welfare service in the ex-prisoners home area.

In case nationals are transferred back to their home country in order to continue their sentence they will be taken under the care of their national prison authority. In the Netherlands only 6% of the Dutch nationals detained abroad are being transferred back on an annual basis. The fact that the Netherlands has a relatively mild sentencing regime towards drug crimes makes other countries more hesitant to agree to a transfer. Once a Dutch national is released and/or transferred back to the Netherlands the contact with the consulate will stop. In practice only the Liaison office of the Dutch Probation remains in contact in case aftercare is facilitated upon return to the Netherlands. Aftercare is limited to offering advice and referral to other professional social workers.

British prisoners returning to the UK after serving their sentence overseas cannot expect any support from the UK Probation Service because they are under no obligation to provide any form of practical assistance. In many cases, without the help of Prisoners Abroad, the ability of returning prisoners to access welfare systems and obtain emergency accommodation would be severely limited. When prisoners return to the UK after the completion of their sentence, they usually arrive at one of the main London airports. At Heathrow airport they can be met by a small British charity called 'Heathrow Travel Care' and at Gatwick airport by a similar, but unrelated charity called 'Gatwick Travel Care'. These organisations provide ex-prisoners if necessary with clean clothes, they can make free phone calls, take a shower and receive instructions on how to find the Prisoners Abroad office. Prisoners Abroad can only offer financial assistance for the first four weeks after arrival back in the UK. Lithuanian citizens detained abroad often do not want to be transferred back to their home country because of the relatively harsh conditions in their national prisons.

In case a foreign national is being expelled, the expelling state takes charge of the expulsion. When a foreign national is being released in the foreign state, the person has to pay personally for his/her return to the home country. Some consulates may cover the transportation expenses, sometimes under the condition of later reimbursement.

4.6 Aftercare

In most EU countries there is no special aftercare for nationals that have been detained abroad. However, in general they are not excluded from social welfare support. However, for many former detainees who after many years come back to their home country it is very difficult to find their way to the social welfare institutions. During their detention abroad none or too little attention is paid to the difficulties and obstacles that foreigner prisoners have to cope with after their return in the home country. In Belgium if an ex-prisoner has no family ties left in Belgium and insufficient financial means, the department of International Judicial Cooperation may ask the Red Cross to support the prisoner upon his arrival and look for housing through the welfare services of his last place of residence. In Ireland the 'Homeless Persons Service Unit' of the Health Service Executive provides information and accommodation for those who have been detained abroad. In Lithuania those nationals that have served a sentence abroad are not excluded from social support but they have to apply within two months and to provide documents to confirm their citizenship, permit of residence and proof of previous conviction. Swedish nationals detained abroad that were interviewed for this study after their return to Sweden expressed a need, especially those who experienced a long and traumatic detention period, for mental and physical support. Although the Swedish social welfare system is well established, this service is not available.

4.7 Public opinion and media

Media attention for the situation of nationals detained abroad is generally low apart from certain exceptional cases that receive special attention. In most European countries, despite the rising numbers of nationals detained abroad, the issue is not a hot topic for the general public. In Lithuania a rather negative opinion prevails about citizens that committed crimes abroad.

However, some individual cases receive a lot of media attention. In these cases the main concern is the well being of the prisoner in severe conditions and extreme long sentences. Cases where French nationals were sentenced for sex-crimes (sexual relations with minors) produced moral condemnation and public exclusion. In principle national authorities like the Ministry of Foreign Affairs and consulates are reserved in putting a prisoners' case in the public light. But very often families and lawyers do while expecting or hoping that public pressure might influence the local justice or politicians. It practice this is often counter-productive and even negative for the prisoner, because local justice or politicians are not willing to be seen as weak under international or diplomatic pressure.

Conclusions

- Not all European countries keep official data on the number of nationals detained abroad.
- Although EU countries shall, according to article 22 of the Council of Europe 'Convention on Mutual Assistance in Criminal Matters', inform other Member States about the number of EU nationals in detention, this is not always applied in practice.
- The total number of nationals of 18 EU countries detained abroad is nearly 23.000 and their number is drastically on the rise. A majority of them are detained within the EU.
- A large majority of the EU nationals detained abroad is male with no or limited educational background and often without an official job.
- In most EU countries foreigners are arrested and held in detention for crimes related to smuggling, trafficking and possession of drugs.
- Nearly all EU citizens that are held abroad are detained under criminal law and not under administrative or immigration law.
- In most European countries there is more than one ministry responsible for the care of nationals detained abroad. In most cases these are the Ministry of Foreign Affairs and the Ministry of Justice in cooperation with diplomatic missions.
- Consular help to foreign prisoners varies per country and per individual case. From hardly no visits to frequent visits and legal / social / and financial support.
- There are limited non-govermental organisations that provide social / pastoral and or practical support to their nationals detained abroad. Some of these organisations are partially of fully financed by the government.
- Despite the existence of bi-lateral and European transfer agreements only a limited number of nationals are enabled to serve the remainder of their sentence in their home country.
- Once nationals are released and return to their home country there are in principle no aftercare or probation facilities available.
- Despite the rising number of foreign nationals detained abroad there is, except for exceptional cases, low media attention.

5 RECOMMENDATIONS

5.1.1 Recommendations with respect to paragraphs 1.1 - 1.6

Recommendation (1)
Foreign sentenced prisoners should either be transferred to their home country in order to properly provide rehabilitative measures and preparation for release in their home country or the host country has to develop special training and vocational programmes that help the integration in the future home country. In cases where the foreigner does not speak the language of the country where he/she will be expelled to, specific language courses could be provided.

Recommendation (2)
Rehabilitation/re-integration is a principal aim for all prisoners. The necessity to provide rehabilitative programmes is laid down in the European Prison Rules which provide rehabilitation as the sole aim of deprivation of liberty for sentenced prisoners (see No. 102.1 European Prison Rules)

Recommendation (3)
At least for those detainees who will stay in the host country alternatives to pre-trial detention and to imprisonment should be further developed. The discrimination and disadvantages of foreigners (often excluded from such community sanctions or alternatives) must be of serious concern. The same is true for conditional (early) release.

Recommendation (4)
Foreign prisoners should get a decision on whether to be expelled or not in the first stage of serving any prison sentence. This will allow planning concrete rehabilitative programmes and the preparation for release in either the host or the future home country.

Recommendation (5)
Foreign prisoners often do not receive sufficient (written) information about their legal rights and duties in a language they understand. Staff in prisons and immigration detention centres should be particularly educated to address the specific needs and language deficits of foreign detainees.
In many countries racism amongst prisoners is a concrete problems that should get more concern by the prison and detention authorities.

Recommendation (6)
Overcrowding is a severe problem in many prisons but also administrative detention centres.
It increases the "normal" problems of foreigners and therefore should be prevented.

5.1.2 Recommendations with respect to the EU - level

Recommendation (7)
From a criminal justice perspective, there are initiatives, which should be developed on a European front that would both meet some of the needs of the humanitarian/welfare agenda and from that of protecting the public and reducing the risk of re-offending, they are not mutually exclusive. These require co-ordination and co-operation between organisations and agencies in the EU.

Recommendation (8)
Meeting the needs of justice and public protection, there should be protocols established amongst EU countries so that previous convictions and other relevant information can be obtained for sentencing. Such information will also be important during the prison sentence to work on offending behaviour, rehabilitation and resettlement issues. The repatriation of EU prisoners to serve their sentence in their own country does have advantages in areas of education, training and general rehabilitation needs.

Recommendation (9)
The number of EU prisoners who voluntarily return to serve their sentence in their country is low and while, in the UK context, only about 20% of FNPs are from EU countries, serving their sentence in their own country has distinct advantages. Depending on EU countries prisoner release arrangements, it might also mean that prisoners are released under supervision as opposed to being released with no requirements.

Recommendation (10)
EU national prisoners, who complete their sentences in the UK (or any other EU country) and are then deported, are not under any form of supervision on release. Protocols should be established between EU member countries to facilitate the transfer of supervision licences on deported prisoners to supervise resettlement and better protect their public against re-offending.

Recommendation (11)
The ability for community penalties and conditional release to be transferred, managed and enforced between EU countries, could also provide courts with sentencing alternatives to imprisonment and thereby reduce the FNP population" (see the recommendation of the UK national report). Social exclusion is likely to have negative impact on successful reintegration into society after release.

5.2 Recommendations with respect to the treatment of foreign offenders

5.2.1 General Recommendation (12)
Prison authorities should acknowledge the vulnerable position of foreign prisoners and should be committed to address their special needs. For this reason prison authorities should introduce special sections in prison regulations and implement special programmes in order to compensate for the disadvantages that foreigners experience in daily prison life.

5.2.2 Living conditions & facilities

Recommendation (13)
Prison authorities should be aware that allocating prisoners of the same national/cultural/religious background can be seen as a 'good practice' as it can elevate the feeling of isolation, it can also create undesirable hierarchical or violent subcultures.

Recommendation (14)
Foreign prisoners should be allowed to penitentiary institutions where they have better chances for successful resettlement, even if they do not stay in the country of detention after release.

Recommendation (15)
Foreign prisoners should be lodged in penitentiary institutions located in the capital city in order to facilitate regular contact with diplomatic missions and relatively easy transportation from the airport when relatives from abroad pay a visit.

5.2.3 Reception and admission

Recommendation (16)
Admission to penitentiary institutions can be seen as an intimidating and dehumanising experience. It is therefore essential that prisoners have a proper understanding of what is actually happening and prison authorities should therefore have information available in various languages. Further prison authorities should at least translate prison rules and house rules in several most common foreign languages and should ensure that they are presented to foreign prisoners upon admission. A good practice can be found in England and Wales where foreign prisoners receive a 'Foreign National Prisoners Information Pack' upon admission. This pack contains information in 20 languages about the rules, prisoners' rights and duties, complaint procedures, how to contact the embassy, how to apply for a transfer etc.

Recommendation (17)
Staff at reception should receive special language training and learn about cultural diversity.

Recommendation (18)
Prison authorities should take into consideration that foreign prisoners often have to make long distance calls and sometimes at odd hours, due to different time zones, in order to notify their families about their detention.

Recommendation (19)
A good practice can be found in England and Wales where 'Foreign National Orderlies' are used to inform new foreign prisoners about prison life, how to find their way and how to reduce their isolation. These Orderlies are foreign prisoners themselves who that have multi language skills and who received a special training.

5.2.4 Work – Education – Training – Sports – Recreation

Recommendation (20)
Being engaged in useful and paid work is essential for prisoners and especially for foreign prisoners because they often do not receive financial support from outside the institution. Prison authorities should ensure that foreign prisoners have equal access to work, education and training programmes. Providing classes for foreigners to become more acquainted with the national language or English could be beneficial for both prisoners and staff.

Recommendation (21)
Prison authorities could seek support from local libraries and diplomatic missions to create a prison library collection of books, magazines and newspapers in various foreign languages.

5.2.5. Food – Religion – Personal hygiene – Medical care

Recommendation (22)
Prison authorities should stock prison shops with cultural specific ingredients or products.

Recommendation (23)
Prison authorities should create a multi-faith room for the use of prisoners of various religious backgrounds.

Recommendation (24)
Prison authorities should make sure that representatives of the most common religions have regular access to foreign prisoners for individual meetings and to hold religious meetings. A good practice can be found in Sweden where the Swedish Prison Service created a network of representatives of different nominations that visit foreign prisoners. This 'Council for Spiritual Welfare' network consists of around 130 persons.

Recommendation (25)
All prisoners should be allowed to wear their own clothing, hair and head dress. Turbans for Sikhs and head scarves for Muslim women should be accepted like in the United Kingdom.

Recommendation (26)
Prison authorities should provide medical care free of charge to all prisoners, so also to foreign prisoners that might not have health insurance.

Recommendation (27)
Requesting interpreter assistance from non-medical staff or other prisoners seems practical but is not desired because of medical confidentiality and the quality of the translation of medical terminology.

5.2.6 Consular help and Legal aid

Recommendation (28)
In order to avoid that foreign prisoners are not made aware of their right to contact their diplomatic mission, prison staff should be informed that foreign prisoners can only refrain from this right if the prisoners requests so in writing.

Recommendation (29)
Diplomatic missions should acknowledge the important role they play or could play for foreign prisoners. In many cases diplomatic mission are their only 'life-line'. The practice of the Prison Service in England and Wales that organises biannual meetings for diplomatic missions to inform consular staff about prison regimes and how to provide a professional service to their imprisoned nationals is worth following.

Recommendation (30)
Another good practice can be found in The Netherlands. The 'Foreign Liaison Office' of the Dutch Probation Service coordinates the visits of 275 Dutch volunteers who live and work abroad in 80 countries and who pay social visits to Dutch nationals in foreign detention. These visits take place every four to six weeks and are organised in close cooperation with Dutch diplomatic missions.

Recommendation (31)
Prison authorities should provide (free) legal assistance to foreign prisoners. Some Belgium penitentiary institutions organise 'Foreign Prisoners' Information Sessions' for lawyers in order to give them more insight in specific foreign prisoners' legal proceedings. In countries like the Czech Republic, Hungary and Malta non-governmental organisations, provide free legal help to foreign prisoners.

Recommendation (32)
Foreign prisoners should be made aware about their status as soon as possible. Are they eligible to remain in the country of detention or will they be expelled after release?

5.2.7 Contact with the outside world

Recommendation (33)
Prison authorities should allow foreign prisoners more flexible visiting schemes in order to allow family and relatives to make the long trip worthwhile. Further prison authorities should allow foreign prisoners to make telephone calls at different hours in relation to different time zones.

Recommendation (34)
Community welfare organisations should be encouraged to pay social visits to foreign prisoners in order to reduce their social isolation. Visits to Dutch citizens detained abroad by volunteers of the 'Foreign Liaison Office' of the Dutch Probation Service can be seen as a good practice. Another example that is worth following are the Spanish non-governmental organisations that provide free stamps and telephone cards to foreign prisoners but also mediation between the prisoner and their families.

5.2.8 Re-integration activities – Prison leave

Recommendation (35)
Prison authorities should acknowledge that re-integration activities and prison leave for foreign prisoners are as important as for other prisoners. Social welfare organisations can play a role in the resettlement of foreign prisoners. An example is Spain where some non-governmental organisations provide secure shelters and dormitories in order to make prison leave possible for foreign prisoners.

5.2.9 Release – Expulsion

Recommendation (36)
The decision of expulsion of foreign prisoners should be made as early as possible (see also recommendation 32) and foreign prisoners should preferably not be put in administrative detention while waiting to be expelled.

5.2.10 Aftercare – Probation

Recommendation (37)
It is advisable that also social welfare services provide assistance to foreign ex-offenders in their re-integration process, like in Portugal and England and Wales.

5.2.11 Staff

Recommendation (38)
Prison authorities should recognise that dealing with prisoners, and foreign prisoners in particular, in a professional, human and personal way requires effective management and great human and technical skills from prison staff. Prison staff should be carefully selected, properly trained, paid as professionals, work under adequate conditions and receive a respected status in society.

Recommendation (39)
Staff working with foreign prisoners should receive special training in language but also on the background of certain cultures, religion etc. A good example is the Swedish prison staff that work directly with foreign prisoners participate in a university level training on 'Intercultural Understanding' and 'Diversity and Dialogue'.

5.3 Recommendations with respect to foreigners in administrative detention

5.3.1 and 5.3.3 Institutions and capacity

Recommendation (40)
Detention of irregular migrants should never be used as a deterrent to put off possible future arrivals.

Recommendation (41)
Detention of foreigners in order to secure their removal or the prevention of unauthorised entry, is only acceptable if it can be shown conclusively that these measures are necessary in order to protect essential public interests and that no other less restrictive methods of achieving these aims are likely to be effective.

Recommendation (42)
Alternative, non-custodial measures which are available to the European states, such as reporting requirements, supervision systems, placement in open centres and the deposit of a financial guarantee should always be considered before detention.

Recommendation (43)
The place and conditions of detention as well as the detention regime should reflect the basic difference that exists between the sanctions and measures of detention that are applied within the criminal justice system and the system of administrative detention that is applied to irregular migrants. Irregular migrants should not be transferred to prisons as a punitive measure unless they are suspect or have been convicted of a criminal offence. As far as possible, an 'open regime' should be maintained within the institution.

Recommendation (44)
All staff in detention centres for irregular migrants should be qualified and trained for the specific needs of irregular migrants, who are detained pending the removal procedure.

5.3.2 The responsible Ministry and legislation

Recommendation (45)
Detention must not be imposed arbitrarily and never purely for the convenience of the authorities. It must be lawful, in accordance with a procedure and based on grounds prescribed by law, reasonably predictable, necessary and applied without discrimination.

Recommendation (46)
The law must define in a clear and concrete way the requirements which have to be satisfied, before detention may be authorised.

Recommendation (47)
The grounds for their detention and their rights while in detention should be communicated to the detainees.

5.3.4 Length of stay

Recommendation (48)
Detention of irregular migrants should be for the minimum period necessary. An absolute maximum duration for any such detention should be specified in national law, which should provide that, as a rule, the detention may not exceed three months. A prolongation should only be allowed if the detainee has not co-operated in facilitating his removal. In no case should the detention exceed six months as stated in the Commission Proposal Returns Directive.

Recommendation (49)
Detention is only justified as a temporary measure. If the aims for which it is used can not be achieved within a reasonable period that is defined by law, it should be terminated.

Recommendation (50)
Foreigners should not be detained for prolonged periods for reasons beyond the detainee's own control, such as states failing to cooperate in the removal process.

5.3.5 The decision procedure

Recommendation (51)
The decision for administrative detention should be issued by judicial authorities. In urgent cases they may be issued by administrative authorities, in which case the order shall be confirmed by judicial authorities within 72 hours from the beginning of the administrative detention as prescribed in the Commission Proposal Returns Directive.

Recommendation (52)
The decision of the judge should always contain clear reasons why other non-custodial measures would be inadequate for the purpose and, in the light of existing alternative measures, there should be clear proportionality between the detention and the end to be achieved. It should be communicated to the detainee in a language and in terms that he understands together with reasons for the decision. They. There should be a presumption in favour of release.

5.3.6 Appeal and review

Recommendation (53)
Administrative detainees should have the right to appeal against the first instance and the review decisions and should be provided with the means, through legal assistance to exercise this right. They must have access to independent and competent legal advice and assistance from the beginning of the detention, irrespective of his ability to pay and they should have the right to attend any appeal hearing and to present their case.

Recommendation (54)
Periodical judicial reviews should be guaranteed by statute in the event of continuing detention. In order to assess the proportionality of the detention, the judge should take into account the conditions of detention. When they are found to be seriously deficient, the judge should have the power to order the release of the detainee on the ground that detention in such circumstances is not proportional, having regard to the aims for which it is being used.

Recommendation (55)
Any review institution should be independent from the detaining authorities. The periodic reviews should take place regardless of whether the detainee has exercised his right to appeal. Detainees and their legal representatives should have the right to attend any review hearings and to present their case. The reviews should include an opportunity for the detainee to refute any assertions made by the detaining authorities.

Recommendation (56)
An effective complaints procedure should be provided relating to the treatment of detainees within the institution, so that problems may be speedily investigated and appropriate remedies provided, in cases where they are warranted. Depending on the different legal traditions and institutional arrangements to be found within each of the countries concerned, such complaints might either be directed to a judge or some other institution such as an Ombudsman or Board of Visitors.

5.3.7 Irregular stay (57)

Illegal entry to the territory of a European state or irregular stay in such a state should in itself not be considered to be a crime punishable with imprisonment.

5.3.8 – 5.3.10 Data and the non-expelled foreigners

Recommendation (58)
National authorities should provide detailed information on relevant statistics, regarding the total number of foreigners in administrative detention, in order to ensure transparency.

Recommendation (59)
Prior to and during detention highest priority should be given to encourage voluntary return through intensive and individualised counselling. Furthermore, the involvement of the International Organization for Migration and other national and international organisations should be stimulated, so they can contribute effectively to the process of voluntary return.

Recommendation (60)
In the case of foreign nationals who can not (or no longer) be lawfully detained, but who have not been granted rights of residence, the law should regularize their status in order to minimise the risks associated with 'social exclusion'.

Recommendation (61)
Persons who are unable to return to their home countries due to the situation in these countries and/or the risk of being 'subjected to torture or to inhuman or degrading treatment or punishment' should not be detained while the host state waits for a change of situation which would allow return.

5.3.11 Detention irregulars under criminal law

Recommendation (62)
Restriction to which criminal offenders are subjected should be applied to irregular migrants as few as possible, especially with respect to restrictions of the right to make phone calls, visits, correspondence, possession of personal goods, disciplinary sanctions, library, free movement inside the holding or detention centre. Therefore, irregular migrants should not be considered and treated as criminals.

Recommendation (63)
Administrative detainees should not be detained together with remand or sentenced prisoners. To accommodate such detainees in an institution which is otherwise integrated into the criminal justice system is acceptable only in exceptional circumstances. Even then, however, administrative detainees should not be in the same building as are used for ordinary criminal prisoners, nor subject to the same restrictions. There should be no co-mingling of the two groups.

5.3.12 Minors

Recommendation (64)
Unaccompanied persons who are under the age of 18 should never be detained and should be released into the care of family members who already have residency within the certain country. Where this is not possible, alternative care arrangements should be made by the competent child care authorities for unaccompanied minors to receive adequate accommodation and appropriate supervision. Residential homes or foster care placements may provide the necessary facilities to ensure their proper development. A legal guardian or adviser should be appointed.

Recommendation (65)
All appropriate alternatives to detention should be considered in the case of children accompanying their parents. Children and their primary care-givers should not be detained, unless this is the only means of maintaining family unity. Such detention should occur only in the most exceptional cases and in the least restrictive conditions. Nursing mothers and women in the later stages of pregnancy should not be detained.

5.4 Recommendations with respect to paragraphs 4.1 - 4.7

Recommendation (66)
Collection of data on nationals detained abroad should be done on a national and European level.

Recommendation (67)
More cooperation between national states and involved authorities is beneficial.

Recommendation (68)
There is an urgent need for the Introduction of minimum standards in consular care for nationals detained within the EU. These standards should contain provisions for social/legal/financial support, assistance to families at home and help with transfer agreements.

Recommendation (69)
Social visits made by volunteers of the 'Liaison Office' of the Dutch Probation Service to Dutch nationals detained abroad can be regarded as a good practice. As are the activities of the non-governmental organisations like the British 'Prisoners Abroad', the 'Irish Commission for Prisoners Overseas' and the Swedish 'Bridges to Abroad'.

Recommendation (70)
Transfer agreements between European countries could be more effective when the procedures are simplified and quicker. The transfer of EU prisoners to their home countries does have advantages for their social, educational and rehabilitation needs. As a result it will better protect the public against re-offending.

Recommendation (71)
The ability for community penalties and conditional release to be transferred, managed and enforced between EU countries, could also provide courts with sentencing alternatives to imprisonment and thereby reduce the EU foreign national prisoners population.

Recommendation (72)
Prison authorities should develop special training and vocational programmes which help the integration of foreign prisoners' into their home country.

Recommendation (73)
Nationals that have been detained abroad should receive access to national aftercare and probation provisions upon return in the home country. Providing practical assistance to nationals detained abroad directly after return, like how to obtain official documents, how to apply for housing, a job, social benefits etc is essential to combat recidivism.

Chapter 2

Austria

Arno Pilgram
Veronika Hofinger

1 INTRODUCTION

1.1 Overview Penalties and Measures

The following types of detention are legally admissible in Austria:
- *police detention (Verwahrungshaft)* (up to 48 hours) to bring someone who is strongly suspected of a criminal offence before the investigating judge (§§ 175-179 StPO);
- *pre-trial detention (Untersuchungshaft)* (up to a maximum of 2 years under special preconditions), proposed by the public prosecutor and decided by a judge (§§ 179-181 StPO);
- *custodial sentence (Strafhaft)* (from 1 day to 20 years, or lifelong, § 18 StGB), after conviction by penal court or after commutation of an irrecoverable fine into a substitute prison sentence (§ 19 para. 3 StGB);
- placement in *preventive custody (Unterbringung)* (in some cases for an indefinite time span) based on penal court's decision against 'mentally abnormal offenders', 'addicted offenders' or 'dangerous recidivists' (§§ 21-23 StGB).
- *administrative penal servitude (Verwaltungsstrafhaft)* (from 12 hours to 6 weeks, § 11 VStG), after sentence by an administrative authority or after commutation of an irrecoverable administrative fine into a substitute penal servitude (§ 16 VStG);
- *police arrest (Polizeihaft)* (up to 24 hours) to ensure an administrative penal procedure (§§ 35, 36 para. 1 VStG);
- *administrative detention of irregular migrants (Fremdenpolizeiliche Haft)* (up to 48 hours) to bring somebody before the immigration authorities (§ 39 FPG);
- *detention pending expulsion (Schubhaft)* (10 months within 2 years at maximum) to ensure administrative procedure to enforce ban of residence and removal (§§ 76 and 80 FPG).[1]

1.2 Overview of the Prison System

Detention can be executed in different institutions:
- *police detention* in cells and detention centres of the police;
- *pre-trial detention* (with some exceptions) in prisons at the location of the courts of first instance. In these court prisons there are separate departments for juvenile and female prisoners;
- *custodial sentences* up to 18 months generally in court prisons, with longer sentences in penitentiaries;
- *preventive custody* in special institutions provided for by the justice administration, but partly also in penitentiaries. Preventive detention of certified insane offenders due to § 21 para.1 StGB to a great extent takes place in general psychiatric hospitals.
- *administrative penal servitude* in police detention centres, in single cases (if following a custodial sentence) also in penitentiaries;

1 Constraints of freedom are also admissible in connection with less severe means: If ban on residence or removal is deferred a directive is possible not to leave a certain area (§ 68, para.2 (1) FPG) or to reside in a place which is designated by the immigration authority (§ 77 para.3 FPG). The strongest restriction can be made according to § 77 para.5 FPG. To ensure the expulsion, forcible return or transition of immigrants they can be demanded not to leave a designated room for at most 72 hours.

- *administrative arrest of irregular migrants* in the police detention centres like police detention of criminal offenders;
- *detention pending expulsion* in the same institutions as administrative penal servitude or police detention of suspected criminal offenders whereas these different detainees are kept in separate cells or departments (following a custodial sentence this custody in some cases can also take place in penitentiaries).

The relevance of these penalties and measures may be assessed by the size of the prison population (daily average): While about 6,000 persons are serving a custodial sentence and 2,500 are kept in pre-trial detention, preventive custody and detention pending expulsion are affecting about 600 persons each and administrative penal servitude another 200. These figures (daily average prison population) correspond to the aggregate number of years of detention imposed.

Institutions under the responsibility of the Ministry of Justice
(*Justizanstalten, JA*): There are 28 JA with 16 small dependent outposts. Of these are:
- 16 court prisons (these are institutions for pre-trial detention and custodial sentences up to 18 months, housing between 50 [*Steyr*] and 1,300 [*Vienna*] prisoners, with separate departments for juveniles and women);
- 9 penitentiaries (for longer custodial sentences and a size between about 120 [youth prison in *Gerasdorf*] and 870 inmates [*Stein*]). One of these penitentiaries is designated for juveniles, another one for women[2];
- Besides these institutions the Ministry of Justice runs three institutions of rather small size for the execution of preventive custody, two of which are designated for mentally ill offenders, one for drug addicts;
- Persons subjected to preventive custody acc. to § 21 (1) StGB are legally under the authority of prisons (one of which is a specialised clinic, *Göllersdorf,)* but most of them are actually placed in psychiatric hospitals. At present there are nine hospitals in eight federal states hosting inmates of this category, partly on closed forensic departments, partly in open sections.[3]

The capacity of justice prisons is 8,068 places (1 Dec 2005). In February 2005 3,630 employees worked there. From this number 2,970 are especially trained guards.Furthermore there are about 300 staff members for special services, about one-third are social workers, another one-third are qualified nurses and the rest are psychologists, physicians or teachers. In 2005 the total budget for these prisons (without building costs) was 255.2 Mio €, of which 133.8 was spent for personnel. These prisons are directly managed and inspected/controlled by the Ministry of Justice.

---

2 These penitentiaries are all closed prisons that partly contain high security departments, partly (semi-) open departments for the imprisonment of first offenders.

3 On 1 Dec 2005 246 mentally ill offenders have been placed acc. to § 21 para. 1 StGB in psychiatric hospitals (or psychiatric departments of general hospitals). There is no information available about the percentage of foreigners in this population.
The hospitals and the health administration of the federal states are responsible for the treatment of these offenders, yet the time of release falls into the responsibility of penal courts that consult psychiatric experts.

Prisoners may address their complaints to the director of the prison (§ 11 StVG); if the complaint is directed against the prison management they may address their complaints to a special chamber of the regional court of appeal (§ 11a StVG) or to the Ministry of Justice as a last resort (§ 121 StVG). In the latter case the prisoner has no entitlement to reply (§ 122 StVG). Prison monitoring committees (*Vollzugskommissionen*) at each regional court exercise some extra supervision over prisons. These committees consist of seven members of the local community appointed by the minister of justice after nomination by the head of the local government and by ministers of some other resorts (§ 18 StVG).[4] The *Volksanwaltschaft* (the national ombudsman-institution) may control the administration of justice, including the management of prisons. It may act on its own initiative (e.g. because of media reporting) or react to citizens' complaints, and make an annual report to the House of Parliament.[5] The *Committee for the Prevention of Torture and Inhumane or Degrading Treatment or Punishment (CPT)* has visited Austria four times since 1990, the last time in 2004.

Institutions under the responsibility of the Ministry of the Interior (*Polizeianhaltezentren, PAZ*): Cells in police stations are for temporary police detention (before admission to police detention centres or to court prisons) and 16 police detention centres are for administrative penal servitude and detention pending expulsion. There are no special centres for juveniles and women, yet care should be taken for their spatial separation according to the law (§ 4 AnhO).

The capacity of police detention centres (PAZ) is 1,118 places, of which 717 are designated for detention pending expulsion and 305 for administrative penal servitude.[6] The smallest institution is located at the Vienna airport in *Schwechat* with 8 places; the largest is also in Vienna the *PAZ Hernalser-Gürtel* with 304 places. There are no figures available on budget and employees, because these institutions use personnel from different local police departments.[7]

---

4 Since the reports of the committees and their recommendations are not published, their impact – if there is any – stays invisible. A draft law from 2000 intended to substitute the committees by advisory boards for each prison. They should also include members of human rights groups and spokesperson for inmates. At the end of the 21st legislative period no more agreement on the bill could be reached.

5 In the 2000-2004 reports a decreasing number of prisoners' complaints is mentioned. The majority of these complaints refer to judicial decrees that are outside the competence of the *Volksanwalt*. There is no evidence from the reports that foreign prisoners complain more frequently, on the contrary. Because of five cases of prisoners' death the *Volksanwaltschaft* in 2001 specifically investigated the penitentiary in Stein. The annual report denies shortcomings and generally acquits the guards stating the growing congestion of the facilities by a 'dramatic change' in the prison population. Apart from a growing readiness to escape, from increasing drug and mental health problems the high number of foreigners among prisoners is seen as a stress factor: 'An additional strain for the personnel results from the high portion of foreign prisoners who do not speak German (presently 30% of prisoners coming from 60 different nations)' (Annual Report of the Austrian Ombudsman Board 2001, p. 13).

6 Information obtained from the Ministry of the Interior (Abt. II/3).

7 After a key date (10 Jan 2001) assessment by the *Human Rights Advisory Council* 458 officials have been busy in police detention centres, thereof 51 women. Social care workers only care for prisoners in detention pending expulsion. According to contracts between the Ministry of the Interior and private organisations there should be two to three care workers for each detention centre with office hours on every working day.

An important control function is exercised by the *Human Rights Advisory Council* (*Menschenrechtsbeirat, MRB*) that resorts under the Ministry of the Interior but is free from its directives. This council has been established through an amendment to the Security Police Act 1999 (introducing §§ 15a/b/c SPG) in compliance with a *CPT recommendation* in 1990, that living conditions in police detention centres should be controlled by an independent body. The real trigger for the establishment of the broad competence of the MRB was the death of a Nigerian citizen during forced removal in 1 May 1999. Besides its annual activity report the council periodically publishes progress-reports on the implementation of its numerous recommendations.[8] The *Volksanwaltschaft* can also be appealed to in matters of police detention and it regularly reports its observations to the House of Parliament.[9]

In principle none of the different types of prisons is reserved for foreigners. In practice, pending expulsion foreigners are detained in police detention centres segregated from the other categories of detainees. There is only one PAZ (in *Eisenstadt*) that exclusively houses detainees pending expulsion. The mean share of foreigners is highest in PAZ (about 75%) and is higher in court prisons (with mainly pre-trial detainees, 50%) than in penitentiaries (40%). The lowest portion of foreigners can be found in institutions (prisons or hospitals) for preventive detention (13%). The regional differences are substantial. The maximum share of foreigners in a prison under justice administration is 70% (*JA Suben*). Compared with their 9.3 %-rate in the whole population[10] foreigners are strongly over-represented in prisons, except in preventive detention measures, yet compared with their rate in the offender population (29% in total, 46% with felony offenders, in 2004) foreigners are only over-represented in pre-trial detention and not in penitentiaries.

There is no department with special responsibilities for foreigners, neither in prisons under justice nor under police administration, except in the largest Austrian court prison in Vienna. There is a foreigners' advisor (*Ausländerreferent*) who may be consulted by prisoners and guards from other prisons and who organizes trainings for officers working with foreign prisoners. Within the new curriculum for the basic training for wardens (enacted in 2004) an extended course 'foreign cultures' is mandatory, but there is also considerable demand for similar courses in further education programmes. The situation is similar in police basic and advanced training courses.

8 *CPT* is demanding an even greater independence of the *MRB* with regard to budget and selection of members and also an extension of its competence to prisons under justice administration (*CTP* 2005, p. 15).

9 In fact only very few complaints against police relate to forcible action or detention measures, even less to actions taken against foreigners. The bulk of complaints refer to police service, respectively to omission of service.

10 In the age group >15-64 the foreigners' rate in 2004 was 10.6% (*Statistisches Jahrbuch Österreichs* 2006, p.191). In addition population statistics are fairly incomplete with respect to non-residents. If we consider a daily average of about 320,000 tourists in the country, the growing number of statistically neglected seasonal workers and the illegally present – estimated at about 80,000 (*Futo/Jandl* 2005, *National Contact Point* 2005) – the rate of foreigners in the population might come up to at least 15%.

Table 1: Prisoners in Austria on 1 December 2005

	total	*Austrians*	*Foreigners*	*% Foreigners*
Court prisons (CP)				
total CP	4918	2406	2512	51.1%
Penitentiaries (P)				
Penitentiaries (men)	3354	2039	1315	39.2%
Gerasdorf (juveniles)	126	60	66	52.4%
Schwarzau (women)	165	105	60	36.4%
total P	3645	2204	1441	39.5%
Facilities for preventive custody (PC)				
total PC	403	350	53	13.2%
total (justice prisons)	8966	4960	4006	44.7%
Police Prisons, by date 23 Nov 2005				
	total	*Austrians*	*Foreigners*	*% Foreigners*
Administrative penalcustody	178	148	30	16.9%
Police detention	14	6	8	57.1%
Detention pending xpulsion	424		424	100.0%
total (police prisons)	616	154	462	75.0%
all prisons	9582	5114	4468	46.6%

Source: IVV-Data (based on prisoners' electronic files), provided by Ministry of Justice, February 2006; Personal communication from Ministry of the Interior, Dep. II/3; own calculations

1.3 Overview Involvement Consulates, Embassies, Ministries Home Country, Probation Service Home Country, NGO's etc

See 2.6

1.4 Overview of Trends

At present the number of prisoners in Austria has reached the highest level since the early 1980s. The marked rise since 2000 is the result of increasing prison input (offenders detected by the police) and inadequate political counter-measures. Such measures have been repeatedly taken between 1987 und 1998, namely a series of penal code and penal procedure law reforms (ranging from the penal law amendment in 1987 to the juvenile court law in 1988 and the so called diversion law in 1998; see: Pilgram 2004).

Even a first crime wave caused by foreigners after the opening of the Eastern borders in the early 1990s was at the time still responded to by liberal reforms (e.g. Penal Procedure Law amendment 1993 and Code of Imprisonment 1993). These could not completely prevent rising numbers of prisoners. Notably the Austrian citizens profited from this policy to avoid pre-trial detention and prison sentences, whereas the growth of the prison population (daily average in justice institutions) from about 5,900 to 7,200 between 1989 and 1993 and from about 6,900 to 8,400 after 2000 is exclusively due to rising numbers of foreigners imprisoned. Criminal policy today, however, propagates imprisonment and prison construction. Criminal policy shows itself as security policy in the face of perceived crime threats originating abroad, and is no longer primarily guided by principles of compensation and re-integration. The increase of foreigners in prisons at the beginning of the 1990s was first effectuated by new 'tourist groups' from the neighbouring countries (Czechoslovakia, Hungary, but also from Poland), second by migrants from the disintegrating Yugoslavia (by people fleeing civil war). Labour migrants to Austria typically originate from these regions (Pilgram 2003a). These groups committed primarily property crimes (occasionally even on a commercial scale).

The increase in the number of foreign prisoners after 2000 can be traced back almost exclusively to citizens from more distant Eastern European regions (e.g. Rumania, Bulgaria, former Soviet Republics) on one hand and to persons from Western African states on the other hand (Pilgram 2003b). They usually only have a provisional residence status as asylum seeker or stay illegally in the country. Almost half of the 20%-increase of the average prison population between 2001 and 2004 (from 7,059 to 8,443) originates from citizens of Eastern European states (n=655, 47%), more than a third (n=508; 37%) of Western African states. Those in the first group invariably get arrested because of recurrent property crimes those in second group because of street drug dealing. While the number in prison of Austrian citizens is falling and that of citizens of states traditionally providing for labour migrants (Yugoslavia, Turkey) remains the same, the portion of prisoners from distant Eastern Europe states rises from 3.9 to 10.3% (maximum 2004) and that of prisoners from Western Africa from 4.0 to 9.1% (2005). (See figures 1-7)

Figure 1 Austrian and Foreign Citizens in Austrian Prisons 1981 – 2005

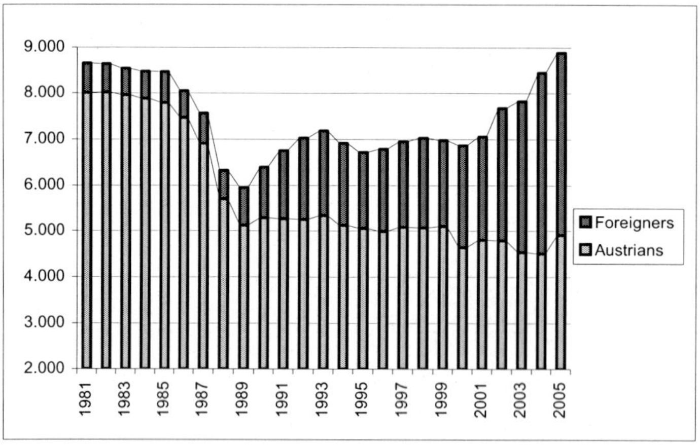

Source: Annual 'Statistische Übersicht über den Strafvollzug'; Bundesministerium für Justiz (1996): Unterlagen zur Budgetdebatte 1997, own calculations; data 2000-2004: personal communication Mag. Gneist (Ministry of Justice); 2005: IVV-Daten, provided by Federal Computing Centre of Austria, March 2006: Mean number of Austrian prisoners; foreign prisoners on key date Sep. 1st (since 2001: Dec. 1st).

Figure 2 Prisoners by Nationality (all prisons)

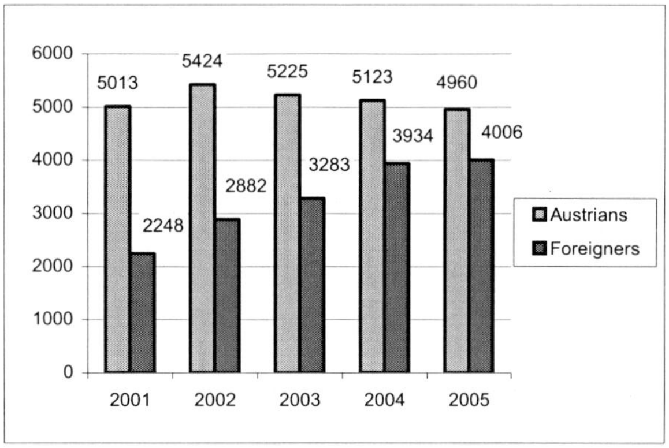

Figure 3 Prisoners in Court Prisons (upper court-district Vienna)

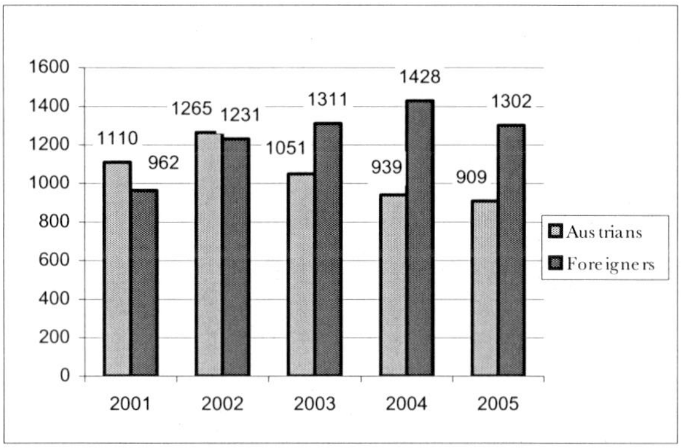

Figure 4 Prisoners in Court Prisons (other upper court districts)

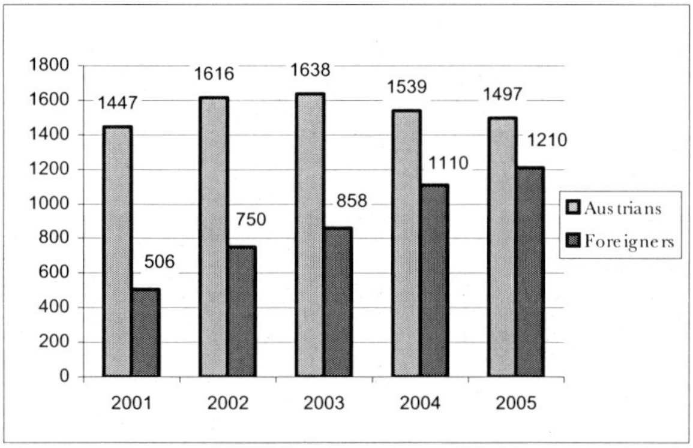

Figure 5 Prisoners in Penitentiaries (for adult males)

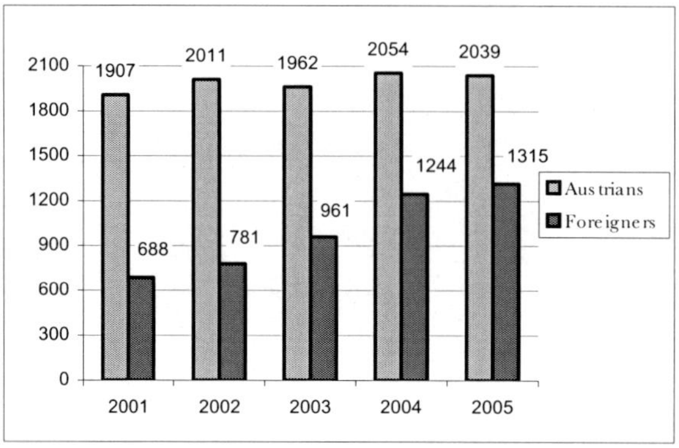

Figure 6 Prisoners in Special Institutions (for juveniles, females, mentally ill)

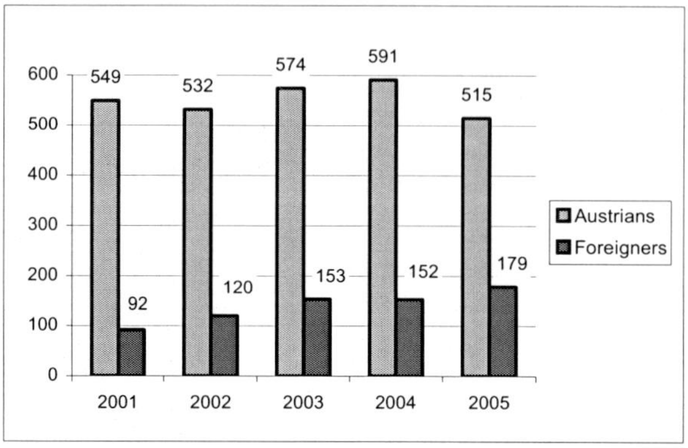

Figure 7a Prison Population* in Austria by Nationality (%) 2001

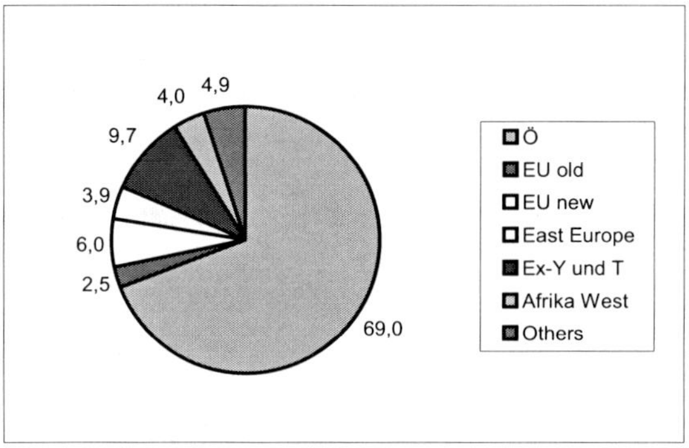

Figure 7b Prison Population* in Austria by Nationality (%) 2005

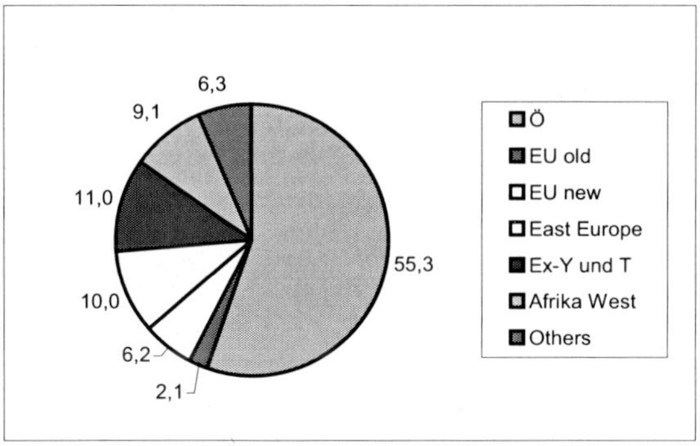

**) Population in prisons under justice administration.*
Source: Figure 2 to 7b: IVV-Data (based on prisoners' electronic files, not including police prisons), provided by Ministry of Justice, February 2006
Nationality:
EU-new: Estonia, Latvia, Lithuania, Malta, Poland, Slovakia, Czech Republic, Hungary, and Cyprus
East Europe: Albania, Armenia, Azerbaijan, Bulgaria, Georgia, Kazakhstan, Bishkek, Moldova, Romania, Russia, Ukraine, Uzbekistan, Tajikistan, Belarus
Ex-Y and T: Bosnia and Herzegovina, Yugoslavia, Kroatia, Macedonia, Serbia, Turkey
Africa West: Angola, Equatorial Guinea, Benin, Burkina Faso, Cote d'Ivoire, Gabon, Gambia, Ghana, Guinea, Guinea Bissau, Cameroon, Congo, Liberia, Mali, Mauritania, the Niger, Nigeria, Senegal, Sierra Leone, Togo, Chad, Central African Republic

Though in the long range a diminishing number of people are sentenced (namely native born and naturalized persons, but even foreigners integrated into the labour market) prison sentences become more frequent – in particular against certain groups of foreigners. They endure more frequently pre-trial detention and short-term prison sentences. Austrians, however, a priori do not experience pre-trial detention and imprisonment as often, but if they do their sentences are longer and more often combined with preventive detention. Criminal policy shows a kind of polarization along the line Austrian – foreign offenders. A slightly growing proportion of juveniles and women among prisoners in recent times is a consequence of the increasing rate of foreigners in prisons. Alternatives to prison sentences are less often used with foreign offenders. (Pilgram 2002; see: Table 2 and 3)

Table 2 Prison Population by Status of Detention and Citizenship

	Austrian					*other EU-citizenship*					*third state citizenship**				
by date 01.12	*pre trial detention*	*penal servitude*	*preventive custody*	*others*	*total*	*pre trial detention*	*penal servitude*	*preventive custody*	*others*	*total*	*pre trial detention*	*penal servitude*	*preventive custody*	*others*	*total*
2001	*769*	*3603*	*532*	*94*	*4998*	*252*	*337*	*6*	*22*	*617*	*555*	*1000*	*32*	*45*	*1632*
2002	*859*	*3862*	*554*	*75*	*5350*	*231*	*372*	*8*	*14*	*625*	*872*	*1159*	*42*	*52*	*2125*
2003	*815*	*3708*	*605*	*76*	*5204*	*262*	*312*	*4*	*15*	*593*	*1074*	*1506*	*48*	*57*	*2685*
2004	*834*	*3578*	*642*	*52*	*5106*	*326*	*441*	*8*	*16*	*791*	*1127*	*1909*	*56*	*45*	*3137*
2005	*703*	*3570*	*657*	*35*	*4965*	*268*	*443*	*16*	*14*	*741*	*935*	*2213*	*59*	*41*	*3248*
percentage															
2001	*15.4*	*72.1*	*10.6*	*1.9*	*100*	*40.8*	*54.6*	*1.0*	*3.6*	*100*	*34.0*	*61.3*	*2.0*	*2.8*	*100*
2002	*16.1*	*72.2*	*10.4*	*1.4*	*100*	*37.0*	*59.5*	*1.3*	*2.2*	*100*	*41.0*	*54.5*	*2.0*	*2.4*	*100*
2003	*15.7*	*71.3*	*11.6*	*1.5*	*100*	*44.2*	*52.6*	*0.7*	*2.5*	*100*	*40.0*	*56.1*	*1.8*	*2.1*	*100*
2004	*16.3*	*70.1*	*12.6*	*1.0*	*100*	*41.2*	*55.8*	*1.0*	*2.0*	*100*	*35.9*	*60.9*	*1.8*	*1.4*	*100*
2005	*14.2*	*71.9*	*13.2*	*0.7*	*100*	*36.2*	*59.8*	*2.2*	*1.9*	*100*	*28.8*	*68.1*	*1.8*	*1.3*	*100*

*Source: Source: IVV-Data (based on prisoners' electronic files, not including police prisons). Provided by Federal Computing Centre of Austria, March 2006, own calculations. *Including stateless persons*

Table 3: Released Prisoners, by Citizenship and Length of Detention, 2005

	citizenship				
	Austrian	*other EU*	*third state*	*foreign state total*	*total*
Released prisoners	6620	1741	5940	7681	14301
after days (mean) of					
pre-trial detention	44	63	60	122	53
penal custody	202	82	110	192	149
total (pre-trial d./penal cust.)	246	145	169	314	202
percentage penal custody	82.2	56.8	64.7	61.1	73.9

Figure 8 Released Prisoners 2005, Citizenship and Length of Detention (days)

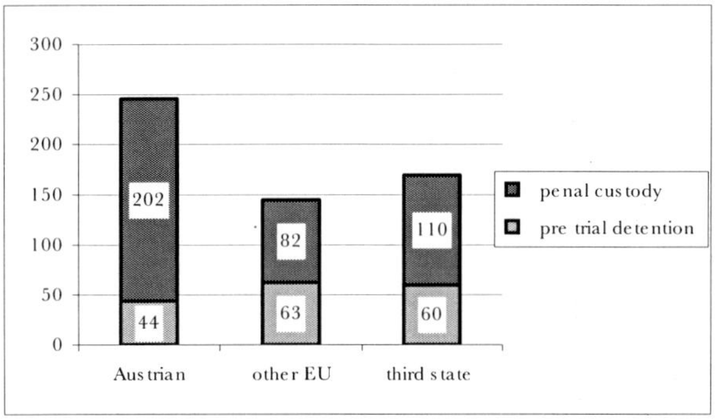

Source: IVV-Data (based on prisoners' electronic files, not including police prisons). Provided by Federal Computing Centre of Austria, April 2006, own calculations

With respect to police detention centres statements of trends cannot be made, because there is no steady data reporting by the Ministry of the Interior. The administration only offered very limited statistics, the total number of detentions in 2003 and 2004 (accession data), and the stock of detainees at two key dates (special inquiry at the turn of 2005/2006). From these sources it can be concluded that more persons are passed through PAZ than through prisons under justice administration, while the average time of detention is rather low there: 14 hours with police detention, 11 days with administrative penal custody and 16 days with detention pending expulsion.

Table 4: Entrances to Police Prisons in 2003 and 2004

			Population in police prisons by		*mean stay (days)**
	2003	2004	23 Nov 2005	23 Jan 2006	
total	26,263	25,889	616	790	9.8
thereof foreigners	18,184	17,807	462	652	11.3
% foreigners	69.2	68.8	75.0	82.5	
thereof % women	13.7	14.2	7.6	14.3	
thereof % juveniles	6.7	6.7	3.0	1.5	
administrative penal custody	5,932	6,212	178	198	11.3
thereof foreigners	1,255	1,307	30	56	12.3
% foreigners	21.2	21.0	16.9	28.3	
thereof % women	7.6	6.8	0.0	21.4	
thereof % juveniles	1.3	2.4	6.7	0.0	
police detention	8,028	8,740	14	13	0.6
thereof foreigners	4,626	5,563	8	4	0.4
% foreigners	57.6	63.6	57.1	30.8	
thereof % women	9.8	7.6	0.0	0.0	
thereof % juveniles	15.8	13.8	0.0	0.0	
detention for the purpose of removal	12,303	10,937	424	592	16.0
% foreigners	100.0	100.0	100.0	100.0	
thereof % women	15.7	18.4	8.3	13.7	
thereof % juveniles	3.8	3.6	2.8	1.7	

Source: Personal communication from Ministry of the Interior, Dept. II/3; own calculations
Comment: Data not including administrative detention facility in Bludenz
** Mean of entrance and population data used for calculation of mean stay.*

Forecasting future trends is quite difficult and risky. Since the last year there are some hints that after 2000 the wave of offences committed by foreigners already might have transgressed its peak. Prison populations might even decrease due to factors like the expansion of the EU and the intensified co-operation in police and justice matters, migration policy agreements within the EU and with accession countries and, last but not least, bi-lateral conventions with third countries. Yet in principle more restrictive regulations concerning residence, occupation, settlement and naturalisation for not privileged nationals, respectively for citizens lacking full citizen status in Austria and migration control by means of criminal law[11] will lead to illegalising of parts of the foreign population. Two

[11] The effects of the Immigration Police Law from 2005 on the numbers of detainees pending expulsion slowly become apparent now according to a press release from the Association for Human rights Austria on 29.01.2006 a doubling of the numbers can be expected in 2006 as compared with the year before.

classes of foreigners with respect to sentencing practice and implementation of prison sentences towards them are a quite presumable scenario for the future.

1.5 Overview of National Legislation

The legal grounds for deprivation of freedom can be:
- Security Police Law (*Sicherheitspolizeigesetz*, SPG) and Penal Procedure Law (*Strafprozessordnung*, StPO) – regulating arrest, police detention and pre-trial detention;
- Penal Law (*Strafgesetzbuch*, StGB) – including principles of sentencing, later modification of sentences and release;
- Code of Imprisonment (*Strafvollzugsgesetz*, StVG) – determining the exertion of prison sentences and of preventive measures;
- Imprisonment Decree (*Vollzugsordnung*) – instructions by the Ministry of Justice for the administration of the code of imprisonment;
- Several administrative state laws or province laws imposing administrative penal custody sanctions on norm violations, or allowing for commutation of irrecoverable fines into penal custody;
- Administrative Penal Law (*Verwaltungsstrafgesetz*, VStG) – determining the imposition and exertion of administrative penal sanctions;
- Police Detention Order (*Anhalteordnung*, AnhO) – instructions by the Ministry of the Interior for the administration of detention in police cells and police detention centres;

All these laws are applicable to Austrians and foreigners. Penal Procedure Law, Code of Imprisonment, and Imprisonment Decree in some articles consider particular requirements for foreigners, therefore the law formally rather entitles than discriminates them. Exclusion from certain rights and benefits usually takes place without reference to nationality, but with reference to rather undefined risk criteria. Actually risk attributions – like inclination to escape or similar assumptions – are more frequently made towards foreigners. While the Administrative Penal Law (VStG) only marginally considers foreign detainees the Police Detention Order (AnhO) acknowledges the situation of foreigners in a similar way as the Code of Imprisonment does. Before an amendment to the Decree of Police Detention which came into force on 1 Jan 2006 detainees pending expulsion in principle, were not treated differently from other police detainees or from persons in administrative penal custody.

- The Immigration Police Law (*Fremdenpolizeigesetz*, FPG) is a law primarily affecting foreigners and it is a significant part of the so-called Immigration Law Package (Fremdenrechtspaket) 2005). It allows arrest of foreigners to bring them before the immigration authority and defines the preconditions for putting somebody into detention pending expulsion.
- Illegal entering and stay in the country are no criminal offence, though an extended range of supporting acts are.

Detention pending expulsion can be applied to assure the administrative procedure for interdiction of residence or removal till enforceability, or to assure rejection, passage in transit or expulsion (§ 76 para.1 FPG). Foreigners can also be detained if the authorities determine that they are not eligible for asylum in Austria, since they have travelled through a so called safe third country (§ 76 para.2 FPG). The use of more lenient instruments can be bound to conditions (adherence to residence and notification obligations) whose violation may also lead to detention pending expulsion (§ 77 para.4 and 5 FPG). Though, in principle, the duration of detention pending expulsion should not exceed two months there are some exceptions. If a procedure is pending whether removal is admissible at all, the custody may take up to six months (§ 80 para.2 FPG), if the detainee is responsible for non-deportability (for instance, because of covering his identity or resisting police force) the custody may be extended to ten months within a period of two years (§ 80 para.4 FPG).[12] Complaints against detention pending expulsion can be brought before the Independent Administrative Senate and have to be decided within one week (§ 83f FPG). Minors in custody have to be separately accommodated, if their parents are also detained, they might be detained with them, except when their well-being demands separate accommodation (§ 79 para.3 FPG).

- The devolution of execution of prison sentences imposed on foreigners by Austrian courts, the take over of the execution of sentences against Austrians imposed by courts abroad and the assistance in law enforcement in general, including extradition[13], is subject matter of the Extradition and Legal Assistance Law (ARHG).

In principle this law under strict conditions also allows the transfer of sentenced persons outside the frame of European conventions and bilateral agreements. Practically this leeway is irrelevant. The large majority of transfers are done on the ground of multilateral and bilateral agreements. The most important legal basis for prisoners' transfer is the European Convention on the Transfer of Sentenced Persons from 1983 (accomplished in a Council of Europe framework and ratified in Austria in 1986). Austria belongs to the states that also ratified the Additional Protocol to the European Convention from 1997 in 2001 which first legalized the transfer without consent of sentenced persons if they had evaded penal execution by escape or got a final and executable ban of residence. While at present no requests for taking over the execution of sentences are made to Georgia or Ukraine, though they already have ratified the Additional Protocol, a memorandum of understanding between Austria and Romania was signed in 2004 to enforce the transfer of sentenced persons by speeding up the procedure through recognizing sentences as a matter of principle.

Further bilateral agreements exist between Austria and Thailand and Cuba. These agreements are of minor relevance and primarily are to ease the execution at home of prison sentences imposed in these countries against Austrians. With substantial groups of convicts in Austrian prisons from Nigeria and other Black-African states, formal interstate agreements with such countries and the prerequisites for transfer requests are inadequate. In 2005 the Austrian Ministry of Justice made 230 requests to foreign states to take over the execution of prison sentences imposed by Austrian courts on their citizens - two to three times more frequent than in the years before - in 76 cases requests were agreed

---

12 Regarding the potential consequences see fn. 11.

13 The documentation of extradition is deficient in Austria. We know about the number of extradition requests from Austria on foreign states and vice versa. On an average 94 requests were made on Austria in the period 2000-2004 (with 215 in 2004). Yet how many persons have been put into custody on request of extradition from abroad, and how many actually have been extradited is still unknown.

to.[14] This corresponds to only about 2% of those foreigners who had been unconditionally sentenced to a prison term of one year or more; with Romanians the transfer rate is 5 out of 43 such cases.

2 TREATMENT OF FOREIGN PRISONERS

The following report on the situation of foreigners in Austrian prisons is based on 14 interviews with experts in selected penitentiary institutions.[15] Managing officials, social workers, a psychiatrist, a psychologist, a pastor, an expert in the field of aftercare and probation as well as an advocate and officials from the Ministry of Justice gave information about the situation of foreigners in Austrian prisons.[16] Whenever possible the qualitative interviews are backed up by quantitative data for the whole of Austria by referring to the statistics of the Austrian penitentiary system, based on electronic prisoners' files, the *IVV (Integrierte Vollzugsverwaltung)*. Unfortunately there are no research projects about the situation of foreign prisoners in Austria. While the *Human Rights Advisory Council (Menschenrechtsbeirat)* of the Ministry of the Interior reports on police detention, no regular public reports exist for the penitentiary system. Information from the *CPT*, the *European Committee for the Prevention of Torture and Inhuman or Degrading Treatment or Punishment* could partly be used for this chapter.[17]

2.1 General

The Penal Procedure Code, the Code of Imprisonment and the Imprisonment Decree are, in general, equally applicable to foreigners and Austrians. Individual paragraphs prescribe special treatment for foreigners intending to compensate disadvantages.[18] In the treatment of foreigners, the wording of the laws in question does not discriminate between those with or without residence permits or whether foreigners are expelled after their detention or not. What does this legal equality or even this form of 'positive discrimination' mean in practice? The interviews showed a typical attitude on the part of

---

14 On top are requests addressing Romania (n=52), followed by Poland (n=36), Hungary and the Netherlands (n=20, each) and to German federal states (n=17, aggregate). The reasons for not making requests or for their failure cannot be figured out statistically. According to expert opinion the main reasons are the duration of the procedure as compared to the length of sentences, the missing consent or undecided residence status of the prisoner (no legally effective ban). From 2000 to 2005 662 requests to foreign states to take over the execution of prison sentences imposed by Austrian courts on their citizens have been made in all. In this period 315 requests (48%) have been agreed to. No accurate figures exist about prisoners having actually been transferred to their home countries. In at least 41 documented cases the transfer did not take place because of the prisoners having already served their sentence or having been paroled in the meantime, or because of revocation of their consent.

15 The interviews were conducted at the largest court prison (*Wien-Josefstadt*), at the largest penitentiary (*Stein*), at the penitentiary with the highest share of foreigners (*Suben*, 70% on 1 Dec 2005) as well as in two other court prisons and one other penitentiary.

16 In the scope of this study it was not possible to hold interviews with foreign prisoners themselves.

17 The CPT has visited several Austrian penitentiaries since 1990. The report cited in this chapter refers to the 2004 visit to *Wien-Josefstadt*, *Linz* and *Wien-Mittersteig*. For the CPT reports as well as the Austrian government's response see http://www.cpt.coe.int/en/states/aut.htm.

18 See also s. 1.5

employees and officials in Austrian penitentiary institutions that can be summarised as follows: 'We do not discriminate; we treat Austrians and foreigners the same way!' It was admitted that there may be a (small) part of the staff with prejudices against foreigners – but basically there *could* actually be no different treatment because of the high share of prisoners of foreign origin.

On a daily basis, however, foreign detainees are disadvantaged in many ways. Often they do not or hardly speak German, they do not have relatives nearby, they are confronted with prejudice, and in addition to their sentencing, they have to face the decisions of the immigration authorities. Even though nationality is no grounds for exclusion from semi-open places, better equipped facilities, courses, work and so on, foreigner status has negative consequences, such as, for example, the assumption that non-integrated foreigners are more likely to attempt escape. Language barriers often lead to information deficits and reduce the chances that individual wishes and needs are respected. Therefore the question arises: *Shouldn't* foreigners be treated *differently* in order to meet their special needs?

In some spheres (as for example religious practice, food, equipping of libraries, or German lessons) concrete steps were taken to fulfil the special needs of foreigners and to compensate disadvantages to a certain degree. When different penitentiary institutions are compared, however, it seems that the implementation of these and other compensating measures depends to a great extent on the atmosphere in the institution, its director, and on the commitment of individuals.

Communication ought to be improved. The language problem is more serious in court prisons than in penitentiary institutions where foreign prisoners usually arrive after having spent some time in the penal system. Particularly with people from former Soviet Republics and Eastern Europe, a common language is often lacking. This leads to mistrust, fear and incomprehension. Some officials scarcely differentiate and refer to Moldavians, Chechens, Georgians, Armenians, Ukrainians simply as 'the Russians', a group that is attributed various bad attitudes and characteristics. Professional translators are not used in daily prison life – too costly and too much effort. Other prisoners or the staffs do most translations. Even at disciplinary procedures professional translators are the exception.[19]

2.2 Living Conditions and Facilities

Pre-trial detainees are held in the prison of the court in charge of the case.[20] Sentenced prisoners are classified by the Ministry of Justice (§ 134 StVG) and assigned a place in a penitentiary somewhere in Austria. There are no special penitentiary institutions for foreign prisoners. The share of foreign prisoners varies according to the type of regime and

---

19 The CPT also criticised this fact after its visit (*Report to the Austrian Government on the visit to Austria carried out by the European Committee for the Prevention of Torture and Inhuman or Degrading Treatment or Punishment (CPT) from 14 to 23 April 2004*, Strasbourg July 2005, s.103, p.46). The Republic of Austria's response refers to a draft decree of the Ministry of Justice: The head of the prison will have to document the approval of the prisoner if another prisoner is translating at a disciplinary procedure (*Response of the Austrian Government to the report of the European Committee for the Prevention of Torture and Inhuman or Degrading Treatment or Punishment (CPT) on its visit to Austria from 14 to 23 April 2004*, Strasbourg July 2005, s.103, p. 43).

20 If necessary the Ministry of Justice may impose detention in another court prison (§ 185 StPO).

differs regionally. The prison in *Suben* is a special case with its high share of foreigners (70 % on 1 Dec 2005). Foreigners (particularly Africans) are sent to this remote prison,[21] since it is presumed that they do not have relatives in Austria and therefore no long journeys for visitors would be necessary (as they receive no visits at all).

Legal regulations for accommodating detainees *in* prisons follow criteria that are not based on nationality. They direct for example that those sentenced for intentionally committed offences are to be accommodated separately from those who had committed offences of negligence; first offenders not together with repeat offenders; pre-trial detainees without prior sentences not together with sentenced prisoners; young offenders separated from adults, men from women, and smokers from non-smokers. Sexual offenders are accommodated separately in some prisons; preventive custody is also spatially separated.

In none of the penitentiaries under investigation were there special sections for foreigners. Allocation depends on the type of regime or the prisoner's workplace. When allocating prisoners to cells, attempts are made to put people of the same provenance and/or the same language together.[22] If possible the prisoners' wishes are considered, but massive overcrowding minimizes the opportunities and makes even legally prescribed separations (such as first offender-repeat offender) sometimes impossible. In practice it comes down to cells with for example only Africans or only Georgians, a fact that is judged differently by the interviewees. While some don't see it as a problem and refuse any kind of 'mixing' as generating further conflicts, others warn against the creation of subcultures. The opinion was occasionally expressed that certain groups of foreigners (e.g. Africans) would actually like to be in cells accommodating eight to ten people, and that they would not mind overcrowded conditions. One interviewee notes that solitary cells – a highly appreciated option in a prison – were inhabited more by Austrians than by foreigners.

2.3 Reception and Admission

The Imprisonment Decree prescribes that prison social services should talk to prisoners with communication problems and 'provenance based adaptation problems' when they are admitted. It is also the role of prison social services to help to establish contact with families or consulates and embassies.

On admission prisoners receive information sheets in different languages – statements on the number of languages available vary from nine (EU) languages up to 'in all languages'. The Austrian government's response to the *CPT* report states that house regulations are available in 13 languages and that the Ministry of Justice regularly reminds the institutions' directors of their duty to hand out these regulations. The *CPT* had reported earlier that prisoners they had talked to on their visits had complained about lack of information.[23]

---

21 *Suben* is a village in Upper Austria. Some years ago the closure of the prison had been discussed.

22 Only in *Stein*, the largest Austrian penitentiary did an interviewee regret that it was no longer possible to separate ethnic groups because of recent overcrowding. It was said that there were still 'mixed' cells.

23 *Report to the Austrian Government on the visit to Austria carried out by the European Committee for the Prevention of Torture and Inhuman or Degrading Treatment or Punishment (CPT) from 14 to 23 April 2004*, Strasbourg July 2005, s.108, p.49.

During pre-trial detention information from the court is of crucial importance, and the question arises whether official notifications and application forms are written in a language the prisoner understands. The current situation has been partly criticised in interviews. While information on court procedures exists in many languages, official notifications are said to be usually only in German (at least as far as Vienna is concerned).

Some prisons have further information materials. The prisons *Wien-Josefstadt* and *Stein* contain special medical departments (so called *Sonderkrankenanstalten*) and in both institutions information sheets on medical issues are available in different languages.[24] A director of a court prison reported on his initiative to provide prisoners with information brochures in 20 languages and with application forms (e.g. for conditional release or for the permission to go out) in languages used in prison.

2.4 Work – Education – Training – Sports – Recreation

The wording of the law concerning allocation of work does not differentiate between nationals and foreigners, but names criteria such as the prisoner's state of health, age, knowledge, duration of the sentence and behaviour in prison as well as preferences and advancement after release (§ 47 StVG). Pre-trial detainees are, unlike sentenced prisoners, not obliged to work. Participation in courses is not bound to the Austrian citizenship either, but for programmes that are conducted in cooperation with the Austrian Public Employment Service (AMS) preferably those detainees are chosen who have permission to work in Austria after release. Austrian prisons are overcrowded[25] which makes work and training positions in prison scarce. The CPT judges the situation as 'far from satisfactory' in the visited prisons and apparently throughout the Austrian prison system.[26] Apart from overcrowding, several prisons and their workshops suffer from lack of orders. Another problem evolves because prisoners often do not have the necessary qualifications. The situation varies greatly in the different prisons, the lowest employment rate is found in court prisons.[27]

Employment in prison is very important for prisoners. Sentenced prisoners who are not able to work receive a small amount of money. Many detainees, and especially foreigners, depend on what they earn in prison, because many of them don't receive money from outside. Employment in prison also entitles a prisoner to unemployment benefit after release. Furthermore many privileges in prison are connected to employment.

It can be said from the interviews that the prisoner's skills and qualifications are the most important criteria for the allocation of work, i.e. a sentenced prisoner with useful qualifications usually gets work in a penitentiary. Prisoners who don't speak German have more difficulties in getting work. One prison director states: 'If I have 200 detainees and only 100 places for work, then the Russian or Georgian prisoners will be the last to get the job.' On the other hand, efforts to give work to all prisoners are made in several institutions. Some groups of foreigners enjoy the reputation that they work hard and do it well. There is a small enterprise in Vienna's court prison where only juveniles and 'young adults' from Africa work. In the prison at *Suben* we were told that only newcomers or

24 See also 2.5 medical care.

25 At a capacity of 8,068 places, an average of 8,885 persons were imprisoned in 2005. In March 2006 more than 9,000 prisoners were reported (*die Presse*, 22 March 2006).

26 Ibidem, s.70, p.35.

27 In Vienna's court prison only about 30% of the prisoners can be occupied.

people not willing to work were unemployed; after three to six months everyone who wanted to work found employment – regardless of their nationality.

The statistics of the Austrian penitentiary system show that foreigners are altogether less often employed than nationals. Austrians earn in average more than twice as much as foreigners per day in prison. The main reason for this difference is that foreigners are more frequently in pre-trial detention.[28] Another index for measuring the difference is obtained when one does not compare the average income earned during the whole period in prison but when income is set in relation to a detainee's time in prison after being sentenced: Austrian sentenced prisoners earn only 1.3 as much as foreign sentenced prisoners.

With regard to training and courses two types have to be distinguished: courses especially for foreigners, i.e. German classes, and courses open to everyone who fulfils certain selection criteria. Nationality is again no reason for exclusion and even when a detainee is expelled from Austria following his release, he is formally not excluded from courses. There are different tests and selection mechanisms, whereof the lack of language competence is a substantial disadvantage. All juveniles and 'young adults' can complete a course of study for a school leaving certificate – a chance taken by foreign young prisoners too. Furthermore computer classes, first aid courses, 'fork-lift truck driving' courses and training in the form of apprenticeships are offered. The supply of training and courses varies a lot from prison to prison; there are no nationwide minimum standards. 'German as foreign language' is offered almost everywhere; English classes for prisoners are provided in some places. Some prisoners are able to study German by themselves on a computer. German classes are in the interest of both sides: not only foreigners but also staff benefit when prisoners speak at least a little German. In most institutions demand is greater than supply.[29] This results mainly from financial problems and shortage of space caused by overcrowding. Some interviewees complained that there were no German courses designed for foreigners from former Soviet Republics.

All prisoners are entitled and obliged to 'exercise' outdoors for one hour a day (juveniles two hours). Gym halls and fitness rooms are mainly for the use of those prisoners who are employed. In many institutions – especially in older penitentiaries – there is a shortage of such facilities. The situation in some prisons is equally bad for all detainees. One disadvantage for foreigners that was mentioned is that jogging-groups organised outside a prison with insufficient facilities are not open to foreigners because of the presumed higher risk of escape.[30]

'Instructive, artistic or amusing' events have to be held once quarterly (§ 65 StVG). In this section the Code of Imprisonment explicitly refers to foreign language prisoners: when organising events and activities their special needs should be taken into account (§ 65a StVG). Examples include concerts, cabaret, slideshows, drum groups, and even belly dancing performances. The penitentiaries under investigation have large libraries (e.g. 16,000 books in *Wien-Josefstadt* or 13,000 books in *Stein*) containing a lot of foreign lan-

[28] The share of foreigners of all pre-trial detainees was 63% in 2005. 89% of all foreigners, who have only been in pre-trial detention, did not work one day in prison. Within the larger group of sentenced prisoners the share of Austrians is higher (57% in 2005).

[29] Even in the largest penitentiary (*Stein*), the demand is estimated to be higher than supply despite German lessons four times a week.

[30] See also 2.8 re-integration activities – prison leave.

guage literature.[31] Furthermore the foreigners' advisor (*'Ausländerreferent'*) sends international magazines to prisons all over Austria.[32] Reading has become less important with the distribution of television.[33]

2.5 Food – Religion – Personal Hygiene – Medical Care

The Code of Imprisonment (§ 38 StVG) regulates that religious guidelines concerning nutrition have to be respected. In all institutions where interviews were conducted, the daily preparation of several different meals was practised (ritual food, diets, vegetarian meals, etc.). The interviewees also reported that certain group preferences were respected (e.g. to serve white bread or rice for Africans). The impression gained from the interviews is that there are relatively few problems in this aspect of daily prison life.

The Code of Imprisonment also regulates the sphere of religious practice within prison walls. § 85 StVG entitles prisoners to take part in religious services and to address themselves to a spiritual advisor. If there is no such contact person sharing someone's religion in a particular prison, the head of the prison may allow the visit of a spiritual advisor. An official of the Ministry of Justice states that supply was generally adequate: On the one hand, there are still a few employed catholic pastors, on the other hand there is an increasing number of spiritual advisors from Austria's recognised religious communities[34] that work in the prisons on a contract basis with the state. A Muslim spiritual advisor visits the two largest Austrian prisons (*Wien-Josefstadt* and *Stein*) once every two weeks. Interviewees in Vienna reported that this was not enough to satisfy demand. Jewish prisoners from all over Austria are brought to Vienna's court prison twice a year to celebrate their highest holidays. The prison houses a synagogue, a Catholic church, a Protestant chapel and for the last few years a mosque. In Stein, there is also a Catholic church and a mosque. This is not the case in all prisons. In one prison visited, religious services are held in the refectory and not all religious groups are attended to. It is argued that there was no demand or that requests to the religious communities to send someone remained unanswered. A widespread attitude is one of not having anything against religious activities per se but it is seen as the churches' and communities' duty to take the initiative. Language barriers play a role in the religious sphere too: there is a demand for religious services in a language the prisoners understand.

For the interviewees there was no doubt that all prisoners would get the same medical treatment. Language difficulties are met in different ways. The institutions partly employ medical staff with foreign language competence. But also other members of the staff or other prisoners translate – a practice that is not without problems, not only because of the lack of medical confidentiality but also because of the quality of the translation (special medical terms). A professional interpreter is hardly ever used. An information sheet in several languages on medical issues exists in the special medical departments (in *Wien-Josefstadt* and *Stein*).

Statistical data (based on the IVV) contains information on the number of transfers to hospitals, to special medical departments of other prisons, and information on the consul-

---

31 § 65a StVG prescribes those foreign prisoners have to be considered when equipping libraries.

32 More about the foreigners' advisor see 2.12 projects.

33 More about television see 2.7 contact with the outside world.

34 At the moment, 13 religious communities are officially recognised in Austria, among them the Muslim and the Jewish community.

tation of a medical specialist or a doctor other than the prison doctor. Analysing this data shows that foreigners are less often taken out (76% of all foreigners are never referred externally in comparison with 68% of all Austrians).

Psychological and psychiatric care is barely possible when the professional does not speak the prisoner's language (or at least a language a prisoner understands). It happens now and then that psychiatrists or psychologists speak (even unusual) languages, but this is more the result of coincidence than of systematic recruitment. The practise of drug substitution seems to vary extensively between the different prisons and depends to a considerable extent on the attitude of the attending physician.

2.6 Consular and Legal Help

The Penal Procedure Law prescribes that prisoners on remand must have a defence lawyer in court (cases of mandatory defence, § 41 StPO). If the accused person cannot afford a lawyer, the court assigns a lawyer to the prisoner on remand (as to all persons who do not understand the language of the court). A lawyer assists nationals and foreigners when it comes to hearings concerning pre-trial detention. In all these cases there has to be an interpreter if the prisoner is not able to speak the language of the court. The interpreter is paid by the court (§ 38a para.2 StPO). In Austria's largest court prison in Vienna we were told that the assignment of a lawyer for foreigners by the court did not usually cause any problems. But again and again some lawyers would come to meet prisoners without an interpreter or too late (right before the trial).

Prisoners can get in contact with the representations of their country if necessary with the support of prison social services. Not everyone wants this contact and not all consulates and embassies are interested in the fate of their fellow countrymen. The extent of co-operation between the detention centres and the representations varies: many interviewees pointed to the good relationships with Western European representatives (esp. the Netherlands, Germany and Britain), with the Turkish embassy and partly with the Romanian. They would come regularly, bring movies and magazines and would 'collaborate'. Little to no contact at all existed with the former Yugoslavian states, the former USSR or with African representations.

2.7 Contact with the Outside World

Prisoners on remand and prisoners serving a sentence are subjected to different regulations with regard to contact with the outside world. In pre-trial detention, the decision over whom a prisoner is allowed to stay in contact with depends on the investigating judge. In the following section we consider contact with the outside world through visits, phone calls, and through TV information.

Prisoners on remand have the right to a 15-minute visit at least twice a week (§ 187 StPO) unless it endangers the aim of detention. Prisoners serving sentences do not need authorisation from a judge. They are entitled to receive longer visits and in the case of relatives having to make long journeys to the prison, the length of visits has to be extended (§ 93 StVG). As expected foreigners receive fewer visits than nationals and many of them none at all. In most of the prisons, visiting hours are extended when relatives come from far away. In the largest court prison we were told that even when the visitor had to make a long trip to the prison, visiting hours were seldom accumulated (to half an hour a week). In the largest penitentiary visiting hours are dealt with generously (prisoners can get up to a whole day of visit). In *Suben*, a prison away from the urban areas, the proportion of foreigners who never receive visits was estimated at 50%. Apart from friends and relatives there are visiting services, partly from organisations specialised in the care for foreigners.

Prisoners on remand who want to make a telephone call have to apply for a permit to the investigating judge (something that according to an interviewee not all foreigners know). Approval is a lengthy process. Difficulties arise because there is not enough telephone boxes in many prisons (especially in the old ones). Mobile phones are forbidden. Calls are only allowed during business hours. Besides that many foreign prisoners (esp. on remand) do not have enough money to make phone calls.

Depending on the prison the number of TV channels differ. Sometimes it varies among the different parts of a single prison. In all detention centres where no foreign language programmes are available at the moment, it is intended to rectify this deficiency.

2.8 Re-integration Activities - Prison Leave

If educational and vocational training measures and incorporation into the working process is seen as re-integration activity, then foreigners and nationals are basically equal, at least in theory. The situation is different when activities are related to leaving prison for a certain time. The wording of the relevant laws does not mention nationality but it is a fact that foreign prisoners are rarely allowed to leave prison (on '*Ausgang*' or '*Freigang*' i.e. to regulate important affairs, to work outside the prison, etc.) especially when they will be expelled from Austria after custody.[35] Foreigners integrated in Austria have better chances of leaving prison for a certain time than foreigners without residence permits or asylum-seekers. During imprisonment the authorities often do not know whether a prisoner will be expelled from Austria afterwards. The interviews revealed that prison directors[36] dealt with this problem differently: while some refused categorically every prison leave in case of uncertainties about expulsion after custody, other prison directors let foreigners leave prison even when the immigration authority has not taken its decision yet. Another precondition for leaving prison for a certain period of time is that prisoners can name specific reasons why they need to go out (e.g. arranging important affairs) as well as a contact address (if they want to stay overnight). If the aim of prison leave is not re-integration and if the prisoner has no social contacts in the country, it will hardly ever be granted.

Statistical information is available about how often a prisoner leaves the prison and for what purpose. A distinction is made between 'Ausgang' (prison leave to regulate important personal, economic or legal affairs, for educational training, etc.; single days, not more than five days) and 'Freigang' (the prisoner works regularly outside prison). 89% of

35 A decision of the Austrian Supreme Administrative Court stated that only concrete indications that the inmate might misuse prison leave to escape justify the refusal of an application for permission to leave prison (Supreme Administrative Court 19 February 2004, decision 2003/20/0502). A blanket refusal of all applications from foreigners is not permitted.

36 The prison director allows prison leave.

all foreigners who have been serving sentence[37] did not get a single day of 'Ausgang' – in comparison to only 36% of nationals in this category. The situation is especially bad for some groups of foreigners: Hardly anybody from the former Soviet Republics left an Austrian prison on 'Ausgang' (1% of all sentenced Georgians, Russians, Moldavians, Ukrainians). Austrians are allowed to leave prison on an average of 3.4 per 100 days while prison leave for foreigners only amounts to 5 per 1,000 days.

Table 5a: Prison Leave ('*Ausgang*')

		no prison leave	*prison leave*	*total*
Austrians	*number*	1,654	2,983	4,637
	%	35.7	64.3	100
EU citizens	*number*	*951*	*60*	*1,011*
	%	*94.1*	*6.0*	*100*
non EU citizens	*number*	*2,988*	*445*	*3,433*
	%	*87.0*	*13.0*	*100*
all foreigners	*number*	3,939	505	4,444
	%	88.6	11.4	100
total	*number*	5,593	3,488	9,081
	%	61.6	38.4	100

Table 5b: Average Number of Prison Leaves ('*Ausgang*')

	number of persons	*mean per 100 days in prison**
Austrians	4,637	3.4
EU citizens	1,011	0.3
Non EU- citizens	3,433	0.5
foreigners	4,444	0.5
total	9,081	2.0

* *Per day in prison after being sentenced*
Source: IVV-Data, provided by the Austrian Federal Computing Centre, April 2006, own calculations

'Freigang' means that a prisoner works outside prison in a factory, a company, etc. without surveillance. 96% of all foreign prisoners (who were not only on remand but have been sentenced) did not work one single day outside prison while 31% of all nationals did leave the penitentiary for work. On average Austrians work outside prison 10 per 100 days but foreigners only 1 per 100 days. There are special departments or even houses

37 Prisoners who were only on remand were not considered in the calculation because prison leave during pre-trial detention is something very atypical.

(the so called '*Freigängerhaus*') for those who work outside the prison – in these semi-open places few foreigners can be found.

Table 6a: Prison Leave to Work outside Prison ('*Freigang*')

		no prison leave	*prison leave*	*total*
Austrians	number	3,199	1,438	4,637
	%	69.0	31.0	100
EU citizens	number	991	20	1,011
	%	98.0	2.0	100
non EU citizens	number	3,276	157	3,433
	%	95.4	4.6	100
all foreigners	number	4,267	177	4,444
	%	96.0	4.0	100
total	number	7,466	1,615	9,081
	%	82.2	17.8	100

Table 6b: Average Number of Prison Leaves to Work outside Prison (F*reigang*')

	number of persons	*mean per 100 days in prison**
Austrians	4,637	9.7
EU citizens	1,011	0.5
Non EU- citizens	3,433	1.1
foreigners	4,444	1.0
total	9,081	5.4

** Per day in prison after being sentenced*
Source: IVV-Data, provided by the Austrian Federal Computing Centre, April 2006, own calculations

All prisoners have the right to parole. Comparing the frequencies of conditional release between nationals and foreigners show that – on a nationwide level and for all duration of sentences – prisoners without Austrian citizenship are released on parole slightly less often than nationals (Pilgram 2005). But there are regional differences and differences depending on the length of a sentence. Nationals with short-term sentences (three to six month) are conditionally released twice as often as foreigners. One reason for this is that Austrians do serve short sentences whereas foreigners often do their time on remand. When medium-length sentences (six to twelve months) are considered there are no noteworthy differences concerning conditional release between nationals and foreigners. Foreigners are more often released conditionally from long sentences (one to three years) than nationals.[38]

2.9 Release - Expulsion

On the occasion of release social workers speak to nationals as well as to foreigners. Prisoners get information sheets with contact addresses. The mission of social workers changes when advising foreigners who are not allowed to live and work legally in Austria. They then have to give legal advice in the field of immigration law, and clarification of what happens after release. Help upon release in the sense of helping to find a flat or a job is not possible in these cases. Social workers get the necessary knowledge in training sessions (at the '*Strafvollzugsakademie*', the Austrian prison staff academy, or at *Neustart*).

Courts and prisons have to inform the immigration police on convictions of foreigners and at the start/end of a sentence. At the latest when the prisoner is released, there ought to be a decision by the immigration police on whether the prisoner will be detained in custody for the purpose of removal or not. Several interviewees pointed to the fact that this decision is not always taken until the end of custody and that there was a lot of insecurity during detention about what might happen after release. The decision to expel or remove a foreigner after imprisonment depends on his or her legal status, the time he or she had spent in Austria before conviction, and on the length of the sentence. The immigration authorities make this decision. In any case the removal to the country of origin must be possible. Even if removal is not possible, a ban on residence can be declared. A foreigner will be expelled (and removed) if he or she is seen as a 'danger to public interest' that is usually assumed after a prison sentence of more than three months or a (semi-) conditional sentence of six months. But also incorrect information given to the Austrian authorities, lack of means of sustenance, illicit work and other (administrative) offences can lead to a ban on residence (§ 60 FPG 2005). For foreigners who have spent much of their lives in Austria the expulsion criteria are less restrictive depending on the extent of integration and on the intensity of family relations. For asylum seekers special regulations are valid (AsylG 2005).

In practice, it very often happens that removal (especially to countries outside Europe) is not possible - people are not removed but at the same time they don't have the right to stay and work legally in Austria. One reason for the rejection of a removal is the existence of a concrete danger in the country of origin, or that the country refuses to 'take back' the person. After release from prison, ex-offenders are often detained in custody for the purpose of removal for a certain time[39] and released after that time because they cannot be removed to their country of origin. The expulsion-decision can be challenged. Legal remedies against expulsion decisions basically have a suspending effect.

---

[38] One reason for this inverted ratio might be that Austrians with long sentences usually have more prior convictions.

[39] The upper time limit has been extended to a maximum of 10-month custody for the purpose of removal as of 1 Jan 2006.

2.10 Aftercare - Probation

In Austria help upon release as well as probation services are provided nationwide by the association *Neustart.* When the proportion of foreigners increased in Austrian prisons the proportion of foreigners also increased in aftercare facilities. This caused difficulties: Apart from increasing numbers of clients the classic social work concepts designed for ex-offenders were no longer appropriate. *Neustart*'s reaction was a minimum programme for foreigners without legal status, which meant no intensive, long-term support and no legal remedies in cases with no chances of obtaining legal status (permission of residence, asylum, etc.). Since a system of basic support for asylum seekers (the so called '*Bundesbetreuung*') was established by the Austrian government, tensions eased and demand was distributed all over Austria. But still the staffs working in aftercare facilities face the difficult situation that they should 'integrate' people into Austrian society who are actually excluded from it, because every legal status is denied to them.

Probation after custody for foreigners is rare. It is difficult in general for social workers to find jobs or flats for foreign ex-offenders (again language barriers, prejudices against ex-offenders and against foreigners, etc). If a foreigner with insecure legal status is put on probation, it is an even more difficult task: How can a social worker find a job for someone who is not allowed to work? How to find a residence for someone without permit to stay?

2.11 Staff

When staff is recruited foreign language competence is not a required criteria. There are very few prison officers with a background in migration. Language competence or migration experience can be an advantage when applying for a job in prison but it remains within the prison director's discretion and is not actively encouraged as criteria. Since 2004, prisons officers-in-training are informed about 'foreign cultures' (16 hours during basic training) and they are taught English (32 hours, technical terminology). As voluntary further training, prison staff can attend courses on migration, globalisation, foreigners in Austrian prisons, a special course on the 'Slav cultural area' and English classes. Many employees attend these seminars.

Over the last few years the increasing presence of foreigners has changed daily prison life. In some prisons more than half the detainees are foreigners from over 100 countries. This meant new challenges for the staff. Information from the interviews points to the presumption that after a period of change and conversion, adaptation to the new situation was achieved. It is admitted that some staff members were prejudiced against foreigners (similar prejudices existed in the rest of the population). But apart from these elements, the treatment of foreigners and relations with them are described as relatively unproblematic. Problems were admitted only in the treatment of people from the former Soviet Republics

2.12 Projects

In 1989 a special department for foreigners (the so called '*Ausländerreferat*') was founded.[40] The project started with a headquarters in Vienna's court prison *Wien-Josefstadt* and there were contact persons in the other Federal States. Today there is only one contact person outside Vienna left and the responsible social worker in Vienna has to divide his time between his work in the court prison (in a section of the prison) and his responsibility for all foreigners in penitentiary institutions in Austria. His aim is to inform people in the justice system on issues concerning foreigners. The last remaining contact person (in *Stein*) sees his duty in managing contacts between the prison and the consulates and embassies of foreign countries.

Special projects for foreigners exist in different prisons to a varying extent. Usually these projects are based on the initiatives of individuals. For example an 'integration group' was mentioned where Austrian and foreign women met once a week to exchange experiences or an information evening about the situation of refugees from the Caucasian region. Repeatedly it was reported that the so called 'group counselling' was successfully held with groups of foreigners. Language courses and cultural events have already been mentioned above.[41] After the CPT had criticised the treatment of foreign prisoners by some staff members and the situation of foreigners in the court prison in Linz in general, the new prison director founded an expert group with representatives from a human rights association (*SOS-Menschenrechte*) and from *Neustart*. They developed a '10-point-programme' listing for example language training for prison officers, TV in foreign languages, and information sheets in a sufficient number of languages. This programme can be seen as an example of how attempts were made to improve the situation of foreigners in the wake of a critical report from an independent committee.

3 ADMINISTRATIVE DETENTION OF FOREIGN PRISONERS

Statistical and administrative reporting on police detention is extremely deficient in Austria.[42] This paper is based on very limited information given by the Ministry of the Interior (Dept. II/3); this information in turn is based on unpublished annual reports from the Security Directorates of the provinces and on two special surveys on two key-days. However, the most profitable data source for this chapter on police detention stems from the *Human Rights Advisory Council* (*Menschenrechtsbeirat, MRB*) because of its proactive and systematic control activities (differing from the singular instance and reactive control by the state ombudsman/*Volksanwalt*). Since its foundation the *MRB* delivered 13-targeted

40 The department was founded by a decree by the Ministry of Justice in 1989. The Imprisonment Decree (1995) describes its function as supporting and advising foreign prisoners with regard to their special needs concerning language problems and cultural differences. They are to be supplied with reading and audiovisual material; special events should be organised for them.

41 See 2.4 Work, Education, Training, Sports, Recreation

42 The annual Governmental Report on Internal Security surprisingly lacks a chapter on police detention centres and a particular one on detention pending expulsion. Correspondingly there is lacking scientific and media attention paid to the issue.

reports, five of which directly focus on matters of police detention.[43] These reports regularly integrate observations made by *CPT*. Moreover, since 1999 annual activity reports of the *MRB* are published. The reports always contain clear recommendations to the minister of the interior. The implementation of the recommendations is periodically evaluated by workgroups of the council.[44] The following *MRB*-reports are directly touching matters of detention. The reports on:

- The problem of minors in custody pending detention (2000)
- Human rights questions in connection with detention of women through police agents (2001)
- The problem of information of detainees (2002)
- Medical care for detainees (2002)
- Conditions of detention and police facilities (2005).

3.1 General

In principle all different categories of detainees in police detention centres are to be treated equally according to the Police Detention Order (AnhO), whereby for detainees pending expulsion a better standard ought to be realized. Even though their separated accommodation from other detainees (in administrative penal custody or in police detention for criminal reasons) has already been demanded by former Decrees on Police Detention (§ 4 AnhO), the revised law of 1 Jan 2006 explicitly introduces for the first time 'custody in open sections' of detainees for the purpose of removal provided there are no objections related to safety such as infectious diseases, aggressiveness, escape attempts, etc. This regulation at least partly takes into account recommendation No. 274 of the *MRB* from Oct 2004. While the administration of detention in open sectors is still legally bound to sufficient spatial facilities and personnel capacities of detention centres the administration of 'custody with temporary open cells' (§ 5a para.4 AnhO) is not yet a binding rule and is not yet realized in each centre.[45] Apart from that only the supervision of phone calls and visits is more generously regulated for detainees pending expulsion than for other inmates. This is also problematic insofar as it actually prevents the common accommodation of spouses and relatives (in particular of children of opposite sex) during detention pending expulsion. This unnecessarily violates the right to have a protected private and family life (that means: recommendation No. 130 of the *MRB* from March 2002 is not yet implemented for lack of spatial and other provisions). While administrative penal custody of juveniles under age 16 is ruled out (§ 7 para.5 AnhO), detention pending expulsion is admissible even with minors of lower age if accommodation and care according to age can be warranted (§ 4 para.4 AnhO). Although the *MRB* from July

---

43 Further general reports of the *MRB* refer to the linguistic usage of police officers, to the use of force by police, or to police training and further education. More significant for this paper are some priority reports of the *MRB* concerning single detention facilities or the report on 'problem-removals' which not at least may result from inadequate preparation and administration of detention pending expulsion. See: http://www.menschenrechtsbeirat.at

44 In particular the last interim report of the *MRB* evaluation-working group (dating from quarter 4/2004) on the recommendations for detention pending expulsion is a very informative one. See: http://www.menschenrechtsbeirat.at/de/index_evaluierung.html

45 This fact was heavily criticised by several NGOs (e.g. refugee service of *Diakonie* and *Caritas*) when they rendered an expert opinion on the draft of the current Police Detention Order.

2000 on (see recommendations no. 33-37) repeatedly denies the existence of appropriate police detention facilities for minors, the numerous invocations of the advisory council to abolish detention pending expulsion with minors under age 14, to restrict it to elder minors, to stipulate the administration of lenient measures, to reduce the maximum time to 2 months and to advance juvenile welfare measures remained without response. The detention of minors and juveniles in detention pending expulsion has been markedly reduced throughout the last years as the co-operation between police and juvenile welfare agencies improved.

A particular problem is identified by the *MRB* when it comes to the joint accommodation of detainees pending expulsion and of criminal prisoners taking place in institutions under justice administration. Though at present no use is made of the rule that detainees in detention pending expulsion may be kept in court prisons or penitentiaries if police detention centres are overcrowded (§ 78 para.1 FPG), detention for the purpose of removal following prison sentences is still practised in general prisons. Detainees are subjected to general prison rules (to the Code of Imprisonment) without relief and have no access to specialized social services like in police detention centres. Because of lacking co-ordination between immigration authorities and justice administration, measures to end residence and stay in the country sometimes cannot be put into effect immediately after the prison sentence.

3.2 Living Conditions and Facilities

The Decree of Police Detention (§ 4 para.1a) requires detention facilities 'worthy of human beings'. Nevertheless the *MRB* in his report on 'Conditions of detention a police facilities' points to the problem of detention in 'historically grown prisons' for the sake of nothing else than to ensure the administrative procedure before immigration authorities (*MRB*, 2005, 8). Though the facilities are not essentially below national and international standards and though there is only sporadic critique by the *MRB* concerning the location, size, occupancy, ventilation, lightening or the sanitary installations (and usually remedying construction measures have been prompted by the critiques) the advisory council recommends better standards in particular for detainees in detention pending expulsion. As non-offenders they would deserve more privacy (e.g. lockable boxes, access to lavatories, washing machines and dryers) as well as more freedom of movement. Detainees pending expulsion appear unreasonably burdened by the living conditions in prisons under police administration. Yet it cannot be decided on the basis of available data, whether foreigners in police detentions centres are discriminated in other ways as well.

3.3 Reception and Admission

In his report 'The problem of information of detainees' (2002) the *MRB* recommends the translation (in additional languages) and availability of more comprehensive and complete information sheets (and as alternative of sound carriers) for detainees in general and those in detention pending expulsion in particular (recommendation no. 131-162). Similar improvements are demanded regarding information policies on the Decree of Police Detention, the house rules, and the social service for detainees pending expulsion (*Schubhaftbetreuung*). Since detainees pending removal are under severe stress the *MRB* has suggested improving the flow of information on matters concerning expulsion. Deportees should be informed in due time and social services should be more easily available to them to prevent situations of crisis and problematic removals. Only a few of these recommendations have been implemented so far.

3.4 Work – Education – Training – Sports – Recreation

Inactivity is a greater problem in pre-trial detention and penal custody in prisons under justice administration compared to relatively short-term detentions in police prisons. Yet also short periods of detention do not justify the denial of meaningful activities. *CPT* complains about inadequate access to recreation areas, books, and games and also to useful domestic work or paid work in Austrian police detention centres. The committee misses an activity regime that is structuring the daytime. Open cells and access to TV alone are not accepted as substitute (*MRB* 2005, 44ff).

3.5 Food – Religion – Personal Hygiene – Medical Care

In 2005 *CPT* recommends to assure free direct access to drinking water for everybody in police custody. The *MRB* urges uniform regulations regarding mealtimes and a general directive for the quality of nutrition, further on the provision of complete cutlery and a more generous absorption of costs for board by the institution. Detainees should have the opportunity to prepare their own meals. The *MRB* also repeatedly concerns about the lack of sufficient clothing for detainees and of clothing that reduces suicide risks. Effective local remedy measures must not belie the defects in central management. This is also true in case of suicide prevention and medical care in PAZ (recommendations 163-222 from May 2002; *MRB*-AG Evaluierung, III. Quartal 2004). On different occasions the lack of sensibility and of special training of the personnel (including police officers and physicians) is pointed out, in particular the lack of regular supervision of and communication (enabled by proper interpreters) with persons at risk and the avoidance of solitary confinement.

With respect to medical care the lacking differentiation between administrative, official expert and medical duties of police doctors is criticised. The same holds true for paramedics. For police detainees the contact with independent medical examiners is complicated. Discrete medical examination and treatment out of sound and visual range of fellow detainees and comprehensible mother tongue clarification as well as medical after care of the released are still not generally granted. Verified by *MRB*, progress has been made in informing about the dangers related to hygiene by the personnel handling hunger striking detainees (communication through social care workers instead of restrictions and punishment) (*MRB*-AG Evaluierung, III. Quartal 2003).

3.6 Consular and Legal Help

Although the right to free access to lawyers also applies to police detainees the practice evidently does not fully comply with the norm. The confidential consultation with a lawyer, the presence of a lawyer in interrogations, the legal assistance free of charge for the destitute, the calling in of a trusted person or lawyer in juvenile cases are not granted without any exception (*MRB* 2005, 70ff). According to *MRB* the social care for detainees pending expulsion is no full surrogate for free of charge legal advice throughout the administrative procedure before the immigration authority (*MRB* 2005, 75f).[46] *CPT* on the occasion of its 2004 visit also argued that the information given to foreign prisoners about the procedure could be substantially improved and that the obligation of external agents (diplomatic missions) to give support does not exempt the state from information duties.

3.7 Contact with the Outside World

According to the Police Detention Order written correspondence is not subject to restrictions (even if some controls are admissible, except with advocates, national administrative and representative bodies of the home country and international organisations for the protection of human rights) and must be made available also for destitute persons. Rights regarding phone calls are at the discretion of the authorities. These rights have to be granted, unless the effort would be disproportionate. The *MRB* (2005, 82ff) argues for the permanent (and not only during a call) availability of mobile phones to detainees pending expulsion, respectively for enabling passive reception of phone calls, particularly because destitute prisoners only may have the first call to relatives free of charge. At least one half hour visiting time per week has to be permitted according to law, detainees pending expulsion should be allowed more visits without supervision as a rule to maintain family and other social relations, however organisational resources and constraints should be considered. (A special recommendation of *MRB* refers to visiting rights of prisoners in hunger strike. These rights should not be restricted even in sickrooms.)

3.8 Re-integration Activities - Prison Leave

Preparation for release is confined to an absolute minimum in police detention centres. According to the new § 25 AnhO released prisoners are at least entitled to an attestation of detention time and documents on medical evidence and treatment. At present the law only provides for some minimum social care through employees of private organisations for detainees pending expulsion. The Ministry of the Interior has been accused of contracting preferably with such organisations that pose advice for returning before counselling in right of asylum and support during asylum procedure. Help for returnees include advice in bureaucratic matters and financial support.

3.9 Release - Expulsion

There are no precise data available and no research has been conducted on measures taken by the immigration police after release from police detention centres or prisons. In 2003 and 2004 11,173 resp. 9,041 imposed custodies compare to 8,073 resp. 5,811 removals carried out (Sicherheitsbericht der Bundesregierung, 2005, p. 331). Since there are no statistics on the reasons for release from detention pending expulsion this difference can hardly be interpreted. We do not know whether the release was because of bad physical condition, so the person could no longer be kept in prison, or whether a transgression of maximum time of detention has occurred, or whether successful legal claims, or postponement of expulsion (§ 46 para.3 FPG), or impracticality or inadmissibility of

---

[46] This is also stated by the UN High Commissioner for Refugees in his written comment on the Police Detention Order (AnhO) 2005.

removal (§ 50 FPG) provide the reason for release. Therefore information about the legal status after release, whether it is a regular, precarious or irregular one, remains unclear too.

3.10 Aftercare - Probation

see 3.8

3.11 Staff

Questions regarding qualification of staff in PAZ have been raised in different contexts. For a long time the *MRB* has been concerned about detention of women (*MRB* 2001). One impact of this concern is the ruling of the now amended Police Detention Order (§ 3 AnhO) that supervision in principle ought to be done by staff of the same sex. In view of insufficient space and staffing in smaller police detention centres the *MRB* recommends to avoid accommodation of females there and to employ more women in the police administration (recommendations no. 93-116, July 2001). Facing the disproportionate high share of women among detainees pending expulsion (18%) foreigners are particularly affected by these deficiencies. According to the latest evaluation (*MRB* Evaluierung I/2004) only 9 out of 16 PAZ have sufficient rooms and personnel to properly accommodate females in separate sections. In particular at small facilities (e.g. border control posts) shortcomings still have to be conceded. The *MRB* several times also recommended training measures, especially for officers enforcing removal and wardens in PAZ, who deal with minors. The improvement of language capabilities and of capacities for intercultural communication through further education courses, the improvement of communication between police officers, social care workers and medical personnel and improved training of the paramedics to recognize mental abnormities and illness were up to now widely neglected recommendations of the *MRB* (Evaluierung I/2004).

3.12 Projects

In nearly every domain concerning spatial arrangements, social and medical care in general and for women in particular, legal aid, and co-operation between professionals and authorities, the committees of the *Human Rights Advisory Council* discovered local models of 'good practise', yet they also see too little exchange, centrally binding standards and quality management.

4 NATIONALS DETAINED ABROAD

By 30 Jan 2006, 151 Austrians had been detained abroad on long-term prison sentences. Furthermore 119 Austrians were imprisoned in short-term detention in 2005.[47] The statistics only contain cases that are reported to the Austrian Federal Ministry for Foreign Affairs. If a national detained abroad does not want contact to be established, the Minis-

---

[47] The Austrian Foreign Ministry (section IV.1) differentiates in its statistics between long-term and short-term detention in relation to custody of under 12 months or more than 12 months.

try is unaware of the detention. Most Austrian detainees are imprisoned within the European Union.

Table 8: Nationals Detained Abroad[48]

	*actual number of long-term detainees **	*short-term detentions 2005*
EU- Europe	92	76
Central and South America	22	4
Asia	15	17
Non EU-Europe	11	7
North America	9	11
Australia and Oceania	2	2
Africa	0	2
total	151	119

Source: Austrian Federal Ministry for Foreign Affairs
** by 30 Jan 2006*

The main reasons for imprisonment are offences related to drugs (smuggling, trafficking and possession). Offences related to drugs account for about 50% of all long-term detentions.

Different ministries support nationals detained abroad: The Ministry of the Interior establishes contact with the prisoners' family; the Ministry of Justice organises transfers to Austria. The Ministry for Foreign Affairs supports the offender in cooperation with the consulates and embassies on-site, coordinates help, stays in contact with the relatives, manages the so called *Depot-Verkehr (*e.g. money transfers from relatives to nationals detained in foreign countries) and the *Red Cross Campaign* (sending presents or money to detainees abroad at Christmas). 60 percent of (officially reported) Austrian detainees are supported by consulates and embassies on-site. Outside the European Union the share of supported prisoners is higher (80 percent). If someone is not cared for, it is usually because he or she does not want any support from the Austrian representations (which often happens when someone is detained in another European country). If support is not possible because there is no Austrian representation in a particular country, the Austrian Foreign Ministry asks embassies or consulates from other (European) countries, or (Christian) NGOs to take care of the prisoner.

The organisation *Neustart* is the nation-wide provider for probation and help on release. They do not support nationals detained abroad unless a detainees themselves get in contact with them (e.g. to inform himself about aftercare facilities or because he or she wants to serve the rest of a sentence in Austria). Back in Austria all aftercare facilities are open to them. There are no bi- or multilateral agreements concerning probation services.

---

48 The number of long-term detentions is available as *stock (prevalence)* data (number of detainees on January 30th 2006) while the number of short-term detentions refers to incoming *flow (incidents)* of short-term detainees in the year 2005. The two statistics therefore must not be merged. For both groups of detainees no statistical information on age, gender or social background is available.

5 EVALUATION AND RECOMMENDATIONS

There is no manifest legal discrimination against non-Austrians with respect to entitlements and living conditions in police or justice prisons. The law on the contrary demands to take into account the particular situation and needs of imprisoned foreigners. As a matter of fact religiously founded claims thereby seem to get more easily accepted while rights to legal information in particular and information in general are less readily respected. Yet general social marginality and the attribution of risks to foreigners become effective in the prison context too and lead to social exclusion. The lack of language competence, non-existing social networks and prospects for social integration also affect social opportunities in prison. Whether it comes to alternatives to detention (in particular to pre-trial detention with its less favourable conditions) or to participation in prison labour, related income and consumption opportunities, leisure time activities, relaxation of prison conditions and preparation for release, the accumulating deficiencies of non-Austrian prisoners operate against them. There are no mandatory standards regarding the institutional duties to compensate for disadvantages of foreigners. It is largely up to the single institution how much it effectively cares about foreigners. There are occasional informal attempts to improve living conditions of foreigners in prison, but no state wide official policy is implemented in this regard.

The growing number of foreigners in severely overcrowded prisons has some contrasting consequences. On the one hand it shows a clearly preserving function. The closing down of old, remote and ill-equipped institutions and departments is interrupted, it becomes more difficult to stop and overcome an un-communicative locking away of prisoners and to simply leave them to the rule of prison subcultures. On the other hand the rising number of foreigners causes a new routine and normality in relations among foreign and native inmates and between foreign inmates and staff, everyday racism is mitigated. Certain challenges through the new prison population also lead to innovations (for instance in the field of medical and social care for prisoners, language education, cable television etc.) and certain groups are even appraised as a 'gain' for the prison system. However, at the same time new unwanted 'problem groups' are identified, with whom communication and co-operation is said to fail – not only because of language barriers. Top ranking among these problem groups are the prisoners from former Soviet Republics. Arguments for a harsher prison regime are explained with this new groups of prisoners.

Bearing the Austrian situation in mind strict separation of administrative detention for the purpose of removal of irregular migrants from other kinds of detention of suspected or sentenced criminals has to be postulated. Detention pending expulsion should be the ultimate resort to enforce the ban on residence and removal, it should be reserved for special risk groups (previously convicted, with disposition to escape or to behave violently) and should exclude minors and traumatised persons. If special institutions for detention pending expulsion are established, their regime should not resemble that of traditional prisons. Open sections and common residence for family members, free access to means of communication with the outside world should be the rule. With every kind of detention of foreigners due information about legal procedures and their respective status has to be granted. The fact of imprisonment should speed up decision making on the residence status of the detainee to reduce uncertainty and psychic stress, to minimize denial of freedom and to prevent critical situations (e.g. in case of unprepared removal). Advice for removal must not curtail legal information and legal aid in asylum and other procedures before the immigration authorities. The transfer of offenders for the execution of sentences to their home country (against the will of the person, according to the Additional Protocol from 1997 to the European Convention on the Transfer of Sentenced Persons from 1983) must not ignore the real social integration in Austria.

The handicaps of many non-Austrian prisoners concerning language and other cultural skills should not be underrated. These handicaps prevent recourse to social, psychological and medical care and to legal grants and they cause social dependencies and disproportional private costs. Multi-lingual information, enhanced language skills of police and justice prison staff (as employment criterion), contracting with private organisations with multilingual personnel for visiting, educational and medical services should be the order of the day.

Considering the low articulation and the conflict potential of foreign prisoners the opening of prisons for independent pro-active control agencies furnished with substantial legal power of audit and resources turns out to be very important. By comparing the activities of the *Human Rights Advisory Council* (competent for police detention centres) and of the Prison Monitoring Committees (for prisons under justice administration) the significance of public presentation of findings and the transparency of administrative reactions to criticisms and recommendations can be demonstrated. Control boards reporting in closed sessions exclusively to the state administration are not a proper solution of the problem. Though the *Human Rights Advisory Council* at the Ministry of the Interior regularly issues focal reports there is a total lack of statistical and political routine reporting by the state administration on the execution of police detention and only fragmentary reporting on justice prisons. The annual Government Report on Internal Security offers a lengthy crime report but pays little attention to institutional detention and penal practise. The current study, anyhow, contributed to cause a redesign of statistical reporting on prisons under Ministry of Justice administration. For the future the data will enable to identify groups of prisoners that are discriminated with respect to access to work, education and training, and to social and medical care. However, the residence status of detained and released prisoners and the administrative measures taken by the immigration police against them still remain undocumented and unreported by the Austrian police and justice administration.

Chapter 3

Belgium

Sonja Snacken

1 INTRODUCTION

Belgium has a positive immigration balance, which means that more foreigners immigrate to Belgium than Belgians emigrate to other countries (+ 12.137 in 2000). The largest groups of immigrants are, in decreasing order, French, German, Moroccan and Turkish nationals. Around 900.000 foreigners live in Belgium legally, i.e. 8.8% of the population. 60% of these are citizens from other EU Member States, in decreasing order from Italy, France, the Netherlands and Germany. The other large groups of foreigners are from Morocco and Turkey. Asylum seekers since 1995 are mainly coming from former Yugoslavia, Russia, Albania and Iran[1]. The largest ethnic minority group in Belgium, the Moroccans, often live in poor neighbourhoods in vulnerable socio-economic circumstances, characterised by high unemployment, and suffer different forms of social exclusion. With the political changes in Central and Eastern European countries in the 1990's and the recent EU enlargement, the presence of immigrants from these countries has also become very visible. Since the topic of "immigration and criminality" gave electoral success in 1991 to an extremist right wing party, these themes have become hot political issues.

In 2004 foreign prisoners represented 44% of the prison population in Belgium. The large proportion of foreign prisoners and the ensuing problems during their detention and upon their release was the subject of a research we carried out for the King Boudewijn Foundation (Koning Boudewijn Stichting) between 1 November 2003 and 31 January 2004, to which we will often refer here[2].

1.1 Overview of penalties and measures

The police under supervision of the public prosecution perform investigation. Only an investigating judge can impose restrictions on fundamental freedoms, such as remand custody. Although provided for in legislation, monetary bail is seldom applied, as it is considered a form of class-justice that discriminates against the poor. In 1990, a new alternative to remand custody was introduced: freedom or release on conditions. Freedom on conditions refers to the decision taken by an investigating judge, within 24 hours of the arrest of a suspect, not to remand the suspect in custody under certain conditions. Release on conditions refers to a similar decision taken, either by the investigating judge or the investigating court, after the suspect has been remanded in custody. Remand custody can only be imposed in case of absolute necessity for the public security and for offences that can be punished with at least 1-year imprisonment. If the punishment for the alleged offence does not exceed 15 years imprisonment, remand custody can only be imposed in case of a risk of recidivism, absconding, collusion or meddling with evidence. Freedom or release under conditions can only be imposed in cases where remand custody is possible.

---

1 Overlegcentrum Integratie Vluchtelingen, Migrants in Europe – Survey Belgium, European Reintegration Networking, www.reintegration.net/belgium/index.htm

2 This research was carried out with two researchers, Jan Keulen and Leentje Winkelmans. This lead to the publication of a report in Dutch and French: S. Snacken, J.Keulen & L. Winkelmans, *Buitenlanders in de Belgische gevangenissen: knelpunten en mogelijke oplossingen (Détenus étrangers dans les prisons belges: problèmes et solutions possibles)* Brussel 2004 (Bruxelles 2004), Koning Boudewijn Stichting (Fondation Roi Baudoin).

At the level of sentencing, the Belgian judge has a variety of penal options: a conditional or unconditional fine (to be accompanied by a substitute imprisonment in case of non-payment), a suspended sentence with or without probation (a declaration of guilt without a formal conviction, which is suspended for a period of one to five years; this decision is not mentioned on the criminal record), conditional imprisonment with or without probation (here a sentence of imprisonment up to five years is imposed, but its implementation is suspended for a period of one to five years; this decision is registered on the criminal record), community service (an autonomous penalty since 2002), imprisonment (from one day to life imprisonment), internment of mentally ill offenders and preventive detention of repeat offenders and sexual offenders. The application of suspended sentences, conditional imprisonment and probation are limited by law to offences punishable by up to five years imprisonment and to offenders whose criminal record does not exceed prison sentences of more than two months for a suspended sentence (brought to six months in 1999) and 12 months for a conditional imprisonment. In case of failure to abide by the conditions of probation or in case of recidivism, the suspended sentence and conditional imprisonment may lead to imprisonment.

1.2 Overview of the prison system

1.2.1. Organisational structure

In the federal state of Belgium, the Prison Administration is a department of the Ministry of Justice, which is a federal ministry. The Prison Administration consists of a central administration, 33 prisons and one institution for "social defence" (i.e., for mentally ill offenders). There are two separate institutions for psychiatric patients and mentally ill offenders, which fall under the joint administration of the federal Ministry of Justice and the regional Ministry of Public Health.

Prisons in Belgium are divided into remand prisons (in each major city), open, half-open and closed prisons for the execution of sentences. Remand prisons have a closed, cellular regime, and are used for pre-trial detention. All major remand prisons have a psychiatric unit for mentally ill offenders and a unit for female prisoners. Most remand prisons are also used for execution of sentences, either by design (subdivisions inside the prison) or due to prison overcrowding (resulting in sentenced prisoners waiting for their transfer).

The division between open, half-open and closed prisons is based on the level of security inside the prison. Open prisons have a dormitory system and prisoners are expected to voluntarily accept prison discipline, while half-open prisons have an open regime during the day and a closed regime at night. Open and half-open prisons are located in more remote areas, where prisoners are deemed unlikely to escape, can work on the surrounding land, or receive educational or vocational training[3]. Since the 1990s, part of the open capacity has been transformed into closed capacity (now totalling 80%), due to a changing prison population and the overcrowding in remand and closed prisons, increasing the need for closed capacity.

---

3 The term "open" therefore does not refer - as in some other countries - to the fact that prisoners are allowed to leave the prison to work in outside society: this possibility exists in Belgium as "semi-detention", but is organized from closed prisons.

The Prison Administration designed a classification of prisoners in 1971, based on legal and administrative criteria such as length of sentence, criminal history, gender, age, and language. In the '80s, attempts to foster the detention of prisoners as close as possible to their homes and social relations (principle of "regionalization") were hampered by the increasing overcrowding issue[4].

Mentally ill offenders remain in the prison system or can be placed in a private psychiatric institution. The decision lies with the "commission of social defence", an administrative commission composed of a psychiatrist and a barrister and headed by a judge. With only three penitentiary institutions specialised in the treatment of mentally ill offenders, all situated in the French speaking part of the country, many of the mentally ill offenders who can not be placed in a private institution find themselves in the psychiatric unit of a remand prison or on normal location, without adequate treatment. This has been severely criticised by both the European Court for Human Rights and CPT[5].

The Belgian juvenile justice system is a combination of a welfare approach towards "children in danger" and a sanctioning approach towards "juvenile delinquents", with possible interactions and transfers between the two categories. Juvenile delinquents can be admonished, receive a community sanction or placed in an open or a closed institution. While the juvenile justice system is part of the federal Ministry of Justice, the juvenile institutions fall under the competence of the regional Departments of Welfare, with the exception of one remand prison for juveniles in Brussels. By Act of 15 May 2006, juveniles between 16 and 18 years old who have committed a serious offence can be brought before a special chamber of three juvenile judges or before an adult court, which can sentence them to a maximum of 30 years imprisonment. A "closed federal centre for juveniles" will have to be built for the implementation of these sentences.

A prison governor and one or several deputies supervise each prison. A majority of them have a university degree in criminology[6]. The majority (85%) of the prison staff consists of prison guards, who – once they are nominated - have the status of public servants. Guard-prisoner ratio in Belgium is 1:2. This figure however does not take into account the fact that staff works in eight hours shifts nor that staff absenteeism ranks high in some institutions. Over the last ten years, financial efforts have been made to ensure that each prison has a "psycho-social team" - at least one full-time social worker, a part-time psychologist and a part-time psychiatrist. Due to the reform of the parole system in 1998, following the Dutroux case, which was highly publicised, these teams are increasingly pressured into a predominantly diagnostic function. Custodial staff was traditionally gender-based (men for male prisoners, women for female prisoners), but the introduction of mixed staff (with a minimum and maximum of 20% "other sex") was decided in 1997 and is now implemented in all prisons. Despite efforts made to improve training of custodial staff, this is still hampered by the prison overcrowding, as staff can hardly be missed in the prisons.

Following the institutional reforms of the Belgian state in 1980 and 1988, all aspects relating to "forensic welfare" (i.e., social aid to offenders, victims and their families) are

---

4 S. Snacken, K. Beyens & H. Tubex, Adult corrections in Belgium. In: *Adult Corrections: International Systems & Perspectives,* edited by John Winterdyk, Monsely, NY 2004: Criminal Justice Press: 21-61

5 ECHR, Aerts v Belgium, Judgement 30 July 1998; CPT reports on Belgium CPT/Inf (94)15, (98)11, (2002)25, (2006)15.

6 Until recently, only criminologists (which is a separate degree in Belgian universities) or professionals already working in a prison could participate in selection examinations for prison governor.

the exclusive responsibility of the regional authorities that are distinguished according to their language base. This has led to "Cooperation agreements" between the Ministry of Justice and the regional authorities, and to the introduction of mixed "welfare teams" in prisons in which internal social workers and external services define their respective tasks[7]. Participation of the community at large in prisons however remains modest and develops unequally between regions.

Internal and external inspection bodies exercise control over the prisons. The two "regional directors" of the central prison administration, who visit the prisons regularly, perform internal inspections. A "Central supervision council" and several local "Supervision committees" perform the external inspection. The central council and the local committees are composed of a minimum of six members, of which at least one acting judge, one medical doctor and one barrister (art. 20-31 Prison Act 2005).

1.2.2. Foreign prisoners

"Foreign" prisoners in Belgium are defined as all prisoners not having the Belgian nationality. They represent around 40% of the prison population since the 1990s, and 44% on 15 January 2004. This definition however covers different categories. As a rule, only foreigners who are suspected of having committed an offence or have been convicted will be placed in a prison. 76% of these have no legal permit of residence, 21% are second or third generation immigrants who did not acquire Belgian nationality and 10% come from neighbouring countries. Recent legislation has made it easier for members of ethnic minorities who are born in Belgium to get the Belgian nationality. This means that on top of the 44% already mentioned, there is a group of prisoners who, although having the Belgian nationality, are of foreign origin. Their problems in prison will be partly similar, partly different from the other categories of "foreign" prisoners (below). Illegal aliens who have not committed an offence and asylum seekers who have been refused refugee status will normally not be placed in prisons but in institutions under the Ministry of Interior. In case of serious disciplinary problems in closed centres an illegal alien may be transferred to a prison. Due to the prison overcrowding, this number has steadily dwindled to a few people.

1.3 Overview of involvement of Consulates and Embassies

See II.1.6.

1.4 Overview of trends

1.4.1. Sentencing trends

Crime statistics in Belgium are hampered by the lack of continuity in registration, due to the partly overlapping competences of the three major police forces (national, judicial, local police) until 1998 and the ensuing police reform (1998-2001). However, the most reli-

7 S. Snacken, Belgium. In : *Imprisonment today and tomorrow. International perspectives on prisoners' rights ans prison conditions (second edition)*, edited by Dirk van Zyl Smit and Frieder Dünkel, Den Haag, London, Boston 2001: Kluwer Law International: 32-81

able figures show that in 1999 46% of crimes registered by the police related to theft and extortion, 11% to destruction and arson, 8% to physical integrity and 5% to drugs[8]. These statistics do not differentiate between nationalities of the suspect.

The number of decisions by investigating judges to remand people in custody fluctuated around 9 000 between 1993 and 2001 (index 108 in 1997, 96 in 1998), but has increased since to around 10 500 (index 115 in 2004)[9]. From research we conducted from 1996 to 2001 on the use of remand custody and its alternatives, it appeared that in most cases remand custody is requested from the investigating judge by public prosecutors (92%). In the majority of cases, the investigating judge followed the request of the public prosecutor: 63 % were dealt with by remand custody, 30 % by a simple release and only 8 % by freedom under conditions. Since then, the limited available data for the whole country and for all offences show a very slow positive evolution in the use of alternatives, but remand custody remains by far the most applied measure[10]. The prison statistics however show a much more important increase in the number and proportion of remand prisoners in Belgian prisons. While incarcerations decreased, the average prison population on remand increased (table 2: index 149 in 2004 compared to 1993, and 248 compared to 1980), indicating an important increase in the length of the remand custodies. The population on remand now represents around 40% of the total average prison population.

At the level of sentencing, the majority of criminal cases are dealt with by the police courts, competent for all petty offences and some misdemeanours (79 % in 2003). The correctional courts, competent for most misdemeanours and for cases of felonies in which mitigating circumstances have been accepted, represented 18.5 % in 2003. Only the most serious felonies are dealt with by the Courts of Assizes, these cases represented only 0.05 % of all judgments in 2003.

Fines are the most applied sanction in Belgium, being imposed in 83 % of petty offences and misdemeanours. Conditional imprisonment is applied in 20 % of misdemeanours and probation in only 4 %[11]. Suspended sentences represent only 4 to 5 % of the decisions, internments of mentally ill offenders only 0.2 %. Preventive detention is used sparingly, but its application has increased after its introduction in the new parole legislation in 1998 for sex offenders[12].

At the level of the correctional courts, sentences to short terms of imprisonment (< six months) decrease while sentences to long terms of imprisonment (> five years) increase. Despite these increases, prison sentences remain predominantly below the one-year limit. In 2003, 82.5 % of prison sentences remain below one year, 97.3 % below three years and only 0.4 % above five years.

The total number of sentences for serious felonies at the level of the Courts of Assizes remains rather low (87 in 1994, 55 in 2001, 75 in 2003). Life sentences fluctuate from

---

8 Algemene Politiesteundienst, Afdeling Politiebeleidsondersteuning, Brussels 2000, Ministry of Interior.

9 Justitie in cijfers (Justice in numbers), Ministry of Justice 2005, p.14.

10 A. Raes & S. Snacken, The application of remand custody and its alternatives in Belgium, *The Howard Journal of Criminal Justice*, 2005 Vol. 43, n°5, December 2004: 506-517.

11 S. Snacken & K. Beyens Alternatieven voor de vrijheidsberoving: hoop voor de toekomst? In: *Strafrechtelijk beleid in beweging*, edited by Sonja Snacken, Brussel 2002: VUBPress, Criminologische Studies: 271-316.

12 Chamber of Representatives 2005: 24 cases in 2003, of which 11 are sexual offenders.

28.7 % in 1994 over 13.6 % in 1999 and back to 32 % in 2003. The other categories, however, indicate a trend towards longer prison sentences. Sentences to more than ten years imprisonment represent 73.5 % of the cases of serious felonies in 1994, sentences to more than 15 years 51.7 %. In 2003, these proportions have increased to 90.6 % for the sentences to more than 10 years and 74.6 % for those to more than 15 years[13].

1.4.2. Characteristics of the (foreign) prison population

While incarcerations decreased between 1980 and 2004 from around 20 000 to 15 500 a year (table 1: index 79), the average daily population increased from 5 700 to 9 300 (index 163), indicating an increase in the average length of detentions.

Table 1 Average daily prison population and annual number of incarcerations (1980-2004)

Year	*Average daily population*	*Index*	*Incarcerations*	*Index*
1980	5677	100	19719	100
1981	5784	102	20153	102
1982	6112	108	20802	105
1983	6450	114	22274	113
1984	6728	119	22166	112
1985	6454	114	19879	101
1986	6695	115	20102	102
1987	6497	118	18437	93
1988	6688	114	17308	88
1989	6549	118	18202	92
1990	6549	115	17406	88
1991	6194	109	18221	92
1992	6869	121	19058	97
1993	7489	132	18261	93
1994	7489	132	16976	86
1995	7693	136	15853	80
1996	7935	140	15660	79
1997	8522	150	14688	74
1998	8707	153	14127	72
1999	8143	143	14434	73
2000	8543	150	14960	76
2001	8536	150	14443	73
2002	8804	155	15695	80
1/3/2003	9308	164	15402	78
1/3/2004	9250	163	15545	79

13 W. De Pauw, e.a De Belgische veroordelingsstatistiek, in: E. Devroe, K. Beyens & E. Enhus (eds.) Criminografie, VUBPress, .2006 forthcoming Criminologische studies.

Source: Prison Administration; Snacken, Beyens & Tubex (2004); Tubex & Strypstein (2006 forthcoming)

During this period, the proportion of foreigners in the prisons however rose from 25% in 1980 to 45% in 1991, and their proportion in the average prison population doubled from 21% in 1980 to 44% in 2004 (index 319 compared to 117 for Belgian nationals)[14]. While the pace of the increase of foreign prisoners in Belgian prisons is fairly steady over these years (index 191 in 1991), we see an even sharper increase since 1998[15]. Since non-Belgian nationals constitute only 9 to 10 % of the registered total population in Belgium, it would seem that they are strongly over-represented in the prison population. We have to remember though that 76% of these foreign prisoners have no legal permit of residence, and only 21% are second or third generation immigrants who did not acquire Belgian nationality.

As far as nationalities are concerned, Belgian prisons were facing not less than 104 different nationalities in 2003, covering all the world continents. The profile of the foreign population has changed however since 1998. Moroccans, who constitute the largest ethnic minority group in Belgium, traditionally represented the largest group within the population of non-Belgians in prison, 38% in 1992, compared to 30% of Western and Southern European foreign prisoners (including 12% from neighbouring countries, 8.6% Italian and 6% Turkish prisoners, the other important minority groups in Belgium) and 10% of Eastern European prisoners. The opening-up of the borders between Western and Eastern Europe has however altered the mix of foreign nationalities in prison. Since the beginning of the 1990s, the number of prisoners with a former Soviet nationality (i.e. Central and Eastern Europe, Russia and Community of Independent States) has steadily increased, and quite sharply so since 1998. In March 2003, both groups represented 28% of the foreign prison population (N= 1.030 Eastern Europeans and 1.043 Moroccans), while the number of prisoners with a Western and Southern European nationality stabilized around 22% (N= 830 prisoners)[16]. The age and gender structure of the foreign prison population is however very similar to the Belgian prison population: in 2003, 65% of foreign prisoners were between 18 and 35 years old, while female prisoners represented only 4%[17].

When we compare Belgian and foreign prisoners with regard to the categories of prison sentences and measures, we see an overrepresentation of foreign prisoners under remand: on 1 March 2003, 48% of the foreign prisoners versus 32% of the Belgian prisoners are imprisoned under remand. Foreigners are underrepresented though in the sentences of more than five years or life for felonies (2% versus 4% for sentences > 5 years, 1% versus 4% for life sentences) and in internment of mentally ill offenders (2% versus 10%) (tables 2 and 3).

---

14 K. Beyens, S. Snacken, C. Eliaerts, C. *Barstende muren. Overbevolkte gevangenissen : omvang, oorzaken en mogelijke oplossingen*, Antwerpen-Arnhem 1993: Kluwer-Gouda, Interuniversitaire Reeks Criminologie en Strafwetenschappen nr. 26; Snacken, Keulen & Winkelmans , ibidem.

15 Snacken, Keulen & Winkelmans, ibidem.: figure 2.

16 For a more detailed overview of the nationalities, see Snacken, Keulen & Winkelmans ibidem.: table 3.

17 Snacken, Keulen & Winkelmans ibidem: tables 4 and 5.

Table 2 Remand prisoners and sentenced prisoners (1980 – 2004)

Year	***Remand***			***Sentenced prisoners***		
	Average daily population –	*Index*	*Proportion of the total population*	*Average daily population –*	*Index*	*Proportion of the total population*
1980	1458	100	26%	2377	100	42%
1985	2004	137	31%	2726	115	42%
1990	1821	125	28%	3236	136	49%
1991	1722	118	28%	2910	122	47%
1992	2191	150	32%	3080	130	45%
1993	2431	167	32%	3723	157	50%
1994	2614	179	35%	3616	152	48%
1995	2546	175	33%	3953	166	51%
1996	2497	171	31%	4344	183	55%
1997	2469	169	29%	4922	207	58%
1/03/	2773*	190	32%	4615*	194	53%
1/03/	2554*	175	31%	4580*	193	56%
1/03/	3023*	207	35%	4900*	206	57%
1/03/	2951*	202	35%	4776*	201	56%
1/03/	3238*	222	37%	4497*	189	51%
1/03/	3680*	252	40%	4807*	202	52%
1/03/	3614*	248	39%			

* Population on March 1st

Source: Prison Administration; Snacken, Beyens & Tubex (2004); Tubex & Strypstein (2006 forthcoming)

Table 3: Foreign and Belgian prisoners: categories of sentences and measures (1 March 2003)

	Foreign prisoners	***Belgium prisoners***
remand custody	48%	32%
1-3y	10%	13%
3-5y	16%	16%
>5y (misdemeanours)	22%	22%
>5y (felonies)	2%	4%
life imprisonment	1%	4%
internment	2%	10%
total	100%	100%

Source: Prison Administration; Snacken, Keulen & Winkelmans (2004)

This overrepresentation of foreign prisoners under remand is a constant feature of the last 15 years[18]. Researchers that explain this overrepresentation have found several mechanisms[19]. A first element is the absence of legal residence for part of these foreign prisoners, which is seen by many investigating judges as enhancing both the risk of absconding and the risk of recidivism; two criteria that allow them to impose remand custody. As this situation usually does not change during the detention, remand custody for this category is also confirmed every month until the person appears before the court. A second element is the poor socio-economic and financial situation of many foreign or ethnic minority offenders, which is again seen as enhancing the risk of recidivism. A third element concerns more particularly offenders belonging to the Moroccan ethnic minority, who were found to be at a higher risk than Belgian or other foreign offenders to find themselves under remand custody or sentenced to imprisonment, due to their "negative" attitude during the procedure. Judges referred more particularly to their sustained denial even in the face of evident proof and their poor use of "earlier offered opportunities for treatment" in case of drug use. Intercultural misunderstandings seem to play a role here. While the denial by Moroccans can be explained in the framework of a more collective culture of shame, in which it allows to save the family's honour, Belgian judges evaluate this attitude within the western framework of individual guilt and responsibility as a lack of insight into the wrongfulness of their behaviour and therefore proof of a higher social danger. It also led some judges to stereotypical thinking of this group as "liars"[20]. On the other hand, judges often assume that drug use is part of the Moroccan culture and accepted by the Islam and therefore see this group again as representing a higher risk of criminality, both because of their assumed acceptance of drug use in itself and because their poor financial situation will lead to other forms of criminality in order to sustain this use[21].

1.5 Overview of national legislation[22]

1.5.1. The legal status of foreign nationals under Belgian law

The administrative legal status of foreign nationals is mainly regulated by the Act of 15 December 1980 on the entry into the country, the stay, settlement and expulsion of foreigners[23], the Geneva Convention of 28 July 1951 on the status of refugees[24] and the Act of 22 December 1999 on the regularization of the administrative situation of certain categories of foreigners[25]. National sovereignty in these matters is of course also dependent on

18 Beyens, Snacken & Eliaerts ibidem: table 25; Snacken, Keulen & Winkelmans ibidem: table 6.

19 Snacken & Raes ibidem; W. De Pauw, *De afhandeling van drugzaken in Brussel in 1993 en 1994*, BRES, Brussel 1996: IRIS; W. De Pauw, *Migranten in de balans*. Brusse 2001: VUB Press. Criminologische Studies.

20 S. Snacken, S. Deltenre, A. Raes, Ch. Vanneste and Paul Verhaeghe, *Kwalitatief onderzoek naar de toepassing van de voorlopige hechtenis en de vrijheid onder voorwaarden*, Onderzoeksrapport VUB/NICC, Brussel 1999.

21 De Pauw (1996, 2000, 2006 forthcoming), ibidem.

22 Snacken, Keulen & Winkelmans ibidem, 29-49.

23 B.S. (Belgisch Staatsblad) 31 december 1980, repeatedly altered since.

24 Act of 26 June 1953, B.S. 4 October 1953; Protocol 31 january 1967 on the status of refugees, New York, act 27 february 1969, B.S. 3 May 1969.

25 B.S. 10 January 2000.

international (cf. European) bilateral and multilateral conventions. The competence over immigration policy was transferred from the Ministry of Justice to the Ministry of Interior in the 1990s (1992-1994).

According to the Act of 1980, entry into the country is dependent upon possession of legal documents. The stay is normally limited to a maximum period of three months. In certain cases, foreigners with legal documents can be refused entry (e.g. when signalled in the Schengen Information System, when seen as a possible threat to public order or national security) or can be ordered to leave the country by Ministerial Decree (e.g. when seen as a threat to public order or national security, in case of insufficient means of subsistence and inability to obtain such means legally). Foreign residents can be expelled by Royal Decree in case of breach of public order or national security, following recommendation by a multidisciplinary "Advisory commission for Foreigners". Orders to leave or decrees of expulsion prohibit re-entry into the country for a period of ten years. In 2000, 50 such Ministerial Decrees and 6 Royal Decrees were issued[26]. Foreign prisoners who have been sentenced to at least six months imprisonment can be expelled after serving their sentence. A special Bureau "D" ("detainees") in the Office for Foreigners' Affairs evaluates the opportunity of expulsion of foreign prisoners on the basis of their situation of residence and the seriousness of the crimes committed.

Foreigners can be recognised as refugees on the basis of a reasonable fear of prosecution for reasons of race, religion, nationality, social group or political conviction (Convention of Geneva 28 July 1951). Asylum seekers who fail to be recognised as refugees can lodge an administrative appeal with the *Conseil d'Etat.*

The Act of 22 December 1999 provided for the regularization of the administrative situation of certain categories of foreigners on the basis of four criteria: asylum seekers submitted to a disproportionate long procedure, foreigners for whom return to the country of origin is impossible, seriously ill foreigners, and finally humanitarian reasons and long lasting social bonds. A more permanent procedure of regularization is based on art.9.3 of the Act of 1980, which allows foreigners "in exceptional circumstances" to request permission of residence from the mayor of the local community, who will send the request to the Minister of Interior[27].

Table 4 shows the administrative situation of the foreign prisoners in Belgian prisons from 1993 to 2003. We can see that in a majority of cases, the Office for Foreigners has not yet taken a decision towards the future legal situation of the foreign prisoners: that was true for 98% of foreign prisoners in 1993, and is still true for 65% of this population in 2003. This has vast implications for their early release (see below II.1.9).

1.5.2. Legal framework for the detention of foreign nationals

a. Administrative detention. In principle, an illegal alien is expected to leave the country on his own initiative. He can acquire help from the International Organisation for Migration, which provides assistance in gathering travel documents, pays a flight ticket and other travel expenses. In case of failure to leave, an illegal alien may be detained for the time strictly necessary for the organisation of the forced repatriation. Such administrative

---

26 Office for Foreigners Affairs, Annual report, Ministry of Interior, Brussels 2000.

27 J. Keulen, Operatie regularisatie, dissertation in criminology, Brussels, Vrije Universiteit Brussel 2003; Snacken, Keulen & Winkelmans, ibidem.

detention normally takes place in a closed centre of the Ministry of Interior. Administrative detention is normally imposed for a maximum of two months, but can be extended to five months. Only when necessary for the protection of public order or national security can it be further prolonged to the absolute maximum of eight months. Appeal against the administrative detention can be lodged with the investigation chamber of the correctional court.

b. Penal la. Belgian penal law is applicable to all crimes committed in Belgium, independent of the nationality of the offender. The fact that a certain deed would not be punishable under the lex personae of the foreigner does not exclude his prosecution and punishment. Remand custody can be imposed in accordance with the Act of 20 July 1990. When the alleged crime is punishable with a maximum of 15 years of imprisonment, remand custody can only be imposed in case of risk of recidivism, absconding, collusion or tampering with evidence. The Directorate General implements sentences of imprisonment for the Implementation of Penalties and Measures. The Bureau "D" of the office for Foreigners' Affairs is responsible for the administrative follow up of foreigners imprisoned for criminal acts, i.e. with regard to their administrative status upon release (permission to stay, order to leave, expulsion.).

c. Prison law. Prison life used to be regulated by the General Prison Regulation, a Royal Decree of 1965 setting only a general framework for the implementation of sanctions and measures involving deprivation of liberty, numerous ministerial circular letters and the house rules of the different prisons. These regulations did not offer substantial or formal rights to prisoners. Although efforts were made since the 1970s to develop prison regimes and open up the prisons to the outside world, most elements of prison regimes remained privileges, which could be withdrawn or refused, with the exception of the right of access to a lawyer and the right to freedom of religion. There was no formal complaint procedure, disciplinary breaches and sanctions were not enumerated and decisions could not be appealed. As a result, situations and regimes differed greatly between prisons and prisoners were uncertain about their rights and duties[28]. After many years of a "hands off policy" by courts towards decisions taken by the Prison Administration, and in accordance with the case law of the European Court of Human Rights, Belgian courts increasingly recognized that prisoners maintain their fundamental rights and that curtailment of these rights must be legitimate and proportionate.

On 12 January 2005, the first Prison Act for Belgium was issued (B.S. 1 February 2005), enumerating for the first time the basic principles that must lead the implementation of sanctions and measures implying deprivation of liberty:

- to guarantee psychosocial, physical and material circumstances of detention which respect human dignity, which allow the prisoner to retain or improve his self respect and which appeal to his individual and social responsibility (art.5.1),
- to safeguard order and security in the prison (art.5.2), through dynamic interactions between prison staff and prisoners ("dynamic security") and a good balance between technical instruments of security and a constructive prison regime (art.105.1),
- no limitations to the political, civil, social, economical and cultural rights of the prisoner will be imposed other than those resulting from the imposed sanction or measure, the inherent consequences of the deprivation of liberty or the law (art.6.1),

---

28 CPT reports on Belgium CPT/Inf (94)15, (98)11, (2002)25, (2006)15.

- detrimental effects of the deprivation of liberty must be avoided as much as possible (art.6.2),
- prisons must strive for a climate of consultation with prisoners (art.7.1),
- the implementation of prison sentences aims at reparation of the harm caused to the victims, the rehabilitation of the offender and the individual preparation of his social reintegration (art.9.2), through the elaboration of an individual sentence plan in collaboration with the prisoner (art.9.3),
- prisons are subjected to independent inspection bodies: a central counsel for central decisions and local supervision committees for decisions taken by the director of the prison (art.20),
- complaint procedures are introduced within these inspection bodies (art. 147-166),
- the disciplinary breaches and sanctions are enumerated in the act; the disciplinary procedure is thoroughly reformed (art.122-146).

Several working groups within the Prison Administration are currently preparing the implementation of this new Act.

d. International conventions. Several international conventions are applicable to foreign prisoners, but are seldom applied in practice.

a) Convention of Strasbourg of 21 March 1983 on transfer of sentenced prisoners (Act of 23 May 1990). Sentenced prisoners can be transferred to their country of origin if certain conditions are fulfilled: the sentence must be definitive, the offence is incriminated in both countries, the prisoner must agree with the transfer, there is no request for extradition and no pending case, the prisoner has at least another six months to serve or has received an indeterminate sentence. The transfer is a favour that will be granted by the Minister of Justice after careful balance of all interests involved and should be decided as soon as possible after the final verdict. Possible counter-indications based on the interests of society are: the request for transfer aims at or will result in a reduction of punishment, e.g. because the country will adapt the sentence to its own maximum punishment or because release can be granted earlier; the prisoner attempts to escape payment of judicial costs or fines or the transfer will hamper such payment. Possible counter-indications based on the victims' interests are: the transfer aims at or will result in hampering payment of civil compensation; the compensation represents an important amount for the victim. These counter-indications will be evaluated on the basis of the efforts made by the prisoner to fulfil his financial obligations, taking into account his personal situation. Transfer can be granted under the condition that (part of) the judicial costs, fines or compensation will be paid; if all these obligations are still open, compensation of individual victims will be prioritised.

The Council of Europe issued an additional Protocol to this Convention on 18 December 1997, in which the agreement of the prisoner for his transfer is no longer obligatory. This Protocol has been signed by Belgium, but not ratified yet. Bilateral Agreements have also been reached with countries outside the Council of Europe, i.e. with Morocco (Agreement of 7 July 1997 on assistance to detained persons and transfer of sentenced prisoners).

b) Convention of Strasbourg of 21 May 1972 on transfer of criminal procedures. This Convention has been signed, but not ratified by Belgium.

c) Convention of Strasbourg of 30 November 1964 on supervision of conditionally sentenced or conditionally released offenders (Act of 15 July 1970). The Belgian state can request the State in which an offender is normally residing to carry out supervision over the offender only, or to carry out supervision and if necessary to enforce the sentence (e.g. in case of revoking an early release), or to assume entire responsibility for applying the sentence (as if it had been imposed by its own court). In complying with a request for supervision, the requested State shall, if necessary, adapt the prescribed supervisory measures in accordance with its own laws. In no case however may this result in more severe measures than those prescribed by the requesting State.

2 TREATMENT OF FOREIGN PRISONERS[29]

2.1 General situation

Imprisonment raises many personal and social problems for all prisoners. On top of this, Belgian prisons face severe overcrowding, especially in remand prisons. This results in additional quantitative and qualitative problems for prisoners and staff: sharing cells designed for one person intensifies feelings of insecurity and possible tensions or conflicts, lack of space hampers normal family visits or prison labour, too many prisoners hinder the possibilities of developing a dynamic security with staff and an adequate preparation of the social reintegration[30]. Being a foreigner can further exacerbate particular difficulties. This will vary however: we mentioned that prisoners in Belgium represent more than 100 different nationalities, which implies a large diversity in language, culture and religion, but also in social isolation and exclusion, depending on the family and social ties of the prisoner in Belgium. Not all foreign prisoners will therefore face the same problems: second or third generation immigrants (mainly Moroccans) will speak the local language and have all their family ties in Belgium, but may still face racism or religious intolerance, while the more recently immigrated Eastern Europeans may not speak any of the languages and find themselves totally isolated.

Language and communication are important in any system, but even more so in prison. Daily interactions between prisoners and staff are seriously hampered if a prisoner does not speak any of the common languages (Dutch, French, and English). Attempts to find a solution will often depend on the goodwill of both partners in the interaction, or the involvement of a fellow prisoner as interpreter. This latter solution may be difficult in more delicate situations (disciplinary procedure, personal information) and will hamper the establishment of a relation of trust with staff (cf. dynamic security). Moreover, many aspects of daily prison life or prison regimes must be asked for in written form (participation in activities, request to see the director or the psychosocial service, etc.). On top of being unable to formulate such requests in one of the local languages, some of the foreign prisoners are also illiterate in their own language. In practice, involving a fellow prisoner or a guard again usually solves this. However, two major risks are mentioned as a result of communication problems: insufficient awareness of the house rules or misunderstand-

---

29 These results of the research carried out for the Koning Boudewijn Foundation are based on interviews with prisoners and prison staff in six prisons, interviews with members of the central prison administration, a parole commission, an external welfare service, the Office for Foreigners Affairs of the Ministry of Interior, and focus groups with officials of the Ministries of Justice and Interior.

30 K. Beyens, S. Snacken & C. Eliaerts, Barstende muren. *Overbevolkte gevangenissen: omvang, oorzaken en mogelijke oplossingen*, Antwerpen 1993, Kluwer Rechtswetenschappen.

ings may lead to more disciplinary sanctions for certain foreign prisoners, while others will retreat in isolation and become "invisible".

2.2 Living conditions and facilities

Foreign prisoners are detained in the same institutions as nationals and have in principle access to the same living conditions and facilities as other prisoners. They are not separated from other prisoners, but some nationalities may sometimes be allocated to the same unit to solve language problems.

Belgian prisons, both for remand custody and for implementation of sentences, are in principle designed for single cell accommodation, with only some cells designed for two, three or four prisoners[31]. However, due to the prison overcrowding of the last 20 years, especially in remand prisons, single cells often have to be shared by two or three prisoners, and multi occupancy cells see their real capacity doubled. In such cases, prison directors may try to allocate foreign prisoners from the same nationality, culture or language to the shared cells, especially when they have serious communication problems. This may facilitate their adaptation to prison rules and internal order, but has on occasion led to external security problems (escape). Criteria applied by the prison directors are however not always in accordance with the individual appreciation by the prisoners. Accommodation on the basis of language or religion has sometimes led to other conflicts, for example between nationals of recently partitioned new states. Other criteria are also taken into account, for example smoking, possession of a TV set. Individual prisoners can request accommodation in a particular cell or with a particular fellow prisoner, which will be granted as much as possible, taking into consideration the overcrowding and security concerns.

The presence of larger cultural subgroups in a prison, such as "North African" (mainly Moroccan) and "Eastern European", is said to increase the development of a group feeling and the risk of group conflicts. Some Central and Eastern European prison systems have large dormitories, in which prisoners' subcultures often develop more easily than in cellular systems. Prisoners from these countries may then import their (sometimes more hierarchical and violent) subculture into the Belgian prisons.

2.3 Reception and admission

Foreign prisoners are submitted to similar procedures on reception and admission as national prisoners. Language problems may arise again here concerning written documents and/or oral interactions. All legal documents in Belgium, including juridical and prison documents, must be written in one of the official languages (Dutch, French or German. Problems may arise at the moment of registration in the prison registry on admission or when explaining the house rules of the prison for foreign prisoners who do not understand these languages. The house rules of the prison inform prisoners about most aspects of daily prison life: discipline, visits, prison labour, activities, use of TV and canteen, etc. Some prisons have taken the initiative to translate the house rules into other languages, usually including English and Arabic, or to show a video, but even these may be insuffi-

---

31 Some of the open and half open prisons have limited dormitory systems.

cient: with 100 different nationalities in Belgian prisons it remains difficult to cover all possible languages.

All incoming prisoners are seen by a prison director and should be seen by the psychosocial service upon admission. The latter however are heavily involved in the preparation/advice on prison leaves or early release, and do not always succeed to see all incoming prisoners. This problem exists for all prisoners, independent of their nationality.

2.4 Work – education – training – sports - recreation

The availability of work and activities varies in different prisons. This is linked to both architectural and policy differences. Most prisons in Belgium were built in the nineteenth or first half of the twentieth century following the so-called "Belgian design", based on the idea of individual isolation and cellular segregation, religion and education. Prison labour was limited to in-cell work. The typical star-shaped prisons had small individual cells and a chapel, but no workplaces or rooms for communal activities. When penological ideas changed, the possibilities for architectural transformations and extensions to existing prisons especially remand prisons that were very often built in town centres were limited. More recently built prisons provide more room for communal activities and specialized forms of prison labour. Policy differences are linked to the division of competences between the regional authorities: the Flemish Community has elaborated a "Strategic Plan for assistance and services to prisoners", offering several educational and socio-cultural activities to prisoners in Flemish prisons, while the provision of services by the other Communities is not systematic yet. On top of this, different priorities may be developed by the local prison directors in collaboration with local NGO's or associations: some will emphasize prison labour, others education or social-cultural activities.

In general though, Belgian prisons face a shortage of labour, resulting in waiting lists, and turning the theoretically legal obligation for sentenced prisoners to work into a de facto privilege. Most prisons are divided in units for "workers" and for "non-workers", with the "workers" having a much better regime combining work, activities and more freedom of movement inside the unit. In remand prisons, large parts of the prison population will remain in their (often overcrowded) cell for 22 or 23 hours a day, with one or two hours of exercise in the open air as only activity. Prison directors will normally not differentiate between foreign and national prisoners when allocating work, but some types of work may require language skills or sufficient knowledge of one of the Belgian languages. Central and Eastern European prisoners are said to be good and hard workers, but will often find themselves in the less demanding manual work because of communication problems. Many foreign prisoners see prison labour as very important, especially if they have no other forms of income to rent a TV, use the telephone, buy goods in the canteen, or if they want to send money home to their families.

Activities such as theatre or movies may be a source of language problems. Some prisons have multicultural music groups or make efforts to provide books in different languages, often in collaboration with the local library. Most prisons also provide forms of vocational training such as language courses or programmes for tackling illiteracy, but usually only to a limited number of prisoners.

2.5 Food – religion – personal hygiene – medical care

As mentioned above, religion was an important feature of the cellular prison regime in Belgium, which lasted from the independence of the country in 1830 to after the Second World War. Catholic chaplains were attached to each prison and were subsidized as part of the prison staff. Units for female prisoners were even staffed by catholic nuns until as late as the 1980s. On the other hand, freedom of religion is an important constitutional right in Belgium, which has lead to some political struggles against the influence of religion and religious groups on Belgian society. As a result, this right to freedom of religion was, with the right of access to a lawyer, the only formally recognized prisoner's right under the General Prison Regulation of 1965. This right has been confirmed by the new Prison Act of 12 January 2005 (art.71 PA), which states that each prisoner has the right to profess his religion or philosophy individually and in community with others, with respect for the rights of others, and has the right to receive religious, spiritual or moral support from representatives of his religion or philosophy attached or admitted to the prison.

Several religions are officially recognized in Belgium, including in Belgian prisons: Catholicism, Protestantism, Orthodox faith, Judaism, Islam and the non-confessional moral philosophy. Representatives of these recognized religions or philosophies are attached to each prison, can visit individual prisoners, can receive uncensored letters and can organize religious/philosophical meetings. Representatives of non-recognized religions can also be admitted to the prison (art.72 PA). Nutritional or other consequences of these officially recognized religions would also be applicable in Belgian prisons: Jewish prisoners are allowed to receive kosher meals; Islamic prisoners can observe Ramadan, etc. On the other hand, freedom of religion also entails the right to be free from religious influence. Therefore, no prisoner can be forced to participate in any religious meeting or to receive the visit of a representative, prisoners can choose freely if and which religion or philosophy they want to turn to and can change course during their detention (art.74 PA).

In practice, not all religions are equally represented in Belgian prisons. Subsidized representatives such as the catholic chaplains and the non-confessional moral advisers are present in all prisons and fulfil an important task of support and guidance. Representatives of the other denominations however are volunteers, and their presence may vary according to regional circumstances. The Imam is generally considered to be very important for the large group of Islamic prisoners, because of his high moral standing and influence. However, as only one or two Imams are currently willing to visit prisoners, they have to cover all 34 prisons over the whole country, resulting in a lower accessibility.

Some religious practices may cause conflicts between prisoners (e.g. a shared cell where one prisoner wants to watch TV while the other is praying) or small forms of disorder (e.g. call for prayer for Islamic prisoners through the whole prison). During the interviews, prisoners were said to be rather intolerant towards other religions.

Personal hygiene or medical care are provided for by the Prison Service independently of nationality or language, but may raise cultural problems. Art. 44 PA states that the prison director must guarantee that prisoners can take care of their personal hygiene on a daily basis. However, hygienic standards may differ personally and culturally, which may raise tensions when cells have to be shared, as is the case in the overcrowded remand prisons. The Central medical Service organizes medical care. It must be of similar (high) quality as outside the prison and adapted to the individual situation of the prisoner (art.88

PA). In reality, psychiatric care is insufficiently provided for in Belgian prisons generally, and for mentally ill offenders more specifically (see above 2). Physical and mental health also has cultural connotations, which will usually not be familiar to the general practitioners and psychiatrists visiting the prisoners. Language problems may also hamper adequate communication in these areas, which may result in some prisoners and their problems becoming "invisible" to medical and other prison staff (e.g. suicide prevention). With the growing presence of prisoners from Central and Eastern European countries, new phenomena such as open TB are also appearing in Belgian prisons.

2.6 Consular and legal help

Foreign prisoners are entitled to contact their consular agency upon admission to prison (one free phone call), with the exception of those remand prisoners whose contacts with the outside world have been restricted by the investigating judge for three days at most (atr.64§2 PA). Correspondence with the consular agencies is confidential and cannot be controlled or censured (art.69 PA). The attitude of consulates or embassies towards their imprisoned citizens varies however: while some will provide help and information, others will remain indifferent and unwilling to provide support.

Prisoners are entitled to all legal help available in society at large, including free legal aid for those who cannot afford to pay for a lawyer (art.104.1 PA). In practice, most foreign prisoners have free legal aid. Many are dissatisfied though, claiming they see their lawyer only in court and receive little information about the procedures ruling their administrative status as a foreigner. Language may again be a problem here. But it is also generally recognized that few lawyers are sufficiently trained in or familiar with the legal aspects of residence permits, asylum seeking and regulations concerning illegal aliens. Some prisons organize information sessions where prisoners can ask questions to a lawyer. However, more and better legal aid was one of the recurrent requests heard during the research.

2.7 Contact with the outside world

Art 58 PA stipulates that, unless otherwise imposed by law, remand prisoners are entitled to daily visits, while sentenced prisoners are entitled to three visits a week. Visits should last at least one hour. Prisoners are also entitled to unsupervised visits once a month, in accordance with conditions determined by Royal Decree. Direct family members (parents, children, siblings, aunts and uncles), and married or cohabiting partners are entitled to visit the prisoner in principle, on proof of their identity, unless specific and individual circumstances endanger the order and security of the prison and cannot take place in a different way, for example through visits behind glass. Other visitors must request permission to visit a prisoner from the prison director (art.59 PA).

Foreign prisoners who have no family or friends in Belgium may find themselves in a situation of serious social isolation. The lack of external support and knowledge of the Belgian system may increase tensions and even aggressiveness. It may also be difficult to ascertain the identity and family relationship of certain visitors. On the other hand, some family members may be unwilling to visit because of their illegal status in the country. Regular transfers of prisoners, for example because of overcrowding, may also hamper the organization of visits. When visitors from abroad have travelled specifically to visit the prisoner, the prison director may adapt visit arrangements accordingly.

Other forms of contact with the outside world may depend on the individual financial situation. All prisoners (unless legal exceptions) are entitled to use the telephone daily, but have to pay for this expense (art.64§1 PA). As the system of "collect calls" was recently abolished in prisons, foreign prisoners may have insufficient financial means to call their family abroad. Similarly, the prisoner can purchase all newspapers or publications legally available in outside society, and radio and television programmes can be listened to and watched in accordance with the house rules (art.77 PA). A television can be rented on a monthly basis, offering access to more than twenty networks, including many foreign programmes (English, Italian, Spanish, Turkish, etc.). Access to the prison library is free though, and many prisons try to diversify the languages available, often in cooperation with outside libraries. Again, this may not cover the whole range of the more than 100 nationalities present in the Belgian prisons.

2.8 Reintegration activities – prison leave

Modalities for prison leave vary with the administrative status of the foreign prisoner. Systematic prison leave, decided by the Prison Administration, allows certain prisoners to leave the prison every month (or three months) for one day (or three days) in order to maintain family and social ties, prepare for social reintegration or in view of a conditional release. A ministerial circular letter of 10 June 1986 regulates the possibilities of prison leave for foreign prisoners:

- Foreign prisoners who are not registered in the Foreigners' Register, in the Population Register or in the Immatriculation (EU) Register cannot be granted prison leave.
- For foreign prisoners who are registered, the decision will depend on their administrative status:
  - If the Office for Foreigners' Affairs has not yet decided on their status, they will be treated like Belgian prisoners.
  - If a proposal to leave the country or be deported has been submitted by the Office to the Advisory Commission, but the latter has advised against expulsion, or has not decided yet and the prisoner has close family ties in the country who are willing to house him, prison leave may still be granted.
  - If the Advisory Commission favours expulsion, the prison administration waits for the definite decision on expulsion.
  - If the prisoner does not appeal against the decision, or if the administrative court does not grant temporary suspension of the decision, no prison leave can be granted.
  - If the prisoner has appealed the decision or the administrative court grants suspension of the decision, prison leave may be granted in case of close family ties in the country.
  - Exceptionally prison leave may be granted in spite of a decision for expulsion, when a combination of conditions are fulfilled: the prisoner serves his term in an open or half open prison, earlier prison leaves were successful, there are no counter indications, the prisoner had a legal permit at the time of incarceration, a certain period is imposed in which to leave to country.
  - If extradition of the prisoner is requested, no prison leave can be granted.

We can conclude that when deciding on prison leave, the Prison Administration takes into account both the legal and the social situation of the foreign prisoner. However, as 76% of foreign prisoners in 2004 had no legal permit to stay, we can assume that a large proportion of foreign prisoners in Belgian prisons will not be granted prison leave.

As far as other forms of prison leave are concerned, only Belgian prisoners or foreign prisoners who have permission to reside in Belgium can be granted incidental prison leave (return the same day), release from prison under electronic monitoring or semi detention (employment, training or therapy outside the prison during daytime, return to prison every night).

2.9 Early release - expulsion

This area is fraught with difficulties for foreign prisoners in Belgium, more particularly due to the combination of criminal and administrative procedures. Criminal procedures of importance here are conditional release, provisional release and provisional release in view of expulsion.

The Act of 5 March 1998 on conditional release does not distinguish between Belgian and foreign prisoners. In practice, conditional release is applied to prisoners serving sentences totalling more than three years. Prisoners are admissible for conditional release after serving 1/3 and minimum three months of their sentences (2/3 and minimum six months for legal recidivists), life sentence prisoners after serving ten years (14 years for legal recidivists). The decision is taken by a "Commission for Conditional Release", a multidisciplinary commission of three members: a specialist in social reintegration, one in prison matters and a judge as president. A commission in the prison where the prisoner serves his sentence, composed of the prison director, members of the psychosocial staff and a senior guard, must discuss all eligible prisoners, including foreign prisoners, except those against whom an order to leave the country or a decree of expulsion has been issued. The latter fall under the system of provisional release in view of expulsion. Prisoners serving between one and three years of imprisonment are provisionally released after serving 1/3 of their sentence[32]. The director of the prison where the sentence is served takes the decision. In case of counter-indications and insufficient prospects for social reintegration, this provisional release can be coupled to specific conditions. If specific conditions are deemed insufficient, the procedure for conditional release will be applied. This form of release is not applicable to foreign prisoners without legal permit of residence. Foreign prisoners, who, due to their administrative situation cannot be released under either of the two previous forms, can be provisionally released in view of expulsion. The minimum terms to be served are the same as for the other forms of early release, depending on whether the total terms exceed three years imprisonment or not.

A first, major problem results from the interaction of these criminal procedures with the administrative procedure of expulsion or order to leave the country. As mentioned above, foreign residents can only be expelled by Royal Decree in case of breach of public order or national security, following recommendation by a multidisciplinary "Advisory commission for Foreigners". Orders to leave or decrees of expulsion prohibit re-entry into the country for a period of ten years. In 2000, 50 such Ministerial Decrees and 6 Royal

32 Prisoners serving less than one year are released after an even shorter term. This system has been introduced in order to cope with the severe overcrowding of certain prisons in Belgium.

Decrees were issued[33]. Foreign non-resident prisoners who have been sentenced to at least six months imprisonment can be expelled after serving their sentence. A special Bureau "D" ("detainees") in the Office for Foreigners' Affairs (OFA) of the Ministry of Interior appreciates the opportunity of expulsion of foreign prisoners on the basis of their situation of residence and the seriousness of the crimes committed. Many non-resident foreign prisoners however have requested asylum status or regularisation of their illegal status. As long as the administrative status of the prisoner as foreigner is uncertain, it is also unclear which procedure for early release must be applied. We have seen that this was the case for 98% of foreign prisoners in 1993, and was still the case for 65% of them in 2003 (table 4).

The Ministry of Justice issued several circular letters to tackle this situation. In a first such letter of 20 May 1981, it was decided that prisoners who had a permit of residence when they were apprehended should be treated like Belgian citizens: i.e. through the normal procedure of conditional or provisional release depending on the length of the sentence. Those who did not possess a permit of residence upon apprehension should be provisionally released with a view on expulsion[34]. The Office for Foreigners' Affairs (OFA) was immediately informed of the start of such procedures, in order to take a decision as to the future administrative position of the prisoner. In case of absence of such a decision at the moment of release, the prisoner was released anyway. In the opposite case, the decision of the OFA was applied accordingly.

One of the consequences of this system is that the procedure for conditional release is sometimes started but can not be finalised in the absence of a decision by the OFA, which means that the prisoner serves more than the minimum of 1/3 or 2/3 imposed by law. Sometimes conditional release is granted by the Commission, but is then followed by a negative decision by the OFA, refusing residence. Transfer of supervision to another country is not always possible, and reintegration or treatment in the country of origin may be difficult to assess. This may hamper granting a conditional release. The same problem arises with mentally ill offenders who can only be released under the condition of adequate psychiatric treatment in their country of origin.

Foreign prisoners without legal permit of residence face serious problems at the time of their apprehension. Pressed by prison overcrowding, the Ministry of Justice issued a circular letter nr. 71 of 20 June 2002, in which prison directors were requested to release prisoners without permit of residence, against whom no decision for repatriation, expulsion or transfer to a closed centre had been taken by the OFA, 15 days after the decision on provisional release in view of expulsion had been reached. The OFA was to be informed of the date of the provisional release as soon as the decision was reached. If a measure of expulsion or repatriation was decided by the OFA within these 15 days, the prisoner could not be held in a prison for more than an additional 15 days on administrative grounds. The total period of additional administrative detention could therefore not exceed 30 days. This policy was revoked however by circular letter of 17 December 2003, following refusals by police forces to be further involved in the transfer or expulsion of foreigners. This was the result of a trial in which police forces were held responsible for

33 Office for Foreigners Affairs, Annual report, Ministry of Interior, Brussels 2000.

34 By circular letter of 28 July 1989, a third category was added, i.e. prisoners against whom a procedure for expulsion has been started and who are awaiting the advice of the Commission for Advice concerning Foreigners.

the death by asphyxiation of a Nigerian woman who was forcefully expelled. According to this latter circular letter, foreign prisoners without permit of residence who could not be transferred to a closed centre for illegal aliens were not to be released anymore. This meant that although these prisoners had served the required proportion of their prison sentence for the Ministry of Justice, they could be further detained in the prison on administrative grounds. It appeared from our research that, in practice, the OFA did not really take into account the possibility of provisional early release after serving 1/3 of the sentence, as this is not a formal right to which prisoners are entitled. The OFA assumed it was sufficient to reach a decision about the administrative status of the foreigner by the end of the prison sentence. As a result, it happened on several occasions that a prisoner was about to leave the prison on provisional release but was held back by a last-minute fax by the OFA requesting his further detention for administrative reasons. This mixture of procedures was sometimes hard to understand for the prisoners involved, and often resulted in dramatic consequences such as hunger strikes, suicide attempts or aggressive behaviour. As a consequence of this research finding, a new cooperation agreement was reached between the Ministries of Justice and Interior, through which the OFA now decides more quickly on the administrative status of the foreign prisoner Circular letter nr. 84 of December 2004 reintroduced the original maximum period of 30 additional days in case of provisional release in view of expulsion. Since September 2005, nine "migration counsellors" (formerly "return agents") from the OFA work inside the prisons in order to hasten the administrative procedure and decision. An information leaflet on the administrative procedures has been developed and is now handed over to all foreign prisoners upon admission to the prison.

That doesn't mean that all problems have been solved. Illegal aliens who will be released provisionally with a view on expulsion, must agree with the expulsion as a condition of release. However, many of them have lived in Belgium for many years and may have a procedure pending on regularisation of their illegal status, sometimes they have no social or family ties left in the country of origin. If they return to Belgium after expulsion and are caught again, they will have to serve the remainder of their prison sentence, without having committed a new criminal offence. This is true even if they come back to Belgium with a legal document, e.g. a tourist visa.

A second problem results from the fact that all these forms of early release require some preparation by the psychosocial service of the prison. Although the number of psychologists in prison has been vastly increased since the Act of 1998 on conditional release, many psychosocial services still find themselves overburdened. This results sometimes in long waiting lists to see prisoners and to answer their queries. This may in its turn postpone the preparation and organisation of the early release and result in longer prison stays. Language problems may arise because of the complexity of the different procedures. But specific cultural problems are also mentioned here. Following the Act of 5 march 1998 on conditional release, the psychosocial service of the prison where a sentence is served must evaluate the possibilities for and efforts towards social reintegration of the prisoner, his behaviour inside the prison, his attitude towards the victims, the risks of relapse into recidivism. For sexual offenders, any form of early release must be coupled to a specialised advice by a psychosocial service and the acceptance of specialised treatment upon release (Act November 2000). Cultural problems may arise due to a different attitude towards certain forms of delinquency, for example linked to matters of honour or to help provided to fellow illegal aliens. The emphasis in the Belgian conditional release system on individual responsibility, guilt and reparation towards the victims of crime may be foreign to more collectivistic cultures, or to foreign prisoners who commit offences to survive. Psychological tests also raise cultural problems: standard tests are based on Western thinking, leading to interpretation problems towards other cultures, and psychologists working in the prisons are trained in Western psychology, with often very little knowledge of ethno psychiatry or –psychology. These cultural problems may subsist even when the pure language problem can be solved.

2.10 Aftercare – Probation

Foreign prisoners who on the basis of their residence permit when apprehended are released under conditional release are entitled to the same guidance and aftercare as national citizens. There are no specific programmes for these prisoners.

2.11 Staff

Prison staff has no special training to deal with foreign prisoners. As mentioned above (II.1.1.) language and communication are very important in prison, where many aspects of prison regime must be asked for, verbally or in written form. Where none of the common languages can help (Dutch, French, English), language problems are solved through the use of fellow prisoners, which may raise other problems.

Staff also mentions cultural problems during the interviews and focus groups. Cultural characteristics are said to influence personal interactions in prison, both between prisoners and staff and amongst prisoners. More patriarchal cultures may lead to refusal by male prisoners to accept the authority of female guards, to talk about personal matters with a female psychologist or to be treated by a female nurse or doctor. Some groups are seen as presenting a more disrespectful, insubordinate and oppositional behaviour, without however resorting to physical violence (e.g. North Africans), while other groups seem rather quiet and well adapted to prison life but become easily violent in case of conflicts (e.g. Eastern Europeans). In some cultures, violent private resolution of conflicts is seen as the norm, with both conflicting parties refusing any interference by prison staff (e.g. Albanians). Some prisoners may also justify their behaviour by referring to their religion, which according to prison staff makes it more difficult for them to assess an infringement on the rules.

Both prisoners and staff mention racism. Prison guards of foreign origin mention institutional racism by the prison administration, as only Belgian citizens can become staff members, and important functions are said to be reserved for native Belgian citizens. The prison environment is described as a very closed field, in which other staff members, despite their positive influence on foreign prisoners, do not accept guards of foreign origin. Expectations are much higher towards guards of foreign origin, and any mistake or fault is said to lead to more extreme reactions by their colleagues. They may also suffer from an additional stigma by foreign visitors of the same origin, who consider them as "traitors".

Foreign prisoners refer to the lack of respect by prison guards, especially the younger ones, and to discrimination in the application of disciplinary reports and sanctions. The more privileged jobs and positions of trust inside the prison are also said to be always granted to Belgian prisoners. Some prisoners assume this is due to the higher level of communication necessary for these jobs, while others mention that foreign prisoners without a permit of residence are automatically seen as presenting a higher risk of escape, and are therefore never granted these positions of trust.

Prison staff also mentions racism amongst prisoners based on nationality. According to a survey of prison directors performed by the "Centre against racism and xenophobia", racism is not very prominent in the prisons though and certainly not a priority problem[35].

2.12 Projects

As a result of this research financed by the King Boudewijn Foundation, the Foundation took several initiatives. At general policy level, a meeting was organised with senior officials of the Ministries of Justice and Interior in order to solve the problems relating to the interaction between criminal and administrative procedures and the ensuing delays in early release of foreign prisoners. This resulted in the above mentioned new cooperation agreement and the introduction of "migration counsellors" working in the prisons in order to fasten the administrative decision-making. The Foundation also financed the translation of a new information leaflet with the rights and duties of the prisoners resulting from the new Prison Act of 2005.

Table 4: administrative status of foreign prisoners – absolute numbers (14 November 1993-2003)

		Uncertain residence	*Residence*	*No residence*	*Residence*
Year	*Total*	*Not mentioned*	*Unknown to OF*	*Expulsion decided*	*Residence granted*
1993	3122	33	3012	19	58
1994	3031	40	2916	22	53
1995	3131	44	3020	20	47
1996	3164	45	3053	17	49
1997	3208	212	2850	54	92
1998	2951	471	2066	88	326
1999	3209	498	2054	82	498
2000	3606	542	2231	96	737
2001	3514	715	1977	89	733
2002	3936	1511	1105	403	917
2003	3917	1411	1115	447	944

Source: Snacken, Keulen & Winkelmans (2004):

[1]. We prefer to use average daily data, but these are not available for the last years. The use of data on a certain date can give a misleading picture since they only refer to the situation on that moment. Calculations are based on the average daily prison population.

---

35 Mentioned by Patrick Charlier of the "Centre against racism and xenophobia" during the focus group on 26 January 2004.

3 ADMINISTRATIVE DETENTION OF FOREIGN PRISONERS

Asylum seekers who have been refused asylum and illegal aliens who have not been granted residence or have not been regularised must leave the country. In case of failure to leave, they may be detained for the time strictly necessary for the organisation of the forced repatriation. Such administrative detention normally takes place in a closed centre of the Ministry of Interior. Administrative detention is normally imposed for a maximum of two months, but can be extended to five months. Only when necessary for the protection of public order or national security can it be further prolonged to the absolute maximum of eight months. Appeal against the administrative detention can be lodged with the investigation chamber of the correctional court.

There are now five closed centres: three for illegal aliens (Merksplas, Brugge, Vottem; the first two are former prisons, capacity around 160 places), one Centre for Repatriation ("127bis", located at Steenokkerzeel, capacity 192 places) and one Transit Centre for asylum seekers arriving at the National Airport ("127", located in the Transit zone of the National Airport, capacity 100 places). To these must be added the "INAD" Centre ("inadmissables"), also located inside the airport zone, taking in persons arriving at the airport without legal documents and who are refused entry into the country (capacity 30 places).

According to the Annual Report 2004 of the OFA[36], 7.622 persons have been detained in the closed centres during 2004. The average number of detainees during 2004 was 513. The different centres had an average population of 105 for Brugge, 145 for Merksplas, 106 for Vottem and 98 for the 127bis. The Transit centres 127 and INAD had an average of 49 and 10 detainees. The average length of stay in these centres was resp. 56, 51, 44, 19, 9 and 2 days. In 2004, 5.612 detainees were expelled, mainly through repatriation (4.065), while 1.866 were released.

The regime and functioning of the closed centres are regulated by a Royal Decree of 2 August 2002 and monitored by the "General Coordination and Control Department" of the OFA. The Royal Decree shows similarities with the Prison Act of 2005, as it was broadly based on an earlier version of the Draft Prison Act. Some examples: right to unlimited correspondence (art.19), daily telephone (art.24), right to and freedom of religion (art.16, 46-50), right to legal aid (art.62).

There are however some notable differences, through which the inmates of the closed centres are entitled to more or broader rights than prisoners: the inmates must receive a leaflet with the house rules, which must be explained to them by a staff member in a language they can understand, if necessary through the assistance of an interpreter (art.17), they can request help with reading or writing of letters (art.22), they are entitled to free writing paper and if necessary stamps (art.23), they must be able to talk undisturbed with their visitors (art.29), they have the right to receive visits by diplomatic or consular agents every day from 8.00 to 22.00 (art.32), they have the right to receive daily visits of minimum one hour from their close family (art.34, except in the Transit Centre 127, located inside the airport), they may call their lawyer every day for free from 8.00 to 22.00 (art.63). The director of the centre must foster the general development of the inmates (art.69) by organising recreational, cultural and sports activities (art.70), every centre must have a library (art.71) and all inmates must have access to the media (art.72). Activities

36 Annual Report of the Office for Foreigners' Affairs, Ministry of Interior, 2004.

can be organised by NGO's if authorised by the Ministry of Interior (art.73). A complaint committee has been established as of 9 September 2003. On the other hand, no work is provided for these detainees.

A remarkable feature concerning staff: nothing is said about the duties and responsibilities of staff (no reference to "dynamic security" as in the Prison Act, nothing about language or communication problems), but religious counsellors and external services or NGO's must have "a neutral attitude towards" or "not act against" the legislation on the closed centres and the legislation on entry and residence of foreigners (art.51, 79). Similarly, the social and medical services must offer counselling to the inmates during their stay in the centre, "prepare them for a possible repatriation" and "guide them into acceptance of the decision concerning their administrative status" (art.68). Many efforts are made by the OFA to improve relations with diplomatic and consular services, in order to foster swifter identification and repatriation of the foreigners and with the International Organisation for Migration in order to stimulate voluntary return to the country of origin[37].

Not surprisingly, life inside the closed centres is rather strained. Frustrations of the inmates run high when their expectations are disappointed (failed appeal against refusal of asylum or regularisation), the communal regime limits individual privacy, despite regulations to the contrary (art.83), and foreigners who have not been involved in criminal activities resent being detained together with former prisoners awaiting their expulsion. Recurrent complaints by staff about verbal and physical aggressions and subjective feelings of insecurity have led to the establishment of a working group on "violence control". Proposals formulated by this working group relate mainly to a better training of staff to cope with aggression and the improvement of some regime aspects for the inmates, thus improving their responsibilities and self-esteem[38]. Several collective protests erupted in the closed centre of Merksplas in 2004, often requiring police intervention, of which one followed a suicide of an inmate of the centre. In the closed centre of Vottem, a few inmates committed arson, thus reducing the capacity of the centre with 1/3. During each of its visits to Belgium, CPT inspected several of these centres:

- the former Repatriation Centre of Walem and the Transit Centre 127 at the airport in 1993 (there were no closed centres for illegal aliens at that time yet),
- the INAD, the Transit Centre 127, the Repatriation Centre 127bis and the closed centre of Merksplas in 1997,
- the forced expulsions of foreigners in 2001 and 2005,
- and finally a follow up visit to the INAD, the Transit Centre 127 and the Repatriation Centre 127bis in 2005.

CPT criticisms were most severe for:

- the Repatriation Centre of Walem in 1993, where material conditions and regime were considered unacceptable and where staff was composed of military conscripts; the centre was closed in 1994;
- the transit zone of the airport in 1993, where material conditions were considered unacceptable;

37 Annual Report of the Office for Foreigners' Affairs, Ministry of Justice, ibidem p.78-79.

38 Ibidem, p. 76-77.

- the INAD and Transit Centre 127 in 1997 and 2005, for their lack of possibilities for visits by family and even by lawyers and the lack of regime;
- the lack of juridical information offered to illegal aliens generally in 1997, and more particularly at the INAD in 2005, concerning the different administrative procedures relating to entry and residence;
- the violence and the techniques used by police forces in 1993, 1997 and 2001 to ensure forced expulsion of foreigners resisting their departure; this had improved by 2005.

Positive aspects were mentioned in 1997 concerning the material circumstances, the regime of activities and the improved staff training in the closed centre of Merksplas, the Transit Centre 127 and the Repatriation Centre 127bis.

Unaccompanied minors (UAM): Belgium has the third largest number of UAM in Europe (1.050 in 2002)[39]. The Act of 1980 on the entry and residence of foreigners does not distinguish between adults and minors. By Act of 24 December 2002, a guardianship service has been established for UAM, defined as "persons younger than 18y, unaccompanied by a person who exercises parental authority or guardianship according to the national legislation of the minor, who is citizen of a country outside the European Economic Area, and who has either requested refugee status or does not meet the conditions for entry or residence inside the country". The guardianship service must identify the UAM, assess their age (if necessary through a medical test), trace their family and coordinate the stay of the UAM in Belgium with the asylum authorities and the reception centres. Guardians are not required to have a specific background, but are trained on the job in several issues concerning children.

The open reception centres are under the competence of the Ministry of Social Integration through the agency Fedasil. According to a policy paper of 21 March 2004 by this Ministry, reception of UAM should follow a dual model. In a first phase, taking 14 days at most, the UAM is brought to a safe place with access to psychological, social, administrative and juridical assistance for observation and orientation. In a second phase, the UAM is transferred to a reception centre of Fedasil or the Red Cross, is placed in a specific centre for UAM created in 2002 or placed in a foster family or in a flat with the help of the children welfare system. The specific centres have multidisciplinary staff and cooperate with other NGO's involved in children's' rights. In reality, many UAM are caught when entering the country at the airport and will be placed in the INAD or the Transit centre 127, or will be placed in an open or closed centre for asylum seekers, which do not always have adequate facilities for children. The disappearance of a number of UAM from these centres illustrates the problem of their vulnerability to organised sexual exploitation.

UAM have the same rights as other children to medical assistance and education. Special classes have been created to help UAM to quickly learn one of the national languages, and all children are entitled to go to school, notwithstanding their illegal status. UAM are entitled to legal assistance free of charge as soon as they arrive at the border. This may however not always be the case in practice, especially during the first stage of the reception. The procedure for asylum seeking is the same for adults or minors, there

[39] European Union 2002, Migration and asylum in Europe: the largest numbers are found in the UK (6.200) and the Netherlands (3.232).

are no specific considerations for their status as UAM and immigration services are not trained to deal with minors[40].

4 NATIONALS DETAINED ABROAD

On the 13 June 2006, 523 Belgian nationals were detained abroad, of which 83% were detained in other Western European countries. The top countries are Spain (27%), France (22%), Germany (12%) and Great Britain (7.5%). Only 1.7% are held in Eastern European prisons. Morocco scores highest within the non-European countries (4.6%), followed by the USA (2.3%). The main reason for detention is drugs (57%), followed by violence (6.3%), theft (4%), sexual offences (3.4%) and murder (2.9%). 3.6% are held in custody in view of extradition[41]. There is no statistical information on the length of the sentences or the personal characteristics of the detainees.

The department of International Judicial Cooperation of the Ministry of Foreign Affairs is responsible for the consular help and advice to these nationals detained abroad. No other organisations are involved. A pamphlet "Help and guidance for Belgians in foreign prisons", with information concerning the possibilities and restrictions for consular help, is issued by the department, can be found on its Website[42] and is distributed by the Belgian embassies and consulates to Belgian prisoners abroad. It explains that foreign authorities do not have an obligation to inform the embassy or consulate of every prisoner, so the prisoner should formally request the local authority to do so on the basis of the Convention of Vienna concerning consular help (1963). If no Belgian embassy or consulate is present in the country of detention, the embassy or consulate of another European Union member state can be informed, within the framework of the Agreement on European Consular Help.

Consular help will vary according to the individual situation and the country. Examples given in the pamphlet are: to inform family and friends of the detention, to help the prisoner to establish and keep contacts with family or with the consular services, to monitor the humane circumstances of the detention (in particular food and medical and dental care) and the absence of discriminatory treatment, to check on the fairness and the speed of the trial in accordance with local legislation and procedures, to inform family on the justice and prison system of the country of detention, the average length of trials, the case law and conditions for early release. Consular help does not include financial help, but can mediate in order to foster the possibilities for the prisoner to buy food or to provide for other basic needs.

Information is also provided concerning the Convention for the transfer of sentenced prisoners of 1983, ratified by Belgium in 1990 (see above I. 5.2.4.). It lists the countries that are party to the Convention and the conditions for its application. The bilateral agreement with Morocco is also mentioned.

No special after care is provided upon return to Belgium, there is no difference with other prisoners released in Belgium. If a prisoner has no family ties left in Belgium and

---

40 C. Joppart, *Separated children in Europe. Questionnaire for country assessment: Belgium*, Brussels 2003, Defence for Children International Belgium.

41 Information provided by the department for International Judicial Cooperation of the Ministry of Foreign Affairs on 13 June 2006.

42 http://www.diplomatie.be/nl/services/prisondetail.asp?textID=659

has insufficient financial means to survive, the department of International Judicial Co-operation may ask the Red Cross to support the prisoner upon his arrival and look for housing, e.g. through the welfare services of his last place of residence. Occasionally, the department advances money to pay the return flight ticket.

Attention to the situation of nationals detained abroad in Belgian media and public opinion is generally low, apart from certain exceptional cases (cf. media attention and public sympathy for a Belgian bus driver imprisoned in Russia for a traffic accident, or another driver supposedly framed for drug trafficking and held for many years in a prison in Tanger, which lead to the recent movie "The hell of Tanger").

5 EVALUATIONS AND RECOMMENDATIONS

Social exclusion is present at different stages and in different forms for foreign prisoners. First, some ethnic minority groups, such as Moroccans, and many illegal aliens live in poor neighbourhoods in bad socio-economic circumstances. Second, this lack of social integration is often seen by actors of the criminal justice system to enhance the risk of criminality or recidivism, resulting in a higher application of deprivation of liberty, at the level of both remand custody and sentencing. Third, foreigners or ethnic minorities face different problems during detention, ranging from severe language and communication problems to religious or cultural conflicts or racism. Fourth, prisoners who have no legal permit of residence will be excluded from some regime aspects such as prison leave or electronic monitoring. Fifth, the combination of criminal and administrative procedures hampers the preparation and swift application of early release procedures. Sixth, when expelled to their country of origin, foreign prisoners may find themselves isolated from their real family and social ties, which may still be in Belgium.

Belgium has a large proportion of foreign prisoners (44% in 2004) and prisons have to cope with more than 100 different nationalities. The King Boudewijn Foundation commissioned the research on which this paper is partly based in 2004, bringing to the fore the difficult situation of foreign prisoners in Belgian prisons. Problems inside the prisons and concerning the procedures of early release were listed and discussed with the relevant authorities. Some of the problems have been tackled since, but many remain. Pressed by prison overcrowding, administrative detention of foreigners who have not committed an offence is now seldom implemented in a prison, and detention in a closed centre of the Ministry of Interior is the norm. These closed centres however also face severe tensions and conflicts. Regime and activities should be further improved for prisoners and detainees, and staff of prisons and centres alike should receive more training enabling them to cope with the multicultural and stressful environment in which they have to work. Transfer of sentenced prisoners to their country of origin for the implementation of the sentences could offer a solution for those prisoners whose social ties are still there. This would however also require sufficient guarantees that living conditions in all prisons and centres respect human dignity.

Chapter 4

Cyprus

Andreas Ellinas

1 INTRODUCTION

Cyprus is a small island in the eastern Mediterranean Sea and it is the closest European country to the Middle East and Asia. It joined the EU as a full member in 2005. Cyprus currently applies the Anglo-Saxon legal system due to the fact that the island was a British colony until 1960. There is only one penitentiary institution in Cyprus (Central Prison Nicosia) which operates under a new comprehensive legislative and regulatory framework that was put in place in 1996 and 1997. This legislation incorporates the European Prison Rules and conforms to the standards contained in the relevant instruments of the Council of Europe.

1.1 Overview of Penalties and Measures

A person can only be deprived of his or her liberty after having been convicted by a court for committing an offence, or when reasons are evident that require a person to be detained while awaiting trial. The penalties that are imposed by the courts in Cyprus depend upon the seriousness of the offence and the likelihood of the offender committing further offences. As far as discipline, security, punishment and penalties are concerned, the Disciplinary Code is applied equally to everyone. According to the law, all prisoners are equal and foreigners have the right to request legal aid if they cannot afford legal representation themselves. In case either Cypriot or foreign prisoners do not have financial means the state shall provide legal aid and - in addition to this - foreigners have the right to an interpreter during police interviewing and through the course of their trial. The Prison Law and regulations are applicable to all prisoners. However, in some cases security issues can make it difficult for foreigners to receive the full benefits of the law, which also include home leaves. In exchange, they receive additional rights to more visits and telephone calls.

1.2 Overview of the Prison System

The issue of foreign prisoners is considered to be of major concern for the Prison Department because of their large number in comparison to Cypriot prisoners. The key factor that influences the proportion of the foreign population in prison is the fact that a greater proportion of foreigners are involved in criminal activity, for a number of reasons:

- The large numbers of tourists, who are unaware of Cypriot law
- Foreign workers (legal and illegal)
- Illegal entries into the country from unauthorised ports
- Foreign residents
- Foreigners taking advantage of the geographical and political setting of Cyprus (financial services etc)

Due to the geographical position of Cyprus, immigrants come in search of a better life. An explanation for the flow of illegal immigrants to Cyprus is the fact that Asian and African countries are very close to the island and migrants can come easily by boat. Based on several sources of information, today there are around 40,000 illegal foreigners (coming predominantly from Pakistan, Sri-Lanka and Bangladesh) in Cyprus, who initially enter the country as students or seasonal workers and then fail to conform to the conditions of their visas. It is often the case that many apply for asylum when their visa is cancelled or expires. In Cyprus, foreign workers are employed as manual or unskilled workers, (for instance in agriculture, farming etc), but also as house servants and in the nursing of elderly people. Many illegal immigrants come from the Turkish occupied areas of Cyprus in which the Cypriot authorities are unable to enforce the law. The Turkish occupied areas are linked with Turkey and do not comply fully with illegal immigration rules, thus allowing movement from the northern part of Cyprus. Furthermore, because of the fact that many illegals have no proof of their personal details, their Embassies often refuse to issue them new travel documents and - as a consequence - they are detained in police custody until their identity has been verified. European citizens are usually convicted for crimes such as drug dealing and possession, assault, burglary and theft. European citizens tend to have fewer problems in organizing new travel documents and as soon as they have completed their sentence the immigration service decides whether they can stay or are to be expelled. The 2006 budget for the Prison Department was approx. 32.000.000 Euros. The Prison Administration includes:

- One Prison Director,
- Two Senior Superintendents
- Four Superintendents
- Eight Inspectors,
- Forty non-commission officers
- Two hundred and sixty one wardens
- Two trainers who are responsible for the prisoners' education program

The wings of the prison have a residential capacity of about 340, and currently hold 577 prisoners. The prison population on 17.4.2006 was 499 convicted prisoners and 78 unconvicted, of whom 340 were foreign prisoners.

1.2.1 Organisational Structure

The central penitentiary institution consists of eight closed prison wings, seven for male offenders and one for female offenders, as well as one wing for pre-trial prisoners. In addition to the above, there are blocks for the accommodation of young offenders, a top security block, an isolation centre (which is used to separate prisoners from the remaining prison population), one open section and one 'Centre for the Guidance and Extra-institutional Employment of Prisoners'. In addition to the central prison in Cyprus, there are detention cells in the police stations in all districts. These are the responsibility of the police and are used to detain suspects of crimes under the courts warrants or any other legal authority, including foreigners who have been arrested for illegal entry or under the order of the immigration official according to the authorization given by the Law on Immigration.

1.2.2 Foreign Prisoners

According to the philosophy of the above law relating to the imprisonment of offenders as a judicial sentence, deprivation of liberty has the purpose not only to keep them in secure conditions, but also to apply various programs in the correctional institution to reform, re-educate and rehabilitate prisoners in order for them to become useful members of society. The Department of Central Prisons is under the administration of the Ministry of Justice and Public Order. Nicosia Central Prison receives all categories of convicted and pre-trial prisoners of both genders and all age groups. No person shall be admitted into the prison as a prisoner unless under a judicial warrant. The prison system places paramount importance in the understanding of different cultures and origins of detainees. There are strict rules and regulations concerning any form of discrimination, whether it is due to racial origin, colour, language, as well as religious, political or other beliefs concerning ethnic or social background. Discrimination is strictly prohibited and severe disciplinary measures are to be imposed if these rules are broken or not adhered to.

1.3 Overview of the Involvement of Consulates, Embassies, Cypriot Ministries and Probation Service, NGO's etc

The prison living conditions, catering, administration practices and everything concerning the prison system are supervised by the Prison Board, the Commissioner of Law and the Ombudsman, who have the right to initiate investigations for wrong practices. In addition to the above, the prison is also subject to frequent visits by the C.P.T., advising for further possibilities of improvement. In order to facilitate communication between prisoners with the above mentioned authorities, the prison administration has installed mailing boxes in various areas of the prison where the prisoners can communicate freely in writing without any censorship.

1.4 Overview of Trends

1.4.2 Characteristics of the Foreign Prison Population

According to prison statistics, in the year 2005 there were 1,187 detainees:

- 650 (54.75%) were foreigners,
- 459 (70.61%) of whom were imprisoned for less than six months
- 37 foreign offenders on drug charges
- 54 foreign offenders for offences against the person
- nine foreign offenders for sexual crimes
- 150 foreign offenders for offences related to property
- 4 foreign offenders for malicious injuries to property / criminal damage
- 31 foreign offenders on forgery charges,
- 365 foreign offenders on other charges, like guns and ammunitions, illegal entry & stay, fines.

Table 1: Foreign prisoners by age (2005).

Age	*Male*	*Female*	*Total*
16-20 years old	46	4	50
21-24 years old	132	7	139
25-29 years old	180	12	192
30-39 years old	172	18	190
40-49 years old	53	9	62
50+ years old	15	2	17
Total	598	52	650

According to the above table the majority of foreign offenders are 25-39 years old.

2 TREATMENT OF FOREIGN PRISONERS

2.1 General Information

According to the constitution, no form of discrimination is allowed against any person. Discriminations on the grounds of ethnicity, language, country of origin, and religion are prohibited and all people are to be treated equally in relation to the law. Therefore, foreign prisoners have the same benefits and same rights as the Cypriot prisoners provided no security issues give reason for differentiated treatment.

The legislator takes into consideration what the Constitution states in respect for Human Rights and the equal treatment of prisoners. The Prison Law and regulations include measures which forbid discriminations of any kind (for example race, colour, language, religion); concurrently, it includes disciplinary penalties for the staff and for the prisoners in cases of non-adherence. Despite the provision in law sometimes there are cases of minor discriminations, which certainly are not deliberate, but rather are subject to special circumstances such as:

- The foreign prisoners do not have six visits per month as is the case for Cypriots because their families live abroad. But, in the event of their families being in Cyprus, special arrangements are made to allow visits every day during their stay in Cyprus. If the foreign prisoners have local friends and acquaintances that can offer them psychological support and help during their imprisonment, they are permitted to visit the prisoners.
- Prisoners from countries that have a bilateral agreement with the Republic of Cyprus for the transfer of convicted prisoners, or which have signed the European Arrest Warrant, are moved to the open prison which is the last stage before their reintroduction into society, provided they meet the necessary requirements.
- All prisoners receive wages according to the work assigned to them and according to the effort and industry they show during their imprisonment, but sometimes this is not enough. Often foreigners apply to the Welfare Committee for financial support. This is examined and assistance is provided based upon the needs of the offender.

- Foreign detainees are permitted to make home visits like Cypriots do, so long as their normal residence or their families are in Cyprus. Such home visits can be both supervised and unsupervised.

2.2 Living Conditions and Facilities

There is the aim of accommodating sentenced and non-sentenced prisoners separately from each in different wings. However, due to overcrowding in the prison this cannot always be fully achieved. The Evaluation Committee, after gathering the relevant information, places the prisoner in a wing and then assigns him/her to working activities. There is no special approach of separation for the placement of foreigners to the wings, and great effort is given to increase socialization and communication among foreigners. In these cases, arrangements are made in order for the foreigner to be placed in a cell with a prisoner of his/her own nationality, so that he/she can communicate and have company.

2.3 Reception and Admission

A general register is kept for every prisoner admitted into the prison, with numbered pages in which personal data are kept such as for instance marital status, the offence of which he/she has been convicted, the courts decision, as well as the date and time of admission and discharge. In addition to the registration information, each prisoner has to go through physical and mental examinations in order to diagnose his/her physical and mental state and to determine whether the person is substance dependent or has a disturbed personality. The results of the examinations are collected and stored in a prisoner's personal record.

On reception, all prisoners - including foreigners - are subjected to a body search and a search of their luggage and belongings. They are then directed to the Admission and Release Office, where each prisoner has to give his/her personal details in order to create a comprehensive database and to further ascertain the needs and requirements of each individual. Foreign prisoners are also informed that they are allowed to be repatriated or to be transferred to their home country to serve their sentence, so long as their country is signatory to the convention for the repatriation of prisoners. They also have the right to apply for political asylum. In such a case assistance is provided for the completion of the application forms.

2.4 Work - Education – Training – Sports - Recreation

The prison administration is bound by law to provide education and training (improving skills) to all prisoners who wish to further their education All prisoners sentenced to imprisonment of more than one month and who wish to benefit from the programs granted by the Prison Law as well as to receive work allowance are in work (classified by the Classification Committee). If they cannot be employed for health reasons due to a recommendation by the Medical Officer or for other reasons after a decision by the director they are excluded from work or sports. The organisation and the methods of the work are as similar as possible to those of free society in order to prepare the prisoners for the conditions of work that they will encounter after release. Detainees awaiting trial are not bound to work. However, they can apply to the Classification Committee and work will be offered to them. They are entitled to receive the appropriate wages once they have been issued a working schedule. This is great assistance to the foreign prisoners who have nobody to look after them.

Prison officers and prison educational staff, in association with departmental psychologists, psychiatrists, general practitioners, nursing staff, and social workers deliver lectures and awareness programs to prisoners. According to law, participation in academic education is voluntary. The overall curriculum is organized by the education staff and other professionals, and it is their responsibility to make the curriculum attractive and interesting, according to the prisoners needs. The prisoners may also borrow books (books are available in foreign languages) from the prison library. Presently, the prisoners' school offers:

- Adult basic education, including literature and maths
- Computer education, (access to the internet is not allowed)
- Expressive arts such as painting, design, copper work, iconography, dance and drama. (The prisoners' theatre team performs both in and outside of the prison. Membership to the group is open to foreigners as well)
- Languages such as Greek (for foreigners), and English
- Traditional education such as history and geography
- Psychology
- Drug and alcohol education
- Health education such as sexually transmitted diseases and other
- First aid
- Cooking, gardening, plumbing
- Chess

Each prisoner has the right to participate in any of the physical exercise programs. Specially trained personnel supervise the prisoners for physical fitness, instrumental gymnastics, team games and contests, both in and outside of prison (a specialized prison officer and a gymnast from the Cyprus Organization of Athletics train a football team). The sporting activities are also available to foreign prisoners.

2.5 Food – Religion – Personal hygiene – Medical care

The food provided to the prisoners is healthy, nutritious, suitably prepared, of reasonable variety, satisfactory in terms of quantity and quality and adjusted in accordance to dietary principles and modern hygiene. The diet is set by the director with close reference to recommendations from the medical officer of the prison, who takes into consideration the age, health, work and – as far as possible - the religious beliefs of the inmates. Every detainee has the right to perform his/her religious duties. Religious representatives are allowed to visit the prisoners in order to offer them guidance. Yet the conversion of a prisoner by another prisoner or by any representative of any religion or doctrine is prohibited. There are both a mosque and a Christian church within the prison. Every Friday - or whenever the case arises - the Muslim prisoners pray in the mosque and the Christians every Sunday in church. They all have the right to celebrate their religious events, religious festivals are observed, and special diets are available to them.

Every effort is made to place prisoners in accommodation where they can be with their fellow countrymen, so that they can speak their own language and share their religious beliefs (if this is what they want). The guards make sure that the prisoners follow the generally accepted code of rules of personal hygiene. These include the cleanliness of communal areas of the prison, of their personal cells and of the public utility rooms. (The department provides all the items that are required for cleaning the prison).

Prisoners have the right to wear their own clothes (in order to reduce stigmatisation, uniforms are abolished). The prison provides every newcomer with a set of clothing as well as toiletries for personal hygiene, and continues to provide them until they are able to buy the items themselves.

Health checks are conducted as soon as possible after admission. They include a full examination, blood tests (non compulsory), registration of the medical history of the family, etc. A general practitioner, qualified nursing personnel, a psychiatrist with assistants, two psychologists, and a work therapist offer their services in the prison on a daily basis. A part time dentist provides his services to the prison. All medical requirements are offered through the medical services of the Republic.

2.6 Consular and Legal Help

Immediately after being admitted to the prison every prisoner is entitled to appoint a legal advisor or to apply to the court for free legal aid. Foreigners have the right to ask for a person who contributes to the amelioration of the special problems that are caused by them being in custody, and especially a person that speaks their own language.

Representatives from the Embassies and the Consulates are notified by the prison administration and are permitted to visit a prisoner at any time as long as they arrange an appointment through the department for suitable hours.

Legal aid is approved for all prisoners in pre-trial detention in court if they are not financially capable to appoint a lawyer. If the court approves a prisoner's request for legal aid, then it will appoint a legal representative. However, after his/her conviction, he/she is not entitled to any form of legal help.

2.7 Contact with the Outside World

The prisoners' communication with the outside world is of vital importance, both to the socialization in prison as well as to the gradual reintegration into the conditions of free society. When a prisoner enters the prison the department is responsible for setting up all the necessary procedures for informing the prisoner's family that their relative has been imprisoned. As far as foreign prisoners are concerned, the prison department informs the Embassy or Consulate.

Telephone communication with the outside world is allowed for all prisoners. Cypriot prisoners are allowed four telephone calls per month, whereas foreign prisoners are entitled to eight, because they cannot receive frequent visits from their families. If required, the department provides free telephone cards to those who can not afford to buy them.

All prisoners are allowed up to six visits per month. There are special procedures for the foreign prisoners regarding family visitors. Also, the monthly number of visits to which they are entitled can be increased to eight, depending on the discretion of the director. This adjustment can be made because the Cypriot prisoners have the advantage of home leaves so long as the Classification Committee approves them – as well as the possibility of being placed in the open prison.

Every day, each wing is provided with local and foreign newspapers (Daily Press) and magazines. Additionally, all cells in the new wings of blocks "five" and "eight" have televisions that receive all of the local television channels. In blocks "one" and "two" prisoners can watch TV in the communal rooms except for offenders who have been sentenced to more than four years imprisonment, who are permitted to have there own television sets in theirs cells. A decision has been made to allow all prisoners, including foreigners to have their own TV in their cell. All prisoners can borrow books and magazines in many languages.

2.8 Re-integration Activities - Prison Leave

The purpose of detention in prisons - besides securing the prisoners - is to attempt to change their behaviour so that they can become capable and respectable members of society. This is to be achieved through social training, work, and support from their families. Foreign prisoners who are granted temporary exit permission or a home leave are divided into three categories:

- Those who will remain in Cyprus after their release,
- Those whose country has signed a statement of intent with the Republic of Cyprus for the transfer of convicted people, and
- Those whose families are permanent residents in Cyprus.

For prisoners who have a criminal or disciplinary offence pending against them, and those who for safety reasons are not permitted to exit the prison, the Classification Committee only decides for a supervised exit permit. The open prison is the last stage before a detainee is discharged. It operates in the outer walls, and prisoners stay, work and move under low security conditions, yet still in accordance with the same principles of conduct, discipline and order that apply to the rest of the prisoners. The privileges of the open prison include free visitations, no locking up during the night and the permission for temporary leave. There is also the guidance centre, which is the last stage before their release, and operates close to the prison. Prisoners who are sent to the centre serve the rest of their sentence in conditions of restricted and controlled freedom with the purpose of their gradual reintegration into free society. Foreign prisoners have the right to be in the centre under the condition that they will remain in Cyprus after their release. There is no parole system currently in place in Cyprus.

2.9 Release - Expulsion

After a foreigner has been convicted, the migration office is responsible for whether or not he is to be expelled. Even European citizens who have committed a serious offence such as murder, drugs offences, robbery or burglary come under the same rule. If the decision of the migration office is for the offender to be expelled from Cyprus, then the offender has the right to appeal before the Supreme Court. In this event the offender remains in custody until the court has made its final decision.

2.10 Aftercare – Probation

Before their release, all prisoners who have been sentenced to more than six months – including foreigners – can request financial assistance before the Rehabilitation Committee. If the latter decides in their favour, they receive a small amount of money as well as a set of clothes to wear on the day of their release. The committee informs those who shall remain in Cyprus about the services and authorities that can assist them in finding employment and in filing applications for financial support, thus helping to gradually reintegrate them into free society.

3 ADMINISTRATIVE DETENTION OF FOREIGN PRISONERS

3.1 Institutions for Administrative Detention

Foreigners who are arrested for offences related to illegal entrance and/or residence in Cyprus, working without permission, or who have applied for political asylum, are kept in prison for the duration of the sentence. If an application for asylum is rejected then they are kept in police detention cells until their removal has been arranged and executed.

3.2 Ministry Responsible and Relevant Legislation

The police detention cells are under the supervision of the chief of the police department which in turn is supervised by the Ministry of Justice and Public Order.

3.3 Capacity of Institutions

The police operate detention cells in all districts. In Nicosia there are two detention cells specially designated for the detention foreigners: one operates inside the prison centre (wing 10) with a capacity for 65 persons, and one is in the district police station of Lakatamia in Nicosia, which is designed to hold up to five female detainees. Unfortunately, in Larnaka, Limasol and Paphos there are no specified cells for foreigners; instead they are held together with criminal offenders. The cells in Larnaka are designed to hold 11 male and three female detainees, while the facilities in Limassol can hold up to 43 male and 12 female prisoners. The cells in Paphos can hold up to nine males and four females.

3.4 Length of stay

Unfortunately, delays occur due to the fact that sometimes Embassies are slow in issuing travel documents and - as a result - the foreigners may be kept in custody for a long time while awaiting their expulsion.

3.6 Appeal Procedure

Foreigners have the right to appeal against the detention order before the Supreme Court within seven days and request their immediate release on the grounds of being illegally held in custody. According to Cypriot law, illegal entrance, residence and work without permission are criminal offences and can be punished with up to two years in prison. Currently, the penalties range from fifteen days to six months for first time offenders, but in cases in which the offender has had previous convictions, the penalty can be up to a year in length.

5 EVALUATION AND RECOMMENDATIONS

The state provides free education especially for those whose native language is not Greek so that they can be in a position to communicate with Cypriots. The government of Cyprus puts great effort into assimilating the foreigners into wider society while attempting to retain their national identity. Schools provide a special curriculum for foreign children in order to assist integration, and the welfare office provides assistance for a fresh start in life.

The Embassies should be more sensitive towards their citizens, and protect and advise them about local laws and customs. More cooperation is necessary when a foreigner is facing expulsion and his travelling papers need to be arranged quickly, in order to avoid unnecessary trouble and worry. Moreover, the government of Cyprus needs to conduct a study to evaluate the living conditions of the foreign prison population.

Foreigners must demand to be treated equally by the local population, but at the same time respect local values, customs and sensitivities. The relevant authorities must increase awareness in the general population concerning cohabitation with foreigners. Last but not least, it is very important to inform all foreigners who want to travel to the island about the penal and penitentiary laws that are in place in Cyprus. Before coming to the island, they must be aware of the laws and legislation, their rights and their obligations in order to avoid committing offences that can result in their imprisonment.

Chapter 5

Czech Republic

Petr Škvain

1 INTRODUCTION[1]

After the fall of the totalitarian regime in former Czechoslovakia at the end of 1989, fundamental social, political and economic changes occurred that subsequently influenced the structure of criminality. In the following years new types of crime emerged and the number of offending foreign nationals rapidly changed. Nowadays, criminality by foreign nationals is considered to be a very contemporary issue of security policy in the Czech Republic.[2]

The issue of how foreign nationals are treated in Czech penitentiary institutions became a priority for the Prison Service after the prison riots in January 2000. On the basis of cooperation with various parties, the basic theses and the most problematic moments in the treatment of foreign prisoners were named in May 2000.[3] Hunger strike, attempted uprising and escape of 'Russian speaking' prisoners accentuated the urgency of this task in November 2001 as well as hunger strike of 'former Soviet Union' prisoners in Praha-Pankrác remand prison in August 2002. Upon_the assignment of the Prison Service of the Czech Republic, the Institute of Criminology and Social Prevention in Prague conducted research concerning foreign nationals in Czech penitentiary institutions in 2002-2003. Its main objective was to characterize the prison population, to determine the main problems concerning the treatment of foreign prisoners, and, on the basis of all information, to state specific recommendations.[4] The main objective of the Czech national study within the frame of the EU 'social exclusion' project on foreign prisoners in European penitentiary institutions is to provide information on the situation and the position of foreign prisoners in the Czech Republic and to state specific recommendations. The outcome of the national study will be used not only for the purpose of this project, but will be also submitted to other involved parties (the Institute of Criminology and Social Prevention in Prague, The Prison Service and Department of Criminal Law at the University of West Bohemia in Pilsen etc.).

1.1 Overview of Penalties and Measures

The penal sanctions provided in the Czech Criminal Code (law no. 140/1961 Coll.) are classified into penalties (punishments) and protective measures. According to Article 39 of The Charter of Fundamental Rights and Freedoms (law no. 2/1993 Coll.)[5], sanctions may be imposed only in accordance with the law. The penalties are exhaustively listed in Article 27 of the Czech Criminal Code (hereinafter the Criminal Code) and include imprisonment, community service, deprivation of titles, honours and awards, loss of a mili-

---

1 Petr Škvain works with the Department of Criminal Law at the Faculty of Law, University of West Bohemia in Pilsen, The Czech Republic.

2 Government of the Czech Republic (2005), Resolution of the Government of the Czech Republic, *The Report on Public Order and Internal Security in the Czech Republic in 2004 (compared with 2003)*, No. 827 of 29 June 2005, Government of the Czech Republic, Prague.

3 Dočekal, M.(2001), *'Koncepce zacházení s vězněnými cizinci'* (*'Conception of treatment of foreign prisoners'*), České vězeňství (Journal of the Czech Prison Service), 1-2, pp. 48-50;.

4 Scheinost, M. at al. (2004), *Výzkum cizích státních příslušníků v českých věznicích* (*Research on foreign nationals in the Czech penitentiary institutions)*, Institut pro kriminologii a sociální prevenci (The Institute of Criminology and Social Prevention), Praha (Prague).

5 Charter of Fundamental Rights and Freedoms (law no. 2/1993 Coll.) is the part of the Czech Constitutional order.

tary rank, prohibition to participate in certain activities, forfeiture of property, fines, forfeiture of good or other property value, expulsion, and the prohibition of residence. The protective measures are listed in Article 71 of the Criminal Code and include protective treatment, seizure of goods or other property value, and protective rehabilitation that may be imposed only upon a juvenile. The objectives of these measures are mainly therapeutic, educational and preventive.[6] Protective measures are imposed irrespectively of the criminal responsibility of an offender, either as a separate sanction or in addition to penalties. In other words, the Criminal Code provides for a bifurcated system of sanctions. In the case of juvenile offenders, the sanctions may be imposed only according to *lex specialis* – The Juvenile Justice Act (law no. 218/2003 Coll.) – and include educational, protective and punitive measures.[7]

There are also cases in which penalties can be replaced by a prison sentence. According to Article 54 para.3 of the Criminal Code and Article 344 para.2 of the Criminal Procedural Code, a court can impose a substitute sentence of imprisonment for up to two years in cases of non-payment of fines. Also, should an offender who has been sentenced to community service not comply with his or her sentence, the court can convert the original sanction into a prison term, the length of which depends on the period of community service that had been originally adjudicated. In this context, two un-served hours of community service equal one day of imprisonment[8].

1.2 Overview of the Prison System

1.2.1 Organisational Structure

The Prison Service of the Czech Republic (hereinafter referred to as the Prison Service) was established according to the law no. 555/1992 Coll. on the 'prison guard' and the 'judicial guard' of the Czech Republic. It is state-financed, is allocated its own budget and is therefore an entity that is responsible for managing and accounting its own funds. The main purpose of the Prison Service is to provide administration and surveillance of both remand and regular prisons. It is responsible for observing the rules and conditions in pre-trial detention and regular imprisonment; for supporting prisoners by means of treatment programmes in detention in order to support their reintegration after release; for conducting research in the field of penology and using scientific findings within the framework of pre-trial detention and imprisonment; for establishing working conditions for prisoners, and providing them with health care etc.[9] The Prison Service consists of the prison guard, the judicial guard and the administrative service.[10] The prison guard patrols, transports and escorts prisoners and provides surveillance for both remand and regular prisons. The judicial guard provides security in courthouses, at public prosecutors' offices and at the Ministry of Justice. The administrative service makes administrative decisions and provides organizational, economical, educational and other

6 Šámal, P., Král, V., Púry, F. (2004), *Trestní zákon – komentář* (*Commentary on the Criminal Code)*, C. H. Beck, Praha (Prague)

7 Šámal, P., Válková H., Sotolář, A., Hrušáková M. (2004), *Zákon o soudnictví ve věcech mládeže – komentář (Commentary on the Juvenile Justice Act)*, C. H. Beck , Praha (Prague).

8 art. 45a para 4 of the Criminal Code and art. 340b of the Criminal Procedural Code.

9 See: Art. 2 of the law no. 555/1992 Coll., on prison and judicial guard of the Czech Republic.

10 The prison and judicial guards have status of armed corps.

professional activities as well as health care.[11] The organizational structure of the Prison Service comprises The General Directorate, remand institutions, prisons and the Institute of Education. The Minister of Justice appoints and dismisses the Director General as head of the Prison Service who is responsible for all of its activities. Governors of both remand and regular prisons are appointed and dismissed by the Director General. At present, the Prison Service administers 35 prison facilities - 11 remand prisons and 24 regular prisons. At the end of 2005, the actual maximum capacity of the prison system was 18.784 places, each providing four square meters of space. 3,258 of these places were in remand institutions, while the remaining 15,526 were in regular prisons. The problem of prison overcrowding was registered particularly in some specific prisons (for example: Heřmanice – overcrowding 20,76 %, Kuřim 27,68 %, Odolov 15,08 %, Oráčov 16,56 %, Teplice 64,71 %, Valtice 24,53 %, Znojmo 35,44 %) and in the remand prisons of Brno (16, 98 %) and Ostrov (38, 55 %). As of 31 December 2005, as many as 10.474 persons were working for the Prison Service, of whom 6.431 were prison guards and judicial guards. A breakdown of the structure of employees reveals that 11,1% were working in educational programs, 58,1 % were active in security and surveillance and 13,7 % were working in administration. At the end of December 2005, 24% of all employees were women.[12]

Penitentiary institutions are classified into four basic categories according to the levels of surveillance and security: minimum security, medium security, high security and maximum security. Additionally, there are special prisons for juveniles, women and mothers with children. Different types of departments can also be located within the same institution so long as the purpose of imprisonment is not endangered.[13] According to the law on the state budget, the budget of the Prison Service for 2005 consisted of income indicators CZK 1,011,080,000 and expenditure indicators CZK 7,507,952,000. During the year 2005 the budget was cut and it was necessary to utilize finances from the reserve fund in order to be able to effectively carry out all tasks and activities. The Prison Service also faced increased expenditures due to increases in the price of materials, medicines and energies as well as a growth of the prison population. The total cost per prisoner per day was CZK 860 (+ CZK 11) in 2005.[14] In comparison to 2004 the prison population of 2005 slightly increased to 18.937 persons.[15] In 2005 the new concept for the development of the Czech prison system up to the year 2015 was introduced.[16]

---

11 See: Art. 3 of the law no. 555/1992 Coll., on prison and judicial guard of the Czech Republic.

12 The General Directorate (2006), Yearbook of the Prison Service 2005, The General Directorate of the Prison Service of the Czech Republic, Prague.

13 The General Directorate (2006), Czech Prisons, The General Directorate of the Prison Service of the Czech Republic, Prague.

14 The General Directorate (2006), Annual Report of the Activities of the Prison Service of the Czech Republic for 2005, The General Directorate of the Prison Service of the Czech Republic, Prague;

15 As of 31 December 2005 (18 343 as of 31 December 2004).

16 The Prison Service of the Czech Republic (2005), The Concept for the Development of the Czech Prison System up to 2015, The Prison Service of the Czech Republic, Prague.

1.2.2 Foreign nationals in the Czech Republic

In 2004 the total population of the Czech Republic was 10,206,923 to an area of 78,866 km². The population density was 129 persons per km². In 2004, the average unemployment rate was 8.3 %.[17] The Czech Republic is administratively divided into 14 self-governing regions. The largest ethnic groups are Ukrainians, Slovaks, Vietnamese, Poles, Russians and Germans.

Table no. 1 – Foreigners by category of residence, sex and citizenship in 2005

Country of citizenship	*Total*	*incl.: Females**	*% of females*	*Residence permits, total*	*Permanent residence*	*Asylum*	*Temporary EU/ Long-term residence*	*90-days-and-over visa*
Total	**280 111**	**112481**	***40***	**258 306**	**110 598**	**1 799**	**145 909**	**21805**
EU 25 total	**87 143**	**34 019**	***39***	**87 089**	**42 202**	**1**	**44 886**	**54**
Belgium	299	67	*22*	299	144	-	155	-
Denmark	205	50	*24*	205	83	-	122	-
Estonia	41	20	*49*	41	23	-	18	-
Finland	127	55	*43*	127	50	-	77	-
France	1 551	488	*31*	1 551	603	-	948	-
Ireland	230	49	*21*	230	91	-	139	-
Italy	1 761	285	*16*	1 761	1 079	-	682	-
Cyprus	42	5	*12*	42	31	1	10	-
Lithuania	223	126	*57*	223	101	-	122	-
Latvia	84	57	*68*	84	54	-	30	-
Luxembourg	15	4	*27*	15	6	-	9	-
Hungary	512	190	*37*	510	386	-	124	2
Malta	17	8	*47*	17	6	-	11	-
Germany	7 187	1 978	*28*	7 182	3 957	-	3 225	5
Netherlands	1 260	350	*28*	1 260	489	-	771	-
Poland	17 810	8 721	*49*	17 798	11 384	-	6 414	12
Portugal	59	16	*27*	59	27	-	32	-
Austria	2 368	505	*21*	2 365	1 161	-	1 204	3
Greece	805	258	*32*	804	752	-	52	1
Slovakia	49 446	20 026	*41*	49 418	20 227	-	29 191	28
Slovenia	184	66	*36*	184	150	-	34	-
United Kingdom	2 234	457	*20*	2 231	986	-	1 245	3
Spain	282	100	*35*	282	162	-	120	-
Sweden	401	138	*34*	401	250	-	151	-

17 See the Czech Statistical Office – www.czso.cz

Country of citizenship	*Total*	*incl.: Females**	*% of females*	*Residence permits, total*	*Permanent residence*	*Asylum*	*Temporary EU/ Long-term residence*	*90-days-and-over visa*
Other countries total	**192 968**	**78 462**	***41***	**171 217**	**68 396**	**1 798**	**101 023**	**21 751**
Other European countries								
Albania	194	74	*38*	175	74	14	87	19
Belarus	3 191	1 758	*55*	2 924	951	171	1 802	267
Bosnia and Herzegovina	1 697	648	*38*	1 656	1 349	13	294	41
Bulgaria	4 586	1 631	*36*	4 153	2 337	35	1 781	433
Croatia	2 143	711	*33*	2 075	1 524	3	548	68
Iceland	14	5	*36*	14	6	-	8	-
Liechtenstein	3	1	*33*	3	1	-	2	-
Macedonia	1 218	254	*21*	1 116	561	3	552	102
Moldova	4 682	1 741	*37*	3 563	678	8	2 877	1 119
Norway	95	26	*27*	95	39	-	56	-
Romania	2 864	1 035	*36*	2 634	1 962	163	509	230
Russian Federation	16 627	8 597	*52*	15 004	6 012	354	8 638	1 623
San Marino	1	-	*0*	1	-	-	1	-
Serbia and Montenegro	3 633	1 119	*31*	3 469	2 306	74	1 089	164
Switzerland	399	122	*31*	399	252	-	147	-
Ukraine	87 834	34 003	*39*	75 663	15 334	45	60 284	12 171
Africa								
Algeria	461	36	*8*	458	369	1	88	3
Angola	194	29	*15*	185	137	22	26	9
Egypt	228	19	*8*	207	159	-	48	21
South Africa	119	55	*46*	114	74	4	36	5
Libya	352	118	*34*	324	61	1	262	28
Morocco	158	17	*11*	150	124	1	25	8
Nigeria	225	24	*11*	220	140	19	61	5
Tunisia	274	23	*8*	272	247	1	24	2
other	794	167	*21*	705	387	96	222	70
Asia								
Afghanistan	359	33	*9*	356	75	241	40	3
Armenia	1 351	583	*43*	1 294	906	83	305	57
Azerbaijan	195	80	*41*	169	52	26	91	26
China	3 587	1 553	*43*	3 331	1 471	7	1 853	256
Georgia	398	167	*42*	360	192	23	145	38

Country of citizenship	*Total*	*incl.: Females**	*% of females*	*Residence permits, total*	*Permanent residence*	*Asylum*	*Temporary EU/ Long-term residence*	*90-days-and-over visa*
India	543	149	27	436	153	2	281	107
Iraq	269	62	23	255	132	86	37	14
Iran	159	27	17	148	55	35	58	11
Israel	614	198	32	529	183	-	346	85
Japan	1 235	543	44	927	105	-	822	308
Yemen	169	45	27	161	95	-	66	8
Jordan	185	19	10	174	120	1	53	11
Kazakhstan	2 289	1 278	56	2 149	1 313	42	794	140
Korea, Republic of	275	150	55	179	38	-	141	96
Korea, Democratic People's Republic of	333	309	93	273	-	-	273	60
Kyrgyzstan	305	168	55	289	65	12	212	16
Lebanon	233	33	14	223	161	1	61	10
Mongolia	2 435	1 583	65	1 965	309	-	1 656	470
Pakistan	251	47	19	247	162	8	77	4
Palestinian Territory	108	13	12	102	42	1	59	6
Syrian Arab Republic	377	84	22	366	285	13	68	11
Thailand	215	189	88	130	42	-	88	85
Tchaj-wan	131	66	50	61	8	-	53	70
Turkey	655	147	22	548	229	20	299	107
Uzbekistan	384	161	42	278	50	21	207	106
Viet Nam	36 902	15 911	43	34 735	23 235	70	11 430	2 167
other	564	215	38	496	172	27	297	68
North America								
Canada	590	247	42	487	310	-	177	103
Cuba	230	56	24	225	175	27	23	5
United States	3 952	1 497	38	3 198	2 051	-	1 147	754
other	184	66	36	144	89	-	55	40
South America								
Brazil	120	60	50	94	64	-	30	26
Colombia	102	53	52	88	48	-	40	14
Peru	108	33	31	101	67	-	34	7
other	293	112	38	256	147	-	109	37
Australia/New Zealand								
Australia	336	137	41	316	238	-	78	20

Country of citizenship	*Total*	*incl.: Females**	*% of females*	*Residence permits, total*	*Permanent residence*	*Asylum*	*Temporary EU/ Long-term residence*	*90-days-and-over visa*
other	85	25	29	75	41	-	34	10
Stateless, not identified	461	150	33	459	419	24	16	2

Source: The Czech Statistic Office – www.czso.cz

At the end of 2005, as many as 258,306 foreign nationals officially held residence permits in the Czech Republic, 110,598 of whom had permanent residence permits, and 167,714 were foreigners with long-term residence permits. Since 1 May 2004 the category of long-term residence has covered persons residing in the Czech Republic by virtue of a visa for more than 90 days, long-term residence permits and temporary residence for citizens of the EU Member States and their family members.[18] Dealing with the problem of integration of foreigners into Czech society, the government has adopted a resolution governing the fundamental principles of migration.[19] Nowadays, the trend is to support legal migration, because the long-term perspectives appear worthwhile and it restricts illegal migration in accordance with international and EU standards.

1.3 Overview Involvement of Consulates, Embassies, Ministry of the Czech Republic, Probation Service, Ngo's etc.

It is obvious that the involvement of 'third parties' is considered to be very important, especially for foreign national prisoners. The involvement of Consulates and Embassies is significant for foreign national prisoners especially in situations in which they have to overcome language barriers. In reality, activity of a diplomatic mission/consulate may also significantly influence the duration of expulsive custody, where a foreign prisoner has to remain while waiting for his/her passport to be issued in order to be expelled. Regarding the role of NGO's, the Czech Helsinki Committee monitors human rights issues in criminal proceedings. The extensive project covered not only the monitoring of conditions in Czech prisons and the cases of individual prisoners, but also training and interactive seminars for prison staff, probation officers and mediators, as well as other activities.[20] The European Committee for the Prevention of Torture and Inhuman or Degrading Treatment or Punishment (hereinafter CPT) adopted the report following its visit to the Czech Republic from 21 to 30 April 2002 and requested that the Czech authorities provide a response setting out the measures that had been taken following its visit report. The report refers to the facts found in police establishments, detention facilities for foreign nationals detained under legislation on illegal residents, in prisons and psychiatric establishments, and states specific actions. The government of the Czech Re-

18 ibidem, p. 17.

19 Government of the Czech Republic (2003), Resolution of the Government of the Czech Republic, Fundamental Principles on the field of Migration of Foreigners, No. 55 of 13 January 2003, Government of the Czech Republic, Prague.

20 See www.helcom.cz

public provided the response to the CPT in 2003 as well as a report on the measures that had been taken following the visit report of the CPT in 2005.[21] Up to the 1 January 2006, there was no authority responsible for executing systematic, preventive and independent supervision and control over all places in which persons are deprived of their personal liberty in the Czech Republic. In accordance to the Optional Protocol to the UN Convention against Torture (OPCAT) it falls under the competence of the Ombudsman (Veřejný ochránce práv). In July 2006, the Office of the Ombudsman released a report on the situation in detention facilities for foreign nationals. It refers to the facts that were found during visits to facilities and states specific recommendations.[22]

1.4 Overview of Trends

1.4.1. Crime and Sentencing Trends

The Czech police statistics of 2005 indicate that the number of police registered crimes has slightly decreased (-2, 2 %) in comparison to 2004. From a long-term perspective, it should be noted that the number of police registered crimes has decreased, while the figure for 2005 was the lowest since 1993, with a total number of 344,060.[23]

---

21 See: Vláda České republiky (2006), Zpráva o plnění doporučení Evropského výboru pro zabránění mučení a nelidskému či ponižujícímu zacházení nebo trestnátní (CPT) v roce 2005, vyplývající z návštěvy tohoto výboru v České republice v roce 2002, Vláda České republiky, Praha *(The Government of the Czech Republic (2006), Report of the Czech Government on measures taken upon CPT visit in 2002 for 2005, The Government of the Czech Republic, Prague).*

22 Veřejný ochránce práv (2006), Zpráva z návštěv zařízení pro zajištění cizinců, Úřad Veřejného ochránce práv, Brno *(The Ombudsmann (2006), Report on Visits in Facilities of Detained Foreign Nationals, The Office of the Ombudsman, Brno).*

23 Ministerstvo vnitra ČR (2006), Informace o zjištěné trestné činnosti v České republice v roce 2005 ve srovnání s rokem 2004, Ministerstvo Vnitra ČR, Odbor bezpečnostní politiky, Praha. *(The Ministry of the Interior (2006), Information on Crimes detected in the Czech Republic in 2005 in comparison with 2004, The Ministry of the Interior, The Department of Security Policy, Prague).*

Figure 1 – The development of crime in the Czech Republic 1989 - 2005

Development of the number of police registered and cleared up crimes in CR in 1989-2005

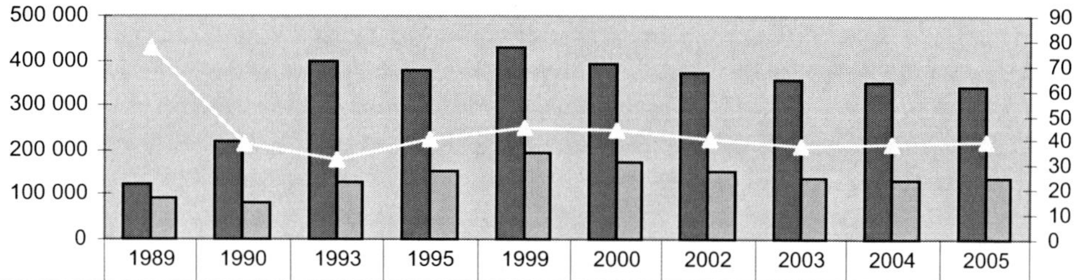

	1989	1990	1993	1995	1999	2000	2002	2003	2004	2005
police reg.crimes	120 768	216 852	398 505	375 630	426 626	391 469	372 341	357 740	351 629	344 060
cleared up crimes	93 542	83 237	126 442	151 842	193 354	172 245	151 492	135 581	134 444	135 281
clear-up rate in %	77,5	38,4	31,7	40,4	45,3	44	40,7	37,9	38,2	39,3

Source: J. Kuchta, H. Válková, *Základy kriminologie a trestní politiky (Foundations of Criminology and Criminal Policy*

The following should be mentioned regarding developments in crime compared to 2004:

- the share of property crime has decreased to 66,6 % (-2,7 %). On the other hand, the proportion of economic crimes increased to 12,8 % (+3,2 %). Violent crimes made up 6,3 % of all registered offences, a very minor decrease of 0,4 %. Robbery still remains a problem. The share of crimes against human dignity stagnated at 0,5 %;[24]
- the number of cleared up crimes increased to 135,281 (+0,6 %), i. e. the clear-up rate reached 39,3 % However, in the capital city of Prague it was only 21 %;
- the sequence of the regions has not markedly changed; the largest number of crimes were committed in the capital city of Prague (share 27,8 %), followed by the Central Bohemian Region (10,8 %), the Moravian-Silesian Region (10 %) and the Ústí Region (9,5 %), followed by the regions of South Bohemia, Plzeň, Liberec, Olomouc and Hradec Králové. The lowest crime rates (up to three percent) were recorded in the Vysočina, Karlovy Vary, Pardubice and Zlín Regions;[25]
- the total number of prosecuted and investigated persons stagnated between 2004 and 2005 (121,511 persons). The age structure of offenders was dominated by the 20 – 30 year olds (34 %) and 30- 60 year olds (49,7 %), while the overall numbers of offenders among children (under 15 years of age) and juveniles groups declined . The proportion of recidivists stagnated (45,97 %), however the figure for 2005 was the highest since 1993;[26]

---

[24] ibidem, p.23.

[25] ibidem, p.23.

[26] It is necessary to mention that according to the police statistics a recidivist is a person who has already been sentenced for another intentional crime, while interpretation of this term differs in the court and prison statistics.

'The passing of a sentence on an offender is probably the most public face of the criminal justice process.'[27] The Criminal Code provides certain general provisions regarding sentencing, most importantly Article 31., which is governed by two fundamental principles: the principle of legality of sentencing, and the principle of individualization of the penalty. Article 31 provides that in sentencing, the court must consider the seriousness of the offence committed, the prospects of whether the offender can be reformed, and the offender's personality. In particular, the court must examine the damage that resulted from the offence, the nature and type of offence, all circumstances of time, place and method of commission and the degree of *mens rea* of the offender.[28] Furthermore, the court has to determine a prognosis on the offender's future behaviour and finally examine his/her personal background.[29]

According to the court statistics, Czech courts lawfully sentenced 67,561 persons for 87,578 crimes in 2005. Compared to previous years, the composition of sentencing showed no major fluctuations. The suspended prison sentence was imposed upon 36,006 offenders (i.e. 53.3%), and was thus the most frequently passed sentence, followed by community service, which was the case for 11, 990 offenders (i.e. 17, 8 %). 2,663 offenders were fined (3,9%), and 10,082 received unconditional prison sentences (14,9%).[30] Regarding the length of the imposed unconditional sentences to imprisonment in 2005, the majority (6,315 offenders; 62.6%) received sentences for up to one year. A further 31,8% (3,210 offenders) received prison terms for between one and up to five years. 539 offenders received unconditional prison sentences for between 5 and 15 years (5,4%), while extraordinary sentences – 15 to 25 years, and life imprisonment - were imposed upon 14 and four offenders respectively.[31]

1.4.2 Crime, Sentencing Trends and Characteristics of the Foreign Prison Population

There are no special prisons or remand prisons for foreign prisoners. The question of specialized institutions for foreigners was also the subject of the research conducted by the Institute of Criminology and Social Prevention in 2002-2003 and is still being discussed. In reality foreign prisoners are usually overrepresented. The most foreign prisoners are imprisoned in the prison of Valtice, Plzeň and Horní Slavkov, while on remand in Praha – Pankrác and Praha – Ruzyně. There are no special controlling mechanisms for foreign prisoners within the Czech prison system (see 1.3 and 2.1.1).

The total number of prosecuted and investigated foreign nationals in 2005 declined (i. e. -3,1 %) to 6, 994 persons compared to the 2004 figures. From a long term perspective, since 1994 the number of prosecuted and investigated foreign nationals has not markedly

---

27 Maguire, M. et al (2002) , The Oxford Handbook of Criminology, Oxford University Press, Oxford, pp. 718.

28 See Art. 3 para. 4 of the Criminal Code.

29 See: Šámal, P., Král, V., Púry, F. (2004), *Trestní zákon – komentář (Commentary on Criminal Code)*, C. H. Beck, Praha (Prague).

30 Ministerstvo spravedlnosti ČR (2005), Statistická ročenka kriminality za rok 2005, Odbor informatiky a statistiky Ministerstva spravedlnosti ČR, Ministerstvo spravedlnosti ČR, Praha; *(Ministry of Justice of the Czech Republic (2005), Statistical Yearbook of Criminality 2005, Department of statistic, Ministry of Justice of the Czech Republic, Prague.*

31 ibidem, p. 30.

changed, averaging roughly 6 % of all prosecuted and investigated persons. In 2005, foreign nationals committed 8,353 crimes (down by 7, 5% in comparison to the previous year).[32] The following should be mentioned regarding the structure of crimes committed by foreign nationals in 2005:

- the most frequently committed crimes were crimes against property in 2,307 cases (i. e. 5 % of the total number of this type of crime), followed by economic crimes in 1, 766 cases (i. e. 7 %), violent crimes in 1,088 cases, i.e. 6,8 % (including 24 murders, i. e. 15 %; intentional injury 302, i.e. 5, 6 %; 291 robberies, i.e. 12,6 %) and crimes against human dignity in 129 cases, i.e. 8, 3 %;[33]
- the highest share of offending foreign nationals is found in the capital city of Prague with a share of 15,1 % of all offenders, followed by the Plzeň Region. The capital is considered to be, from a long-term perspective, the most vulnerable area in the Czech Republic;
- Concerning nationality, citizens of Slovakia are the most frequently prosecuted foreign nationals (34, 5 %), followed by Ukrainians (21, 6 %), citizens of Vietnam, Poland and Russia;
- The offence types with the highest shares of prosecuted foreigners were obstructions of the execution of an official decision (14,5 %), pick pocketing (14,4 %), murders (15,5 %) and robberies (9,6 %);
- there is a link between selected serious crimes committed by foreign nationals and organized crime[34].

According to court statistics, 4,223 foreign nationals were sentenced in 2005 (i. e. 6, 3 % of all convicts); the majority of all sentenced foreign nationals were sentenced by the Courts in the capital of Prague (1, 685), followed by West Bohemian (581) and North Moravian Courts (530).[35] The nationalities that were most strongly represented among sentenced foreign nationals were Slovaks (1, 239) and Ukrainians (1, 129).

---

32 Ministerstvo vnitra ČR (2006), Zpráva o situaci v oblasti veřejného pořádku a vnitřní bezpečnosti na území České republiky v roce 2005 ve srovnání s rokem 2004, Ministerstvo Vnitra ČR, Praha. *(The Ministry of the Interior (2006), Report on Public Order and Internal Security in the Czech Republic in 2005 compared with 2004, The Ministry of the Interior, Prague.*

33 ibidem, p. 32.

34 Ministerstvo vnitra ČR (2005), Zpráva o situaci v oblasti veřejného pořádku a vnitřní bezpečnosti na území České republiky v roce 2004 ve srovnání s rokem 2003, Ministerstvo Vnitra ČR, Praha. *(The Ministry of the Interior (2005),Report on Public Order and Internal Security in the Czech Republic in 2004 compared with 2003, The Ministry of the Interior, Prague.*

35 It has to be noted that the court districts differ from the administrative regions of the Czech Republic.

Table. 2 – Foreign national offenders, by nationality

Prosecuted, accused and convicted persons by nationality in 2004

	Prosecuted	Accused	Simplified proceedings	Moved for punishment in simplified proceedings	Convicted
Total	**89 288**	**75 861**	**18 773**	**18 569**	**68 443**
European countries, total	**88 513**	**75 206**	**18 493**	**18 292**	**67 756**
EU 25, total	**87 605**	**74 416**	**17 392**	**17 239**	**66 133**
Belgium	5	3	-	-	1
Czech Republic	85 760	72 894	16 648	16 508	64 344
Denmark	2	1	4	3	3
Estonia	-	-	3	3	1
France	25	22	10	7	10
Ireland	4	3	3	3	9
Italy	24	17	10	10	10
Lithuania	54	48	49	49	77
Latvia	3	2	3	3	4
Hungary	9	6	3	3	3
Germany	92	76	10	10	69
Netherlands	18	14	-	-	5
Poland	187	127	71	71	183
Austria	31	25	1	1	21
Greece	9	8	-	-	8
Slovakia	1 160	971	448	439	1 132
Slovenia	4	1	1	1	1
United Kingdom	20	17	4	4	12
Spain	3	2	1	1	3
Sweden	2	1	4	4	4
Other European countries, total	**908**	**790**	**1 101**	**1 053**	**1 623**
Russian Federation	111	87	54	52	111
Ukraine	526	469	858	821	1 164
Other	271	234	189	180	348
Asian countries, total	**634**	**534**	**193**	**190**	**544**
Viet Nam	427	360	109	107	368
other	207	174	84	83	176
African countries, total	**82**	**75**	**53**	**53**	**103**
American countries, total	**35**	**27**	**8**	**8**	**29**
Czech and other citizenship	21	16	21	21	3

Citizens of more states	-	-	-	-	4
Stateless	1	1	2	2	3
Not identified	2	2	3	3	1

Source: The Czech Statistic Office – www.czso.cz

The penalty of expulsion was imposed on 2,068 foreign nationals in 2004. Other numbers and the structure of the penalties to which foreign nationals were sentenced are not available at the moment.[36] In 2005, the total prison population slightly increased to 18,937 prisoners (+ 594 prisoners, i.e. + 3,2 %) compared to 2004. From a long term perspective, the total prison population has rapidly decreased since the fall of the totalitarian regime in 1989, which was directly affected by the amnesty of the president of former Czechoslovakia in 1989 and 1990. This drop has to be exemplified by the data. At the end of 1989 there were 22,365 prisoners in former Czechoslovakia prisons, whilst at the end of 1990 there were 'only' 8,231. In the following years the prison population was on the permanent increase until 1999 (23,060 prisoners), while 2002 showed the lowest (16,213 prisoners) figures. In 2003 the prison population began to increase again, however not to a profound degree.

Table 3 – Development of the Prison Population

Development of the Prison Population in 1989 - 2005										
Situation on 31.12. of respective year										
	1989	*1990*	*1991*	*1993*	*1995*	*1999*	*2002*	*2003*	*2004*	*2005*
on remand	2 537	4 172	5 373	7 810	8 000	6 934	3 384	3 409	3 269	2 860
in imprisonment	19 828	4 059	7 357	8 757	11 508	16 126	12 829	13 868	15 074	16 077
Total	22 365	8 231	12 730	16 567	19 508	23 060	16 213	17 277	18 343	18 937

Source: The Prison Service of the Czech Republic

The total prison population of foreign nationals decreased to 1,578 prisoners (- 134 prisoners, i.e. 8,5 %) in 2005 compared to 2004. If one looks at long-term trends, the total number of foreign prisoners was on the increase in the early 1990's, primarily the number of foreigners on remand. On the other hand, it has to be noted that the low number of foreign prisoner might have also been affected by the amnesty of the president of former Czechoslovakia in 1989 and 1990. The major increase of foreign prisoners is apparent in 1994, because former Czechoslovakia was split into two independent states – the Czech Republic and the Slovak Republic - on 1 January 1993, and consequentially from that time onwards imprisoned citizens of Slovakia were registered as foreign prisoners.

[36] It has to be mentioned that foreigners are not a separate category in the available judicial statistics.

Table 4 – The Prison Population of Foreign Nationals

Foreign prisoners on remand/in imprisonment in 1989 - 2005										
Situation on 31.12. of respective year										
	1989	*1990*	*1991*	*1994*	*1997*	*1999*	*2000*	*2002*	*2004*	*2005*
on remand	60	69	159	1301	1594	1656	1405	757	792	663
in imprisonment	129	34	75	1406	1730	1309	1129	917	920	915
Total	189	103	234	2707	3324	2965	2534	1674	1712	1578

Source: The Prison Service of the Czech Republic

Up to 1996 the number of foreign nationals in Czech prisons had been on the increase. From 1997 onwards it continuously and steadily decreased, and between 2000 and 2003 it comprised about 7 % of the total prison population. In 2005, this share dropped to 5, 7 %.[37] The number of foreign prisoners on remand was on the increase until 1999[38], but in the following years it started to continuously decline. The current population of foreign prisoners detained on remand is the lowest since 1994. On the other hand, it has to be noted that the relative share of foreign prisoners on remand has not rapidly changed in total number of prisoners on remand and ranged between 23 %. The reason for the drop in the foreign prison population could also be attributed to legislative changes in 2000 and 2004 concerning the residence of foreigners as well as to fundamental changes of remand conditions in the Criminal Procedural Code. Concerning the composition of the foreign prisoner population in 2005 it has to be noted that the most represented nationalities were citizens of Ukraine (412 persons, i.e. 26, 1 %) followed by citizens of Slovakia (330, i.e. 20, 9 %), Vietnam (159, i. e. 10 %), Serbia and Monte Negro (79, i.e. 5 %) and Russia (62, i.e. 3, 9 %).

37 See: Kuchta, J., Válková, H. (2005), *Základy kriminologie a trestní politiky (Foundation of Criminology and Criminal Policy)*, C. H. Beck , Praha (Prague).

38 Except 1998, when the number was probably affected by the amnesty of the President.

Table 5 – Prisoners on remand/in imprisonment: by citizenship, 31 December 2005

Prisoners on remand/in imprisonment: by citizenship; 31 December 2005

Citizenship		Accused			Convicted		
	Total	Total	Males	Females	Total	Males	Females
Total	**18 937**	**2 860**	**2 697**	**163**	**16 077**	**15 336**	**741**
Czech Republic	17 122	2 116	1 990	126	15 006	14 305	701
Outstanding[1)]	237	81	75	6	156	142	14
Foreigners, total	1 578	663	632	31	915	889	26
EU 25, total	**469**	**169**	**158**	**11**	**300**	**282**	**18**
Belgium	2	1	1	0	1	1	0
Estonia	2	2	2	0	0	0	0
France	1	1	1	0	0	0	0
Italy	5	3	3	0	2	2	0
Lithuania	49	21	20	1	28	27	1
Latvia	1	0	0	0	1	1	0
Hungary	2	0	0	0	2	2	0
Germany	21	17	14	3	4	4	0
Netherlands	3	3	3	0	0	0	0
Poland	42	10	10	0	32	30	2
Austria	6	4	4	0	2	2	0
Greece	2	0	0	0	2	2	0
Slovakia	330	104	97	7	226	211	15
United Kingdom	1	1	1	0	0	0	0
Sweden	2	2	2	0	0	0	0
Other countries	**1 109**	**494**	**474**	**20**	**615**	**607**	**8**
Other European countries							
Belarus	32	11	11	0	21	21	0
Bosnia and Herzegovina	6	3	3	0	3	3	0
Bulgaria	42	18	18	0	24	23	1
Romania	58	24	18	6	34	34	0
Russian Federation	62	32	32	0	30	29	1
Serbia and Monte Negro	79	39	39	0	40	40	0
Ukraine	412	152	146	6	260	258	2
Macedonia	26	16	16	0	10	10	0
Moldova	39	13	10	3	26	26	0
other	6	3	3	0	3	3	0
Africa							
Algeria	18	5	5	0	13	13	0
Tunisia	18	5	5	0	13	13	0
other	24	14	13	1	10	10	0

Asia							
Armenia	11	3	3	0	8	8	0
China	41	27	25	2	14	14	0
Georgia	17	8	8	0	9	9	0
Viet Nam	159	91	89	2	68	65	3
other	48	25	25	0	23	23	0
North America, total	3	0	0	0	3	3	0
South America, total	2	2	2	0	0	0	0
Australia, total	1	1	1	0	0	0	0
Stateless	5	2	2	0	3	2	1

1) Refers to persons whose citizenship (Czech or Slovak) is not evident from available documents

Source: The Prison Service of the Czech Republic

A very peculiar and particular problem has arisen concerning the issue of nationality within the prison population of the Czech Republic. There are still 237 prisoners who are ex – nationals of the Czechoslovak Federation for whom the available documents do not clearly indicate whether they are in fact Czech or Slovak nationals. Taking this issue into consideration, the overall prison population in the Czech Republic can be divided into the following groups:[39]

- Czech nationals
- Ukrainians
- Slovaks
- Vietnamese
- Nationals of the ex – Soviet Union excluding Ukrainians
- Nationals of the Balkan states Albania, Bosnia and Herzegovina, Bulgaria, Croatia, Serbia and Monte Negro, Macedonia
- Nationals of the Islamic states Afghanistan, Algeria, Bahrain, Egypt, Iraq, Iran, Jordan, Kuwait, Libya, Morocco, Pakistan, Palestine, Syria, Tunis
- Other foreign nationals
- Stateless
- Ex – nationals of the Czechoslovak Federation for whom available documents do not clearly indicate whether they are Czech or Slovak nationals

1.5 Overview of National Legislation

1.5.1 Criminal Law and Criminal Procedure, Penitentiary Legislation

Criminal law in the Czech Republic is predominantly codified into the Criminal Code (law no. 140/1961 Coll.), the Criminal Procedural Code (law no. 141/1961 Coll.) and

39 See: Scheinost, M. at al. (2004), *Výzkum cizích státních příslušníků v českých věznicích* (*Research on Foreign Nationals in the Czech Penitentiary Institutions)*, Institut pro kriminologii a sociální prevenci (The Institute of Criminology and Social Prevention), Praha (Prague).

the Juvenile Justice Act (law no. 218/2003 Coll.). The recodification of Czech criminal law began over 14 years ago; the Criminal Code (law no. 140/1961 Coll.) was originally adopted in 1961 and provides the basis of criminal law in the Czech Republic. It has, of course, been amended many times in the course of its existence, but due to fundamental economic, political and social changes that since the fall of the totalitarian regime in 1989, it is necessary to adopt a new Criminal Code that will provide society with better protection against criminality.[40]

The proposal for a new Criminal Code was introduced in the Parliament of the Czech Republic in July 2004. It was discussed for more than one and half years and finally passed in the Lower House; however, it was rejected by the Upper House and subsequently rejected by the Lower House as well.[41] Although the new Criminal Code has not been adopted yet, progress was made when the so called "great amendment" (law no. 265/2001 Coll.) of the Criminal Procedural Code and the Juvenile Justice Act (law no. 218/2003 Coll.) were adopted in 2001 and 2003 respectively.[42] The Council Framework Decision on the European Arrest Warrant and the Surrender Procedures between the Member States (2002/584/JHA) were finally implemented into the Criminal Code and the Criminal Procedural Code by the laws no. 537/2004 Coll. and no.539/2004 Coll. and came into effect on 1 November 2004. There is no code on the execution of sanctions, while detention in remand prisons is governed by the law no. 293/1993 Coll. and specified by the Ordinance of the Minister of Justice no. 109/1994 Coll. Imprisonment is governed by the law no. 169/1999 Coll. and specified by the Ordinance of the Minister of Justice no. 345/1999 Coll. The execution of other sanctions is regulated in the Criminal Procedural Code.

1.5.2. Criminal Law, Criminal Procedure, Penitentiary Legislation & Foreigners

Regarding the special sections in national legislation that apply to foreigners, the following should be noted:

- According to Article 57 of the Criminal Code the court expel foreign nationals or stateless persons - except those who bear the legal status of a refugee - but only in cases where it is necessary for public safety or other public interest. Expulsion may be imposed for a period of one up to ten years or *ad infinitum*,[43] either as a separate sanction or in addition to penalties. The court may not impose an expulsion in cases in which the nationality of an offender is unknown, the offender has been granted asylum, the offender is staying in the Czech Republic on a long-term residence permit, has a social and working background and the imposition of such a penalty will be inconsistent with the interest of family integrity[44]. Also, a person may not be expelled when an offender

---

[40] See: e. g. Šámal, P. (2002), *'K úvodním ustanovením připravované rekodifikace trestního zákona'* (*'Commentary to the front provisions of prepared codification of Criminal Code'*), Trestněprávní revue (Criminal Law Revue), 12, pp. 349 ff.

[41] See: Škvain, P. (2004), *'Nad probíhající kodifikací trestního práva hmotného'* (*'Codification of substantion criminal law in motion'*), Trestněprávní revue (Criminal Law Revue), 10, pp. 304 ff.

[42] For more detailed information about the national legislation see: e. g. Z. Karabec et al. (2002), The Criminal Justice System in the Czech Republic, Institut pro kriminologii a sociální prevenci, Praha;

[43] See Art. 26 para. 3 of the Juvenile Justice Act (maximum for five years).

[44] See Convention on the Rights of The Child.

faces persecution in the country he/she will expelled to on grounds of his/her race, nationality, ethnic origin, affiliation with a certain social group, political opinion, religion, or will be exposed to torture or inhuman and/or degrading treatment or punishment.

- According to Article 350c of the Criminal Procedural Code the court may decide to place a convict in expulsive custody when there is a danger that he/she will abscond or in any way obstruct the imposed expulsion and when there are no grounds to replace such a decision by a guarantee / promise of a convict or by bail.[45]
- There are special sections dealing with the foreign prisoners in remand prisons within the law no. 293/1993 Coll., Articles 27, 28 as well as in the Ordinance of the Minister of Justice no. 109/1994 Coll., Articles 79, 79a, 80.[46]
- There are special sections dealing with the foreign prisoners in imprisonment in the law no. 169/1999 Coll., Article 72 as well as in the Ordinance of the Minister of Justice no. 345/1999 Coll., Article 98 [47]
- Article 375 and following of the Criminal Procedural Code on the process of liaison with other states governs in particular the procedure of extradition and the European Arrest Warrant.
- The administrative detention of foreign nationals is governed by Articles 124-149 of the law no. 326/1999 Coll. on residence of foreigners in the Czech Republic.

It is necessary to mention that the Czech Republic is a signatory of many bilateral treaties with European and non-European states that were ratified before 1989 but are still in power. Multilateral international treaties ratified by the former Czechoslovakia were also succeeded by the Czech Republic. There is no information available on the actual application of these international agreements. However, it remains to be mentioned that a very characteristic phenomenon within the foreign prison population is the lack of interest in serving their prison sentences in their home countries.

2 TREATMENT OF FOREIGN PRISONERS

Introduction: Facts about the Research on Social Exclusion of Foreign Prisoners realized in Plzeň (Pilsen) Prison in March 2006.

The objective of this project is to address the issue of social exclusion of prisoners detained in European penitentiary institutions outside their country of national origin. Although the problem of social exclusion was not the objective of the research realized by the Institute of Criminology and Social Prevention, a very important step has been made in that foreign prisoners have become the subject of the first relevant study in the Czech Republic. [48] The objective of the Czech national study - to provide information on the situation and position of foreign prisoners in the Czech Republic - may not be realized properly without awareness of the foreign prisoner's opinion. In order to know more facts about the 'real' treatment of foreign prisoners, the research was conducted in Plzeň (Pilsen) prison. It was executed via questionnaires that were distributed to both foreign pris-

45 Compare Art. 350c and Art. 67, Art. 73 and 73a of the Criminal Procedural Code.
46 See chapter 2.1 on General Facts about Treatment of Foreign Prisoners.
47 ibid., p. 46.
48 See Introduction.

oners as well as members of prison staff. The Tilburg University in the Netherlands provided the foundations of both questionnaires. The questionnaires were edited and finalized at the end of February 2006 and then submitted to the Prison Service. Both questionnaires were structured into sections, while some of the questions were intentionally repeated within different sections in order to validate previous answers. The Research was executed at the beginning of March 2006 and at the end of April 2006 in the prison in Plzeň (Pilsen)[49]; the first questionnaire was submitted to convicted foreign prisoners while the other was handed to employees of the Prison Service working with foreign prisoners. Their willingness to cooperate was one of the most important factors for the successful completion of this task. The Prison Service selected voluntary foreign prisoners while taking the structure of the current prison population into consideration. For safety reasons my personal presence was not permitted, but both foreign prisoners and the employees of the Prison service working with these prisoners were free to answer all of the questions of the submitted questionnaires without interference from others.

Regarding the evaluation of the research, a total of 32 questionnaires were returned. One can say that the vast majority of respondents generally understood the questions, and some of them were able to illustrate and elaborate their answers. All 22 questioned foreign prisoners were male citizens of either Ukraine, Algeria, Afghanistan, Bahrain, Tunisia, Kazakhstan, Moldavia, Russia, Macedonia, Serbia and Monte Negro, Rumania, Slovakia, Mexico or were stateless; 77 % of them were sentenced to expulsion. The prison of Plzeň was targeted for various reasons. Firstly it has the fourth largest population of foreign prisoners within Czech penitentiary institutions. Furthermore, the research could be accomplished within one month not least due to the helpful and professional approach of Mr. Šefl, the Governor of Plzeň prison.

49 For more detailed information about Prison Plzeň, see www.vscr.cz

Table 6 – Local Prison Population in the prison of Plzeň (Pilsen)

Local prison population in the Prison Plzeň on 5 May 2006	
Citizenship	***Prisoners***
Afghanistan	1
Algeria	6
Austria	1
Bahrain	1
Serbia and Monte Negro	3
Bulgaria	3
Belarus	4
China	2
Croatia	1
Czech Republic	911
Germany	1
Iraq	1
Kazakhstan	1
Lithuania	5
Mexico	1
Moldova	5
Morocco	1
Nigeria	1
Poland	3
Romania	8
Russian Federation	4
Slovakia	15
Viet Nam	8
Tunisia	4
Turkey	2
Ukraine	40
Former Republic of Yugoslavia	6
Macedonia	3
ČSFR (ex - Czechoslovakia nationals)	5
Total	**1047**

Source: T he Prison Service of the Czech Republic

At the end of February 2006 there were 23 foreign prisoners on remand, 146 prisoners in imprisonment and eight persons in custody awaiting expulsion in the prison of Plzeň. Given the facts about the structure of the prison population in the Czech Republic, the responding foreign prisoners were categorized into the following groups:

- Ukrainians (seven prisoners);
- Nationals of the former Soviet Union except Ukrainians: (three prisoners) Russia, Kazakhstan, Moldavia;

- Nationals of Islamic states: (five prisoners) Afghanistan, Algeria, Bahrain, Morocco, Tunisia;
- Nationals of Balkan states: (two prisoners) Serbia and Monte Negro, Macedonia;
- Slovaks:(two prisoners);
- Other foreign nationals: (two prisoners) Rumania, Mexico;
- Stateless: (one prisoner) ethnic origin Albanian.

The following is a breakdown of the data on the foreign prisoners who responded in our research according to the categories of nationality listed above:

Ad a) Ukrainians (seven prisoners):
- serious crimes were committed by the respondents in six cases (rape, murder, attempted murder, robbery);
- average age of the respondents is 32, 9 years;
- average term of the imposed prison sentence is 10 years;
- penalty of expulsion imposed upon all seven respondents.

Ad b) Nationals of the former Soviet Union, except Ukrainians (three prisoners)
- Two of the respondents in this group were imprisoned for violent offences (robbery), one for embezzlement;
- the average age of the respondents is 30,6 years;
- the average term of the imposed prison sentence is six years;
- penalty of expulsion imposed upon all three respondents.

Ad c) Nationals of Islamic states (five prisoners)
- three respondents of this group were sentenced for drug trafficking, and one each for fraud and theft;
- the average age of the respondents is 37,8 years;
- the average term of imprisonment is 5,7 years;
- two of the respondents are to be expelled.

Ad d) Nationals of Balkan states (two prisoners)
- one respondent was imprisoned for violent crime (murder), the other for theft and blackmail;
- the average age of the respondents is 33 years;
- the respondents were sentenced to 10 and two and a half (2, 5) years of imprisonment respectively;
- penalty of expulsion imposed upon both respondents.

Ad e) Slovaks (two prisoners)
- One prisoner was sentenced for obstructing the execution of an official decision together with endangering under the influence of an addictive substance, the other for grievous bodily harm;
- the respondents were 22 and 32 years old;
- sentenced to 16 months and five years of imprisonment;
- one respondent of this group is to be expelled.

Ad f) Other foreign nationals (two prisoners) Rumania, Mexico
- One prisoner was sentenced for drug trafficking, the other for fraud and forgery ;
- respondents were 31 and 35 year old;
- both respondents sentenced to five and half years of imprisonment;
- penalty of expulsion imposed upon one respondent.

Ad g) Stateless (one prisoner) ethnic origin Albanian
- sentenced to prison for murder;
- respondent is 60 year old;
- sentenced to 13 years of imprisonment;
- penalty of expulsion was imposed.

Concerning the second group of respondents - the employees of the Prison Service working with foreign prisoners- they are all Czech nationals working for the Prison Service in the prison of Plzeň. Seven of them are men and three are women, with an overall average age of 45,8 years. Three of the responding employees have a university degree and one of them is working with foreign prisoners on remand.
They are active in the following professions:
- Psychologist
- Pedagogue
- Educationist and therapist
- Prison guard
- Inspector of prison guards
- Educationist
- Social worker

2.1 General Facts about the treatment of Foreign Prisoners

2.1.1 Theoretical situation

There are special sections dealing with foreign prisoners in remand prisons in the law no. 293/1993 Coll., Articles 27, 28 as well as in the Ordinance of the Minister of Justice no. 109/1994 Coll., Articles 79, 79a, and 80. These provisions mainly concern a different reception and admission procedure; in other issues foreign prisoners on remand are subject to the same rights and obligations as Czech prisoners. There are special sections dealing with foreign prisoners in regular imprisonment in the law no. 169/1999 Coll., Article 72 as well as in the Ordinance of the Minister of Justice no. 345/1999 Coll., Article 98. These provisions mainly provide for special procedures of reception, admission and for the accommodation of foreigners with fellow foreign prisoners. In other issues foreign prisoners serving prison sentences are subject to the same rights and obligations as Czech prisoners. It is necessary to emphasize that Article 98 para. 2 of the Ordinance of the Minister of Justice no. 345/1999 Coll., states that it should be taken into consideration whether the penalty of expulsion has been imposed while drawing up a sentence plan for foreign prisoners.

There are no special controlling mechanisms for foreign prisoners. The public prosecutor regularly inspects the places of remand and imprisonment. He/she is entitled to visit all locations where prison sentences are being served at any time, to access prison documents, to speak with prisoners without the presence of other persons and to request relevant explanations from the Prison Service. He/she has the power to order the release of a person who has been illegally remanded or imprisoned. The supervision of the public prosecutor does not override the obligation of the Prison Service to perform its own control activities. The Ministry of Justice, through the minister's general inspectorate, is also directly involved in control and supervision activities.[50]

2.1.2 Actual situation

2.1.2.1 Generally, the majority of the responding foreign prisoners perceived no differences in their treatment compared to Czech prisoners. However, some respondents highlighted the problems of healthcare delivery and language barriers as the most significant. Two foreign prisoners felt that they are treated differently by some of the prison guards, while three felt to be treated differently by doctors in medical care. Three foreign prisoners believed that the reason for these differences in treatment may well lie in their nationality and in language barriers; one foreign prisoner was unable to pinpoint any reason. Two prisoners think that they are being socially excluded because of the difficulties in language. The most frequent/common problems in the everyday life of foreign prisoners were found in health care delivery, an unprofessional approach of prison staff (lack of respect), health problems and other prisoners. To overcome language barriers, some of them can speak Czech, while others rely on help from their fellow prisoners, study the Czech language, use dictionaries etc.[51] Six foreign prisoners gave information that referred to their stay in other Czech penitentiary institutions.

2.1.2.2 The vast majority of responding prison staff spoke of potential differences in the treatment of foreign prisoners compared to national prisoners due to language barriers. One respondent illustrated his answer as follows: 'Knowledge of language plays the key role; otherwise a prisoner does not have the opportunity to communicate with others and it will be easier to end up in social isolation. Such a prisoner is not able to understand what his/her obligations are in prison and he/she is treated differently not only by prison staff, but by his/her fellow prisoners too.' Because all responding staff members work with imprisoned foreigners, it is very important to show their awareness of the most frequent/usual problems that foreign prisoners face. Nine respondents answered positively, while language barriers are considered to be the most frequent/usual problem as well as differences in mentality, culture and religious environment. In order to overcome language barriers, some of them can speak foreign languages, while the others rely on help from their colleagues and from other foreign prisoners.

---

[50] See law no. 293/1993 Coll., Art. 29; law. no. 169/1999 Coll., Art. 78.

[51] It has to be noted that for Slovak prisoners the problem of language barriers practically does not exist, because the Czech and Slovak languages are very similar.

2.2 Living Conditions and Facilities

2.2.1 Theoretical situation

According to the law, foreign prisoners on remand have access to the same living conditions and facilities as Czech prisoners. Foreign prisoners on remand who speak the same language are to be placed together. Foreign prisoners in custody awaiting expulsion are placed in a section with a more relaxed regime, together with other eligible prisoners on remand. According to the law, foreign prisoners in imprisonment have access to the same living conditions and facilities as national prisoners. Foreign prisoners are not placed separately; those with the same nationality or who speak the same language are placed together.

2.2.2 Actual situation

2.2.2.1 The majority of the foreign prisoners within the sample feel that they have access to the same living conditions and facilities as Czech prisoners. Foreign prisoners are not placed separately and they usually share cells with other foreign nationals, however some also reported to be accommodated with Czech prisoners. This in turn did not, however, result in any complaints. It was ascertained that nearly all respondents have the opportunity to meet and speak with other foreign prisoners of the same nationality.[52] Some of the foreign prisoners are allowed to spend approximately 16 hours a day outside their prison cells.[53]

2.2.2.2 The view that foreign prisoners have access to the same living conditions and facilities as Czech prisoners was confirmed by all of the prison staff in the study. They stated that foreign prisoners are usually placed together with prisoners of the same or different nationality. Prisoners of the same nationality or those who speak the same language have the opportunity to meet regularly in the course of their activities (e. g. club of the Russian culture, sport, watching TV, work etc.).

2.3 Reception and Admission

2.3.1 Theoretical situation

According to the law, foreign prisoners on remand/in imprisonment have to be appropriately instructed upon arrival about their rights and duties in their native language or in a language that they understand. Foreign prisoners have to be especially instructed about their right to contact the diplomatic mission or consulate of their home country. Instructions of rights and duties are currently available in 25 foreign languages.

---

52 Other citizens of Mexico are not placed in The Prison Plzeň.

53 Depending on the level of security.

2.3.2 Actual situation

2.3.2.1 Nearly all responded foreign prisoners are not aware of different reception procedures for foreigners. Four prisoners were instructed in languages they did not understand. The vast majority of prisoners were instructed in the Czech language that they supposedly understand, and some of them in Russian. Five respondents had no opportunity to contact the diplomatic mission or consulate of their native country; nor could they call their family members upon arrival in the institution. This inability *could* be due to the fact that the use of the telephones was often problematic (see also section 2.7.1).

2.3.2.2 The vast majority of responding prison staff assumes that there is no special reception procedure for foreigners; some of them find the instruction of a foreign prisoner to be most problematic due to language barriers. All of the respondents answered that foreign prisoners are instructed upon arrival about their rights and duties in their native language or in a language that they understand, and that they have the opportunity to call to their family members. All foreign prisoners have the opportunity to contact the diplomatic mission or consulate of their native country as well.

2.4 Work – Education – Training – Recreation

2.4.1 Theoretical situation

A prisoner may be employed while he/she applies for a work and the prison may provide with a suitable work. According to the law, foreign prisoners are allowed to have access to books written in their native/understandable language. Depending on the period of imprisonment the Prison Service shall provide suitable conditions for Czech language lessons.

2.4.2 Actual situation

2.4.2.1 According to the research, 16 prisoners are physically able to work (for instance in terms of their state of health), while eight of them are in fact currently working and are paid (gross salary varies according to the occupation from CZK 4, 500 to 6, 750).[54] One prisoner stated that foreign prisoners are not entitled to work. All responding foreign prisoners reported to be participating in educational and vocational training classes; only one respondent mentioned his participation in the Czech language course for foreigners. Four prisoners claimed to have no access to books in an understandable language, while pointing out that the selection of these books is very limited. Foreign prisoners participate in the following recreational activities: PC, TV, video club, relaxation, painting club, table tennis, chess, body building or darts.

2.4.2.2 The second group of respondents - prison staff - assumes that foreign prisoners utilise the possibility to participate in educational and vocational training classes, have access to the books in a language they understand and are entitled to participate in all recreational activities.

---

[54] approx. 150 – 225 Euros.

2.5 Food – Religion - Personal Hygiene - Medical Care

2.5.1 Theoretical situation

The Prison Service provides regular food for all prisoners and takes their cultural and religious traditions into consideration. A prisoner may refuse the provided food on the grounds of his/her dietary habits. In such cases 'additional' food is provided at his/her own expense.[55] The Prison Service provides freedom of religion according to the law.[56] 'The prison religious service is currently composed of 29 prison chaplains (persons in an employment relationship with the Czech Prison Service) from 10 state-registered churches with authorisation to execute special rights (in accordance with Act no. 3/2002 Coll.); they are active in 22 prisons and remand prisons in the Czech Republic. Their activities are primarily directed towards the ensuring of religious services in individual facilities and co-operation with clerics, who travel to prisons as part of the activities of the Prison Religious Care (PRC) civic association and voluntary activities of the churches and religious associations.'[57] 'Prison Religious Care (PRC) is a non-governmental organisation providing broad ecumenical services, traditionally sharing in activities with charged and convicted persons. In its existence and in practice it is a guarantee of the constitutional right to practise one's religious faith.'[58] The Prison Service shall provide for penniless prisoners basic hygiene requirements. The delivery of health care is regulated in the law no. 20/1966 Coll. However, it should be noted that foreign national prisoners without health insurance have to pay for medical care except in cases of emergency.[59]

2.5.2 Actual situation

2.5.2.1 The issue of religion as well as medical care is considered to be the most problematic for foreign prisoners. For example, foreign prisoners from Ukraine (Orthodox Catholics) find that freedom of religion as well as cultural requirements are equally respected inside the prison, while some of the foreign prisoners of another religion, for example Muslims, feel that they are hindered because of prescribed dress (wearing a habit is not allowed), personal hygiene (the need for everyday hygiene before prayer) and food (Muslim food is not prepared properly according to the rules of *Cheriáa*). Meeting with qualified religious representatives is very important for many prisoners, yet only some of them actually have that possibility. Concerning medical care, 14 respondents think that foreign prisoners are treated differently compared to Czech prisoners, because they do not have health insurance. Therefore, they are apparently not entitled to receive any

---

55 In the Prison of Plzeň so called "Muslim food" is provided as basic food free of charge.

56 Law no. 3/2002 Coll., on churches and religious associations.

57 Generální ředitelství Vězeňské služby ČR (2006), Výroční zpráva Vězeňské služby České republiky za rok 2005, Generální ředitelství Vězeňské služby ČR, Praha , pp. 103-104. *(The General Directorate of the Prison Service of the Czech Republic (2006), Annual Report of the Activities of the Prison Service of the Czech Republic for 2005, The General Directorate of the Prison Service of the Czech Republic, Prague, pp. 103-104), bilingual version;*

58 ibidem, p. 57.

59 See: The Council of Europe (2004), *Report to the Czech Government on the visit to the Czech Republic carried out by the European Committee for the Prevention of Torture and Inhuman and Degrading Treatment or Punishment (CPT) from 21 to 30 April 2002*, The Council of Europe - CPT/Inf 4, Strasbourg.

treatment or medicine. However, some responses from working prisoners indicate the contrary.

2.5.2.2 Awareness of religion and cultural requirements may be essential to prison staff working with foreign prisoners. The vast majority of the prison staff believes that freedoms of religion as well as other cultural requirements are well respected in the prison. Only two respondents are aware of the problem with prescribed dress for Muslims.[60] Concerning health care delivery, only two respondents highlighted the problem with health insurance mentioned above.

2.6 Consular and Legal Help

2.6.1 Theoretical situation

Foreign prisoners have to be especially instructed about their right to contact the diplomatic mission or consulate of their native country upon their arrival or to admit a visit of a representative of the respective diplomatic mission or consulate. The Prison Service has the legal obligation to inform the respective diplomatic mission/consulate when a foreign prisoner has been transferred. The Czech Helsinki Committee also provides free legal aid to foreign prisoners within the bounds of observance of human rights in the Czech Republic.[61]

2.6.2 Actual situation

2.6.2.1 The vast majority of foreign prisoners stated that they have the opportunity to communicate with officials of the diplomatic mission or consulate of their native country, while two foreign prisoners (a citizen of Macedonia and a stateless person) claimed that this had not been possible. Only five foreign prisoners were visited by a lawyer, embassy or consular official of their country of origin. The vast majority of foreign prisoners have had access to (free) legal aid. However, it has to be noted that some of them claimed to have experience with *ex offo* lawyers in criminal proceedings, whose service is basically not for free. Good cooperation with an embassy or consulate is especially necessary when a foreign prisoner has to stay in expulsive custody while waiting for his/her travel documents. I am personally aware of a case, when a citizen of Serbia was forced to spend more time in custody awaiting expulsion than necessary, because the Embassy failed to issue his travel documents.

2.6.2.2 The vast majority of prison staff respondents claim that foreign prisoners stay in touch with officials of their diplomatic mission or consulate and that they have access to (free) legal help.

---

60 See: B. Spalek, 'Muslims in British Prisons' / www.hmprisonservice.gov.uk

61 See: www.helcom.cz

2.7 Contact with the Outside World

2.7.1 Theoretical situation

According to the law, foreign prisoners are allowed to receive and to send correspondence without any restriction at their own expense.[62] However, correspondence is subject to inspection of its contents. The inspection of mail is inadmissible in a number of cases enumerated in law, for example written correspondence from a defence attorney. Foreign prisoners (except those in 'collusive' remand) are entitled to call to their close relatives should they have a legitimate reason for doing so. Should very important reasons arise, access to the telephone may be allowed for communication with persons other than close relatives. A foreign prisoner is obliged to cover the costs for the calls that he/she makes. The Prison Service is allowed to listen in to and record calls except those with enumerative bodies and persons. Foreign prisoners on remand have the right to one 90-minute visit (no more than four persons) once every 14 days. They may also use a radio or TV set under prescribed conditions and purchase (foreign) daily press and magazines so long as it is generally distributed and available in the Czech Republic. Foreign prisoners in regular imprisonment are entitled to visits that amount to three hours per calendar month. Some persons (e.g. barristers, clerics, representatives of embassies/consulates, NGOs etc.) may visit foreign prisoners without any limitation or upon agreement with the Prison Service. Books, daily press and magazines may be sent to foreign prisoners by mail without any restriction. A TV set or radio may be owned only upon the decision of the Governor of the prison.

2.7.2 Actual situation

Nearly all foreign prisoners claim that they are enabled to stay in contact with their relatives. The vast majority of the foreign prisoners we questioned stated that they have received visits from their relatives, friends and other persons, whilst seven prisoners have not been visited yet. Only a few prisoners made any statement on the frequency with which they received visitors. For example, a stateless 60 year old man with a total sentence of 13 years imprisonment received roughly ten visits in a period of eight years. Regarding means of communication, all prisoners use written correspondence as the most frequent connection with the outside world, followed by visits and phone calls. Only one foreign prisoner stressed the problem of not having the financial means to use the telephone, but we can assume that more foreign prisoners in fact face this problem. One foreign prisoner stated that his source of information about the outside world is TV and radio broadcasting.

62 The costs of correspondence with a barrister are covered by the Prison Service when a foreign prisoner is insolvent.

2.8 Re-integration activities, Prison leave

2.8.1 Theoretical situation

According to the law, a prisoner's sentence plan is prepared on the basis of all available information about a foreign prisoner with respect to the total term to be served, the offender's personality as well as the circumstances of and the reasons for committing the crimes. While following the plan, suitable conditions for resettlement into society after release shall be established for all prisoners at least three months before their release. The Governor may decide (on the basis of recommendation of qualified prison staff) to transfer a prisoner to a 'release' department within the same prison. This usually occurs six months before release. It is necessary to emphasize that Article 98 para. 2 of the Ordinance of the Minister of Justice no. 345/1999 Coll. states that it should be taken into consideration whether the penalty of expulsion was imposed while drawing up a sentence plan for foreign prisoners.

2.8.2 Actual situation

2.8.2.1 All 22 foreign prisoners are familiar with their right to apply for parole; six respondents applied for parole, five applications were refused, one has not yet been decided on. None of the foreign prisoners were placed to another prison department to prepare them for resettlement into society after release, and nobody was eligible according to the law.[63] However, it has to be noted that one Ukrainian prisoner who had been sentenced to six years of imprisonment and expulsion, claimed that he had not yet been subjected to any 'preparation' for release six months before his release. In general, the preparation for release is usually implemented in a special section of a prison called 'výstupní oddělení' ('release department') and is primarily focused on prisoners who have been imprisoned for three years or more. The conditions in the release department differ from prison to prison, but its main objective is to prepare prisoners for activities of every day life, such as for instance cooking, laundry, applying for a job and social support.

2.8.2.2 Somewhat miscellaneous answers were registered when the responding prison staff answered the question on whether foreign prisoners are transferred to other prison departments in order to prepare them for resettlement into society. Five respondents stated that such transfers in fact take place, while two members of staff answered to the contrary. One respondent stated that such a placement is only possible if a foreign prisoner requests it. Respondents were not able to illustrate their answers about differences in 'release' departments (e.g. conditions, regimes, programs etc.).

---

63 See: Chapter 2.8.1.

2.9 Release, Expulsion

2.9.1 Theoretical situation

The Criminal Procedural Code regulates the execution of expulsion.[64] Respective prisons shall be notified by the Court that the penalty of expulsion that has been imposed upon a foreign prisoner is to be executed following his/her release. The police of the Czech Republic (hereinafter the police) are responsible for the ensuring that an expulsion is in fact carried out. Where necessary, the Court can also require of the police to provide a foreign prisoner with the necessary travel documents (usually a passport) so that expulsion can be executed immediately after his/her release. The Court can also annul the expulsion of a foreign prisoner should new consequences/circumstances arise. The Court shall decide about releasing a foreign prisoner from serving the penalty of expulsion if new circumstances / consequences are present and, should this be the case, the penalty of expulsion may not be imposed.[65] Regarding the general procedures of release from penitentiary establishments in the Czech Republic, the same provisions apply to foreigners as to Czech inmates.

2.9.2 Actual situation

According to the court statistics, 4,097 foreign nationals were sentenced in 2004. Also, in the same year the penalty of expulsion was imposed upon 2,068 foreign nationals.[66] Of the foreign prisoners who participated in our study, 17 were to be expelled from the Czech Republic after their release from prison (77%). Foreign prisoners - including all citizens of Ukraine who responded to the questionnaire - were sentenced to both imprisonment and expulsion when serious and violent crimes were committed. This is in line with the established judicial practice that is in adherence to the purpose and aims of punishment (individual and general prevention) which make it necessary to impose the penalty of expulsion alongside imprisonment when a foreign national has committed a serious crime of violent nature or against property *(R 42/1994-II)*.[67] Some foreign prisoners try to 'prevent' being expelled by applying for asylum. According to the Highest Court of the Czech Republic, an asylum applicant can be expelled, and the responsible court need not await the decision on the application for asylum. Also, it can decide that an expulsion is not possible due to legal obstacles that can also lie in issues of internationally recognized human rights *(Tpjn 310/2001 from 17 April 2003).*

2.10 Aftercare – Probation

'In co-operation with the Probation and Mediation Service of the Czech Republic, concrete steps were initiated [in 2005] towards the implementation of the Parole project, which utilises European Union funds; continuing to work towards tools for prisoner assessment. Training was subsequently carried out by workers at remand prisons and pris-

---

64 See: Law no. 141/1961 Coll., the Criminal Procedural Code, art. 350b and following.

65 See: Chapter 1.5.2 Criminal Law, Criminal Procedure, Penitentiary Legislation & Foreigners.

66 See: Chapter 1.4.2 Crime, Sentencing Trends and Characteristics Foreign Prison Population.

67 Of course other legal requirements also have to be fulfilled – ibid., p. 65.

ons and centres of the Probation and Mediation Service, which resulted in the creation of several working groups for the purpose of preparing and launching a pilot cognitive-behavioural program for prisoners before and after their conditional release. Based on the analysis of current experience, work continued on the Risk and Need Assessment project, which, apart from the requirement for individualisation of treatment, will lead to a better prediction of results of re-socialisation activities. A methodological paper was published as part of the gradual implementation of the concept of risk and needs assessment into the methodology of the handling of imprisoned persons. This paper updates the content and structure of comprehensive reports in an effort to seek possibilities for the formulation of treatment programs so that they logically relate to the risk and need assessment system.'[68] It has to be noted that nowadays the role of mediation within imprisonment is being increasingly discussed, when successful mediation helps to remedy the relationship between the convict and victim.[69]

2.11 Staff

2.11.1 Theoretical situation

'Lifelong learning remained an integral part of the fulfilment of the main objectives of personnel work. Through it, the Prison Service endeavours improved development of its employees in their professions, or the possibility of their occupying managerial positions, and last but not least the enhancing of their responsibilities and performance.'[70] This enhancement is to be achieved through special courses that the Prison Service organizes.[71]

2.11.2 Actual situation

Nearly all responded prisoners have positive or neutral relationship with prison guards and other prison staff; twenty foreign prisoners claim that prison guards and other prison staff do not treat them differently compared to Czech prisoners.[72] All respondents answered that prison staff communicates with them in Czech language, and that the prisoners try to speak Czech as well.[73]

One member of prison staff who participated in the study assumes that prison guards treat foreign prisoners differently, which can however be predominantly attributed to communication difficulties. All ten respondents claim that prison guards speak only in Czech with foreign prisoners. Somewhat miscellaneous answers were registered in comparison with foreign prisoners, while six respondents supposedly speak with foreign pris-

---

68 Generální ředitelství Vězeňské služby ČR (2006), Výroční zpráva Vězeňské služby České republiky za rok 2005, Generální ředitelství Vězeňské služby ČR, Praha pp. 19. *(The General Directorate of the Prison Service of the Czech Republic (2006), Annual Report of the Activities of the Prison Service of the Czech Republic for 2005, The General Directorate of the Prison Service of the Czech Republic, Prague, pp. 19), bilingual version;*

69 Bernard, J. et al (2005), '*Mediace v rámci výkonu trestu odnětí svobody*', ('*Mediation within Imprisonment*'), Příloha časopisu České vězeňství (Supplement of the Journal of the Czech Prison Service), 1, p.p. 5-14.

70 ibid p. 68, pp. 26 ff.

71 See: www.ivvs.cz/vzdelani/kurzy *(Czech version only).*

72 See: Chapter 2.1.

73 See: Chapter 2.1 – solving the problem of language barriers.

oners in foreign languages.[74] Merely one respondent participated in the special course – Treatment of Foreign Prisoners – that is organized by the Prison Service, and only one respondent took part in the special language course that aims to improve communication with Russian speaking prisoners.

2.12 Projects

As mentioned above under section two the Institute of Criminology and Social Prevention in Prague conducted the research concerning foreign nationals in Czech penitentiary institutions in 2002-2003. Its main objective was to characterize the prison population, to name the main problems concerning treatment of foreign prisoners and to state specific recommendations on the basis of all information.[75] The Czech Helsinki Committee realized the project focused on the Czech Prison Service in 2003-2005. The research also includes the monitoring of Czech prisons and case agenda.[76] This project is not primarily focused on foreign prisoners. Nowadays a three year project 'Šance' ('Chance') is being realized. The project focuses on the reintegration of prisoners after their release. The prison in Plzeň (Pilsen) provides a special Czech language course for foreign prisoners.

3 ADMINISTRATIVE DETENTION OF FOREIGN PRISONERS

Illegal migration is considered to be a serious problem in the Czech Republic. The term 'illegal migration' comprises two basic categories:

- Illegal migration across the national border into the territory of the Czech Republic
- Breach of residency rules

In 2004 a total of 9,433 persons illegally crossed the Czech national border (7,555 foreign nationals were obliged to have a visa when entering the Czech Republic), which was a decrease of 19% compared to the previous year.. Most illegal migrants came from the Russian Federation (3,725 persons), China (1,009), Ukraine (878), Georgia (564), Moldova (294) and Vietnam (237).[77] The number of asylum-applicants declined after the EU accessions of May 2004. In that year, 2,728 asylum-applicants were registered, the most of whom were citizens of Ukraine (29,3 %), the Russian Federation (27,4 %), Vietnam (7,1 %), China (5,9 %) and Belarus (4,1 %). 142 foreigners were in fact granted asylum (i.e. 2,6 %). According to the report the trend of illegal migrants abusing asylum procedures continues, while 417 persons were transferred from detention facilities for foreigners to asylum facilities.[78] The total number of persons breaching the residency rules in the Czech Republic dropped to 16,696 persons (-21, 8 %) in 2004. Illegal residence of

---

74 ibid., p. 73.

75 See Introduction.

76 See www.helcom.cz

77 Ministerstvo vnitra ČR (2005), Zpráva o situaci v oblasti veřejného pořádku a vnitřní bezpečnosti na území České republiky v roce 2004 ve srovnání s rokem 2003, Ministerstvo Vnitra ČR, Praha; *(The Ministry of the Interior (2005), Report on Public Order and Internal Security in the Czech Republic in 2004 compared with 2003, The Ministry of the Interior, Prague).*

78 ibidem, p. 77.

foreign nationals usually goes hand in hand with other illegal activities such as work without permission, obstruction of the execution of an official decision (which is a criminal offence)[79], pick pocketing or thefts. According to the law, an administrative decision of expulsion was imposed upon 15,194 foreigners, predominantly concerning citizens of Ukraine (66,9 %), China (7 %) and the Russian Federation (5 %).

The conditions of detention facilities for foreign nationals were subject to repeated critique from the CPT and the Ombudsman among others.[80] In concordance with recommendations, the law no. 326/1999 Coll. on the residence of foreigners in the Czech Republic was amended in order to establish appropriate regimes in such facilities. Since 1 January 2006 the issue of administrative detention has fallen within the competence of The Administration of Refugee Facilities (*Správa uprachlických zařízení*) within the Ministry of the Interior. The conditions for administrative detention of a foreign national are regulated in Articles 124-149 of the Law on Residence of Foreigners. A detained foreign national has the right to a judicial review of the administrative decision. The maximum duration of such administrative detention may not exceed 180 days (90 days for minors). The police are legally obliged to inform a respective diplomatic mission/consulate as well as a relative should the individual in question request this. Currently, 305 persons (249 men, 56 women, 11 minors) are detained in four administrative detention facilities in the Czech Republic - Poštorná, Frýdek-Místek, Velké Přílepy and Bělá-Jezová. [81]

The asylum issue has been a matter for the Ministry of the Interior since 1990. Nowadays, the issue more specifically lies in the competence of the Department of Asylum and Migrant Policy and is directed by the first deputy of the Minister of the Interior. The Administration of the Refugee Facilities *(Správa uprchlických zařízení)* was established in 1996 as a structural unit of the Ministry of the Interior. The main objective is to provide accommodation, food, health care, social and other services for asylum-applicants.[82] According to the law we recognize three types of asylum facilities: entrance, stay and integrative facilities.[83]

The objective of entrance facilities is to provide new asylum-applicants with accommodation and basic surroundings until the entrance procedure has been completed. This procedure involves the identification of a person, complex medical examinations and the initiation of administrative proceedings. All asylum-applicants must undergo such a procedure in a closed facility. It is necessary to emphasize that applicants are not allowed to leave such a facility, because they could pose 'health hazards' to the general population. There are two main entrance facilities in Vyšní Lhota with a capacity of 580 places and a transit area in airport Praha- Ruzyně with a capacity of 16 places. There is also a reserve capacity of 167 places in the asylum stay facility in Červený Újezd. After the entrance procedure has been completed, the asylum-applicant has the right to arrange his/her

79 See: Art. 171 of the Criminal Code, e. g. Failure to leave the Czech Republic after administrative expulsion decision was imposed.

80 See: The Council of Europe (2004), *Response of the Czech Government to the Report of European Committee for the Prevention of Torture and Inhuman and Degrading Treatment or Punishment (CPT) on its visit to the Czech Republic from 21 to 30 April 2002*, The Council of Europe - CPT/Inf 5, Strasbourg.

81 Veřejný ochránce práv (2006), Zpráva z návštěv zařízení pro zajištění cizinců, Úřad Veřejného ochránce práv, Brno; *(The Ombudsman (2006) , Report on Visits in Facilities of Detained Foreign Nationals, The Office of the Ombudsman, Brno).*

82 For more detailed information see www.suz.cz *(Czech version only).*

83 See law no. 325/1999 Coll., o azylu.

own accommodation, or will be placed in a facility of stay. Basic surroundings as well as other services are provided for 'waiting' asylum-applicants, too. Such asylum facilities are open, so asylum applicants are able to move outside of the facility, however their movement is still regulated by the law, for example applicants have a right to leave the facility for a maximum period of ten days per calendar month. Any leave longer than 24 hours has to be notified in writing to the Ministry of the Interior. Furthermore, leaves or three days or longer have to be notified to the Ministry 24 hours in advance..[84] It is also necessary to mention that such facilities are internally divided into first and second round sections. The first round sections are for asylum-applicants who are awaiting a decision from the Ministry of the Interior about their application, while the second-round sections accommodate those applicants who have lodged an appeal to the court because their application for asylum has been turned down. There are ten facilities of stay in the Czech Republic – Bělá pod Bezdězem, Červený Újezd, Zastávka u Brna, Kostelec nad Orlicí, Havířov, Bruntál, Kašava, Stráž pod Ralskem, Seč and Zbýšov.

Facilities of integration serve as temporary accommodation for persons who have been granted asylum. People whose applications for asylum have been accepted have the same legal position as Czech nationals in the labour market and in the social security and health-care systems. Their accommodation is regulated by lease, and rent has to be paid until a person has acquired permanent accommodation from the state integrative program or private accommodation. There are four facilities of integration in the Czech Republic – Předlice, Hošťka, Jaroměř a Zastávka u Brna. The Administration of the Refugee Facilities *(Správa uprchlických zařízení)* cooperates with a number of international and national organizations (e. g. UNHCR Prague, IOM Prague, Hessisches Sozialministerium, Office for Repatriation and Illegal Residents etc.)[85]

4 NATIONALS DETAINED ABROAD

The Ministry of Justice is not able to provide any information on Czech nationals detained abroad. In case that there is no international treaty on assistance in criminal matters Czech nationals might be imprisoned without awareness of the Czech authorities. Some cases of Czech nationals who have been imprisoned abroad have been highlighted by the media (for instance Emil Novotný and Radek Hanykovics case of drug smuggling in Thailand) while other cases remain unknown both to the public and to the Czech authorities. It has to be noted that those cases of Czech nationals who have been imprisoned abroad that the Czech authorities are aware of usually seek to serve their sentences in their home country, because of inhuman imprisonment conditions in some countries.

---

84 art. 82 of the law no. 325/1999 Coll., o azylu.

85 http://www.unhcr.cz; www.iom.cz; www.sozialministerium.hessen.de; www.uric.gov.pl, www.minv.sk/mumvsr/; www.fedasil.be; www.asylum.redcross.dk; www.justice.ie; www.coa.nl; www.hero.no; www.migrationsverket.se; www.bmbah.hu

5 EVALUATION AND RECOMMENDATIONS

Information obtained through this research is necessarily evaluated as preliminary, because it is the first time that the specific issue of social exclusion of foreign prisoners in Czech prisons has been debated. It is obvious and it should be recognized that foreign national prisoners have different needs than Czech prisoners do. The research, even though it was conducted within two months and with a limited scope, objectively revealed that some groups of foreign prisoners are socially excluded. One of the findings of the research is that medical care is considered to be the most problematic issue for foreign prisoners. The vast majority of responding prisoners claim that they are treated differently, because they do not have health insurance. Accordingly, they are allegedly not entitled to receive any or proper treatment or medicine. The situation is based on the legislation that is in force, which indicates that only necessary and urgent medical care is provided 'free of charge' for foreign prisoners on remand/in imprisonment without health insurance. It shall be noted that the Prison Service has to cover all costs of such provided medical care with its own budget. Difficulties with the freedom of religion have also been highlighted. Some Muslim prisoners claim that they feel to be disadvantaged because of the prescribed prison dress (wearing *habits* is not allowed), personal hygiene and food (dietary needs in concordance with *halal* are not properly adhered to). Foreign Muslim prisoners have no access to qualified religious representative (*Imam*), although this is very important to many of them.

I would like to propose to the Prison Service that a Muslim adviser be appointed whose work would involve the preparation of a directory and guide on religious practices to enable prison staff to know more about religious needs of foreign prisoners. Such a book should provide information about the Muslim religion as well as the corresponding diet, dress, the role of personal hygiene and families etc. Members of other religious groups have the same right to practise their religion (e.g. Christian prisoners), so it is also necessary for the Prison Service to provide access to a qualified Muslim religious representative (*Imam*) for all Muslim prisoners.

Other findings of the Research are that although progress has been made, the Prison Service is still heading to its objectives with overcoming language barriers. It will be worthwhile to prepare special booklets (not only a translation of the laws on execution of remand/imprisonment) designed for foreign prisoners in the most common foreign languages. These booklets should contain information on his/her rights and duties and contacts to embassies /consulates. Furthermore, it should deal with issues of asylum, prison regimes etc. It would also be appropriate to provide brief information for visitors (e.g. family members of foreign prisoners) in most common foreign languages. More things have to be changed, for instance regarding the professional training of prison staff who works with foreign prisoners. Without any doubt it is absolutely necessary that prison staff undergo a special course as well as foreign language courses that are currently provided by the Prison Service.[86] Another finding has to be necessarily mentioned. The procedure of access to the telephone shall be regulated as more transparent, while the term 'legitimate' reason may be interpreted different ways.

In conclusion I would like to mention that evaluation as well as other relevant information stemming from this research should be submitted to all involved and relevant par-

86 See: Chapter 2.11 Prison staff.

ties in order to address the issue of social exclusion of foreign prisoners within Czech penitentiary institutions.[87]

[87] E.g. The Prison Service, The Institute of Criminology and Social Prevention in Prague, University of West Bohemia /Faculty of Law/ Department of Criminal Law, The Czech Helsinki Committee etc.

Chapter 6

Denmark

Anette Storgaard

1 INTRODUCTION

Article 71 of the Danish Constitution of 1953 requires the legality of any deprivation of liberty. Subsections 1-5 regulate criminal procedure while subsections 6-7 are concerned with administrative detention. Detailed rules are given in different, more specific legal sources. In this context the Penal Code, the Code on Legal Procedure and the Code on Foreigners are the most relevant to mention. Deprivation of liberty is never the one and only legal solution. An individual may only be deprived of his/her liberty when it is provided for in law and, firstly, if no less intrusive mean is sufficient in order to reach the aim and, secondly, if the the principle of proportionality applies.[1]

The following article focuses primarily on Danish rules, practices and procedures. International and European conventions shall only occasionally be mentioned. Focus is also concentrated on the deprivation of liberty, which means that other forms of legal interference, like for instance taking fingerprints or orders to stay in contact with the police, are not regarded here. Furthermore, other issues that are of relevance to foreigners in Denmark are not elaborated on here, such as for example residence and permits, citizenship and so on.

An attempt to describe and discuss the issue of nationality in relation to the criminal system cannot be based on one single statistical source or piece of research. One consequence of the fact that experiences must be collected from a number of different sources is that – when observed together – the individual pieces do not form a homogeneous and coherent picture of the actual situation.

There is no difference between foreigners and Danish citizens in terms of legal definitions and the legal framework of charge, offence and imprisonment. According to the Danish Ministry of Justice and to Statistics Denmark, 84,7 % of all charges[2] and 89,9 % of all criminal dispositions in the year 2004 were against Danish citizens.[3]

1.1 Overview of penalties and measures

According to section 31 of the Penal Code fines and imprisonment are the two ordinary sanctions. Although both fines and prison sentences can technically be ordered in both a suspended as well as an unsuspended form, in practice only sentences to imprisonment are in fact suspended. Imprisonment as a response to a criminal offence may only be imposed by the court. Fines may be imposed by the courts or agreed upon between the respective person and the police. Furthermore, according to section 722 of the Code on Legal Procedure, the decision on whether a charge is to be withdrawn (in specific cases, for example for young offenders who come to the attention of the police for the first time) lies in the hands of the police and is consequently confirmed by the court.

In the period from 2001 to 2004, between 100.000 and 150.000 fines (which shall not be further discussed in this article) were imposed annually, if one includes all fines without making any distinction between which rules were violated and which authority – either the police or the court – imposed the fine.

1 Foreign Right, p. 782-783.

2 Sigtelser 2004 fordelt efter indvandrerbaggrund og oprindelsesland. www.jm.dk

3 Criminal Statistics 2004, p 27.

Beside a number of possible conditions for suspended sentences that are regulated in section 57 of the Penal Code, two interventions are stated as alternatives to imprisonment. Firstly, the Community Service Order (CSO) has been gradually introduced into and implemented in the Danish sanctioning system since 1982. Initially, CSOs were introduced in specific geographical regions, but from 1984 onwards they were introduced at the national level. In 1992[4] the status of the CSO was changed from being an experiment to an ordinary penalty that is regulated in sections 62-67 of the Penal Code. The CSO is described as an alternative to imprisonment but is imposed by the courts as a condition of a suspended sentence. Secondly, in 2005 electronic monitoring[5] with „bracelets" or „tags" ("serving sentences at home"; "home curfew") was introduced as an alternative to imprisonment for cases of drunk driving, in sections 78A-78F of the CEP. In April 2006, the scope of application for electronic monitoring is to be extended to cases of juveniles (aged 15-17) who have committed less serious offences.

Section 74a of the Penal Code provides for the so-called Youth Sanction as a specific intervention for juveniles. The Youth Sanction is a two-year measure that incorporates both institutional as well as social training. It may be applied when juveniles are convicted of a crime for which the most appropriate sanction is imprisonment of at least three months.

Both the CSO and the Youth Sanction can only be imposed by the court, while electronic tagging is an administrative measure. These alternatives are viewed as ordinary elements of the sanctioning system. The criteria for their application are general, like for instance age and the crime committed, while nationality is not a formal criterion.

1.2 Overview of the Prison System

1.2.1 Organisational Structure

With only few exceptions[6], any detention that stands in connection with (the suspicion of) crime in Denmark takes place in institutions that are governed, controlled and supervised by the Department of Prisons and Probation. There are two main categories of penal institutions in Denmark. Firstly, there are pre-trial-prisons, which are located in the close vicinity of the court-buildings. They are designed to house persons awaiting trial as well as sentenced persons either serving a relatively short sentence (six months or less) or awaiting placement in a prison. The latter category is "prisons", which solely accommodate convicted offenders serving a sentence.

The decision on whether a person is to be placed in pre-trial detention or in prison mainly depends on the degree of suspicion and on the sentence that is to be served. Neither gender nor national background is explicitly taken into account in the legal framework, neither in formal law nor in administrative instructions. But if a suspect or

4 Supplement to the Penal Code, no. 6 of 3 January 1992.

5 Supplement to Code on Execution of Penalties, no. 367 of 24 May 2005 and Parliamentary instruction no 506 of 17 June 2005.

6 The exceptions where a punishable person may be detained in an institution that is governed and controlled by other authorities or services are mainly when persons suffering from a mental disease before or after conviction are placed in a secure hospital for the mentally ill; and juveniles, who should be placed in institutions for juveniles under the Social Services in stead of in pre-trial detention centres or prisons. These groups, however, are not central to this article.

sentenced person is aged between 15 and 18, the authorities are obliged to make an effort to find an alternative institution[7]. After having been sentenced the prisoner is allocated to either a closed or an open institution. The majority of the closed prisons are located in the cities whereas open prisons are predominantly based in the countryside. The pre-trial-detention facilities and the closed prisons have the same levels of security. They all have perimeter walls supplied with video cameras and separated wards. An open prison is more like a campus in which the prisoners can move relatively freely during the daytime.

In the mid 1990s a number of open prisons established semi-open departments. The Department of Prisons and Probation justified this decision by pointing to a lower utilization rate in the open prisons than in the closed institutions, which was said to be due to the fact that a smaller proportion of the convicted persons were suitable for open prisons. In other words an upcoming proportional imbalance between the number of prisoners and the capacity of the prisons was foreseen. An inmate may only be placed in a semi-open ward if he or she is "qualified" for closed prison but need not necessarily be transferred to such an institution.[8] While the courts decide on the length of the sentence, the type and location of the prison is determined by the Department of Prisons and Probation.

Ultimo 2005 the total capacity of the Danish prisons system was 4.316. Though the borderline between closed and open prisons is becoming unclear because of the semi-open and semi-closed units it is still meaningful to describe the capacity as follows: closed capacity: 939 places distributed in five closed prisons and two closed units in open prisons, and 1.659 places distributed in 12 open prisons. The rest of the capacity is distributed in about 40 pre-trial prisons, which in terms of security are to be compared with closed prisons.

As is mentioned below (section 1.4) the prison capacity is and has been under pressure for several years. In order to ease the pressure, defeat drugs among prisoners and decrease absence owing to sickness among staff the budget of the penalty sector was increased as a result of a political agreement in 2004. According to this political agreement the budget of the sector was increased with totally 1.556 million Dkr over the years 2004-2007. This brings the annual budget up to a little more than 2 billion Dkr.[9]

There is, however, another category of persons who are detained in institutions under the Department of Prisons and Probation without in fact having committed a crime (or being under the suspicion of having done so). This group comprises foreigners who are seeking asylum and who may be detained according to one of the reasons listed in the Code on Foreigners[10] while awaiting a decision on their case.

1.2.2 Foreign Prisoners

Foreign prisoners who are to be expelled after having served their sentence are always placed in closed prisons (see section 2.9 below). But foreigners are not placed in separate units or wards in the closed prisons. The placing of foreign prisoners is administered like

7 It happens, though only once in a while, that a 15-17 year old person is placed in prison.
8 Department of Prisons and Probation, Yearly Reports 1999 and 2000.
9 Year 2007: 2.066 billion Dkr. (1 Euro = 7,50 Dkr). Kriminalforsorgen, marts 2004.
10 Code on Foreigners, no 826 of 24 August 2005.

the placing of prisoners in general, which implicates that normally prisoners serve their sentence as close to important relatives as possible.

On 4 November, in 2005 there were 12.906 prisoners and other clients in the Danish criminal system out of whom 2 % were foreigners, 82 % were Danish and the rest were immigrants (13%) or descendants (3%).[11] The proportions are equivalent to the proportions in May 2004. However, the groups are not evenly dispersed in the different subgroups. All foreigners are either to be found in the closed prisons, or the pre-trial prisons. In the closed prisons Danish prisoners form 68 %, immigrants 20 %, descendants 4 % and foreigners 8 %, whereas there are no foreigners among the clients under supervision by the probation service, a group in which the Danish clients form 85 %.

A little less than half of all immigrant prisoners (309 out of 760) come from Asia (mainly Lebanon and Iraq), whereas among the imprisoned descendants in 2005 94 out of 177 came from Europe (mainly Turkey).

In the decade 1995-2005 the average yearly number of imprisoned asylum seekers were between 72,4 and 107,7. Averagely throughout the year 2005 74,4 asylum seekers were imprisoned.[12]

1.3 Overview over the involvement of Consulates, embassies, Ministries of the home country, Probation Service of the home country, NGO's etc.

It is not possible to describe the concrete involvement of different consulates and embassies. Neither the media nor reports from the Ombudsman, NGOs or the like indicate major problems in relation to prisoner's rights to meet embassy representatives (described below).

The most important NGOs in Denmark in the field of foreigners are the Red Cross and the Danish Refugee Council. Their efforts are mainly concentrated on general issues, for instance the situation of children in asylum centres. The NGOs do not focus much on individual cases.

The Danish Red Cross offers visits to lonely people in general. Among others the organisation offers visits in prisons. This service as well as the efforts to support children of prisoners, however, is not in any way dedicated to foreigners.

The Red Cross offers translation services in more than 20 languages. The price is 400 Dkr per hour no matter if the interpretation is oral or written. The court-language is Danish but persons who do not understand Danish have the right to have everything, including documents, interpreted. Interpretation is needed (and prescribed in the Procedural Code section 149) in all criminal cases involving foreigners. If the the accused is found guilty, he is also obliged to refund all costs to the state, including defence, interpretation etc. This is one of the very important explanations why prisoners are often deeply in debt. Foreign prisoners are no exception in this question, except for the additional costs that arise from the necessary translations.

Normally interpretation is only in use during the investigation and in court. Afterwards when a person is in prison interpretation is no daily or regular occurrence. It may even happen that a prisoner is transferred from one prison to another without being pro-

11 Department of Prisons and Probation, Yearly Report, 2005, page 32.
12 Department of Prisons and Probation, Yearly Report, 2005, page 37.

vided with any understandable explanation. Such a transfer can take place for different reasons, among others in order to use the total prison capacity as well as possible.

1.4 Overview of trends

1.4.1. Sentencing trends

The number of criminal dispositions has not been developing continuously over the years. However, the general impression when comparing dispositions according to the Penal Code and the Traffic Code is that the share of the former is declining while the latter share is on the increase. This trend goes on as for 2005 where 62 % of all criminal dispositions were related to the Traffic Code and 25 % were related to violations of the Penal Code.[13] Furthermore, the proportion of sentences to unsuspended imprisonment appears to be declining slightly while the imposition of suspended sentences and fines tends to be slightly increasing. The proportions between males, females and companies are almost stagnant. See tables 1.A, 1.B and 1.C below.[14]

Table 1.A Penal dispositions by violated code

	1994	*1995*	*2000*	*2001*	*2002*	*2003*	*2004*
Absolute number of criminal dispositions	172.946	165.566	165.487	164.872	148.903	161.714	194.926
Type of Code (%)	100	100	100	100	100	100	100
Penal Code	37	37	32	32	36	33	29
Traffic Code	51	51	58	58	54	55	59
Other spec. Codes	12	13	10	10	10	12	12

Table 1.B Penal disposition by type of disposition in %

	1994	*1995*	*2000*	*2001*	*2002*	*2003*	*2004*
Type of disposition	100	100	100	100	100	100	100
Unsusp.imprisonment	9	8	7	6	7	7	6
Susp. Imprisonment	5	5	6	8	8	8	7
Fine	74	75	76	74	71	71	76
Other[15]	12	12	12	12	14	14	11

13 Criminal Statistics, Yearly Report 2005, page 21.
14 Concerning tables 1.A-1.C: Criminal Statistics Yearly Report 2004, page 19.
15 Withdrawal of charge, neglect of charge and verdict of not guilty.

Table 1.C Penal disposition by gender

	1994	*1995*	*2000*	*2001*	*2002*	*2003*	*2004*
Gender	100	100[16]	100	100	100	100	100
Male	84	84	82	83	84	84	82
Female	15	15	16	15	14	14	16
Companies	1	2	2	2	2	2	2

Table 1.D below shows an increasing number of inmates in all the main categories of imprisonment. This is the case for males as well as for females.

Table 1.D Average number of inmates per day[17] - main[18] categories

	Custody/pre-trial Male/Female	*Closed imprisonment Male/Female*	*Open imprisonment Male/Female*	*Secure imprisonment Male/Female*
2001	805 / 44	1047 / 44	963 / 53*	24 / 0
2002	956 / 46	1119 / 55	1097 / 54*	23 / 0
2003	1005 / 55	1170 / 51	1191 / 53	23 / 0
2004	1028 / 61	1220 / 51	1254 / 58	26 / 0

* a special type of imprisonment, "lenient imprisonment", was phased out at the beginning of this decade. In 2001 the average number of male and female inmates in lenient imprisonment was 96 and four respectively. In 2002 the figures were 16 and two. As lenient imprisonment was almost comparable to open prisons the number of "leniently imprisoned" people should be added to the number of inmates in open prisons to complete the information.

Table 1.E shows that as the number of convicted persons admitted to prisons mainly seems to have been declining, the number of unsuspended sentences more severe than fines appears to have been increasing. The majority of all unsuspended sentences to imprisonment are shorter than six months.

16 The counting error is copied from the source.
17 Criminal Statistics Yearly Reports 2001, p. 124, 2002, p. 122, 2003, p. 122 and 2004, p. 122.
18 The categories which are not included are unpaid fines, imprisonment for breaches of the Code on Foreigners, to which we will return below, and for 2001 and 2002 also lenient imprisonment.

Table 1.E Admission to prison, unsuspended sentences and their length[19]

	Convicted persons admitted to prison		*Unsuspended sentences greater than fine*		*Sentenced to 6 months or less*
	Abs	*Pr. 100.000*	*abs.*	*Average length*	
1985	15007	360	6306	7,0	4582 (72%)
1990	13878	325	7432	6,4	5729 (77%)
1995	17746	410	8074	5,8	6607 (81%)
2000	11700	269	7561	7,4	5821 (76%)
2004	9602	219	10722	6,1	8643 (80%)

From 2004 to 2005 the average length of all unsuspended sentences declined from 6,1 months to 5,7 months. Unsuspended sentences for violations of the Traffic Code declined from 1,5 months to 1,4 months on average, whereas the average concerning violation of the Penal Code declined from 7,3 months to 6,8 months. The only crime for which the average length increased was minor violence for which the average length of the unsuspended part of the sentences increased from 2,7 to 2,9 months.[20]

If we focus on the share of criminal dispositions and the share of sentences to imprisonment and compare 1995 with 2005 it becomes obvious that there are less convictions for violations of the Penal Code (1995: 1.405/100.000 and 2005: 1.284/100.000) but more prison sentences (1995: 388/100.000 and 2005: 410/100.000). The trend is almost opposite regarding violations of the Traffic Code (1995:1.908/100.000 and 2005: 3.089/100.000) and the share of resulting prison sentences (1995: 99/100.000 and 2005: 100/100.000).[21]

Each year on a random day in December the Department of Prisons and Probation creates an overview of the crimes for which the prisoners are serving their sentences. Table 1 F below shows a few of the crimes which changed by 1,0% or more from 2001 to 2005.

Table 1.F Crime committed[22]

	27th Dec 01	20th Dec 02	2nd Dec 03	27th Dec 04	27th Dec 05
Prisoners[23]	2.146	2.440	2.709	2.567	2.994
Murder %	8,8 %	6,9 %	6,3 %	6,6 %	5,7 %
Violence %	20,2 %	20,3 %	22,4 %	24,0 %	23,7 %
Drugs %	16,0 %	15,7 %	15,0 %	17,8 %	17,3 %
Theft %	13,8 %	13,8 %	13,8 %	12,8 %	15,6 %

19 Criminal Statistics Yearly Reports; 1985, p 56 and 58, 1990, p. 62 and 65, 1995, p. 59 and 64, 2000, p. 65 and 67, 2004, p. 45, 73 and 74.

20 Criminal Statistics, Yearly Report 2005, page 23.

21 Criminal Statistics Yearly Report, 2005, page 22-23.

22 Department of Prisons and Probation, Yearly Report, 2005, page 26.

23 The number of prisoners is the total number of convicted prisoners on that random day, whereas the information about each crime shows how many % of the total number of prisoners were convicted for this specific crime.

Since 1994, the average utilization of the prison-capacity has increased almost every year, from 91.3 % in 1994[24] to over 97 % in 2005. The Department of Prisons and Probation finds a utilization of averagely 92 % normal in relation to manpower and physical facilities within the prisons.[25] A Danish prison director describes occupation and leisure-facilities as insufficient when occupancy levels are so high. One of his points is that marginal clients (by which he may mean women or foreigners) can not possibly be occupied, and that relevant considerations in matching the right prison for the right person can not be properly taken into account.[26]

Overcrowding in prisons has self-evident negative consequences. Especially in the closed prisons even a small conflict could escalate if there is no empty cell to which a prisoner can be transferred. Since the total numbers of employees as well as technical equipment are intended and provided for lower occupancy levels, there is less time and less energy per inmate in relation to prison-life and in relation to their preparation for release, for instance organising future accommodation or employment. Furthermore, as release on parole cannot take place if the inmate does not have adequate housing, overcrowding may result in a person being in prison for a longer period of time than is in fact necessary.

In the periods of high utilization another tendency has been dominant in the Danish prison system. That is a tendency of developing different types of special units, like family-units, treatment-units for drug addicts respectively alcoholics, semi-closed units in open prisons and others. Today every prison has at least one – and more often several – special units. From an adminstrative and efficiency oriented point of view, these two tendencies do not combine with each other very well.

Recently, the Department of Prisons and Probation announced that due to an increased institutional capacity and to the introduction of electronic monitoring the backlog of persons waiting to serve a prison sentence will have nearly disappeared at the beginning of 2006.

1.4.2 Characteristics of the Foreign Prison Population

In combination, overcrowding and specialization result in prisons with less resource for prisoners, who are not immediately motivated, and who do not need or who are not taken in to one of the special units. For instance foreigners will be at risk of being "dumped" into the prison-places without receiving any special or specific attention.

In the year 2005 the Department of Prisons and Probation published a report on ethnic minorities within the prison population.[27]

It appears that foreigners account for 23 % of the imprisoned population and they are mainly placed in the ordinary units, which house about two thirds of all prisoners. Additionally, interviewed staff members have stressed that inmates belonging to ethnic minorities often band together and to a certain degree form groups which seem to be powerful in a problematic way.

---

24 Department of Prisons and Probation, Yearly Report, 2004, page 23.

25 Department of Prisons and Probation, Nyt fra Kriminalforsorgen, no. 6, 2005, page 5.

26 Engbo, Hans Jørgen in WWW.helsinki-komiteen.dk

27 http://www.kriminalforsorgen.dk (publikationer/rapporter og undersøgelser/Undersøgelse og anbefalinger vedrørende etniske minoriteter i kriminalforsorgen 2005).

In the light of this background, the publishers of the report recommends that foreigners should be spread out across more units in more prisons in order to avoid the development of problematic groups and to promote their integration (those who are not expelled after having served the prison sentence) into Danish society. Furthermore, the report stresses that a better distribution requires that (more) foreigners be placed in the treatment units which again challenges both the motivation of the prisoners as well as the capacity of treatment places in the prisons.

Apart from the recommendation of including more foreigners in the treatment units, the report stresses the importance of a successful mentoring concept (also mentioned below under 2.8). Further still, reference is made to inspiring experiences from using consultants from ethnic minorities, and it recommends more common prison-activities where Danish as well as foreign prisoners and staff members are active together, for instance team sports or the like. More organised contacts between the foreign prisoners and the "external" employment service, educational establishments and, for instance, relatives and former teachers are also recommended.

The authors of the departmental report were not the first to suggest that more foreigners should be admitted to the treatment units. Earlier evaluations had already indicated a very low proportion of foreigners in these units, as is elaborated under section 2.8 below.

In spite of the fact that – in principle – there are no legal differences between foreigners and Danes, two Danish researchers, Holmberg and Kyvsgaard, find it relevant to raise the question: "Are immigrants and their descendants discriminated against in the Danish criminal justice system?"[28]

Part of the background for their question is an overrepresentation of foreigners in the penal system which can be illustrated through one of the statistics from Statistics Denmark that is not published on a regular basis. Every now and then statistics on the registration of crime for national groups compared to their respective share in the overall population are published. The latest publication covers the period from 1995 to 2002.[29] The proportion of penal sentences for male foreigners increased from 1995 to 2000 but it was stable from 2000 to 2002. In 1995 the proportion of sentences was 24 % higher for foreign men than for men in general, and in 2000 and 2002 it was even 38 % higher. The increase is markedly higher for foreign descendents than for immigrants. In 1995, male descendents had 64 % more sentences for crimes and in 2002 they had 98 % more sentences than all men sentenced in Danish courts. For immigrants the sentences were 21 % and 30 % above the general level in 1995 and 2002 respectively, including a modest decrease from 2000 to 2002. Descendents form 10 % of the foreign men between 15 and 64 years olds, so the difference is much more significant when observed in relative terms rather than in absolute numbers. The same can be observed for women, however at a much lower level. Women found guilty of at least one crime form 1 % of the population

28 L. Holmberg and B. Kyvsgaard, "*Are Immigrants and Their Descendants Discriminated against in the Danish Criminal Justice System?*" Journal of Scandinavian Studies in Criminology and Crime Prevention, 2003 vol. 4, no. 2., pp. 125-142.

29 New statistical information is expected for May 2006. Unless stated otherwise, the statistics refer to the male population between 15 and 64 years. The minimum age of criminal responsibility in Denmark is 15.

but 1,8 % of the female descendant population and 1,4 % of the female immigrant population.[30]

It is a general experience that criminal activity varies considerably by age, urbanization and other social and economic conditions, such as for instance their affiliation with the labour market. Since the conditions of immigrants differ from those of the general population, these differences may account for some of their overrepresentation in the statistics.

1.G Overrepresentation of male immigrants and descendents with a penal disposition, corrected for different conditions.[31]

	Overrepresentation in percent
Not corrected	+ 49 %
Controlling for differences in age	+ 38 %
Controlling for differences in age and urbanization	+ 35 %
Corrected for differences in age and income	+ 19 %
Corrected for differences in age and socio-economic background	+ 8 %

Holmberg and Kyvsgaard consider that this could very well not solely explain the overrepresentation of foreigners. Rather, they could also tend to have a higher probability of being detected and apprehended. According to the authors this assumption corresponds with research experiences from other countries.

Beginning with charges in combination with arrests (a charge is sometimes, but not always, combined with an arrest) and subsequently convictions, Holmberg and Kyvsgaard find a clear trend: "for immigrants, the event of an arrest not leading to a conviction is 39% more frequent than for persons with a Danish background. For descendants, the difference is even greater (73%). For all persons with a foreign background the difference is 45%."[32]

Out of a total number of 2,690 custody cases not resulting in a subsequent conviction, 2,115 involved persons with a Danish background, while the remaining 575 were against foreigners. The 2,115 of these cases against Danes constituted four percent of all custody cases against Danish citizens. The 575 cases against foreigners formed eight percent of all custody cases against foreigners.[33]

Turning their attention to all penal dispositions, Holmberg and Kyvsgaard[34] indicate that while 3,3 % of the population with a Danish background have had a penal disposition passed against them the same goes for 5,0 % of the population with a foreign background (4,7% of immigrants and 7,9% of their descendants).

30 www.dst.dk/ Nyt fra Danmarks Statistik, nr. 235, 27 May 2004.

31 L Holmberg and B. Kyvsgaard, 2003, pp. 127. The authors use information from Statistics Denmark but regret that the figures are not corrected simultaneously for all the differences, namely age, urbanization, income and socio-economic background. Further recent data (published June 2004) show an overrepresentation at 50 % with no correction and at 4 % with correction for age and socio-economic background, http://www.jm.dk/image.asp?page=image&objno=72137

32 Holmberg, L. and Kyvsgaard, B. 2003 p. 129.

33 Holmberg, L. and Kyvsgaard, B. 2003, p. 132.

34 Holmberg, L. and Kyvsgaard, B. 2003, p. 127.

The authors conclude that: "Persons with a foreign background are, in fact, more likely to be arrested and remanded in custody without a subsequent conviction than are persons with a Danish background, even when their age, gender and crimes are readily comparable."[35] But they do not claim to have found the explanation for it. Rather, they stick to what they can tell from their own research, which besides the statistics also contains their observations from taking part in police patrols: "[A]ll previous studies on Danish police work regarding minorities agree that persons with a foreign background will often attract a disproportionate amount of police attention. They also agree that confrontations between the police and members of such groups are not entirely uncommon." And further: "Based as it is on group probability rates, this kind of police practice is self-reinforcing: the more control, the more illegal acts will be discovered. Police targeting on certain groups will yield evidence that can only reinforce the notion that these groups are worthy of special attention-and will contribute to their overrepresentation in the criminal justice system. This problem seems impossible to solve; it is inherent in proactive policing, and it does not only concern ethnic minorities."

The major part of the overrepresentation of foreigners within the penal system relates to violations of the Penal Code, mainly theft (178 %), whereas in the cases of rape (110 %) and violence (130 %) – which attract more media attention – the degree of overrepresentation is lower. Two thirds of all penal dispositions are reactions to breaches of the Traffic Code. Here the overrepresentation of foreigners is 8 %.[36]

1.5 Overview of national legislation

1.5.1 Penitentiary Legislation

Being locked up in prison results in lonesomeness, but it also implies a lack of or weak access to public services, information, debate, and so on. Consequently it is of common interest for both the prisoners and the prisons to be well aware of prisoners' legal rights. For the people in prison, legal rights are essential in order to prevent arbitrariness in the fulfilment of the sentence, while for the prisons adhering to and providing legal rights is extremely important in order to obtain respect from and generate confidence among the population.

The penalties are regulated in the Penal Code[37] as is the extent to which they should be imposed. In the year 2000, the first Danish Code on the Execution of Penalties[38] (CEP) was passed. Prior to this legislation all matters of prison life had been regulated administratively through circulars and instructions given by administrative authorities at different levels. Such circulars and instructions are still used complementary to the Code. Further, the European Prison Rules[39] as well as the UN Standard Minimum Rules are viewed as components of the legal basis of the Danish prison system.

35 Holmberg, L. and Kyvsgaard, B. 2003, p. 137.

36 www.jm.dk. Notat vedrørende Kriminalitet og national oprindelse. 2002.

37 Penal Code, no 126 of 15 April 1930. Latest revised edition Consolidate Act no 909 of 27 September 2005.

38 Code on the Execution of Penalties, no 432 of 31 May 2000. Latest revised edition Consolidate Act no 207 of 18 March 2005.

39 Rec(2006)2.

Within the framework of the CEP the Department of Prisons and Probation is responsible for the running of the prison system. Circulars and instructions are given by the Minister of Justice or the Department or by a lower authority under direction from the Minister or the Department.

Up until the CEP was passed, prisoners had no possibilities for bringing any decisions made by the prison authority before a court. Conflicts had to be solved administratively in the prisons (before the director) or by the Department of Prisons and Probation. Very few kinds of conflicts might (and may still) be brought before the Ombudsman. Complaints are now regulated in chapter 22, sections 111-123 of the CEP, according to which conflicts must firstly be stated before the prison director and subsequently before the Department of Prisons and Probation. When a decision is final it may in a limited number of cases - which are explicitly listed in section 112 CEP - be challenged before the courts. Practically the only question which has been brought before the courts since the introduction of this rule is when release on parole has been denied, and the court has to date always confirmed such refusals of parole.

The European Convention on Human Rights was incorporated into Danish law in 1992.[40] This provides the possibility to file claims of infringements of the Convention before the European Human Rights Courts.

Finally the Programme of Principles (Principprogram) for the Department of Prisons and Probation should be mentioned. The Programme was published in 1993 and was the very first official definition of principles and functions for the prison sector. The programme lays down that the main task is the execution of penalties and that this task consists of two parallel components: first, to exercise the control necessary for executing the penalty, and secondly to support and motivate the sentenced person to lead a life without crime by supporting his social and personal development through work and education. This programme can be seen as the beginning of an increased focus on education and social/cognitive training in prisons. Additionally, the societal trend of 'decentralisation' implies that in the following years the prisons developed different concepts for supporting and motivating their prisoners.

1.5.2 Penitentiary Legislation & Foreigners

As has already been mentioned above there are no formal differentiations between Danish and foreign prisoners in institutions for convicted persons. Consequently, an introduction to foreigners in Danish prisons is more or less an introduction to imprisoned people in Danish prisons in general.

There are cases, however, in which foreigners are mentioned explicitly in the law. These are situations in which it is evident that by simply applying the same rules and practices to both Danes and to foreigners the latter would be treated unequally. When foreigners are mentioned explicitly in the legal sources the intention is not to create or maintain different conditions for foreigners and Danes but - on the contrary - to prevent unequal conditions from arising; in other words, to place individuals in unequal positions on an equal footing. It may, however, be worth some extra thought to enlighten some

---

40 No 285 of 29 April 1992, revised in no 750 of 19 October 1998 and in Governmental Order no 749 of the same date, CEP with comments, page 247.

further aspects of everyday life in prison in order to secure a higher degree of actual (not just formal) equality.

2005 Denmark codified the European Warrant of Arrest[41], which implicates broader extradition possibilities/duties than before, of Danes as well as foreigners from within Europe. Also, there are a number of bilateral agreements between Denmark and the Nordic countries, USA and a few others. Traditionally the Nordic Countries including Denmark do cooperate very much in the protection of citizens but until now it is not possible to tell to which degree the European Arrest Warrant is going to influence the practices of extradition. The fact is that Denmark often tries to make a Dane who has been convicted abroad serve his sentence in Denmark, whereas foreigners convicted in Denmark do not always want to go to their home country in order to serve the sentence there.

2 TREATMENT OF FOREIGN PRISONERS

Originally there were no general restrictions for foreigners who wanted to stay in Denmark so long as they did not cause problems in relation to public order or demanded help from the social security system. In 1926 a legal demand for residence and work permits for foreigners who wanted to stay in Denmark for more that 3 months was implemented. The approach witnessed a shift from individual control of foreigners geared towards keeping problematic individuals out to a general form of control directed at everybody who is not a Danish citizen. Consequently, everybody now requires their own personal residence and work permits. Thus, permission – not prohibition – must be concrete and individual.

Since the 1970ies there have been two overall tendencies in the developments: some groups - mainly citizens from the Nordic countries and EU-citizens - are privileged, while the possibilities for others are restricted. Unemployment and more recently terrorism are the main arguments for strengthening the control and practice of issuing permits.[42]

2.1 General

A prisoner has the right to be informed of his rights, duties and the prison conditions as soon as possible. It is a general main rule that imprisonment is served in open prisons, unless the sentence is of five years or more. A prison sentence over five years in length, however, can also be served in an open institution insofar as it is considered unproblematic to do so. On the other hand, if – in spite of a sentence being shorter than five years – the sentenced person is a foreigner who is to be expelled after release, the term will always be served in a closed prison (see more under 2.9 below).

Furthermore, a person may always be placed in a closed prison instead of in an open institution for security reasons if the prisoner is classed as being dangerous to himself or to others. More than 90 % of all persons, who are imprisoned, are allocated to an open prison.[43]

---

41 Code no 833 of 25th of August 2005, revised in Code no 538 and 542 of 8th of June 2006.

42 Foreign Right, pp. 3-5.

43 CEP with comments, p. 65.

In general, the open prisons have better possibilities to vary and develop both work-facilities and treatment programmes due to the space available and the different category of inmates that they house in comparison to those that are located in the closed prisons. But overall funding is a major problem. Different practical skills such as painting, brick-laying, farming, driving licenses and carpentry to name but a few are taught within the prison system as a whole. Besides basic school each prison has individual occupation and treatment programmes for the prisoners.

In the prisons - both open and closed - a ward typically comprises eight to 12 cells. Should the institution also house women there will be wards in which the sexes are separated and other wards where they are mixed. Each ward has a kitchen and toilets as well as shower and washing facilities that are adequate for the respective number of persons.

Taking into account factors such as housing, guarding, occupation and so on, a cell in an open prison costs about half as much as a cell in a closed prison. The daily costs for a cell in an open prison are 727 Dkr , while the daily expenses that arise from a cell in a closed prison lie at 1.576 Dkr.[44]

2.2 Living conditions and facilities

In general, it is intended that all prisoners have a cell of their own. But several prisons also retain the possibility of using cells for up to five or six persons in case of a temporary lack of places. Apart from one totally new prison the prisons in Denmark are relatively old and - due to a lack of funds - many prison buildings are in need renovation. A indication of this is given in a new study on imprisoned women[45] where 41% of the respondents state that the temperature in their cells is not appropriate, which obviously implies that the cells tend to be too warm in the summer and too cold in winter.

A very fundamental principle in the management of prisons is *normalization*. This principle contains the ambition to create general prison conditions and facilities that resemble life and conditions in wider society as closely as possible. Normalization is not – which some might believe – a question of "normalizing" the prisoners but of "normalizing" life in prison. A logical consequence of this principle is that because deprivation of liberty is not normal it should never take place to a larger degree than is required due to security reasons.

The principle of normalization consists of at least two core elements, namely the principles of *self management* and *supplying oneself with provisions*, as laid out in section 43 of the CEP. The idea is a kind of de-institutionalization of the prisons which means that even if the prisoners confined they are neither sick nor unable to take care of their own needs in the course of an ordinary day. In other words, individual daily routines, such as for instance cooking, cleaning, washing clothes, beddings etc, are to be carried out by every single person. Consequently, every prison houses a drug-store where prisoners at specific times can buy what they require to cover their daily needs. The above mentioned new research on imprisoned women (of all nationalities) showed a great deal of frustration

---

44 1 Euro=7,50 Dkr. Department of Prisons and Probation, Yearly Report, 2003.

45 The report is coordinated by the Department of Criminology at the University of Greifswald, Germany, and the information regarding Danish prisons can be ordered from the author. The report is not published as a whole.

among the respondents about the stores which were described as being too expensive, selling old goods and offering a very "limited" assortment.

In the pre-trial prisons or the prisons there are sets of "Guidelines for detainees & remand prisoners" in several languages as for instance: Arabic, Czech, Estonian, Farsi, Finnish, French, German, Greenlandic, Italian, Latvian, Lithuanian, Polish, Russian, Serbian, Spanish, Turkish and Urdu [46]. The guidelines are not very detailed but do contain information on rights of defence, duty to work and of course means for contacting the relevant embassy.

2.3 Reception and admission

Once a person has been convicted he/she will either be taken (back) into custody to await information on which prison he shall be serving his sentence in, or he/she returns home to await this information. Practice is mainly dependent on the crime committed and on whether he/she was held in pre-trial detention or not.

As soon as possible after being admitted to prison an action plan[47] for the person's stay in prison and for the initial time period after release must be elaborated. The plan must be made and revised on the basis of dialog and cooperation between the prison and the prisoner. The demand for the elaboration of such an action plan is common for all prisoners[48] except for prison sentences of 60 days or less. An action plan must also be elaborated for the short-term convicted if a Danish prisoner is 18 years old or younger or a foreigner is 26 years old or younger.

2.4 Work – Education – Training – Sports – Recreation

Every prisoner under any kind of deprivation of liberty has the right and the obligation to take part in *work, training/treatment or school* every day (section38, subsection 1 CEP). Before the CEP was confirmed and implemented, the question was only about actual work, but now more forms of constructive occupation are accepted – sometimes even recommended – and consequently remunerated like work. The standard rate of pay for prison work is 8 Dkr per hour, while extraordinarily good or demanding work can be remunerated with an increased salary of up to 12 Dkr per hour (2005).[49]

If a prisoner participates in an education programme or has to interrupt his/her daily work routine in order to attend a cognitive skills programme, the time for which he/she is absent is not deducted from the basic salary. However, on the other hand no bonuses can be achieved. Similarly, full time school education - either in the prison school or in educational institutions outside the prison in some cases - or full time participation in a structured treatment programme are financially rewarded at the same rate as for ordinary prison work. Also, more individual activities can also be financially rewarded, for instance if a prisoner is working as a spokesperson for the prison.

---

46 The Guidelines may be downloaded from http://www.kriminalforsorgen.dk/

47 This is solely a plan on developing social skills. Newcomers are not regularly taken to medical and dental checks (see section 2.5 below).

48 Section 31 CEP, CEP with comments p 82, Instruction no 367 of 17 May 2001, circular no 166 of 29 June 2001 and instruction no 155 of 29 June 2001.

49 Engbo, p. 211.

It is stressed in a report by the Department of Prisons and Probation on ethnic minorities in the prison and probation system, that more attention should be given to prepare (not least the young) prisoners for the labour-market, that the needs and wishes of ethnic minorities should be taken into account and that external partners should be increasingly included. "External partners" refers to professional as well as non-professional partners like for instance local job-consultants or mentors.[50] In the report on imprisoned women mentioned under section 2.2 above the need for relevant and constructive occupation is also stressed.

Regarding education and training - like for instance cognitive skills - it is stressed in the report on ethnic minorities that the prisons need to know more about the levels of basic education and knowledge of the foreigners in prison. In order to develop adequate programmes the foreign prisoners' knowledge of Danish society, behaviour and the language should be more enhanced. Also, the development of specific cognitive programmes should take cultural, societal and linguistic differences into account.[51]

In relation to foreigners in the prisons the departmental report[52] highlights the following issues as being the most important: information, communication and ensuring that decisions by the prison staff or director have been understood by the prisoners. In order to assist in addressing these issues the authors of the report suggest that persons from the prisoners' network outside the prison be consulted, for example former teachers, parents or social workers.

The fact that there is no proper contact between foreign prisoners and the staff is stressed in interviews with foreign prisoners, referred to in the report. The departmental report points out the importance of common spare time activities as a remedy for the integration of foreign prisoners with Danish prisoners and staff members.

In order to meet the very remarkable and expressed common message from all the prisoners that education is needed the state prison of Ringe piloted the approach of admitting an imam[53] to the institution. In general the foreign prisoners are not experienced by the prison system as being open-minded towards the Danish treatment system for drug addicts, but they are always interested in conversing with the imam.[54]

According to the Code on Execution of Penalties, section 58, prisoners must be able to read newspapers, listen to radio and see TV to some (yet not defined) degree. Further they must be given the possibility to borrow books etc in the public libraries –also to a not defined degree. Finally, the section states that foreign prisoners should – as far as possible – be given the opportunity to read papers, magazines and books in their own languages. The comments to this subsection state, however: "The term "as far as possible" means that there are not only practical but also economical limitations of the prisons duty to make this possible[55].

---

[50] www.kriminalforsorgen.dk/publikationer/rapporterogundersøgelser/Undersøgelse og anbefalinger vedrørende etniske minoriteter i kriminalforsorgen 2005, page 5.

[51] www.kriminalforsorgen.dk/publikationer/rapporterogundersøgelser/Undersøgelse og anbefalinger vedrørende etniske minoriteter i kriminalforsorgen 2005, page 4.

[52] www.kriminalforsorgen.dk/publikationer/rapporterogundersøgelser/Undersøgelse og anbefalinger vedrørende etniske minoriteter i kriminalforsorgen 2005, page 6.

[53] See more under section 2.12 below.

[54] Nyt fra Kriminalforsorgen , December 2005, p 18-19. (News from the Prison and Probation Service, December 2005, p 18-19).

[55] CEP wih comments, page 137.

2.5 Food – Religion – Personal Hygiene – Medical care

It follows from the principles of self management and providing for oneself (CEP section 43) (see above section 2.2) that every prisoner takes care of cooking, personal hygiene and so on. All necessities must be bought in the prison store - including food, soap, toothpaste and whatever else might be needed except for clothes. All prisoners receive 51 Dkr per day (about 7 Euro) (2005) – if they are working or not – to cover their personal needs in this respect (section 42, subsection 2, CEP).[56]

The report on imprisoned women (see section 2.2 above) is very convincing in relation to food at least regarding female prisoners. They are all satisfied with both the quality and quantity of the food provided.

Food-supplies in the stores, however, are not satisfactory. The stores (which obviously have a monopoly in the prison) are expensive and offer products which are not fresh, very one-sided and monotonous. According to the prisoners the special offers that are available in the main department of the same store in the local city never reach the prison store. When a prisoner is out – either on leave, or in order to frequent a job or school– he/she can see the special offers in the local store. However, due to various limitations stemming from the rules – and maybe also due to the prisoner's own financial limitations– it is not possible to bring an unlimited supply of goods from the local store into the prison.

Section 35 CEP states the right to freedom of religion. This implies that prisoners have the right to practice their religion in relation to - for instance - attending services, praying and living in accordance with other religious customs that are important to each individual, like food or work.

This is, however, a rule that was formulated before the number of foreigners and the focus on foreigners reached level that they are at today. Originally, this rule was intended for Christians, but now almost one fourth of the prisoners belong to another religion, and 15-20 % of the prisoners are Muslims. This fact presents new – and still more perceptible - challenges for the principle of religious liberty. Most prisons offer facilities organised for use as churches and staff include full time or part time priests. Also, prison staff also includes an imam in a number of prisons.

Newly published research on the practice of religion in prison concludes that Danish prisons are open to and tolerant of religion. The researching sociologist assumes that an important motive for prisons to be highly aware of religion is that the presence of religion has a positive influence in the prisons. Not least the priests' or the imams' role as a spiritual adviser to all the prisoners who desire it is a very important factor. Contrary to the other staff members, members of religious staff adhere to professional secrecy.[57]

A newspaper article that referred to a PhD on the sociology of religion by Lene Kühle pointed out that the prison staff needs to be better and more frequently instructed on how to handle Muslim prisoners. It is the experience of the author that some prisoners are tending to overemphasize the meaning of their religion in order to obtain power. For instance, food may be an issue in this respect. It is well known that Muslims do not eat

56 Engbo, p. 154.

57 Kristeligt Dagblad (Christian Daily) 16 of May 2006, Karitte Lind Bejer is the journalist who interviews Lene Kühle about the anthology "Straffens menneskelige Ansigt?" ("The human face of the penalty") and her PhD on the role of religion in the Danish Prisons.

pork. The author refers to an example where Muslim prisoners have attempted to deny Danish prisoners access to the prison kitchens because Muslim food could not be prepared in the same kitchen where pork had been prepared. The same article also states that a new set of treatment guidelines and instructions are on the way.

The existing guidelines for prisoners on serving custodial sentences state the following on religion: "Church services are held in penal institutions and some local prisons. You have the right to speak to the penal institution's/local prison's priest, who belongs to the Danish Lutheran Church. The priest can also arrange for contact with a priest from another faith."

If a prisoner belongs to a recognised faith which forbids him to be working on certain days, he is to be exempted. Concerning food (for a religious perspective): "If you are a vegetarian or belong to a recognised religious faith, special requirements regarding food can be followed. Ask the section's staff or the priest." However, the interviewed foreign prisoners[58] are not satisfied with the limited assortment and the prices in the prison stores, just like the interviewed female prisoners in the above (section 2.2) mentioned report on imprisoned women.

With this background in mind, and according to my personal experience with prison-life, it is reasonable to conclude that the formal rights of the prisoners are modest and in terms of practising religion as well as other essential questions the conditions in reality are often better than the minimum rights that are prescribed in the sources prescribe. This may have different reasons. One reason may be the wish to generate a better atmosphere in the prison (like Lene Kühle suggests). Another may be that each prison has a professional interest in doing a good job by fulfilling legal needs and legal rights to the highest possible degree.

A doctor is associated to every prison and upon reception to the institution a prisoner will always have the opportunity to speak with the doctor or a nurse. Until recently, it was common practice that every prisoner saw the doctor at least once after reception to the institution, but for economical reasons practice has been adapted so that this formerly compulsory visit to the doctor is now only offered.. Also, a prisoner can always ask to be seen by a doctor or nurse and the doctor decides if treatment is required. Should treatment be deemed necessary, it is performed in the prison or in a hospital. Prisoners do not have the right to choose their own doctor or to administer their own medicine as is the case for regular citizens.

An administrative instruction on health care[59] states that if a female prisoner is pregnant the staff must inform the doctor and make it possible for the prisoner to see him/her as soon as possible. Furthermore, if the woman is still in the prison three months or less prior to the expected date of delivery, it has to be agreed in which hospital the child is to be born. It is to be ensured (as far as possible) that children are not born within the prison (sections 10 and 11). There are no special or supplementary provisions for foreigners in this respect.

Each year a number of persons who are guilty of a crime but are suffering from a mental illness are acquitted and sentenced to treatment. Foreigners form 23,5 % of those sentenced to psychiatric treatment after having been found guilty of a crime, compared to

---

58 www.kriminalforsorgen.dk/publikationer/rapporterogundersøgelser/Undersøgelse og anbefalinger vedrørende etniske minoriteter i kriminalforsorgen 2005, page 39.

59 No 374 of 17 May 2001.

the 23 % of the prison population for which they account (see part A2 above). This takes place in accordance with sections 16 and 68 or 69 of the Criminal Code. On average, 330 persons were sentenced to treatment per year in the period of 2001 to 2004.[60]

Prisoners (both male and female) who are suffering from psychiatric and mental illnesses, but nonetheless are sentenced to imprisonment, will – if they are not (temporarily) placed in a hospital - be allocated to the closed state prison of Hersted Vester. This prison houses mentally ill prisoners as well as serious sex-offenders, those sentenced to secure (time unlimited) imprisonment (forvaring) and the Greenlanders, who are sentenced in Greenland but in accordance with the Greenlandic criminal law have to serve their sentence in Denmark. Hersted Vester is the only penal institution where psychiatrists belong to the basic staff and where the prisoners can receive continuous psychiatric treatment while serving their prison sentences. From 2002 to 2004 the number of prisoners who were waiting for a cell in Hersted Vester increased from 10 to over 20. The former peak in the number of imprisoned persons waiting for a place there was 18 in 2000. [61]

It is certainly stressed in the report from the Department of Prisons and Probation on ethnic minorities, which has been mentioned several times above, that cooperation between the psychiatric system and the prisons regarding diagnostics and treatment should be expanded and improved. In the same context, it is explicitly suggested to ensure that the interpreters, who are assisting the communication between the foreigner and the prison system, doctors etc, have deep knowledge of both the language as well as the cultural background of the foreign prisoners.[62]

Psychiatric treatment as well as imprisonment may both involve a certain legal restraint towards the patient respectively the prisoner. The psychiatric system and the prison system have different sets of rules on restraint and the choice of rules depends on the institution in which the person is staying at the moment where restraint is necessary. This implies for instance that a prisoner can not be forced to stay in the hospital unless medical indicators prescribe this. However, as long as the prisoner is serving a sentence of imprisonment, he/she returns to prison if he/she does not stay in hospital.

For years, drugs have been an issue of great attention in the Danish criminal system. In 1994 the state prison of Ringe opened the very first drug treatment unit in a Danish prison, the so-called contract-unit. An evaluation of this special unit was conducted in 1998, and revealed that 7,1 % of the prisoners who were treated in there were foreigners, while at the same time foreigners accounted for 49 % of the total population of the institution.[63] A further treatment unit was opened in the state prison in Vridsløselille in 1997. A report on this unit covering the first five years of its operation showed that of the 193 prisoners who had been treated in the examined period, only 13 (6,7 %) were foreigners. [64]

---

60 Psychiatric diseases and crime (Psykisk sygdom og kriminalitet), p 76. 2006. The Ministry of Social Affairs, The Ministry of Justice and The Home Office.

61 Psychiatric diseases and crime (Psykisk sygdom og kriminalitet), p 102.

62 www.kriminalforsorgen.dk/publikationer/rapporterogundersøgelser/Undersøgelse og anbefalinger vedrørende etniske minoriteter i kriminalforsorgen 2005, page 8.

63 Anette Storgaard: The contract in the State Prison of Ringe, p. 32. Centre for Alcohol and Drug Research, University of Aarhus, Denmark. 1998.

64 Anette Storgaard: The Import model in the State Prison of Vridsløselille, Appendix 1, p. 2. The Department of Prisons and Probation. 2003.

It must certainly be stressed that neither all Danish nor all foreign prisoners are necessarily in need of treatment for a drug or substance addiction. However, the situation remains that foreigners only account for a very small proportion of those prisoners who receive drug-treatment in the prisons compared to their share of the total prison population. The new and more widespread report published by the Department of Prisons and Probation which is mentioned above[65] concludes that the foreign prisoners are still more frequently placed in ordinary (non-treatment) units than Danish prisoners. Furthermore, the report encourages efforts to determine how foreigners can be more efficiently motivated to participate in drug treatment during their time in prison. Although interviews have shown that Danish prisoners more frequently suffered from addiction problems than their foreign counterparts, still roughly one third of the foreign inmates are assumed to be (ab)users of drugs.

What the drug treatment report might have stressed more clearly is that there may be structural and cultural barriers in the organisation of the programmes (for instance language, methods, approach etc.) that could very well make the concept seem less inviting and relevant to foreigners.. Furthermore, there may be the issue of motivating the prison staff to better motivate the foreign prisoners as firstly: foreigners are often expelled after having served their sentence. Since treatment in prison is more expensive and requires more resources than imprisonment without treatment the staff may find it more plausible to offer one of the few treatment-places to a Dane. Secondly, treatment units are very often funded through short-term financial grants. Such grants are more likely to be extended if it can be proven that the provided treatment is successful. Since the treatment programme was developed in Denmark with Danes in mind, the degree of its success may appear to be greater if predominantly Danish persons are admitted to it.

In July 2006 the Danish Ministry of Justice published a draft proposal for a change of the CEP which intends to guarantee access to treatment for drug addiction for more prisoners and in more prisons than is the case today.[66]

2.6 Consular and legal help

Visits in the prisons as such may among others be paid by The Ombudsman, the Standing Committee on Legal Matters of the Parliament (Folketinget) and the European Committee for the Prevention of Torture and inhuman or degrading Treatment or Punishment (CPT). The prison authorities are obliged to respond to any questions or queries that they may have, and their comments and questions as well as the responses from the prison authorities are published. The Ombudsman provides the Parliament with annual reports on the prison situation. He can take up issues of all kinds, general as well as specific, legal as well as procedural. Traditionally, the Ombudsman is very much aware of prison conditions and his statements are taken very seriously. However, neither the Ombudsman nor the other two mentioned bodies can give orders or prescriptions in relation to prison life.

It occasionally occurs that other groups or bodies arrange visits to the prisons, for example the Danish Institute for Human Rights or groups of lawyers, law students, judges

65 http://www.kriminalforsorgen.dk (publikationer/rapporter og undersøgelser/Undersøgelse og anbefalinger vedrørende etniske minoriteter i kriminalforsorgen 2005).

66 www.jm.dk

and others with a special or professional interest in the prison system. Though these last mentioned visits do ensure some public contact to the world behind the bars they cannot be categorized as parts of the formal control.

Apart from this and without a defined limitation of duration, every prisoner has the right to receive unsupervised visits from his defence lawyer. Furthermore, foreign prisoners have the right to receive visits from consulates and embassies of their home country.[67] Such visits may – as is the case for all of the previously stated visits with the exception of visits from defence lawyers – be attended by members of staff for security reasons.[68]

According to section 56 CEP all prisoners (national and foreign) have the right to continued correspondence with different national and international organisations and authorities, which all intend to exercise legal and legality control as for instance the Ministry of Justice, the Department of Prisons and Probation, the Ombudsman, Members of Parliament (Folketinget), The European Human Rights Court, the CPT and the defence lawyer of the prisoner.

Foreign prisoners have the right to correspond in unlimited secrecy with diplomats and consulates from their home country .[69] Letters between a foreign prisoner and a diplomat or consular representative may not be opened, damaged or retained. If there are reasons to believe that a letter from one of the mentioned senders contains illegal substances (drugs) it may be screened. Also, if there are reasons to believe that the intended sender is not the actual sender of a letter, the prison may either contact the authority in question (the intended sender) to ensure that they did in fact send the letter, or return the letter asking the authority to confirm that it was sent from there.

2.7 Contact with the outside world[70]

It is a most fundamental principle in section CEP that during the execution of the penalty restrictions cannot be imposed apart from those laid out in the law or resulting as a direct consequence of the penalty.

Nevertheless, prison life is definitely lonesome irrespective both of which country the prison is located in and of the nationality of the prisoner. In practice, imprisonment intervenes in customary access to persons and authorities outside of the penal institutions. Consequently, prisoners are provided with a set of minimum rights to enable them to remain in "contact with the outside world" through, for instance, visits and written correspondence.

These rights are - to some extent -adequately extended for foreign prisoners. The CEP confers to prisoners the right to one visit of at least one hour – and as far as possible two hours – every week.[71] As a main rule prisoners receive visits without the presence of members of the prison staff. But it may be decided by the Ministry of Justice or the prison

---

67 Section 51 CEP which is related to art. 36 of the Vienna Convention where it is laid down that consulate representatives have the right – though not if it is against the wish of the prisoner – to see prisoners from their country.

68 CEP section 53 and CEP with comments p 128.

69 Instruction on letters no. 377 of 17 May 2001.

70 The following strictly applies to convicted prisoners but rules and conditions are to a very large extent the same for prisoners in pre-trial prison so long as they are not in solitary confinement.

71 CEP section 51.

director (upon authorization from the Ministry of Justice) that a staff member must be present during the visit.

In closed prisons visits take place in cells, which are located side by side and connected by a corridor. If a visitor needs to visit the WC during the visit he or she must pass the other cells. The women from the state prison of Hersted Vester, who were interviewed in relation to the report on imprisoned women (see section 2.2 above) felt that this was problematic when for instance children or grandchildren might glimpse a "famous" sex-offender or murderer.

As the open prisons are predominantly located in the countryside, their accessibility by public transport may be an issue of relevance. Some of the respondents in the above mentioned research on imprisoned women (see section 2.2 above) expressed much frustration over the fact that public busses do not pass the prison. This means that relatives coming to the nearest train station must travel several kilometres by taxi. In spite of a flexible practice on behalf of the prison regarding the planning and duration of visits, this complicates the efforts to maintain good contact with children and other close relatives.

In relation to visits it should finally be mentioned that the general protection of individuals' protection of homes[72] is in force in prisons as well as in private homes. That means that investigative monitoring of a cell in which a visit takes place requires permission to do so from the court and must be in accordance with the conditions in sections 780 and 781 of the Law of Procedure. On the other hand, it is the prison that is informed about monitoring having taken place, not to the prisoner whose visit was in fact monitored. The reason for monitoring is typically that the prisoner is under the suspicion of having committed a new offence.

The right of prisoners to send and receive letters is another aspect of the issue of securing the possibility of "contact with the outside world" as it is prescribed in Article 24 of the European Prison Rules.

A basic right to correspondence does exist for foreign as well as Danish prisoners. The reasons for the limitations that are laid down in sections 55 and 56 CEP are justified mainly in terms of the security of the prison and the security of the victim of the crime for which the prisoner is serving a sentence. The ways of legally breaching the secrecy of correspondence in accordance with the mentioned sections also concern letters sent to the prison that are addressed to the prisoners as well as letters sent to the prisoners' private address that are subsequently forwarded to the prison. The CEP defines different degrees of breaching the secrecy of correspondence. The less radical intervention is the opening and closing of mail with the prisoner present. This takes place when there is the suspicion that the letter may contain drugs. It is by far more intrusive when a staff member actually reads a letter. This is only justifiable if there is a fear that the security of the institution or the victim of the offence are in jeopardy. The decision to read a letter/letters may be made specifically for one letter or for all letters that are sent to a prisoner. The prisoner must be informed when a letter has been read but such a notification may be given up to four weeks after the letter has been read by the prison staff. The most radical intrusion into secrecy is when a letter is retained and not handed over to a prisoner. In this case it must normally be returned to the sender. But for the reasons of security mentioned above, a letter may also not be returned but simply retained by the prison. In such cases the sender must be informed within four weeks.

---

72 Section 72 of The Danish Constitution.

Section 56 CEP mentions a number of authorities the secrecy of whose written correspondence with a prisoner – both national and foreign – cannot legally be breached. That is for instance the Ministry of Justice, the Department of Prisons and Probation, the Ombudsman, Members of the Parliament (Folketinget), The European Human Rights Court, the CPT, the solicitor of the prisoner and other public and international authorities.

The Administrative Instruction no. 377 of 17 May 2001 on letters states that foreign prisoners have the right to correspond in unlimited secrecy with diplomats and consulates from their home country. In these cases the letters may be neither opened nor broken nor kept back (see above). If there are reasons to suspect that a letter from one of the mentioned senders bears illegal contents (for instance drugs) it may be screened. Also, if there are reasons to suspect that the apparent sender is not the original sender the prison may either contact the authority in question (the apparent sender) to secure that they did in fact send the letter or return the letter asking the authority to confirm it was sent from there.

Another way to stay in contact with "the outside world" is by telephone. However, prisoners are not allowed to be in possession of mobile phones and the possibilities of using telephones in the prisons depend on "practical conditions". On the one hand it is not impossible and not illegal for prisoners to make phone calls while on the other hand they can not stay in telephone contact with the outside world to an unlimited extent. "Practical conditions" concerns the availability of staff who need to be present during the phone call or who listen to a taped conversation afterwards. The possibility of using telephones may be denied for the same reasons that also justify a breach of the secrecy of correspondence as mentioned above. In general prisoners in open prisons have better telephone facilities than prisoners in closed prisons. An aspect that is of specific relevance for foreigners is that the staff may demand that the conversation be held in an understandable language.[73] The prison can only deny a prisoner the right to call one of the persons or authorities with whom he is granted uncontrolled correspondence by the CEP or the administrative instruction in exceptional circumstances.

The possibilities of sending or receiving emails and faxes are extremely limited as prisoners have no explicit rights to posses or demand access to computers or fax machines. The only exception from this is that in a few cases the prison-schools in open prisons allow prisoners to use email. This is seen as a privilege rather than a right.[74]

Finally, it should be mentioned that prisoners have the right to access literature from public libraries and to read newspapers, listen to the radio and watch television. In order to comply with this prisoners have the right to bring their own televisions with them or to rent one from within the prison. In section 58 subsection 3 CEP it is laid down that as far as possible foreign prisoners should have access to newspapers and other written media in their own language.

Another aspect of having access to the media is the right of prisoners to participate in interviews with media representatives, according to section 59 CEP. Prisons may only deny this for concrete security reasons. A lack of staff resources may have the consequence that interviews must be held in special parts of the prison or at a time when it is

73 CEP article 57 and Instruction on the use of telephone no. 378 of 17 May 2001.
74 Instruction on articles no. 208 of 18 March 2005.

possible and convenient for the staff. It is not legal to make photos of other persons than the prisoner who has agreed to it.

2.8 Re-integration activities – Prison leave

In principle all training and educational programmes as well as occupations and activities in the prisons all fall within the category of preparation for release. The same must be said for efforts to stay in good contact with relatives outside the prisons, i.e. visits in the prisons and temporary leaves for the prisoners. The latter is not possible for prisoners who are to be expelled after their prison sentence. However, the majority of the other prisoners do have a systematic possibility to have temporary leaves from the institution every three weeks.

In each individual action-plan release must be prepared as well as possible, which includes the provision of housing, occupation and so on prior to release. Release on parole can be postponed until these issues have been resolved. But when the whole sentence has been served the prisoner must be released whether there is housing and occupation for him or not. The probation service can only supervise a released prisoner if he/she has been released on parole. Supervision is not possible when the full sentence has been served (see below section 2.9).

2.9 Release - Expulsion

Release must be prepared in accordance with the prisoner-specific action plan that is continuously revised in the course of the stay in prison and according to section 38 (section 41 for life sentences) of the Criminal Code. Prisoners are normally released on parole when 2/3 of the custodial sentence has been served. This only applies, however, if the sentence is for a total period of at least three months. In exceptional cases a prisoner can be released after having served between 1/2 and 2/3 of the sentence. Either the prison or the Ministry of Justice (Department of Prisons and Probation) decides whether a prisoner is to be released on parole. Parole can be denied if it is judged that there is a risk of reoffending. Furthermore, it can only be granted under the condition that the prisoner has been provided with appropriate housing and occupation.[75]

Upon release on parole a probationary period will be set. If a crime is committed during this period of probation, the remainder of the previous sentence will normally be added to the new custodial sentence resulting from the new offence. In some cases parole can be supplemented with the condition of being under the supervision of the probation and after-care system. In addition, there can be special supplementary conditions, for example treatment for alcoholism. If the conditions are breached the Ministry of Justice (Department of Prisons and Probation) may decide that the released prisoner must return to prison in order to serve the rest or part of the rest of the sentence. The rules described above are supplemented with more specific details on release requirements and procedures – including special provisions for foreigners – which are contained in the "Guidelines on serving custodial sentences".

The issue of expulsion is of pivotal importance for some foreigners, and the guidelines state the following: "If the court has decided that you are to be expelled upon your re-

75 Criminal Code section 38, subsection 5.

lease, you must normally serve your sentence in a closed prison. If you are to be expelled, you have the possibility of being released on parole when 7/12 of your custodial sentence has been served. Even if you do not want release on parole, for example because you are trying to have a sentence of expulsion changed, you will be released after 2/3 of the punishment. You can seek advice from the staff or your defence lawyer. The police decide how you are to be expelled. If you have the money, you must pay for the transport home yourself. Ask the staff if you are in doubt about anything concerning expulsion."

The rule on release after 7/12 is explained by the fact that foreigners who are to be expelled are not granted temporary prison leave (normally every three weeks). 7/12 of a sentence without any interruption is estimated as being equivalent to 2/3 of a sentence when ordinary leaves are included.

Regarding the possibility for foreigners to be transferred to their home country the guidelines state the following: "In certain cases it is possible for you to serve your custodial sentence in your home country. Ask the staff". It is never an obligation for any authority – courts or others – to expel a foreigner – on the contrary. The expulsion of a foreign national who is legally residing in Denmark requires a legal basis, for example a criminal conviction.

* A refugee, who has obtained a residence permit as well as a foreigner who has legally been staying in Denmark for seven years or more may be expelled:[76]

- if he/she is sentenced to unsuspended imprisonment for four years or more (for one crime as a first conviction),
- if he/she is sentenced to unsuspended imprisonment for two years or more (for several crimes sentenced at the same time but as a first conviction),
- if he/she is sentenced to unsuspended imprisonment for two years or more (for one crime but he/she has been sentenced to imprisonment before),
- if he/she is sentenced to unsuspended imprisonment for an attack on the security of the State, drugs offences, trafficking in human beings, forcing somebody else to marry against his/her own will or for certain crimes which are deemed more serious and (possibly) more severely punishable in the Criminal Code, for instance sexual offences, arson, robbery and murder.

* A foreigner who has legally been staying in Denmark for three years or more may be expelled in the following cases:[77]

- for the same reasons as mentioned above
- if he/she is sentenced to unsuspended imprisonment for two years or more (for one crime as a first conviction)
- if he/she is sentenced to unsuspended imprisonment for one year or more (for several crimes sentenced at the same time as a first conviction),
- if he/she is sentenced to unsuspended imprisonment for one year or more (for one crime but he/she has been sentenced to imprisonment before).

* Other foreigners may be expelled:[78]

---

[76] Code on Foreigners, section 22 and Foreign Right, p 660 ff.

[77] Code on Foreigners, section 23.

[78] Code on Foreigners, section 24.

- for the reasons mentioned above,
- if he/she is sentenced to suspended or unsuspended imprisonment.

If a person is sentenced to reside in a psychiatric institution, he/she may also be sentenced to expulsion alongside the rules described above about prison sentences.

The question of expulsion must be raised in court by the prosecutor simultaneously with the accusation for the committed crime. Consequently the accused has a defence lawyer; he/she has the right to appeal and the right to a fair trial. It is up to the courts to decide whether or not the foreigner is to be expelled and if so, for what period of time. Expulsion is to be considered in the light of issues of the enforcement of law (whether the crime so grave that we want the person out of the country) and of legal protection (considerations of the necessity to protect wider society against future offending by the person in question). [79]

Further, the courts have to balance the arguments for expulsion against arguments drawing in the opposite direction. Section 26 of the Code on Foreigners mentions the arguments that are to be considered; the degree to which the foreigner is involved with somebody or something in Denmark, age, state of health, consequences of possible expulsion for relatives, involvement in the home-country and possible safety risks in home-country.

Even if the courts are free to decide within the legal framework, an indication whether or not to expel someone is given in section 26 subsections 2. Here it is stated that if the crime committed is related to drugs, trafficking, national security or another of the serious crimes mentioned above, the reasons *not* to expel a person should be very strong. It has not been possible to find authoritative statistics on how many foreigners are expelled when convicted for a crime. But it is possible to attain an impression of practice in the Supreme Court.[80]

According to the 2003-2004 annual report by the public prosecution service, the Supreme Court had 94 cases – involving 107 persons - in which expulsion was an issue from 1 January 1997 to the end of June 2005. It must, however, be stressed that Supreme Court practice does not provide statistical proof. Mentioning them here merely serves the purpose of illustrating judicial prejudices.

Out of these 107 persons 76 were expelled. In turn, of the 76 persons who were expelled two were expelled for a period of five years and one for ten years, while the remainders were expelled indefinitely.

This part shall be concluded by referring to a few examples of Supreme Court decisions in which expulsion was an issue. The intention behind the examples that I have chosen does not lie in proving homogeneity but rather to illustrate how difficult it is to foresee whether a case will result in the issuance of an expulsion or not.

U99.1394 H. Drugs offence. 3rd conviction. Imprisonment for four months. Had been living in Denmark for 23 years. All relatives in Denmark. Not expelled.

---

79 Foreign Right, p 641 ff.

80 Annual Report 2003-2004 from the Director of Public Prosecutions (Rigsadvokatens årsberetning), pp. 193-216.

U2003.56 H. Serious violence. 1st conviction. Imprisonment for four months. Had been living in Denmark a little less than 7 years. Job but no relatives in Denmark. Expelled for five years.

U2000.546 H. Drugs offence. Previously sentenced to six years imprisonment in 1985. Imprisonment for five months. Had been living in Denmark for 21 years. Divorced. Was living with his mother in Denmark. Expelled for five years.

U2004.2772 H. Serious violence. 1st conviction. Imprisonment for five months. Had been living in Denmark a little less than 8 years. Some relatives in Denmark. Not expelled.

2.10 Aftercare – and Probation

The general release and after care procedure is common for everybody who is released from prison and is described above (section 2.9). Furthermore, a few additional projects for the reintegration of foreigners have been implemented in the last few years. They are mentioned in section 2.12 below.

2.11 Staff

Roughly 70 % of the budget of the Department of Prisons and Probation is spent on wages.[81] Including housing, security, occupation and so on, a cell in an open prison costs about half as much as a cell in a closed prison. The daily costs of a cell in an open prison lies at roughly 820 Dkr, while a cell in a closed institution is 1.640 Dkr. The prison guards undoubtedly constitute the largest group of staff and employees in the prisons and prison administration – 2.950 of the 4.400 prison staff members are prison guards. 650 to 700 people are engaged in management and administration. The remaining roughly 1000 persons are social workers, teachers, nurses or other specialists such as for instance psychiatrists, priests, imams or the like.[82] It takes a person three years to become a trained prison guard. The largest share of the training period is practical and takes place within the prisons. Theoretical education is concentrated in a period of 26 weeks, where knowledge of society, psychology, conflict resolution and self defence are trained.

It is a fact that the proportions of foreigners among prisoners and prison staff are unequal. Altogether 15 % of the clients in the prison and probation services (23 % of the imprisoned clients, 12 % of the clients in the probation service) are of foreign background, whereas in the third quarter of 2004 1% of the staff in the prison and probation service had a foreign background. But as it is a part of the official policy to try to secure a broad representation in terms of age, gender and ethnic background among prison staff efforts have been made to recruit more guards with a background other than Danish. Firstly, special courses for foreigners aspiring to start the ordinary education for prison guards have been offered from 2000 to 2004. Out of 38 pupils in these courses 32 went through the total program, 16 passed the tests successfully and in April 2005 six of them were still appointed to the prison system. Secondly, a preparatory school (introductory

81 http://www.kriminalforsorgen.dk. 1 Euro=7,5 Dkr.

82 http://www.kriminalforsorgen.dk

course) for foreign aspirants was opened in 2006. The first group of ten persons who passed the preparatory school consisted of one woman and nine men from Pakistan, Turkey, Serbia and Lebanon.[83] Furthermore, a small number of special days and five-day courses are arranged in the ordinary education for prison staff. This applies both to ordinary basic training as well as to senior training. It is not explicitly described what the aim and content of these courses are. In the light of their extension the ambition cannot be to teach languages to the staff but rather to present some basic cultural and maybe religious background.

The trainees receive a modest salary during the education period. The average yearly wages that a skilled prison guard receives is equivalent to that of "other guards", for example car park attendants, and lies at about 270.000 Dkr, but is lower than the average salary of for instance police officers, who earn about 356.000 Dkr per year.[84]

2.12 Projects[85]

In the year 2000 a mentor programme was introduced for released young foreign prisoners. A mentor is an external adult who is not part of the authoritative system but who does cooperate with it and whose task it is to support the released person during the final stages of the prison sentence and the initial period of time after having been release. The programme has been evaluated by a Danish University and in 2004 it was the winner of the "International Community Justice Award" in the category of the "Social Inclusion Award". The prize is given by the English National Probation Service.

The state prison of Ringe (which accommodates female prisoners and young male prisoners) introduced a possibility for foreign prisoners with a Muslim background to spend evenings of study and debate with an Imam and a researcher. The experiment shows that in spite of coming from different home countries many ethnic prisoners share common experiences about being born into the culture and lifestyle of another country. Starting with a sentence from the Koran the group discusses both religious and practical everyday issues.[86]

The Probation Service has one consultant for the reintegration of ethnic minorities into the society. The tasks of this person are to try to establish contact between labour-market representatives and foreigners being released as well as to assist the education of the staff.

During 2006 and 2007 the state prisons in Nyborg and Horsens plan to establish special units for foreigners who were gang members. The inmates in these units shall attend more intensive education on Danish culture and the unit staff shall receive support from a representative of the department.[87]

---

83 www.kriminalforsorgen.dk/publikationer/rapporterogundersøgelser/Undersøgelse og anbefalinger vedrørende etniske minoriteter i kriminalforsorgen 2005.

84 http://www.oes-cs.dk/PUBLIKATIONER/LSTATISTIK/2005/

85 On projects for staff see section 2.11 above.

86 Nyt fra Kriminalforsorgen , December 2005, p 18-19. (News from the Prison and Probation Service, December 2005, pp. 18-19).

87 Information received from a prison director personally.

3 ADMINISTRATIVE DETENTION OF FOREIGN PRISONERS

3.1 Institution

As mentioned in the introduction any deprivation of liberty needs to be explicitly legalised. Further, the deprivation of a person's liberty is never an obligatory mean. The principles of proportionality between mean and aim must be kept in mind both by the courts and the administrative decision makers.

3.2 Ministry Responsible & Legislation

The competent superior authority in relation to the asylum centres is the Ministry for Refugees, Immigrants and Integration, which is often simply called the Ministry of Integration. According to the specialization within the Ministry a Foreigners' Service is taking care of most of the questions in relation to the asylum centres and the asylum seekers. When a foreigner is confined by force he/she is under the authority of the Department of Prisons and Probation.

The legal possibilities of depriving a foreigner of his liberty are mentioned exhaustively in section 36 of the Code on Foreigners.[88] But of course the police (the responsible authority) are left with a wide scope of discretion. The largest share of this group are asylum seekers who have no address in Denmark and who are in a situation where the police find it necessary to detain them in order to be able to lead them out of the country as soon as all necessary formalities have been achieved.. See more about the legality and legal control in section 3.5 below.

3.3 Capacity Institutions

In February 2006 there were a total number of ten asylum centres, eight of which are run by the Danish Red Cross. The other two institutions are run by local municipalities. At the same time, 2.479 individuals were located in the centres. The biggest and most famous asylum centre in Sandholm houses not only persons seeking asylum but also constantly about 70-100 foreign persons (mainly asylum seekers) who are confined on the basis of an administrative (police) decision (see section 3.2 above and section 3.5 below).

3.4 Length of Stay

The average time that a person spends in an asylum centre is 1000 days. This has increased from 300 to 1000 within a short time. The situation in the centres is described as very tense by politicians, the media and the director of the Red Cross. Among experts it is a wide spread opinion that the longer a stay in a centre is the more traumatic the experience. Not least the children are suffering from the lack of normal socialisation, and first and foremost from the lack of proper possibilities to frequent schools. An illustration of the tension is the number of (attempted) suicides which has been increasing the latest

[88] Code on Foreigners, no 826 of 24 August 2005.

years. In the year 2001 seven attempts were registered per 1000 residents over the age of 17. Four years later in 2005 the figure had increased to 15 per 1000.[89]

3.5 Decisions procedure

Under certain circumstances, foreigners may be denied entry to Denmark at the border by the police (section 48, Code on Foreigners). If the foreigner claims to be seeking asylum the competence is transferred to the Ministry mentioned above in section 3.2. It is common that persons who are seeking asylum or residence permits and are waiting for a decision to be made stay in one of the ten asylum centres.[90] If the person has another place to stay (for instance with relatives) – and there is no legal justification to detain him/her – he/she may stay there.

Detention for the purpose of ensuring a person's presence for the time when an expulsion is to be executed (pursuant to article 36) must be brought before a local court within 72 hours from the moment when the person is locked up. If the court accepts the legality of the deprivation of liberty a time limit must be fixed. This time limit may be extended as many times as the court deems necessary for up to four weeks each time. The foreigner must be provided with a defence counsel. The police are obliged to inform the foreigner about his rights, including the right to unlimited contact with diplomatic representatives of his home country. [91]

All of the legal reasons for the administrative detention of a foreigner are related to the actual execution of the expulsion, refusal of admission, transfer or other means of removing the person from Denmark. The main idea of the rules is that a foreigner can be detained if he/she does not cooperate with the authorities who are treating his/her case and if other restrictions of his/her behaviour do not fulfil the need. The legal definition of not cooperating with the authorities consists for instance of withholding information, not appearing when the authorities summon him/her for interviews etc. Furthermore, a released prisoner, who is sentenced to be expelled, will most typically be detained in the closed unit in Sandholm until his/her expulsion can be executed.[92] According to section 36 subsection 1 of the Code on Foreigners, a foreigner who has a permanent address in Denmark may only be detained if he/she poses a threat to national security. As mentioned above, a foreigner who is under the suspicion of or who is convicted for having committed a crime is treated in accordance with the general rules of criminal investigation and procedure. But as a supplement to these rules the Code on Foreigners stipulates more possibilities for taking a foreign suspect into custody. The intention behind section 35 is to secure the possibility of retaining a foreigner until his conviction is final if there is a possibility that the conviction will include expulsion, the foreigner has no permanent address and there are firm reasons to believe that he/she might abscond before the expulsion can be executed.

---

89 http://nyhederne.tv2.dk

90 http://www.udlst.dk/asyl

91 Code on Foreigners section 37.

92 This information is given via telephone by the Department of Prisons and Probation and seems to be part of a not all that clear rule in the Code on Foreigners section 25b.

3.6 Appeal Procedure

Decisions on refusal of entry to Denmark or expulsion may be executed immediately. If the foreigner/asylum seeker wishes to contest the decision, an appeal may be lodged with the Minister of Integration. However, such an appeal has no delaying effects on an expulsion order and does not make it possible for the foreigner to enter the country again. Up to now it has not happened that an appealed expulsion was changed in favour of the foreigner/asylum seeker.[93]

3.7 Irregular stay

Without a valid visa or residence permit, in principle a foreigner has no right to stay in the country and should leave. However, he/she may be granted so-called procedural residence as long as his/her case is being addressed by the authorities, in which case his stay is not illegal or irregular. If the application is turned down the foreigner has to leave the country within a fixed time-limit whereafter his residence in the country is illegal and he may be expelled by the use of police force. Under certain circumstances, namely most typically if the foreigner is in danger of being victimised in the country to which he/she is to be expelled, he may stay in Denmark in accordance with section 31 of the Code on Foreigners. The foreigner's residence in Denmark is then tolerated so long as this danger exists.[94] In accordance with section 59 of the Foreign Code and section 125a of the Penal Code it is seen as a crime to cross the border illegally as well as organising illegal border crossing (trafficking). But the fact that a person does not leave the country though ordered to do so by the court is not seen as a crime and may be executed by the help of the relevant authority, in this case the police.

3.8 Numbers

In February 2006 the total number of individuals in the ten Danish asylum centres was 2.479. The number of rejected asylum seekers who do not want or who are unable to leave Denmark is increasing (see section 3.7 above on tolerated residence). In October 2005 this was the case for 1.620 persons, and by April 2006 the number of foreigners who had been refused residence permits but who were still not leaving had increased to 1.940[95]. In reality, this group is not allowed to reside anywhere else but in the asylum centres. If they cooperate with the authorities they can stay in one of the open units and when not, they may be locked up[96]. This of course makes the problems of capacity in the centres even worse. Especially the children are suffering socially, educationally and emotionally from this situation.

93 Foreign Right, pp. 111-112.
94 Foreign Right, pp. 14-15.
95 http://www.dr.dk/P1
96 Code on Foreigners sections 34, subsection 3, 36, subsection 7 and 42a, subsection 8.

3.9 Expulsion

According to section 36 of the Code on Foreigners there is a close connection between the execution of decisions of expulsion and administrative detention. The Danish police are the responsible authority for the execution of all expulsions and at the same time the police are the competent authority to decide whether or not a foreigner should be detained.
In May 2003 the Danish government decided to be more effective in the execution of expulsion once it was formally decided. In other words it was the wish to reduce the number of persons staying in the country after a legal and final decision on expulsion.

According to the police there has been a systematic decrease in the number of asylum seekers who were formally in a position of leaving the country but remained in Denmark nonetheless. From January 2005 to December 2005 the number decreased from 1.928 to 1.468 and by ultimo September 2006 there were 1.252 asylum seekers who were ordered to leave Denmark but who were still present.

In the whole period from January 2005 to September 2006 between 500 and 600 individuals out of the total number of asylum seekers, who were ordered to leave Denmark, were from Iraq. The group from Kosovo is also numerous but it has steadily decreased over the 21 months from 400 in January 2005 to 184 in September 2006. From Afghanistan there were 161 in January 2005 and 20 persons in September 2006. It has not been possible to reduce the number of asylum seekers from Somalia with a final order to leave Denmark. In January 2005 there were 63 individuals in that position and in September 2006 the number had increased to 77. [97]

3.10 Not-expelled prisoners

In principle, a foreign prisoner who is convicted of a crime but who is not expelled serves his/her sentence in accordance with the same rules and practices as everybody else. Decisions on release on parole also occur within the same legal framework. Foreigners can be detained while their application for asylum is being dealt with. If the application is turned down the person in question has to leave Denmark and will most typically be expelled very quickly, if necessary by force (see section 3.7 above). Should asylum be granted the person is released from the closed unit in Sandholm (see section 3.5 above) and transferred to an open section until he can be situated normally.

3.11 Detention irregulars under criminal law

Under certain circumstances irregulars may be taken into custody without being encompassed by the rules on custody in the Code on Legal Procedure. This is a consequence of section 35 of the Code on Foreigners which lays down the following main conditions: custody should be a necessity to secure the person's presence while his case or his appeal is treated or until a conviction to expulsion can be enforced; the foreigner is suspected of having committed an offence which may result in an expulsion; the foreigner is already expelled and has entered the country regardless. The general rules on duration and the

[97] Rigspolitiet, oktober 2006.

prolongation of custody are in force when foreigners are taken into custody under section 35 of the Code on Foreigners.

3.12 Minors

In November 2005, 1.060 children were living in Danish asylum centres. They were either waiting for their family's application for asylum to be approved, for a decision on their appeal against the refusal of asylum, or they were simply waiting for the Danish police to come and take them to the airport. There are examples of children who have been living under this pressure for ten years and more[98]. This situation is very much criticised by different experts, among others a child psychiatrist who claims that Denmark is breaching the UN Convention on Children's Rights by treating children in the asylum centres worse than Danish children in general, who would have been taken into foster homes if they had been living under similar conditions[99]. In 2005 the Danish Red Cross reported to Danish city authorities (councils) about 52 children in the asylum camps who did not thrive well - mentally and/or physically. An extra appropriation of 37 million Dkr to improve living conditions in the asylum centres – mainly those of children – in May 2006 was immediately followed by a reduction in the budget of the same amount[100].

4 NATIONALS DETAINED ABROAD[101]

4.1 Numbers and composition group

In February 2006, 97 Danes – including immigrants to Denmark who have been granted Danish citizenship – were imprisoned abroad. The length of the sentences varied very much from a few months to life sentences.[102]

4.2 Detention countries

Only 23 of the 97 persons, who were imprisoned abroad primo February 2006, were imprisoned in a non-European country. Also, 28 of the 97 Danes, who were imprisoned abroad, were detained in a German Prison. [103]

Further the Foreign Ministry website informed in April 2006 that eight Danes were in penal institutions in America and a small part was distributed around the world, with seven in Asian prisons, four in Africa, and three in the Middle East and finally two in South America.

---

98 In Norway a new rule gave asylum to everybody who had been waiting for the administrative procedure for more than 3 years.
99 http://programmer.tv2.dk/article.php?id=3164437
100 Newsletter from Danish Refugee Council 03/2006.
101 http://www.dr.dk/nyheder
102 Information via telephone from the Foreign Ministry on the 5th of February 2007.
103 Information via telephone from the Foreign Ministry on the 5th of February 2007.

4.3 Reasons for detention & sentencing

More than half the Danes in foreign prisons are detained for drugs offences and they are serving sentences that range from a few months up to life sentences. This also goes for those imprisoned in Germany, which can be seen as the southern entrance to Denmark and with similar restrictions on drugs as Denmark has.

4.4 Involved organisations

The Danish Foreign Ministry states[104] that everybody who is imprisoned in a foreign country has the right to see a representative of the embassy. The latter will offer assistance in finding a defence solicitor as well as in establishing contact with relatives in Denmark. However, Danish embassies do not offer assistance if the imprisoned person is both a citizen of Denmark as well as of the country in which he/she is being detained. The Danish Foreign Ministry is not able to cover the costs of defence, travel or the like for the prisoner or his/her relatives. All forms of financing , for instance of living costs if a person is retained by foreign authorities, must be covered and organised by the person in question. However, support in communication and transfer costs are usually covered by the respective Embassies. This practice applies for criminal cases as well as civil cases.

4.5 Release and reception home country

If a Dane arrives in Denmark after having served the full sentence abroad he/she will normally be free. The only exception is if the crime committed was threatening to the national security of Denmark[105]. If he/she is transferred due to either a convention, a bilateral agreement or a concrete agreement before the time of release, the sentence is to be fulfilled in a Danish prison and in that case in accordance with Danish rules and routines.

4.6 Aftercare

It depends on concrete agreements between the country where the person was imprisoned and Denmark if there will be a period of probation if the prison sentence is served abroad. But if the prisoner is transferred to a Danish prison during the period of imprisonment, he will be released on similar conditions to Danish prisoners.

4.7 Public opinion and media

Danes in foreign prisons is not a very hot issue in the media. It is a wide spread impression that the conditions in foreign prisons are tougher than in the Danish prisons.

---

104 http://www.um.dk/CMS

105 Criminal Code section 6-12.

5 EVALUATION AND RECOMMENDATIONS

Being a minority excluded from societal existence individuals deprived of their liberty are undoubtedly in a vulnerable position. This is the case for Danes as well as foreigners in (foreign and Danish) prisons. The presentation above raises the question whether detention has the same meaning and implications for all who experience it. Basic principles of equality as well as section 4 of the CEP presuppose, however, that prisoners are mainly equally vulnerable. Contrary to this some sections in the CEP define special rules for foreign prisoners (for instance access to embassies). This legislation can only be a token of realisation of the extra vulnerability of foreigners being imprisoned abroad.

The legal differences between national and foreign prisoners are founded on international human rights conventions or basic principles of equality. It may be questioned if equality is achieved to a sufficient degree within the CEP. The practice of religious liberty may be discussed. The right to see a Lutheran priest is obviously of different relevance for Christians, Catholics and Muslims. Resources, traditions as well as capacity of room and staff surely cause limitations for practising religion. Historically there has been no reason to consider religious matters in relation to the prison budgets. Today the choice is between a (relatively) high budget for one religion, or common low budgets for several or all religions of relevance. It is a "hot issue" in the political arena that foreigners do commit crime and do go to prison. But it has not become an issue of similar interest how to offer foreign prisoners religious services.

Apart from those serving in the state prison of Hersted Vester there are no authoritative statistics on prisoners suffering from psychiatric diseases and of course also not on foreign prisoners in need of psychiatric or psychologist assistance. But a report on the occupation of prisoners from the Department of Prisons and Probation which was published 2002[106] states: "A relatively large share of the prisoners has acute or permanent psychiatric problems, which often are expressed in huge problems of behaviour or self-destruction [...] there is a massive need of psychologist treatment in the institutions." There is no reason to believe that foreign prisoners should not be (at least proportionally) represented among those in need of treatment and it should be considered whether problems of language and culture come more into the foreground than in connection with somatic health problems.

Alcoholism and drug-addiction are multifactoral occurrences which demand consideration in the light of somatic and psychiatric/psychological health as well as language, culture, tradition and other "soft" aspects. According to Danish experiences the capacity of and access to alcohol and drug treatment while serving a prison sentence requires much awareness while discussing prisoner equality.

Occupation (work, education, and training/treatment) as well as daily routines like cooking and spare time in the prisons are organised on the basis of the national way of organising daily life, education and production. It is taken for granted that the prisoners are familiar with (or rather an integrated part of) the Danish society and the perspective is to (re)integrate the prisoners into Danish society.[107] The conditions are equal for everybody though everybody is not equally familiar with them nor are they equally motivated

---

[106] Beskæftigelse af indsatte, Kriminalforsorgen, 2002, p. 92. (Occupation of prisoners). My translation.
[107] Beskæftigelse af indsatte, Kriminalforsorgen, 2002, p. 94. (Occupation of prisoners). My translation.

to adapt to the Danish way of working, learning and living because their chances of being released into the Danish society are not equal.

There is no possibility in the prisons to prepare for a future in another country. Foreigners may have their duty to work modified for religious reasons but apart from that the prisons do not offer any program or job that has been created specifically for foreigners. The committee behind the Report on Occupation recommended firstly to find out how many foreign prisoners are going to be expelled after their sentence and secondly to study the experiences from a Swedish prison that runs a special program for prisoners who are to be expelled. The prisoners who are to be expelled do often have long sentences.

Release is seen as the ultimate aim for prisoners but it is also the ultimate challenge for many of them. Prisoners who have to leave the country do often not know what awaits them, and prisoners – foreigners as well as Danes – who are released in Denmark are familiar with some places and people outside the prison but not necessarily the most desirable ones.

In relation to release (on parole) the Criminal Law and the CEP leaves the impression of uniformity but instructions beyond the law in the judicial hierarchy put other perspectives forward. In order to prevent the prisoner from re-offending it is a general requirement for release on parole that the prisoner will have appropriate occupation and housing.[108] There is no exception from this, neither in the law itself nor in the comments or the remarks on it. Nevertheless the instruction on release[109] says in section 39 that when a foreigner who is to be expelled is being released on parole the only condition is a probationary period. Though if the prisoner is from another Nordic country there is a possibility, due to specific Nordic agreements, of asking the Probation Service of his home country to take over the supervision. And the instruction says that if a Nordic prisoner denies co-operating with the Probation Service of his home country, he should not be released on parole.

To put it short: a Danish prisoner, who most typically wants to get out of prison, must be considered for release on parole after 2/3 of the sentence but may be forced to serve it in full for some (more or less well) defined reasons. Whereas a foreigner who has to leave the country permanently (and more typically even prefers to stay in prison), will be forced to the leave the prison and the country after at least 7/12 and no later than 2/3 of the prison term have passed. Since 2003 foreign prisoners who are to be expelled indefinitely may be (forcedly) released after ½ of the time. This decision was part of authoritative efforts to use the prison places more efficiently.[110] About release and expulsion it is even more contradictory that after having been forcedly released from prison the person may be forced to spend some time in one of the overcrowded asylum centres or in some cases even in custody until the expulsion can be executed. Expulsion is decided by the courts – not the prisons. Supreme Court practice does not raise doubt about the formal legality of the expulsions. However, nobody will deny that official and popular attitudes towards foreigners in Denmark has become more negative in recent years, and many experts and engaged professionals claim that not only the tone but also practice have become harsher.

108 Criminal Law section 38, subsection 5.

109 Instruction no 29 of 19 April 2006.

110 Engbo, p. 358. The Ministry of Justice estimated that this change would free 10-15 prison places per year.

Overrepresentation of foreigners in the penal system may prove that foreigners tend to commit more crimes than Danes. But criminologist experience shows that some social factors do correspond with the crime level and if the figures on foreigners are corrected for some of the well known factors the degree of overrepresentation tends to decrease. Without correction the overrepresentation is 49 % but corrected for age and socio-economic background it falls to 8 %. The major part of the overrepresentation of foreigners within the penal system relates to violations of the Penal Code, mainly theft (178 % overrepresentation), whereas rape (110 %) and violence (130 %) – which attract more media attention – both have a lower degree of overrepresentation. Two thirds of all penal dispositions are related to breaches of the Traffic Code. Here the overrepresentation of foreigners is 8 %. The description above may leave an impression of an intolerant police, intolerant prisons or even an intolerant society, but conclusions should not be drawn too early.

In some prisons great efforts are made to create humane and tolerable conditions. A few examples are the newly published research on practising religion in the prisons, which concludes that Danish prisons are open and tolerant towards religion; one prison has introduced visits by an imam and a researcher with the intention to study and debate issues on specific importance for Muslims; the Department of Prisons and Probation has introduced a mentor programme for young foreign prisoners who are released. The impression is far from unambiguous: on the one hand attempts are made to secure humanity and equality while on the other hand equal rules do not automatically secure equal living conditions or even equal chances for everybody.

It is documented in this article that in important issues like preparation for the labour market and drug-addiction-treatment equality between Danish and foreign prisoners has not yet been established. Attention is also paid to pre-time release from prison. It is argued that from an equality point of view there are evident discrepancies between foreigners who are expelled and Danish prisoners. Danes cannot obtain pre-time release without housing and adequate occupation whereas expelled foreigners cannot avoid pre-time release after 2/3 time (often already after ½ of their sentence). These rules are laid down in the law and cannot be changed by the prisons.

Finally we must conclude that while the borders are opened for some of the inhabitants of the world other inhabitants are not welcomed warmly. The problem is not (always) that they have ever hurt the Danish society but that they started the travel from the wrong place and very often were in a situation where they could hardly afford the ticket. The debate on foreigners is strong in Denmark and divides the population markedly. It is worthwhile to remark that while the government and its supporting party stick to a restrictive course, large shares of the population as well as local politicians find that the enough is enough.

Chapter 7

Estonia

Piret Liba

1. INTRODUCTION

1.1 Overview of penalties and measures

According to the Estonian Penal Code, offences are categorized into criminal offences and misdemeanours.[1] A misdemeanour is an offence for which the principal punishment prescribes a fine or detention. For a misdemeanour, a court may impose detention for a term of up to thirty days. An imposed fine could also be substituted by detention, if an offender fails to pay it. Ten fine units (600 EEK/ 40 EUR) correspond to one day of detention. In the case of substitution of a fine by detention, the minimum term of detention shall be one day. A criminal offence is an offence for which the principal punishment prescribes a pecuniary punishment or imprisonment in the case of natural persons and a pecuniary punishment or compulsory dissolution in the case of legal persons. A criminal offence in the first degree is an offence for which the maximum punishment is prescribed which is imprisonment for a term of more than five years, life imprisonment or compulsory dissolution. A criminal offence in the second degree is an offence for which imprisonment for a term of up to five years or a pecuniary punishment can be imposed. For a criminal offence, the court may impose imprisonment for a term of thirty days to twenty years, or life imprisonment. Imprisonment for a term of more than ten years or life imprisonment will not be imposed on a person who, at the time of commission of the criminal offence, is less than 18 years of age.

If a convicted offender fails to pay the amount of the pecuniary punishment imposed on him or her, the court shall substitute the punishment by imprisonment or, with the consent of the convicted offender, by community service. Three daily rates (not less than 150 EEK/ 10 EUR) of a pecuniary punishment correspond to one day of imprisonment. In the case of substitution of a pecuniary punishment by imprisonment, the minimum term of the imprisonment shall be ten days.

One principal punishment and one or several supplementary punishments may be imposed for one offence. Supplementary punishments for criminal offences imposed on natural persons are:

- occupational ban;
- deprivation of driving privileges;
- deprivation of the right to hold weapons or ammunition;
- deprivation of hunting or fishing rights;
- a fine to the extent of assets;
- expulsion.

If a court convicts a citizen from a foreign state of a criminal offence in the first degree and imposes imprisonment, the court may impose expulsion on the convicted offender with a ten year prohibition of entry as a supplementary punishment. If the spouse or a minor child of the convicted person lives with him or her in the same family in Estonia on a legal basis, the court shall provide in its judgment reasons for an imposition of expulsion. Expulsion shall not be imposed on a convicted citizen of a foreign state who, at the time of commission of the criminal offence, was less than 18 years of age.

---

1 Penal Code.

According to the Penal Code a punishment can either be substituted by community service or be suspended. If a court imposes imprisonment of up to two years, the court may substitute the imprisonment by community service. One day of imprisonment corresponds to two hours of community service. Imprisonment shall be substituted by community service only with the consent of the convicted offender. The duration of community service shall not exceed eight hours a day. If an offender performs community service during the free time from his or her other work or studies, the duration of community service shall not exceed four hours a day. A convicted offender shall not be remunerated for community service. The term for the performance of the service shall not exceed twenty-four months. If a convicted offender evades community service, fails to comply with supervisory requirements or to perform the obligations imposed on him or her, the court may, on the basis of a report prepared by the probation officer, enforce the imprisonment initially imposed on the convicted offender. In the case of execution of the imprisonment, the sentence shall be deemed to be served to the extent of the community service, whereas two hours of community service correspond to one day of imprisonment.

If a court – taking into consideration the circumstances relating to the commission of a criminal offence and the personality of the offender – finds that service of the imprisonment imposed for a specified term or payment of the amount of the pecuniary punishment by the convicted offender is unreasonable, the court may order suspension of the sentence on probation. In such case, the court shall order that the imprisonment imposed shall not be enforced in full or in part if the convicted offender does not commit a new intentional criminal offence within the period of probation determined by the court and complies with the supervisory requirements and obligations imposed on him or her for the term of supervision of conduct. If the court decides that an imposed imprisonment is partially not enforced, the court shall determine the part of the imprisonment to be borne immediately and such part of the imprisonment which is suspended on probation. Probation shall be ordered for a period of three to five years. In case a convicted offender has been subjected to supervision of conduct, probation shall be imposed for a period of eighteen months to three years.

Besides principal and supplementary punishments there are some other sanctions, for instance confiscation, coercive psychiatric treatment and sanctions applicable to minors. The court shall order coercive psychiatric treatment of the person:

- if at the time of commission of an unlawful act the person lacks capacity or if he or she becomes mentally ill or feeble-minded or suffers from any other severe mental disorder, after the making of the court judgment but before the service of the full sentence;
- if it is established during preliminary investigation or the court hearing of the matter that the person suffers from one of the aforementioned conditions and therefore his or her mental state at the time of commission of the unlawful act cannot be ascertained and he or she poses a danger to himself or herself and to the society due to his or her unlawful act and mental state and is in need of treatment,

The coercive psychiatric treatment shall be provided by a psychiatric institution which is issued with a corresponding licence. Coercive psychiatric treatment will be applied until the person recovers or ceases to pose a threat. Termination of treatment will be ordered by the court. If a punishment is imposed on a person after coercive psychiatric treatment, the period of treatment will be included in the term of the punishment. One day of treatment corresponds to one day of imprisonment.

Taking into account the level of the moral and mental development of a person between 14 and 18 years of age and his or her ability to understand the unlawfulness of his or her act or to act according to such understanding, the court may release the person from punishment and impose the following sanctions on him or her:
- admonition;
- subjection to supervision of conduct;
- placement in a youth home;
- placement in a school for pupils who need special treatment due to behavioural problems.

A person under the age of 18 is placed in a youth home or a school for pupils who need special treatment due to behavioural problems for up to two years, taking into consideration the end of the academic year. The court may extend the term of stay in a youth home or a school for pupils who need special treatment due to behavioural problems by up to one year, taking into consideration the end of the academic year.

Detention can also be a preventive measure which is applied with regard to a suspect or an accused or convicted offender which means deprivation of a person of his or her liberty on the basis of a court ruling. A suspect or accused person may be arrested at the request of a Prosecutor's Office and on the basis of an order of a preliminary investigation judge or on the basis of a court ruling if he or she is likely to abscond from the criminal proceeding or continue to commit criminal offences. In pre-trial procedure, a suspect or accused shall not be kept under detention for more than six months.[2]

Provisional custody will be included in the term of a punishment. One day of provisional custody corresponds to one day of imprisonment or three daily rates of a pecuniary punishment. If a person is held in custody in the course of misdemeanour proceedings, this will be included in the term of a punishment. Twenty-four hours of custody corresponds to one day of detention or to ten fine units.

Detention and up to three months imprisonment is to be served at a house of detention on the location of the court that adjudicated on the matter or in the residence of a detained person.[3] Custody pending trial shall be served in wards prescribed for pre-trial detention in maximum-security prisons or in houses of detention. Imprisonment is applied in maximum-security or open prisons. A maximum-security prison is a prison with a guarded wall or other barrier which enables the constant supervision of prisoners. An open prison is a prison with a territory marked by clearly visible signs. A house of detention is a part of police prefecture within the area of administration of the Ministry of Internal Affairs.[4] A prison is a government agency in the area of government of the Ministry of Justice.

As of 4 April 2006 there were 4,803 detained persons in a house of detention and prisons. There were 4,397 persons held in custody in closed prisons - 3374 convicted prisoners and 1023 pre-trial prisoners – and 55 in open prison departments. In Estonia there is one prison for women with 159 prisoners (04.04.06) and one prison for juveniles

2 Code of Criminal Procedure.

3 Imprisonment Act.

4 Police Act.

with 103 prisoners (04.04.06). There are 33 prisoners serving life imprisonment in maximum-security prisons. The coercive psychiatric treatment is provided by a psychiatric institution which has been issued a corresponding licence. There is one hospital (Viljandi Hospital) in Estonia with a special department for coercive psychiatric treatment, with a capacity of 71 places.

In order to complete expulsion, the person to be expelled can be placed in an expulsion centre until his or her expulsion has been executed, but for no longer than two months, this at the request of the governmental authority who is applying and enforcing the expulsion of the foreigner and on the basis of a judgment of an administrative court judge. When a person is to be expelled and is to be placed in an expulsion centre, he or she may be detained in a police detention house for up to thirty days instead of an expulsion centre. The expulsion centre works under the administration of the Ministry of Internal Affairs. In 2005 31 persons were placed in the expulsion centre.

1.2 Overview of the Prison System

1.2.1 Organisational Structure of the Estonian Prison System

A prison is a government agency in the area of government of the Ministry of Justice, its task being the implementation of custodial sentences and pre-trial imprisonment.[5] The Prisons Department is the administrative management unit of the prison system the main task of which is the work arrangement, development and supervision of prisons. The department is managed by the deputy secretary general on prisons of the Ministry of Justice and it is sub-divided into three divisions: sentence implementation, social welfare and a legal and development division. In addition, the staff of the department also includes an advisor-head chaplain, a secretary and an assistant to the deputy secretary general. There are 21 officials working in the prison department of the Ministry of Justice in Estonia.

5 Imprisonment Act.

Management structure of the prison system as of January 1st, 2006

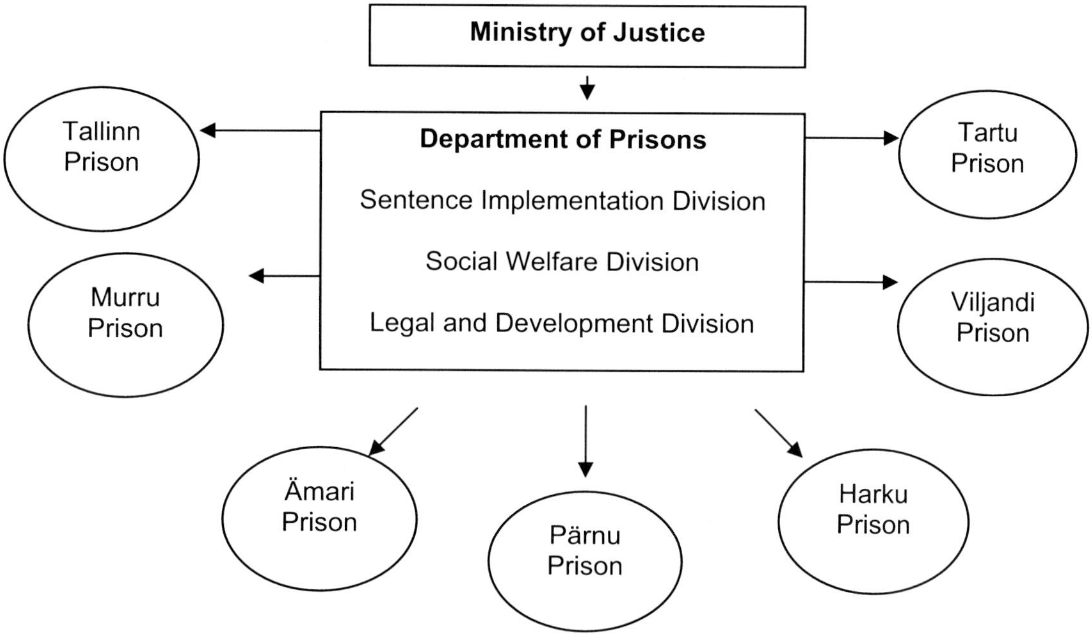

Supervisory control over the prisons is executed by the Minister of Justice. The Minister of Education and Research and the Minister of Social Affairs exercise professional supervision over the performance of duties in the areas of education, social welfare and health care in prisons. Activities of prisons or ministries can also be supervised by the State Audit Office (SAO) as an independent external auditor. The main task of the SAO is to inform Parliament about how money has been spent to achieve any given results. Control can also be performed by the Chancellor of Justice whose main function is to exercise supervision over the constitutionality and legality of legislation passed by the legislative and executive powers and by local governments. The second main function of the Chancellor of Justice is to serve as an ombudsman and to verify whether agencies and officials who perform public functions comply with the constitutional rights and freedoms of persons and the principles of good governance. The agencies whose activities the Chancellor of Justices supervises are the ministries, the boards and inspectorates and their local subordinate bodies, as well as local governments.

The population of Estonia is 1 344 000 (01.01.2006). As of 1 January 2006 there were 4,410 people held in custody in prisons, 3,386 convicted prisoners and 1,024 pre-trial prisoners. There are 328 prisoners per 100 000 inhabitants.

At the moment, there are seven closed prisons and two open prison department in Estonia. Prisons differ in size and groups of persons held in custody:

Prison	*Group of persons held in custody*	*Number of persons*
Harku Prison	Female adult and juvenile convicted prisoners	137 (including 1 juvenile)
Murru Prison	Male adult convicted prisoners, in open prison department	1485 34
Pärnu Prison	Male adult convicted prisoners	100
Tallinn Prison	Male adult pre-trial prisoners, female adult pre-trial prisoners and male adult convicted prisoners	605 44 416
Tartu Prison	Male adult pre-trial prisoners, female adult pre-trial prisoners, juvenile pre-trial prisoners and male adult convicted prisoners	295 27 53 563
Viljandi Prison	Male juvenile convicted prisoners in open prison department	103 8
Ämari Prison	Male adult convicted prisoners	540

According to the Internal Rules of the Prison approved by the Minister of Justice there should be at least 2.5 m^2 per prisoner. Hence the estimated capacity of prisons is 4,499 places: 3,107 places for convicted prisoners and 1,392 places for pre-trial prisoners. Thus the general capacity utilisation of prisons is 99% although facilities for convicted prisoners are overcrowded (with a capacity utilisation of 110%).[6]

In the year 2005 the operation costs of prisons were 20 553 772 euros. Personnel costs constituted the biggest share of the prison budget (66%). The average cost per prisoner per month was 381 euros. To draw a parallel, the average monthly gross wages in the last quarter of 2005 were 555 euros in Estonia.

As of 1 January 2006 there were 2,013 job positions in prisons, of which 1,620 were staffed. Among the prison staff you will find prison officers, public officials and support staff. A public official is a person elected or appointed to the office of the staff of an administrative agency. Support staff are clerical staff employed under employment contracts in support staff positions of the staff of an administrative agency.

According to the Public Service Act, an Estonian citizen who has reached the age of eighteen, who has at least a secondary education and who has an active legal capacity and is proficient in Estonian to the extent provided by or pursuant to law, may be employed in the service of a state or local government official. A citizen of a Member State of the European Union who conforms to the requirements established by law may, on the basis of the law, also be appointed to a position. Only Estonian citizens can be appointed to positions which involve the exercise of public authority and protection of public interest.[7] Prison officers are officials in the prison service who are divided according to the

6 Internal Rules of the Prison.

7 Public Service Act.

complexity of duties, the directing function and scope thereof. This is related to positions which correspond to the given official ranks specified in the following descending order:
- chief inspector of prison;
- class 1 prison inspector;
- class 2 prison inspector;
- class 1 guard;
- class 2 guard.

Persons who comply with the requirements stipulated for public officials and who have undergone a preparatory service for prison officers and who have complied with the obligation of military service, may be appointed to office as prison officers. A prison officer who has undergone preparatory service will be appointed to a position in the lowest official rank which corresponds to his or her preparatory service. Persons who fall within any of the following categories are not admitted to the preparatory service for prison officers or appointed to positions as prison officers:
- persons without active legal capacity or with restricted active legal capacity;
- persons convicted of intentionally committed criminal offences;
- persons who have served imprisonment sentences;
- persons who are suspects, accused or accused at trial in criminal matters or
- persons who are divested of the right to work as prison officers by court judgments entered into force.

Preparatory service for prison officers consists of practical and theoretical professional training. The prison officer candidates undergo preparatory service in prison where the candidates participate in practical training and in an institution of applied higher education for public defence. To become a prison guard, one year of training is required of which at least one half is spent in practical training. To become a prison inspector, three years of training are required in the course of which the person acquires applied higher education.

A person undergoing preparatory service for prison officers is referred to as a prison officer candidate. The latter will be admitted to preparatory service by the executive officer of the educational institution carrying the said service out. A prison officer can be appointed to office by the director of a prison or by an official authorised by the director. A director of a prison shall be appointed to office by the Minister of Justice.

Approximately three quarters of the job positions in the prison system are prison officers (imprisonment, also management). Administration (finances, personnel, and correspondence) takes up 15% of all the positions and social welfare (social workers, psychologists, chaplains) and health care accounts for 10 % of all the job positions in prisons (Figure 1).

Figure 1: Breakdown of job positions on 1 January 2006

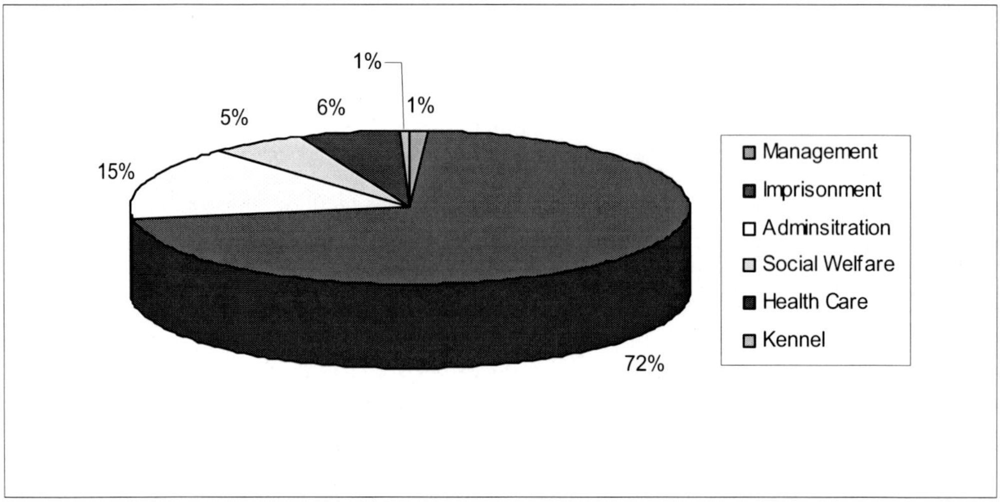

Since the re-establishment of the Estonian prison system (after the Soviet army had left), the number of female prison officers has increased. The former closed military system has become more open and humane. 42 % of all employees are women and 58 % are men. Employees with higher education constitute nearly one-third of the staff. Five percent of employees have a basic education (Figure 2), while more than half of the staff is older than 40 years.

Figure 2. Education of employees on 1 January 2006

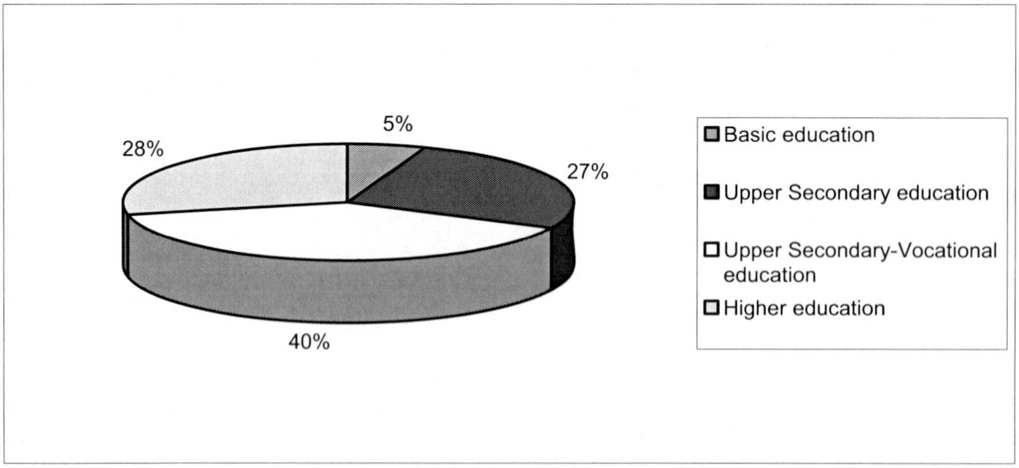

41-50 year-olds constitute the largest age group among employees (31%), followed by 51-60 year-olds (26%) and 31-40 year-olds (21%) (Figure 3).

Figure 3. Age of employees on 1 January 2006

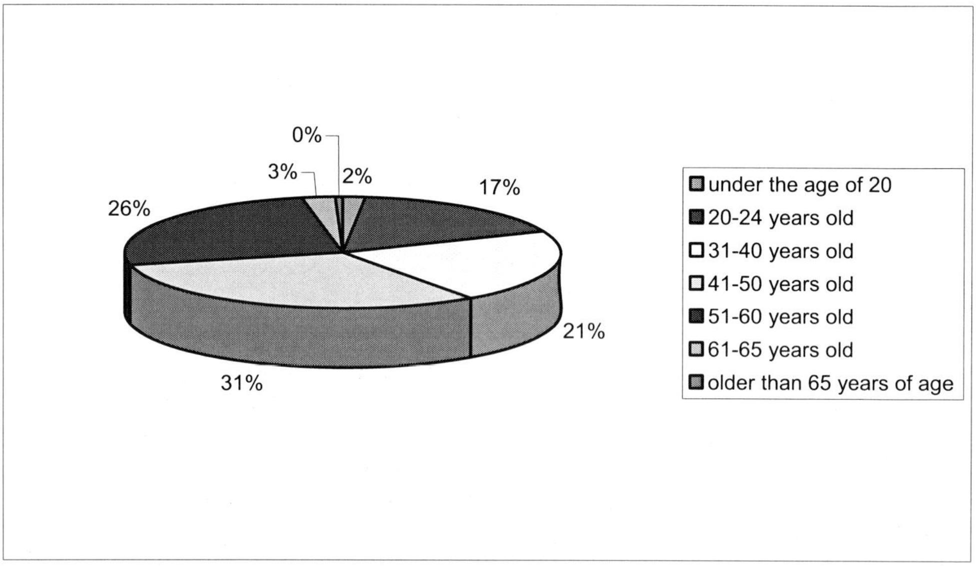

1.2.2 Foreign Prisoners

As of 4 April 2006 there were 1,941 foreigners detained in police houses of detention and prisons, which is 40% of all the detainees held in such institutions. More than half of the prisoners are Russian or other ethnic nationalities from the territory of the former Soviet Union. Thereby most of the Estonian prison population is Russian speaking.

In Estonia foreign prisoners are not kept separately from others. There are no specific institutions for foreign prisoners and no specific section of the prison service is responsible just for foreigners. As a part of preparatory service prison officers are taught about different cultures and their customs, and it is mandatory to learn the Russian and English language.

Most of the foreign prisoners are persons with undefined citizenship, mostly born in Estonia or in Russia or other former Soviet Union countries. According to the Citizenship Act Estonian citizenship is acquired by birth if at least one of the parents of the child holds Estonian citizenship at the time of the birth of the child.[8] Presumptively prisoners with undefined citizenship or their parents hold a citizenship of a country of the former USSR. It is very likely that most of these prisoners with undefined citizenship held in custody in Estonia actually have the right to acquire Russian citizenship by birth.

According to the Citizenship Act of the Russian Federation all citizens of the former Soviet Union who were born in the territory of the Russian Federation since 30 December 1922 and after, had acquired Russian citizenship by birth. According to the order of

8 Citizenship Act.

the Constitutional Court of the Russian Federation from 21 April 2005 the same also applies to their children wherever in the territory of the former Soviet Union they were born.

There are several conditions for the acquisition of Estonian citizenship by naturalisation, among others the requirement for knowledge of the Estonian language and knowledge of the Constitution of the Republic of Estonia and the Citizenship Act. This knowledge is assessed by way of examination which can also be prepared and taken while in prison.

On 1 January 2006 the population of Estonia was 1 344 684.[9] According to the Statistical Office of Estonia the number of ethnical Estonians is 921 908, which constitutes 68,6 % of the total population. The proportion of Estonians is lowest among 40 – 60 year olds and highest among 5 – 15 year olds and persons older than 80. [10] In 1992 almost one third of the Estonian population consisted of foreigners with undefined citizenship i.e. persons who had during the past 50 years arrived from the territory of the former Soviet Union and settled in Estonia. According to the Estonian Citizenship and Migration Board 82% of the Estonian population are Estonian citizens, 10% are with undefined citizenship and eight percent are citizens of other countries. [11] The proportion of foreigners among the prison population (40%) is more than twice as high as in the national population (18%).

1.3 Overview of the involvement of Consulates, Embassies, Ministries and the Probation service, NGO's etc

In Estonia, the organisation of international judicial cooperation has been placed within the competence of the Ministry of Justice. The International Judicial Cooperation Division of the Courts Department is responsible.

International judicial cooperation means proceedings of requests for assistance from judicial authorities (courts, prosecutor's offices) by a competent legal authority in the territory of another country. International agreements allow mutual recognition of court judgements and the performance of procedural acts (delivery of documents, collection of evidence, legalisation of documents issued abroad) as well as the resolution of various legal issues with the help of the public authorities of another country. International judicial cooperation includes both civil and criminal matters. The competence of judicial authorities in international communication depends on the laws of the state and on international agreements (conventions, legal assistance agreements, EU legislation). As a rule, in the framework of an international agreement, one authority is assigned to coordinate the provision of legal assistance. Usually, this is the Ministry of Justice, but depending on the judicial system of the state in question, this function may be performed for example by the public prosecutor's office or other judicial authorities.

International legal assistance includes the performance of several procedural acts, including mutual legal assistance in criminal matters, which lies in the exchange of infor-

---

9 The main Social and Economic Indicators of Estonia. 12/06. /2006).Statistical Office of Estonia. www.stat.ee

10 Tiit, E.-M. (2006). The main indicators of Estonian population in 2005—2006 in the background of Europe. Office of the Minister for Population and Ethnic Affairs, Tartu University, Statistical Office of Estonia.

11 Citizenship and Migration Board Yearbook. (2006). Tallinn. www.mig.ee

mation as well as in the extradition and surrender of people in the framework of criminal proceedings.

Estonia ratified the Convention on the Transfer of Sentenced Persons (ETS 112) on 28 April which into force on 1 August 1997. The Additional Protocol to the Convention on the Transfer of Sentenced Persons came into force on 1 June 2000. The transfer of sentenced prisoners is organised according to the conditions and rules of the convention. Although 41% of the prison population and 39% of all convicted prisoners are foreigners, most of them have undefined citizenship. As of 21 February 2006 there were 201 prisoners with the citizenship of a foreign country, including 174 Russian citizens. As Russia has not ratified the European convention and Estonia does not have a bi-lateral transfer agreement with Russia, no Russians have been transferred. During the last few years Estonia has transferred five Latvians to Latvia and one Finn to Finland.

In 1992 the Estonian Migration Foundation was established by the Estonian government. The Migration Foundation consults and, if necessary, supports migrants financially. The foundation also collects and analyses information about migration and migrants, conducts research on migration, integration and asylum, and organizes events where migration topics are discussed. In the year 2005 the Estonian Migration Foundation supported the remigration of 217 foreigners to their ethnic countries of origin with nearly two million croons, mainly to Russia, Byelorussia and Ukraine. Among the supported migrants there were 33 former Soviet military personnel and their family members, 81 retired persons and 47 unemployed persons. The Migration Foundation also supported the return of 12 Estonians to Estonia with nearly 200,000 croons. In comparison, in 2004 such remigration support was given to 235 persons in amount of 2.4 million croons and with about 400,000 croons the return of 36 Estonians to their homeland was supported. In 2005, the Estonian Migration Foundation also assisted with the expulsion of 12 illegal residents from Estonia.

Financial support from the Foundation is also available for foreign prisoners, but there were only a few cases where such support was used. Many foreign prisoners are not motivated to leave Estonia because they prefer applying for Estonian citizenship or a residence permit.

Regarding the involvement of Embassies and Consulates, it can be noted that there has been some cooperation with representatives from the Russian Federation, Latvia and Lithuania. Their involvement has predominantly been in the areas of providing documents and passports in order to enable their citizens to be able to leave Estonia once they have been released.

1.4 Overview of trends

1.4.1 Sentencing Trends

The official statistics on sentencing and committed criminal offences do not make distinctions according to nationality. Since nearly half of the Estonian prison population are foreigners, the following trends and figures basically apply to both foreign and Estonian prisoners. Over the past ten years, the number of prisoners in Estonia has not changed significantly, ranging from 4,200 – 4,800 per year. There were 3,386 convicted prisoners and 1,024 pre-trial prisoners in Estonian prisons in early 2006. The percentage of pre-trial prisoners among persons held in custody in prisons has decreased during the past ten years from 32% in 1997 to 23% in 2006 (Figure 4).

Figure 4: Number of convicted and pre-trial prisoners in prisons

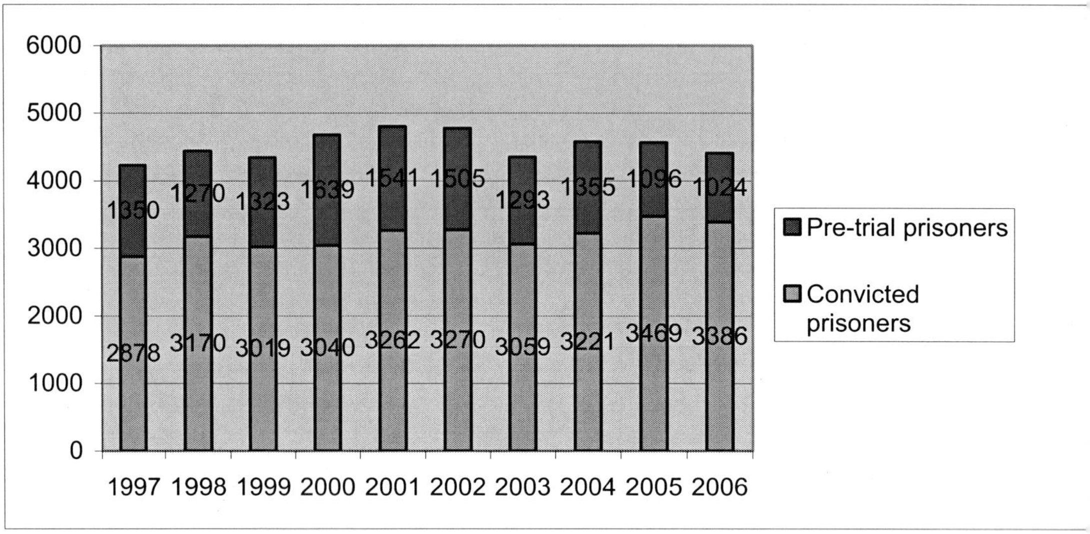

95% of prisoners are adult men, four percent are adult women, and juvenile men account for one percent of all convicted prisoners. Most of the prisoners are relatively young, about half of the convicted prisoners are younger than 30 years, 78% of all convicted prisoners are younger than 40 years. 22 – 29 year olds constitute the most numerous group among prisoners (36%), followed by 30 – 39 year olds (30%) and 40 – 49 year olds (14%) (Figure 5).

Figure 5: Convicted prisoners by age on 1 January 2006

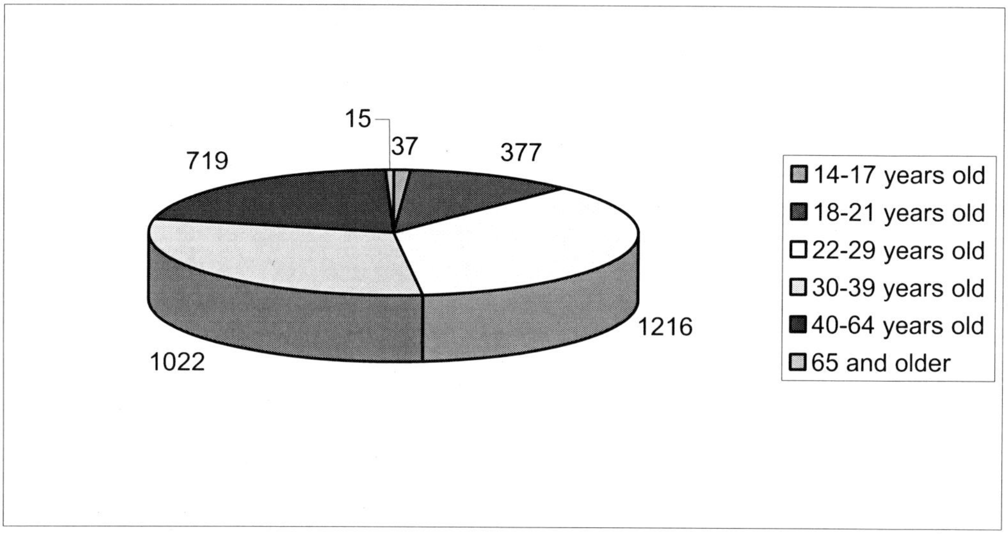

During the period 1991 – 2001 an increase in the percentage of 22 – 30 year olds (42% in 2001) and a decrease in the percentage of 31 – 40 year olds (26% in 2001) could be regarded as the most important change. The age composition of prisoners became somewhat younger in the years 1994 – 2001.[12] During the few last years the percentage of 22 – 29 year olds has decreased and the percentage of 30 – 39 year olds has increased a little but both stayed in the same magnitude during 2004 - 2005.

As of 1 January 2001 persons with a secondary education constituted the largest group among prisoners (43%), followed by persons with a basic education (37%). When looking at the change in the level of education of prisoners during the period 1991 – 2001, we can see a definite decline, a trend that is in fact ongoing. This is particularly evident in the approximate tripling of the number and percentage of persons with the lowest level of education.[13] Still, in 2003 prisoners with secondary education constituted the largest group among the prison population (36%). Currently the largest group are prisoners with basic education (37%), followed by prisoners with secondary education (31%). Approximately one-fifth of the prisoners have primary education or less (19%) (Figure 6). The share of persons in Estonian prisons who have a low level of education is growing.

---

12 Saar, J., Markina, A., Ahven, A. jt. (2002). Crime in Estonia 1991 – 2001. TPÜ Rahvusvaheliste ja Sotsiaaluuringute Instituut; EV Justiitsministeerium.

13 Ibid.

Figure 6. Convicted prisoners by educational background on 1 January 2006

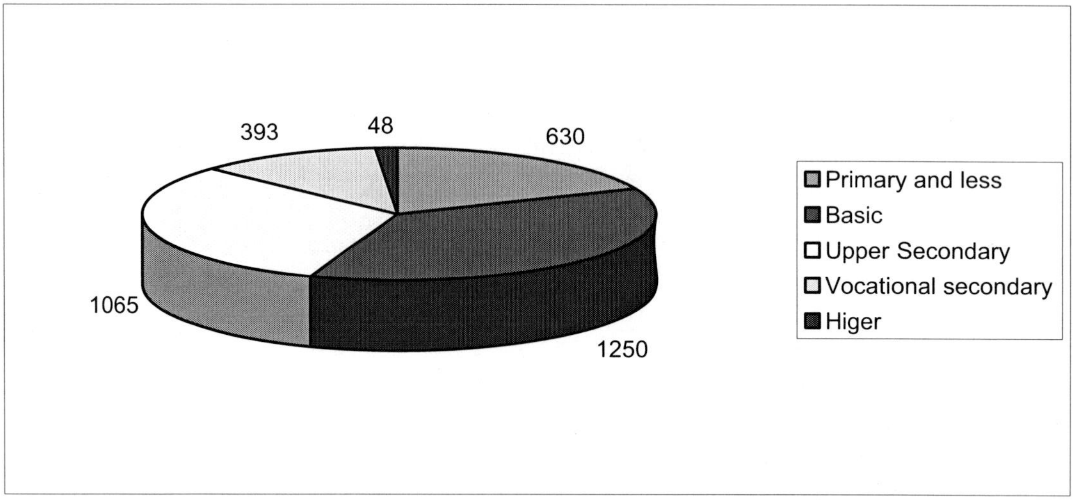

The main type of criminal offences for which prisoners are being punished is property offences (50%). Approximately one-fifth are serving sentences for offences against persons (21%) (Figure 7).

Figure 7: Types of criminal offences for which prisoners are imprisoned 1 January 2006

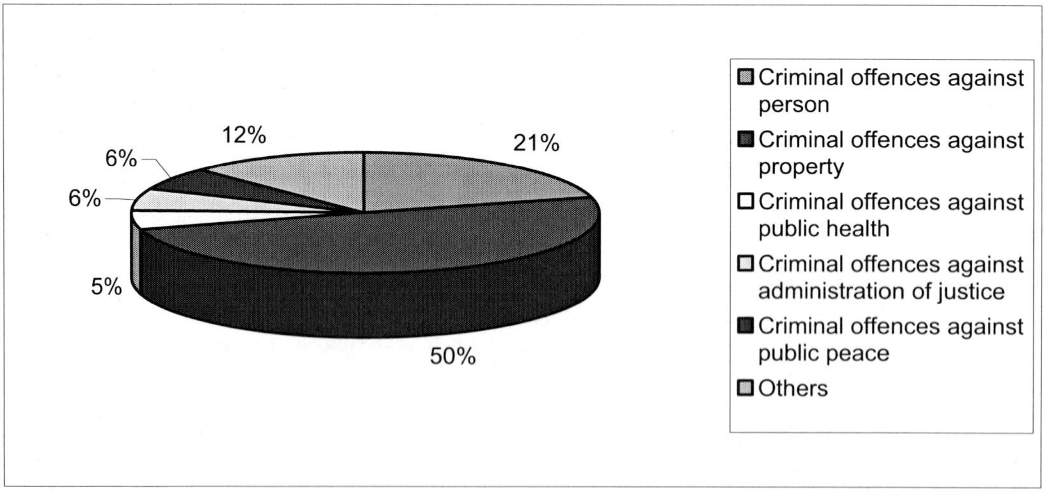

A trend that is apparent in the period from 1991 to 2001 is a decrease of the percentage of offences against property (58% in 1992; 51% in 2001) and an increase in the percentage of offences against persons (23% in 1992; 32% 2001). The percentage of offences against persons was the highest in the mid-1990s (36% in 1994-95).[14] Since 2001 the percentage of such offences has decreased from one-third to one-fifth; at the same time the share of offences against property has stagnated at about half of all offences. Many prisoners serve sentence for both – offence against property and offence against persons. The proportion of prisoners who have committed violent crimes is at 54% (Figure 8).

Figure 8: Breakdown of convicted prisoners by the main offence 1 January 2006

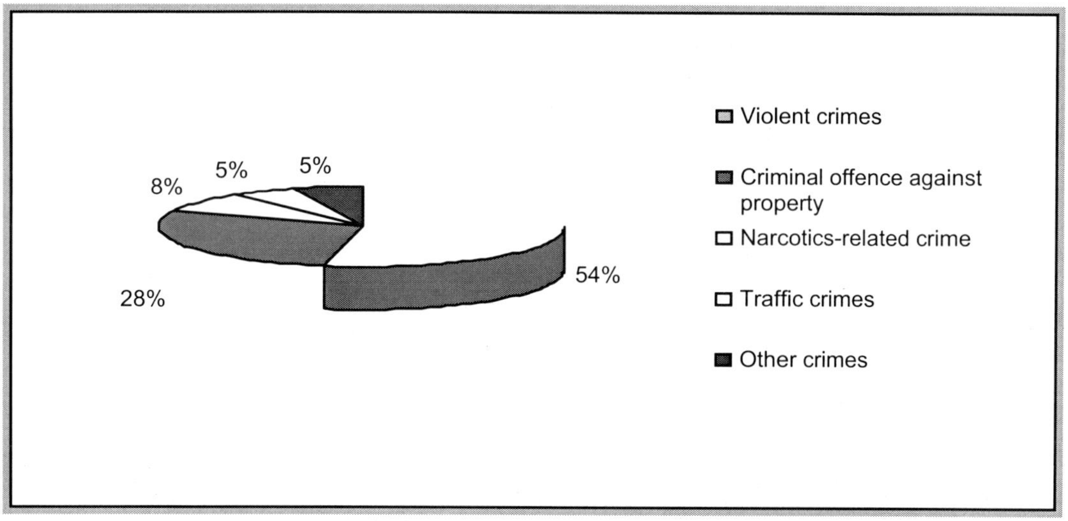

Roughly 50% of the prisoners in Estonia are serving sentences of between one and five years, while approximately one-third have been sentenced to five to ten years in prison. 10% of prisoners have sentences up to one year. There are 33 prisoners serving life sentences, which accounts for roughly one percent of the overall prison population (Figure 9).

[14] Ibid.

Figure 9: Convicted prisoners according to length of sentence on 1 January 2006

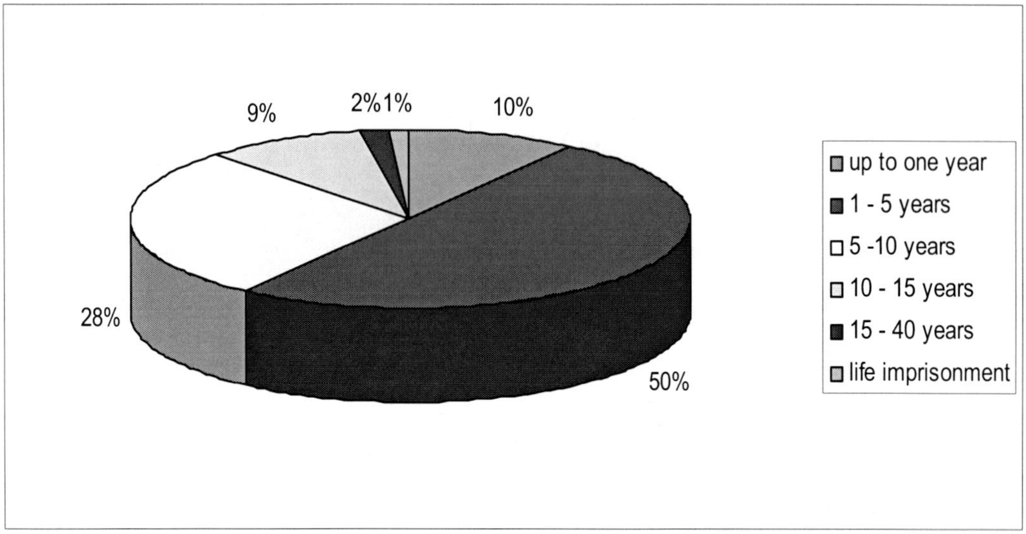

Since 2001 there have been no remarkable changes in the percentage of prisoners who are serving sentences to ten years or more. The share of long term prisoners has been 12% to 14%. From 2001 to 2006, the proportion of prisoners serving short prison terms of up to one year has doubled from five to ten percent. Over the same period, the percentage of prisoners serving sentences with the length one to five years has increased from 43% in 2001 to 50% in 2006. Also, there has been a ten percent decrease in the proportion of prisoners who are to serve five to ten years, from 38% in 2001 to 28% in 2006. These developments are in line with an ongoing trend supported by state criminal policy to shorten the length of sentences.

1.4.2 Characteristics of the Foreign Prison Population

45% of all prisoners are Estonians; more than half of the prisoners are Russian speaking (Russians and other ethnic nationalities from the territory of the former Soviet Union) (Figure 10). Already in 1992 there were fewer Estonians than non-Estonians in prisons and Estonians have been a minority among prisoners throughout the whole period of re-independence.

Figure 10: Breakdown of convicted prisoners according to nationality on 1 January 2006

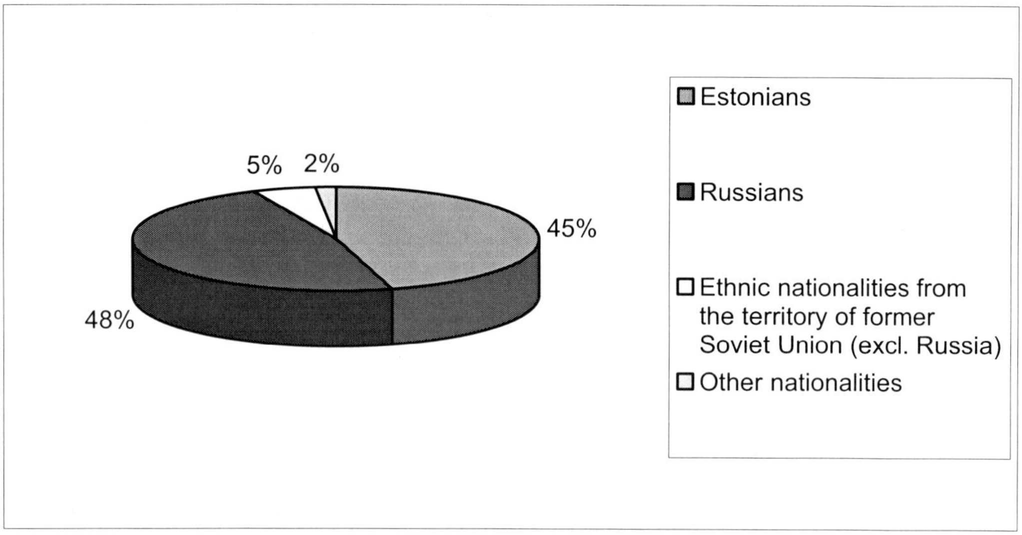

When considering the citizenship of prisoners, until 1999 the percentage of persons without citizenship was the highest (66% in 1999). The number of persons with Estonian citizenship has increased very quickly since then. As of 1 January 2006, Estonian citizens already constituted 61% of the prison population (31% in 1999) (Figure 11).

Figure 11: Convicted prisoners by citizenship

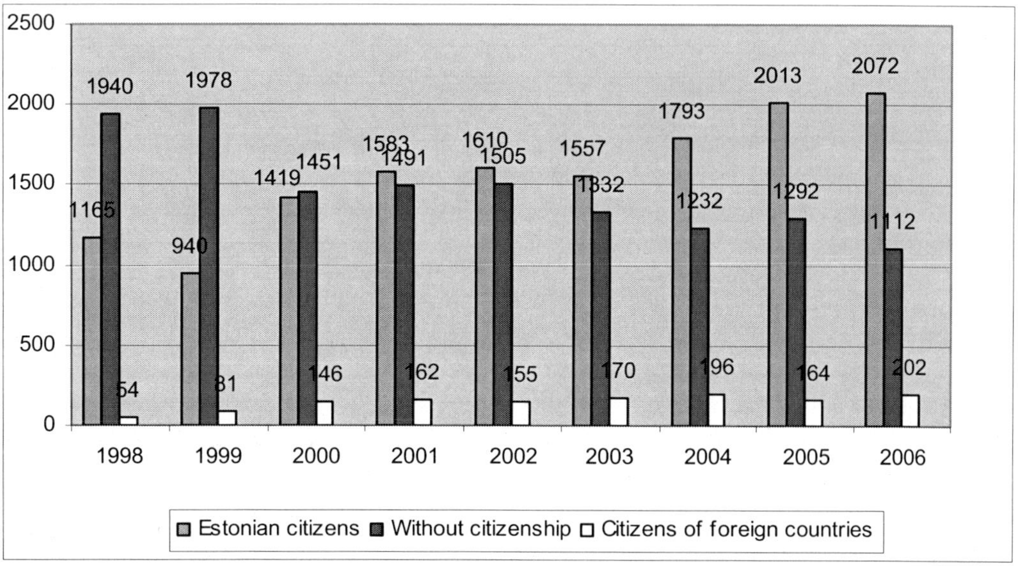

According to the database of persons held in custody as of 21 February 2006 there are 2,624 Estonian citizens (59%) and 1,823 foreign prisoners (41%) in Estonian prisons:

	Pre-trial prisoners (1,057)	Convicted prisoners (3,390)
Estonian citizens	561 (53% of pre-trial prisoners)	2,063 (61% of convicted prisoners)
Foreign prisoners	496 (47% of pre-trial prisoners)	1,327 (39% of convicted prisoners)
Including prisoners with undefined citizen-ship	417	1,126

Prisoners with undefined citizenship constitute 85% of all foreigners held in custody in prisons:

Citizenship of foreign prisoners	Pre-trial prisoners (496)	Convicted prisoners (1,327)
Azerbaijan	1	1
Dominican Republic	0	1
Israel	2	0
Canada	1	0
Lithuania	1	7
Latvia	6	12
Moldova	0	1
Nigeria	0	1
Peru	1	0
Germany	1	0
Finland	1	0
Turkey	1	0
Ukraine	3	3
Byelorussia	0	1
Russia	57	174
Undefined	417	1,126
No data	4	0

79% of prisoners with undefined citizenship were born in Estonia, 13% in Russia, seven percent in other former Soviet Union countries and one percent in other Baltic States:

Place of birth of prisoners with undefined citizenship	Pre-trial prisoners (417)	Convicted prisoners (1,126)
Armenia	1	1
Azerbaijan	4	6
Estonia	333	883
Georgia	1	1
Kazakhstan	6	6

Place of birth of prisoners with undefined citizenship	Pre-trial prisoners (417)	Convicted prisoners (1,126)
Kyrgyzstan	1	2
Lithuania		2
Latvia	6	11
Moldova	2	1
Mongolia		1
Germany		1
Tajikistan	1	
Czech		1
Turkmenistan		1
Ukraine	8	38
Uzbekistan		4
Byelorussia	6	14
Russia	48	146
No data		7

89% of prisoners with undefined citizenship who are born in Estonia are ethnic Russians; five percent are other ethnics of former Soviet Union; one percent is Finns and a further percent is gypsies. In the future there is the intention to decrease the number of persons with undefined citizenship. It is very likely that most prisoners with undefined citizenship held in custody in Estonia are actually entitled to Russian citizenship by birth.

1.5 Overview of national legislation

1.5.1 Penitentiary Legislation

The Penal Code defines and provides offences and the punishments that can be imposed in response to criminal behaviour. The Code of Criminal Procedure provides the rules and provisions for the pre-trial procedure and court procedure for criminal offences as well as the procedures for the enforcement of decisions made in criminal matters. The procedures for and organisation of the execution of imprisonment, detention and pre-trial custody as well as the definition and conditions of the prison service are provided in the Imprisonment Act.

1.5.2 Penitentiary Legislation relevant to Foreigners

Generally there are no differences between citizens and foreigners in terms of the punishments to which they can be sentenced, but there are two exceptions:

- according to § 54 of the Penal Code, if a court convicts a citizen of a foreign state of a criminal offence in the first degree and imposes imprisonment, the court may impose expulsion with a prohibition to enter Estonia for ten years as a supplementary punishment on the convicted offender;
- according to § 260 of the Penal Code a foreigner who is caught residing in Estonia without a legal basis at least twice within one year shall receive a pecuniary punishment or be sentenced to up to one year of imprisonment.

Currently, there is only one convicted prisoner in prison who has been punished according to § 54, and none according to § 260.

According to § 416 of the Code of Criminal Procedure a judge in charge of execution of court judgments may rule to waive the enforcement of a sentence to imprisonment for a specified term if the convicted offender is extradited to a foreign state or is expelled. Also, the responsible judge may enforce a sentence of imprisonment for a specified term if the convicted offender who has been extradited or expelled returns to Estonia earlier than ten years after his or her extradition or expulsion.

According to § 75 of the Imprisonment Act, a prisoner who is a foreigner and who has no residence permit shall be expelled from Estonia upon release. If immediate expulsion from Estonia is not possible, the foreigner shall be placed in an expulsion centre upon release.

The Citizenship Act provides procedures for the acquisition, resumption and loss of Estonian citizenship. According to § 21, Estonian citizenship shall not be granted to or resumed by a person who among other things:
- does not observe the constitutional order and Acts of Estonia;
- has acted against the Estonian state and its security;
- has committed a criminal offence for which a punishment of imprisonment of more than one year was imposed and whose criminal record has not expired or who has been repeatedly punished under criminal procedure for intentionally committed criminal offences.

The Foreigners Act regulates the entry of foreigners into Estonia, their stay, residence and employment in the country and the bases for legal liability of foreigners. For the purposes of this Act, a foreigner is a person who is not an Estonian citizen. § 5 stipulates rights and duties of foreigners:
- foreigners staying in Estonia are guaranteed rights and freedoms equal to those of Estonian citizens unless the Constitution, this Act, other Acts or international agreements of Estonia state otherwise;
- foreigners are guaranteed the rights and freedoms arising from the generally recognised rules of international law and international custom;
- foreigners staying in Estonia are required to observe the constitutional order and legislation of Estonia.

According to § 12, a residence permit shall not be issued to or extended for a foreigner if among other criteria:
- he or she does not observe the constitutional order and laws of Estonia;
- he or she has committed a criminal offence for which he or she has been sentenced to imprisonment for a term of more than one year and his or her criminal record has neither expired nor been expunged, or the information concerning the punishment has not been expunged from the punishment register;
- he or she has been repeatedly punished pursuant to criminal procedure for an intentionally committed criminal offence;
- there is information indicating or good reason to believe that he or she belongs to a criminal organisation, that he or she is connected to the illegal trafficking of narcotics, psychotropic substances or persons across the border, that he or she is a member of a

terrorist organisation or has committed an act of terrorism, or that he or she is involved in money laundering.

Exceptionally, temporary residence permits may be issued to foreigners on certain conditions. In practice, temporary residence permits are granted to most foreign prisoners prior to their release.

The Refugees Act regulates the legal status and bases for stay in Estonia for applicants for asylum and refugees, based on the United Nations Convention relating to the Status of Refugees and the Protocol relating to the Status of Refugees of 31 January 1967 (hereinafter the Convention). For the purposes of this Act, a refugee is a foreigner who has been issued a residence permit on the grounds that the foreigner is deemed to be a refugee pursuant to the Convention.

The Obligation to Leave and Prohibition on Entry Act provides the bases and procedure for the application to foreigners of the obligation to leave Estonia as well as the prohibition to enter the country. This act also stipulates conditions for detention in an expulsion centre, which is discussed under section three below.

2 TREATMENT OF FOREIGN PRISONERS

2.1 General Information

In the Estonian prison system only nine citizens from countries other than former Soviet Union or other Baltic States are being held in custody. Thus, the majority of the prison population is Russian speaking and not as multi-cultural as is the case in the prisons of Western European countries. There are no provisions that foreign prisoners are to be treated differently compared to national prisoners.

According to the Penal Code, in imposing a punishment the possibility to influence the offender not to commit further offences in the future shall be taken into consideration. The aim is to develop a flexible and individualised system of punishment. The reasons for behaving in a criminal fashion in each individual case are at the centre of attention of imprisonment. Each prisoner has an individual sentence or action plan, the objective of which is to plan the work that is to be conducted with every prisoner individually, to identify possibilities to reduce his or her risk of re-offending (the need to provide education, opportunity to work, working skills etc.) and to determine a time schedule for the implementation of these measures. Hence, every prisoner is being treated as an individual and thus the treatment of offenders can differ and vary. However, this differential treatment is based rather on individual risks and needs and not on nationality. Generally there are no different rules regarding the implementation of sentences in legislation.

As almost all prisoners and members of prison staff can speak Russian, which in turn reduces the problems that could in fact arise from language barriers in practice. However, when placing prisoners into cells or rooms, the nationality and mother tongue of the prisoners is also to be taken into account. There are also many employees and prisoners who speak English, so communication with those two convicted prisoners who are not from any former Soviet Union country is not a problem (one is from the Dominican Republic and one is from Nigeria; both have been resident in Estonia for a long time and are known as former pop-singers, convicted for drug trafficking). In cases in which there is someone in prison who does not speak Estonian, Russian or English (there have been few cases in practice) an interpreter will be roped in.

2.2 Living conditions and facilities

First of all, it should be pointed out that the same living conditions and facilities as well as access thereto apply to both foreign and Estonian prisoners. The respective relevant provisions make no differentiation according to nationality in this regard.

Regarding accommodation, a maximum-security prison has cells which allow for prisoners to be constantly visually and electronically monitored. Prisoners are permitted to move about freely within the territory of a maximum-security prison at locations that are stated in the internal prison rules, from the time of rising until the time of retiring. During sleeping hours, prisoners are separated in their individual locked cells. Since the majority of Estonian penitentiary institutions are colonies from Soviet times, usually more than one prisoner is allocated to each cell. In some cases, more than ten persons are accommodated together, however usually there are between two and six persons to a cell. In 2002 a new prison was opened in Southern Estonia (Tartu Prison) and a further new institution is planned to be put into operation in Eastern Estonia by the end of 2007.

An open prison has residential buildings with rooms for the accommodation of prisoners. Prisoners are permitted to move about freely within the territory of an open prison from the time of rising until the time of retiring. With the permission of the director of a prison, prisoners are also permitted to move outside of the territory of an open prison in connection with their studies or work. At nighttimes, prisoners are to retire to their individual rooms which can be locked if necessary. With the permission of the director of a prison, prisoners are permitted to stay within or outside of the territory of the open prison in connection with their work from the time of retiring until the time of rising. Currently there are open prison facilities only in Murru prison and Viljandi prison. However, it is planned that there will be open prison facilities in every prison.

Prisoners will be placed to prisons pursuant to the treatment plan, taking into consideration the length of the actual sentence imposed, their age, sex, state of health and personal characteristics. Prisoners are separated according to their age, gender, and whether they are convicted or pre-trial prisoners. Men and women are split, as are minors and adults. Furthermore, there are special accommodation provisions for persons whose previous professional activities could put them at risk of acts of revenge or retaliation.

2.3 Reception and admission of Foreign Prisoners

According to the Code of Criminal Procedure, a preliminary investigation judge or court shall immediately give notification of a person's arrest to a person close to him or her and to his or her place of employment or study. If a foreign citizen is arrested, a copy of the arrest warrant or court judgment shall be sent to the Ministry of Foreign Affairs. If a convicted offender was not held in pre-trial detention during the court proceedings, the county court enforcing the court decision shall send a notice to the convicted offender, setting out by which time and to which prison the convicted offender must appear for the service of the sentence.[15]

A person is received into a prison on the basis of a copy of a court judgment or court ruling entered into force and the identity document or, if the person has no identity document, on the basis of identification documents prepared by the police. Upon arrival in a prison, a prisoner and his or her personal effects are thoroughly searched by a prison officer of the same gender as the prisoner is question, which is followed by a medical examination. Also, arriving inmates are photographed and their fingerprints are taken. No later than on the day following the date of reception into an institution, a prisoner shall meet with the director of the prison or with a prison officer appointed by the director, who then explains the rights and obligations that a prisoner has within the institution. He or she is then provided with written information concerning the Acts and legislation that regulate the application of his or her imprisonment, the internal rules of the prison and the submission of complaints. The largest part of this documentation is available in Estonian, Russian and English. Some regulations that are not available as translated and written information will be interpreted and explained to the prisoner.

Persons sentenced to more than one year of imprisonment are placed in the so called reception ward, where their biographical data is verified, a socio-psychological prognosis is made, and other information is ascertained that is needed in order to prepare an individual action and treatment plan. Prisoners can not stay in a reception ward for longer than three months. A personal file of a prisoner is opened upon his or her reception into a prison. Documents pertaining to the grounds for the detention of a prisoner, disciplinary sanctions imposed on the prisoner and the time and reason for imposition thereof, information on the conduct, studies and work of the prisoner and other information and documents provided for in the internal rules of the prison will be recorded in this personal file. Furthermore, the photographs and fingerprint cards that were taken upon arrival are attached to the personal file. One set of photographs will be forwarded to the pre-trial investigation authority which requested that the person be taken into custody where it shall be annexed to the criminal file and one fingerprint card will be forwarded to the Police. If a prisoner is transferred to another prison, his or her personal file will be forwarded accordingly.

Upon reception into prison, a prisoner will receive counselling with regard to ensuring social security to the people close to him or her, as well as the retention of his or her property. Prisoners shall also be provided with legal assistance. All abovementioned requirements and provisions apply equally to foreigners as well.

2.4 Work - Education – Training – Sports - Recreation

According to the law the objective of providing prisoners with an opportunity to further their education is to ensure that they have adequate knowledge, skills and ethical principles which should allow them to continue their education and work after release.

Education activities in prisons are organised pursuant to the Republic of Estonia Education Act, the Basic Schools and the Upper Secondary Schools Act and the Vocational Educational Institutions Act and legislation issued on the basis thereof. A prison administration will ensure that general premises, classrooms and workshops necessary for the

15 The Code of Criminal Procedure.

acquisition of general education, vocational education and for carrying out vocational training exist, as well as the possibility to receive practical training in the areas of specialisation taught in the prison.

The acquisition of education is organised during working hours. A prison administration will direct and encourage prisoners to acquire an and / or further their education. They have the opportunity to attain (and build on) basic education on the basis of national curricula. This implies that prisoners can attend basic education, and/or further this by attending secondary education should they request to do so. A prisoner will be ensured preliminary vocational training within the framework of elective subjects prescribed by national curricula for basic schools and upper secondary schools and according to the national curricula for preliminary vocational training according to the Vocational Education Institutions Act. Prisoners may, at their request, be permitted to study at educational institutions located outside of prisons.

Educational institutions providing basic and general secondary education as well as secondary vocational education within the premises of a prison are state schools, municipal schools or their structural units operating in the prison. They are funded by the state budget on the bases of and pursuant to the procedures provided by the Basic Schools and Upper Secondary Schools Act and the Vocational Educational Institutions Act respectively. The costs related to and arising from the furnishing, repairs and operation of the premises that educational institutions are allowed to use are covered by the budget of the prison. Additionally, prisoners are provided with the opportunity to acquire secondary vocational education and can participate in vocational training according to their wishes and aptitude. Those areas of vocational specialisation are preferred that are in the highest demand in society, most commonly metal- and woodworks, construction and sewing.

Educational degrees can be achieved both in Estonian and in Russian. The provision of education in prison is arranged by the Ministry of Education and Research. Prisoners who are not proficient in Estonian can – at their request – be provided with the opportunity to study Estonian. With the aim to integrate non-Estonians to the Estonian society, Prisons organise courses in Estonian language and citizenship studies that aim at integrating non-Estonians into Estonian society.

The study work is supported by the prison libraries. There is a social pedagogue in the juvenile prison who offers counselling and support to the juvenile in their studies. Estonian prisons employ so-called education-organisers with the aim of improving the cooperation between the prison and the schools, as well as providing the prisoners with counselling in education related questions.

According the Imprisonment Act, all convicted prisoners under the age of 64, who are not participating in educational courses and who have no medical contraindications, are obliged to work. Working prisoners are categorized into prisoners who are engaged in prison maintenance work – support staff, cleaners, kitchens, laundry etc. – and prisoners who work in production. In 2001 a state company PLC Estonian Prison Industries (AS Eesti Vanglatööstus) was established in order to increase the number of prisoners in employment, improve the competitiveness of production and to decrease prison expenses. Prisoners' working conditions are in compliance with the requirements established by the labour protection law, with the exception of the specifications arising from the Imprisonment Act. A prison administration is required to ensure that prisoners are guaranteed working conditions which are safe to life and health. Prisoners may be required to work overtime, however on their day's off and on public holidays this is only possible with the consent of the prisoners. Prisoners participating in the maintenance of the prison are required to work according to the nature the work at the discretion of the prison administration. On the order of the prison director, prisoners can be required to participate in the prevention of a natural disaster, epidemic, accident, catastrophe or other emergencies, or in the elimination and alleviation of the effects thereof. In such an event, the prison administration will ensure the security and safety of the prisoners. All of these provisions and requirements apply to Estonians as well as to foreigners.

A prisoner – both national and foreign – with regard to whom there is adequate reason to presume that he or she will not re-offend can, with his or her consent, be allowed to work outside a prison without supervision or under supervision if this complies with the objectives of imprisonment and the individual treatment programme of the prisoner.

Provisions of Labour Law – including those concerning entry into employment contracts, remuneration and holidays – apply to the unsupervised work of prisoners outside of a prison. A prisoner's employment contract shall not indicate that he or she is serving a sentence. An employer will transfer an externally employed prisoner's wages to the bank account of the respective prison. Prisoners who work receive remuneration, which also applies to prisoners who are required to participate in the maintenance of a prison. The remuneration of a prisoner will be at least twenty per cent of the minimum wage rate established on the basis of the Wages Act, and is calculated on the basis of the nature of the work and the amount of time that the prisoner has actually worked. The director of a prison may reduce the remuneration of a prisoner working in the prison by up to 60 per cent for unsatisfactory work results for which the prisoner is at fault. The prisoner will be informed in writing of the amount of his or her remuneration.

Prisoners are provided with the opportunity to engage in sports. There are indoor and outdoor sports facilities in every prison. Hobby, educational, cultural and sporting events in prisons are arranged by free-time counsellors. Prisoners are allowed at least one hour of walking in the open air daily. These requirements apply both to foreigners and national prisoners.

2.5 Food – Religion – Personal hygiene – Medical care

The dwellings of prisoners are in conformity with the requirements of construction technology, health and hygiene, and have windows to ensure that the premises are suitably lighted. Prisoners are required to clean their cells and furnishings and keep them tidy. The provision of food for prisoners is organised in conformity with the general dietary habits of the population with a view to meet the food requirements necessary for survival. Food shall be provided for prisoners on a regular basis and it will meet the requirements of food hygiene. The medical officer of a prison supervises the preparation of the prison's menu and the provision of food. As far as possible, prisoners are permitted to observe the dietary habits of their religion. A prison administration will ensure that prisoners are provided with an opportunity to satisfy their religious needs. Prisoners have the unrestricted right to receive visits from representatives of their religion. Such visits are to take place without any interruption or disturbances of any kind.

Prisoners must take care of their own personal hygiene. Prisoners are given the opportunity to have a sauna, bath or shower at least once a week and upon reception into prison. Furthermore, they have access to hairdressing and barber's services. It is permitted to shave a prisoner's head only with a respective prescription of a doctor or at the

prisoner's own request. The director of a prison may impose coercion to ensure compliance with hygiene requirements if a prisoner fails to sufficiently tend to his or her personal hygiene and when this has brought about actual danger to his or her health or to the health of other prisoners. However, the imposition of coercion may not pose s danger to the life or health of a prisoner.
Health care in prisons constitutes a part of the national health care system. Health care in prisons is organised pursuant to the Health Care Services Organisation Act. Provision of health services to prisoners is financed from the state budget though the Ministry of Justice. There are no restrictions for foreign prisoners. Members of the prison's medical staff are required, among other duties, to supervise the state of the prisoners' health on a constant basis. They must treat the inmates within the prison to the extent that the facilities and their fields of specialisation allow and, if necessary, refer them to medical care institutions prescribed for the required treatment. The prisoners are guaranteed that emergency care is available to them twenty-four hours a day. Prisoners who are in need of treatment for which the facilities within the prison cannot provide shall be referred to medical care institutions prescribed for the respective purpose. A prison ensures the guard of prisoners during the time when they are in medical treatment. Any time spent in medical treatment is classed as time served in prison.

2.6 Consular and legal help

According to the Imprisonment Act prisoners have the unrestricted right to receive uninterrupted visits from their criminal defence counsel. Any written materials that a legal representative brings to the meeting are not allowed to be reviewed or read. Prisoners who are citizens of foreign states have the unrestricted right to receive visits from consular officers of their countries of nationality. There have been some contacts with Embassies of Russian Federation, Latvia and Lithuania for support in attaining passports and travel documents. Contact to Embassies is usually established by prison employees, either by telephone or in writing. Prisoners also have the possibility to send written correspondence and use a telephone for these purposes. In practice, it has occurred that a prisoner has visited the Embassy of the Russian Federation during prison leave to arrange the documents that are necessary for acquiring passport.

2.7 Contact with the outside world

According to the Imprisonment Act, prison administrations must facilitate the prisoners' contact with the outside world. Primarily, such contact is supposed to facilitate staying in touch with family, relatives and close friends in order to prevent that a prisoner's social links and ties break while he or she is in prison. Prisoners are permitted to receive at least one supervised visit per month from their family members. Visits from other persons are allowed so long as with regard to whose reputation the prison administration has no reasonable doubts regarding their reputation. A short-term visit can last for up to three hours. A prisoner is allowed to receive long-term visits from his or her spouse, father, mother, grandfather, grandmother, child, adoptive parent, adoptive child, brother or sister. A long term visit from a cohabitee is also allowed under the condition they have a common child or a shared household or that they had been cohabiting for at least two years before the prisoner began to serve his or her sentence. Long-term visit means that the prisoner and the visitor are allowed to live together without constant supervision in specially designated prison premises for a period of one up to three days.

Prisoners have the right to written correspondence and the use of a telephone (except mobile phones) if the relevant technical conditions are fulfilled. The prisoner has to bear any costs arising from letters and telephone calls. The director of a prison may restrict these rights if they endanger the security or violate the internal rules of the prison or damage the objectives imprisonment. Such restrictions are not applicable to communication with state agencies, local governments or their officials, or with the prisoner's legal defence counsel. Costs related to a prisoner's correspondence with the Chancellor of Justice; Ministry of Justice, Office of the President, prosecutor, investigator or court will be borne by the prison.

A prison officer can open letters sent by or to a prisoner in the presence of the prisoner – except letters addressed to the persons and agencies mentioned above – and may confiscate any items the possession of which is prohibited by the internal rules of the prison. The contents of a prisoner's correspondence and messages forwarded by telephone may be examined only with the permission of a court and on the basis of and pursuant to the procedures provided for in the Surveillance Act. It is prohibited to examine the contents of prisoners' letters and telephone messages to the legal defence counsel, prosecutor, and court, the Chancellor of Justice or the Ministry of Justice. It is prohibited to refuse to forward a prisoner's letters to state agencies, local governments and the officials thereof, to his or her legal defence counsel and respective consular officers.

Prisoners are provided with the possibility to read national daily newspapers and national periodicals in a prison. In practice there is at least one daily newspaper in Estonian and one in Russian available in every prison. In addition a prisoner is permitted to subscribe to a reasonable number of newspapers, periodicals and other pieces of literature at his or her own expense unless the subscription endangers the objectives of imprisonment, the security of the institution, or violates the internal rules of the prison.

Prisoners are allowed to listen to radio broadcasts and watch television broadcasts in prison. With the permission of the director of a prison, a prisoner is allowed to possess a personal radio, television set, audio tape recorder, video tape recorder or other such leisure time equipment unless the use of such items violates the internal rules of the prison or disturbs other inmates. In practice, those who do not have their own radio or television sets are provided with the opportunity to listen to the radio or watch TV by the prison. In these cases, the channels are changed after every couple of hours to change the language of the broadcasts so that the majority of prisoners can in fact listen to or watch TV in a language that they understand.

2.8 Re-integration activities - Prison leave

The preparation of a prisoner's release includes the organisation of social welfare support, the granting of privileges or a prison leave, or a transfer to an open prison. Furthermore, the prisoner is provided with assistance in resolving issues related to the management of his or her financial affairs and personal life, and in the preparation of documents. A prisoner is informed of the possibility to receive social benefits provided by the general social welfare system.

In preparation of the release of a prisoner, information concerning the prisoner's need for social welfare services after his or her release are forwarded to the rural municipality or city government of the prisoner's residence, and the prisoner's possibilities to receive specific aid will be ascertained. If the residence of a prisoner or his or her family is not known or if a prisoner does not wish to return to his or her former place of residence, information concerning the prisoner will be forwarded to another rural municipality or city government considering, if possible, the prisoner's wishes concerning his or her choice of residence. At the request of a rural municipality or city government, a prison is required provide them with the information and documents necessary for the provision of a released person with social welfare services. When a person is released from prison before having served the full sentence (early release), information concerning the prisoner will be forwarded to the probation supervision department of the residence of the prisoner or his or her family. If the residence of a prisoner or his or her family is not known or if a prisoner does not wish to return to his or her former residence, information concerning the prisoner shall be forwarded to another probation supervision department considering, if possible, the prisoner's wishes concerning his or her choice of residence. At the request of a probation officer appointed by the court, a prison can be required to forward information and documents necessary to initiate and conduct probation.

Prison leave can be granted by the director of a prison under a number of different conditions. In general, such leaves are for an overall length of 21 calendar days per year. Firstly, they are granted to prisoners who are serving their sentence in a maximum security prison and who have already served at least one year of their prison terms. Prisoners who are serving sentences for at least the second time for an intentionally committed crime in the first degree can be granted leave if they have already served at least half of their total sentence. In the case of open institutions, permission to leave the prison for 21 days per year can be granted regardless of the proportion of the total prison term that a prisoner has already served. Whether or not a person is in fact granted prison leave depends on a number of factors. The responsible prison director has to take facts relating to the commission of the criminal offence into consideration, the progress that a prisoner has made in his or her individual treatment and action plan, and whether the granting of leave is compatible with the objectives of imprisonment.

It is also possible for a prisoner to be allowed to go on prison leave for up to seven days should the prisoner's spouse, father, mother, grandfather, grandmother, child, adoptive parent, adoptive child, brother or sister become terminally ill or pass away, or in the case of other family emergencies. The duration of prison leave granted in the case of a family emergency is not subtracted from the total of 21 days to which a prisoner is entitled each year. Prisoners serving a life sentence and prisoners who are likely to abscond are not granted permission for prison leave. Any costs arising from a leave period are carried by the prisoner him/herself. The time spent by a prisoner on prison leave will be included in the duration of the prisoner's total sentence.

If the objectives of imposing imprisonment rule out the possibility of normal prison leave, the director of a prison may grant permission to leave the institution under supervision for up to three days. As is the case with regular prison leave, the arising costs are to be covered by the prisoner in question, and the period of leave is included in the total sentence, and thus counted as days of imprisonment. The decision making procedures and criteria are the same for foreigners and national prisoners. Since during the implementation of a sentence the prisoners are not allowed to leave Estonia – except in cases of transfer – prison leave is not possible if they have no place to go outside the prison, which in turn can have negative implications for the probability of a foreign prisoner actually being granted leave.

2.9 Release - Expulsion

Prisoners are released as early as possible on the last day of their sentence, however, no later than 12 a.m. If the release date of a prisoner falls on a public holiday or a day off, the prisoner will be released on the last working day before the public holiday or day off. When released, prisoners are returned their belongings, documents and personal clothing that had been deposited in the prison. If the prisoner has no personal clothing or if the prisoner's personal clothing is not suitable for the time of year, the prison will provide the prisoner to be released with clothing without charge. Furthermore, the deposited savings fund accrued from the funds deposited in the personal account of the prisoner are handed out. If the amount deposited as a savings fund is less than one month's unemployment benefit, the prisoner will be paid a lump-sum benefit to the extent of the difference between the savings fund and the amount of unemployment benefit.

A prisoner who is a foreigner and who has no residence permit shall be expelled from Estonia upon release. If immediate expulsion from Estonia is not possible, the foreigner will be placed in an expulsion centre upon release. In practice it rarely ever happens that a foreigner prisoner is released without a residence permit; usually this is decided prior to the end of imprisonment. If he has been refused a residence permit, the prison informs the Citizenship and Migration Board. Between 10 March 2003 and 31 March 2006, 24 foreign prisoners were expelled after having served their full sentence. Since 1 January 2007, it has been possible for a foreign prisoner to be released early without supervision of his/her conduct if he/she is to be expelled. However, there has not yet been such a case in practice. According to the Obligation to Leave and Prohibition on Entry Act, expulsion may be contested before the administrative court. Parties and third persons have the right to appeal against a judgment of an administrative court to a circuit court pursuant to appellate procedures. The parties and third persons have the right to appeal against a judgment of a circuit court to the Supreme Court in cassation proceedings.[16]

Pursuant to the Penal Code, prisoners can be released on parole before they have completed their full sentence. An early release proposal is submitted to the court by the prison director together with the personal file of the prisoner in question. The court then considers whether or not to grant early release on the basis of whether a prisoner has successfully completed his or her individual treatment plan, and while taking material characterising the prisoner which is documented in the personal file of the prisoner into account. If a court refuses early release, another such proposal cannot be filed for at least six months. Should a person in fact be released on parole, the prison administration may transfer a part of the prisoner's savings fund to a special account of the probation supervision department of the residence of the prisoner that is then to be paid to the released prisoner in instalments. Parole is also possible for foreigners if they have a place to live in Estonia. Early release cannot be granted without subsequent supervision of conduct.

16 Code of Administrative Court Procedure.

2.10 Aftercare – Probation

According to the Penal Code, if a person has been convicted of a criminal offence in the second degree, or of a criminal offence in the first degree through negligence, the court may release the convicted offender on parole if he or she has actually served at least half but not less than six months of the total term of the imposed punishment. If a person has been convicted for an intentional criminal offence in the first degree, the court may release the person on parole if the convicted person has actually served at least two-thirds of the total sentence. In its decision on whether to release a prisoner on parole, the court shall take the circumstances relating to the commission of the criminal offence, the personality of the convicted offender, his or her previous personal history and his or her conduct in prison into consideration, as well as his or her living conditions and the consequences which release on parole may bring about for the convicted offender. If a person has been sentenced to life imprisonment, the court may release the person on parole if the convicted offender has actually served at least thirty years. Probation shall be ordered for a period of five to ten years. During the period of probation, the person shall be subject to supervision of conduct. This means that a convicted offender is required to comply with the following supervisory requirements:

- he or she has to reside in a permanent place of residence determined by the court, and has to report to the responsible probation supervision department at intervals determined by the probation supervisor;
- he or she has to submit to the supervision of the probation officer, and provide him or her with information relating to the performance of the offender's obligations and means of subsistence;
- he or she has to obtain the permission of the probation officer before leaving the place of residence for longer than fifteen days;
- he or she has to obtain the permission of the probation officer before changing residence, employment or place of study.

Taking into consideration the circumstances relating to the commission of the criminal offence and the personality of the convicted offender, the court may impose the following obligations on the convicted offender for the period of supervision of conduct:

- to remedy the damage caused by the criminal offence within a term determined by the court;
- not to consume alcohol or narcotics;
- not to hold, carry or use weapons;
- to seek employment, acquire general education or a profession within the term determined by the court;
- to undergo the prescribed treatment if the offender has previously consented to such treatment;
- to perform the maintenance obligation;
- not to stay in places determined by the court or communicate with persons determined by the court;
- to participate in social assistance programmes.

In supervising probation, probation officers shall monitor the performance of obligations specified in court orders, assist and advise probationers in the performance of such obligations and provide assistance in their social adjustment. Probationers will receive assistance in finding employment, admission to an educational institution and a place of residence, as well as in the resolution of other personal problems. Probation officers will promote the probationers' ability to cope independently in everyday life. In supervising probation, probation officers will respect the dignity of probationers. After the entry into force of a court order, a probation officer will prepare a plan for the performance of the obligations specified in the court order and for the supervision of probation. Probationers are involved in the preparation of supervision plans. Probation supervisors have the right to amend supervision plans as necessary. There are no specific aftercare facilities or probation activities for foreigners. If they have a residence permit and a place to live, they attend the same programmes as national offenders do.

2.11 Staff

There are no language barriers and no serious cultural difficulties as most foreigners in Estonian prisons are Russian speaking and many officers are Russians as well. However, Russian and English courses are a part of the preparatory service. The staff does not receive any specific training to deal with foreign prisoners.

2.12 Projects

There are several activities related to the rehabilitation of offenders, but no specific project for foreign prisoners. It is possible to attend Estonian language courses, but these are also available for citizens, whose mother tongue is not Estonian and who want to learn it.

Various inmates' rehabilitation programmes are being implemented and developed in Estonia. The aim is to develop them to be more effective and research based. All programmes, which are currently in the test phase, have been developed as a result of a specific need and are directed towards reducing various risk factors. An overview of different programmes is available in compendium "A Selection of Rehabilitation Programmes in Prisons 2005".

3 ADMINISTRATIVE DETENTION OF FOREIGN PRISONERS

3.1 Institutions for Administrative Detention

According to the Obligation to Leave and Prohibition on Entry Act, foreigners are prohibited from staying in Estonia without a legal basis. The legal bases for a foreigner to stay in Estonia are:

- an Estonian residence permit;
- a residence permit issued by a competent agency of a member state of the European Union, a member state of the European Economic Area or the Swiss Confederation, except Estonia;
- an Estonian visa;
- a uniform visa issued by a competent agency of a member state of the European Union, a member state of the European Economic Area or the Swiss Confederation, except Estonia;

- the right to stay in Estonia arising from an international agreement;
- the right to stay in Estonia arising from a resolution of the Government of the Republic to forego the visa requirement;
- the right or obligation to stay in Estonia directly arising from law, a court decision or an administrative act;
- a residence permit or a return visa issued by a competent agency which belongs to the common visa area.

A precept to leave Estonia shall be issued to a foreigner who is staying in Estonia without a basis for stay. A foreigner shall be expelled from Estonia upon expiry of the term for compulsory execution of a precept to leave. If it is not possible to complete expulsion within the term provided for in the Obligation to Leave and Prohibition on Entry Act (described in section 3.4. below), the person to be expelled shall be administratively detained in an expulsion centre until his or her expulsion can be carried out.

Administrative detention is carried out in a so called expulsion centre. Expulsion centres are structural units of the Citizenship and Migration Board. Its function is to enforce the judgments on the detention of persons to be expelled. An expulsion centre is a guarded enclosed territory which is marked by clearly visible signs and which enables the constant supervision of persons who are to be expelled. Officials of an expulsion centre can exercise supervision over persons to be expelled by visual and electronic surveillance. Persons to be expelled can not the centre without supervision and without the permission of the head of the institution.

A person to be expelled is admitted to an expulsion centre on the basis of a transcript of the judgment of an administrative court and an identity document or, in the absence thereof, an identification document. Upon arrival in the centre, administrative detainees and their personal effects are searched by an official of the expulsion centre who is of the same sex. If necessary, a medical examination will be conducted. A person to be expelled who has been placed in an expulsion centre will be photographed and fingerprinted, unless this has been done beforehand in the course of proceedings relating to expulsion. Upon reception into an expulsion centre, a detainee's cash, documents and personal effects – the possession of which is not permitted in the expulsion centre – are deposited with the expulsion centre. As is the case with persons who are admitted to regular penal institution, a personal file of the person to be expelled is be opened which includes the documents and information on which a person's placement in an expulsion centre is based, documents and information transferred to the expulsion centre by the agency which arranged for the detention of the foreigner, photographs, a fingerprint card and other relevant documents and information. Upon arrival in an expulsion centre, a detainee's rights and obligations are explained in a language which he or she understands and, upon request, legal aid and language services can be provided for him or her at his or her own expense. A person to be expelled will be given written information concerning legislation regulating the enforcement of his or her expulsion, the internal rules of the expulsion centre and the submission of complaints.

An expulsion centre has a residential building with rooms for the accommodation of persons to be expelled. Male and female persons to be expelled are accommodated separately and family members are placed together. They could be accommodated in separate rooms if a family member acts violently towards other detainees. Minors are accommodated separately from adults except if this is evidently in conflict with the interests of the minor.

Persons to be expelled are permitted to move about in the residential building of the expulsion centre in the rooms prescribed by the internal rules from the time of rising until the time of retiring. Persons to be expelled may enter other rooms and move about within the territory of the centre in the cases and at times prescribed by the internal rules of the institution. During sleeping hours, administrative detainees are required to stay in their rooms which can be locked if necessary. They can wear their own personal clothing, and if a person to be expelled lacks suitable clothing, the expulsion centre will provide him or her with clothing without charge. There is the obligation for administrative detainees to wear a name tag. Furthermore, they are required to clean, keep in order and regularly change their clothing.

Detainees awaiting expulsion are provided with an opportunity to satisfy their religious needs if the expulsion centre has possibilities therefore and this is not in conflict with the provisions of the internal rules.

The provision of food in expulsion centres is organised in conformity with the general dietary habits of the population of Estonia with a view to meet the food requirement necessary for survival. Food is provided on a regular basis and it will be such as to meet the requirements of food hygiene. The provision of food for minors will be organised taking into consideration the needs resulting from their age. As far as possible, persons to be expelled are permitted to observe the dietary habits of their religion at their own expense. The person who ensures the provision of medical care in an expulsion centre will supervise the preparation of the menu and the provision of food at the expulsion centre.

Administrative detainees awaiting expulsion must take care of their personal hygiene. At least once a week and upon reception into an expulsion centre, persons to be expelled are provided with an opportunity to use a sauna, bath or shower. Once a month, hairdressing and barber's services will be provided. On the command of the head of an expulsion centre, coercion may be imposed to ensure compliance with hygiene requirements if a person to be expelled fails to take care of his or her personal hygiene to a necessary extent and when this has brought about actual danger to his or her health or to the health of other persons in the centre. The imposition may under no circumstances endanger the life or health of a detainee. Toiletries will be provided by the institution if someone does not have these or the funds to purchase them.

Expulsion centres ensure the provision of emergency medical care and have permanent treatment facilities for the supervision of the detainees' state of health. Medical workers are required to constantly supervise the health of persons to be expelled and to place them in treatment in medical care institutions if their medical condition does not allow their detention in the expulsion centre or their expulsion from Estonia. The medical expenses of emergency services and treatment of persons to be expelled are covered by the state budget.

Detainees in expulsion centres can be visited by the following persons:

- consular officers of their country of nationality;
- legal counsels;
- religious representatives with regard to whose reputation the head of the expulsion centre has no reasonable or justifiable doubts.

With the permission of the head of an expulsion centre, an administrative detainee awaiting expulsion is allowed to receive short-term supervised visits of personal, legal or commercial interest in matters that cannot be resolved through third persons, unless such a visit would impede the enforcement of an expulsion. The detainees are permitted to receive visits only from persons with regard to whose reputation and motives the head of the expulsion centre has no reasoned doubts. Officials of an expulsion centre have the right to search visitors and their personal effects. It is, however, prohibited to review the content of the written material brought along by a legal defence counsel. The searches are conducted by an official of the same sex as the visitor. Items the possession of which is prohibited in an expulsion centre shall be temporarily deposited for the duration of the visit, which shall not exceed three hours. Persons to be expelled will be visited in the presence of an official of the expulsion centre. Visits from a legal defence counsel or a religious representative are allowed within sight but not within hearing distance of officials of the expulsion centre.

Persons to be expelled have the right to send and receive written correspondence and to the use of telephone and other public communication channels if the relevant technical conditions exist in the expulsion centre. An official of an expulsion centre will open letters sent to a person to be expelled in the presence of the person to be expelled and confiscate any impermissible items. The actual content of written correspondence and of messages forwarded by telephone or other public communication channels by or to a person to be expelled may be examined only with the permission of a court and on the bases of and pursuant to the procedures provided for in the Surveillance Act. The head of an expulsion centre may restrict the correspondence and use of telephone and other means of communication if it could violate the internal rules of the expulsion centre or impede the enforcement of the expulsion. Written correspondence with state agencies, legal defence counsels, ministers of religion and consular officers will not be restricted. Costs arising from written, telephonic, and other public means of communication will be borne by the detainee. For correspondence with Estonian state agencies, legal defence counsels, ministers of religion and the respective consular officers, a person to be expelled will be provided with stationery and postal charges will be covered if he or she cannot afford them.

Persons to be expelled may, by the mediation of the expulsion centre, purchase food, toiletries and other permitted items, in an amount that is accordance to the procedures and provisions of the internal rules of the expulsion centre. They are also allowed to receive packages. An official of the expulsion centre will examine the content of a package before it is handed over in the presence of the recipient of the package. Parcels are not allowed to contain food and medicinal products. An official of an expulsion centre is required to seize impermissible contents.

3.2 Ministry responsible and relevant legislation

The Citizenship and Migration Board is a government agency within the Ministry of Internal Affairs and its main tasks include:

- the determination of persons living in Estonia either as Estonian citizens or foreigners and the issuance of identity documents to residents of Estonia;
- reception and processing of applications for acquiring and restoring Estonian citizenship, as well as for exempting from Estonian citizenship, and preparing the respective

materials for the government of the Republic to make decisions on these applications;
- receiving and processing applications for residence and work permits of foreigners who wish to settle or are living in Estonia, and making decisions on whether to grant or refuse such permits;
- processing of asylum applications and making decisions on whether or not to grant asylum;
- confirming visa invitations and extending the allowed period of stay in Estonia;
- processing of misdemeanours committed by foreigners illegally staying or working in Estonia, issuance of precepts to leave Estonia or to apply for a residence permit in Estonia, organising the expulsion of foreigners from Estonia;
- making decisions on the requests of foreign countries for the readmission of Estonian citizens and foreigners whose habitual residence is in Estonia;
- maintenance of the relevant state registers and databases.

The entry of foreigners into Estonia as well as their stay, residence and employment in the country and the bases for legal liability of foreigners are stipulated in the Foreigners Act. The bases and procedures for the application to foreigners of the obligation to leave Estonia and the prohibition to enter Estonia are provided in the Obligation to Leave and Prohibition on Entry Act. This act also stipulates conditions for detention in an expulsion centre. The internal rules of an expulsion centre are established by the Ministry of Internal Affairs.

3.3 The Capacity of Institutions for Administrative Detention

There is one expulsion centre in Estonia, opened in March 2003. Before that time, persons to be expelled were placed in prison, however in a section separated from criminal offenders.

In the report to the Estonian Government on the visit to Estonia carried out by the European Committee for the Prevention of Torture and Inhuman or Degrading Treatment or Punishment (CPT) from 13 to 23 July 1997 it was stressed that "a prison is not an appropriate place in which to detain someone who is neither suspected nor convicted of a criminal offence. In those cases where it is considered necessary to deprive persons of their liberty for a prolonged period under aliens' legislation, they should be accommodated in centres specifically designed for that purpose, offering material conditions and a regime appropriate to their legal situation and staffed by suitably qualified personnel. Obviously, such centres should provide accommodation which is adequately furnished, clean and in a good state of repair, and which offers sufficient living space for the numbers involved. Further, care should be taken in the design and layout of the premises to avoid as far as possible any impression of a carceral environment. As regards regime activities, they should include outdoor exercise, access to a day room and to radio/television and newspapers/magazines, as well as other appropriate means of recreation (e.g. board games, table tennis). The longer the period for which persons are detained, the more developed should be the activities which are offered to them. The CPT invites the Estonian authorities to review their policy concerning immigration de-

tainees, in the light of the above remarks."[17] The CPT recommended that immediate steps shall be taken:
- to remedy the shortcomings observed in the sanitary facilities used by immigration detainees;
- to offer a wider range of activities to the detainees, in particular to those held for prolonged periods.

Since 2004 there have been 42 places in expulsion centre for persons to be expelled: 16 places for women and families and 26 places for men.

3.4 Length of stay

A precept to leave issued to a foreigner who is staying in Estonia without a basis for stay shall be subject to compulsory execution after the seventh day as of the date of issue of the precept. A precept to leave issued to an illegal resident who is staying in Estonia without a basis for stay, whose residence permit is revoked or whose residence permit has expired shall be subject to compulsory execution of the precept after the sixtieth day as of the date of its issuance.

A foreigner shall be expelled from Estonia upon expiry of the term for compulsory execution of a precept to leave. Expulsion shall be completed within forty-eight hours after the foreigner is detained.

If it is not possible to complete expulsion within the term provided for in the Obligation to Leave and Prohibition on Entry Act, the person to be expelled shall, at the request of the governmental authority which applied for or which is enforcing the expulsion of the foreigner and on the basis of a judgment of an administrative court judge, be placed in an expulsion centre until his or her expulsion, but for not longer than two months. A person to be expelled who is to be placed in an expulsion centre may be detained in a police detention house for up to thirty days instead of an expulsion centre.

Should it not be possible to enforce an expulsion within the term of detention in the expulsion centre, an administrative court can, at the request of a competent official of the Citizenship and Migration Board, extend the term of detention by up to two months at a time until expulsion is enforced or until the foreigner is released.

In practice the average length of stay in the expulsion centre is 129 days, approximately four months.

3.5 Decisions procedure

Foreigners are prohibited from staying in Estonia without a legal basis. A precept to leave Estonia shall be issued to a foreigner who is staying in Estonia without a basis for stay. Precepts shall be issued by the Citizenship and Migration Board.

Judgments concerning the detention of persons to be expelled and extensions of the term of detention shall be made by an administrative court. Placement in the expulsion centre and extension of the term of detention are decided in a court session.

---

17 CPT/ Inf (2002) 26 Visit 13/07/1997 - 23/07/1997.

3.6 Appeal procedure

A person to be expelled has the right to appeal against a judgment of an administrative court to a circuit court. A written notice of the filing of an appeal shall be submitted to the administrative court which adjudicated the matter within ten days after the court judgment is pronounced or made public. An appeal shall be filed through the administrative court which made the judgment within thirty days after the judgment is pronounced or made public.

3.7 Irregular stay

According to § 260 of the Penal Code a foreigner who is detected in Estonia at least twice within a year without a legal basis shall be punished by a pecuniary punishment or up to one year of imprisonment. Currently, there is no one who is being punished in prisons or the expulsion centre according to this paragraph.

3.8 Numbers

During the period from 10 March 2003 to 31 December 2005 68 persons were administratively detained in the expulsion centre, among them four women and 64 men:

Citizenship of persons placed in the expulsion centre	
Armenia	2
Azerbaijan	7
Bosnia-Herzegovina	1
Estonia	2
Finland	1
Georgia	8
Iraq	1
Latvia	1
Romania	1
Serbia-Montenegro	1
Turkey	1
Ukraine	2
Uzbekistan	1
Russia	25
Undefined	14

In 2003, 23 persons were placed in expulsion centre: two women and 21 men. In 2004 the figure decreased to 14 persons, among which there was only one woman. The year 2005 witnessed an increase in the number of people who were administratively detained, to 31 persons in total. In this year, too, there was only one female detainee. No minors have yet been detained in the centre.

3.9 Expulsion

A person to be expelled shall be expelled to the state from which he or she crossed the Estonian border, to the country of his or her nationality, to his or her country of habitual residence, or to a third state with the consent of the third state. If more than one of these options could in fact apply, the reasoned preference of the person to be expelled shall be the primary consideration, so long as this preference does not significantly impede the enforcement of the expulsion.

A foreigner may not be expelled to a state where he or she could face the consequences specified in Article 3 of the Convention for the Protection of Human Rights and Fundamental Freedoms or Article 3 of the United Nations Convention against Torture and Other Cruel, Inhuman or Degrading Treatment or Punishment, or the application of the death penalty. The expulsion of a foreigner shall comply with Articles 32 and 33 of the United Nations Convention relating to the Status of Refugees.

Once it is possible to actually implement the expulsion of a foreigner who is staying in administrative detention, the person is released from the institution and is expelled at the request of the governmental authority that is responsible for enforcing the expulsion (either the Citizenship and Migration Board or the police). Around 76% of the persons who are placed in the expulsion centre are in fact expelled from Estonia.

3.10 Not-expelled prisoners

An administrative detainee who is not expelled from Estonia is released from the centre if:

- He or she is taken into custody as a suspect or an accused in a criminal matter;
- if a precept is annulled or declared invalid; or
- a decision is made to grant a foreigner the legal basis to stay in the country.

18% of all persons who are placed in the expulsion centre have been released because they have been granted a residence permit. Four percent of the persons to be expelled were taken into custody as a suspect or an accused in a criminal matter, and were consequently released from the expulsion centre on the basis of a ruling to take him or her into custody. Two percent are released because the expulsion proceedings are terminated.

3.11 Detention of Irregulars under Criminal Law

According to § 260 of the Penal Code a foreigner who stays in Estonia without a legal basis at least twice within a year shall be punished by a pecuniary punishment or up to one year of imprisonment. To date there are no known cases of persons being punished in accordance with this legal provision.

As already stated above, administrative detention is performed in expulsion centres, which are structural units of the Citizenship and Migration Board under the Ministry of Internal Affairs. Administrative detainees can not be placed together with criminal convicts who are serving sentences in prisons under the Ministry of Justice.

Minors
According to the Obligation to Leave and Prohibition on Entry Act, if a foreigner to whom a precept is issued is accompanied in Estonia by his or her minor foreign child or ward (hereinafter minor), and if the minor does not have a basis for residing in Estonia, an obligation to organise compliance with the precept with respect to the minor shall be imposed by the precept on the parent, guardian or other person responsible for the minor (hereinafter parent). A precept is issued to a minor staying in Estonia without a parent and compliance therewith shall be organised by a guardianship authority. The expulsion of a minor shall be organised in co-ordination with the competent state agencies of the admitting country and, if necessary, of the transit country and protection of the rights of the minor shall be ensured. However, in practice there have not yet been any minor administrative detainees in the expulsion centre.

4 ESTONIAN NATIONALS DETAINED ABROAD

To date there is no adequate information about Estonian nationals detained abroad, and nobody is known to be collecting such information as official data. Presumably there are quite a few Estonian nationals detained in Finland and Sweden but also in Germany, Austria and Spain. According to the media the main reasons for detention are drug trafficking, robbery and serious theft.

Estonia has ratified the Convention on the Transfer of Sentenced Persons (ETS 112) and its additional Protocol to the Convention on the Transfer of Sentenced Persons. The transfer of nationals detained abroad is also arranged in the framework of this convention and according to the conditions and rules thereof. Additionally there is a bi-lateral agreement between Estonia and Thailand.
Estonians have been transferred back to Estonia from the following countries:
- 12 prisoners in 2003: six from Sweden, one from the Czech Republic and five from Thailand;
- 14 prisoners in 2004: 12 from Sweden and two from Latvia;
- 26 prisoners in 2005: ten from Sweden, 12 from Finland, two from Latvia and two from Germany.

In 2006 at the time of writing, seven Estonians had been transferred home from foreign countries. Three involved prisoners in Austria, while the remaining four came from Sweden. Additionally, there were eight applications for transfers of prisoners back to Estonia, of which seven were to be sent from Sweden and one person had been imprisoned in Finland.

5 EVALUATION AND RECOMMENDATIONS

Foreigners constitute almost half of all people held in custody in police detention houses and prisons (40%). In Estonia, foreign criminal offenders are not kept separately from other prisoners, which can be greatly attributed to the fact that the vast majority of foreigners in Estonian prisons and police detention units speak Russian. Persons to be expelled are kept in the expulsion centre on the basis of administrative law. Compared to

Western European countries the Estonian prison population is not that multi-cultural. More than half of prisoners are Russian or other ethnic nationalities from the territory of former Soviet Union (54%). Thereby most of Estonian prison population is Russian speaking. As many of the prison officers are Russians too, there are no serious cultural or language barriers in communication with foreigners. Even so, as younger people in Estonia are not so fluent in Russian, it is necessary to have Russian language courses in preparatory training. Although the percentage of prisoners with undefined citizenship has decreased, they still constitute the most numerous group among foreigners in prisons (85%). Considering the decision of the Constitution Court of Russian Federation from 21 April 2005 it is very likely that most prisoners with undefined citizenship actually have a right to acquire Russian citizenship by birth. It is one of the main challenges in criminal policy to decrease the number of foreign prisoners (including prisoners with undefined citizenship) in Estonia. There are several possibilities in different stages of detention.

At the beginning of criminal proceedings, these should be increasingly discontinued (or not even initiated). Instead, the provisions of the Penal Code and the Code of Criminal Procedure on the expulsion of foreigners should be more widely applied. Also, expulsion should be more frequently imposed as a supplementary penalty which includes a prohibition to enter Estonia for a fixed period, as provided for in the Penal Code.

Once a foreigner has in fact been admitted to a prison, there should be an improved exchange of information between the involved penal institution and the Citizenship and Migration Board in order to attain a more complete picture of the prisoner's status, which in turn allows for the drafting of a more appropriate individual treatment and action plan. While a foreigner is imprisoned, they should be provided with more information on the possibilities and procedures for acquiring Estonian citizenship or a residence permit. Finally, in preparing foreign prisoners for release, they should receive more and improved support in applying for the necessary documents. Also, correspondence between the prisons and the Citizenship and Migration Board should be improved so that the latter is informed of foreign prisoners who are soon to be released and who do not (yet) hold a permit for legal residence in Estonia.

Chapter 8

Finland

Tapio Lappi-Seppälä

1 INTRODUCTION

Foreigners and immigrants in Finland: historically, Finland has been a country characterized by emigration rather than immigration. A remarkable change in this respect has occurred during the 1990s. Although the amount of immigrants living in Finland is still low by European standards (ca. 2% of the population are foreign nationals, or circa 100,000 persons of which circa 20,000 are refugees), relative increase of foreign nationals is among the highest in Europe. The number of foreigners has quadrupled during the last 10 years: from circa 25,000 in 1990 to more than 100,000 in 2003.

Table I Foreigners in the whole population

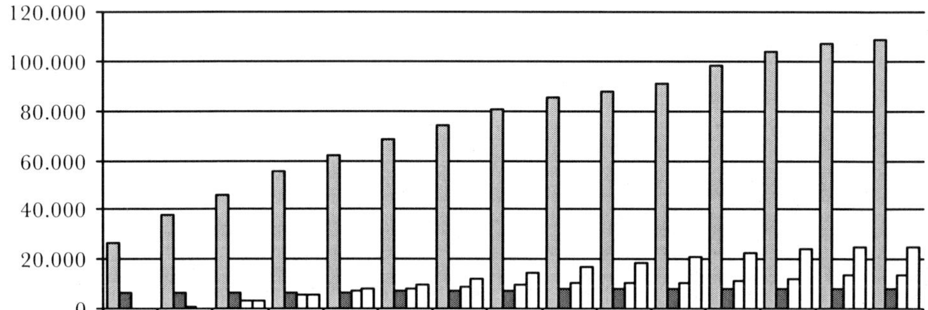

	1990	1991	1992	1993	1994	1995	1996	1997	1998	1999	2000	2001	2002	2003	2004
Foreigners	26.255	37.579	46.250	55.587	62.012	68.566	73.754	80.600	85.060	87.680	91.074	98.577	103.682	107.003	108.346
Sweden	6.051	6.277	6.456	6.528	6.685	7.014	7.291	7.507	7.756	7.809	7.887	7.999	8.037	8.124	8.209
Estonia	0	720	3.380	5.893	7.472	8.446	9.038	9.689	10.340	10.652	10.839	11.662	12.428	13.397	13.978
Russia	0	0	3.448	5.828	7.785	9.720	11.810	14.316	16.861	18.575	20.552	22.724	24.336	24.998	24.626

A little less than 40% of these people are under 30 years old, and 25% are under 21. The largest groups according to citizenship[1] are Russians (25 000), Estonians (14 000), Swedes (8 000), and Somali people (5 000). Nearly half of the foreign citizens live in the capital area (Helsinki, Espoo, Vantaa, and Kauniainen) Even if Finland can be considered a new country of immigration, the question of cultural diversity is not a new phenomenon: Finland has a long history of "old national minorities" in particular Sami and Roma people living in Finland. However, the multicultural landscape of Finland has changed substantially during the last 10 years and has been taken up as an important political topic first in the 1990s – although in a contradictory way. The debate in Finland focused firstly on concerns about national security and maintaining social order as well as the conditions under which immigrants could enter and be included in Finnish society. More recently, this viewpoint has been challenged because of concern over the social integration of im-

1 The concepts of nationality and citizenship are often used interchangeably in the Finnish language. For example the law regulating citizenship is called a *Nationality Law*. In the Finnish language there is only a one letter difference between these terms (nationality=kansallisuus, citizenship=kansalaisuus), which may contribute to the conceptual ambivalence.

migrants. The Finnish debate on immigration has emphasized more demographic changes and the fact that European countries like Finland need more immigrant workers in the future.

Official debate and policy reforms have led to partly new approaches to the management of immigrants. At the same time, Finnish asylum practices are still rather strict. There were 3,221 asylum seekers in 2003 (compared to the number of asylum seekers in Sweden 31,355 or Norway 15,859 in the same year). The Directorate of Immigration (working under the Ministry of the Interior) gave asylum or residence permits to 501 persons; 2,443 persons were rejected (more than 80% of all requests for asylum and residence permits).

Legislative reforms: many reforms related to immigration and non-discriminatory legislation have been made during the last couple of years. The new *Aliens' Act* has been enacted in 2004. The Act formulates the conditions under which permanent residence can be refused, as in the case of a person suspected or convicted of a crime[2]. A new *Nationality Law* was implemented in 2003. Among the reforms, a possibility to grant dual citizenship was launched which can be seen as a welcome reform. Constitutional rights are rights that are granted to all persons living in the country. In a reform of the *Form of Government Act* in 1995, foreigners living in Finland were guaranteed the same constitutional rights as Finnish citizens – with the exception of the right to vote, eligibility for parliament and freedom of movement beyond national borders. A new *Constitution of Finland* was introduced in 2000. The law addresses, among other things, action against discrimination and equal treatment of different groups of persons. According to this law (6 §), everyone is equal before the law. No one shall, without an acceptable reason, be treated differently from other persons on the ground of gender, age, origin, language, religion, conviction (religious belief), opinion, health, disability, or other reasons concerning his or her person. A new *Equality Act* was introduced in 2004. The law can be seen as a signal of more active policy steps within Finnish legislation in the fight against discrimination, partly due to recent changes of immigration and partly due to the pressure from international agreements. To apply the law in practice, new administrative actors (including the Ombudsman for Minorities and Discrimination Board, working in connection with the Ministry of Labour) have been implemented whose role is to give guidance, advice or recommendations to a person who considers her/himself to have been the victim of discrimination

---

2 Section 57 – *Obstacles to issuing permanent residence permits*

(1) A permanent residence permit may be refused if the alien:
1) is found guilty of an offence punishable by imprisonment;
2) is suspected of an offence punishable by imprisonment;
3) is found guilty of two or more offences; or
4) is suspected of two or more offences.

(2) The sentence passed for an offence need not be final. When the obstacles to issuing a residence permit are being considered, the nature and seriousness of the criminal act and the length of the alien's residence in Finland shall be taken into account. If an alien has been sentenced to unconditional imprisonment (for the clarification of sentences, see the section 2.1.2), a permanent residence permit may be issued if, on the date of decision on the application, three years have passed since the alien served his or her sentence in full. If the alien has been sentenced to conditional imprisonment, a permanent residence permit may be issued if more than two years have passed since the probation ended. In other cases, a permanent residence permit may be issued if the offence was committed more than two years before the date of decision on the application.

on ethnic grounds, and to participate in societal discussion and concrete discriminatory cases. Thus, the aim for the Ombudsman for Minorities is to improve legal protection related to ethnic minorities. In the course of recent years, public discussion in Finland has moved from focusing solely on "recognition of differences" to more active steps to combat discrimination and inequality on ethnic grounds. At the international level, Finland has taken part in the EUMC (European Monitoring Centre on Racism and Xenophobia) and has been active in the implementation of the European Commission's *Community Action Programme to Combat Discrimination.* Finland is also taking part in implementing Article 13 of the Amsterdam Treaty, which gives the European Union a new competence for combating discrimination based on sex, ethnic origin, religion or belief, disability and age. In addition to this Treaty, there are several international legal instruments directly or indirectly dealing with discrimination, such as the United Nations Convention on the Elimination of all forms of Racial Discrimination, and the European Convention of Human Rights. (Bousetta & Modood 2001).

One of the most dominant judicial and policy steps of the Finnish immigration policy during the 1990s was the *Integration Act* introduced in 1999 concerning persons who have been in Finland for less than 3 years. Immigrants are provided with a three-year integration period during which time they should acquire language skills as well as knowledge of the society necessary for living in the country. Municipalities are responsible for the preparation of integration programmes as well as integration plans for each immigrant person and family living in their area.

Regardless of new legislation and agreements related to immigration policy, there is a gap between the formal level and the practical level. For example, according to an international evaluation in 2002 done by ECRI (the European Commission against Racism and Intolerance), Finnish officials frequently failed to follow new regulations. This may happen in the working place, at schools, etc. In the international evaluation, one central doubt was whether the Finnish police process discrimination cases properly, i.e., whether Finnish anti-discrimination legislation is effective in practice. The ECRI's concern that the Finnish police investigations would discriminate on ethnic or racist grounds is essential from the perspective of this research project as well.

1.1 Overview penalties and measures

Principal punishments in Finland are unconditional and conditional prison sentence, community service, fines and juvenile punishment for young offenders.

Unconditional imprisonment is either for life or fixed term. It is possible to sentence life imprisonment for very few crimes. A fixed-term prison sentence may be 14 days at the shortest and 12 years at the longest. When passing a combined sentence the maximum length is 15 years. When sentences are enforced, the aggregate punishment may be 20 years in maximum.

A prison sentence of two years in maximum can be passed as *conditional.* Besides that a fine can be passed. If conditional sentence is longer than a year, 20-90 hours of community sentence can be passed. A young offender, who has committed his/her crime while being under 21 years of age, may be sentenced to supervision to boost up the conditional prison sentence. The enforcement of conditional imprisonment is postponed for probationary period that is at least one year and at most three years. If the convict commits a new crime during his/her probationary period for which an unconditional imprisonment should be sentenced, the court may decide that the conditional sentence should be executed. The court may also decide that the conditional sentence is enforced only partly, when the sentence remains for other part as conditional with the original probationary period.

Community service can be sentenced instead of an unconditional prison sentence not exceeding eight months, 20 hours in minimum and 200 hours in maximum. Community service is unpaid work carried out under supervision. *The Probation Service* assesses the suitability of the suspect for community service before the sentence is passed and it acquires a service place and supervises the performance of the service.

Fine is sentenced as day fines, the minimum amount of which is one and the maximum 120-day fines. The amount of fines depends on the level of seriousness of the crime. The monetary value of the fine depends on the financial standing of the convict. District court converts unpaid fine in a separate proceedings into imprisonment. Two unpaid fines correspond to one day's imprisonment. Conversion is at least four days and at most 90 days of imprisonment. Petty fine is a fixed currency property fine. It cannot be converted into imprisonment.

Juvenile punishment consists of supervision (4-12 months) and different types of programs. Juvenile punishment may be imposed on a young person who has committed a crime while being under 18 years old, if fine is considered to be too lenient a sanction and no weighty reasons demand unconditional imprisonment. The use of different sentencing alternatives is described in table II.2 below.

1.2 Overview of the Prison System

1.2.1 Organisational Structure

Prisons: sentences of imprisonment are enforced either in closed prisons or in open institutions. Finnish prisons are not formally classified according to their security status, nor are the prisoners classified according to any security grading. However, the intensity of supervision varies to some extent also between closed prisons.

If the sentence of imprisonment is at most two years in length, the sentence may be ordered enforced in an open institution. A further requirement is that the offender is capable of working or participating in training offered at the institution and that he or she presumably will not leave without permission. Open institutions hold about one-fourth of the current prison population. The regime in open institutions is more relaxed. Prisoners receive normal wages for their work. One quarter of their wages is deducted towards their maintenance. Open institutions are in practice prisons without walls: the prisoner is obliged to stay in the prison area, but there are no guards or fences. All open institutions are drug-free institutions in which an inmate is required to controlled commitment not to use any intoxicants.

Prisoners in closed prisons are obliged to work or to take part in vocational training or other activities unless they are relieved from that duty on the grounds of health, studies or for other reasons. Prisoners may also receive permission to pursue other studies either within or outside the institution. Part of the prison sentence may be served also outside the prison in a rehabilitation institution for substance abuse. For those serving sentences in excess of two months, a prison furlough may be granted. A prisoner may be furloughed from prison for a maximum of six days over a four-month period.

Release from prisons. In Finland all prisoners except those few dangerous violent recidivists who serve their sentence in (approximately 20 prisoners at any given day) are released on parole. In practice this means that 99 % of prisoners released every year are released on parole. The director of the prison makes the decision in question. In general, recidivists are always released after they have served two-thirds of their sentence, and first-time prisoners are released after they have served one-half of their sentences. Offenders between 15 to 20 are released either after 1/3 (first offenders) or after ½ (recidivists). In all cases, a further condition is that the prisoner has served at least fourteen days.

The duration of parole reflects the amount of time remaining in the sentence, however, at least three months and at most three years. About one fifth of those released on parole are placed under supervision. The supervisor may be the Probation Service or a private individual appointed by the Service. In principle, the supervision involves both control and support.

The court decides on revocation of parole if the offender commits an offence during the period of his or her parole and on the grounds of a behavioural infraction. In practice all parole revocations are based on new offences, and only such an offence that would normally lead to a prison sentence may serve as a reason to revoke the parole order.

Organization: prison and probation services belong to the administrative field of the Ministry of Justice. *The Prison Service* enforces the prison sentences judged by the courts of justice and detentions and apprehensions connected to trials. The Prison Service has altogether over 30 prisons located in various parts of Finland: 16 closed institutions, 19 open institutions and two hospital units. In 2006 the total budget of the prison service was 166 billion euros. *The Probation Service* is in charge of community sanctions, which include the enforcement of community service, juvenile punishment, the supervision of conditionally sentenced young offenders and conditionally released prisoners (parolees). The Probation Service has 15 district offices and 5 local offices.

Controlling mechanisms; the Ombudsman of the Parliament has a general responsibility to overview also prisons. The ombudsman carries out regular visits to prison-facilities and reports the findings in the annual reports. Another task of the Ombudsman for minorities (since 2001) is to overview the treatment and the conditions of these groups, also of those in detention.

1.2.2 Foreign Prisoners

There are no specific penal institutions for foreigners. Foreign prisoners are mixed with the national prison population. In practice majority of the foreign prisoners are concentrated in the Southern parts of Finland and in the Helsinki region. The Kerava and Helsinki prisons hold half of the 200 foreign prisoners serving a sentence in 1.6.2006. Over half of the 110 remand-prisoners are held in the Vantaa prison (near Helsinki).

In 1.6.2006 the total number of foreign prisoners was 317. Of these 207 were serving a sentence and 110 were on remand. This corresponds some 8 % of the total prison population foreigner are over-represented in the Finnish prison as the share of non-national foreigners is about 2,2 % of the total population. Part of this is explained by the skewed demographic distribution among the foreigners (over-representation of younger age-groups and males).

There is no specific section of the Prison Service responsible for foreigners. However, their affairs are being concentrated in the department of foreign affairs in the Ministry of

Justice. Currently there are no NGO's operating in Finland that are concentrated solely on assisting foreign prisoners. However, the services provided by these organisations are accessible to foreign prisoners as well.

The purpose of the *Probation Foundation Finland* is to support probation service and its development, to foster measures that reduce recidivism and its side effects and to organise and make available services that reinforce the aims of the foundation. The foundation aims to help people who have been convicted of a crime, are in a crisis situation because of a crime or are facing social ostracism. The operation of the Foundation is financed by the income from real estate and stocks owned by the foundation as well as financial aid from the Finland's Slot Machines Association (RAY).

Bridge-Supportorganization produces nationally significant services in the fields of rehabilitation, education and work-life oriented services for people in danger of becoming socially ostracized, such as prison inmates and clients of probation and after-care.

Prison Fellowship Finland is operated by the Finnish Evangelican Lutheran Church and is based on voluntary work. The mission of Prison Fellowship is to mobilise and assist the Christian community in its ministry to prisoners, ex-prisoners, victims, and their families; and in the advancement of restorative justice. The volunteers of the organisation assist needy ex-prisoners with the practical challenges of re-entry into the community. Also the *Finnish Red Cross* trains volunteers to visit those prisoners who have no family of friends to stay in contact with while in prison.

KRIS-Finland and *Support for released prisoners'* target groups are ex criminals and addicts who have decided to start a new life and get back into society. The idea is to help people who are released from prison to stay away from crime and drugs by offering them a new; drug free social network. Vapautuvien Tuki ry also offers help to the families of prisoners during and after the prison sentence.

Back to Life Association does supporting and preventive special youth work among children, young people and young adults who have become alienated or live under the threat of becoming alienated. For example, the "Free...Choice to the future" project aims to prevent repeated offences of young people and by that prevent alienating. With the help of Free Choice project, 17 - 26 year olds who have drug/alcohol problem and lawbreaker backgrounds are supported to return to society. It is carried out by developing e.g. personally co-ordinated activity. The project makes it possible to build "low threshold" services and leisure time activities for specific target groups and tries to develop cooperation between customer service providers and activity networks.

The Guarantee Foundation helps people in difficulties due to huge debts to manage their debts independently. A condition of eligibility for a guarantee is that the amount of the debts is reduced to a sum equal to the clients' ability to pay. The aim is to achieve this reduction through negotiation among the parties concerned if the shortfall problems are beyond the debtor's ability to pay. The Guarantee Foundation was established in 1990 primarily to help people who have been in prison or in a hospital for the mentally ill. Of the guarantees that are made available a total of 50 % are provided for loans made to ex-patients of hospitals for the mentally ill, 13 % for loans made to ex-alcoholics and 9 % for loans made to ex-prisoners. Main financier of the Foundation is the Finland's Slot Machine Association (RAY).

1.3 Overview involvement Consulates, Embassies, Ministries home country, Probation service home country, NGO's etc

See above 1.2.2. and below 2.6. and 3.B.6.

1.4 Overview of trends

1.4.1 Sentencing Trends

a) Foreigners and the criminal justice system

Table II.1. Foreigners (* in the Finnish criminal justice system

	POPULATION (1000)			*SUSPECTED OFFENDERS*			*CONVICTED IN COURTS*			*PRISONERS*		
	Total	*For. N*	*For. %*	*Total*	*For. N*	*For. %*	*Total*	*For. N*	*For %*	*Total*		*For.%*
1990	4 986	26	0,5	697 918	..		81 716	..		3441	20	0,6
1997	5 138	81	1,6	564 415	..		57 892	2197	3,8	2974	116	3,9
1998	5 154	86	1,7	569 384	..		58 732	2421	4,1	2809	130	4,6
1999	5 166	88	1,7	557 530	13316	2,4	59 651	2738	4,6	2743	138	5,0
2000	5 176	91	1,8	580 266	14273	2,5	64 417	2940	4,6	2855	173	6,1
2001	5 195	99	1,9	580 222	14783	2,5	66 605	3339	5,0	3135	248	7,9
2002	5 206	104	2,0	564 306	15758	2,8	64 791	3511	5,4	3433	293	8,5
2003	5 220	107	2,0	589 179	16621	2,8	64 872	3630	5,6	3578	291	8,1
2004	5 236	108	2,1	633 408	17314	2,7	69 765	3723	5,3	3577	284	7,9
2005	5 256	114	2,2	643 647	19346	3,0	68 856	..	..	3888	282	7,3

*) Foreigners having residence in Finland. Excludes foreign born nationals

In 2005, 19 300 foreigners who had residence in Finland, were suspected of some offence. This rate was 3.0 % out of all persons suspected of offences known to the police in Finland. The number of offences committed by foreigners has increased 79 % since 1996. In 2005, about 114 000 foreigners (2,2 % of the whole population) had residence in Finland. In addition about 16 100 foreigners not having residence in Finland, tourists and other visitors were suspected of offences in 2005.

23 per cent of all foreigners suspected of crimes were Russians, 18 per cent were Estonians, and 8 per cent were Swedes. Foreigners were most typically suspected of traffic offences (45 % in 2005). Forcible rapes and robberies were offences where foreign suspects were most clearly over-represented in 2005 (forcible rapes 21 per cent and robberies 27 per cent of all suspects).

Majority of foreign offenders are suspected of minor offences that lead to summary fines (usually for traffic offences). In 2004 15 441 foreigners received summary fines, while 3635 were sentenced in the courts either to fines or other penalties. The distribution of penalties in 2004 is in table II.2.

Table II.2. Penalties imposed for foreigners 2004

	All		*Foreigners*	
	N	%	N	%
Summary fines	232 613	77,4	15441	80,9
Courts				
Fines	39420	13,1	2161	11,3
Conditional	16165	5,4	1089	5,7
Community service	3621	1,2	95	0,5
Prison	8530	2,8	290	1,5
Total	300349	100	19077	100

Of all foreigners sentenced to imprisonment in 2005, over one-fourth (27 %) were Estonians, and about one-fifth (21 %) were Russians. The number of foreigners in Finnish prisons has been increasing rapidly in last ten years, from about one per cent to 7–9 per cent of the average daily prison population. Foreigner participation in the growing narcotics markets is a central factor in this development.

b) General trends in prisoner rates 1995-2005

The number prisoners in Finland have – after a long decline –again started to increase. Between 1999 and 2005 the number of prisoners has increased in Finland by 40 %. This change can be analysed in terms of different prisoner groups (for example remand, fine defaulters, foreigners, females, juveniles etc.) and in terms of the principal offence (the trends in prisoner rates is examined in more detail in *Lappi-Seppälä* forthcoming).

Figure 1 Prisoners by **Principal offence 1990-2005**

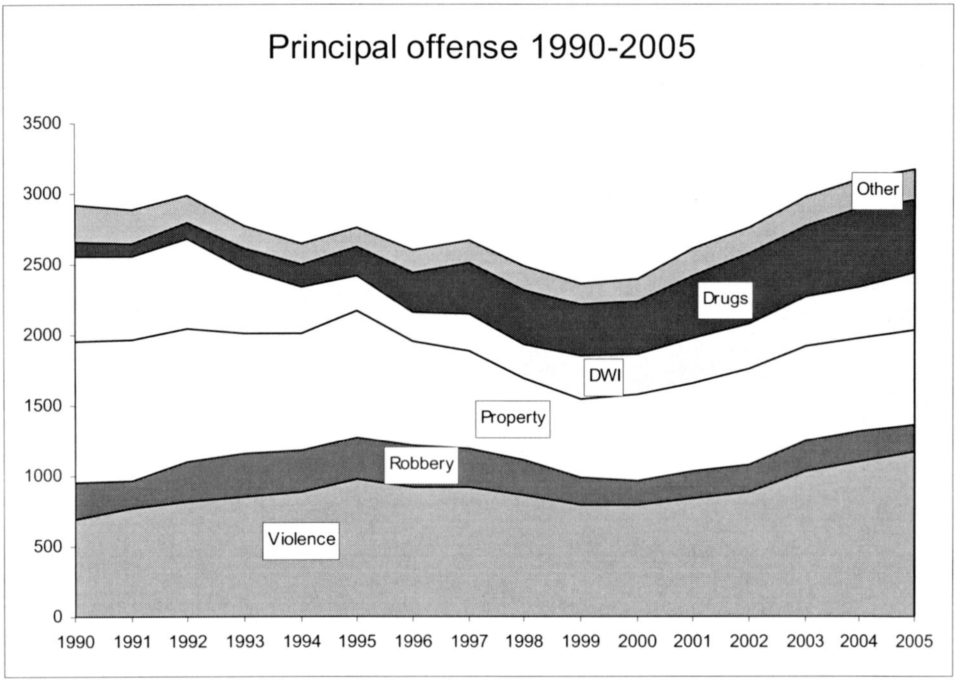

Source: Criminal Justice Agency

Table II.3 Prisoners on 1 May by type of offence in Finland (remand and fine defaulters excluded)

					Change %	
	1.5. 1999	1.5. 2002	1.5. 2005	1.5. 2006	*1999-2005*	*2005-2006*
Property	746	875	864	827	*15,8*	*-4,2*
Violence	794	951	1254	1349	*57,9*	*10,0*
Drunk Driving	312	313	409	386	*31,1*	*-7,3*
Drugs	360	498	512	484	*42,2*	*-5,6*
Other	149	125	134	140	*-10,1*	*4,8*
Total	2361	2762	3173	3186	*34,4*	*0,5*

Property offenses include robberies

Violence crime shows the most rapid increase (58 %) followed by drug offenses (42 %). The number of prison sentences imposed byt the courts for aggravated drug offences have doubled and the sentences have become longer by one third. However, rather than changes in the sentencing traditions, this increase reflects changes in the crime structure (especially in the quantity of the drugs). The good news is that after 2002 the situation seems to have been stabilised and between 2005-2006 the number of drug offenders in prison decreased by 6 %. The bad news is violent offences -- the largest prisoner group – still show an increase of 10 % between 2005 to 2006. This is a result of deliberate overall tightening in the official control of violent offences (in reporting, apprehension and sentencing level).

Table II.4. Prisoner rates according to prisoner groups in Finland 1990–2006

Prisoners serving a sentence by prisoner-group 1990-2005. Annual averages.

	Serving a sentence	*Remand*	*Fine defaulters*	*All*
1998	2421	292	96	2809
1999	2287	354	102	2743
2000	2358	376	121	2855
2001	2529	457	149	3135
2002	2765	478	190	3433
2003	2888	492	198	3578
2004	3023	473	81	3577
2005	3190	519	179	3888
2006	..	..	..	3790

Source: Criminal Justice Agency

The number of remand prisoners has almost doubled in 1998–2005 (but it still modest in the comparative perspective). Fine-defaulters are a specific problem for the Finns. The share of fine defaulters corresponds to some 5 % of the Finnish prison population (while Sweden manages to do without this group altogether). [3]

3 The short-term decline in 2004 is explainable by the fact due to a computer program failure (!) the enforcement of fine-default penalties was interrupted for most part of the year 2004. Unfortunately the programs were fixed, and the number of fine-defaulters rose back to their original level.

Figure 2 The Length of Sentences 1985-1995 (1 October) and 2000-2005 (1 May)

THE LENGTH OF SENTENCE IN 1985-1995 (1 October) AND 2000-2005 (1 May)

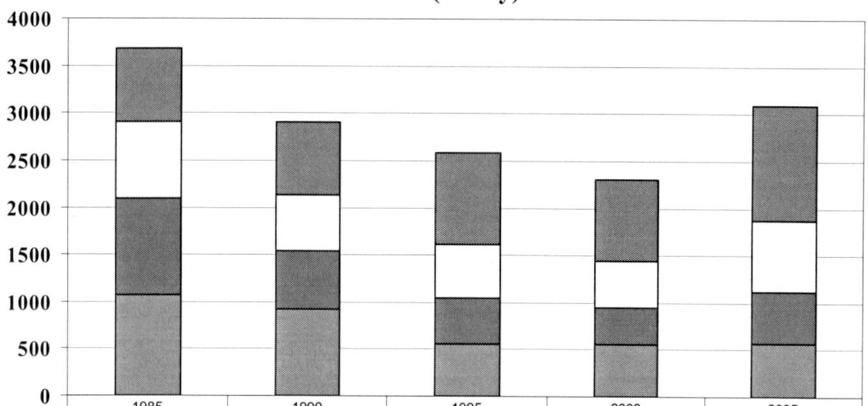

	1985	1990	1995	2000	2005
2 years-	783	775	971	853	1218
1<2 years	816	591	568	503	753
6<12 months	1019	614	494	390	556
<6 months	1068	923	551	553	565

<6 months 6<12 months 1<2 years 2 years-

Source: Criminal Justice Agency

The increase of prisoner rates in Finland in 1998–2004 is a summary effect of five major factors, each affecting in slightly different times: (1) An increase in the number of foreign prisoners (mainly from Russia and the Baltic countries), (2) an increase in drug trafficking (often linked with the former groups), an increase in the number of (3) fine defaulters and (4) prisoners in remand, and (5) an increase in violent offenders (towards the shift 1990/2000).

1.4.2 Characteristics Foreign Prison Population

During the 1990s foreign population living in Finland increased by some 250 % (from 26 000 to 114 000). This change has reflected also in the prisoner rates. The number of foreign prisoners increased from a near zero to a figure that corresponds to about 8 % of the Finnish prisoner rates.

Figure 3 Foreign prisoners rates in Finland 1976-2005

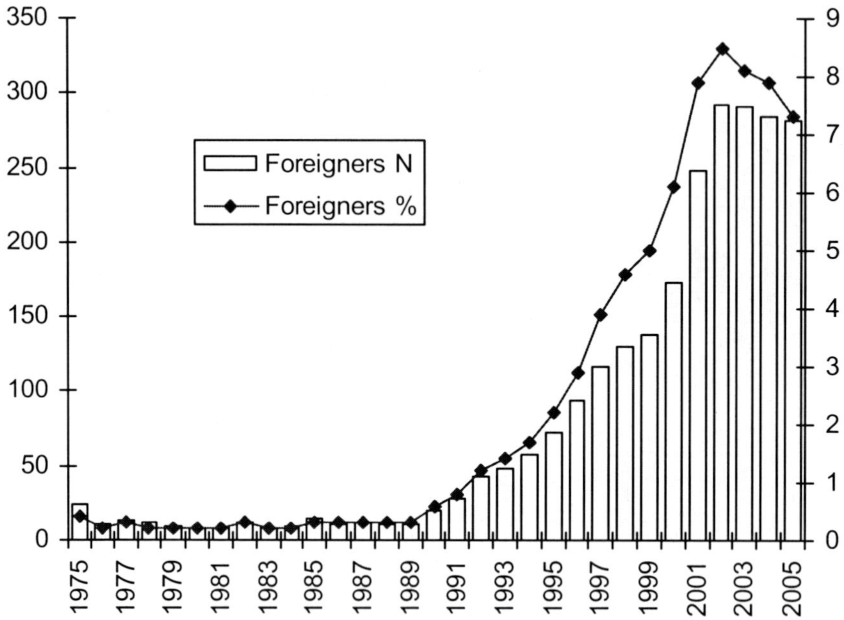

Source: Lappi-Seppälä (forthcoming)

Figure 4 Foreign prisoners by nationality 1995 - 2005

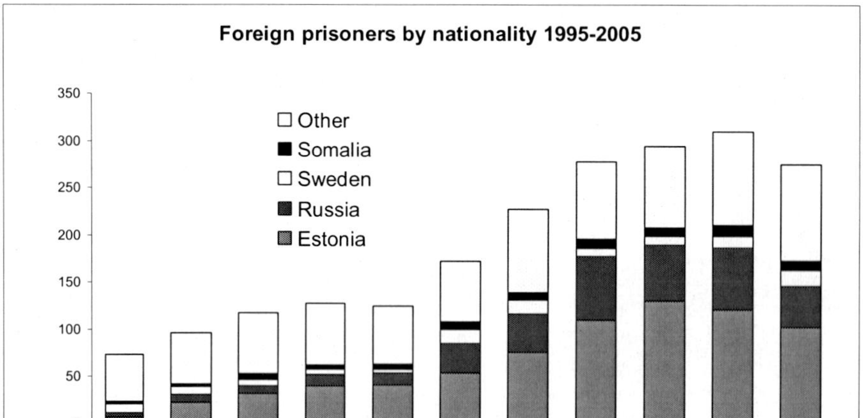

	1995	1996	1997	1998	1999	2000	2001	2002	2003	2004	2005
□ Other	49	54	64	65	62	64	88	82	86	99	102
■ Somalia	3	3	6	4	5	8	8	10	9	12	10
□ Sweden	9	8	7	6	4	15	15	8	9	12	16
■ Russia	5	8	8	12	13	31	40	68	60	66	44
■ Estonia	7	23	32	40	41	54	76	110	130	121	103

Source: Criminal Justice Agency

Half of the prisoners are detained for drug offences.

Figure 5

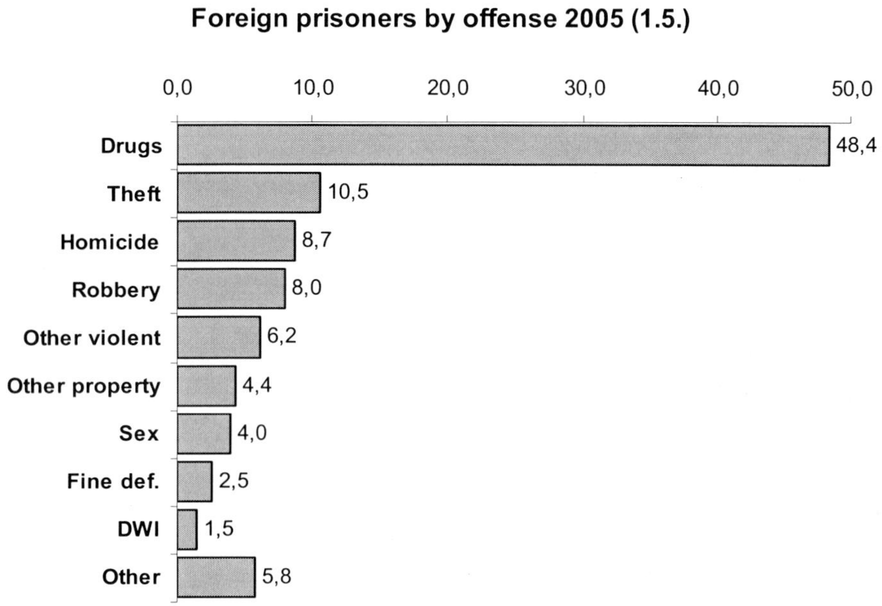

Source: Criminal Justice Agency

About 10 % of FP are women. Half of them are between the ages of 25-39 years.

Figure 6 Foreign prisoners according to their age in 2001-2005 (1 May)

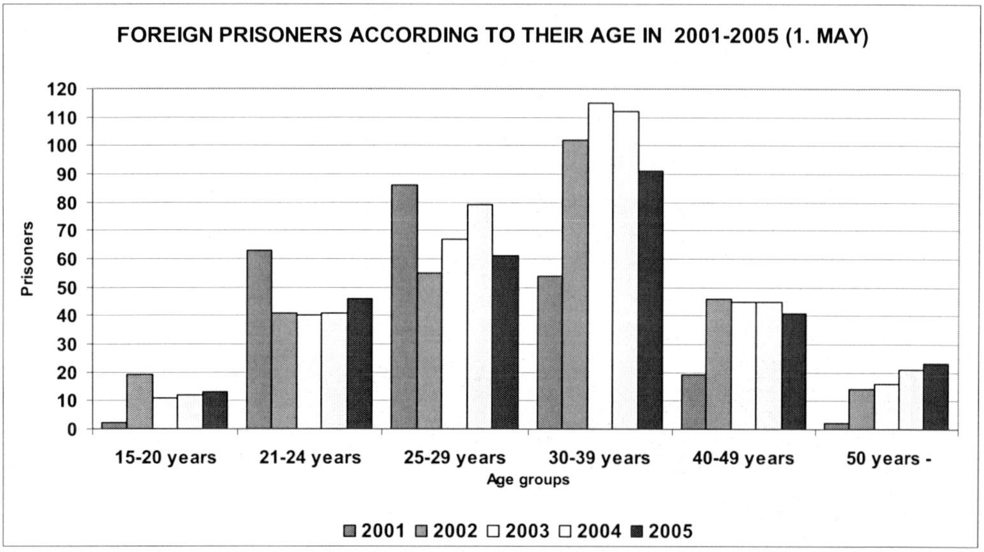

Source: Criminal Justice Agency

1.5 Overview of national legislation

1.5.1 Penitentiary Legislation

Provisions related to prisoners and the executions of sanctions are gathered in the new Penitentiary Law in force 2006. New Penitentiary Law gives high priority for the constitutional rights of prisoners. Leading principles in the enforcement include the following starting points (Penitentiary Law sections 2-4):

- "Goal of the enforcement of imprisonment is to increase the ability of a prisoner to a life without crime by promoting the prisoner's potential to cope and his adjustment to society as well as to prevent the committing of offences during the term of sentence."
- "A sentence of imprisonment shall be enforced so that it is safe to society, prison staff and prisoners."
- "The enforcement of imprisonment may not restrict the rights or circumstances of a prisoner in any other manner than that provided in the law or necessary due to the punishment itself."
- "The authorities in charge of the enforcement of imprisonment shall ensure that, during the imprisonment, no person will unjustifiably violate the personal integrity of the prisoner"
- "The conditions in a prison shall be arranged, to the extent possible, so that they correspond to the living conditions prevailing in society" (The principle of normalization)
- "The possibilities of a prisoner to maintain his health and functional ability shall be supported. The goal is to prevent any detriment resulting from the loss of liberty." (The aim of harm-minimization)
- "Prisoners shall be treated with justice and with respect for their human dignity. Prisoners may not, without a justifiable reason, be placed in an unequal position due to race, national or ethnic origin, colour, language, sex, age, family status, sexual orientation, state of health, disability, religion, social opinion, political or professional activity or other reason relating to the person".
- "When enforcing the imprisonment of juveniles, who have committed their offences when under 21 years of age, special attention shall be paid to the needs arising from the age and stage of development of the prisoner."

These principle apply also to foreign prisoners. They have the same legal position as other prisoners and they have the same legal rights and obligations, so the law applies to both groups on similar basis.
Provisions for all types of sanctions as well as crime definitions are in New Penal Code revised in several stages during the 1990s. Foreigners are not excluded from any specific sanctions. However, the use of community service seems to be underrepresented among the foreigners. This may partially result from the fact that to be able to carry out the sentence usually requires some language skills (if not Finnish then at least in Swedish or English). In addition to these provisions there are several special sections in national legislation that are applicable for foreign prisoners and minorities. These have been listed in section A above.

1.5.2 Penitentiary Legislation & Foreigners

Finland has ratified all the main human rights documents that influence the system of sanctions, sentence enforcement, and the treatment of those who are deprived of their liberties. The United Nations International Covenant on Civil and Political Rights entered into force in Finland in 1976 and the European Human Rights Convention (ECHR) in 1990. National courts can apply the provisions of the Convention. All the international agreements that Finland has adopted are part of the Finnish judicial system after having first been incorporated by the decision of the parliament.[4] There is a long lasting tradition of Nordic co-operation in legal matters. This co-operation has produced several legislative acts in each country since the 1960s onwards. In many cases, these Nordic agreements and acts go further than other European instruments. Still, the latter ones are, of course, also applied in relation to other countries. Finland has been active in ratifying agreements drafted within the EU, for instance, the Convention on the Protection of the European Communities' Financial Interests (1995) and the Convention relating to Extradition between the Member States of the EU (1996).

Extradition between the Nordic countries follows simplified rules, as compared to extradition to/from other countries. Between the Nordic countries there is no requirement of double criminality, and also Finnish citizens may be extradited to other Nordic countries. Both are exceptions from those principles that apply currently to other European countries. The Framework decision (11483/02) of the European Union on European arrest warrant and the surrender procedure between Member States will bring changes in both of these aspects (the general demand of double criminality and the obligation to extradite Finnish citizens to other European countries). These extensions are to be included in a bill that will be passed to the parliament in September 2003.

Nordic Agreement on Mutual Assistance between the Nordic states regulates the procedure in situations where a Nordic state needs assistance concerning the service of summons or the collection of evidence. The Agreement involves only certain fairly limited deviations from the European Convention on Mutual Assistance in Criminal Matters and presupposes that the Nordic co-operation shall be governed also by the Convention. In June 2003, the Government passed a bill to the parliament in order to implement the European Convention for Mutual Assistance in Criminal Matters (EYVL C 197, 12.7.2000).

The enforcement of *economic sanctions* follow simplified rules between the Nordic states, and judgements according to which such sanctions (for example fines) are imposed can, on request, be enforced in Finland without further formal conditions. A Nordic judgement on *imprisonment* may be enforced in Finland if the sentenced person, at the time of

---

4 However, these documents, such as the European Human Rights Convention (ECHR) do not have a general or absolute precedence over other statutory law in Finland. Still, in cases where the provisions of the convention and the contents of national law contradict each other, a doctrine of interpretation known as "human rights friendly interpretation", was adopted in Finland by the Constitutional Committee of the parliament: the interpretation and application of laws shall always aim at obtaining a result that as closely as possible corresponds to the international obligations of Finland in the field of human rights. The same principle has also been declared in the new Finnish Constitution which entered into force in 2000. According to section 22, the public authorities shall guarantee the observance of basic and human rights. As a result, the Finnish courts have more and more often referred to the articles of the convention in their decisions.

enforcement, is a Finnish citizen or is domiciled in Finland. Such a judgement may also be enforced in Finland if the sentenced person is present in Finland and it is considered appropriate that the sentence is enforced here. Consent from the convicted person is, in principle, not needed but his or her opinion is generally respected. Finland can, on request, *supervise offenders sentenced to a suspended (conditional) sentence*. No prerequisites are explicitly stated in the Nordic Act but, in principle, the criteria used with regard to sentences of imprisonment apply (supervision shall be enforced by another state than the one which passed the sentence only when the convicted person resides or plans to reside in the former state). Supervision of persons *conditionally released* in other Nordic states can be executed in Finland. The rules regarding the supervision of conditionally released persons and the rules regarding the supervision of offenders who have received a suspended sentence are very much the same.

These rules, in comparison with those applicable in relation to non-Nordic states, are simpler and contain fewer pre-conditions. However, the Framework decision (10710/01 COPEN 37) of the European Union on the application of the principle of mutual recognition to financial penalties would bring changes in this respect. Under current structure, the financial penalties imposed in other European countries outside the Nordic-region cannot be enforced in Finland. The Finnish government supports this expansion and wishes to extend it also to summary fines. The government also support the proposal for a new Framework decision concerning the enforcement of confiscation order within the EU-countries.

2 TREATMENT OF FOREIGN PRISONERS

2.1 General

Foreign prisoners are treated according to the same principles as national prisoners. However, other prisoners often discriminate those other prisoners, which differ from the Finnish and Europeans by their outlook (race, colour). This discriminated are being placed to sections where the prisoner are not mixed with other prisoners or where also other discriminated prisoners (based on crime or other reasons) are being placed. There are now security classifications but the distinction between open and closed prisons. Low risk prisoners who are capable to work are placed to open prisons (about 23 % of all). About the same percentage (20 %) of foreigners are placed in open prisons.

In autumn 2005 the Finnish prison service nominated a working group to examine whether ethnic minorities (basically foreigners and gypsies) are receiving equal treatment both in legal provisions, administrative guidelines and enforcement practices. In the work two groups of offenders receive the main attention: Foreigners (around 300 prisoners) and gypsies (around 200)n prisoners. These groups cover about 12 % of the daily prison population.

2.2 Living conditions and facilities

Foreign prisoners have access to the same living conditions and facilities as national prisoners. When placing the prisoner within an institution the individual traits of the prisoner, his or her chances to participate the prison activities (work, education etc.) must be taken into account. The prisoners own wishes regarding his or her placement must be considered as well.

Based on the prisoners own request he or she can be isolated from the other inmates if there are reasonable grounds. However, according to the Ombudsman of the Parliament isolating a prisoner must not be exercised as an additional punishment, but the objective can only be either to ensure that the prisoner remains in the facility or to maintain prison safety and security. "Isolation at one's own request" takes place often in cases when prisoner feels to be threatened by fellow prisoners. This group "fearing prisoners" has received attention during the last years in Finland. As it also seems, prisoners of ethnic origin and gypsies are over-represented among this prisoners. In 2004 a specific section was established in Helsinki prison for "fearing prisoners". Among those 142 prisoners who were replaced in that unit, 25 had ethnic background and 18 were gypsies (30 % in contras to overall 12 % see above).

2.3 Reception and admission

Reception procedures are the same for nationals and foreigners. Prison-rules have been translated into English, Russian and Estonian. Prisons have also translated the daily programs into those languages needed. In Helsinki prison additional information is arranged for Russian and Estonian prisoners. Prisoners are entitled to communicate with a representative of their diplomatic mission (consulate). They can also call their families, provided they have money for the telephone. The practical measures regarding phone calls vary in different institutions. The most common procedure is that prisoners can purchase telephones cards to be utilised in the prison telephones during a separately designated time (usually 1-2 hours per week).

There are no separate 'telephone funds' directed to prisoners without money. However, every prisoner is entitled to a prisoner's allowance, which is 0, 20 □/hour both in closed and in open institutions. The prisoner allowance is paid to those prisoners who cannot participate in prison duties (work, education, action programmes). Private telephone calls and other personal expenses are expected to be covered with the allowance. Financial benefit can be received from the social services for official calls such as calls for attorney. If the prisoner is without funds, he or she is also eligible to make a free 'homecoming' phone call when released from prison to a Finnish address he or she is registered (if available).

2.4 Work - Education – Training – Sports - Recreation

Foreign prisoners attend to work and to the educational and vocational training in classes, sports and recreational activities as all other prisoners. However the lack of language skills causes difficulties especially in programs that are based on communication. Russian prisoners have been arranged with outside help health- and service info courses in Kerava. Helsinki and Kerava provide lessons in the Finnish language. The prison libraries have some books in foreign languages. The libraries may order books and videos in other languages if such material is available.

2.5 Food – Religion – Personal hygiene – Medical care

Religion: over 90 % of the Finnish population belong to the Evangelic-Lutheran church. Also the majority of prison priests represent Evangelic-Lutheran church, although every foreign prisoner has a right to a priest of his or her own religion. All prisoners have in principle the right to practice their own religion alone and together with others, provided that this does not breach "the law, good manners and prison order". According to the law, "care must be taken that the prisoners do not have to take part in religious occasions against their own will." The law also obliges the prison to reserve a suitable facility for joint religious ceremonies for those prisoners who form the majority. For other prisoners facilities will be provided "according to practical possibilities". Furthermore, prisoners have the right to discuss privately with a person belong to his/her own religion. Arrangements have been agreed upon with the Orthodox Church to take care of the Russian prisoners (part time orthodox clerks). In Kerava the Muslim prisoners have a prayer-hour once a week.

Diet and food: the Prison Service arranges special diets according to the religions demands. Enforcement appreciates the diet requirements as well as the Ramadan-period. The Cantinas are also provided with ethnic food.

Medical care: medical and the healthcare are organized on similar principles for all prisoner groups. In practice language problems and the lack of interpreters may cause problems. Also personal hygiene requirements are the same for all prisoners. The prisoners are eligible to shower as often as they wish. The inmates may keep their personal clothes.

2.6 Consular and legal help

The prisoners are informed about their choice to take contact with the representatives of their diplomatic mission. They decide themselves, whether they will use this option or not. The income limit to receive free legal aid in Finland is 650 □ per month. Up to the income limit of 1400 □ per month a person is entitled to partially free legal aid. Also non-nationals without legal resident permits are eligible for free legal aid. Interpreters shall be designated for foreign prisoners when needed. In practice difficulties in finding the interpreters have been encountered with prisoner from the African countries.

2.7 Contact with the outside world

Foreign prisoners may stay in contact with their relatives and also receive visits. Telephone is the most frequently used means of communication. Prisoners who cannot read nor write are granted help with their letters and correspondence. Newspapers in different languages (mostly English) are available in some prisons, as well as cable television with various channels. Consulates assist often in providing the reading-materials (newspapers etc).

2.8 Re-integration activities - Prison leave

There are no special programs for foreign prisoners in order to promote the resettlement into society after release. Foreign prisoners are allowed to go on furlough according to individual discretion. Normal rule for parole also apply. Parole is being used on routine-basis after ½ or 2/3 of the sentence has been served.

2.9 Release - Expulsion

Upon release foreign prisoners are being sent to their country of origin depending on the seriousness of their offence and the length of the sentence. The criteria for overall consideration of expulsion are defined in the Aliens Act.

A foreigner who has resided in Finland under a residence permit may be expelled if: 1) he or she resides in Finland without the required residence permit; 2) he or she is found guilty of an offence punishable by imprisonment for a maximum of a year, or if he or she is found guilty of repeated offences; 3) he or she has shown, through his or her activities that he or she is liable to endanger other people's safety; or 4) he or she has been engaged in activities that endanger Finland's national security or relations with a foreign state or on the basis of his or her previous activities and for other reasons, there are grounds to suspect that he or she may engage in such activities. A refugee may be expelled in the cases referred to in 2-4 above. A refugee may not be expelled to his or her home country or country of permanent residence against which he or she still needs international protection. A refugee may only be expelled to a State that agrees to admit him or her.

In the Act it is stated that when considering refusal of entry, expulsion or prohibition of entry and the duration of the prohibition of entry, account shall be taken of the facts on which the decision is based and the facts and circumstances affecting the matter otherwise as a whole. When considering the matter, particular attention should be paid to the best interest of children and the protection of family life. Other facts to be considered include at least the length and purpose of the alien's residence in Finland, the nature of the residence permit issued to him or her and the alien's ties to Finland. Should a refusal of entry be based on any criminal activity of the alien, account shall be taken of the seriousness of the act and the detriment, damage or danger caused to public or private security. This applies mutatis mutandis to IV.9. See below ('Administrative detention of foreign prisoners'). Alien's act is applied to both prisoner groups.

Competentauthorities: police or authorities at the border shall take action to refuse an alien entry or expel an alien who does not meet the requirements for entry into or residence in the country. After that period, police or authorities at the border shall submit a proposal to the Directorate of Immigration to the effect that the alien be refused entry or be expelled, unless the Directorate of Immigration has already taken action to remove the alien from the country.

Police or authorities at the border may order a maximum of two years' prohibition of entry for an alien if he or she is refused entry. Police or authorities at the border shall submit a proposal to the Directorate of Immigration to the effect that the alien be refused entry if they are not competent to refuse entry or if they consider that the alien should be prohibited from entering the country for more than two years.

The Directorate of Immigration decides on refusal of entry upon proposal by the District Police or authorities at the border or on its own initiative. The Directorate of Immigration always decides on refusal of entry if more than three months have passed since the alien's entry into the country, or if the alien has applied for a residence permit on the basis of international or temporary protection. The Directorate of Immigration decides on expulsion upon proposal by the District Police or authorities at the border or on its own initiative. The Directorate of Immigration may prohibit entry of aliens for a fixed term or until further notice. The Directorate of Immigration decides on abolishing a prohibition of entry.

2.10 Aftercare – Probation

In case foreign offenders stay after release in the host country, are they allowed to make use of aftercare facilities and support from the probation service as offered to national ex-offenders. In practice, however, much depends on the language skills of the offender. For Russian and Estonian prisoners special programs related to drugs and alcohol have been arranged.

2.11 Staff

There are some 2700 full time officials working in the Prison Service. More than half of them work in supervising and guarding duties, the majority are on uninterrupted three-shift work. During recent years, the structure of the personnel has been developed and job descriptions broadened for instance by directing the personnel's work input more on various prisoners' activity programmes and close work. The Probation Service employs some 300 civil servants. Most of them are client workers: social workers and instructors whose duty is to enforce community sanctions. Also the assistant directors and a great deal of directors of the district offices carry out client work. At the end of the year 2004 there were 330 private supervisors at the service of the Probation Service. Private supervisors supervise in the direction of the district offices conditionally sentenced young offenders and conditionally released prisoners (parolees). For supervision work a nominal fee is paid. The basic training of the prison staff includes also courses in English. There is no other special training to deal with foreign prisoners.

2.12 Projects

There are no specific projects funded by the Government for foreign prisoners inside or outside penitentiary institutions in Finland. Some of the support services offered by Non-Governmental Organisations have been described in section I. 4 above.

3 ADMINISTRATIVE DETENTION OF FOREIGN PRISONERS

A. General questions
The provisions dealing with the administrative prisoners are in The Aliens Act (301/2004) and the Act on the Treatment of Aliens in Custody and on a Custody Unit (116/2002).

3.1 Institution

Finland has only one custody unit for aliens referred to in the Aliens Act. In 2005 the previous Helsinki Unit was transferred to a new Custody Unit in Metsälä near Helsinki. The new facility has a capacity for ca. 40 detainees.

The detention of an alien is specifically meant to safeguard the clarification of the preconditions of entry of an alien or the enforcement of expulsion in cases where another safety measure, for example the duty to report, cannot be deemed sufficient.

The basic training of the staff is good. Many have degrees from a college, a polytechnic or a vocational institution in the fields of health care, social studies or a corresponding field. In addition, the Custody Unit arranges and acquires additional training for example in safety issues.

The Metsälä Custody Unit also hosts a small reception centre for asylum seekers (46 places) as well as an information/service point for asylum seekers with private accommodation. The aim is for the children and spouse of the detained, where possible, to be accommodated in the premises of the open reception centre. On the other hand, the custody unit can also use the services of the reception centre. The new premises comply with the Finnish standard for institutions, in addition to which the special features and requirements of custody operations have also been observed. In connection with the changes in 2005 the conditions of the customers improved considerably; there is more room for free time activities and hobbies. The outdoor exercise premises will be much more pleasant than at present and there also is a special outdoor area for i.e. smoking, which the customers will have free access to.

A detained alien may exceptionally be placed in police detention premises if the custody unit is full. Another reason for placing a person in police detention premises is that an alien is detained far away from the closest custody unit. In the latter case, the detention may not last more than four days.

3.2 Ministry responsible & legislation

The Custody Unit operates subordinate to the Ministry of Labour. Its operation and the treatment of persons in custody there are governed by the Act on the Treatment of Aliens in Custody and on a Custody Unit (116/2002).

3.3 Capacity institutions

The institution has a capacity of 40 inmates.

3.4 Length of stay

There are no written norms on the maximum length of the stay. The district court decides on the continuation of the detention in two- week intervals. In actual practice the maximum length of stay is, however, 3 months. The average length of stay was in 2005 17 days. The period of detention depends on the progress of the investigation and other authorities. The matters involving a detained person are handled as urgent.

3.5 Decisions procedure

In the first instance the police or border guards take the decision for detention but the district court will decide on further detention. The assessment of the justification and necessity of detention is performed by the District Court at the latest within four days from the apprehension under section 124 of the Aliens Act. Also an asylum seeker who has been given a negative decision can be detained before expulsion.

3.6 Appeal procedure

The decision of the District Court is not subject to appeal.

3.7 Irregular stay

Illegal stay in the country is criminalized as an intentional crime and punishable with fines.

3.8 Numbers

The number of detained irregular foreigners varies from single cases to some 20-30 at any given day.

3.9 Expulsion

No statistics are available on those foreigners that have been expelled after administrative detention. However a rough estimation varies between 70-80 %.

3.10 Not-expelled prisoners

Non-expelled foreigners will be released. In case they receive the status of asylum seeker they are moved under the jurisdiction of asylum seekers centre.

3.11 Detention irregulars under criminal law

Under certain conditions Category 3 prisoners may also be placed in police facilities (see above), which usually hold also prisoners who are detained under criminal law. Minors (under 18 years) may be held in the detention unit. In this case they are immediately appointed a representative to take care of their interests.

The powers of the police to enter the premises of the Metsälä Custody Unit and to impose restrictions on detainees are very limited. In cases involving the safety of the custody unit, the director of the Custody Unit or his deputy contacts the police. These cases involve the safety of the persons in custody and the police act on request of the Custody Unit.

The police have been reserved premises in connection with the Custody Unit, where they can meet with an alien in issues relating to the application of the Aliens Act, such as the reason for entry, travel itinerary and removal from the country. This is done to avoid the transportation of detained aliens and to decrease costs arising from transportation.

It would be contrary to the principle of the least harm and more restrictive of the rights of the detained to transport him separately to police premises solely to hear him if the custody unit has premises where the hearing may take place causing the smallest possible harm to the customer. In some cases, for example to take comparison fingerprints, it is necessary to transport the detainee to the police station for the procedure. In that case, it is also well founded to hear him in the premises of the police.

The hearings are recorded using computer-based forms. Both a pending pre-trial investigation and a police investigation relating to asylum are confidential. In order to ensure data security and the legal protection of both the detained person and the police, no outsider can be allowed access to the premises where the police keep their computers and forms.

Visits of the police to the Custody Unit are agreed upon. The police do not have free access to the premises of the Custody Unit. Nor do the police have authority with regard to the operations and personnel of the Custody Unit.

The independent powers of the police with regard to an alien detained in a custody unit are restricted to the following cases: (1) The police may forbid contacts with an outsider if, for a well-founded reason, the contact is estimated to endanger the clarification of the entry preconditions of an alien taken into custody and his identity or if there is a justifiable reason to assume that the meeting will contribute to a crime. (2) The police make the decision on segregation in a custody unit if segregation is necessary as an exception to safeguard the clarification of the preconditions of entry into the country or identity.

B COMPARISON TO IMPRISONMENT

1. General. Detention units for foreign administrative prisoners are closed social units that differ in many respects from prison. The conditions are often more comfortable and the relationships with the staff and the wards are based on co-operation. The staff consists mainly of tutors, not of guards. Security aspects are not forgotten, but the wards are motivated by the fact that the conditions are more relaxed than in prison and this is also appreciated by the wards themselves. In case of violence and attempted escapes, the ward may temporarily be placed in isolation or in police-premises.

2. Living conditions and facilities. Foreign administrative prisoners have basically access to better and more relaxed living conditions and facilities than normal prisoners (see above).

3. Reception and admission. Upon arrival foreign administrative prisoners receive information on the prison rules in their own language both verbally and, if possible, in writing. They are entitled to communicate with a representative of their diplomatic mission, their family and legal aid instances (e.g. The Refugee Advice Centre). The wards may also keep their own mobile phones, provided that these do not have the camera-facility.

4. Work - Education – Training – Sports – Recreation. There are no educational or vocational training programs available. The wards may participate daily in different kinds of sports and recreational activities. There is a small library with books with foreign languages as well as access to internet and TV.

5. Food – Religion – Personal hygiene – Medical care. Foreign administrative prisoners are able to practice their own religion. For that purpose the unit has a small room for religious duties. However, no visits of qualified religious representatives have been organized. Dietary restrictions based on religious or cultural reasons are appreciated. Issues concerning clothing are not interfered with provided that it is in accordance with the general standards of decency. The Custody Unit has attended to arranging acute dental care. Appropriate treatment and therapy will be acquired for those needing psychological or psychiatric help either by calling in a psychiatrist or a psychologist to the Custody Unit or by transporting the person in need of the help outside the Custody Unit for treatment.

6. Consular and legal help. The unit itself has not established direct contacts with foreign representatives of their diplomatic mission. The foreign prisoners can directly be in contact with consular officials and lawyers and they may meet basically any visitors they wish. Asylum seekers have access to free legal aid.

7. Contact with the outside world. The wards have the right to receive any visitors they prefer and to communicate with the outside world. They may have their own mobile phones, provided that these have no camera-function. They may, further, have access to the Internet, TV and some foreign newspapers. The telephone may be used on condition that the detained alien gives notice of whom he intends to contact. The use of the telephone may be denied if, for a well-founded reason, it may be estimated to endanger the clarification of the preconditions of entry into the country or identity or if there is justifiable reason to assume that the use of the telephone will contribute to a crime. (17 §). The right to be in contact with someone outside the custody unit by using telecommunications, other electronic communications or other such technical connection may be restricted on the grounds provided for in section 17 by confiscating the mobile phone or other means of communication from the alien for the duration of the ban.

8. Re-integration activities - Prison leave. Foreign administrative prisoners are not provided with specific activities that prepare them for resettlement into society after release. Neither are there any intermediate steps, such as furloughs or parole. However, an alien may be granted permission to leave the custody unit in order to visit or bury a seriously ill close relative or other close person or for other similar reasons of special significance.

9. Release – Expulsion.
See above III.9:

4 NATIONALS DETAINED ABROAD

The Legal Register Centre of Finland is the authority responsible for collecting and maintaining statistics regarding sentences imposed abroad on a Finnish national or a foreigner permanently living in Finland. The Criminal Records Act states that information from the criminal records shall be delivered to a State Party of the European Convention on Mutual Assistance in criminal matters. Furthermore, provisions on the delivery of data from the criminal records to another Nordic country shall be issued by Decree. However, according to the officials of the Legal Register Centre the procedure of receiving data from abroad is not realised in practise (except for data exchange between the Nordic countries). This means that there is no valid information available on the numbers and characteristics of the Finnish prison population detained abroad.

Nationals detained abroad are not an issue in Finland. Therefore, there is no media or general public opinion on this particular topic. However, individual cases may receive sometimes quite a lot of media attention. In these cases the main concern is on the well being of the prisoners and then fact that detention times are in many cases much longer in other countries and also usually in much worse conditions.

5 EVALUATION AND RECOMMENDATIONS

Both *legal and material conditions of foreign prisoners* are deemed to be in a fairly satisfying level. The new prison law (in force 1.10.2006) rectifies most of the existing shortcomings in the penitentiary legislation. The problems faced by the foreign prisoners are to large extent similar to those faced by national (minority group) prisoners. *Fear of fellow prisoners* is among those problems (although in international comparison fear in Finnish prisons is relative low. Among those groups suffering most from the pressures and intimidation from fellow prisoners are sexual offenders of "wrong colour". The prison administration faces a serious challenge in order to secure the proper standard of security and safety for foreign prisoners as well as other minority groups.

The CPT carried out in 2003 its third periodic investigation of the Finnish prisons (http://www.cpt.coe.int/documents/fin/2004-20-inf-eng.htm). Foreign *nationals detained under aliens legislation* were among the key topics under consideration. The report was generally positive with relatively few critical remarks. Since the visit of CPT a new custody unit for aliens had been established in order to overcome the earlier shortcomings with the older unit regarding outdoor exercises and medical care. CPT reported also shortcomings regarding the instructions according to which the police and the Frontier Guard establishments should provide detained foreign nationals with a written account of their rights in a language they understand. The Finnish authorities referred to these shortcomings in their report (paragraph 53). Along with the entry into force of the new Aliens Act (301/2004) on 1 May 2004, the procedures have been improved in order to enhance the legal protection of persons under the Act. In all decisions made under the Aliens Act, the person in question is issued a written decision in his case with appeal instructions. All the decision forms of the Frontier Guard relating to alien issues have been renewed and translated into different languages, such as Swedish, Russian, German, Spanish, French and English.

The *accelerated asylum procedures* in Finland have been widely criticized. The legal safeguards are not sufficient considering the interests of asylum seekers. The timeframe of eight days for the execution of the expulsion decision is too short for applicant to prepare the appeal, including appropriate legal and linguistic assistance. Within eight days the Helsinki Administrative Court should process the application and also give the decision. NGOs have presented that the timeframe of eight days should be given up and the expulsion should not be executed before the Administrative Court has dealt with the case. (The Refugee Advice Centre 2006.)

Chapter 9

France

Pascal Décarpes

I INTRODUCTION

Foreign national prisoners have never been high up on the French political agenda[1]. Social and economic difficulties – e.g. a 10% unemployment rate - a persistent and influential xenophobic political minority and a constantly rising prison population partially explain this lack of attention for such a serious issue. In order to observe and analyse the situation of foreign nationals in French prisons, researchers have had quarterly statistics at their disposal since the early 1970's, and the 'individual prisoner file' since 1993 including socio-demographic, penal and release data. The rate of foreign prisoners among the prison population has gone up from 18% in 1975 to 29% in 1995.[2] The absolute growth between 1975 and 1999 was an increase from 4,645 up to 12,164 foreign national inmates. It corresponds to a 162% rise in comparison to 91% for French inmates.

Figure 1: Foreign national prison population in regard to nationalities since 1992 *France-continent and France-overseas*

Year	*Total all foreign nationals*	*Europe*	*Africa*	*America*	*Asia*	*Oceania*	*Non-defined nationality*
1992	15 044	16,3 %	70,0 %	5,1 %	7,9 %	0,1 %	0,7 %
1998	13 557	23,5 %	62,0 %	5,8 %	8,3 %	0,1 %	0,3 %
2004	13 123	28,5 %	52,3 %	9,1 %	9,6 %	0,1 %	0,4 %

Source: Prison administration statistics, Paris

1.1. Overview of penalties and measures

In total, 82% of all releases (2,859 persons between 1 January 1996 and 30 April 1997) have not benefited either from a conditional release, or from a sentence in the community. In 2004, only 5.8% of released prisoners benefited from conditional release. In this context, foreign prisoners cannot expect much from these rarely applied measures. Moreover, irregular foreign detainees are excluded from measures such as prison leaves, furlough or electronic monitoring. Concerning more specific penal features, 41.7 % of foreign prisoners are pre-trial detainees (vs. 31.3% among the French prison population). About 85% of the foreigners first entered prison through pre-trial detention (69% among French prisoners). 58% of the foreign nationals in pre-trial detention were sent to prison through a 'fast track' procedure (47%), which in turn increases the probability of being sentenced to imprisonment because of the poor trial conditions. 6% of the foreign nationals were imprisoned through a criminal procedure (11%). One fourth was sentenced for drug offences.

1 There is also no mention of foreign nationals in the last CPT-Report (31 March 2004) on French prisons after its visit between the 11 and the 17 June 2003.

2 All further references and data are, when not mentioned, issued from the Ministry of Justice.

Figure 2: Comparison French / foreign nationals in regard to number of convictions and main sentence

Nature of the main sentence	*Total*	*% Total*	*Foreign nationals*	*% Foreign nationals*
Imprisonment	258257	54	37188	59.6
(partly)	74783	30	17839	47.9
Partly on probation	24899	9.6	2923	7.8
All on probation	158575	61.4	16426	44.1
Fine	148411	31	17930	28.7
Alternative sentence	49900	10.4	5394	8.6
Other	21367	4.5	1840	2.9

Source: National criminel file 2002, Paris

1.2 Overview of the Prison System

No particular kind of institution is used to detain foreigners - foreign prisoners are allocated to general prisons. Nor is there a specific section of the prison service (or another authority) that is responsible for foreigners. Furthermore, there is no special controlling mechanism for foreign detainees (this also applies to general prisons; most control is performed by judicial bodies).

1.2.1 Organisational structure

Under the authority of the Ministry of Justice, the organisational structure of the prison service is based on a central prison administration (the DAP) which is situated in Paris. There are nine regional administrations and one overseas 'mission' that implement national policies. The responsible authorities are the national head officer, ten regional executives and the local prison directors. There are 188 prisons and one "public facility of national health" (in Fresnes). There are three main types of institutions: 115 pre-trial and short sentence prisons ('maison d'arrêt', hereinafter referred to as MA) and 29 corresponding sections located in other prisons; 24 long[3] sentence prisons ('centre de détention', hereinafter referred to as CD) and 31 corresponding sections; and five prisons for prisoners with very long sentences ('maison centrale') and 8 corresponding sections. There are also 13 semi-liberty centres and four corresponding sections (underused to only 60% of their capacity). Social and judicial care and monitoring are performed by 101 'probation and insertion service' headquarters. The first semi-private prison was opened in the late 1980s, and since then the number of such public-private partnerships has increased to 27. The overall prison budget in 2005 was about 1.654 billion euros, a rise of 3.9% compared to 2004, and accounts for 30.3% of the budget of the Ministry of Justice. On the other hand, the prison staff numbers grew 5.7% in one year, reaching a total of 30,238 employees.

All members of prison staff are public servants. Directors, probation officers, guards, technicians and members of the administration all receive training at the 'National

3 Based on the Recommandation of the Council of Europe Rec(2003)23 on the mamagement by prison administrations of life sentence an other long-term prisoners.

School of the Prison Administration' (ENAP) in Agen. The school budget for 2004 was roughly 26.5 million euros. 238 persons work at the school and each year over 700 non-residents give lectures. In 2005, 5,813 participants - of whom 1,040 were guards - took part in the educational programme.

In July 2006, the prison capacity was 50,332 places. 5,000 new places were created between 2002 and 2006. Four new prisons with 600 places each opened in 2004 and 2005. 13,200 places are planned_in the 2002 law, and the first are to be available in 2007. Eight MA - with 700-800 places each - are planned for 2008, three prisons with 400-700 places each for 2009 and 7 prisons for juveniles, with 60 places each, are scheduled from 2007 on. On 1 July 2006, there were 61,413 prisoners (down 1.6% since July 2005), which represents 97.4 prisoners per 100,000 of the resident population. 1,568 prisoners have been supervised with electronic monitoring and 357 have been placed externally without accommodation; consequently, there was a ratio of 118 inmates per 100 places. There were 20,999 pre-trial detainees (34% of the total prison population). On 1 July 2006, in 13 prisons or prison sections the rate of overcrowding was 200% or more. In a further 51 prisons or prison sections, the rate was between 150 and 200%, and between 100 and 150% in yet another 74 prisons or prison sections. The overcrowding is only in pre-trial prisons ('MA'), in which short prison sentences of less than 1 year are served, and of whom most are foreign prisoners.

To sum up, between 1980 and 2006, we can observe a rise from 66 up to 97 prisoners per 100,000 of the resident population. The development of the French prison population rate follows the same trend as all other European countries (with the exception of Finland). As to alternative sanctions, on 1 January 2005, 125,437 persons were under judicial monitoring and supervision in the community. On 1 January 2006, 1,221 were in semi liberty (6,440 measures in 2005), 525 in placement outside (2,310), and 871 were being electronically monitored (4,025). 5,916 benefited from conditional release in 2005 and 16,885 were working for the community on 1 January 2005. At the same time, 108,528 persons were on conditional probation (78% of all measures in the community).

In regard to prison population numbers, on 1 December 2005there were 2,129 women (3.6%) and 744 minors (1.1%) in French prisons. About half of the prison population is under 30 years old. On 1 January 2006, 2,242 prisoners were older than 60 (3.8% of prison population, twice the figure of a decade earlier). 59.5% had received an education, only 44% had a job.

1.2.2 Foreign prisoners

There were 4,645 imprisoned foreign nationals in 1975, 15,507 in 1993 (30.8 %), and most recently 11,125 (20 %) on 1 January 2006. On the one hand, the growth of the foreign prisoners' population between 1982 and 1996 is mainly due to a rise in offences against immigration laws. Concerning other offences, the increase remains equal to the French prisoners' figure[4]. On the other hand, foreign nationals are imprisoned more than French nationals because of a lack of different guarantees or resources[5], such as a home, an income, locally residing family, work, etc. Besides, in 1998, 28.5 % of foreign nationals in prison were detained in relation to immigration offences (illegal residence, refusal of

4 see *Kensey/Tournier* 2002, p. 24-25.

5 see *Mary* 1998.

removal, refusal to give name and citizenship in order to oppose expulsion). Between 2000 and 2003, there was a 32% increase in such sentences to prison, from 2,345 up to 3,085. They were sentenced for immigration- and/or other immigration related offences such as the use of false documents or food theft. A major problem in studying specific groups of inmates is the French citizenship approach of the 'universal citizen'. The prison administration invokes little information on foreign nationals because of the discriminatory aspects of such data. Additionally, there is little information as well as contradictory assertions on ethnic sorting[6]. Moreover, the expulsions and removals should be taken into account within prison population figures. Unfortunately this is seldom the case.

Concerning our studied group, 21.5% are foreign nationals: 29.4% of all foreign prisoners come from Europe, 10.1% from the American continents, 9.6% from Asia, and 50.4% from Africa. Foreign prisoners are clearly over-represented because foreign nationals constitute only around 3.5% of the French population. Among foreign prisoners in 1998, 5.2% were women (4.9% among French prisoners), the average age was 31.1 years (30.3 in the case of French prisoners), 22% were married (11%), 66% had no children (65%), 14% were analphabetic (3%), 50% were unemployed (35%), and 22% were in employment (28%). Among foreign prisoners, 92% of illegal foreign nationals who enter prison come from precarious circumstances vs. 57% of legal foreigners[7].

1.3 Involvement of Embassies, Consulates, NGOs etc.

There is currently no detailed information on the actual involvement of Embassies, Consulates or NGOs in issues relating to foreign prisoners.

1.4 Overview of trends

A key-date concerning the prison population is the abolition of the death penalty in 1981 and its 'replacement' with the life prison sentence. This is one of the reasons for the rise of the average duration of detention between 1982 and 1998 by 54% for French prisoners and 80% for foreign prisoners (around nine months). The penal climate has become harsher. High rates of unemployment, populist and xenophobic discourses, and pressure from the mass media are some reasons for harsher sentences, for instance through tougher drug legislation. The drug law of 31 December 1970 is conservative and punitive as a reaction to the 1968 movement. It has been amended (and strengthened) several times - in 1986, 1987, 1992 and 1996.

In regard to all sentenced offences, French and foreign nationals exhibit the same offending structure. Both groups committed around 0.7% serious offences, 82% misdemeanours, and 17% petty offences (National Criminal File 2002). It indicates that nationality is not a criminogenic characteristic. However, the more an offence is elucidated, the more foreign nationals are among the suspects[8]. This is indicative of the fragility and the visibility of their situation, which in turn facilitate the activities of the police. In 1998, 14% of the convicted and 24% of detainees were foreign nationals[9]. At the same time,

6 see *Oip* 2005, p. 14.

7 see *Lamy* 2004.

8 see *Lévy, R.* (1987), Du suspect au coupable, le travail de la police judiciaire, Médecine et Hygiène, Klinsieck, Genève, 53-54.

9 "Les condamnations en 1998", Etudes et Statistiques Justice (2000), n° 16, minsitère de la Justice.

15% of foreign nationals were sentenced to prison solely for a drug offence in comparison to 9% for French persons (52% vs. 37% for burglary)[10]. For handling stolen goods as a sole offence, 16% of prison sentences were less than three months in length for foreign nationals vs. 30% for French nationals[11]. Since the 1992 reform of the penal code, more than 200 offences can result in an 'Interdiction from entering French national Territory' (hereinafter referred to as an ITF). In 2004, 8.750 such ITFs were passed: 1,518 as the main sentence, and 7,232 as a complementary sentence. The public prosecutor demands the ITF - almost systematically - when a drug or an immigration offence has been committed. For common offences, it can occur that the judge imposes an ITF, although the public prosecutor did not demand it (for instance in the judicial districts of Rouen and Pontoise)[12]. The ITF is ruled under article 131-30 CP. An immigration offence can lead to a three month prison term with a complementary 3 year ITF sentence. The Rouen court refuses all ITF appeals for drug offences, "even if the person has been living in France for 40 years and has 5 children"[13]. In some cases, public prosecutors were asked by the préfet (local State head officer) to charge illegal foreign nationals with prison sentences in order to have sufficient time to prepare their removal. Many court decisions are in favour of foreign nationals against public authorities' policies in issues such as asylum, removal, expulsion, social security, citizenship and family rights. Still, few foreign nationals are actually aware of their rights. Moreover, the political pressure is permanent. In November 2005, the Minister of the Home Office announced the expulsion of foreign nationals who were arrested during the urban guerrilla in France last spring, even those holding a legal permit of residence.

1.5 Overview of national legislation

Foreign prisoners have about the same legal position as other prisoners as well as the same legal rights and obligations. The main national legislation on foreign nationals is comprised in the 'Code of entry and stay of foreign nationals and of asylum rule' (CESEDA), which contains all rules from ordinance n° 45-2658 of 2 November 1945 and law n° 52-893 of 25 July 1952, as well as new codification relevant to Article 92 of the law of 26 November 2003. With regard to foreign prisoners, there is no specific penitentiary law. Prison rules are comprised in the Criminal Code ("Code Pénal", 'CP') in articles 714 to 803-4; and in the Code of criminal procedure ("Code de Procédure Pénale", 'CPP')[14]: Some are in "Rule part-State council" Articles R.55 to R.61-6 but most of them are in "Rule part-simple decrees" within 'Book V procedure of execution, Title I execution of criminal sanctions'.

It is striking that most prison legislation is made of simple decrees in the CPP. Thus, the classical legal hierarchy is adapted since notes, circulars, orders and decrees play a major role in prison rules. For instance, the foreign prisoners' regime is partly documented under the 'Rule Part-Simple Decrees', Title II on detention, Chapter XI on different categories of inmates, Section II on foreign national inmates. Article D.505 (decree

[10] Couret, F:, Masson, M.-F., "Français-étrangers : l´écart se resserre", Journal La Croix, 27 December 2000.

[11] see *Mary* 1998.

[12] see *Gisti* 2001, p. 17.

[13] see *Gisti* 2001, p. 19.

[14] Without further mention, all articles mentioned in the text are issued from the CPP.

n° 98-1099 of 8 December 1998) stipulates that "under reserve of particularities relative to conditional release, foreign national inmates are under the same regime as national inmates belonging to their penal category. Particular precautions are required concerning [placement on the outside, semi-liberty and prison leave]". On the other hand, Article D. 506 specifies that "under reserve of application of dispositions of the second clause of Article D. 250-4, redress to an interpreter is valid only in case of absolute necessity, if the inmate can not speak or understand the French language and if there is nobody present who would be able to translate. Visits and correspondence can proceed in their language, under reserve of dispositions of Articles D. 407 and D. 418". Finally, Article D.507 indicates that "inmates detained on an extradition-demand expressed by a foreign government are under the regime of pre-trial detainees. Visit permits and correspondence control are issued and conducted by the public prosecutor".

Additionally, a recent circular (CRIM.06.5/E1 from 21 February 2006) sent to préfets and public prosecutors concerning illegal foreign nationals states that "pragmatism, resoluteness and briskness" shall be the key-words of ITF procedures. Even if an ITF is considered as an "exceptional sentence" and should not be applied to some immigration offences (irregular entry, illegal residence), it will still be required in many cases connected to other offences.

2 TREATMENT OF FOREIGN PRISONERS

Although the difference between a pre-trial detainee (D.50) and a convicted inmate (D.491, D.568 and D.50) is clearly defined, foreign prisoners face the same difficulties being either on remand or sentenced to prison. Still, bad prison conditions in MAs strain the already existing drawbacks of foreign nationals. Furthermore, prison administration does not feel to be responsible for the situation of irregular migrants, since they are detained for immigration offences and will be 'removed' after release. As a matter of fact, foreign prisoners – both with or without a legal residence permit - are often isolated from social and economic resources.

2.1 General situation

Theoretically, foreign prisoners and national prisoners are not to be treated differently. However, prison is per se an unequal structure where the 'strongest' and the 'richest' benefit more from the system than others. As mentioned above, in general foreign prisoners are a burdened population in many issues. To schematise, one could say that they are poor, they are poorly educated, they have no family, relatives or friends nearby and they do not speak French. As a whole, they often have to face discriminations or simply a lack of attention. Prison staff, for instance, is not trained to deal with the cultural and judicial complexity of foreign nationals. Moreover, irregular foreign nationals awaiting expulsion or removal are not seen as 'real' prisoners, but more as 'transit' detainees. Prison staff opinion regarding their situation would rather be "it's none of my business". As far as other prisoners are concerned, communication and common understanding are difficult.

Social exclusion among prisoners may occur during group activities or congregational events. It is often the case that foreign prisoners spend their time either alone or with prisoners from their home country. Large communities of foreign nationals join together in prison and generate a sort of 'home identity'. This natural need for personal acknowledgement is unfortunately perceived by staff and nationals as a refusal of contact and integration. Thus, foreign prisoners do not find much support in or from the general public. There is the wide-spread opinion that foreign criminals broke the trust of France which welcomed them as guests and therefore they should be sent back to their country of origin. Another issue is religion. In times of international terrorism, public opinion and mass media manufacture confusion between Islam believers and Al Qaeda partisans. Tolerance is challenged and foreign prisoners who wish to practice their religion face prejudices and mistrust among European individuals. Unfortunately, we have no data at our disposal concerning racist violence in detention amongst prisoners.

Language is also a key issue. Article D. 407 stipulates that "inmates and visitors must speak in French. When one of them can not speak the language, surveillance must be ensured by a staff member who is able to understand them. Without such a member, visits are only authorised under the condition that the visit permit stipulates clearly that the conversation can be held in a foreign language". Actually, interpreters are rarely consulted in prisons because this is not covered by the budget. Neither interviews between the new prisoner and the members of the prison staff nor interviews with social workers, healthcare staff or psychiatrists are considered as an "absolute necessity". Language is a major problem because prison staff has no translation system at its disposal to communicate with foreign prisoners. Mostly the translations are performed by another inmate. This is obviously problematic concerning the guarantee of medical secrets during a visit to the doctors. Social workers can hardly discuss problems in prison because the inmate could feel pressured through the translation by another inmate. This translation system could also give the interpreter a disproportionate degree of power. Probation officers and inmates may translate, but confidentiality and professional secret must be guaranteed.

2.2 Living conditions and facilities

Foreign prisoners legally and theoretically have access to the same living conditions and facilities as other prisoners. Furthermore, the allocation of a foreign prisoner to a prison establishment should not be effected on the grounds of his nationality alone. However, one fourth of all foreign prisoners are in the three big Parisian prisons (Fleury-Mérogis, La Santé, and Fresnes) and 16 prisons have a proportion of foreign nationals 25% above the national average. One of the reasons for this overrepresentation is the foreign nationals' population density around the capital Paris. In this context, foreign prisoners are placed in these prisons more often and thus more often together. Still, there is criticism concerning the institutionalisation of discrimination in so called 'ethnic units'. Already criticised 30 years ago by the Information Group on Prisons (GIP), this system is in effect for instance in the pre-trial prison "La Santé" in Paris. There, the proportion of foreign inmates is 55 %, with 86 nationalities represented. Inmates are placed in four units: Unit A hosts the "Europeans", Unit B the "Africans", Unit C the "North Africans", and Unit D the "rest of the world". The prison head office justifies this selection as being an aim to limit conflicts and with the reason that inmates wish to be grouped by "affinity" such as common language or religion.

Actually, a Christian English inmate might be placed in the same cell as a Muslim French inmate. French of African origin (often born in France, not knowing the country where his parents or grand-parents are from) are also placed in units B "Africans" and C "North Africans". We also see the problem of citizens from former Yugoslavia being placed together. In Fresnes, an English prisoner spent one week alone in a cell; the prison staff pretended that they did not understand what he said, and asked him to write down his demands[15].

2.3 Reception and admission

All first receptions in a French prison are in MA institutions. Reception procedures are the same for nationals and foreigners. Upon arrival they seldom receive information on the prison rules in a language that they can understand. Theoretically, they are entitled to communicate with a representative of their diplomatic mission. However, they hardly know their rights and prison staff cannot (or do not want to) inform them properly; or they omit to do so. Moreover, because of cultural or legal reasons, many foreign prisoners do not want their embassy to know about their criminal situation, especially those awaiting removal or expulsion. Some problems do arise when it comes to contacting their family: they have no financial means to make a telephone call, the relatives could be irregular migrants and thus not be reached, or prison staff refuses conversations in any language other than French.

Reception is partly regulated by article D.284: arriving prisoners will go to a "waiting cell". But in July 2003, only 75 of the 139 'reception prisons' had 'arriving cells', with a total of 700 places. Foreign prisoners face overcrowding on their very first day. Then, the prison director or his/her representative will meet the detainee either on their day of arrival or the following day. The prisoner will receive a medical examination with the "shortest possible delay", he will meet a probation worker "as soon as possible" and he will be issued information about religious practice. But language barriers are present. For instance, if a Tunisian arrives and receives the house rules in French; it is up to him to seek help from his co-detainees[16]. Prison house rules meet Article D.255 and circular DAP 88-16 G2 of 27 December 1988. They are compiled by the prison director, are often obsolete and sometimes missing. They contain orientations from the CPP (D.247), but are barely binding for the prison administration. House rules are often different from one prison to another, very dense and complicated and not always published. They should be translated into different languages but very few probation agencies offer a complete or even summarized translation.

2.4 Work – Education – Training – Sports – Recreation

Foreign prisoners have the opportunity to work and to participate in educational and vocational training classes, sports and recreational activities (socio-cultural activities are under D.440-D.449-1). However, language and cultural barriers are rarely addressed. There are no data available on the proportion of foreign nationals participating in such programmes. Article D.450 stipulates that "inmates shall acquire or develop necessary knowledge after release in regard to better social adaptation".

---

15 see *Oip* 2005, p.17.
16 see *Oip* 2005, p.17.

There are around 1,500 teachers active in prisons. 38,000 inmates took part in school in 2004 and roughly 5,000 took an exam. In article D.452 it is mentioned that special programmes are organised for those who are unable to read or speak French. Still, training courses against illiteracy are overcrowded or rarely offered. On the other hand, 152 prisons provide vocational teaching, in which 18,500 inmates were involved in 2005.
21,500 inmates were paid for work or training in 2005: 6,600 for house work (180 euros per month), 1,200 for a penitentiary workshop (560 euros), and 9,000 for the private market (350-500 euros). House work is often allocated to national prisoners because co-operation and closed relations to prison staff are often required. This is in fact quite an absurd paradox that should be underlined: whereas work outside the prison constitutes an offence for illegally resident foreign nationals, they can work inside the prison

Physical and sporting activities (D.459-1 – D.459-3) are the main opportunity for foreign prisoners to leave their cell and to make contacts, in addition to article D.359 "every inmate shall have the opportunity to walk one hour per day in open air".
Finally, socio-educative intervention done by the probation service (SPIP) must prevent the dissocialising effects of imprisonment (D. 460). This is, however, rarely the case with foreign prisoners.

2.5 Food – Religion – Personal hygiene – Medical care

Foreign prisoners are entitled by law to practice their own religion ("spiritual assistance", D.432-D.439). However, there are not enough special facilities available for prisoners to devote themselves to their religious duties. There is also a lack of qualified religious representatives who have access to foreign prisoners (69 Islam religion officers). On 1 January 2003, there were 918 religion officers working in prison, of which 323 were paid: 513 were Catholics, 267 Protestants, 69 Muslims, 64 Jewish, 3 Orthodox, and 2 Buddhists. To illustrate the problem, a big prison like Fresnes (637 foreign prisons in 2004) could not find an imam[17]. Prison Service deals with dietary restrictions 'as far as possible'. There are no dress requirements.

There are neither special health-care provisions for foreign prisoners nor special care for inmates with mental problems. Since a 1994 law, health care in prison has been under the authority and responsibility of the Ministry of Health. There is a 'Unit of ambulatory consultation and care' (UCSA) in every prison (except in semi-liberty centres) as well as 93 psychiatric sections. Personal hygiene requirements are common to all prisoners (D.348-1 until D.359): "as far as possible, inmates shall be allowed to take a shower three times a week". The inmate may keep his personal clothes (D.61, D.338 and D.348) or ask for a fresh set if so required.

As to alimentation, "the composition of the alimentary regime is done by the prison administration" (D.342). Article D.354 stipulates that "the food shall, as far as possible, take into account inmates´ philosophical or religious convictions". The Jewish inmates can receive food for Easter, New Year's Eve (Rosh-ha-Shana) and Yom Kippur. Muslim inmates can celebrate Ramadan (Aid El Fitr) and Ail El Kebir with the appropriate and respective food. Otherwise, food packages are prohibited. Still, article D.343 specifies the possibility to buy food inside the prison but the offer remains centred on French-

[17] Michel Saint-Jean, Head officer of Fresnes Prison, *Journal du dimanche*, 4 April 2004.

European products. Moreover, prices are decided by the prison director (D.344), and are often 10% (sometimes up to 50%) more expensive than in a normal supermarket.

Since a law passed on 18 January 1994, all inmates are affiliated to the social security system. Foreign nationals are also automatically and compulsorily affiliated, for up to three years after release. Their family benefits only under the precondition that they are legal residents. For illegal foreign nationals, the affiliation concerns them only during their time in detention (D.366).

2.6 Consular and legal help

Legal help is regulated by articles 2, 3 and 4 of law n°91-647, passed on10 July 1991. On 1 January 2004, the income limit in order to receive the complete amount is 830 euros per month, and 1,244 euros for partial help. The request has to be stated before the TGI by the legal help office; the lawyer fees will then be covered. EU citizens and non-EU legal residents in France can benefit from legal help. Exceptionally, some other groups are also eligible when the situation appears worthwhile. Legal help is allowed without conditions for minors as well as persons within the procedure of Articles 18bis, 22bis, 24, 35bis and 35.4 of ordinance from the 2 November 1945 relative to conditions of entry and stay of foreign nationals in France. In 2002, 41,000 admissions for legal help concerned administrative or foreign nationals' cases, which represent only 6% of all admissions[18].

On the other hand, Article 24 of law n° 2000-321 from 12 April 2000 as well as other texts stipulate that an interpreter shall be designated by the prison's chief officer in case of a disciplinary procedure in order to prepare the defence of the prisoner. But the availability of a three hour preparation delay – to be extended by the lawyer – is unknown, too short, or useless for a foreign national. Moreover, the procedure is – predominantly - a written one.

Additionally, the 'offices for legal access' (PAD) can provide prisoners with help. At the end of 2004, 38 PAD were functioning within 52 prisons. In Fleury-Mérogis, the PAD is managed by the association 'ARAPEJ Ile de France'. Among 1,384 consultations in 2004, 44% dealt with foreign national law: 14.95% concerned the stay in France, 18.57% were about administrative procedures and 10% involved penal procedures.

2.7 Contact with the outside world

Foreign prisoners can stay in contact with their relatives and they can receive visitors. The telephone is often used, but is prohibited in pre-trial detention centres where most foreign prisoners are detained. Written correspondence is problematic because many foreign prisoners are analphabetic. Although some can read, many cannot write. Moreover, letters written in a foreign language can be required to be translated in order to be checked (D. 418). As to correspondence (D.413-D.419), no text prohibits sending and receiving letters in a foreign language. Correspondence with diplomatic and consular authorities is subjected to supervision.

Newspapers, magazines and books in a foreign language should be available (D.444), but prison directors are often unwilling to fund media that they can not understand. Few libraries contain books in appropriate foreign languages; most of the books are in English.

---

18 see *Oip* 2004, pp.69-70.

Newspapers in foreign languages have to be approved and ordered by the prison authorities. Television programs are often kept to a minimum, with only five channels, all of which are in French. Different channels in other languages could be received via cable or satellite television. This is seldom the case, because it is expensive and prison authorities would not be able to control the program content.

Visitors (D.403-D.412) must speak in French, or in another language under certain conditions (D.407). Actually, the rule is not too strictly applied. Still, the soft legal context is a source of discretionary control for the prison services. A problem that remains is that the family members of many foreign nationals are afraid of or mistrustful towards the prison services, especially if they are irregular migrants. On the other hand, 'family relations' (D.420-D.423) implies that they have the right to keep their wedding ring, photos, and to receive money, clothes and books. They can also attend family events and receive prison leave (D.424-D.426) for weddings, death or in cases of illness. However, a foreign prisoner would not be allowed to go abroad within such a measure.

2.8 Re-integration activities - Prison leave

No specific community agency is responsible for the resettlement of foreign prisoners and providing then with aid and support. The foreign nationals participate in the same programmes as all other prisoners do. The law of 26 November 2003 states the possibility for foreign prisoners to benefit from these alternatives during the execution of their prison sentence, yet many inmates believe that such measures give them no benefit[19]. Social workers are not completely informed on foreign prisoners' rights. The prognosis is based on behaviour in prison and prospects of reintegration. Within and during a conditional release, the removal decision is suspended. But during this period the irregular migrant is the titular of a "release card under conditions" and may not work. In this context, semi freedom, placement outside or electronic monitoring may be delivered in order to enable a request for the removal to be revoked. In some regions, judges implement these measures, while others do not. However, there is no possibility for foreign nationals awaiting removal to benefit from such alternatives because the 'judge for the execution of sentences' (JAP) or the probation officer can not provide aftercare and monitoring outside of French territory.

Moreover, according to the 'National consultative commission of human rights' (CNCDH) in its report from 18 November 2004, the JAP tends to estimate a foreign national's chances of obtaining a stay permit in order to allow him to benefit from a sentence arrangement. Since 1 January 2001 (law from 15 June 2000 on the presumption of innocence), the JAP must justify his decisions and a prisoner can file an appeal. A lawyer can assist the inmate in this. In addition, foreign prisoners can apply for a 'composed sentence' in order to ask for the erasure of the removal sentence. The JAP can order a conditional release for a foreign national under a secondary sentence of removal, which will be deleted in the case of no further offence. The CNCDH criticizes the criteria to obtain this composition, since in most of the cases the sentence is only the consequence of the impossibility to regularise his or her administrative situation.

---

19 see *Trombik* 2005, p.37.

The Court of Cassation decided that a ITF sentence is incompatible with the benefit of a leave permit[20], even if it infringes family relations in regard to Article 8 § 1 ECHR, because the ITF measure is necessary for public safety. It leads to difficulties in the preparation of the removal or - simply - to organise the departure from France. Besides, some local head-offices representing the State (prefecture) refuse to register a demand of regularisation (the allocation of a legal residence permit) before the prisoner's release. Without a legal status, one can not apply for a job or accommodation. In order to exemplify one of many problematic situations, the Oip related the issue to a prisoner living in Belgium, who received no prison leave because - according to the judge - he might have escaped from the French authorities, although his situation abroad was regular. Therefore, he could not prepare his defence before trial[21].

Figure 3: Proportion (%) of conditional release among all releases in regard to the offence: comparison between French and foreign nationals.

Nature of offence	*French conditionally released (%)*	*Foreign national conditionally released (%)*
Homicide	36.4	16.7
Violence	11.7	7.7
Sexual offence	16.3	13.3 (only 2 persons)
Drugs	19.1	21.5
Robbery	13.1	5.9
Theft	30.4	10.0
Immigration	16.7 (only 1 person)	6.8

Source: Tournier/Kensey 2000

Foreign nationals have less opportunity to receive a conditional release than nationals. Moreover, more than 92% of persons who serve a sentence in the community are French, and only 7% are foreign nationals[22].

2.9 Release - Expulsion

There are no special requirements and procedures regarding the release of foreign prisoners. Article 729-2 specifies that "when a foreign national, condemned to a prison sentence, is under a measure of expulsion, removal, or ITF, his or her conditional release is dependant on the implementation of the measure. This measure can be executed without his or her agreement. In exception to the precedent clause, the JAP or the TAP can issue a conditional release to a foreign national under ITF. The measure is suspended until the end of the monitoring period. If this has been duly executed, the ITF is automatically revoked. If not, the measure is applicable".

Here is an exemplary situation of a foreign prisoner[23]. A man is married to a French public servant, has held a regular stay permit since 1980 and is the father of one child. He has been sentenced to ten years in prison and three years 'interdiction from the French

[20] Cass. Crim, 25 mars 1987, *Gaz. Pal.* 1987, 398, note X.
[21] see *Oip* 2005, p. 17.
[22] see DAP 2000.
[23] see *Oip* 2005,p. 24.

territory' (ITF). He had one year of his term left to serve. His first demand of revocation of the ITF measure was rejected because his "projects of conjugal life do not imply a life in France". Under the law of 26 November 2003, he demanded leave permits. The JAP refused this because the application decrees were not published. The second demand invoked the conservation with family relations. It was rejected because "the ITF can not allow such a demand". After a demand of conditional release, which automatically revokes the ITF once the sentence is duly served, he was again refused because "according to article 78 clause 1 of the law from 26 November 2003, a leave permit can be given to a prisoner under ITF only within the procedure of preparation of revocation of ITF". Also, the prison direction claimed to have "little information about this law".

Another example[24]: a pregnant prisoner wants to give birth while being with her family in a European country. Therefore, she demands a 'conditional release-expulsion'. The expulsion order is signed by the local State service. However, the JAP could not decide because they forgot to ask for psychiatric opinion. Thus, she will have to give birth alone.

A third example deals with a foreign prisoner who arrived in France in 1973 and was condemned to life imprisonment in 1977. He demanded a conditional release four times. The last one was rejected because the préfet signed an expulsion order. He comes from former Yugoslavia, has no more family there but in France instead, and the Serbian government does not recognise his nationality. He feels condemned to spend the rest of his life in prison.

On the other hand, taking into consideration the example of German prisoners, transfer to their native country is not often used[25]. Many expelled foreign prisoners fear spending more time in prison once they are back in their home country.

In 1998, 18,314 foreign prisoners were released (of 72,886 releases, 25.1% of the total). 4,133 thereof involved an immigration offence (22.6%). For an immigration offence only, they served 4.7 months detention (half of foreign nationals' detention length). Regarding releases related to immigration offence, 30% were removed (10% in other cases). Less than 10% of illegal foreign prisoners were released by the judge (20% of legal foreign nationals, 26% of French). Only two percent benefited from conditional release.

A recent text formulates improvements in the coordination between prisons and the Ministry of the Interior in the implementation of the removal and expulsion of foreign nationals (21 January 2004, "AP-2004-02 EMS1/21-01-2004"). Local and regional coordination groups are asked to improve removal measures since these are not statistically satisfying. As soon as a foreign national enters detention, the prison administration has to inform the police services. The prison administration then delivers to the latter all documents concerning the foreign national who is under a measure of removal. All releases and transfers will be immediately communicated. A prison administration circular of 18 April 2003 stipulates that foreign national inmates under a removal measure with less than six months to spend in prison shall only exceptionally be transferred, in order for the police to proceed with their removal. However, it must be taken into account that when an inmate is ill he or she is protected against removal since his or her health status requires treatment that can not be provided should he/she be removed (Article 26-5 of law from 26 November 2003). Finally, a bi-annual conclusion with results and difficulties shall be sent to the central prison administration.

---

24 see *Oip* 2005, p. 24.

25 see *Trombik* 2005.

2.10 Aftercare – Probation

In case foreign offenders (can) stay in the host country after release, they are allowed to make use of aftercare facilities and support from the probation service as offered to release French nationals. The two conditions are that they benefit from a stay permit and that they are not under a removal or expulsion measure. Otherwise, there are no special provisions for foreign offenders within the aftercare period. There were no available statistics on this issue.

An irregular migrant can not work, has neither access to social welfare nor benefits from housing and reintegration facilities. Still, a foreign national can benefit from a 'relèvement': removal, as a complementary sentence, might be stopped; the sentence remains but not its effect. The foreign national must wait six months after the sentence is passed; he or she has to be either placed at home or in prison or outside the territory.

2.11 Staff

On 1 January 2005, there were 23,265 guards, 2,322 probation officers, 2,810 administrative employees, 742 technicians, and 426 head officers. 4,000 new jobs have been created since 2002, 700 of which are for probation services. 2,026 new jobs are predicted for 2006.

Prison staff receives little special training to deal with foreign prisoners. All courses are given by the National school of prison administration (ENAP). Language skills are still secondary knowledge and their importance in a prison environment with one fourth 'foreign clientele' is undermined. As to appropriate training among guards, only 'basic guards' are taught about the "problematics of ethnic minorities". There is no specific training for chief guards and supervising guards. Probation staff receives a nine hour course on "foreign nationals" among other specific groups (women, minors, old people) even though foreign prisoners represent a larger population than all other groups together (25% vs. 10%). There is no specific training for chief probation officers. Direction staff also receives some information about "foreign nationals" among other specific groups (women, minors).

Guards have a memento at their disposal, in which legal dispositions concerning foreign prisoners are available[26]. As regards the language issue, the principle is to prohibit communication that guards do not understand. In practice, there are severe discrepancies between individual prisons. From a sociological point of view that takes organisational and work theories into account, a foreign national inmate represents an additional burden of tasks. In this context, some guards are not willing to help foreign nationals who have language difficulties.

Christine Joffre, a social worker in Fresnes prison for ten years, described some difficulties of his job with foreign prisoners[27]. First of all, one shall consider different situations in detention: the stay permit may expire in prison or a person was irregular before sentence or was sentenced to territory ITF. According to Joffre, in such situations, it is "very complicated, almost impossible" to obtain a regular stay permit during detention. Therefore, probation workers need help from specialised associations because they do not know

26 see *DAP* 2005, pp. 108-112.

27 see *Oip* 2005, p. 22-23.

how to deal with foreign national legal texts. Such training exists, albeit not systematically. Besides, local State services require a release in order to handle the procedure of regularisation. It often means that a pre-detained person with a regular permit may leave prison without a legal status because it was not possible to renew the permit during detention. Joffre concludes by saying that "when we know that regularisation is not possible, we reach the limits of our work". Moreover, some housing and social integration centres ("CHRS") refuse persons with an irregular legal status.

In addition, probation work is mainly based on interviews and discussions with prisoners on their situations and projects. Without a common language, this task can not be fulfilled.

2.12 Projects

There are no significant specific projects for foreign prisoners inside or outside penitentiary institutions. We have little information at our disposal about local activities towards foreign prisoners. For instance, in the MA Fleury-Mérogis it has been encouraged to have prison visitors who speak similar languages as the foreign prisoners.

Interesting information became public in May 2006. The prison administration made a proposal to financially support a study on "foreign prisoners". It will tackle their qualitative and quantitative situations, face their problems, address staff problems associated with this group and analyse answers given by the institution. The research period is 20 months. The time limit for project completion was 31 May 2006. This study would be the first exhaustive research on foreign prisoners in France. It is not excluded that our contemporary European research has played an exemplary role in this decision.

3 ADMINISTRATIVE DETENTION OF FOREIGN PRISONERS

Administrative detention is a deprivation of freedom for the time until the foreign national is removed or expelled. There are 18 administrative detention centres ('CRA') in continental France with between eight and 160 places each. Moreover, there are many smaller local facilities (LRA) on which no information is available. Since 2001, the list of permanent centres has been set by ministerial order. Some are under the control of "regional public security" (SPD), some under the border police and some under the gendarmerie. The logistics are ensured by the prison administration or outsourced to private firms. Administrative detention centres have existed since 1981. They are intended for foreign nationals under administrative measures – removal because of threat to public order, refusal of asylum under judicial decisions – expulsion and/or ITF sentence for an offence as well as illegal residence. All information at our disposal is issued by the CIMADE report. The Cimade is an ecumenical care service and the only association that has access to CRAs (but not LRAs). Created in 1984, it works in cooperation with the State in order to provide social and legal support. The Cimade deplores in its annual report (2004) that not all statistics are available and that there is a possibility of error or impreciseness in the figures.

In 2004, Cimade's employees and volunteers met with 26,000 persons in administrative detention centres. A short and schematised overview of administrative detention leads to one main conclusion: the detention conditions are, in all respects, worse than in prison. Problems are numerous: overcrowding, more and more persons suffering from psychological ailments, violence, self-mutilations, suicide attempts, hunger strikes, no leisure opportunities; etc. The restriction of smoking times (9.00, 11.00, 14.00, 17.00, 21.00) in CRA Coquelles[28] illustrates partially one of the many structural and organisational complexities and absurdities of administrative detention. Moreover, the health situation of administrative detainees is worsening. This statement was issued at the first national congress of medical units for administrative detention centres held on 7 and 8 October 2004. All CRAs have been obliged to provide medical service since 1999. Medical staff does not receive any particular training for the treatment of foreign detainees.

According to the provisional planning of the inter-ministerial committee for immigration control, 1,438 new places are planned for January 2006 (2003: 739 places, 2004: 969 places, 2005: 1,300), 1,718 for June 2006, 2,383 for June 2007, and 2,700 for June 2008. In 2003 and 2004, the Ministry of the Interior compiled instructions setting an amount of removals. A decree from 30 May 2005 foresees that new centres with 140 places shall be built, and that foreign nationals in administrative detention applying for asylum have to pay the interpreter - required for the completion of applications in French - themselves. Asylum application forms have been required to be written in French since August 2004. Furthermore, the creation of centres with family facilities indicates that more and more children are expected. Facilities must be improved but delays are not concretised. A decree from March 2001 proposes to fulfil new material and equipment norms within a three year period. In 2004, the government postponed this obligation for one year. Another decree from 30 May 2005 set the most recent limit to the 31 December 2006.

3.1 Institutions for the Administrative Detention of Foreign Prisoners

There are two types of institutions used for administrative detention: the detention centres (CRA) and detention rooms (LRA).

3.2 Ministry responsible & relevant Legislation

The Ministry of the Interior is responsible for administrative detention facilities. Administrative detention is ruled under dispositions in the CESEDA, Book V "removal measures", Title V "retention of a foreign national in facilities that do not depend upon prison administration". According to Article L.551-2, the administrative authority is responsible for placement decisions. Two more decrees (N° 2004-1215 from 17 November 2004 and N° 2005-617 from 30 May 2005) complete the legal framework.

3.3 Capacity of institutions for Administrative Detention

In 2004, 969 places were distributed across 20 Detention centres (without overseas regions): the largest ones are Paris-Vincennes and Mesnil-Amelot with 140 places each, Paris-dépôt with 96, Coquelles with 79, Lyon with 78, Bobigny with 52 places, and Marseille and Bordeaux with 24 places.

3.4 Length of stay

28 see *Cimade* 2005, p. 126.

A law, passed on 26 November 2003, prolonged the retention delay from 12 to 36 days and somewhat improved the flexibility of the procedure of translation. The average length of stay in administrative detention has almost doubled from 5.3 days in 2003 to 9.9 days in 2004. The time spent varies from 6.7 days in Rivesaltes up to 12.9 days in Paris-Vincennes.

3.5 Decisions procedure

Since a law from 26 November 2003, administrative detention has been decided on by the préfet, who within the first 48 hours must request from the 'judge of liberties and detention' ("juge des libertés et de la détention" – JLD) the authorisation for the prolongation of detention by 15 more days. Once the 17 days have expired, the préfet may request a new extension of up to 15 days. According to Articles L.552-7 and L.552-8 of CESEDA, a foreign national can be put in administrative detention "in cases of absolute emergency or particular major threat to public order" or "when diplomatic documents are not available".

3.6 Appeal procedure

The appeal against the decision of the JLD to prolong the length of detention ("appel 35bis") is to be filed before the "cour d´appel - CA". To contest the legality of the removal decision, in most of the cases, it deals with a "préfectoral arrêté" against which an appeal before the administrative court (TA) ("recours 22bis") is possible within 48 hours. In 2004, there were 1,354 appeals (non exhaustive) before the CA against JLD decisions. In 73% of cases, the CA confirmed the JLD decision; and in 15% detention was revoked; in four percent of cases, home placement was ruled until the removal had been executed. On the other hand, in 2004, there were 2,364 appeals (non exhaustive) before the TA against removal decisions. In 65% of cases, the TA confirmed the removal; in 12%, it was revoked; and in one percent, the country of destination was annulled.

3.7 Irregular stay

No permanent or temporary residence permit, refusal to board a plane during removal[29], use of false identities, refusal to give identity or nationality to oppose removal, false weddings, etc are criminal offences. More than 200 immigration related offences lead to expulsion or removal. For example, in Lyon, a foreign national has been sentenced to six months prison and ten years ITF for "drug purchase for personal use", this because of seven grams of cannabis[30]. In 2003, there were 5,606 sentences for immigration offences, of which 3,085 were prison sentences. An irregular migrant – illegal entry or stay - can be handed a prison sentence of up to one year. In 2001, there were 4,295 foreign nationals in prison for immigration offences. In many cases, imprisonment serves as 'second hand administrative detention'. Besides, ITF is often a complementary sentence. On average, there are around 3,000 to 4,000 expulsions per year ("arrêté d´expulsion"), ordered by the préfet or by the Ministry of the Interior because of "threat to public order". There are

---

29 average sentence of one up to three months prison and three years ITF, see *Cimade* 2005, p. 141.

30 see *Cimade* 2005, p. 136.

around 20,000 removals per year ("arrêté de reconduite à la frontière"), ordered by the préfet for irregular stay.

3.8 Numbers

25,828 persons were detained in 2004. 20,571 foreign nationals were from known nationalities. 4,135 were from Algeria, which represents the biggest group with 20.10% of all administrative detainees. 2,352 were for instance from Morocco (11.43%), 1,814 from Rumania (8.82%), 1,403 from Turkey (6.82%), 1,101 from Tunisia (5.35%), and 901 from Mali (4.38%). In 2003, 1,524 women were detained in administrative centres, accounting for 6.83% of all administrative detainees. In 2004, they were 1,824 (8.87%). 262 female foreign nationals were for instance from Rumania (17.19% of all detained women), 104 from Algeria (6.82%), 101 from China (6.63%), 95 from Morocco (6.23%), and 82 from Ecuador (5.38%).

3.9 Expulsion

The objective for 2005 is 23,000 removals. Previously, removal efficiency rose up from 44% in 2003 up to 55% in 2004, which stands for 10,341 persons (without 'Paris-dépôt', nor 'Paris-Vincennes', nor 'Nantes'). According to statistics covering a ten year period (1992-2002), around 50% of detained foreign nationals are removed. The rate fell from 61% in 1992 to 39.6% in 2002, but the length of detention rose from seven days in 1992 to 12 days in 2002. The average length of detention while awaiting a ruling on the removal or release of a foreign national is four days. 70% of removed or expelled foreign nationals were removed or expelled within the first 12 days, and 23% between the 13th and the 17th day. Concerning the home countries, 67 foreign nationals from Bolivia were removed or expelled, which represents 93.06% of Bolivian detainees in administrative detention centres. The other 7% were released. Among other removed or expelled foreign nationals, there were for instance 382 from Bulgaria (80.76%), 1,259 from Rumania (79.48%), 123 from Ecuador (79.35%), 882 from Turkey (65.97%), 2,237 from Algeria (60.35%), 1,119 from Morocco (54.77%), 425 from Tunisia (44.27%), and 11 from Palestine (9.09%).

3.10 Not-expelled prisoners

8,026 administrative detainees were released in 2004 (statistics without Paris-dépôt, nor Paris-Vincennes, nor Nantes). Among them, 44% remained in detention for more than 12 days. A second prolongation was issued for 13%. Some of them were "déférés", what means that - according to Article L.624.1 CESEDA - they were put before the penal judge because of infringements to the removal procedure. The préfet can demand that the public prosecution take legal action against a released irregular foreign national because of supposed 'refusal of removal'. The foreign national will then be brought before the penal judge and often sent to prison before his or her case is examined before court.

3.11 Detention of Irregulars under Criminal Law

Foreign nationals under measures or procedures of removal or expulsion can be detained with prisoners who are detained under criminal law, thus not in separate sections.

3.12 Minors

Four centres are adequate and qualified for the accommodation of minors. Parents can choose whether to keep their children with them, and they all in fact do so. In 2004, more than 90 foreign nationals in administrative detention declared being minors. Many of them were removed or expelled. In Lyon, 139 children were in administrative detention in 2004. Five other centres are also used for the detention of minors. However, since there is no legal disposition about children, some centres lack adequate facilities or equipment.

3.13 Waiting Zones

Waiting zones ('WZ') were introduced in 1992. They are legally defined as places where "the foreign national arriving in France [...] who is not authorised to enter the French territory or who seeks asylum" will be detained "during the strict necessary time for his leave and, as an asylum seeker, for a check of his demand". The placement of a foreign national is an administrative decision and is evaluated after 72 hours by a judge who will decide on its prolongation. Waiting zones are located near judicial borders – airports, sea-ports/harbours or railway stations. Foreign nationals are only "maintained" and not "detained" because they are free to leave the French national territory. Therefore, the judicial protection is weaker than in other confinement institutions. Foreign nationals can be held in waiting zones for up to 20 days. After this period, if they have not been removed, the boarder authorities must release them, even if they consequentially become irregular migrants. There are more than 100 waiting zone facilities, most of them are small rooms, for instance police stations, hotel rooms, administration offices. The waiting zone Roissy – Charles De Gaulle represents the two international airports in Paris. 95% of the foreign nationals are in the WZ Roissy-CDG. There are 250 beds available; in addition to overcrowded rooms with sometimes more than 200 persons. The law requires "hotel-like conditions", which are not fulfilled. Regular human rights associations have no access to WZs. The association ANAFE ("National Association for Assistance at Borders to Foreign Nationals") is the only one to publish visit reports.

4 NATIONALS DETAINED ABROAD

According to the latest available data, roughly 1,500 French persons are currently being detained abroad[31]. One association has specialised on nationals detained abroad – the so-called FIL ("Français incarcérés au loin" # 'Far off imprisoned French'). Unfortunately,

[31] source: 'European Group for Prisoners Abroad' EGPA.

its activities are reduced at the moment. There have been no more volunteers for the last three years. Therefore, most of our information is from FIL 2001.

4.1 Numbers and Composition of French Nationals detained abroad

In 2001, 1,368 French nationals were prisoners abroad: These figures are probably an underestimation. Some prisoners do not contact the embassies because they fear prosecution by the French authorities upon their return to France. We may assume that figures concerning the rest of the world are more reliable given the need for outside contact due to the distance and the harshness of the imprisonment conditions. There are very little data available on personal and social structures of this group. FIL reported that in Caracas nine out of 18 French prisoners are from the Ivory Coast. This is the case for two out of three in Lima and every second in Rio de Janeiro.

4.2 Countries of Detention

905 nationals were detained in Western Europe; 86 were to be found in North America, 13 in Japan, nine in Australia, 405 in Spain, 169 in Belgium, 85 in Germany, 77 in the USA, 77 in Morocco, 44 in Italy, 25 in Madagascar and 23 in Thailand.

4.3 Sentencing and Reasons for Detention

Half of French prisoners abroad were convicted for misdemeanour or serious drugs-related crimes. This was the case for 307 French nationals detained in Spain, 50 in Morocco, 36 in Belgium, 31 in Great-Britain, 23 in Germany, 22 in Italy, 20 in the United-States, 18 in Venezuela, 13 in Brazil, 12 in Japan and 11 in Thailand.

Three prisoners were sentenced to the death penalty and 14 to life sentences, of whom most were charged with murder. Inmates awaiting death sentences are to be transferred back to France. Nine were imprisoned for political reasons. Some are 'victims' of an argument in which prison is used as a tool of pressure.

Sex tourism is a growing cause of imprisonment, but French prisoners tend to be ashamed of their crime and therefore do not contact the French authorities. Moreover, many countries like Indonesia, Malaysia or Venezuela have hardened their legislation, resulting in longer prison sentences.

4.4 Involved Organisations – Tasks and Activities

The consular protection is based on the 1963 Vienna Convention on consular relations. As soon as a foreign national is arrested or committed to prison, the judicial authorities have to inform him/her of his/her right to contact the embassy/the consulate. Once contact has been established, both prisoner and consular post have the right to converse and correspond, and the consular staff can visit the prisoner. The consular officer informs the prisoner about the local justice system and provides him/her with a list of French speaking lawyers. Consular officers are present at the trial in order to make sure that it is conducted fairly. The consular post deals with money, mail and medicine transfer, which are all sent with the 'diplomatic bag', which has to be prepared and transported. It corresponds also with French local, regional and national authorities concerned by the prisoner's situation.

Nationals detained abroad complain about local prison conditions: lack of food, poor hygiene and health care. Some prisoners feel unsafe and thus pay other detainees to insure their own safety. Some must buy drinkable water. However, in few cases, regarding the rather constraining prison conditions in France, some prisoners prefer to spend their time abroad.

4.5 Release and Reception in France

The reception in France after release is mostly organised on a private and voluntary basis, since the French Justice is not responsible for a foreign sentence. There is no French organisation comparable to 'Prisoners Abroad' in the UK or the 'Liaison Office for Dutch Prisoners Abroad and International Contacts' in the Netherlands.

4.6 Aftercare

When the person being released is expelled, the expelling State takes charge of the expulsion. When the person has been released in the foreign State, he or she has to pay the transportation to France himself or herself. The French State may cover the transportation expenses under the condition of later reimbursement. The consular post informs individuals or associations in France to take care of this person at the airport or train station at which they are arriving.

4.7 Public Opinion and the Media

Nationals detained abroad are not an issue. Therefore, there is no media or general public opinion on this particular topic. The situation of French individuals who have been sentenced abroad for sexual crimes – most of them because of sexual relations with minor prostitutes – may be described from time to time in newspapers or shown on TV. However, the discourse on such cases would rather produce moral condemnation and public exclusion.

The Ministry of Foreign Affairs does not put the prisoner's case on the public scene in opposition to what many families and lawyers do, expecting or hoping that public pressure might influence the local justice or politicians. It is often counter-productive and even negative for the prisoner, because local justice or politicians are not willing to be seen as weak under international or diplomatic pressure. Furthermore, a media campaign let believe that justice abroad might be influenced and partial, whereas French justice is thought to be independent and fair.

To conclude, since FIL stopped its work some years ago, there has been no more systematic legal care and monitoring for French prisoners who are or have been detained abroad.

5 EVALUATION AND RECOMMENDATIONS

Although the proportion of foreign prisoners has been quite stable within the last 25 years (between 20 and 30%), foreign nationals, especially irregular ones, still face disadvantages and discrimination inside French prisons, since their problems have not been addressed consistently. The cultural, social and economic background, in addition to low education, illiteracy and French language deficits, formed a weak individual, to whom prison services can neither offer skills, nor time and provisions in the budget. However, we believe that a positive political attitude towards this issue would enable important improvement.

A first step should officially tackle the problem in order to stop the process of media criminalisation against foreign nationals[32]. Secondly, a proposition of the CNCDH is to abolish prison sentences for immigration offences, or to limit sentences to a maximum of one month. A clearer and fairer procedure shall be implemented in order to simplify and facilitate access to residence permits. Access to asylum right meets similar difficulties, and thus could benefit from similar recommendations. Modalities of expulsion, including administrative detention centres, shall attend further to human care and humanitarian monitoring. Voluntary return shall be facilitated or foreign prisoners shall be allowed to serve their sentence in their home country. More professional interpreters and more language courses shall be hired and offered. The item "absolute necessity" shall be erased from the CPP Unique prison house rules shall help prisoners and reduce translation costs. On the other hand, local councils or centres for legal advice shall be encouraged. 16 projects concerning 23 prisons are planned with a total of 75. One hundred prisons or penitentiary centres are to be "equipped". Finally, prison administration shall hire more foreign staff or migrant nationals in order to facilitate cooperation, communication, and cultural understanding.

---

32 see *Tsoukala* 2002.

Chapter 10

Germany

Frieder Dünkel
Andrea Gensing
Christine Morgenstern

1 INTRODUCTION

1.1 Overview of penalties and measures

In 1969 the German system of penal sanctions was thoroughly overhauled by the 'great reform of criminal law' of that year. This reform intended to strengthen the preventive purposes of punishment as opposed to its purely retributive aspects, and in this way to reduce the significance of imprisonment, in particular, as a form of punishment. Section 47 of the Penal Code (*Strafgesetzbuch* - StGB), which has since been in force , makes provision for prison sentences of less than six months, but only if the offender's personality or the special circumstances of the offence require such a sanction in order to influence the offender or to protect the legal order. Non-custodial sentences have absolute priority. They range from the dismissal of proceedings combined with the imposition of obligations (for example, compensation or an administrative fine), through pecuniary penalties coupled to a warning that further punishment may be imposed, to the suspension of sentence on probation. Since 1969, the administration of justice has, to a great extent, put these epoch-making changes to the law into practice. Therefore, in comparison with non-custodial measures, the prison sentence currently fulfils only a minor role in the system of sanctions. Only about seven percent of all sentences are unconditional prison terms, whereas fines (80 per cent) and probation coupled with suspended sentences (13 per cent) predominate. The fact that the prison sentence functions as an *ultima ratio* becomes even clearer if one also considers the informal decisions of the public prosecutors who dismiss, perhaps with the imposition of an administrative fine, 52 per cent of all cases[1]. All facts considered, one finds that prison sentences account for a mere three to four percent of all sanctions. Although the official crime rates have increased considerably during the last 30 years and the average length of prison sentences has also increased (*inter alia* because of more violent crime) the incarceration rates have been rather stable until recently. The stability has been achieved by extending the application of fines and suspended sentences, especially for property offenders.

Since the death penalty was abolished constitutionally in 1949 in West Germany by article 102 of the Basic Law (*Grundgesetz* - GG), life imprisonment is the most severe sanction that may be imposed by the state. This sanction still embodies the notion of retribution in its pure form. The Federal Constitutional Court has confirmed that it is constitutional under the condition that persons sentenced to life imprisonment retain the prospect of eventually regaining their liberty.[2] Therefore, where such a sanction is imposed the state has to guarantee an execution of the life sentence that provides for effective forms of rehabilitation (resocialization). As implemented in practice, this type of sanction can be regarded as a prison sentence of an indeterminate duration[3]. In terms of s.57a of the Penal Code, a court may place a prisoner sentenced to life imprisonment on parole once the prisoner has served 15 years, if the prognosis is favourable and the crime was not particularly heinous (for example, parole is not granted easily to repeat murderers or persons

---

1 Mostly petty offences, but also cases of economic and environmental crimes, see *Heinz* 2004.

2 Decisions of the Federal Constitutional Court, *Bundesverfassungsgerichtliche Entscheidungen* – BVerfGE 45, 187ff.

3 see *Kaiser* 1997, p. 423.

convicted of hate crimes). The Federal Constitutional Court has restricted the discretion whether to execute the life sentence for longer than 15 years by demanding that the courts state that the case is particularly heinous at the trial[4]. Annually there are less than 100 persons sentenced to life imprisonment. Approximately 1,800 persons are serving this sentence at any given time (2005). The number of prisoners serving life imprisonment has increased in the last 15 years. The period of time served prior to release averages between 18 and 20 years.

The use of short-term prison sentences is an equally controversial issue. Although it was the stated aim of the 'great reform of criminal law' to abolish the short prison term completely, it is still an essential component of the execution of prison sentences. The reasons for this include: the reduction of the prison sentence by the period of pre-trial detention; the revocation of probation or parole with the result that short, conditionally suspended sentences are brought into operation; imprisonment for failing to pay a fine; and the lack of alternative, non-custodial measures. The annual proportion of persons who serve a prison term of less than six months is much higher than the proportion of such terms actually imposed - it has been estimated to be up to six times higher[5]. In recent debates about penal policy more significance has been attached to short-term imprisonment than at the time of the original legislation, which was heavily influenced by the principle of resocialization.

Recently, however, the debate of the early 1980s about possible penal law reforms in order to shorten the average prison sentences[6] has been replaced by a shift in official crime policy to strengthen penal law. In 1998 two penal law reforms were introduced that increased the penalties for violent and sexual offenders considerably. Furthermore, the possibilities for parole have been restricted. This new penal policy pays more regard to public opinion and pressure for public security more than in the past.

A prison sentence of up to two years may be suspended and an offender placed on probation. Such probation has become an important non-custodial sentence in its own right and is no longer regarded as a type of prison sentence[7]. The law provides that conditions of probation may include both restitution orders and directives prescribing how the probationer should conduct his life. In addition, provision is made for the appointment of a qualified probation officer where this is deemed necessary for the resocialization of the offender (the same rules apply to prisoners released on parole.) About one-third of adult probationers are assigned a probation officer. At present, about 70 per cent of all prison sentences are suspended on probation. This non-custodial sanction therefore clearly outnumbers unconditional prison sentences. The extension of suspended sentences contributed greatly to the fairly stable incarceration rates during the 1970s and 1980s. At the end of 1991, 145,000 probationers were allocated to about 2,100 full-time probation officers. The high ratio of probationers to probation officers (70 : 1) is a considerable problem and the improvement of this ratio is a major concern of penal policy. In spite of these difficulties, the probation service can claim that the recidivism rate of ap-

---

4 see BVerfGE 86: 288ff.

5 see *Weigend* 1986, p. 261.

6 see also the 'memorandum' of a group of academics and practitioners to abolish or reduce long-term imprisonment in 1994, *Jung* and *Müller-Dietz*, 1994.

7 See *Jescheck* and *Weigend*, 1996.

proximately 35 per cent, with an average probation period of three years, is much more favourable than the rate of recidivism for those released from prison. Parolees – even when one controls for selection criteria – generally re-offend less often than prisoners released after serving their full sentences[8] .

Numerically the fine is the most important penal sanction as it is imposed in about 83 per cent of all cases. The Penal Code has created a day-fine system in which one 'day-fine' corresponds to one day spent in prison. Section 43 of the Penal Code makes provision for a maximum of 360 day-fines and for up to 720 day-fines in exceptional cases, for example for an accumulation of offences. In practice, 96 per cent of all fines do not exceed 90 day-fines. The amount imposed for a day depends on the financial capacity of the offender. Approximately 6 to 7 per cent of the fines are converted into prison sentences because of non-compliance[9]. Since the early 1980s 'free work' (community service) may be imposed as an alternative to imprisonment for failing to pay a fine. Such a substitution may be made by the judicial administration (s. 293 of the Introductory Act to the Criminal Code - *Einführungsgesetz zum Strafgesetzbuch* – EGStGB). Generally, the administration of this alternative is the duty of the social workers who are attached to the courts and who provide for and arrange community service. One day-fine is regarded as the equivalent of six to eight hours of community service[10]. Since the late 1980s the problem of fine defaulters has increased considerably, especially in the new federal states of the former German Democratic Republic[11]. In 1996 about 10 per cent of all adult prisoners served a period of imprisonment in lieu of a fine (*Ersatzfreiheitsstrafe*): 13 per cent in East Germany; in West German federal states seven per cent[12]. The bad economic situation with concomitant high unemployment rates especially in East Germany, is the main reason for this development. Some efforts at reorganizing and intensifying the social services arranging community service have diminished the proportion of fine defaulters in East Germany to 8 per cent of the daily adult prison population in 2004. A special project in Mecklenburg-Western Pomerania had particularly positive effects by reducing the number of fine defaulters serving prison sentences by 50%[13] .

1.2 Overview of the prison system

1.2.1 Organisational structure, prisons and numbers of inmates

The German prison system provides a total of 222 prisons with a capacity of 80,000 places. The Federal Prison Act as well as some of the administrative rules (*Verwaltungsvorschriften*) are the same in all federal states. However, as the federal states are responsible for the construction of buildings and the funding of the personnel, great differences between the federal states have emerged. In June 2006 the Federal Parliament (*Bundestag*) – despite heavy criticisms by almost all academics and a large majority of practitioners – decided to transfer the legislation for prisons to the federal states. This was part of a new

8 see *Dünkel*, 2004; *Dünkel* and *Spiess*, 1992.

9 see *Kaiser* 1997, p. 436.

10 for details see *Jehle*, *Feuerhelm*, and *Block* 1990; *Feuerhelm* 1997.

11 see *Dünkel* and *Scheel* 2004; 2006.

12 see *Dünkel* and *Kunkat* 1997.

13 see *Dünkel* and *Scheel* 2006.

distribution of power between the federal states and the central government. Consequentially, in future there could possibly be up to 16 Prison Acts of the "Länder".

Prison administration belongs to the ministry of justice of the federal states. The budgets vary from state to state, as do the numbers of prison staff. The education of regular prison officers in Germany is comparatively good as they are trained for three years in special schools run by the Länder. Privatization is not a major issue in Germany, as privatization would be in contradiction to the Constitutional restriction of coercive power and restriction of freedom only to public services. Therefore, privatization has only been used to build new prisons and to outsource certain services like laundry, transportation of prisoners or medical services. On the other hand the German prison system has proven its openness and readiness for reform by new public management strategies[14].

The prison system provides open and closed facilities. About 20% of the prisoners on a given day are accommodated in open prisons or departments. The proportion varies between more than 30% in some northern states and less than five percent in Bavaria.

Each *Land* provides social-therapeutic treatment for difficult or dangerous offenders, particularly sex offenders (about 2.500 places in total). The treatment programmes include various forms of individual and group therapy in a milieu therapy setting. The results of treatment programmes are encouraging[15].

The controlling mechanisms of individual complaints procedures are well developed in Germany. Extensive jurisdiction on all issues of daily prison life has contributed to extensive publications and commentaries to the Prison Act. The possibility to submit individual complaints to the Constitutional Court (*Bundesverfassungsgericht*) is a further important guarantee to implement the prison system in accordance to the rule of law and principles of human rights (human dignity etc.). The Constitutional Court has issued important decisions on the principle of resocialisation as a constitutional principle (1972, 1973, 1975, 1998 etc.), on the remuneration of prison labour (1998), accommodation in communal cells (2002), preventive detention (2004), and the "unconstitutionality of the present youth prison legislation" (2006). Regular inspections take place only by the ministry of justice itself, not by independent bodies. However, there are parliamentary control mechanisms similar to prison ombudsmen (the Green party and other oppositional parties regularly submit parliamentary inquiries). Furthermore, the so-called "Anstaltsbeiräte" (an independent citizens' board in the neighbourhood of each prison) exercise some control, although they are obliged to work confidentially with the prison directors.

Looking at the prison statistics it can be determined that, after a notable decrease in the 1980s, a serious increase of incarceration rates can be seen from 1989. In 1998 there were 96 prisoners per 100,000 inhabitants, 98 in West and 84 in East Germany. In 2005 East and West-Germany had about the same prison population rates with 97 per 100,000 inhabitants (see *Figure 1.1*). In this respect Germany ranks in the middle of those European countries with the highest imprisonment rates[16]. The comparatively high imprisonment rate, compared to Scandinavian countries, results from the fact that the average period of time served is relatively long. The number of individuals actually sentenced to unconditional prison sentences are not greater than, for example, in the Scandinavian coun-

[14] see *Flügge*, *Maelicke* and *Preusker* 2001.

[15] 10-20 percent reduction of serious recidivism, see *Dünkel* and *Drenkhahn* 2001.

[16] see the actual world wide data published by Kings College London under www.prison.org.

tries. The sentencing practice in these countries is, however, characterized by very short prison terms, which result in a lower average daily prison population.

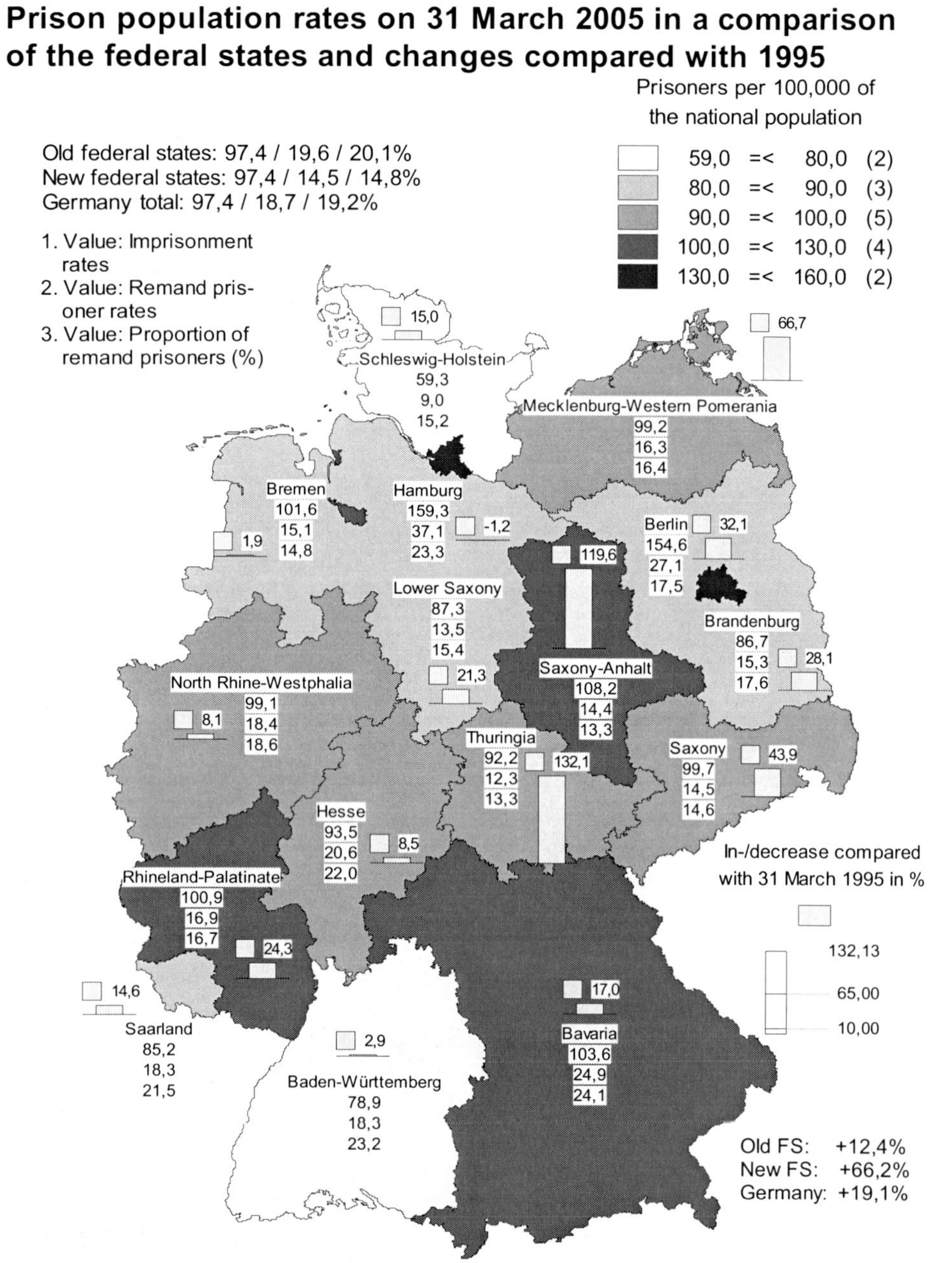

Figure 1.1

The importance of incarceration also varies among the different federal states which is only attributable to a minor extent to different crime rates. The so-called 'city states' of

Berlin, Bremen or Hamburg apparently have higher incarceration rates because of their urban structure and criminality. However, here too, considerable differences can be seen. Bremen, in 2005, had a total prisoner rate of 102 for every 100,000 inhabitants, Berlin had a ratio of 155, and Hamburg a ratio of 159. These remarkable differences are partly the result of a very low pre-trial detention rate in Bremen. Looking at the larger ('mixed' rural and urban) states we find a variation between 59 prisoners per 100,000 of the population in Schleswig-Holstein and 108 in Saxony-Anhalt. In general the southern federal states (with the exception of Baden-Württemberg) have higher incarceration rates than the northern states (see *Figure 1.1*), which seems to be particularly interesting when considering that the official crime rates in general, and those for violent crimes are higher in the northern states. Again we find indications of different policies of incarceration with a more repressive sentencing practice in southern states, like Bavaria or Saxony.

Administrative deprivation of liberty does not exist in Germany. Police custody is restricted to a maximum of 48 hours, after which a judge has to impose pre-trial detention or the person has to be released. The police laws of the different federal states provide for police detention in cases of disturbances of public order, for example, in cases of hooliganism in Bavaria. Up to two weeks are permissible, but - also in these cases - this decision has to be confirmed by a judge within 48 hours.

The prison population rate in West-Germany has been somehow stable, notwithstanding the fact that there have been quite important increases and decreases over time (see Figure 1.2). The first sharp decrease at the end of the 1960ies was the result of a major penal law reform replacing short term imprisonment with fines. The increase in the 1970ies up to the mid 1980ies was partly due to an increase in crime and a more punitive climate influenced by a difficult political situation caused by the Red Army Fraction terrorists. In the early 1980ies a campaign against the extensive use of pre-trial detention was even supported by the federal minister of justice at that time. The result was a decrease in the numbers of pre-trial and sentenced detainees. Other factors were the extension of community sanctions particularly for young offenders under the Juvenile Justice Act (14-21 years old) and of suspended sentences (probation) in the general penal law. Crime rates - including violent crimes - decreased. The opening of the eastern borders and the civil war conflicts in the early 1990ies created a severe burden also for the criminal justice system. Foreigners and migrants from Southern and Eastern Europe contributed to an increase of the prison population rate. But also an increase in violent crimes by young males in general resulted in this development. Since the mid 1990ies the prison population rate remained relatively stable although prison sentences for violent and sexual offenders have been increased due to legislative reforms.

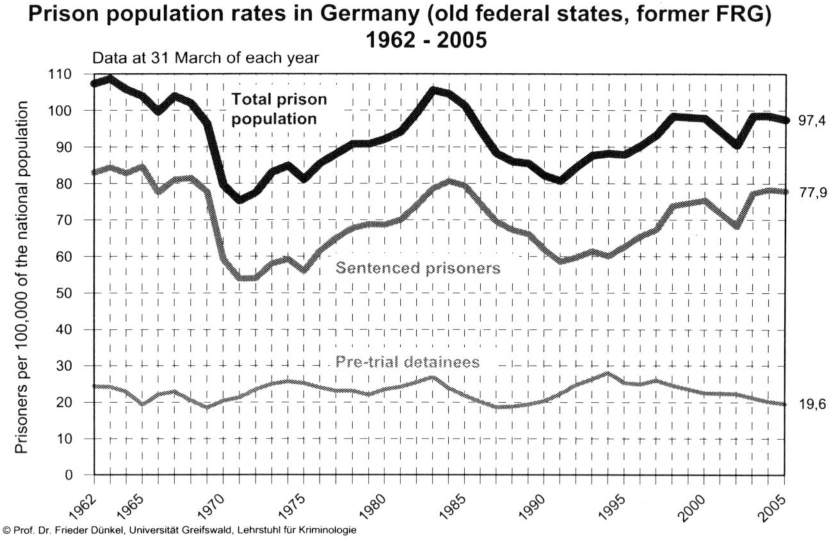

Figure 1.2

1.2.2 Institutions for foreigners and proportion of foreign prisoners

Foreign prisoners in Germany are mixed together with national prisoners. There are no separate wings or prisons as one feels that integration is better achieved by mixing foreigners and Germans. However, the prison administration is aware of the problems of different nationalities and ethnicities. Therefore, Turkish and Kurdish prisoners will not be accommodated in the same cell – and if possible wing – of a prison. The number of foreign prisoners has been stable during the last 20 years (20-25%).

As will be shown below (see 1.4.2), particularly young migrants and members of ethnic minorities have become a major problem and challenge for the prison system. The prison statistics available from the statistical central office at Wiesbaden (*Statistisches Bundesamt*) only show part of the problem, as they only differentiate between persons with and without a German passport. Some "new" groups of immigrants like the so-called Russian Germans (who are naturalised Germans because of the specific German immigration legislation) cause serious crime problems[17] and are also highly over-represented in prisons. Other groups like refugees, citizens of former Yugoslavia as well as asylum seekers (who suffer from particular living conditions as they are not allowed to work and move freely) have influenced the development of prisoner rates. This can be seen when one takes the pre-trial detention rate into account, which increased with the rise of the number of asylum seekers at the beginning of the 1990s by several thousand persons, and decreased after the new immigration legislation in 1993, which reduced the number of asylum seeking immigrants considerably (see below 1.4.2).

The statistical data regarding "foreigners" in German prisons reveal that in the adult prison system the proportion of foreigners is 24%, compared to 19% in youth prisons (2005). The proportion of foreigners has particularly increased in the 1980s and 1990s (from 7% to about 24% in the prisons for adults and from 6% to temporarily over 30% in

[17] see *Kerner* 2001; *Grundies* 2000; *Weitekamp*, *Reich* and *Bott* 2002; *Reich* 2003 with the explanation for their increased delinquent behaviour by the negative experiences of immigration.

the youth prisons (see *Table 1.1*). Youth prisoners are juveniles (14-17 years) or young adults (18-21years) who are sentenced to a youth prison sentence (six months up to five years, in serious cases or in the case of young adults up to ten years of imprisonment). They can stay in the youth prison until the age of 25. Therefore, almost 90% of the daily youth prison population consists of 18 to 25 year old "adults"[18]. Foreigners are even more over-represented in the age groups of 18-21 years, but also 21-30 year olds in the general prison system and in the very young age group of juveniles in the youth prison system (see *Table 1.2*).

Table 1.1: Proportion of foreign prisoners in Germany in adult and youth prisons 1976-2005

Year	*Prisoners in prisons for adults (> 18 y.)*	*Proportion of foreigners (%)*	*Youth prisoners (14-25 y.)*	*Proportion of foreigners (%)*
1976	31,592	6.0	5,967	4.8
1980	35,537	7.2	6,490	6,0
1985	41,852	9.7	6,360	9.4
1990	34,799	12,6	4,197	18.5
1995	41,353	21,6	4,980	31.5
2000	53,183	23,7	7,396	21.7
2002	52,988	23,0	7,455	18.6
2005	52,781	24.2	6,913	18.8

Source: Bundesamt für Statistik: Strafvollzugsstatistik 1976-2005, www.destatis.de

Table 1.2: Prisoners of foreign nationality in German prisons according to different age groups (on 31 March 2002)

Sentenced prisoners	*n =*	% of foreigners
Prisons for adults	52,988	22.3
Age groups		
18-21	214	45.8
21-25	5,619	25.6
25-30	11,292	29.8
30-40	19,697	25.1
40-50	10,801	16.2
50-60	3,979	11.8
60 and more	1,386	7.5
Youth prisons	7,455	18.6
Age groups		
14-18	849	24.0
18-21	3,540	18.4
21 and more	3,066	17.4

Source: Statistisches Bundesamt, Strafvollzugsstatistik 2002.

[18] see *Dünkel* 2003a; 2006.

The over-representation of foreigners in German prisons and particularly in youth prisons is considerable (see *Figures 1.3* and *1.4*). Another striking result in this context is that in East Germany, where the foreign population is very small, foreign prisoners are even more over-represented (about six times higher than their proportion of the general population) than in West-Germany (two to three times higher)[19]. These facts raise the question as to which selective practices of the justice system explain the elevated prisoner rates.

19 see *Winkler* 2003, 70 ff.; also *Dünkel* and *J. Walter* 2005.

Figure 1.3

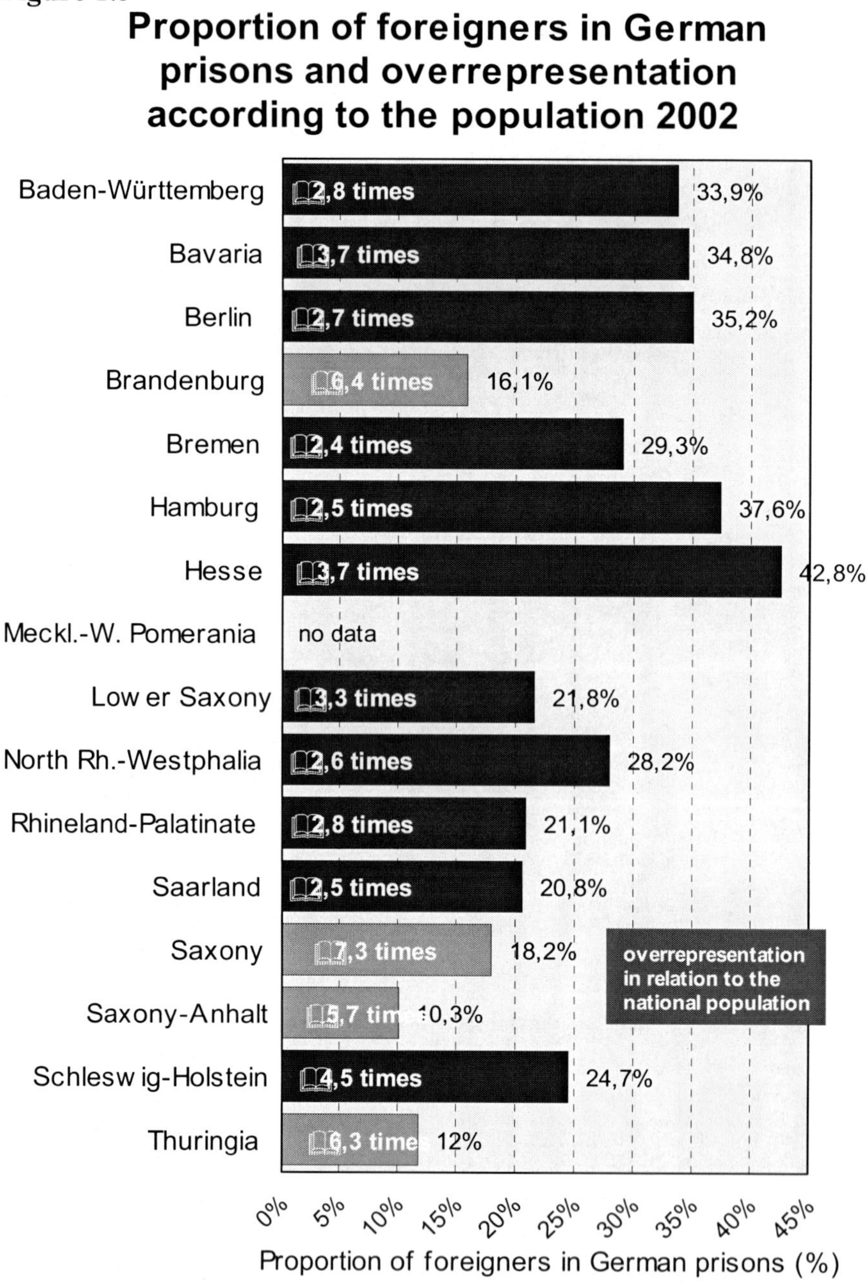

Source: Winkler, 2003, 76 ff.

Figure 1.4

Prison staff has often received no special training for dealing with foreigners, and special controlling mechanisms for foreign prisoners do not exist. The prison administration is making efforts to provide foreign prisoners with the same treatment as Germans (see 2.8. concerning the problems with re-integration activities and prison leaves).

1.3 Overview of the involvement of consulates, embassies, ministries of the home country, NGO's etc.

There is no systematic information about the involvement of foreign consulates and embassies, but in individual cases exchange of information is given, particularly if the extradition is a question of concern. The supervision and care of foreign prisoners is at least one of a number of focal points of various NGOs who campaign for the support of convicts. For example, the protestant pastoral care service in prisons (*Evangelische Gefängnisseelsorge*[20]) has a respective special unit that is in active opposition to the "obligation of removal" in cases of foreign prisoners who are enrooted in Germany. There are also initiatives at the regional level (see for example the *Straffälligen- und Bewährungshilfe Berlin e. V.* which aims to assist foreign prisoners, and has developed a respective information-flyer[21]). The associations of defence attorneys also have sporadic respective initiatives. The creation of a network, as aspired for by the international NGO of the *European Group for Prisoners Abroad*[22] – which bears no permanent German member – is, however, an initiative that is not visible in Germany.
There are more activities that show a greater degree of networking at the federal level when regarding people detained under Foreign Nationals Law, especially for refugees[23]. An important example of such work is the *Jesuite Refugee Service*, based in Berlin[24] that carries our advocacy work for refugees and forcibly displaced persons, e. g. by visiting detainees in the detention centre of Berlin-Köpenick.

1.4 Overview of trends

1.4.1 Trends in sentencing, numbers of prisoners, composition of prison population etc.

The general trend of the German sentencing practice has already been described under 1.1. Fines and suspended prison sentences are the predominant penalties in the German adult penal law system, unconditional prison sentences are considered as a measure of "last resort" ("ultima ratio"). However, there has been a major shift in the composition of the German prison population. There has been an increase of violent and drug offenders, especially of robbery and assault offenders, whereas the proportion of property offenders (theft, larceny) decreased. The extension of community sanctions for property offenders

---

20 see online under www.gefaengnisseelsorge.de.

21 see online under www.sbh-berlin.de.

22 see www.egpa.org for detailed information.

23 see for example the initiatives by *Pro Asyl*, www.proasyl.de.

24 see www.jesuiten-fluechtlingsdienst.de.

contributed to the above mentioned rather stable prison population even in times where violent crimes were on the increase and resulted in more prison sentences (see *Figure 1.5*).

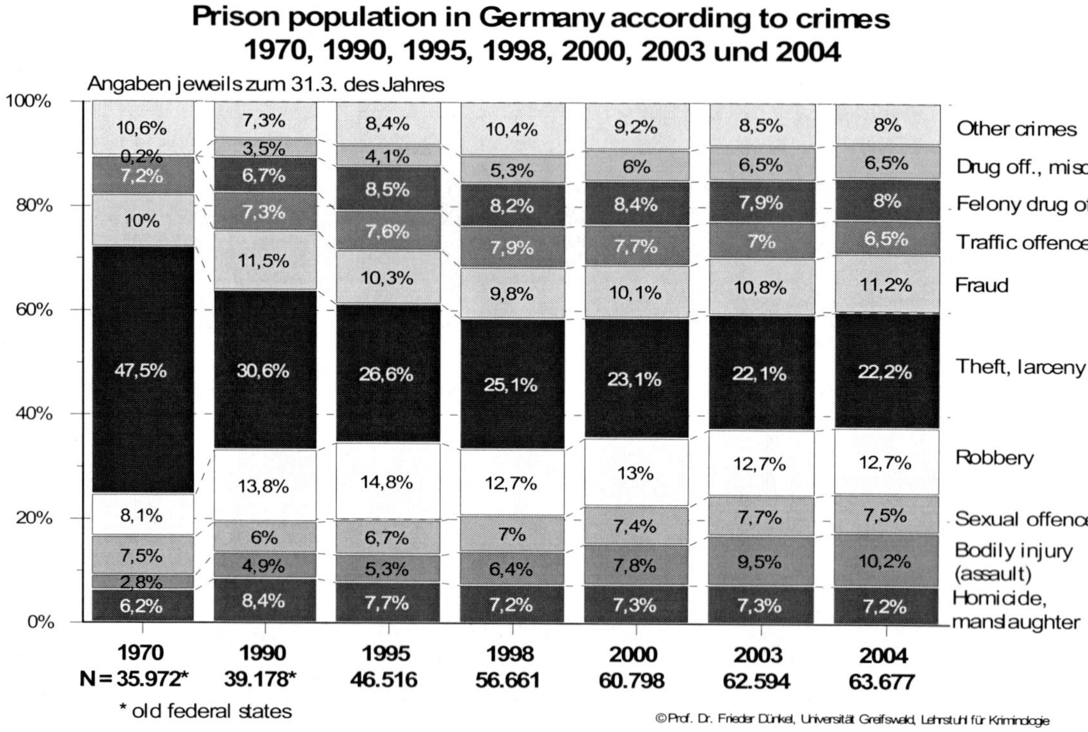

Figure 1.5

Tables 1.3-1.5 demonstrate that the length of prison sentences has also increased, however this is not so much the result of a harsher sentencing practice, but of an increase in the number offenders convicted for more serious crimes like robbery, serious bodily injury and sexual offences. The proportion of sentences of more than two years is still very low (less than 8% of all prison sentences see *Table 1.3*). The increase of sentences of more than one and the decrease of less than one year has been compensated by an extended practice of suspended sentences (probation) also for the longer sentences. In the last years, however, the use of life sentences for homicide has increased considerably. The daily prison population (31 March of the year) for life imprisonment developed as follows:

- 1980 956
- 1985 1.062
- 1990 1.149
- 1995 1.314
- 2000 1.598
- 2003 1.774
- 2004 1.794 (= + 88%)

The number of convictions per year until 1995 was around 70 and then increased to about 110 (2003: 105). The increase of „lifers" in prison is, however, mainly the result of a more restrictive release practice according to § 57a Penal Law (StGB, which in general provides a release after having served at least 15 years of the life sentence).

Table 1.3: Sentenced adult offenders according to the length of prison sentence, 1975-2003 – all crimes

Year	*Sentenced adults total*	*Prison sentence abs.*	*Pris. sent. % of. 2*	*Suspended p. s. % of 3*	*PS – 6 m., % of 3*	*– 6 m. susp. p. s. % Sp. 6*	*6 m. – 1 J., % Sp. 3*	*6 M. – 1 y., susp. p. s., % of 8*	*1 – 2 y. % of 3*	*1 – 2 y. susp. p. s. % of 10*	*2 – 3 y. % of 3*	*3 – 5 y. % of 3*	*5 – 10 y. % of 3*	*10 – 15 y. % of 3*	*life sentence % of 3*
1975	567.606	94.018	16,6	61,6	50,2	73,8	37,9	62,8	7,7	10,1	total 3,5		total 0,7		0,07
1980	599.832	104.850	17,5	65.7	48,0	79,3	39,1	66,9	8,0	18,3	2,4	1,5	0,8	0,11	0,05
1985	600.798	111.876	18,6	66,3	44,0	80,1	40,3	68,5	9,7	35,7	2,9	1,9	1,0	0,14	0,08
1990	615.089	102.454	16,7	68,0	45,8	77,8	37,8	70,5	10,8	54,1	2,8	1,9	0,8	0,11	0,06
1995	683.258	115.767	16,9	69,6	39,8	79,4	39,5	74,7	13,6	62,5	3,4	2,4	1,1	0,15	0,09
2000	638.893	125.305	19,6	67,5	37,1	75,2	41,1	74,0	14,3	64,8	3,7	2,5	1,1	0,16	0,09
2003	634.735	127.511	20,1	69,1	36,5	75,9	40,9	76,1	14,9	68,8	3,6	2,7	1,2	0,13	0,06

Table 1.4: Sentenced adult offenders according to the length of prison sentence, 1975-2003 – serious bodily injury (assault)

Year	*Sentenced adults total*	*Prison sentence abs.*	*Pris. sent. % of. 2*	*Suspended p. s. % of 3*	*PS – 6 m., % of 3*	*– 6 m. susp. p. s. % Sp. 6*	*6 m. – 1 J., % Sp. 3*	*6 M. – 1 y., susp. p. s., % of 8*	*1 – 2 y. % of 3*	*1 – 2 y. susp. p. s. % of 10*	*2 – 3 y. % of 3*	*3 – 5 y. % of 3*	*5 – 10 y. % of 3*	*10 – 15 y. % of 3*	*life sentence % of 3*
1975	7.085	2.090	29,5	62,3	37,9	72,3	49,9	68,0	8,8	10,4	total 3,1		total 0,3		0,0
1980	8.467	2.720	32,1	67,3	33,0	82,1	52,9	72,7	10,4	17,3	2,7	1,0	0,07	0,0	0,0
1985	8.593	3.099	36,1	66,3	29,5	80,9	54,3	71,1	12,4	31,5	2,7	0,9	0,2	0,0	0,0
1990	8.157	2.844	34,9	68,3	28,3	79,8	56,9	73,3	12,3	46,2	2,9	1,3	0,07	0,0	0,0
1995	9.384	3.616	38,5	73,5	26,2	86,9	53,1	79,1	15,3	57,4	3,7	1,5	0,2	0,0	0,0
2000	10.139	7.176	70,8	78,0	10,8	89,2	69,2	86,5	14,7	60,2	3,3	1,6	0,3	0,0	0,0
2003	11.045	8.370	75,8	79,9	10,0	89,7	70,2	87,5	15,1	64,0	2,9	1,7	0,2	0,01	0,0

Table 1.5: Sentenced adult offenders according to the length of prison sentence, 1975-2003 – drug offences

Year	*Sentenced adults total*	*Prison sentence abs.*	*Pris. sent. % of 2*	*Suspended p. s. % of 3*	*PS – 6 m., % of 3*	*– 6 m. susp. p. s. % Sp. 6*	*6 m. – 1 J., % Sp. 3*	*6 M. – 1 y., susp. p. s., % of 8*	*1 – 2 y. % of 3*	*1 – 2 y. susp. p. s.. % of 10*	*2 – 3 y. % of 3*	*3 – 5 y. % of 3*	*5 – 10 y. % of 3*	*10 – 15 y. % of 3*	*life sentence % of 3*
1980	9.960	6.804	68,3	54,4	13,7	81,6	48,3	76,6	23,2	27,0	6,7	5,5	2,6	0,04	–
1990	17.399	8.777	50,5	60,3	20,5	76,3	38,3	75,9	25,2	61,6	8,6	5,6	1,6	0,2	–
1995	25.748	13.582	52,8	62,0	20,4	77,2	35,2	66,8	25,1	68,8	8,4	5,3	2,0	0,2	–
2000	34.354	16.773	48,8	61,0	20,4	71,3	33,6	77,1	28,2	72,8	9,6	6,0	2,1	0,2	–
2003	35.952	16.378	45,5	61,4	20,2	69,3	30,4	79,4	30,4	76,9	9,7	6,7	2,5	0,1	–

There are no systematic statistical data available for the sentencing practice concerning foreign offenders. However, some individual studies give a somewhat contradictory picture.

Prima vista there is much evidence that some discrimination takes place at the different levels of the criminal justice system[25].

The fact that the police are aware of more than 90% of "classic" crimes is a result of the victim's or witness's reporting behaviour. The rise of crime figures of foreigners in the early 90s according to the lower Saxony study of youth violence is attributed to the fact that foreigners also report violent conflicts to the police more often, as increasingly violent conflicts are not restricted to intra-cultural problems, but also incorporate inter-cultural problems. If Turkish and German youngsters have problems with each other, they are more likely to report than if Turkish or German youngsters have conflicts that are restricted to persons of their national peer group[26] (see 2.3 below). According to several studies in Germany, there seems to be greater risk of being reported to the police for foreigners or those who look like them than for native Germans. I. e. the level of tolerance with regard to deviant behaviour is different[27].

At the police level several research studies show discriminative and sometimes hostile practices, whereas one cannot say that the police in general exhibit xenophobic attitudes. It is, however, the situation of suspecting a person, and sometimes young foreigners at least have the feeling of generally being suspected of having committed crimes. Therefore, their chance of being detected might be greater than for young Germans. Looking from the prosecutor's perspective, an interesting observation can be made: More cases of foreign suspects are dismissed by the public prosecutor than in cases of German suspects (diversion according to §§ 153 ff. Criminal Procedure Act, *StPO*, or §§ 45, 47 Juvenile Justice Act, *JGG)*[28]. This is particularly true for juveniles (14-18 years) and young adults (18-21 years). The result is that the prevalence rates of foreign compared to German offenders are still higher, but not as significantly as the police data would suggest[29]. This means

25 see e. g. *Hamburger*, *Seus* and *Wolter* 1981, p. 168; *Geißler* and *Marißen* 1990; *Walter* and *Pitsela* 1993, p.12; *Mansel* and *G. Albrecht* 2003, p. 679 ff.

26 see *Pfeiffer* and *Wetzels* 2000, p. 107; *Wilmers et al.*, 2002, p. 37.

27 see *Walter* 1993, p. 349; *Schwind* 2003, p. 471 with further references.

28 see in general *Dünkel* 2003.

29 see *Mansel* and *G. Albrecht* 2003, p. 687 ff.

that prosecutors somehow "de-dramatise" (petty) offences of foreigners to a more "realistic" level. *Mansel* and *G. Albrecht* in their comprehensive nation-wide statistical analysis furthermore demonstrate offence related and regional variations and conclude that the considerable differences between federal states can be understood by different strategies of crime control (including different rates of reporting to the police) and not so much by the relevant respective behaviour of foreigners[30].

The research study of *Steffen* in Bavaria revealed, however, that the risk for foreigners of being convicted increased in the 1990s. The proportion of foreigners, particularly those under 21 years of age, measured as a percentage of all (German an Non-German) police suspects resp. all formally sentenced offenders, increased, whereas the proportion of Germans decreased[31], due to an extended application of diversionary procedures (§§ 45, 47 Juvenile, Justice Act, *JGG*). So at least in Bavaria the "de-dramatising" process of earlier years has disappeared. This could be the result of intensive crime policy debates about (illegal) immigrants in the 90s and the strong pressure of public opinion for a tougher policy approach.

The most important stage of discrimination is at the level of pre-trial detention[32] . The legal preconditions are constructed in a way that foreigners – due to the in practice predominant reason "risk to abscond" - a priori run a greater risk of being held in pre-trial detention. This is at least the case for those who do not dispose of a place of permanent residence, like asylum seekers, or other travelling persons. The definition of a risk to abscond and not to stand trial is much greater than for domestic residents. The research evidence is quite clear. *Jehle* (1995) stated in his comprehensive report on pre-trial detention that he found many cases of foreigners being sent to pre-trial detention "who, if they had been Germans, would not have been detained." The negative consequence of this practice is that those having been sent to pre-trial detention run a much greater risk of receiving an unconditional prison sentence than those who stayed outside detention. This might be one of the reasons why foreigners are so over-represented in prisons[33]. On the other hand a *contemporary* empirical study of suspected and sentenced young burglars in Bavaria indicates no negative discrimination of foreign suspects, particularly concerning the sentencing decisions of the courts[34]. The most important factors were confessing to the crime, prior convictions, the value of the stolen good(s) and the fact of being in pre-trial detention. Pre-trial detention in these cases, however, did not correlate with the status of nationality. On the other hand, an indirect effect of "nationality" could be found as foreigners tended more likely to confess to the crime than Germans[35].

Other studies concerning Turkish and Yugoslavian offenders clearly demonstrated that they received harsher punishments than their German counterparts[36]. Foreign recidivists were exposed to more severe punishment, particularly imprisonment[37]. A study was conducted on behalf of the German Association of Probation Workers that concen-

30 see *Mansel* and *G. Albrecht* 2003, p. 713 f..

31 see *Steffen* 1998, 676 ff.; 2001, 259 ff..

32 see *Schott* 2004, p. 391; *Pfeiffer* et al. 2005 p. 82 ff.

33 see *Dünkel* and *J. Walter*, 2005.

34 see *Dittmann* and *Wernitznig* 2003, 195 ff.

35 ibid. p. 203.

36 see *Ludwig-Mayerhofer* and *Niemann* 1997; see also *Mansel* and *G. Albrecht* 2003.

37 see *Hartmann* 1995.

trated on the typical problems and situations of clients of the probation Service The study stated that although foreigners are overrepresented amongst those convicted (in relation to the population), they are under-represented in the group on probation in most of the Federal States[38].

	Foreigners	*Germans*
Population	8%	92%
Convicted persons	26%	74%
Probationers	17%	83%

(Source: Engels and Martin 2002)

A reason for this might be the fact that foreign criminals are less often brought under the supervision of the probation service than Germans "because they are either expelled after the conviction or because language problems seem to make successful probation supervision impossible"[39]. A similar under-representation – partly due to specific immigration regulations and pending expulsion – can be found with regard to prison leave and placement in open institutions[40] (see 2.8. below).

Although there are clear indicators for a discrimination of (some groups of) foreigners or at least a more restricted access to non-custodial dispositions of the courts, the database is limited and further research is necessary[41] (). On the other hand there is also evidence that the overrepresentation of foreigners in prisons partly can be explained by a more violent behaviour of certain foreigner groups[42] .

1.4.2 Overview on issues concerning the general population of foreigners and of foreign suspects of crime

Foreigners, migrants and ethnic minorities constitute a heterogeneous phenomenon in Germany which is partly a result of specific regulations of traditional immigration laws. Migrants from the former Soviet countries or other countries who can claim to be of "German" ancestry are legally seen as Germans and have the right to bear a German passport (see Article 116 of the Constitution, "*Grundgesetz*"), whereas third generation Turkish youngsters, although their parents are born in Germany, have until recently been seen as "Foreigners". They often no longer speak the language of their grandparents, whereas the young Russian migrants in many cases have serious problems with the German language.

The problem of defining different groups of ethnic minorities is strongly related to the criminal political debate, as particularly right wing extremist parties, but also the conservative Christian Democratic Party in election campaigns repeatedly run for more restrictive immigration laws in order to fight "imported" criminality of foreigners etc.

---

38 see *Engels* and *Martin* 2002.

39 see *Engels* and *Martin* 2002, p. 22.

40 see *Schott* 2004, p. 385.

41 see *Suhling* and *Schott* 2001, p. 78, *Walter* and *Trautmann* 2003, 66 f.

42 see *BMI/BMJ* 2001.

In the political debate populist arguments often emphasise asylum seekers and young male migrants who are prejudiced as being involved more in violent crime than the German residents. In addition, the recent discourse has been greatly influenced by the problems of terrorism and of organised crime where foreigners are over-represented (particularly in drug offences, trafficking young females for prostitution etc.).
As the subject of ethnic minorities and crime is often abused in the political debate for promoting xenophobic attitudes, some go so far to argue that statistics shouldn't even differentiate between Germans and foreigners, a question of political correctness that is emphasised particularly in Sweden. This would, however, result in a loss of knowledge concerning social integration and even disguise discrimination that takes place nonetheless. The differentiation of specific groups of ethnic minorities can support group related integration and therefore crime prevention strategies.

In general, the situation of migrants in Germany has changed considerably since the late 1980s. The absolute numbers of foreigners increased from about 4.5 million foreigners in the 1980s to a stable number of 7.3 million since the mid 1990s (see *Figure 1.6*). A recent calculation of the foreign population revealed, however, that the numbers of foreigners had been overestimated in the past years: There are only about 6.7 million foreigners living in Germany. In addition to foreigners, the number of "German" immigrants from former states of the Soviet Union or empire since the end of the 1980s rose to almost 400,000 annually (in 1990). From 1991 to 1995 the annual numbers were slightly more than 200,000 and then sharply dropped to about 31,000 in 2005 (see *Figure 1.7*). The new Immigration Law from 1999 permits the naturalisation of foreigners who have lived in Germany for longer periods and who are integrated into German society. Moreover, the new Immigration Law changes the concept towards a "ius soli", i. e. "foreign" children born in Germany are by definition "Germans", if the parents have lived in Germany for at least 8 years and have a "right" to live there. The absolute numbers of naturalisation of adult foreigners, however, are unexpectedly low. Only less than 150,000 in 1999 and between 150,000 and 190,000 in the years 2000-2002 were naturalised and consequentially received a German passport, in 2004 the numbers dropped to less than 130,000 (see *Figure 1.8*).

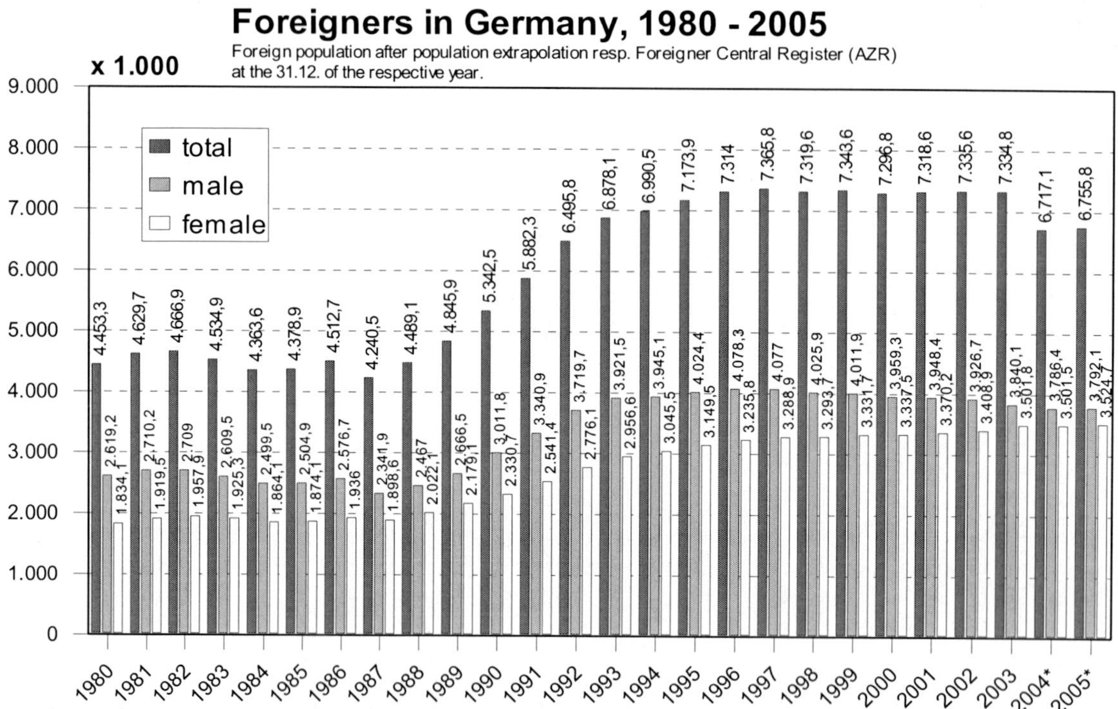

* The data of the population extrapolation for 2005 refer divergently from it to 30.9.2005. The details for the number of the foreigners to the AZR for 2004 and 2005 are not directly comparable with those of the previous years because of the register clearing up carried out in 2004.
Source: Statistisches Bundesamt Deutschland, 2006, http://www.destatis.de

Figure 1.6

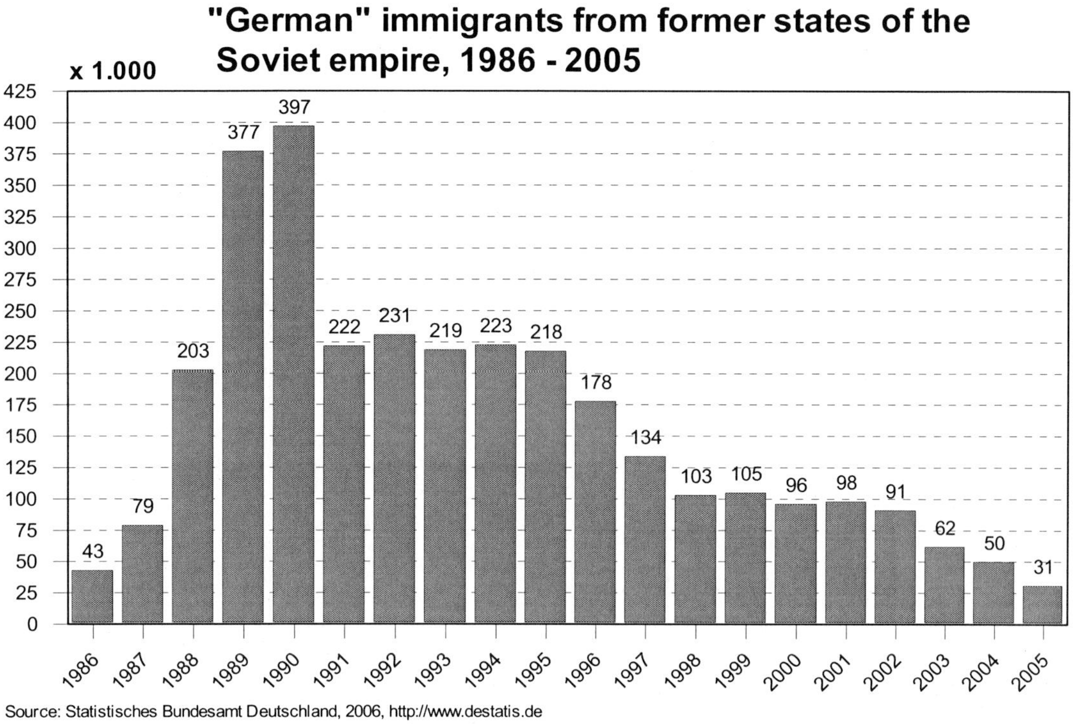
"German" immigrants from former states of the Soviet empire, 1986 - 2005
x 1.000
425
400
375
350
325
300
275
250
225
200
175
150
125
100
75
50
25
0
43
79
203
377
397
222
231
219
223
218
178
134
103
105
96
98
91
62
50
31
1986
1987
1988
1989
1990
1991
1992
1993
1994
1995
1996
1997
1998
1999
2000
2001
2002
2003
2004
2005
Source: Statistisches Bundesamt Deutschland, 2006, http://www.destatis.de

Figure 1.7

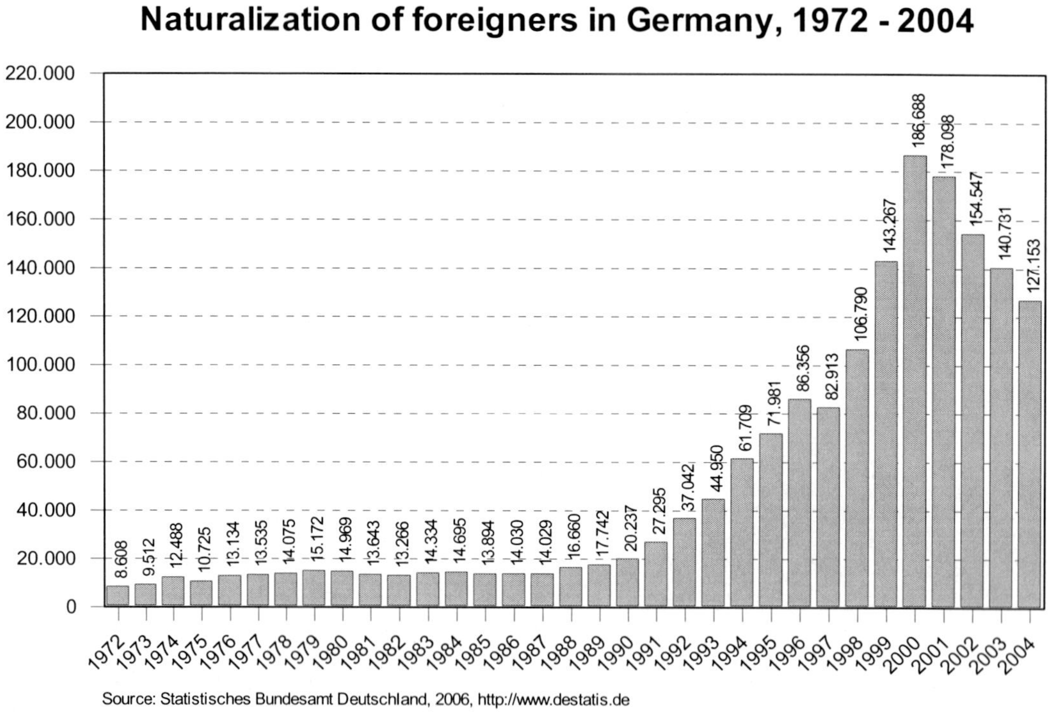

Figure 1.8

The crime rates of foreigners and ethnic minorities on the basis of registered police data suffer from a number of specific shortcomings. In consequence the police themselves publish the statement that the crime rates per 100.000 are not comparable. The crime rate is at first glimpse about 5 times higher than that for Germans. If we look thoroughly at the shortcomings of the statistical database the picture changes totally.

First we have to consider that certain offences as those against the immigration laws can only be committed by foreigners. The group of foreigners in the population is underestimated as many are not statistically registered (tourists, members of army forces, illegal immigrants). Germans and foreigners differ according to age, gender and social structure. So e. g. almost half of foreigners live in bigger cities against only 29% of the German population.

The risk of being reported to the police and of being prosecuted, sent to pre-trial detention and being sentenced differ considerably (see also 1.4.1 above). A differentiated analysis by the Bavarian police (*Landeskriminalamt*) shows that the relation of 4.9: 1 drops to only 2.7 : 1 if only the registered population of foreigners is taken into account. It further drops to 2.4 if offences that cannot be committed by Germans are deducted. Finally the ratio is 1.9 : 1 if only 14-21 years old male juveniles and young adults are considered. The crucial point is the social structure. No empirical approach so far has successfully eliminated all influential distorting factors. It may well be that the crime rate of really comparable groups will show no difference between foreigners and the domestic national population[43]. The majority of German criminologists claims a real higher crime rate of some groups of foreigners and of the so-called *Spätaussiedler* (Russian immigrants since 1993 with a German passport), which is caused at least in part by more intensive social control by the police and justice system[44].

Whereas the first generation of foreigners, the so-called guest workers of the 50s and 60s, showed no increased crime rates[45], studies in the 70s and 80s already revealed that young foreigners of the second and third generation of immigrants had considerably elevated crime rates (about twice as high as their German counterparts[46]). The hypothesis of cultural conflicts seemed to be somehow plausible. The data of the federal police statistics show that the proportion of foreigners amongst 14-25 years old young offenders is between 17% and 33%, whereas the proportion of foreigners in the total population is between 10% and 16%[47].

A study of the Lower Saxony criminological research institute demonstrated that 83% of the increase of crime rates for the 14-21 years old age group during the period from 1984-97 (in the old federal states) was caused by foreigners[48].

The development until 1993 was also greatly influenced by the increase in the number of asylum seekers and refugees who faced serious discrimination and social control. When the Immigration Law was changed in 1993 the number of asylum seekers dropped considerably (see *Figure 1.9*).

---

43 see *Geißler* and *Marißen* 1990, p. 633 ff.; *Walter* and *Trautmann* 2003, p. 75 ff., 77.

44 see *BMI* and *BMJ* 2001, p. 315

45 see *Schüler-Springorum* 1983; *H.-J. Albrecht*, 1997; perhaps as the social control and pressure to adapt to the new living conditions were felt so strongly.

46 see *P.-A. Albrecht* and *Pfeiffer* 1979; *Gebauer* 1981; *Villmow* 1983; *Karger* and *Sutterer* 1990; Schöch and *Gebauer* 1991; *Kubink* 1993.

47 see also *Schwind* 2003, p. 465.

48 see *Pfeiffer et al.* 1998.

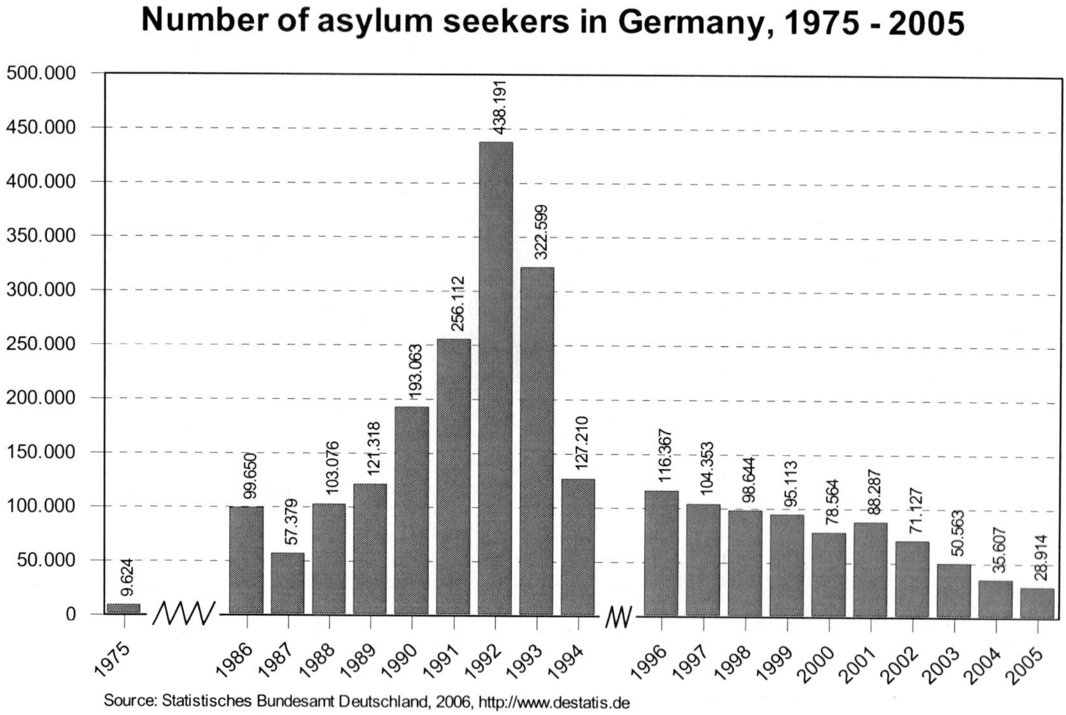

Figure 1.9

The proportion of foreign suspects of crime with respect to the total number of police recorded suspects of crime dropped from 34% in 1993 to 22.5% in 2005 (if one excludes offences against Immigration Laws, which cannot be committed by Germans, from 27% to 19.5%; see *Figure 1.10*). This development is remarkable as the number of police recorded German suspects continued to rise since 1993. A differentiation of the groups of foreigners involved in police registered crime is given in *Figure 1.11*. It shows that the proportion of so-called guest workers (foreign employees) has decreased from 33% of Non-German suspects in 1984 to around 17-18% in the years 1998-2005. On the other hand, the proportion of asylum seekers (although it has dropped considerably in the late 1990ies) with 10% in 2005 is still higher than in 1984 (8%). A maybe unexpected group are foreign students, who still contribute about 8% to the Non-German group of criminal suspects (in 1984 they even accounted for 15%, see *Figure 1.11*).

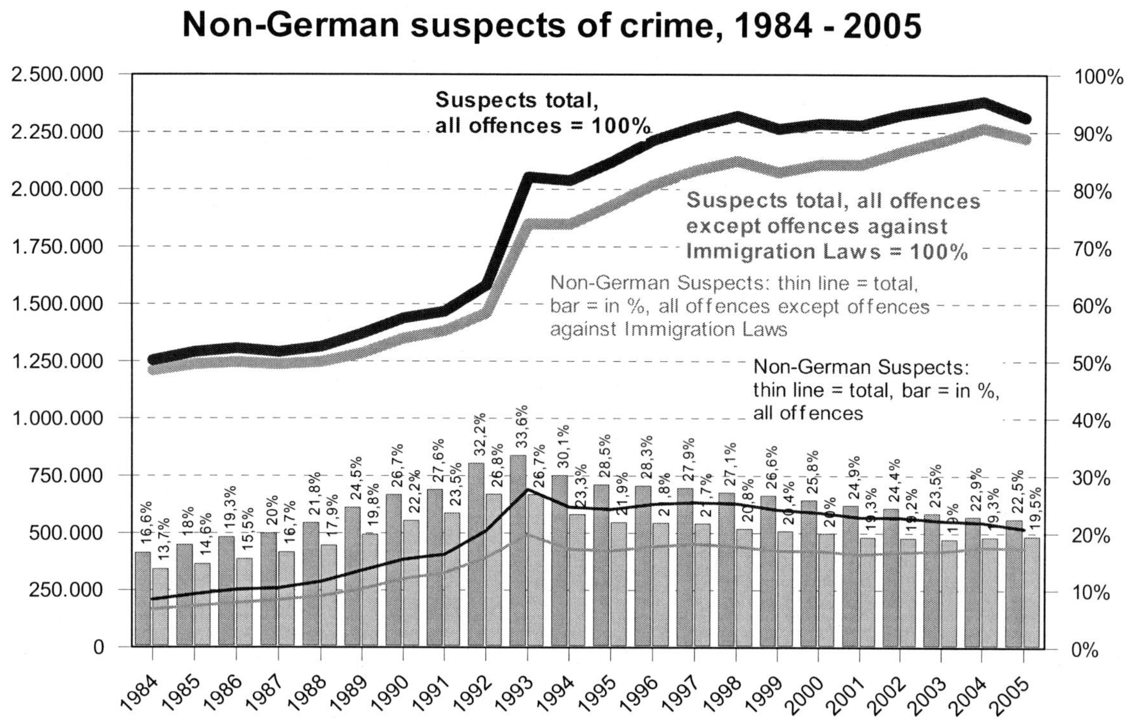

Source: Bundeskriminalamt (BKA), Polizeiliche Kriminalstatistik, 2004 and 2005, http://www.bka.de

Figure 1.10

Non-German suspects of crime according to the reason of stay; 1984 old Federal States, 1998 - 2005 Germany total

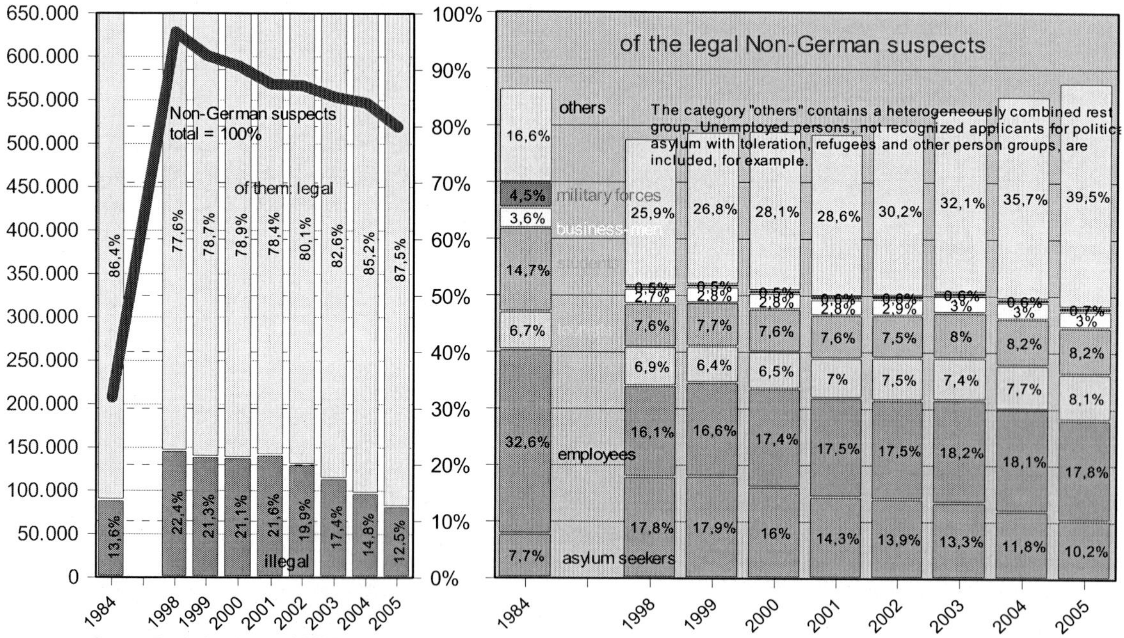

Source: Bundeskriminalamt (BKA), Polizeiliche Kriminalstatistik, 2004 and 2005, http://www.bka.de

Figure 1.11

1.5 Overview of national legislation

1.5.1 Constitution, Penal Code, Criminal Procedure Act

Foreigners are generally protected against discriminatory acts by the basic right of equal treatment before the law (allgemeiner Gleichbehandlungsgrundsatz), Article 3 GG because their cases concern disadvantage by state authorities. The much debated Anti-Discrimination Act (Antidiskriminierungsgesetz) (which has in the meantime been passed as the General Equal Treatment Act (Allgemeines Gleichbehandlungsgesetz (AGG)) which came into force on 18.8.2006) is meant for the protection of minorities within labour law and civil law. It thus has no direct meaning for the protection of foreign criminal prisoners from discrimination. A general anti-discrimination agency – as required by European guidelines - is planned to be founded in the Federal Ministry for Family Affairs, Senior Citizens, Women and Youth. It needs to be stated, however, that there are already active institutions that advocate the rights and interests of foreigners – whether or not specialization is more appropriate in this sense remains to be answered. For example, in their annual reports on the position of foreigners in Germany[49] these delegates often also look into the activities and behaviour of state agencies and can, for example, take sides against the above stated changes to the European Convention on the Transfer of Sentenced Persons.

With the final decision of a court the convict – in principle – knows whether he has to serve a sanction of imprisonment and how long this will be. This is different for foreigners: it is still not clear, when and if the execution of the sanction starts, how long it will continue and whether it will be executed in Germany or not.

As stated earlier, some measures can be taken by the public prosecution agency against foreign suspects or – in its capacity as the enforcement agency (*Vollstreckungsbehörde*) – the foreign convict: § 154b StPO (Criminal Procedure Act) as well as § 456a StPO open up the possibility to refrain from the execution in cases of extradition or expulsion[50]. The conditions for the expulsion are laid out in the new "Residence Act", see below 3., while extradition is regulated by the IRG. It is important to note that the decision to refrain from the execution is at the *agencies discretion*. § 17 of the Code on the Execution of Punishment (*Strafvollstreckungsordnung*) prescribes some criteria that the agency has to consider: No waiver of prosecution /execution is possible when "the personality of the convict or the nature of the crime" do not allow this. Arguments in favour of the waiver are that - as a rule - convicted foreigners are not allowed to leave the prison (Administrative Directives for the Code of Penal Execution; *Verwaltungsvorschriften zum Strafvollzugsgesetz*, Nr.5 and 6 on § 11 Code of Penal Execution) etc. (see 2.8. below), and that family contact is restricted by the external circumstances etc. The German jurisdiction[51] therefore approves the concept of a higher degree of "Strafempfindlichkeit" (*penal sensitivity)* when dealing with foreigners. One aim of these regulations was to return foreign criminals to their home country as soon as possible[52], while also paying regard to an easier reintegration into society. It was also planned to reduce the strain on the prison administrations, given the fact that dealing with foreign inmates is often more difficult. But the implementation of these regulations often bears problems for the persons concerned: § 456a StPO stipulates that in case of the return of this person (legally or illegally) the sentence can be executed later. This is a problem in particular for those who have family members in Germany.

Often foreign nationals see no more perspective of staying in Germany once they have been convicted, so they often have the wish to return to their home country. For some cases the possibility of a "Vollstreckungshilfe" exists in the form of bilateral agreements to execute a sentence of imprisonment. They provide a relatively flexible and quick procedure. In other cases the foreign prisoner can be transferred to his home country on the basis of the European Convention on the Transfer of Sentenced Persons (ETS no. 112, 1983) and its additional protocol (ETS no. 167, 1997). Originally – and this is the case also for Article 71 of the German "Act on International Cooperation in Criminal Matters" (IRG) – this transfer was only possible when the prisoner consented. The 1997 additional protocol gave up the precondition of consent of the prisoner. Rather, the in-

49 *Beauftragte der Bundesregierung für Migration, Flüchtlinge und Integration* 2005 p. 393 ff.

50 see *Tzschaschel* 2002, *Boese* 2003.

51 e.g. OLG Celle, *Strafverteidiger* 1981, p. 407 ff.

52 for an (older) international comparison see *Plachta* 1993.

strument now sets out the rules applicable to transfer of the execution of sentences, firstly where sentenced persons have absconded from the sentencing state to their state of nationality, and secondly where they are subject to an expulsion or removal order as a consequence of their sentence.

Contemporarily, there is much political debate in Germany on a proposed simplification of the prerequisites for the extradition of foreign prisoners by law enforcement agencies. This direction *was particularly* purposed by conservative groups but was then also included explicitly in the coalition agreement of the new two-party-government. Accordingly, in the near future an amended bill for the implementation of the European Convention on the Transfer of Sentenced Persons and its supplementary protocol shall come into force. The amendments shall effect the removal of the requirement for consent from German Law, while on the other hand aiming to safeguard standards of German Basic Rights by ordering *a judicial review of legitimacy* of the extradition abroad[53]. The verifiability of such extradition rulings (which could affect Basic Rights) was approved by the Federal Constitutional Court in a landmark decision on 18.6.1997 (BVerfGE 96,100). The German Federal Council (*Bundesrat*) only plans for the retroactive defeasibility of the decision through 23 EGGVG (introductory act to the Penal Code). This safeguard is by far too slack, even if the precondition for the transfer decision by the enforcement agency lies in the fact that the prisoner shall subsequently and definitely be expelled from Germany under Immigration Law. Government's bill plans to provide for an alternative, which is in itself seen as the minimum requirement. This alternative implies an examination according to § 71 IV IRG through which the regional court when dealing with extraditions has to check the foreigner's personal circumstances in their entirety as well as whether or not he/she faces political persecution in the ‚receiving' country. Additionally, a parallel provision must be made to § 80 III IRG, which states that foreigners who are enrooted in Germany may not be extradited to another EU-country against their will. In this context, the legal situation is generally obscure, because these new tendencies do not necessarily suit the direction that has been pursued by, for instance, the German Law on the European Arrest Warrant, which has – as is generally known – been deemed entirely unconstitutional. It did, however, contain the better safeguards in the field of execution for foreigner whose roots lie in Germany.

At this point, reference must also be made to the problems with the trans-national execution of punishment, especially when a foreign detainee who is *transferred* to Germany to serve a sentence has already been remanded to pre-trial custody in another country. Not only does the general rule apply which permits the time served in pre-trial custody abroad to be deducted from the prison sentence. Rather, the ratio need not be 1 to 1, but is at the courts discretion (§ 51 IV StGB). Respective case-law in this context is inconsistent, because evaluation criteria on the conditions in the foreign institution are often missing or are assessed very differently by the courts. Therefore, it can occur that a prisoner, who has spent six months in pre-trial detention in Spain, can have this period deducted from the pending full three year sentence, while another court – taking the conditions of detention in the respective country into consideration – could have deducted one year or even 18 months[54].

---

53 Source: *Draft Law of the Federal Council, Bundesratsdrucksache* 356/06 of 26.5.2006.

54 survey of the relevant case-law in Münchener Kommentar-*Franke* § 51 Rn. 24.

1.5.2 Penitentiary law; Legislation for foreign prisoners

The German Prison Act in general does not provide different treatment for foreigners compared to German nationals. However, administrative rules exclude those foreigners from prison leaves and the transfer to open prisons (see the administrative rules to §§ 10, 11 and 13 StVollzG), who are to be or who are in danger of being expelled. On the other hand, the rules for food and religion provide for the peculiarities of foreign prisoners to be taken into consideration. For foreign prisoners as well as for the prison administration the difficulties and specific problems arise more from practical questions than from legal provisions. (see more specifically under 2.5 below).

2 TREATMENT OF FOREIGN PRISONERS

2.1 General

The problems of foreigners and members of ethnic minorities in prisons have recently been the focal point of a study by the University of Bielefeld. This study involved the questioning of experts of the federal state ministries. On the one hand, this revealed the possibility of differentiated structural problems within the prison system as well as its lack of appropriate programmes. Furthermore, problems of the prisoners themselves were also revealed, for example motivational factors and language deficits. A specifically East-German problem seems to be the emergence of the treatment of young neo-nazis and xenophobic offenders as a new challenge for the youth prison system. Another study shows that the main goal of the German *Strafvollzugsgesetz* - the rehabilitation of the offender - comes into an unresolvable conflict with the consequences of criminal behaviour in the German immigration laws, i. e. the expulsion of the foreign prisoner[55]. The following table summarises the results of the Bielefeld-study mentioned above.

---

55 see *Boese* 2003.

Table 2.1: Problems of foreign prisoners and members of ethnic minorities and specific treatment programmes and opportunities for these groups (Questioning of Prof. *Britta Bannenberg*, University of Bielefeld, from September 2002, see *Bannenberg*, 2003; *Winkler*, 2003)

Federal states (Länder)	*Problems*	*Treatment programmes*
Baden-Württemberg	• Language problems • Increasing numbers of "German" immigrants from Russia • Problems of the "Russian" subculture	• Language courses for foreigners and "*Aussiedler*" from Russia • Regular school classes in Italian language • working groups and conferences concerning "Russians" in some prisons • Consideration of religious practices (food etc.)
Bavaria	• Language problems complicate individual treatment and care • Increasing numbers of "German" immigrants from Russia • Problems of the "Russian" subculture (resistant to treatment offers, abuse of group activities, specific language problems, etc.)	• Language courses for foreigners and "*Aussiedler*" from Russia • General foreign language courses • Leaflets in foreign languages • Consideration of religious practices (food etc.) • Foreign language courses for staff members • Employment of staff of foreign nationality or with foreign language knowledge (particularly Russian) • Suppression of subculture developments
Berlin	• No information	• Language courses for foreigners and "*Aussiedler*" from Russia • Leaflets in foreign languages
Brandenburg	• Language problems • Proportion of foreigners who participate in work programmes is considerably lower	• Language courses for foreigners and "*Aussiedler*" from Russia • Leaflets in foreign languages
Bremen	• No information	• No specific programmes for foreigners
Hamburg	• No information	• No information
Hesse	• No information	• No information
Mecklenburg-Western Pomerania	• No information	• No information

Federal states (Länder)	*Problems*	*Treatment programmes*
Lower Saxony	• Only language problems cause difficulties with foreign prisoners • Instead: sincere difficulties with "German" immigrants from Russia (subculture, extortion of other prisoners, forcing other *Aussiedler* to participate in drug dealing, assaults against other prisoners and prison staff, hunger strikes etc.)	• Language courses for foreigners and "*Aussiedler*" from Russia • Employment of foreigners as staff members • Project "searching social case work", external volunteers contacting foreign prisoners with special need of care • Work-group for problems with *Aussiedler*, developing a treatment and security concept
North Rhine-Westphalia	• Multicultural, multiethnic structure of inmate population causes serious problems with prison subcultures • Language problems • Increasing numbers of "German" immigrants from Russia • Problems of the "Russian" subculture	• In general equal treatment of German and foreign prisoners resp. *Aussiedler* • Consideration of religious practices (food etc.) • Efforts to diminish language barriers and to integrate foreigners into general treatment programmes • Foreign literature in the prison library
Rhineland-Palatinate	• no information	• no information
Saarland	• No specific problems with foreign prisoners • Increasing numbers of "German" immigrants from Russia (subculture problems, hierarchical structure, resistant to treatment offers, strong group cohesion)	• No concrete solutions or programmes
Saxony	• Only few "German" immigrants from Russia, therefore no specific problems	• No information
Saxony-Anhalt	• Language problems with foreign prisoners	• No information
Schleswig-Holstein	• Language problems as a hindrance for integrating foreigners and *Aussiedler* in schooling/vocational training and therapeutic programmes	• Language courses for foreigners and "*Aussiedler*" from Russia • Consideration of religious practices (food etc.) • Counselling and leisure time activities by external foreign volunteers for Turkish, Polish and Russian prisoners

Federal states (Länder)	*Problems*	*Treatment programmes*
		• Leaflets in 12 foreign languages • Since 2002: in Neumünster a central office for the work with foreign and *Aussiedler* prisoners was opened (offering language courses for staff members, employment of foreign staff members, further vocational training seminars for staff members
Thuringia	• Proportion of foreign prisoners is very small, therefore no serious problems • In single cases language problems	• Some general measures (not described in detail) to combat language problems

In general we may conclude that the East-German federal states do not face a serious problem with foreigners or members of ethnic minorities in prisons, whereas most West-German states reported language problems in general and the increasing numbers of (young) "German" Russians as a violence-oriented group creating a problematic subculture in prison.

The study by *Winkler*[56] reveals that most federal states offer some language training courses, but besides that have not developed specific treatment programmes for foreign prisoners or members of ethnic minorities (see Table 3 above). Insofar the "German" Russians (*Aussiedler*) are perceived as a particularly problematic group in some West-German states, where they are highly over-represented as indicated before[57].

With respect to the general treatment efforts in prisons in Germany, one can state that particularly in youth prisons young foreigners are integrated into school and vocational training programmes quite well. They are also integrated into anger-management programmes, developed in some institutions for violent offenders in general or in so-called socio-therapeutic units.

An exception must be made in the case of those who are sent back to their country of origin after having served their sentence partially (in general, they are extradited after two thirds of the sentence). They are not granted home leaves or other forms of the relaxation of the prison regime (including the transfer to an open prison).
In some prisons the recruitment of staff with foreign background (e. g. Turkish social workers) has started which simplifies the involvement and commitment of foreign prisoners.

Xenophobic or right-wing extremist offenders have, until recently, not been seen as a specific problem and some prison directors still deny having difficulties with them. In some of the new federal states these (regularly violent) offenders are now a matter of concern as they promote their extremist ideas and by that contribute to the development of a specific subculture which can be as explosive as that of young immigrants from Russia.

---

56 see *Winkler* 2003.

57 see *Grundies* 2000; *Reich* 2003.

One experiment which could be interesting in this context is the "just community" project in a department unit of the Adelsheim youth prison in Baden-Württemberg. Its focus lies on developing democratic structures and of educating young prisoners towards tolerance and democratic attitudes[58]. It could be of particular importance for young persons with a social background of former totalitarian systems as well as for young anti-democratic nationalists of the neo-nazi scene. Although an empirical evaluation on its outcome concerning later recidivism has not yet been conducted, there is some evidence that the prison climate has improved and that a culture of democratic conflict resolution can be established even under the particularly difficult situation in youth prisons.

First empirical results have also shown that the level of development of moral judgement[59] of most participants in the pre-post comparison increased significantly, mostly by about half a stage. There is also a visible shift from pre-conventional to conventional levels of development of moral understanding[60]. As negative effects did not occur and as the reported experiences allow confidence, it is now important to integrate the model into the "grey routine" of the total youth prison. At least there is evidence that social and moral learning is possible even under the conditions of the juvenile penal system[61]. The presupposition is therefore that we summon up our courage to dare more democracy, even in prison. The project seems to be of major importance also for the living together of different ethnicities and nationalities in prison. The climate insofar has improved under the rules of the "just community" model, as well.

2.2 Living conditions and facilities

The living conditions of foreign prisoners do not differ from those for Germans as they are not separated from them. Foreign prisoners often prefer to be accommodated in communal cells, if possible with other inmates from their home country. As they are less often in open prisons, their possibilities to freely move around inside prisons are restricted.

2.3 Reception and Admission

Reception and admission procedures are the same as for Germans. In cases of foreigners coming from abroad the prison authorities regularly inform the embassies of the home country.

2.4 Work, education, training, sports, recreation

Foreign sentenced prisoners are obliged to work (see § 41 StVollzG). There is no information available about any form of discrimination towards foreigners if the prison administration cannot provide work for every prisoner. Each prisoner has to save some money during his time in prison (so called "Überbrückungsgeld"). This money can not be seized

---

58 see *Dünkel* and *Walter* 2004.

59 in the sense of *Kohlberg's* model of moral development, see *Kohlberg* 1987.

60 see *Brumlik* and *Sutter* 1996: 46 ff.; see also *Sutter* 1996; *Sutter*, *Baader* and *Weyers* 1998.

61 see *Weyers* 2003, p. 106 ff.

for any reason (§ 51 StVollzG). Accordingly, it is not possible for the immigration authorities to use this money to cover the expenses of extradition[62]. Foreign prisoners can take part in all training, sports and recreational activities. The Prison administration is obliged to offer social welfare measures (Soziale Hilfe, § 71 StVollzG) for every prisoner who needs and desires help. Such measures for foreign prisoners can include language classes and special job training.

2.5 Food, religion, personal hygiene, medical care

§§ 53 ff ; 157 StVollzG puts the freedom of worship as laid out in the German constitution (Article 4 GG) into effect. The prison administration is therefore obliged to provide for special dietary and religious food rules (e. g. during Ramadan). Foreign prisoners are allowed to exercise their religion and possess goods to practice their religious duties. It is not always possible for a foreign prisoner to have regular access to a qualified religious representative, e. g. an Imam for Muslim prisoners.

2.6 Consular and legal help

Germany ratified the Vienna Convention on Consular Relations from April 1963. Art. 36 of the Convention requires that foreign nationals who are arrested or detained be given notice "without delay" of their right to have their embassy or consulate notified of that arrest.

2.7 Contacts with the outside world

There are no different regulations for foreign prisoners (the minimum length of visit is one hour per month, see § 24 StVollzG). However, the prison administration may grant long term visits of several hours if a prisoner receives a visit from a relative from abroad. The writing and receiving of letters is in no way restricted at all. Telephone calls can be made subject to supervision by an interpreter. The regulation in § 31 StVollzG that enables the prison administration to seize letters that are written in a foreign language “without compelling reason” usually excludes letters written by foreign prisoners. If nevertheless the prison administration wants to control a letter written in another language, it has to provide for the translation; it must be paid by public means

2.8 Re-integration activities, prison leave

If the foreign prisoner is not to be expelled, he may be granted the same re-integrative activities and prison leave up to the integration into work release programmes. If the foreigner is to be extradited he is generally excluded from prison leaves etc., except those that are accompanied by prison guards. A study by *Tzschaschel*[63] revealed that 58% of all German prisoners but only 18% of all foreign prisoners in the sample were granted the opportunity to leave the prison. Only 10% of all foreign prisoners in the sample were eli-

---

62 see *Fluhr*, 1989, 103 ff.

63 see *Tzschaschel* 2002, p. 42 ff.

gible for the placement in an open institution (28% of the German prisoners). On the other hand foreign prisoners may be eligible for internal training programmes preparing for release. In fact, prison administrations tend to exclude foreigners from such rehabilitation programmes when there are not sufficient places for all prisoners.

2.9 The removal of criminal foreign detainees

Detained foreign nationals whose detention functions solely a means for safeguarding their administrative removal in accordance with § 62 AufenthG – as presented under 3. below – are to be held separately from imprisoned foreign nationals who are to be expelled as a response to their perpetrated criminal offences. But there is also the possibility to remove foreigners who have committed crimes or who pose a threat to public order and security. The foreign nationals' department is also responsible for removals in these cases. In cases where grave or repeated premeditated criminal offences specified in § 53 AufenthG (including for example: offences with a conviction to at least three years detention, or deprivation of liberty without probation due to breaches of the German Drugs Act (Betäubungsmittelgesetz, BtMG); for the individual regulations see the appendix) have been committed, a removal is obligatory as stated in § 53 AufenthG. Also, § 54 AufenthG specifies criminal offences (including: leading to sentences of imprisonment without probation; juvenile detention of at least two years for all offences) the perpetration of which normally results in the foreign offender's expulsion from German federal territory. Additionally, certain circumstances are stated in § 55 AufenthG – especially concerning threats for public security and order – under which the decision on removal is a matter of discretion. However, in these cases § 55 III AufenthG requires that the duration of prior legal residence and (other) family ties be taken into account.

Foreigners who are approved asylum seekers or who are otherwise legitimately residing in Germany (e. g. through a settlement permit, *Niederlassungserlaubnis*) are specially protected against removal by § 56 AufenthG. This protection is, however, put into perspective by § 56 I 2, 3 AufenthG when there are profound grounds. This precondition is normally fulfilled in the above mentioned cases of convictions for offences specified in §§ 53, 54 AufenthG. However, a removal order must take into account the restrictions of § 60 AufenthG. This states that persons may not be removed should they be at risk of being tortured in their home country. Also, § 60 V AufenthG forbids that a removal infringe the ECHR, for example Article 8 ECHR (Right to Respect for Private and Family Life).

In addition one needs to consider that, fundamentally, an expulsion lasts indefinitely (§ 11 I 1,2 AufenthG. However, § 11 I 3, 4 AufenthG specifies that a limitation of the removal period can be considered, should the respective application be made. The resulting decision must take the principles of the ECHR into consideration, as has been exemplified by a ruling of the EGMR (www.coe.int/t/d/menschenrechtsgerichtshof/dokumente_auf_deutsch/volltext/urteile/20051027-Keles-U.asp#TopofPage). In fact, in many cases in which the foreign nationals department orders a removal, the person in question is in penal detention.[64]. The course of action regarding the actual departure from Germany has to be determined by the authority responsible for the execution of punishment (Strafvollstreckungsbehörde)

64 see www.gefaehrdetenhilfe.de/download/ 150_abschiebung_aus_untersuchungs_und_strafhaft.pdf.

- in this case the prosecution service,. § 456a StPO allows the latter to decide whether the sentenced foreigner is to be removed immediately, or whether he/she is to serve the sentence in whole or in part in Germany. In any case, the foreign national shall be expelled "out of custody".

In most of the *Länder* the expulsion is considered after the enforcement of half of the sentence (§ 456a StPO), in some cases two thirds of the term of imprisonment are executed before an expulsion. *North hine-Westphalia* even checks the preconditions of an expulsion according to § 456a StPO right at the beginning of the execution of the foreigner´s prison term[65].

2.10 Aftercare, Probation

There are no laws or regulations that provide for a different treatment of foreigners concerning their access to probation or aftercare. As mentioned above, fewer foreigners are supervised and supported by the probation service than Germans. This is party due to the fact that foreign criminals are more often expelled, but it is assumed that another reason lies in the expected difficulties with foreigners as probationers (in particular those who do not speak German).

2.11 Staff

Some West-German prison units recruit prison staff from the most common home countries of foreign prisoners, like Turkish social workers etc. One example is Hamburg, where 40% of all prisoners are not German nationals; they come from 94 different countries. Three prisons employ so called "*Ausländerberater*" (foreigner´s aides). However, given the massive job cuts in prison staff in Hamburg this is probably merely a drop in the ocean.

2.12 Projects

See 2.1 (the just community project in Adelsheim)

3 ADMINISTRATIVE DETENTION OF ILLEGAL RESIDENTS IN GERMANY

Asylum Law and Law concerning Foreign Nationals have been continuously gaining relevance. In this field there have been numerous landmark decisions, and one should also bear the compromise on asylum ('A*sylkompromiß')* in mind. One subject area is the ,removal / expulsion' as well as the 'administrative detention of irregular migrants' ('*Abschiebungshaft*'). Originally, removal/expulsion was regulated in the Foreign Nationals Act (*Ausländergesetz*; AuslG). However, there has been a series of legal amendments especially in the last 15 years. Changes have been made to provisions that concern, for example, the subsequent immigration of dependent family members. However, removal/expulsion was

---

[65] see *Tzschaschel* 2002, p. 11 ff.

also facilitated, penal prescriptions intensified, and § 57 AuslG, which regulated the administrative detention of irregular migrants, was broadened.

On 1st January 2005, the Foreign Nationals Act was replaced by the so called Residence Act (*Aufenthaltsgesetz*; Law on the Residence, Occupation and Integration of Foreigners in the Federal Territory of Germany; AufenthG). Administrative detention of illegal residents is now regulated in § 62 of the Residence Act[66].

3.1 What type of institution is used for this kind of administrative detention?

Expulsion is the enforcement of a foreigner's duty of departure by means of removal from Germany's federal territory[67]. It is a measure of administrative execution in the form of directly exerted compulsion. Such administrative detention acc. to § 62 AufenthG is a measure of liberty-deprival under Civil Law that serves to safeguard the implementation of this compulsive departure[68]. Such detention is neither a sanction for improper conduct nor a means of directly coercing a foreign national to leave the country. Thus, it is not of a punitive nature and merely serves safeguarding purposes[69].

There are three different models for the accommodation of detainees pending expulsion: allocation to special establishments for the administrative detention of illegal residents; in regular penitentiary institutions ('*Justizvollzugsanstalt*', JVA) or in special departments of such a JVA[70]. Special establishments for the administrative detention of irregular migrants can only be found in a select few German Federal States, for example Berlin, Brandenburg and Bremen, and are within the responsibility of the Ministry of the Interior / the administration of justice of the respective Federal States[71]. In Rhineland-Palatinate, the Ministry of the Interior runs special detention establishments for detainees awaiting removal[72]. Accordingly, these states have special ‚Laws on the Execution of Detention pending Removal'. Yet in general the prescriptions of the Law of Prison Administration (*Strafvollzugsgesetz*, StVollzG) are deemed to apply respectively, with the exception of judicial legal protection.

In the other federal states, with the exception of Rhineland-Palatinate, the justice administration assumes responsibility for execution through administrative assistance acc. to § 8 II of the Act on Court Proceedings relating to Deprivation of Liberty, FEVG[73]. In part, for example in Northrhine-Westphalia, there are extra penitentiary establishments that are designed solely and especially to accommodate detainees awaiting expulsion, while on the other hand a proportion of these detainees is also accommodated in regular prisons alongside criminally convicted prisoners or pre-trial detainees. Thus, in these cases the norms of the StVollzG on the execution of liberty-deprivation are applicable, so long as they do not impede the peculiarity and purpose of administrative detention._Thus,

66 For a detailed commentary on the legal regulations on administrative detention for foreigners see *Melchior* 2006.

67 see *Hailbronner* 2006, p. 197.

68 see *Beichel-Benedetti* and *Gutmann* 2004, p. 3016.

69 see *Heinhold* 2004, p. 15.

70 ibid. 2004, p. 28.

71 see *Horstkotte* 1999, p. 34; *Heinhold* 2004, p. 94.

72 see *Heinhold* 2004, p. 236.

73 see *Horstkotte* 1999, p. 34.

different institutions and establishments - that are associated either to the administration or to the prison system - are used for the detention of illegal residents awaiting removal.

Concerning the quality of living conditions in the respective institutions or units it is important to bear in mind the reports of the Council of Europe's Committee for the Prevention of Torture and Inhuman or Degrading Treatment or Punishment (CPT). The CPT´s remark in its report of the visit in the year 2000 is particularly interesting: "For its part, the CPT considers that to hold immigration detainees in prison is a fundamentally flawed approach, even if the actual conditions of detention for the persons concerned in a given prison establishment are adequate. As already emphasised in paragraph 76 of the report on the 1996 visit, a prison is, by definition not an appropriate place in which to detain someone who is neither suspected nor convicted of a criminal offence."

Delegations of the CPT visited Germany five times, and on several occasions special institutions or units for foreigners/immigrants were visited. Some of the visited institutions gave rise to criticism; in particular visits to the unit at the Frankfurt am Main Airport, as well as the institution in Eisenhüttenstadt. The visit to Frankfurt in 1998 was a so-called ad-hoc visit as a response to reports that the CPT had received which were critical of the conditions under which immigration detainees were being held there. Those reports also contained a series of allegations of ill-treatment of such persons; more particularly, allegations were made of the use of excessive force during the enforcement of removal orders. Certain allegations were also made that non-medically qualified staff had administered tranquillizers to the persons concerned. The delegation itself found no evidence of ill-treatment but requested reports on the investigations by the German authorities. The Delegation had several comments on poor ventilation, monotonous food, poor facilities and activities for younger persons and children, on insufficient medical and psychological/psychiatric care and on the need to improve training for those officials dealing with foreign detainees at the airport[74]. Some of these shortcomings had still not been remedied before the follow-up visit by the CPT in the year 2000. During the same visit, the CPT inspected the Eisenhüttenstadt detention centre. Among several rather minor shortcomings, the CPT had strong objections to some of the discipline and security measures employed there, such as the withdrawal of outdoor exercise that was applied occasionally by staff as a disciplinary measure. The delegation found conditions in one of the two security cells totally unacceptable. This cell was fitted with four metal rings anchored to the floor, in order to secure a person's hands and feet while lying prone and spread-eagled. It recommended a completely different approach to agitated detainees than in intimidating security cells.

A delegation of the CPT carried out a visit to Germany from 20 November to 2 December 2005, the CPT's fifth visit to this country. In the course of the visit, the CPT's delegation followed up a number of issues examined during previous visits, in particular the fundamental safeguards against ill-treatment offered to persons deprived of their liberty by the police and the situation of immigration detainees. Three out of the 17 visited institutions or units were designed for foreigners. A report of that visit is not yet available.

---

[74] Ref.: CPT/Inf (99) 10 [EN] (Part 1) - Publication Date: 27 May 1999; all reports are available under www.cpt.coe.int.

Table 3.1: Foreign detainees pending removal in penitentiary establishments 1990-2006

Count on Jan. 1. of the year	*1990*	*1991*	*1992*	*1993*	*1994*	*1995*	*1996*	*1997*	*1998*	*1999*	*2000*	*2001*	*2002*	*2003**	*2004*	*2005*	*2006*
*Germany total ** *	302	430	557	1.242	2.600	2.322	1.690	1.849	2.283	1.938	1.924	2.001	1.824	1.786	1.582	1.302	947
Males total	274	399	503	1.130	2.373	2.135	1.564	1.738	2.034	1.727	1.681	1.758	1.627	1.571	1.346	1.101	820
Females total	28	31	54	112	227	187	126	111	249	211	243	243	197	215	236	201	127
Baden-Württemberg	34	68	37	80	115	220	166	164	174	113	145	164	134	142	136	111	76
Bavaria	104	94	137	205	512	476	333	423	554	465	435	402	388	351	340	314	181
Berlin			9	16	14	18	1	-	15	-	-	1	1	4	3	3	3
Brandenburg				14	9	4	4	4	1	1	-	-	-	1	-	-	-
Bremen	-	-	1	5	14	2	4	3	1	1	-	-	1	-	-	-	-
Hamburg	13	33		33	83	103	54	80	95	79	83	92	93	94	75	55	82
Hesse	14	29	27	35	160	154	84	141	158	188	214	183	206	205	224	137	122
Mecklenburg-Western Pomerania			6	13	33	43	21	24	13	11	14	24	14	19	12	18	10
Lower Saxony	24	58	94	201	283	239	160	177	238	202	206	245	212	188	135	94	55
North Rhine-Westphalia	76	132	160	357	872	696	559	532	705	659	633	676	609	650	513	411	322
Rhineland-Palatinate	18	24	18	67	50	46	22	17	10	1	1	-	6	4	1	-	-
Saarland	8	13	13	23	58	58	43	35	49	40	47	31	1	4	-	1	1
Saxony			30	73	118	71	59	88	56	80	56	109	87	43	63	64	37
Saxony-Anhalt			2	29	94	24	52	42	64	41	39	30	34	30	27	22	20
Schleswig-Holstein	8	8	21	72	140	111	95	83	113	14	8	11	16	32	35	39	26

Count on Jan. 1. of the year	*1990*	*1991*	*1992*	*1993*	*1994*	*1995*	*1996*	*1997*	*1998*	*1999*	*2000*	*2001*	*2002*	*2003**	*2004*	*2005*	*2006*
Thuringia			2	19	45	57	33	36	37	43	43	33	22	19	18	13	12

Source: Statistisches Bundesamt: destatis
** as of 2003 cut-off date on March 31 of the respective year*
*** as of 1992: All of Germany including the new Federal States*

3.2 Which Ministry is responsible and which laws/regulations are applicable to this category?

The regulations that are decisive for expulsion/removal as well as for the administrative detention of illegal residents are contained within the Residence Act. The procedure is regulated in the Act on Court Proceedings relating to Deprivation of Liberty and in the Act on Non-Contentious Proceedings (FGG). Regarding the implementation of detention, the norms of the StVollzG and respective special regulations at the Federal State level apply. Decisions and measures relating to residence issues – which includes removal/expulsion – are matters for the respective local 'Foreign Nationals' Registration Offices' (*Ausländerbehörden)* (as stated in § 71 I AufenthG). In accordance with § 106 II 1 AufenthG and § 3 S.1 FEVG, these agencies also initiate the procedure of administrative detention pending removal by filing the application for detention. The Foreign Nationals' Registration Offices are directly responsible to the Federal State Ministry of the Interior. Under certain circumstances, such an application for detention can also be filed by customs and excise (§ 71 III Nr.1 AufenthG) as well as by the police forces of the individual Federal States (§ 71 V). Whether or not the application is allowed is decided by the District Court in accordance with § 3 FEVG in the procedure of non-contentious proceedings.

3.3 How many of these institutions exist and what is their capacity?

The number of applicable institutions varies among the Federal States - each State makes use of multiple penitentiary establishments, and the capacities thereof also exhibit a degree of variation. In Germany, roughly 2250 foreign detainees awaiting removal can be accommodated. A detailed listing of the individual Federal States, their institutions and capacities up to the year 2002 can be found in the book „Abschiebungshaft in Deutschland" ("Administrative detention in Germany") by *Heinhold* 2004; see also table 3.2.

Table 3.2: Institutions for the Administrative Detention of Irregular Migrants in the individual Federal States of Germany

	Responsibility	Placement in:	Particularities	Capacity
Baden-Württemberg	JVA in administrative assistance for the Administration of the Interior	JVA Mannheim; JVA Rottenburg	Special section in Mannheim; Accommodation in containers located in yard; surrounded by walls / screened from view	104 places in Mannheim
Bavaria	JVA in admin. Assistance for the Bavarian Ministry of State for the	JVAs	in JVA Nürnberg (and München-Stadelheim) special section	Flexible
Berlin	Ministry for Internal Affairs	Establishment for detainees awaiting expulsion in Köpenick	Police are responsible for custody pending expulsion	340 places, of which 50 for women
Brandenburg	Ministry of the Interior	Establishment for administrative detention in Eisenhüttenstadt		108 places, 30 of them for women
Bremen	Senator for Interior Affairs and Sport	Administrative custody pending removal in the "Vahr76"	In Police Custody; single- and double cells	18 places for men and 10 for women
Hamburg	Ministry of the Interior	Establishment for administrative detention in Glasmoor; JVA Holstenglacis, JVA Suhrenkamp; JVA and Juvenile Detention Centre Hahnöfersand	Containers in Glasmoor	84 places in Glasmoor, 15 for juvenile male detainees in Hahnöfersand, 5 for female and 16 for adult male detainees in pre-trial detention centre
Hesse	Ministry of Justice	Establishment for admin.detention in Offenbach; JVA Fulda, JVA Kassel; JVA Frankfurt/Main for Frauen; JVA Wiesbaden and JVA Rockenberg for male juveniles and young adults		50 places in Offenbach
Mecklenburg-Western Pomerania	Ministry of the Interior	JVA Bützow, men only	special expulsion-department, if overcrowded then transfer to Eisenhüttenstadt;	11 places

	Responsibility	Placement in:	Particularities	Capacity
			Women always to Eisenhüttenstadt or to other Federal States.	
Lower Saxony	Ministry of the interior	JVA Langenhagen; JA Hameln; other JVAs		185-245 places (emergency capacity) in Langenhagen; of which 45 for women
North Rhine-Westphalia	Ministry of the Interior	JVA Büren; Det. Centre Moers; Det. Centre in Neuss; other JVAs		530 places in Büren; 144 for men in Moers, 80 for women in Neuss
Rhineland-Palatinate	Ministry of the Interior and Sports	detention centre for detainees pending expulsion (*Gewahrsamseinrichtungen für Ausreisepflichtige* GfA); Ingelheim; GfA Birkhausen		150 places for men in Ingelheim, 51 for men and 19 for women in Birkhausen
Saarland	Ministry of the Interior and of Sports	GfA Ingelheim a. Zweibrücken/Birkhausen (in Rhineland-Palatinate); JVA Zweibrücken, JVA Ottweiler	GfA for women a. men	GfA has 50 places
Saxony	Ministry of the Interior	JVA Bautzen; JVA Chemnitz; JVA Dresden; JVA Görlitz; JVA Leipzig; JVA Plauen, JVA Stollberg, JVA Zwickau, u.a.	No special penitentiary establishments	Total of 115 places
Saxony-Anhalt	JVA in administrative assistance for the Ministry of the Interior	JVA Volkstedt for men; JA Raßnitz; JVA Halberstadt for women and female juveniles		roughly 50 places
Schleswig-Holstein	Ministry of the Interior; with admin. assistance from the Ministry of Justice	establishment for administrative detention in Rendsburg for men; JVA Lübeck for women	Support from establishment for administrative detention in Eisenhüttenstadt or Glasmoor	56 places in Rendsburg
Thuringia	Ministry of the Interior	JVA Goldlauter for men; JVA Chemnitz for women		45 places in Goldlauter

Source: Heinhold 2004.

3.4 What is the legal length and average length of detention?

Firstly, it should be noted that there are two different forms of administrative detention in Germany. On the one hand, there is so called *preparatory detention* acc. to § 62 I AufenthG., which serves to prepare a removal/ an expulsion according to §§ 53 ff AufenthG. The duration of preparatory detention may not exceed six weeks in accordance with § 62 I 1 AufenthG. An extension shall only be applicable in exceptional cases. On the other hand, there is actual *administrative detention to safeguard removal* which is regulated in § 62 II, III AufenthG. This form of detention serves to secure the successful removal of the detainee from the federal territory (§ 62 II 1 AufenthG). One key precondition for *administrative detention to safeguard removal* is that the detainee's expulsion is beyond any doubt. The maximum period of time for which a person can be detained in this form is six months (§ 62 III 1 AufenthG). In cases in which the foreign national impedes his expulsion, the period of detention can be extended by a further 12 months (§ 62 III 2 AufenthG).

However, § 62 II 4 AufenthG states that, in general, administrative detention while awaiting removal should not exceed three months[75]. If the departure deadline has passed and if it is clear that the detainee's removal can actually be implemented, then the term of *admin. detention to safeguard removal* should not exceed two weeks (§ 62 II 2 AufenthG).

§ 62 III 3 AufenthG stipulates that a period of time spent in preparative administrative detention shall be deducted from the total duration of *administrative detention to safegaurd pending removal.* Additionally, there are two further forms of detention, so called 'Zurückweisungshaft' (when an illegal resident is apprehended upon entry at the border) and 'Zurückschiebungshaft', to which the provisions of § 62 AufenthG also apply (acc. to §§ 15 IV 1, 57 III AufenthG). The average duration of administrative detention is roughly six weeks. However, such a statement could be misleading, not least in the sense that many detainees are only briefly in custody, while others are detained for considerably longer periods[76]. The proportion of detained illegal residents awaiting expulsion who spend more than six months in custody lies at roughly 10 to 20%[77].

3.5 Who makes decisions for administrative detention?

First of all, the local 'Foreign Nationals' Registration Office' has to examine whether the foreign national is to be expelled from Germany or not. Should an expulsion be deemed possible, the office can file an application for administrative detention at the County Court (§ 3 S.1 FEVG), as long as grounds for expulsion/removal in terms of § 62 II 1 AufenthG are affirmed. Article 104 II of the German Constitution stipulates that decisions concerning the deprivation of liberty can be made solely and only by a judge. The County / Civil Court Judge or judge responsible for ordering administrative detention as a sole residing judge then decides whether or not administrative detention is to be ordered in non-contentious proceedings. However, the district judge only reviews whether the application itself is admissible and justified (whether the application was filed by the responsible authority, whether there are grounds for removal, and whether administra-

---

75 see Heinhold, 2004, p. 304.

76 see *Hagenmeier* 2000, p. 11.

77 see *Horstkotte* 1999, p. 36.

tive detention pending expulsion is a proportional measure)[78]. The district judge is not required to examine whether the foreign national is fact obliged to be removed and whether the preconditions for an expulsion are given. An examination of whether the content of the administrative act that justifies the expulsion is proper lies – according to prevailing opinion - only in the competence of the administrative court[79].
The Judge responsible for ordering administrative detention is naturally not limited in his function to being merely the executive body of the Foreign National's Registration Office. Rather, he is also obliged to independently review the individual case (so called "*Amtsermittlungsgrundsatz*"of § 12 FEVG) and to preserve the rights of the affected. In particular, the affected person is to be heard, and the judge is to comprehensively review the foreign person's case file[80].

The right to a hearing as stated in § 5 FEVG also implies the right to an interpreter[81] . Additionally, the right to legal representation also applies. The procedure for administrative detention pending expulsion is not a fast-track procedure. An interim deprivation of liberty (§ 11 FEVG) can only be ordered in exceptional cases. Moreover, one should consider that the judge assumes full responsibility for his decision on administrative detention, and could possibly be held officially liable, because in FGG proceedings the protection of judges from liability for their decisions (so called '*Spruchrichterprivileg*') does not apply[82]. The actual execution of detention is in turn a matter for the Foreign Nationals' Registration Office[83].

3.6 Which body can be appealed to and within how much time?

There is the permission to immediately file an appeal at the Regional Court (acc. to § 7 I FEVG, § 19 FGG) against both general and interim decisions of the County Court. § 22 I FGG sets the time limit for such an appeal at two weeks after the decision has been proclaimed. According to § 27 I FGG, decisions of the Regional Court – being an appellate court – can be immediately appealed against, which falls into the jurisdiction of the Higher Regional Court (§ 28 I FGG). According to a ruling of the German Constitutional Court, an affected detainee awaiting removal has a legally protective right to determine the illegality of his detention even if the measure has already been served (Article19 IV GG), for being deprived of ones liberty through imprisonment is indicative of a need for redemption[84] . Should immediate execution of administrative detention awaiting removal be ordered in accordance with § 8 I 2 FEVG, then a regular appeal is possible in the terms of § 19 FGG, however, without having a postponing effect[85]. Ordering immediate execution/implementation is – contrary to the intentions of the Law – often the case in practice[86].

---

78 see *Heinhold* 2004, p. 291, 298 f.; *Beichel-Benedetti* and *Gutmann* 2004, p. 3017.
79 see *Beichel-Benedetti* and *Gutmann* 2004, p. 3017; *Heinhold* 2004, p. 297.
80 see *Beichel-Benedetti* and *Gutmann* 2004, p. 3017; *Heinhold* 2004, p. 276.
81 see Heinhold, 2004, p. 278.
82 see *Beichel-Benedetti* and *Gutmann* 2004, p. 3016.
83 see *Laubenthal*, 2003, p. 431.
84 *BVerfGE*, 2 BvR 2266/00 on 24.07.02. See www.bverfg.de.
85 see *Heinhold* 2004, p. 286.
86 ibid. 2004, p. 282 f.

There are possibilities of legal protection during the period of detention depending on the circumstances. One the one hand, should an illegal resident be administratively detained in a JVA on the foundation of administrative assistance, he can file an application as stated in §§ 109 ff. StVollzG. Another means is filing a suit to the Administrative Court (§§ 40 ff. VwGO) if a detainee is being held in an establishment of the Administration of the Interior[87].

3.7 Is illegal/irregular residence a criminal offence? If yes, what is the minimum/maximum penalty?

In many cases, illegal entry and illegal residence in the Federal Territory of Germany constitute a criminal offence (see § 95 I, II AufenthG). The cases stated in § 95 I Nr.1-8 AufenthG are punishable with liberty-deprivation of up to one year or a fine. Breaches of § 95 II Nr.1-2 AufenthG can result in detention for up to three years or a fine. According to § 95 III AufenthG, even the attempt is liable to prosecution. Some cases (see § 98 I – III AufenthG) ‚merely' constitute misdemeanours, which are punishable with an administrative fine of up to 5.000 Euros (§ 98 V AufenthG).

3.8 What is the number of detained irregular foreigners?

There are by all means numerous detainees who were convicted due to breaches of the Residence Act and/or the Asylum Procedure Act. These detainees are, however, predominantly young adults and adults, and only rarely young people sentenced to juvenile imprisonment. One needs to take into consideration that penal detention takes priority over administrative detention pending removal, and that interim pre-trial- or penal detention temporarily suspends administrative detention. For more detailed data see table 3.3.

Table 3.3: Illegal residents in detention

Count on 31. March in Germany	*Detainees for breaches of Residence Act provisions*	*Of those, youth imprisonment*	*Detained for breach only of § 95 Residence Act*	*Of those, youth imprisonment*	*Detained for breach of Law on the Procedure of Asylum*	*Of those, youth imprisonment*
1998	483	5	no data	no data	76	2
1999	639	9	464	9	45	-
2000	674	13	546	12	42	2
2001	683	14	489	6	36	2
2003	605	8	493	7	45	-
2005	440	4	325	3	26	-

Source: Statistisches Bundesamt: www.destatis.de

87 see *Laubenthal* 2003, p. 364.

3.9. What is the percentage that will be expelled after administrative detention?

There is a considerable number of administrative detainees who are in fact not expelled from Germany. The true proportions of expelled or non-expelled foreign detainees cannot be accurately stated due to a lack of respective statistics from the individual Federal States. Estimates assume that roughly 80% of administrative detainees pending removal are actually expelled; figures from other sources are at around 60%[88].

3.10 What happens with non-expelled foreign prisoners?

Those who are ultimately not expelled are released from custody, for which there are several different reasons. Normally, no further supervision or support follows. The released foreigner merely remains in contact with the Foreign Nationals' Registration Office, provided that this is deemed necessary.

3.11 Can Category 3 prisoners also be detained with prisoners who are detained under criminal law? And if so, are they detained in separate sections? What happens with minors (under 18 years)?

In the Federal German States that have no special establishments for foreign detainees awaiting expulsion, they are allocated to regular prisons where they live alongside prisoners convicted of criminal offences as well as pre-trial-detainees. Such practice is criticised especially for its criminalising effect on detainees awaiting removal, who are precisely not deprived of their liberty as a means of punishment but rather in order to safeguard their pending expulsion. When foreign detainees awaiting removal are placed in normal penitentiary establishments, they can in principle be accommodated with other prisoners. Partly there are separate sections within the prison. In cases involving smaller numbers of people, they are usually accommodated together with the other prisoners of the establishment.

The detainees are fundamentally separated according to gender[89]. They are placed predominantly in shared dormitories, sometimes in single cells, and in part there is the problem of overcrowding. The size and facilities of the cells vary from establishment to establishment.

Since the proportion of women among administrative detainees is rather small they are predominantly placed in regular detention facilities[90]. The German Residence Act (§ 80 I AufenthG) states that juveniles aged 16 and above are generally capable of acting and capable of participating in proceedings. Juveniles and minors are, however, especially in need of care and protection and this needs to be taken into consideration throughout the entire process. Accordingly, young people aged 16 and above can still be detained for the purpose of later expulsion[91]. Special establishments for the detention of

---

88 see *Heinhold* 2004, p. 59.
89 see *Heinhold* 2004, p. 30.
90 ibid. 2004, p. 49.
91 ibid. 2004, p. 47.

illegal residents pending removal often incorporate special juvenile sections. Should this not apply, however, then the young person is, in general, accommodated in the respective penitentiary establishment. There, he is usually jointly accommodated with prisoners who have been convicted of criminal offences[92].

4 NATIONALS DETAINED ABROAD

4.1 How many German Nationals are detained abroad and what is the composition of this group?

In 2005 there were 3.100 German citizens in foreign penitentiary establishments[93], serving both short-term and long-term periods of detention. In comparison, in 2004 this figure was 2.435. However, estimates also suggest a considerable dark-figure. Overall it is assumed that the number of German nationals detained abroad has increased drastically in recent years. This rise could be accounted for by an increased urge to travel in connection with more criminal offences having been committed. One also needs to assume that these German detainees are predominantly males.

4.2 What are the main countries of detention?

More than half of these German detainees were being held in prisons of the European Union. For example, 657 Germans were detained in Spain, 364 in Great Britain, 246 in France and 150 in Poland[94]. Roughly 301 Germans were in prisons in the United States of America. German nationals can also be found in prisons in Asia, for example in Thailand, where roughly 70 are in prison[95]. Imprisonments are also known to have occurred in Africa.

4.3 What are the main reasons for detention (e.g. drugs) and what sentences do they receive?

Due to a lack of relevant data and information it is difficult to determine which criminal offences were perpetrated. It is, however, evident that drugs-offences play a significant role. Furthermore, it is likely that offences concerning personal injury, property- and sex-crimes are included. It is also probable that there are German nationals in administrative detention awaiting expulsion/removal. Overall, the majority are likely to be in prison due to fines or being sentenced to deprivation of liberty. However, in some countries there is the possibility of being sentenced to death. Contemporarily, there are four Germans on Death Row in the United States, and a further six in Kenya, the Lebanon, Thailand, Taiwan and in the Philippines[96]. The situation becomes increasingly problematic in cases

---

92 ibid. 2004, p. 46.

93 see http://presseportal.de/story.htx?firmaid=61201.

94 see http://presseportal.de/story.htx?firmaid=61201.

95 see *Neef* and *Novy* 2004, p. 155.

96 see http://presseportal.de/story.htx?firmaid=61201.

of torture. Moreover, the Foreign Offices in Tunisia, in Egypt and in Syria are looking into cases in which Germans were possibly tortured during their period of detention. A detained national in Brazil is said to have died as a result of having been tortured while in detention.

4.4 Which organisations are involved and what are their responsibilities and activities?

The German Embassy is responsible for caring with and supporting German nationals – especially those detained in penitentiary establishments – in the respective countries. § 5 I of the Consular Act (*Konsulargesetz;* KonsularG) stipulates that in the case of emergencies German citizens are entitled to aid and assistance from the German Embassy. § 7 of the Consulate Act states that the responsible consulate officers are to give support – most importantly legal protection - to those German pre-trial- and criminal detainees who request such aid.

In general, the authority responsible for making the arrest should give the suspect the opportunity to contact the German Embassy. A number of countries are even obliged to do so under the Vienna Convention[97]. The primary duties stated in § 7 KonsularG are the provision of an initial legal counselling session and a German-speaking lawyer. It is also often the embassy that informs relatives of an arrest.

It is not a matter of course for an employee of the embassy to observe the proceedings. Such an assignment is however at the discretion of the embassy, and is / should be made in cases in which nationals are facing punishments that – in comparison to our legal understanding – are disproportionately severe. Experience has shown that criminal proceedings are generally conducted more thoroughly when observed by a foreign diplomat[98]. There is also the possibility of financial support, for example by covering the costs of the trip back to Germany. However, financial support from the German State is subsidiary to the detainees / suspect's own financial means[99]. Also, the recipient is obliged to rebate any disembursements as stated in § 5 V KonsularG.

The German Department for Foreign Affairs (*Auswärtiges Amt*) has issued a leaflet with the respective information (also available in the internet). Most prominently, it recommends that German Nationals who are being detained should urge the police that they be allowed to inform the respective German consulate or embassy.

4.5 Who is responsible for the reception in the home country alter release?

Should a German national be extradited prior to having served the full sentence abroad, then he must, in general, serve the sentence in a German penitentiary establishment in accordance with respective existing extradition treaties, thus handing the case over to the court or to the Public Prosecution Office[100].

---

97 see *Neef* and *Novy* 2004, p. 157.
98 see *Neef* and *Novy* 2004, p. 157.
99 Ibid. 2004, p. 159.
100 see *Neef* and *Novy* 2004, p. 158.

4.6 What kind of aftercare is provided and how is this organised?

Support for nationals who have been held in a foreign prison is generally provided by non-profit organisations, human rights organisations and other similar bodies. The State itself only rarely provides aftercare.

4.7 What is the opinion of the media and general public?

This topic receives relatively sparse interest from the media, thus information is hard to come by. Rather, only dramatic individual cases that involve the possibility of the death penalty or the life imprisonment of a juvenile / young adult tend to attract public and media interest. In this respect it is difficult to determine any predominant opinions and views. The work of the embassies is partly deemed dedicated and good; however there is also room for improvement in certain areas[101].

5 EVALUATION AND RECOMMENDATIONS

In Germany, as in many other European countries, foreigners are overrepresented in prisons. Particular problems emerged in the late 1980s and early 1990s, when the proportion of foreigners increased considerably. Since then the situation has stabilized or even de-escalated by a reduction in the number of foreign prisoners. Their overrepresentation can partly be explained by some groups of younger and more violent foreign offenders compared to the German population. However, empirical research has also revealed that particularly those foreign offenders who have not yet been granted a right of residence according to the German immigration laws are also discriminated by the justice system. Alternative sanctions are less often used than for foreigners with a right of residence and still less than for German residents.

The legal situation of foreigners in prison is not all that different from that of German prisoners. However, they are regularly excluded from relaxations of the prison regime (prison leaves, work release etc.), particularly if they are to be expelled after serving their prison sentence. Some federal states (Länder) provide language courses for foreign prisoners, but the majority of states does not provide specific programmes for foreigners. Foreigners are not disadvantaged regarding internal leisure time and other programmes. The very problems of foreign prisoners result from the more and more restrictive immigration laws, which constitute an obligatory or at least regular expulsion of foreigners if they have committed a crime resulting in an unconditional prison sentence. This is particularly problematic as the traditional German law (until 1999) created severe difficulties for the naturalization of foreign residents, even when they have lived in Germany for years or generations.

The situation of foreign asylum seekers or illegal residents who are detained under administrative law is even more problematic. They are sometimes detained in departments of normal prisons, sometimes in separate detention centres of the ministries of interior. In both cases the protection of human rights and the living conditions in general

---

101 see Neef/Novy, ZfStrVO 2004, issue 3, p.157; http://presseportal.de/story.htx?firmaid=61201

have to be criticized. The most extreme cases (Frankfurt am Main airport, Eisenhüttenstadt detention centre) have even been a case for the Torture Committee of the Council of Europe. These examples confirm the importance of the work of the CPT, especially when concerning such un-visible groups such as foreigners who are to be expelled for whom subsequently filed appeals are basically pointless. One can suspect that their circumstances would not have improved had the visits and follow-up visits described above not been conducted.

In criminal policy, efforts to enable a quicker transfer of foreign criminal prisoners to their home country without the prisoners' assent are beginning to emerge. This thwarts the notion by which transfers were originally meant just to provide better prospects of rehabilitation. This in itself was the reason why such transfers were subject to the prisoners' consent / application. This, too, exemplifies the problems that foreigners face who actually have their roots in Germany. The soon to be passed law on the creation of the premises for the ratification of the supplementary agreement on the European Convention on the Transfer of Sentenced Persons (currently in the closing stages of legislation, see above) is a real step backwards.

Furthermore, it is lamentable that the courts apparently bear so little knowledge of how to evaluate the harshness of the detention experienced abroad, which can in turn result in non-uniform and possibly unfair rulings.

Chapter 11

Greece

M. Akritidou
A. Antonopoulou
A. Pitsela

1 INTRODUCTION

1.1 Overview of Penalties and Measures

The Greek penal system is based on custodial sanctions. According to the Greek Penal Code (hereinafter: PC), the main penalties are the following categories of deprivation of liberty:

Detention is the deprivation of liberty that involves a minimum duration of one day and a maximum of one month (Article 55 PC). In special cases, the maximum duration of detention can be increased to six months (Article 94 paragraph 1 PC). This type of penalty is provided for contraventions (Article 18 PC). It is rarely served since it is usually suspended or converted into a pecuniary sentence (fine).

Imprisonment is a deprivation of liberty for at least ten days and for a maximum term of five years (Article 53 PC). Any offence punishable by imprisonment is a misdemeanour (Article 18 PC). This penalty, as a rule, is usually suspended or converted into other non-custodial sanctions (pecuniary penalty or community service). In special cases, the maximum duration of imprisonment can be raised to ten years (Article 94 paragraph 1 PC).

Confinement in a penitentiary institution can either be incarceration for life or for a period between five and 20 years (Article 52 PC). This sanction is provided for felonies (Article 18 PC). In special cases, the maximum duration of temporary confinement in a penal institution can be increased to 25 years (Article 94 paragraph 1 PC). According to the penal law about conditional release (Article 105 PC), life confinement actually ranges between 16 and 20 years. Confinement in a penitentiary for an indeterminate period is provided for habitual recidivists (Article 90 and 91 PC). It should be noted, however, that in practice confinement in a penitentiary for an indeterminate period has never been imposed. Confinement in a young offender institution for juveniles between 13 and 18 years of age (Article 54 PC) is a *sui generis* form of imprisonment served in special institutions. Confinement in a psychiatric institution is imposed on (dangerous) offenders with limited imputability (Article 37 et. seq. PC).

Pecuniary sanctions are also central penalties, which exist in two forms: proper pecuniary penalties (150.00-15,000.00 Euros) and fines (29.00-590.00 Euros). They are directly imposed only about 5% of the convicted persons (see Table 7). For some specific offence types, the PC and special penal laws provide that the pecuniary sanctions can also be imposed additionally to the sanctions of deprivation of liberty.

Greek Penal Law provides for a number of non-custodial sanctions that are not main penalties, but which are essentially alternatives to serving custodial sentences. Firstly, custodial sanctions not exceeding one year (detention, imprisonment) can be converted into pecuniary sanctions (Article 82 paragraph 1 PC). As a rule, the court also orders the conversion of imprisonment up to one year but less than two years unless the defendant is a recidivist and the court finds that the sentence must not be converted. Sentences to imprisonment for more than two but less than three years can also be converted if the court adjudges this as appropriate (Article 82 paragraph 2 PC). Community service is legally provided for in two forms and by two different kinds of legislation. Firstly, a sentence to imprisonment for two up to three years can be converted into community service at the stage when the sentence of imprisonment is imposed. In addition – at the same stage - community sentences can be served as a further conversion of imprisonment sentences that have already been converted into pecuniary penalties (Article 82 paragraph 6 PC). Secondly, community service can also be imposed as an alternative measure for prisoners who are already serving a sentence of imprisonment that had initially been converted into a pecuniary sentence, but which was in fact never paid (Article 64 of the Penitentiary Code). Community service is granted on the condition that the person convicted requests or accepts the conversion of his/her sentence. This measure was first instituted at the very beginning of the 1990s and is still applied only very sparingly.

The suspension of a sentence – either with or without supervision (probation) - is also not considered a main sentence according to the PC. Suspension (Article 99 and 100 PC) is imposed on the majority of sentences of up to three years[1] under the condition that the convicted person has not been previously convicted to a sentence longer than six months. Suspension of sentence with supervision is imposed on sentences from three to five years (Article 100A PC). However, due to a lack of technical and human resources (i.e. because probation officers for adults have not been hired as yet), this institution is not enforced. Through the wide application of converting sentences to imprisonment into pecuniary sanctions and the less often applied suspension of sentences, every year only four convicted offenders out of 100 actually serve their sentence in prison[2].

The following supplementary penalties are provided and imposed alongside the main penalties: the deprivation of civil rights (Articles 59-66 PC); The prohibition to exercise a profession that requires special permission from the authority (Article 67 PC); the publication of the sentence (Article 68 PC); the expulsion of a foreigner (Article 74 PC); the confiscation of instruments or products of an offence (Article 76 paragraph 1 PC).

In addition to these supplementary penalties that are provided by the PC and rarely imposed, special penal laws also provide for other supplementary penalties, such as the withdrawal of a driving license (Articles 103 and 106 of Code of Traffic regulations - Law 2696/1999), or the temporary or permanent suspension of a license to operate a business. The PC includes not only penalties but also *security measures* irrespective of the imputability of the defendant in order to protect the public order. Security measures are provided either as substitutes for main penalties for persons who are not criminally responsible, or in addition to penalties for persons who *are* criminally responsible. The security measures consist of:

- *Custody of offenders in a public therapeutic institution.* This measure is applied to convicts who, due to mental illness or deafness/muteness, cannot be punished for a criminal offence that they have committed but who still pose a threat to public safety (Article 69 PC). Its application is rare.
- *Committal of alcoholics and drug addicts to a therapeutic institution* (Article 71 PC). This security measure has never been imposed, primarily because appropriate therapeutic institutions have not yet been established. Since 2002, a pilot program has been running in a therapeutic institution for drugs addicts, not as a security measure but rather as a treatment programme for convicts serving their sentence.
- Offenders whose acts may be attributed to laziness or to a tendency towards vagrancy and irregular life can be *referred to a workhouse* (Article 72 PC). This measure has also never been applied. Furthermore, its character is not in accordance to the Greek

---

1 Up to two years the suspension is obligatory. Up to three years, the court has the possibility to suspend the sentence.

2 This finding is based on data on the period 1980-1996.

Constitution. According to Article 22 paragraph 4 of the Greek Constitution "any form of compulsory work is prohibited"[3].

- *The prohibition of residence in certain areas* as well as the notification of the place of residence (Article 73 PC).
- *The expulsion of a foreigner* (Article 74 PC).
- *The confiscation of instruments or products of an offence* (Article 76 paragraph 2 PC);
- These two last security measures, mainly expulsion of foreign criminals upon their release from prison, are often imposed.

Pre-trial detention is a measure of penal procedure that is decreed in order to ensure the attendance of the accused person in court. It is provided only for persons accused of having committed a felony (crime punishable by law with confinement in a penitentiary for between five and 20 years or for life), and only under conditions that are restricted by the law (Article 282 Code of Penal Procedure). In practice, this measure is imposed in the majority of felony cases. Pre-trial detention for juveniles (13 to 18 years of age) is provided only for persons accused of having committed a felony punishable by law with confinement in a penal institution for between ten and 20 years or for life.

1.2 Overview of the Prison System

1.2.1 Organisational Structure

According to the provisions of Chapter 14 of the Code of Basic Rules for the Treatment of Prisoners on the prison staff and its duties (Law 1851/1989) - the only chapter which has not been nullified by the Penitentiary Code in force (Law 2776/1999) - the organisation of the prison administration includes a Governor, social work service, health service (including a medical doctor, a dentist, a psychologist, nurses etc.), the administration or secretariat, a number of correctional officers (guards) supervised by a chief correctional officer, and the necessary technicians and other staff (see Article 97). Prison institutions are administrated by Governors who are accountable to the Direction of Crime Prevention and Correctional Treatment of Juveniles and to the Direction of Correctional Treatment of Adults of the Ministry of Justice[4]. The health and social work staff is also accountable to the relevant directions of the Ministry of Justice. Teachers and other educational personnel are provided by the Ministry of Education and accountable to the relevant direction of the Ministry. Certain institutions are staffed with additional specialised personnel, e.g. the psychiatric hospital for inmates with psychiatric staff, the agricultural prisons with specialists in Agriculture.

The Greek Prison System comprises 30 institutions of various kinds that are dispersed all over the country. They are all run by central government, more specifically by the Ministry of Justice. According to Article 19 of the Penitentiary Code, the Greek prison system consists of: a) general institutions of detention b) special institutions and c) therapeutic institutions. The general institutions are categorized into type A institutions for pre-trial detention, people detained for debts and inmates sentenced to short-term im-

---

[3] for the English text of the Greek Constitution see www.parliament.gr/english/politeuma/syntagma.pdf.

[4] Presidential Decree 36/2000, Organisation of the Ministry of Justice.

prisonment, and type B for the remaining inmates (Article 11 of the Penitentiary Code). Women are held in separate sections of male institutions or in the only closed prison for females (Article 13 of the Penitentiary Code) in Korydallos. Special institutions include those for juveniles (Article 12 of the Penitentiary Code) and the semi-open prisons (Article 19 of the Penitentiary Code). The Ministry of Justice, in practice, distinguishes five categories of penitentiary institutions: agricultural prisons, correctional institutions for minors, closed prisons, therapeutic institutions and judicial prisons.

The composition of the prison population in Greece on 16 June 2005 is shown in the tables below.

Table 1: agricultural prisons for adults

Location	*Capacity*	*Number of inmates*
Agya	146	231
Kassandra	300	255
Tyrintha	200	255

Table 2: correctional institutions for minors and young adults

Location	*Capacity*	*Number of inmates*
Avlona	308	242
Kassavetia (agricultural institution)	250	184
Volos	65	92

Table 3: closed prisons, one of them for females

Location	*Capacity*	*Number of inmates*
Alikarnassos	105	251
Kerkyra	160	192
Patra	343	724
Trikala	125	216
Chalkida	120	224
Korydallos for females	270	561

Table 4: therapeutic institutions

Location	*Capacity*	*Number of Inmates*
Hospital in Korydallos	60	122
Psychiatric Hospital in Korydallos	160	301
Detoxification in Theben	300	52

Table 5: judicial prisons

Location	*Capacity*	*Number of Inmates*
Thessaloniki	370	620
Ioannina	80	264
Komotini	105	239
Korydallos	640	2,194
Kos	45	86
Larissa	363	740
Nafplion	314	463
Neapolis	45	103
Amphissa	100	283
Tripolis	65	132
Chania	67	130
Chios	100	142
Corinth	60	48
Korydallos (semi-open)	38	51
Malandrino	280	269

As of June 2005, 9,598 inmates (adults and juveniles) were detained in the prison system, while there were only 5,584 available places. Thus, it is observed that the occupancy rate in Greek prisons amounts to 172%. As far as the state budget for the prison system is concerned, the estimations - according to the information of the Greek Ministry of Justice - are as follows: 86,127,319.00 € for the year 2003, 96,398,000.00 € for the year 2004, 103,150,000.00 € for the year 2005, 104,460,000.00 € for the year 2006. Two thirds of the estimated funds go to the state employees of the correctional services.

Regarding the prison staff, 3,836 public servants work in Greek prisons today, despite the fact that the Ministry of Justice provides that the total necessary number for covering the needs of the Greek Prison System should be 7,062; thereby, only roughly 54.3% of the necessary posts are covered. It is worth noting that there are only 16 doctors (out of 76 that are deemed necessary), one criminologist (of a recommended 13) and four psychologists (out of 48 that the Ministry considers necessary). The great majority of the prison staff is guards; 2,076 guards for internal supervision and 1,246 guards for external safekeeping, while the recommended numbers given by the Ministry of Justice are 3,024 and 3,040, respectively. Thus, out of the total number of prison staff that is provided as needful by the Ministry, 42.8% should work in internal supervision and 43.0% in external safekeeping. The corresponding percentages of the actual situation, though, are 54.4% and 32.4%, respectively.

All prison personnel have the obligation to attend special educational seminars during the first two years of work in a penal institution. Furthermore, the training needs of the prison staff may be covered by several training programmes provided by the Institute of Durable Education of the National School of Public Administration[5], or by other spe-

5 www.ekdd/ESDD/esdd.htm

cial programmes organised by the Ministry of Justice - as long as the respective funds are available[6].

The Greek prison system it is monitored both directly and indirectly, through the Greek Ombudsman or the Body of Inspection and Control of Detention Establishments respectively. The Greek Ombudsman is a constitutionally established Independent Authority that was founded in October 1998 and operates under the provisions of Law 3094/2003. The Ombudsman provides its services to the public free of charge and received more than 41,865 complaints during its first five years in operation (from October 1st 1998 to December 31st 2002). The Greek Ombudsman investigates individual administrative actions or omissions or material actions taken by government departments or public services that infringe upon the personal rights or that violate the legal interests of individual or legal entities. The aim of the Greek Ombudsman is to mediate between public administration and private individuals, in order to protect the citizens' rights, ensuring compliance with the rule of law, observing the rule of law and combating maladministration. In addition, the objectives of the Greek Ombudsman include the protection and promotion of the rights of the child and migrants. The Ombudsman does not have the power to impose sanctions or to annul any illegal actions of public administration. The complaints that citizens submit are investigated in terms of thematic categories, which correspond to five different areas of activity in the institution:

- The Human Rights Department
- The Health and Social Welfare Department
- The Quality of Life Department
- The State-Citizen Relations Department, and
- The Children's Rights Department

Many times prisoners have submitted complaints to the Ombudsman about the conditions and the violation of human rights in Greek prisons. As a result of these complaints, the Ombudsman has visited a number of institutions of detention and has pointed out the declinations of the reality in Greek prisons in comparison to the directions and provisions of the law. The most recent example of such research is described in the Annual Report of the year 2005, where problems with the regular leaves and the social reintegration of prisoners are underlined. Even though the Greek Ombudsman is a relatively new authority, its operation is considered very important and its overall role in the relations between the state and its citizens is estimated as being very positive. It is worth mentioning that a large proportion of the complaints that this authority receives are filed by foreign persons living in the county. For this reason, a special section for the rights of migrants offers its services to foreign nationals in the Human Rights Department.

The Body of Inspection and Control of Penitentiary Institutions (Article 3 Law 3090/2002) acts under the direct supervision of the General Secretary of the Ministry of Justice, and has the following goals: (a) To conduct regular and irregular controls any time of the day in order to confirm the conditions of detention, the maintenance of order, and the observance of safety measures in the penitentiary institution. In addition, the Body inspects the application of the arrangements of the Penitentiary Code and the

6 As far as it concerns the prison staff, the Direction of Correctional Treatment of Adults of the Greek Ministry of Justice has provided us with the relevant information. For our investigation, the general support of the responsible officers of the Ministry of Justice has been valuable.

proper implementation of the regulations of the penitentiary institution. (b) To research and to hunt down ex *officio any crime* that takes place in penitentiary institutions in the entire country. Furthermore, the Body selects, analyses and exploits the information and elements that document these actions. In every case the results of the investigation are compiled in a written report. Additionally, every year in December a report with observations and recommendations for the improvement of the organisation and the function of the penitentiary institution is submitted to the General Secretary of the Ministry of Justice.

1.2.2 Foreign Prisoners

Before the 1990s, less than 20% of the prison population were not Greek nationals. Nowadays, in the year 2006, more than 40% of the prison population in Greece are foreign prisoners, mostly Albanians, followed - at a great distance - by nationals from the former USSR, Iraq, Rumania, Turkey etc.
Table 6 shows the augmentative trend of their proportion over the last 20 years.

Table 6: Proportion of foreign prisoners in Greek penitentiary institutions in selected years

Year	%
1986	17,7
1990	20,9
1996	35,6
2000	48,4
2005	41,0

Source: Council of Europe. Penological Information Bulletin, No. 10 (1987), 28; No. 12 (1988), 22; Nos. 13 & 14 (1989); No. 15 (1990), 16.; No. 16 (1992), 28; No. 17 (1992) 23, No. 18 (1993), 20; No. 21 (1998), 67; No. 22 (2000), 25, 63; No. 23 & 24 (2002), 72. The data for the year 2005 has been provided by the Direction of Correctional Treatment of Adults of the Greek Ministry of Justice.

This high percentage becomes even more impressive if one considers the fact that foreigners account for only approximately 10% of the general population in Greece as well as of the total number of criminal suspects (excluding traffic offences). Many reasons can be referred to in order to explain this impressive change of the composition of the prison population. The most important reason seems to be the high level of immigration of the 1990s after the geopolitical changes in Europe and the Middle East. Additionally, the age and gender composition of the migrants of the last 15 years have been in line with those most commonly attributed to being liable to and active in criminal activities. The vast majority of them are men between 17 an 50 years of age, and among some nationalities, such as Iraqi, Afghan and Pakistani, there is an impressive absence of women. Furthermore, the social living conditions , concentration in big urban centres, ghettoization, social exclusion, xenophobia of the host society, and prejudice on behalf of the police and criminal justice are some of the factors that contribute not only to the rise of crime attributed to foreigners but also to the punitiveness of the administration of justice. Last, but not least, procedural problems like for example the fact that the migrants do not always have a lawyer or witnesses for their defence make their convictions before criminal courts more often in comparison to Greek offenders. There are no specific establishments for the detention of foreigners; thereby, they are not separated from the other prisoners. Rarely, they are detained in separated wings of the prisons: because of some incidents between Greek and Albanian prisoners in Neapolis, for example, the administration of this prison has decided to keep foreign prisoners in a special wing. The only exception to the unity of penitentiary establishments between Greek and foreign prisoners is the penitentiary institution for young prisoners at Volos, where only young foreigners are detained. The prison staff of this institution is very impressed by the special abilities of young prisoners to quickly learn the Greek language. Theoretically, the prison staff should be afforded with programmes that aim to improve their understanding of the hardships and cultural backgrounds of the prisoners. In practice, however, no special training programme is provided to the prison staff.

1.3 Overview of the Involvement of Consulates, Embassies, Ministries and the Probation Service of Greece, NGOs etc.

Upon their admission into a penal establishment foreign prisoners will be informed of their rights, obligations and of the regulations. They shall be provided with the relevant informative printed matter in a language that they understand (Article 24 paragraph 2 of the Penitentiary Code). They have the right to contact their embassies as well the right to procure information about the possible help that can be provided to them by the competent authorities (Article 52 paragraph 6 of the Penitentiary Code). If a foreign prisoner wishes to seek help from diplomatic or consular representatives, and this help includes procedures concerning social re-integration in case of release, the diplomatic authorities must be informed at once about these requests. An information pamphlet with the address and the phone number of the closest embassy/consulate must be provided to the foreign prisoner upon his/her admission into the penitentiary institution.

Furthermore, the prison authorities in cooperation with NGOs (organisations that are responsible for providing help in the area of rehabilitation) must give their special attention to the foreign prisoners (see Article 52 paragraph 2 of the Penitentiary Code). The latter shall be informed about the help that can be provided to them through the NGOs, and prison authorities have to ensure access to this information as well as making contact with the above organisations. The prison authorities are also obliged to facilitate visits by and correspondence with the NGOs so that the foreign inmate can avail himself/herself of their help, of course so long as the inmate agrees to this. In practice however, members of NGOs often denounce the Greek Prison management's unwillingness and lack of flexibility regarding their intention of visiting penal institutions and prisons in order to communicate with foreign prisoners. The Greek Ombudsman has criticized the Greek Prison System many times for this bad practice [7].

---

[7] For example, the 28 November 2002 letter to the Ministry of Public Order- number of protocol 12393.02.1.

1.4 Overview of trends

1.4.1 Sentencing Trends

The following statistics in table 7 give a general and representative image of the sentences imposed in Greece for the years 1996[8] and 2001:

Table 7: Offenders sanctioned for misdemeanours or felonies according to the type of sanction in Greece for the years 1996 and 2001

Sanctions	1996		2001	
	Convicted persons N	%	Convicted persons N	%
Imprisonment for up to one year (usually suspended or converted)	71,830	82.66	48,043	81.07
Imprisonment 1-5 years	4,673	5.38	3,073	5.19
Pecuniary sentence (imposed as such)	4,648	5.35	3,902	6.58
Temporary confinement in a penitentiary	472	0.55	369	0.62
Confinement for life in a penitentiary	44	0.05	22	0.04
Confinement in a psychiatric institution	17	0.02	31	0.05
Confinement in a young offender institution	164	0.19	88	0.15
Educational/therapeutic measures (only for minors)	5036	5.79	3,555	6.00
Non reported sentence	8	0.01	179	0.30
Total	86,892	100	59,262	100

Source: National Statistical Service of Greece. Statistics of Justice 1996. Table B:19. www.statistics.gr, Table VII:12.

During the 1980s, only a small proportion of offenders were actually admitted to prison which resulted in a general decrease of the prison population in accordance to the general trend of de-institutionalization in Europe. In the decade that followed, despite the introduction of more lenient legislation this proportion increased. Notwithstanding of the wide application of the institutions of suspension of sentence and of conversion of custodial into pecuniary sanctions ("front-door" strategy) as well as conditional release

8 The year 1996 was the last year in which data on the number of convictions and the type of the sanctions imposed were published by the National Statistical Service of Greece. See the website: www.statistics.gr

("back-door" strategy) that targeted the solution of the prison overcrowding problem, the population in penitentiary institutions remained at a high level. This general increase in the prison population is partly related to the increase in the committal of particular offences. More specifically, while the total number of crimes recorded by the police showed a slight increase, there was a dramatic increase in particular offences, e.g. drug offences and robberies. Drugs, some forms of organised crime, clandestine immigration and the exploitation of women became a social issue after 1990. The augmentative trend in the number of prisoners is furthermore associated with the increasing proportion of foreigners among convicted offenders and pre-trial detainees in the last 15 years, as well as with the increase in the overall number of suspects actually being held in pre-trial detention.

Since the turn of the millennium, despite the fact that the proportion of convicted offenders who are given sentences that can be converted to pecuniary ones is quite high, as well as the ample use of conditional release, the prison population has continued to increase. The detention rate in Greece doubled between 1980 and 2001. In 1980 there were 41 prisoners per 100,000 inhabitants, while in 2001 the figure had increased to 79 prisoners per 100,000.

Table 8: Total number of prisoners in Greek penitentiary institutions in selected years

Year	Prisoners = n
1980	3,419
1986	3,780
1990	4,747
1996	5,304
2000	8,038
2005	9,598

Source: Council of Europe. Penological Information Bulletin, No. 2, 1983, 17, 25; No. 4, 1984, 34; No 5, 1985, 23; No. 6, 1985, 25; No. 8, 1986, 22; No. 15 (1990), 11 ff.; No. 16 (1992), 28 f.; No. 17, 23; No. 18, 18 ff.; No 21, 1998, 64. Data from the Greek Ministry of Justice.

The state's responses to the abrupt social changes and changes in crime patterns since 1990 are ongoing. Personnel and resources of the criminal justice system are constantly increasing. The same is also true with respect to selection, hiring and education of police personnel, members of the judiciary - public prosecutors included - and correctional staff. However, the number of prosecutors and correctional staff that actually work is still low because of the great number of vacant posts.

1.4.2 Characteristics of the Foreign Prison Population

Table 9: Characteristics of the prison population on 16.6.2005:

Prison capacity	5,584
Total number of prisoners	9,598
(Prisoners convicted and untried)	
Untried prisoners	2,725
Foreign prisoners	3,934 (40.98%)
Female prisoners	602
Young prisoners	366
Detained for drug law violations	3,952

Table 10: Convicted prisoners according to the kind and duration of the deprivation of liberty in Greece on 16 of June 2005

penalties of liberty deprivation	*Convicted prisoners = n*	%
Life confinement	620	9.2
Temporary confinement	(3,947)	(58.3)
a) 5-10 years	1,838	27.2
b) 10-15 years	1,170	17.3
c) more than 15 years	939	13.9
Imprisonment	(2,198)	(32.5)
a) up to 6 months	324	4.9
b) 6-12 months	297	4.4
c) 1-2 years	459	6.8
d) 3-5 years	1,118	16.5
Total number	6,765	100

Source: Data of the Ministry of Justice.

Until the 1990s Greece was a homogeneous society: 99% of the population had Greek as a mother tongue and 98% were of the Greek Christian Orthodox religion, 1% were Muslims and 1% were of other religious denominations. After 1990, an influx of refugees and (clandestine) immigrants began, predominantly from countries of Central and Eastern Europe. Thus, Greece developed from a country of emigration to a country of immigration, and was totally unprepared for the reception of immigrants. Neither the relevant legislation nor the required social structure and institutions existed. Hence, the exact figure of illegal immigrants or the total number of non-nationals is unknown.

The Ministry of Labour estimates this number to be roughly 500,000-600,000, while the U.S. Department of State sees it as being closer to 1,000,000. In January 1998 a legislation process for clandestine immigrants was initiated and as of June 1999 approximately 50,000 green cards were granted, while the Greek government planned to issue another 200,000 approximately by the end of 1999. Once again, on 2001 a great number of clandestine immigrants received a green card. During the year 2005, another effort for their regularisation took place, and they were allowed to apply for a green card under some specific conditions named in the new Foreigners Act[9]. The bureaucratic process has not yet been completed. It is estimated that the total number of migrants who shall be issued a green card will not be more than 40,000 to 60,000 (out of more than 100,000 applications). However, due to the geographical position of the county, its enormous coastline, land boundaries and the political situation in the region, there is a continuous influx and outflow of people. The most important nationalities represented among foreigners in Greece are people coming from Russia (although many of them of Greek origin) and Albania, Egypt, Poland, Ukraine, Iraq, Palestine, the Philippines, Nigeria, Pakistan, etc.

1.5 Overview of National Penitentiary Legislation

1.5.1 Penitentiary Legislation

In theory, a shield with various layers of protective legislative provisions covers the body of prisoners in Greek custodial institutions. The first layer compromises provisions of the Greek Constitution (hereinafter: GC) that refer to the human rights of i) Greeks and ii) any person living within the Greek territory. Needless to say, the most fundamental right of every human being is the respect of his/her dignity, even if he/she is deprived of liberty (Article 2 paragraph 1 and Article 5 paragraph 1 of the GC). The second layer of protection is provided by the European Convention of Human Rights (hereinafter: ECHR) and its First, Fourth, Sixth, Seventh and Eighth Protocols that Greece has signed and ratified. According to Article 28 paragraph 1of the GC all of these ratified international norms constitute an integral part of national law, prevailing over any contrary national legal provisions (other than the GC). The ECHR, like the GC, makes no explicit statement on the rights of prisoners. Yet, the European Court of Human Rights, as already pointed out, guarantees the application of the ECHR to convicted individuals as well. The third and most direct layer protecting persons serving custodial sanctions is constituted by the Greek Penitentiary Code, which replaced the older Code of Basic Rules for the Treatment of Prisoners (except for Chapter 14 on staff duties that still remains). This code, enacted in 1999, contains 14 chapters and 87 Articles and aims at safeguarding the human dignity of detained persons on the one hand, and the orderly function of custodial institutions on the other, by regulating the rights and duties of the prisoners.

Under the prevailing legislative norms, detained persons in Greece, therefore, enjoy three sets of rights stemming from: i) the GC, ii) the ECHR and iii) the Penitentiary Code. Taking a closer look at the human rights protected by the Penitentiary Code, it should be pointed out that functional theorists of Constitutional Law share the widespread opinion that persons deprived of their liberty upon a lawful sanction during the execution of their sentence retain all human rights (Article 4 Penitentiary Code) except

[9] Art. 90 paragraph 11 of Law 3386/2005.

for that of personal liberty (free movement). The basic safeguarded prisoners rights– in accordance to Article 3 about the equal treatment of prisoners and Article 6 about the legal protection of prisoners of the Penitentiary Code - are: the right to make written complaints to the Prison Council first and then to the — never established — Court of Execution of Sentences (in the meantime, however, the Misdemeanours Court Council of the area where the sentence is executed performs this duty); the right to communicate in writing with any public authority and the prison administration has the corresponding duty to expedite the communication without delay and without inspecting its content; the right to satisfy the prisoners' religious needs and customs with no discrimination for of any reason. It should also be added that obligatory/forced work is absolutely forbidden according to the GC (Article 22 paragraph 3 GC), a provision which also encompasses work in prison.

Furthermore, prisoners have the right to be represented by an advocate in disciplinary hearings. In Greek prisons, in principle, there are no prohibitions against receiving books and newspapers (however at the prisoners' own expense). Prisoners may also purchase various goods from the prison shop. Detained persons may also be visited by a physician or a psychiatrist of their choice under certain circumstances. Finally, the GC and the Greek Code of Penal Procedure recognizes a prisoner's right to compensation in case of unlawful detention, a right which is seldom exercised and even more rarely satisfied.

The last and most recent shield of protection lies in the European Convention for the Prevention of Torture and Inhuman and Degrading Treatment or Punishment that Greece ratified in 1991 (Law 1949/1991). Among others, the so-called anti-torture Convention in Article 1 provides for a European Committee that through inspection may prevent or correct breaches of human rights in the context of imprisonment.

1.5.2 Penitentiary Legislation and Foreigners

Foreign prisoners have the same legal position, legal rights and obligations as national prisoners (Article 3 Penitentiary Code). According to the Law 1708/1988[10] it is possible for foreign prisoners to be transferred to their country in order to serve the remainder of their term if:

- the country has signed a convict transfer agreement with Greece or has acceded to the current convict transfer agreement of the European Council;
- they are nationals of the country to which they request to be transferred;
- the sentencing judgement is irrevocable or they have waived all legal remedies (appeals, etc.);
- the sentence they shall continue serving in their country, after their transfer, shall not be greater that the one imposed in Greece;
- the remainder of their term in Greece is not be less than six months, and
- their country consents to such a transfer.

Until recently, foreign prisoners rarely, or never, availed themselves of the possibility of being transferred to a prison in their own country, possibly because living conditions in the prisons of Greece are better than those in their home country. In the meantime,

[10] This law ratified the European Convention for the Transfer of Prisoners of 1983.

more and more foreign prisoners – mainly from Albania – have begun to express a desire to serve their penalty in their own country. While inmate relationships are developed among prisoners of the same ethic group, foreign prisoners do not seem to interact either positively or negatively with Greek prisoners. There have of course been some incidents between Greek and Albanian prisoners – like for example in Neapolis, at it mentioned above - that force the administration to keep them separated.

2 TREATMENT OF FOREIGN PRISONERS

2.1 General Information

In responding to section 2 appropriately, for the theoretical part the writers used the Internal Operation Regulation of General Detention Establishments of Type A and B[11] (hereinafter: Internal Regulation), in accordance with the similar Articles of the Penitentiary Code.

It was very difficult to provide answers to the actual situation of foreign prisoners, because information and data on this topic are very limited. The Greek law does not foresee a separation of Greek prisoners from foreign prisoners. For any prisoner, no other right than the right to personal freedom shall be limited. All prisoners may exercise the rights conferred to them by the Constitution and by the special rules of law, in person or by proxy.

2.2 Living Conditions and Facilities

Foreign prisoners have the same access to facilities and they have the same living conditions as Greek prisoners.

Every prisoner may have objects or articles of immediate and daily use that do not exceed in volume the size of a regular suitcase in his cell or in his ward, without metal foils.

2.3 Reception and Admission

The foreign prisoner will be informed upon his/her admission to the establishment by the director of the institution about his/her rights and obligations in a language he/she understands (Article 24 paragraph 2 of Penitentiary Code). If the individual does not understand any commonly known language (i.e. English, French, Spanish, etc) it is foreseen that he/she seek help from a familiar consulate. Under Article 52 paragraph 6 of the Penitentiary Code, the foreign detainee has the right to contact his/her consulate or embassy.

In addition, in case that a foreign prisoner is submitted to a disciplinary procedure because of a disciplinary offence, an interpreter must be provided if the prisoner does not speak the Greek language (Article 71 paragraph 2 of Penitentiary Code and Article 31 No. 37 of Internal Regulation).

---

[11] Ministerial Decision 58819/7.4.2003 by the Ministry of Justice. For this project the formal translation in English by the Ministry of Justice of this regulation was frequently used.

2.4 Work – Education – Training – Sports – Recreation

All prisoners have the right[12] to participate in and co-operate in educational, cultural, sporting, artistic and recreational events and other creative activities during the detention period. They can work in the establishment on their own account. More specifically, the prisoners have the right:

- To exercise under the supervision of guards and coaches for at least one hour daily, on the playing fields of the establishment or on other fields, as long as there are appropriate facilities, as well as in roofed sports facilities located outside the detention areas (Article 17 of Internal Regulation and Article 36 of Penitentiary Code about Sports). The department of social work in co-operation with the Office of Physical Education of the Prefecture Government may organise programs of group exercise for the prisoners by forming athletic teams, as long as suitable facilities exist and the smooth operation of the establishment is not jeopardized. In fact, one of the greatest problems in every detention facility in the whole of Greece is the lack of exercise facilities.
- To be informed by: a) watching television and listening to and radio programs through devices that belong either to them or to the prison service, pursuant to Article 19, paragraphs 2-4 of Internal Regulation, b) reading the daily press and magazines as well as books of their choice, subject to the condition that their content is not indecent, c) lectures and discussions by special scientists and agents, and d) any other convenient way by decision of the Prison Council (Article 18 of Internal Regulation and Article 37 of the Penitentiary Code regarding Information). A lending library shall operate in the establishment, constantly enriched at the initiative of the department of social work and the sociologist. If it is possible, the library of the establishment shall be associated with the library of the Municipality to which the establishment belongs and the operation thereof shall be defined in co-operation with a special librarian. The library shall be open all working days for at least two hours, both in the morning and in the afternoon. All prisoners shall have access thereto, as long as the communication between prisoners from different wings or departments of the establishment is precluded. In fact, there are some books available in foreign languages, yet certainly not enough to cover the needs of all foreign inmates. However, there are neither newspapers nor magazines available in foreign languages.
- To participate, if they wish, in group or individual recreational or artistic events that shall be organised by the Prison Council in a suitable indoor or outdoor part of the establishment (Article 19 of Internal Regulation and Article 38 of the Penitentiary Code on Recreation). In every cell or ward there shall be at least one television set. The operating hours shall be subject to the condition that fellow prisoners are not disturbed and no tensions are created between them. Upon decision of the Prison Council, it is also possible for a pay TV channel to be available for the projection of sports events or films of recreational or cultural content. The interested prisoners have to cover the any expenses that arise. The prisoners may use, upon inspection by the service, a small radio or private television set with earphones, in order to

12 Chapter "Rights and Obligations of the Prisoners", art. 31 "Rights of the prisoners" of the Internal Operation Regulation of the General Detention Establishments of Type A and B.

avoid disturbing their fellow prisoners. The use of computers and games shall be prohibited, unless there are special educational reasons, which depends on the discretion of the Prison Council. In the detention areas the use of computers and games is strictly prohibited. There are some non-governmental organisations, such as ARSIS[13] (Social Support of Youth), that come into prison and organise recreational activities, for example making mosaics. .

- To attend any education units operating within the detention facilities (primary school; junior high school; second opportunity school) or secondary and tertiary education establishments or vocational training institutions outside the detention facilities through educational leaves (Article 20 of Internal Regulation and Article 35 of the Penitentiary Code concerning Education, Vocational Training and Work of the prisoners). In every establishment, education and vocational training programs for small groups of prisoners shall be organised in co-operation with special training centres, under the supervision of the department of social work, the sociologist and the Educational Council. In any case, at least one guard shall be present to accompany and supervise the prisoners. The Prison Council shall take care of the elaboration of programs: for example a) for illiterates, b) second opportunity school, c) for vocational training, d) foreign languages. The continuation of the prisoners' studies outside the establishment shall take place at recognized and certified educational institutions and schools in which they shall be enrolled. The enrolment and study or apprenticeship at such institutions and in schools of any degree shall be ensured by the granting of educational leaves. Good use of these leaves shall be monitored by the specialized scientific personnel and the public prosecutor-supervisor. The work of the prisoners shall be carried out in various sectors of the operation of the establishment. The posts in which prisoners may work have to be approved by the Ministry of Justice, and their work shall be supervised by the authorised employees, with beneficial counting of sentence days. It is not permitted for a prisoner to be employed in a post different from the one to which he has been officially placed. Article 35 paragraph 4 of the Penitentiary Code provides for the education of the foreign prisoners. According to this article, if it is possible special measures for their training can be taken at any establishment. In practice, however, this task seems to have been left to the few NGOs[14] that are active in the Greek prisons. The overall expenses of education and recreation of the total prison population in Greek prisons are extremely low. It is worth mentioning that during the debates of the Greek Parliament on 1 December 1999 about the Penitentiary Code, it was mentioned that the state budget for books for the prisoners in 1999 and 2000 was not more than 3,000 euro annually. Roughly the same amount was disposed for educational and for athletic material.

2.5 Food – Religion - Personal hygiene - Medical care

According to Article 14 of the Internal Regulation in accordance with Articles 35 and 39 of the Penitentiary Code:

- The state is responsible for the provision of food.

---

13 www.arsis.gr

14 With the financial support of the European Union.

- All prisoners shall be served daily breakfast, lunch and dinner pursuant to the daily operation program of the establishment at the following hours: 07.30, 12.00 noon and half an hour before sunset.
- The menus shall be prepared at the end of each week by the financial department based on known dietetics programs. The content of the weekly menu must provide for dietary diversity and shall be signed by the doctor and members of the Prison Council. The observance of the program and the quality of the food shall be inspected every day by the doctor and the governor of the establishment.
- Poorly prisoners shall be issued special diets that are prepared by the doctor of the establishment. If it is not possible to cover all cases that require such special dietary needs, the patients, upon recommendation by the doctor and agreed opinion of the Prison Council, shall obtain at their own expense foodstuffs from the contractual suppliers of the establishment and shall also be provided with food for religious purposes.
- Prisoners are allowed to purchase foodstuffs and other goods at their own expense (a) from the shop/canteen/buffet operating in the establishment, or (b) through the supplier who shall be appointed by tender, or, finally (c) from free trade outside of the establishment, care of the prison service. The provision shall be limited to quantities that are deemed sufficient for the covering a person's needs. Upon decision of the Prison Council, the delivery of meals and foodstuffs that can be checked easily by the personnel of the detention establishment may be permitted up to twice a month during the visits.
- The prisoners are not permitted to receive fruits from visitors.
- The quality of all of the foods (fruits, vegetables, fishes, meat etc.) shall be checked by the competent committee of collection.
- The food that the prisoners obtain and the goods that are brought into the establishment for them shall be subject to examination and search. If prohibited goods are found during such examinations and searches, they shall be retained and the fact shall be immediately reported either to the director of the establishment, to his legal substitute or to the chief guard when the former are hindered or absent.
- On the holidays of New Year, the 25th of March, Easter, the Assumption of Virgin Mary (15th of August), the 28th of October and Christmas, as well as on local national and religious holidays, the prisoners shall be permitted to consume beverages with a low alcoholic content (beer or wine). The shop-canteen or buffet of the establishment shall be paid with chips or coupons or with the use of personal booklets or cards. These chips, coupons and cards are intended to serve as means of limiting the amount of sweets, ice creams and soft drinks that prisoners can purchase. A prisoner may spend no more than 20 euros per week on these goods (Article 13, paragraph 4 of the Internal Regulation). The purchase of goods on credit is not possible.

The detainees shall be entitled to exercise their religious duties and communicate with recognized representatives of their religion and dogma. The exercise of the religious duties shall take place regularly, at the church or another suitable room of the establishment, upon decision of the Prison Council (Article 31, No. 22 of the Internal Regulation). In practice, those prisoners who do not belong to the Eastern Orthodox Christian Church seem to have very limited opportunities to perform their religious duties properly, with the exception of the followers of the Roman Catholic Church.

Article 15 of the Internal Regulation about personal hygiene and cleaning of shared areas states:

- Newly admitted prisoners shall be provided with bedding and the necessary toiletries including, soap, shaving foam, cotton, a disposable razor, toothpaste, a toothbrush and shampoo.
- Soap and toilet paper are provided by the prison service for the entire period of detention, while other toiletries are provided to indigent prisoners through the social service of the establishment.
- The prisoners may purchase personal toiletries from the shop/canteen of the establishment or from the contractual supplier of food and other goods at their own expense.
- Each prisoner is provided with a mattress, a pillow, two pillow-cases, four sheets, two face towels and two bath towels. Such Articles shall be returned to the service by the prisoner on the day of his/ her transfer from the establishment for any reason. Prisoners are allowed to use their own blankets, sheets and towels that may differ in colour from the ones provided by the service, after having previously unsown the hems. In this case the prisoner is obliged to return the relevant linen that he/she no longer requires to the prison service.
- The bedding and linen mentioned above shall be washed by working prisoners, at the laundry of the establishment under the supervision of authorised employees.
- The prisoners shall be obliged to observe the personal hygiene and cleaning conditions and to keep their clothing, blankets and living facilities clean.
- The prisoners shall be provided with hot water in the bathrooms as well as in the laundry on a daily basis. The working hours of such facilities shall be fixed by order of the day by the director of the establishment, upon recommendation of the chief guard.
- The shared areas shall be cleaned every day by the shifts of working detainee cleaners, under the supervision of authorised employees. In addition, the service shall use the appropriate disinfectants in drains and other critical points every day.

Article 16 of the Internal Regulation which concerns Medical Care and Article 44 of the same regulation concerning the duties of sanitary personnel in accordance with Articles 29 and 30 of the Penitentiary Code state the following:
1. Medical personnel, doctors and nurses, as foreseen in Articles 44-49, shall ensure medical and pharmaceutical care for the prisoners at a level corresponding to that of the rest of the population
2. In rendering its services to the prisoners the medical and nursing personnel shall utilize all information available through modern science and their professions, and shall apply the principles of ethics and deontology, relating to the practice of medicine and nursing. In fact, many of the inmates, both Greek and foreign, have complained about considerable delays in seeing a doctor. Due to staff shortages, it is almost impossible to adequately care for all of the prisoners.

2.6 Consular and legal help

According to Article 33 of the Internal Regulation about legal aid, prisoners have the following rights:

- If the prisoner states that he/she is financially unable to exercise his/her rights to defence, specialised professional personnel of the penal establishment shall be informed, whereupon the detainee shall be requested to file an application with the supporting documents of financial need (tax returns and a statement of income from the revenue office; a certificate of financial need; certificate confirming the granting of a welfare allowance; certificate of unemployment subsidy from the Manpower Employment Organisation; records of proceedings from judicial authorities; documents from which previous appearances without a defence counsellor or ex officio appointment of a counsellor can be concluded; previous failure to comply with pecuniary penalties, etc)
- Such an application is to be addressed to the public prosecutor-supervisor and the notes of the departments of social work and finances of the detention establishment regarding the probable indigence or financial need of the applicant are to be attached thereto.
- The application and the relevant supporting documents are checked by the public prosecutor-supervisor (hereinafter: p.p.s.) with assistance from the specialised professional personnel of the establishment with the stipulation that either additional supporting documents (solemn statements, statements of personal accounts, etc.) be presented or, when this does not apply, they be forwarded to the competent judicial authority by the p.p.s. with relevant indication in order to examine the application for ex officio appointment of a counsellor or rendering of legal aid due to financial need. In any case effort shall be made for the application to be forwarded at least fifteen days before the investigation of the judicial act for which the ex officio appointment of a counsellor and the rendering of legal aid in general is requested.
- The applying prisoner shall be informed of the outcome of his/her application at least fifteen days before the investigation or the date of hearing. Should the application be dismissed, he/she shall be entitled to file an appeal before the immediately higher authority within three days.

2.7 Contact with the outside world

According to Article 21 of the Internal Regulation in accordance with Article 52 of the Penitentiary Code the prisoners have the following rights concerning visits:

- Sentenced prisoners are entitled to receive visits from spouses and relatives up to the fourth degree at least once a week, with each visit lasting a minimum of 30 minutes. The Prison Council shall set the maximum number of visits and the duration thereof.
- Prisoners awaiting trial shall be entitled to have visits from spouses and relatives up to the fourth degree at least twice a week, with each visit lasting a minimum of 30 minutes. In exceptional cases, when the harmonious operation and the safety of the establishment as well as the smooth conduct of the investigation justify it, it is possible for restrictions to be imposed through decisions of the public prosecutor-supervisor.

- The chief guard notifies the prisoners of the dates and times of the visits as well as of any possible changes for extraordinary reasons. Notification occurs through notices that are posted in the visiting rooms as well as on the prisoners' notice board.
- Representatives of social agents, members of parliament, and members of scientific societies, cultural, religious or other associations may visit prisoners upon permission of the Prison Council. The Prison Council shall duly inform the Minister of Justice, who then decides within three days whether or not permission is to be granted. If this term expires without any action having been taken, permission is considered to have been approved.
- Foreign prisoners shall be granted the means to communicate with the diplomatic or consular representatives of their home countries. At the discretion of the Prison Council, these means shall also be granted to other persons and agents who contribute to the solution of special problems caused by detention. Such visits by prisoners shall be reported to the Ministry of Justice by the director of the establishment on the following working day, by forwarding the particulars of both the visitor and the detainee who was visited.

Foreign prisoners have the same visitation rights as Greek inmates. The only problem is that foreigners detained in Greek prisons rarely have relatives who live in the country, which in turn results in a lower number of visits actually taking place. One can infer from the CPT report of 2001 that the conditions in which visits are conducted were not satisfactory at that time. For example, the prisoners' entitlement to 30 minutes of visits per week was not always respected. Many prisoners stated (and the prison staff in fact confirmed) that they were allowed only two visits per month lasting a mere 20 minutes each. The facilities revealed shortcomings such as the fact that prisoners and visitors had to shout to make themselves heard, they could hardly see each other, and they were rarely provided with seats.

2.8 Re-integration activities - Prison leave

According to Article 24 of the Internal Regulation in accordance with Articles 54-58 of the Penitentiary Code, regarding leaves prisoners have the following entitlements and rights:

- Prisoners are to be granted regular and educational leaves by the Disciplinary Council. A special log shall be kept registering the date and time when prisoners on leave exit and return to the institution in order to check their return time. The prosecutor-supervisor, pursuant to the provisions of Article 7 paragraph 2 (3) shall grant the special leaves hereof.
- Upon returning from leaves, the prisoners shall be obligatorily searched for any possible contraband in accordance with the provisions of Article 10, paragraph 5.
- In cases of transgression of leaves, the competent judicial and police authorities as well as the Ministry of Justice shall be informed immediately.
- Every month a list containing particulars regarding: a) the submitted applications for leave, b) any form of leaves that have been granted, and c) any possible transgressions of leaves shall be sent to the Ministry of Justice.

No special activities are provided for preparing prisoners for their resettlement into society, neither for foreigners nor for nationals. There is no probation service in Greece.

In order to be granted conditional leave a prisoner must have an address in Greece. This precondition makes it very unlikely that a foreign prisoner shall be granted conditional leave for they rarely have a fixed address within the country. Theoretically, however, these leaves are still allowed. According to Article 54 paragraph 4 of the Penitentiary Code, the right to leaves cannot be annulled only due to the fact that a prisoner is foreign.

The 2005 annual report of the Greek Ombudsman states that foreign prisoners have great difficulties in actually drawing any advantage from this right. According to the report, even though the foreign prisoners theoretically do have the right to apply for leave and no discrimination issue comes up, the necessary requirements –stable residence in Greece, family ties for example - are very rarely fulfilled in their case.

2.9 Release- Expulsion

According to Article 35 of the Internal Regulation that concerns preparation for release, the prisoners have the following rights:

- From their admission into the detention establishment and during the entire period of their stay prisoners are subject to treatment that is orientated towards ensuring a fair hearing of their case if they are awaiting trial, and their adaptation into legal social life if they are convicts.
- Within the frameworks of section 1 of this Article: a) the prisoners awaiting trial shall be assisted in the preparation of their defence before the judicial authorities, b) the prisoners shall collaborate, if they so desire, with the specialised professional personnel in the design of a treatment program (participation in education, work, vocational training, special therapeutic groups, etc), in order to limit further debasement of their actual and legal status and of the position of the persons depending on them.
- The responsible authorities of the detention establishment shall ensure that all prisoners have the opportunity to be incorporated into institutions for service of sentence (participation in education, work, vocational training, therapy etc.) by which the period of detention is creatively exploited and the prisoners' bonds with the wider social environment are strengthened, especially when the time for their final or conditional release approaches.

According to Article 61 of the Internal Regulation in accordance with Articles 78 and 79 of the Penitentiary Code concerning release, the prisoners have the following rights:

- When a period of detention has been completed, the director of the establishment or his/her substitute shall be informed by the head of the administrative department and shall see to the immediate release of the prisoner. If this day coincides with a holiday or any other exceptional occasion, release shall occur on the working day prior to the initially intended day of release.
- Release occurs through the issuance of release papers from the administration department of the establishment. These papers are signed by the secretary and confirmed by the director. The reasons for detention and the duration thereof shall be stated in these release papers and a recent photo of the detainee shall be affixed.
- The prisoner shall receive a copy of the release papers and if he/she so desires, the specialised professional personnel shall inform him/her about the agencies and ser-

vices that offer support after release and he/she shall be referred accordingly. Such information may also take place after release.

Article 74 PC deals with the expulsion of foreigners and provides that if an offender sentenced to confinement in a penitentiary or to imprisonment for not less than one year is a foreigner, the court may order his expulsion from the country after final release from the penitentiary or, in (rare) cases of conditional release, immediately after his release from the penitentiary. The court may also order the expulsion of any foreigner upon whom the security measures under Article 69 PC (custody of offenders in a public therapeutic institution), 71 PC (committal of alcoholics and drug addicts into a therapeutic institution) or 72 PC (referral to a workhouse) have been imposed. In such cases, expulsion may be ordered in lieu of such measures. Foreigners who are expelled under these circumstances may return to the country three years after their expulsion, provided that the Minister of Justice grants them permission to return. If the foreign prisoner has been conditionally released according to Article 105 PC (or Article 129 PC in case that the prisoner is a juvenile), the expulsion imposed according to Article 74 takes place, unless it is infeasible (Article 105 paragraph 4 or Article 129 paragraph 5 PC). In this latter case the released foreign prisoner is not obliged to leave the country, but must only comply to the conditions imposed during his/her early release, as is also the case for released Greek prisoners.

2.10 Aftercare-Probation

There is no probation or after care service for adults in Greece. A probation service for minors has existed since 1954 (Law 2793/1954 especially as amended by Law 378/1976). By contrast, such a service for adults – although provided by Art. 100A PC introduced by Law 1941/1991 – has not been established as yet. Therefore, the law provides that until the creation of a body of probation officers for adults, supervision duties are to be exercised by the public prosecutor of the court that ordered supervised suspension of sentence (Art. 100A paragraph 8 PC).

2.11 Staff

There is no special training for the staff that specialise in the treatment of foreign prisoners. This obviously results in the impossibility to provide prison personnel capable of communicating in a language comprehended by the foreign inmates. Thus, communication of non-Greek speaking foreigners with prison staff and the public prosecutors is rarely direct. Many respondents, however, mention the assistance of informal interpreters i.e. of fellow inmates acting as mediators who facilitate communication. As in many other parts of the prison system (i.e. medical care), empirical knowledge is referred to in order to cover needs due to lack of human agents and resources. According to the prison staff, Albanian prisoners who pose the vast majority of foreign prisoners in Greece seem to have a good knowledge of the Greek language.

2.12 Projects

There are no specific projects in the penitentiary institutions. The only efforts are made by the few NGOs that have access to prison life, and these encompass all prisoners without specifically dealing with the problems of foreign prisoners. Only very few prisons offer Greek language courses.

To sum up, prison overcrowding, a negative psychological climate, pessimism, lack of confidence and difficulties in communication between prisoners and staff are some of the most important problems of prison life. The gap between prison legislation and reality and the lack of social support complete the list of the major problems that have already been stated. The multiple shields of protection offered by the international and national legal norms are not enough to adequately safeguard the fundamental rights of the prisoners. The available domestic and international mechanisms guaranteeing the enforcement of these rights involve complex and bureaucratic procedures to which the average detainee, and especially prisoners from ethnic minorities, has no easy access. As a consequence there is a great discrepancy between the law in writing and the law in action. Furthermore, the provisions of the ECHR do not specifically concern detained individuals, and therefore, these provisions, approached from the angle of prisoners' protection, are vague and set minimum standards only.

3 ADMINISTRATIVE DETENTION OF FOREIGN PRISONERS

3.1 Institutions for Administrative Detention

Any foreign person who has been arrested under an administrative decision of detention and expulsion must be detained in a special institution of detention, according to the Foreigners Act (Law 3386/2005). According to Article 81 of this law, he/she remains detained at the police station of the locality that he/she was initially detained in. Until the proceedings for his/her expulsion have been completed, he/she is to be detained in special institutions that were yet to be established – when the law was passed – by a Ministerial Decision. The same decision will define the terms of operation of these special institutions. The responsibility for these institutions lies with the Greek Police. Until today, no such decision has been made. New special institutions have not yet been added to the already existent[15] special centres for migrants (mentioned below).

3.2 Ministry Responsible and Relevant Legislation

The Ministry responsible for these detention institutions is the Ministry of Public Order and not the Ministry of Justice, as is the case for the rest of the Greek Prison System.

As a result, the Penitentiary Code and all regulations concerning prisoners in Greece do not apply to this category of foreign prisoners. The application of these rules can only be analogical. Generally, the legal status quo of foreigners from third countries[16] is regu-

15 They were established with previous ministerial decisions, under the directions of the previous Foreign Act (Law 2910/2001).

16 That means non-EU nationals.

lated by the Foreigners Act. At the beginning of the 1990s, after the great migration wave that followed the collapse of the socialist regimes of Eastern Europe, the Greek state was obliged to react by creating a completed Foreigners Act in order to organise its policy towards the massive wave of migration. The Law 1975/1991 was the first legislative reaction to this – at least for Greek society - new phenomenon, with a very restrictive character, corresponding to the general guidelines of intergovernmental agreements of the EU. Ten years later, this law was substituted by a new Foreigners Act (law 2910/2001) in an effort to correct the deficiencies and impasses of the old law. However, this law also failed to correspond, to the expectations of an effective migration policy. One year ago the new Foreigners Act was enacted. The new Law 3386/2005 is based in the same philosophy as the previous one. In general, it is considered more detailed and – in some points - more restrictive. It contains provisions that concern the entrance, stay, expulsion and detention of nationals from outside of the EU.

3.3 Capacity of Institutions for Administrative Detention

The special centres for the detention of illegal migrants are located in the following towns[17]: Chios, Lesbos, Samos, Evros, Athens (Amigdaleza and Ellinikon for women and minors), Piraeus and Thessaloniki. Since only a small number of such special centres of detention exist, every police station detention room - all over the country - constitutes *de facto* an institution of administrative detention for foreign prisoners. In practice, a vast majority of the foreign prisoners under administrative detention is kept at the police establishment of the town near which he/she had been detected and arrested by the police. No published data on the capacity of these two types of institution exist, though. Finally, ad hoc reception centres may be established in different parts of the country (more often on the islands) should a large number of illegal migrants arrive.

3.4 Length of stay

Any foreigner of a third country who has entered the country legally (with a legal visa) can stay in Greece for three months. If he has residence permission, he/she can stay for one year. This permission can be renewed for two years under very specific terms described by the law.

Any foreigner who has violated legal provisions and regulations on legal entrance and the legal stay in Greece can be detained upon an administrative decision. The maximum length of such administrative detention is three months[18]. If the foreign person is not expelled within this period, he/she must be released immediately. However, NGOs in the region state that there are a significant number of cases in which foreign prisoners are being unlawfully held in detention beyond this maximum period of three-months.

3.5 Decisions Procedure

According to the Foreigners Act (Law 3386/2005), any third country national who has violated the rules and the procedures for legal entrance into Greece and who has no

---

17 According to the Greek Permanent Representation to EU on 18-04-2005.

18 See art. 76 of Law 3386/2005.

valid (permanent or temporary) residence permit shall be expelled on the order of the commanding police officer authorized to this purpose by the Ministry of Public Order (decision of administrative expulsion). According to the third paragraph of article 76 of the Foreigners Act, the illegal migrant can be detained (decision of administrative detention[19]) until the expulsion has been implemented, especially if the suspect is perceived as likely to abscond or as dangerous for the public order. The Law underlines the obligation of the authorized officers to inform the foreign detainee of the reasons for his/her detention and to facilitate the communication with his/her lawyer.

In general, all registered asylum seekers cannot be arrested and detained as illegal entrants. According to a Ministerial Decision of 1992[20] (the conformity of which has been questioned in relation to the Constitution) as well as the Foreigners Act, asylum seekers who have applied for asylum after having been arrested for illegal stay in Greece, and who have been detained by an order of the police authorities because an expulsion order has been issued against them should remain in detention until a final decision on their application for asylum has been reached or until the period of their detention exceeds the maximum length of three months. If the foreigner lodges an asylum application after the issuance of the expulsion and detention order, his/her expulsion and/or any measure of return will be suspended. However, the foreigner remains in detention. After three months have passed, the asylum seeker must be released from detention if within this detention period a positive decision on his/her asylum application is not reached; if within this detention period a positive decision on his/her asylum application is reached he/she must immediately be released from detention and cannot be deported as a refugee (other than under the cessation and withdrawal grounds provided for by the Geneva Convention).

If an application for asylum is rejected during the three-month period of detention the authorities have to execute the expulsion of the detainee before the three months have expired. Otherwise, as stated above, the detainee is to be released immediately.

3.6 Appeal Procedure

According to the provisions of paragraphs 3 and 4 of Article 78 of the Foreigners Act, an appeal against the decision of administrative detention may be lodged by any detained illegal migrant or asylum seeker before the President of the First Instance Administrative Court in the area of his/her detention. Should the President consider that the detained foreigner is not a threat to public order and that there is no strong likelihood of him/her absconding, he/she is to be immediately released. In practice, only a minority of foreign prisoners - mainly those who have applied for asylum while in detention- has been released through this procedure after having claimed that they do not pose a threat to public order since their only offence was illegal entry, and that there is no strong likelihood of absconding.

---

19 Also with an order of the Commanding Police Officer authorized to this purpose by the Ministry of Public Order.

20 Ministerial Decision No 4803/13/7a-1992 by the Ministries of Foreign Affairs, Justice and Public Order.

3.7 Irregular stay

According to Article 83 of the Foreigners Act, any national of a third country who illegitimately crosses or attempts to cross the Greek border is punishable with a penalty of imprisonment of at least three months[21] and a pecuniary penalty of at least 1.500 euros. However, the public prosecutor of the first degree can abstain from the penal prosecution after referring to the public prosecutor of second degree (There is a form of collaboration between the two public prosecutors before the decision to abstain from prosecution is made. The public prosecutor of the first degree needs the approval of the public prosecutor of second degree). In this case, the commanding officer of the police / the coast guard service by which the foreigner had initially been detected is informed of the abandonment of prosecution. Thereupon the commanding officer orders the administrative expulsion of the foreigner. After three months - but not later than one year - if the illegal foreigner has not yet been expelled, the public prosecutor can pursue penal prosecution. The illegal stay of foreigners who have entered the county legally and whose residence permit or visa subsequently expires is not classed as a criminal offence. However, he/she must be expelled with an administrative decision.

3.8 Numbers

The exact number of foreign prisoners being held in administrative detention and awaiting expulsion is very difficult to calculate or even estimate, for a number of reasons. Firstly, the detention facilities of the police stations in which such prisoners are held also accommodate criminal suspects, persons who have been transferred to attend court proceedings or who are in transit to other establishments, as well as persons serving sentences with a total duration of up to 30 days. Secondly, a large number of foreign prisoners are expelled almost immediately within a few days of their arrest. In addition to the great fluctuation of this category of prisoners, the lack of published information on behalf of the Ministry of Public Order makes the determination of exact number of this category even more difficult.

3.9 Expulsion

The vast majority of the foreign persons who have no legal papers and who are detected by the police are detained in order to be expelled back to their countries of origin. The foreign illegal migrants who come from the countries bordering Greece -for example Albania or Bulgaria- are detained for a sort period (for an average of one week), and their expulsion is executed directly as they are transferred without serious delay to the borders by the Greek police officers.

3.10 Not-expelled prisoners

The foreign illegal migrants who come from distant countries - especially Afghanistan, Iran, Iraq, Pakistan and Nigeria in the case of Greece - are usually detained for a period much longer than one week. They either remain in detention for the whole three month

---

[21] As it already has been mentioned above, the maximum length of imprisonment is five years.

period or they are released prior to the expiration thereof, but usually not earlier than one month- as their expulsion is considered infeasible (for example because they have no passport and the country that they claim to come from does not accept them back, or because they have no diplomatic representative in our county, like for instance the case of Afghanistan). In both cases they are released and are ordered to leave the country on their own account within approximately 30 days. If they are still residing illegally in Greece once this period of tolerance has passed, it is possible for them to be detained for another three month period should they be detected again by the police. As a result, many foreign migrants move in and out of detention again and again, a cycle that continues until they apply for asylum and obtain temporary residence permission as asylum seekers.

3.11 Detention of Irregulars under Criminal Law

Detention can also be ordered by a court as a consequence of a decision of expulsion according to criminal law (Article 74 PC). In that case he/she is detained in prison together with other criminal prisoners, and must be expelled not only because he/she has violated the provisions of the Foreigners Act on illegal entrance or stay but also because he/she has committed an act punishable by Greek penal law. Thus, he/she is kept detained in prison together with the other prisoners who have been sentenced under criminal law. According to a Ministerial Decision of 1992[22], if a foreigner is detained after a court (and not the police authorities) has ordered his/her expulsion, there is no precise time limit for the duration of his/her detention. There are general limits, however, provided by the Greek Constitution on lawful conditions for arrest and detention. When the expulsion ordered by a court is impossible or cannot take place in due time for reasons related to 1) international embargos, 2) violations against Article 3 of the European Convention on Human Rights and/or of Article 3 of the UN Convention against Torture etc., or 3) other material obstacles to the expulsion, an appeal against the expulsion order can be submitted before the competent judicial authority.

3.12 Minors

Regarding the general proceedings of expulsion and administrative detention, the Foreigners Act does not distinguish minors as a separate category. Minors can be detained and expelled under the same conditions and regulations as adult illegal foreigners, and they actually are, despite objections of the Greek Ombudsman on this matter. Generally, for the territory of Attica, they are detained in Amigdaleza detention centre for women and minors. If they were detected elsewhere - mainly in northern Greece- and they are older than 13 years, they are detained separately in special rooms of the police establishment. If they are younger than 13 years old and are accompanied by their mothers, the family members are detained together, usually only for a few days. Those minors who are not yet 13 years old and who have no relatives in Greece cannot be detained and must be accommodated in special hostels or institutions while the Greek authorities

---

[22] Ministerial Decision No. 4803/13/7a-1992 by the Ministries of Foreign Affairs, Justice and Public Order.

attempt to locate their family. The treatment of illegal foreign minors poses a significant problem and the role of NGOs is very crucial.

The actual situation of institutions for foreign prisoners under administrative detention in Greece can be characterised presented by the investigations of two international organisations, the NGO Human Rights Watch and the Committee for the Prevention of Torture of the Council of Europe. These two visits took place five and four years ago respectively, yet the general situation has not changed dramatically since then. The prisoners of this category are exposed to worse conditions than the foreign prisoners who are detained under criminal law.

Human Rights Watch conducted research in Greece during a visit in November 2000. With the full co-operation of the Ministry of Public Order, on 18 November 2000 the researchers visited the Attica General Police Directorate on Alexandras Avenue in Athens to monitor the conditions of detention for undocumented migrants held there in a special detention centre for foreigners. The men detained in Alexandras Avenue facility where foreigners detained for entering and/or living in Greece without valid travel documents or residence permits which is in violation of Greece's Foreigners Act. Police authorities insisted that the facility of this establishment was not a prison and that the people were held only temporarily while awaiting expulsion. However, Human Rights Watch interviewed prisoners who stated that they had been detained for five, six, eight and twelve months respectively. Numerous prisoners had been held there for over five months. Those held at the Alexandras Avenue centre and all foreigners held under similar circumstances in police facilities in Greece are in detention as defined by the UN Body of Principles for the Protection of all Persons under Any Form of Detention or Imprisonment (Body of Principles). That is, they are persons deprived of their liberty without a conviction under Greek criminal law. The research team from Human Rights Watch were immediately struck by the degree of overcrowding when they first entered the facility. Dirty mattresses lined the floors of the corridors and large groups of prisoners were seated on them, crammed into individual rooms and milling about in the limited available floor space in hallways. According to police officials, the Alexandras Avenue facility houses approximately 150 men in a space designed for 80 prisoners. There were 19 narrow rooms in two large blocks, each room approximately 12 square meters or 130 square feet and a small cell in which a mentally disturbed detainee was held. According to police officials, each room could sleep four people. Numerous prisoners actually live and sleep on the floors of the inner corridors of the blocks. As many as twelve prisoners shared four single mattresses in the corridor of one section of the centre. The mattresses were thin and narrow and clearly designed for a single person.

Here are a few examples of the conditions that the research team from Human Rights Watch found in the facility: Due to the overcrowding, the average room sleeps between seven and twelve prisoners. Some mattresses were on frames but most of them were on the floor, which left no walking space on the floor for prisoners to move about when other prisoners were lying down. This situation forced the prisoners to walk on each others bedding to get to and from their mattresses during sleeping hours. During the day, the mattresses are piled against the wall in some rooms to allow a passage for walking. Persons living in the hallways routinely tolerate other prisoners walking across their bedding. The corridors in each of the blocks were dimly lit but there were no lights at all in any of the individual rooms. The corridor lights provided minimal lighting in the rooms after sunset, certainly not enough to read. The lights in the corridors and the toilet

/shower rooms were kept on twenty-four hours per day. Prisoners living in the corridors complained that the constant light made it difficult to sleep. There was no natural light at all during the day in the inner corridors where these prisoners stayed. Windows in the outer corridors provided some light in the individual rooms during the day. Despite the best efforts by prisoners, the cells and individual rooms of the detention centre were filthy, and the severe overcrowding in the centre had led to unsanitary conditions that could pose a serious threat to their health.

The centre was roach infested and the researchers even viewed roaches crawling on the walls, on the water fountain and on the prisoners themselves when they were giving the interview. The prisoners also complained of finding them in their bedding both during the daytime and during the night.

Each detainee was responsible for washing his own clothes. Piles of laundry littered the bathroom and lines of drying clothing were hung in the rooms. The prisoners had to purchase soap and toilet paper with their own money and many claimed that police officers selling these products charged them excessive amounts. They even had to provide and launder their own sheets. Prisoners complained of insufficient amounts of food and that the type of food served was nutritionally deficient. The prisoners were not permitted to exercise outdoors or in an indoor facility nor were they granted regular access to fresh air. Despite long periods of detention, they had no access at all to educational programs or social services. One telephone was available for use by all prisoners in both blocks, and consequentially the line to the phone was always extremely long. They could use it at any time but had to purchase their own phone cards. . It was nearly impossible to receive a phone call because the phone was in constant use. Therefore, lawyers and non-governmental organisations working with prisoners were forced to appear in person in order to maintain contact. Although the prisoners could meet with their lawyers at any time, the facilities did not permit privacy.

There is no state supported general legal aid scheme for the indigent in Greece, although asylum seekers can access free legal counsel if they know which organisations offer representation. Prisoners awaiting expulsion at the Alexandras Avenue detention facility had to pay for their own legal counsel. Numerous prisoners complained that they and their families could not afford the high costs that the appointment of legal representation brings with it.

Finally, prisoners at the Alexandras Avenue facility did not, in general, complain about physical abuse by police officers in the course of the daily life at the detention centre. Physical abuse in the process of expulsion, however, was reported to be more common. The substandard conditions of detention in the Alexandras Avenue detention facility detailed above violate many of the requirements of both internationally and regionally recognised, basic, minimum standards for the treatment of prisoners. Moreover, the Standard Minimum Rules is an authoritative set of guidelines for interpreting Article 7 of the International Covenant on Civil and Political Rights (hereinafter: ICCPR) prohibiting cruel, inhuman or degrading treatment or punishment, and ICCPR Article 10 states that "all persons deprived of their liberty shall be treated with humanity and respect for the inherent dignity of the human person".

Prisoners at the Alexandras Avenue detention centre are sometimes held there for many months—even up to a year—and some are held for indefinite periods. The long periods of detention in combination with the conditions endured by prisoners (overcrowding, lack of adequate sleeping accommodations, no access to fresh air or exercise, a dirty, roach-infested environment, questionable access to medical care) raise serious concerns that this situation may amount to cruel, inhuman or degrading treatment.

In pursuance of Article 7 of the European Convention for the Prevention of Torture and Inhuman or Degrading Treatment or Punishment, a delegation of the CPT carried out a visit to Greece in October 2001. The last visit of the Committee that took place was on August of 2005. During this visit, the Committee focused particular attention on detention facilities for foreigners, but until today the respective report has not yet been published.

During the visit in 2001, the visited establishments were: police establishments in the Attica region, Crete, and north-western Greece, as well as coastguard, customs authority, prison and military establishments. Regarding ill-treatment, a considerable number of persons interviewed by the delegation in the course of the visit alleged that they had been ill-treated by law enforcement officials. The allegations concerned mainly the police, however, some of them also related to Coast Guard officials. The alleged ill-treatment consisted mostly of kicks and blows with hands, fists, batons or other objects, often inflicted during questioning. Certain allegations also involved the use of excessive force at the time of arrest or ill-treatment of prisoners during transfers.

Regarding the conditions of the detention establishments, the CPT research team reported the following results: Though the detention facilities in these establishments are designed to hold criminal suspects for short periods, in practise they are frequently used to hold persons for prolonged periods, in particular immigration prisoners. With regard to the establishments designed for detaining persons undergoing ordinary administrative removal procedures (i.e. for a maximum of three months), Amigdaleza Holding Centre, which was designed for women and minors, offered good material conditions. The premises were spacious, clean, had good lighting (including access to natural light) and ventilation, and were adequately albeit sparsely furnished.

The situation at Hellenikon and Piraeus Holding Centres for Foreigners was far less favourable: inmate accommodation was in a poor state of hygiene and devoid of furniture, artificial lightning was insufficient, and there were problems with the water supply, particularly hot water. At Hellenikon, sleeping arrangements consisted of mattresses placed directly on the concrete floor. Furthermore, the Piraeus centre was in need of repair, especially in the toilet and shower areas.

A feature common to all three holding centres was the total absence of organised activities. In addition, inmates were not provided with newspapers, magazines, or books, and could not watch television or listen to the radio. Admittedly, this state of forced idleness was mitigated to some extent by the open door policy practised, and by generous visiting possibilities and access to telephones. However, minors held at the Amigdaleza centre were being offered no outdoor exercise; in addition, no outdoor exercise facilities were available at Piraeus and the exercise yard at Hellenikon was still not open for use. These are particularly serious shortcomings given the possible length of detention in those facilities. Furthermore, the CPT is concerned by the admission of border guard officers to the delegation that they were under no obligation to inform persons subject to immediate readmission procedures (i.e. expedited removal to a neighbouring country) of their rights and more particularly, that such persons did not have the rights of notification of custody and access to a lawyer. It should be noted that the CPT delegation received many complaints from immigration prisoners that very little or no information had been provided to them about their situation and the procedures applied to them.

In their report about Greece "Out of the Spotlight", Amnesty International (2001) writes that they are very concerned about the conditions in the country with regard to immigrants and asylum seekers. Specifically, the organisation is concerned that authorities, especially in border areas, may actively be impeding refugees' access to asylum through the refugee's inability to communicate in Greek. Prisoners interviewed by the organisation's representatives claimed that upon arrival at the detention centres where they were held, police officers asked them to sign papers which they could not read but perceived to be documents relating to legalisation of their status

4 NATIONALS DETAINED ABROAD

The Greek Ministry of Justice provided no information about this category of prisoners and there are no statistics or studies available that are relevant to this part of the project.

5 EVALUATION AND RECOMMENDATION

The most important suggestion is the establishment of probation and after care services, as found in most European countries. A great deal of research regarding the foreign population in Greek prisons needs to be conducted. In particular, matters concerning the foreigners' social backgrounds and families, and their criminal profiles need to be addressed. Furthermore, since there is currently no information available about Greek prisoners abroad, research should be undertaken to fill this gap.

The recommendations of Amnesty International (2005) are as follows:
Conditions of detention for foreigners should conform to international and regional standards, including the *U.N.* "Minimum Rules for the Treatment of Prisoners, U.N. Body of Principles for the Protection of All Persons Under Any Form of Detention, and the European Prison Rules". In particular, at a minimum each detainee should have reasonable sleeping space in an environment conducive to restful sleep, his/her own bed, and adequate toilet/bath facilities and the provision of toiletries; access to reading lights at night and natural light during the day; effective access to medical care and psychological services; adequate means to contact and facilities to meet in confidence with legal counsel; one hour of exercise per day; and access to educational and social service programs.

Asylum seekers, in general, should not be detained. Exceptions to this general principle should be applied on a case-by-case basis only and as a matter of last resort. Asylum seekers must have a prompt and effective opportunity to challenge a detention order before a judicial or administrative body independent of the detaining authorities. Periodic reviews of continuing detention should be conducted and asylum seekers and their representatives should have the right to be present at such reviews.

Undocumented migrants must have a prompt and effective opportunity to challenge the lawfulness of both their detention and expulsion order in a judicial proceeding or before another competent authority. Continued detention should be subjected to periodic review.

Information bulletins detailing the rights of prisoners to minimum standards of treatment and due process guarantees should be made available to every person in a language that he/she can understand. In the case of prisoners who cannot read, this information should be presented orally in a language they can understand. Prisoners should be informed in a language they can understand of their right to seek asylum, the procedure for filing an asylum claim, and the contact numbers of appropriate agencies that provide free legal representation for the asylum procedure;

A complaints procedure regarding conditions of detention should be developed and implemented. All prisoners should be informed of the existence of a complaints procedure in a language he/she understands. Prisoners should have access to a judicial remedy for abuses suffered in detention (e.g. police abuse) that amount to torture or cruel, inhuman or degrading treatment or punishment;

Prisoners should have access to legal counsel. Those who cannot afford counsel should be provided with counsel at no cost. Lawyers should have unhindered access to their clients in detention facilities.

Non-governmental organisations that provide legal assistance and representatives from UNHCR should have unhindered access to all detention facilities for foreigners.

Migrants awaiting expulsion and asylum seekers in detention should be housed in facilities separate from persons in custody for violations of Greek penal law. Furthermore, regarding the Greek prison system, the repletion of vacant staff posts is necessary, mainly within the social services of prisons and other scientific posts. It is also necessary to expand Greek language programs in prisons.

Finally, emphasis must be placed on the training of the staff of the Greek prison system and of the police officers. Existing training programs and any new programs to be introduced should be subject to regular review, to ensure that law enforcement officials are given practical training in how to implement national and international human rights legislation both in their daily duties and in situations of emergency, with particular emphasis on non-violent measures of law enforcement. This training should reinforce measures specifically designed to promote race-awareness and combat racist or xenophobic attitudes amongst police officers and prison staff, in order to prevent the social exclusion trends in the Greek Prison System.

Chapter 12

Hungary

Tímea Szabó
Balázs Tóth
Gábor Győző
András Kádár

1 INTRODUCTION

1.1 Overview of penalties and measures

In the Hungarian legal system are several forms of punishments and measures as a consequence of which someone can be lawfully deprived of his/her freedom. The forms of detention relevant for the purposes of this study can be divided into the main categories of detention for criminal reasons and detention for non-criminal reasons. The most important form of non-criminal detention is alien policing detention. The forms of detention for criminal (or quasi-criminal) reasons are the following:

- *Short-term custody*: the police may take into short-term custody – inter alia - those who are caught in the act of committing an intentional criminal offence; those against whom a warrant of arrest has been issued based on a law or international treaty; those whose custody or pre-trial detention has been ordered; those who escaped during the implementation of custody, pre-trial detention or imprisonment; those who are unable or unwilling to prove their identity; and finally those who are suspected of having committed a criminal offence. Short-term custody is ordered by the police, and may not last longer than 8 (in exceptional cases 12) hours.[1]
- *Custody:* the police, the prosecutor or the court can order the custody of a person in the event that there is a well-founded suspicion that he/she has committed a criminal offence punishable with imprisonment, if the subsequent pre-trial detention of the person is likely to be ordered. Custody may last for no longer than 72 hours (including any form of detention preceding the custody).[2]
- *Pre-trial detention:* in the case of an offence punishable with imprisonment the defendant may be subjected to pre-trial detention if – inter alia – he/she escaped or remains hidden from the court, the prosecutor or the investigative authority; taking into account the risk of his/her escape or any further reason, there are well-founded grounds to presume that his/her presence at the procedure can not be secured in any other way; well-founded grounds justify the presumption that if not taken into pre-trial detention, he/she would frustrate, hinder or threaten the procedure; there are well-founded grounds to presume that if not taken into pre-trial detention, he/she would accomplish the criminal offence he/she attempted or commit another offence punishable with imprisonment. Pre-trial detention – with certain exceptions - may not last longer than three years. It can only be ordered and extended by the court.[3]
- *Imprisonment:* Imprisonment may be imposed on the defendant if he/she is found guilty of a criminal offence for which Act IV of 1978 on the Penal Code ("Penal Code") prescribes this form of punishment as a possible sanction. The minimum length of imprisonment is two months, the maximum duration is fifteen years (in case of cumulative or consolidated sentences twenty years) or a life-sentence.[4] There are three main regimes for the execution of imprisonment: low-security regime, medium-security

1 Art. 33, Act XXXIV of 1994 on the Police ("Police Act")
2 Art. 126, Act XIX of 1998 on Criminal Procedure ("CCP")
3 Art. 129, CCP
4 Art. 39, Penal Code

regime and high-security regime.[5] In the sentence the court defines under which regime the defendant shall serve the prison sentence.
- *Compulsory medical treatment:* "Compulsory medical treatment" is applied with regard to those mentally ill perpetrators who have committed violent crimes against other persons or crimes that have endangered public safety, where there is a danger that they may commit similar crimes in the future, provided that the initial offence would be punished by imprisonment exceeding one year. This treatment is under regular supervision. The first review takes place eight months after the admission, and after that once a year.[6]
- *Reformatory education:* According to the Penal Code, the court may sentence a juvenile offender to serve time in a reformatory institution (reformatory education) if it regards this as necessary for the juvenile offender's development.[7] The minimum length of reformatory education is one year, the maximum time is three years. No parole is possible until one year is served.[8] Reformatory education shall be distinguished from prison sentence served in juvenile penitentiaries (low- or medium security). While these are integrated within the general prison system (under the Ministry of Justice), reformatories are under the Ministry of Youth, Family and Social Affairs and Equality.
- *Forms of detention related to petty offences:* 1. Petty offence arrest: arrest of those presumably having committed a petty offence punishable with petty offence detention. The maximum duration of petty offence arrest is 72 hours. 2. Petty offence detention: an Act of Parliament can prescribe the detention of those having committed a petty offence. The minimum length of petty offence detention is one day; the maximum duration is 60 days.[9]

Detention related to the alien policing procedure may take the following forms:
- detention for refusal (in order to implement the readmission agreements)
- detention in preparation for expulsion
- alien policing detention

Detention for refusal may be ordered by the Border Guards for five days, detention in preparation for expulsion and alien policing detention may be ordered by the Office for Immigration and Nationality (OIN) also for five days. After the initial five days, the court is entitled to prolong the detention. In case of the first two types for a maximum of 30 days, in the case of alien policing detention for a maximum of altogether 12 months. The different forms of the detention shall be summed up, but their total length may not exceed 12 months.

The most frequent of the above is alien policing detention that may be ordered by the OIN with the purpose of securing the subsequent expulsion of a foreigner who hid from the authority or hindered the execution of expulsion in any other way; who refused to leave the country or it is presumable on any other grounds that he/she would hinder or

---

5 Art. 41, Penal Code

6 Art.74, Penal Code and Article 13 of Decree of Minister of Justice 36/2003. (X. 3.) on the Implementation of Forensic Compulsory Treatment, Temporary Forensic Compulsory Treatment and the Tasks and Operation of the Forensic Observation and Psychiatric Institution ("IMEI Regulation")

7 Art. 118, Penal Code

8 Art. 454, Penal Code

9 Art.14, Act LXIX of 1999 on Petty Offences

frustrate the execution of expulsion; who committed a petty offence or a crime during the temporal scope of expulsion; who seriously offended the behavioural rules of the place where he/she is obliged to stay on the basis of the OIN's decision or otherwise hindered the alien procedure; finally if he/she has served a prison sentence imposed for having committed an intentional criminal offence.[10]

There are some other forms of detention applicable in Hungary that will not be mentioned in this study, because they are not applied frequently. The most frequent forms of detention are imprisonment and pre-trial detention (see below). The above-mentioned punishments and measures are executed in penitentiary institutions (imprisonment, pre-trial detention, petty offence detention), the Forensic Observation and Psychiatric Institution (compulsory medical treatment), reformatory institutions (juveniles' pre-trial detention, reformatory education), police jails (criminal custody, pre-trial detention for a maximum of 60 days, petty offence arrest, petty offence detention) and alien police jails (detention related to the alien policing procedure).

1.2 Overview of the Prison System

The different institutions where detention may be implemented are under the scope of authority of different organizations. Below the authors will outline the most important ones, and then go on to deal in more detail with the status and structure of the penitentiary administration.

Institutions under the authority of the Ministry of Justice (and managed directly by the National Penitentiary Administration) include penitentiary institutions (32); the Forensic Observation and Psychiatric Institution (IMEI), where "compulsory medical treatment" is implemented; and the Central Prison Hospital in Tököl, where medical treatment is provided for (not mentally) ill criminal detainees

Institutions under the authority of the Ministry of Interior include police jails (police jails are managed directly by the County Police Headquarters, subordinated to the National Police Headquarters); and alien policing jails, where non-Hungarian citizens can be detained (alien policing jails are managed directly by the Border Guards) (5).

Reformatories for juvenile offenders are under the authority of the Ministry of Youth, Family, Social Affairs and Equality (there are four reformatories – three for male and one for female juveniles).

The status and organization of the Hungarian penitentiary system is set out in Act CVII of 1995 on the Penitentiary System ("Penitentiary Act"). The top unit of the system is the National Headquarters of the Penitentiary System (NHPS), which is financed by the central state under the supervision of the Ministry of Justice since 1963. The basic organisational structure is defined by the Penitentiary Act, but the details are determined by the Minister of Justice who approves the organisational chart and approves of the number of the staff. The NHPS's annual budget is determined by the Parliament in the annual law on the budget, within the budgetary chapter of the Ministry of Justice. Within the framework of the approved budget, the NHPS may autonomously use the resources but it has to comply with the general state budgetary guidelines. The NHPS is a fundamentally military structure headed by the National Commander who directs the penitentiary administration autonomously within the framework created by the laws and

[10] Art. 46, Act XXXIX of 2001 on the Enrty and Stay of Foreigners "Alien Policing Act"

regulations in force, as well as the decisions of the Minister of Justice. The Ministry of Justice performs professional supervision through its Department of the Supervision of Penitentiary Matters and the Deputy State Secretary responsible for the penitentiary administration.

The average number of prison population in 2005 was fluctuating between 16,000 and 17,000 (convicted prisoners: around 12,500, pre-trial detainees: 4,000, persons under compulsory medical treatment: 280, persons in petty offence detention: 100). The composition of prisoners on 12 May 2005 was: 15,510 males and 1,011 females. Out of the 16,521 inmates 482 were juveniles and 625 foreigners. The full official capacity of the prison system was 11,253 on 12 May 2005, therefore, the average rate of overcrowding is around 150%, while in certain penitentiaries (especially in ones serving primarily remand purposes) the rate of overcrowding can be as high as 220%. On 12 May 2005, the number of penitentiary personnel was around 8,600 with approximately 6450 uniformed and 2150 non-uniformed staff.[11]

There are three main types of mechanisms controlling detention conditions in Hungary. A specific department of the regional prosecutor's office is regularly supervising the lawfulness of detention in all possible places of detention (including penitentiaries and police jails as well). Prosecutors have access to all kinds of data, may talk to prisoners and other detainees, and may receive written complaints from them as well.[12] The organs implementing detention shall be obliged to comply with any instruction given by the prosecutor. They may challenge the instruction with the prosecutor's superior, this however may not delay the implementation thereof.[13] Another important form of control is the Ombudsman. There is no specific ombudsman for detention matters, but detainees may turn to the General Ombudsman if they think that their fundamental rights have been infringed during detention. While investigating into the complaint, the Ombudsman may request information, a hearing, written explanation, declaration or opinion from the competent official or demand that an inquiry be conducted by a superior. When finding a violation, the Ombudsman issues recommendations, to which the examined authority shall respond within 30 days.[14] The third form of control of detention is civil monitoring carried out by non-governmental organizations. Based on its agreement of cooperation with the NHPS, the Border Guards and the National Police Headquarters, the Hungarian Helsinki Committee has been monitoring detention in penitentiaries, police jails and alien policing jails for years.

Foreigners can be detained in all the institutions listed above. The institution where only foreigners can be detained is the alien policing jail where nationals obviously may not be placed. In terms of Article 223 of Decree 6/1996 (III. 6.) of the Minister of Justice on the Implementation of the Rules of Imprisonment and Pre-trial Detention (hereafter: Penitentiary Regulation), when detaining a foreign prisoner, it should be assured if possible that the detainee be placed in a cell where such other detainees are placed who speak both Hungarian and the language the foreigner speaks and understands. In practice this regulation leads to a situation whereby foreigners from the same country or the same region are placed in the same cells if the rules requiring the separation of

[11] Data in this section were provided by the Department of Detention Affairs of the NHPS.
[12] Art. 11, Act V of 1972 on the Prosecutors of Hungarian Republic ("Prosecutors Act")
[13] Art. 12, Prosecutors Act
[14] Art. 18, Act LIX of 1993 on the Ombudsman

detainees do not prevent this (e.g. women shall be separated from men, and accomplices from each other in terms of the pertaining legal provisions). Consequently, so called "foreigners' cells" are established in practice. Within the organizational structure of the NHPS there is no special department responsible for foreigners. One reason for this might be that the proportion of foreign detainees in the whole prison population is less than 4%. This might also offer an explanation as to why prison staff does not receive any kind of special training on how to deal with foreigners special problems.

In the experience of the HHC's civilian monitors, the members of the penitentiary personnel usually do not mention problems specially related to foreign detainees, and monitors do not receive significantly more or substantively different complaints from foreign detainees either.[15] The issue of the detention of foreigners is not regarded as one of the central problems within the penitentiary administration. Another reason for the lack of a special unit responsible for foreign prisoners could be that according to the Hungarian legal regulation,[16] foreign detainees can have unrestricted access to the consular authorities of their respective countries. This means that they could in theory receive all the necessary help they need during detention from their country of origin. However, if their own consulate does no provide them with the necessary – or any – help (which does happen in practice) they might face serious problems as shall be seen below.

1.3 Overview involvement Consulates, Embassies, Ministries home country, Probation service home country, NGO's etc

The Penitentiary Regulation[17] prescribes that "foreign prisoners may keep contact with the embassy or consulate of their country of origin in accordance with the rules laid down in the international convention on consular contacts and in international agreements signed by the concerned countries." The penitentiary institution has an obligation to immediately notify the competent embassy or consulate upon the admission of a foreign inmate. The institution may only refrain from this if the inmate requests so in writing.[18] If the foreigner requests that a member of the consulate' personnel visit him/her, or send him/her a parcel or money, this request shall be forwarded to the consulate immediately. The number of visits with or packages sent by the consulate cannot be restricted,[19] whereas with regard to Hungarian nationals there are restrictions in this regard (usually one visit and one parcel per month is allowed). In practice, the actual involvement of consulates in providing detainees with assistance depends on their financial resources and other possibilities. The monitors of the HHC met on a number of occasions with foreigners in police jails or prisons who complained that their respective consulates were not actively supporting them. It also happened occasionally that the HHC turned to a consulate asking for some kind of help but received no reply at all. There are of course positive examples as well. Certain embassies have direct, well-established contacts with the penitentiary institutions where their own citizens are detained. This means that they

15 See: IHF Report 2006 on Hungary, Events of 2005 in: *Human Rights of the OSCE Region, International Helsinki Federation for Human Rights* (to be published).
16 Art. 226 of the Penitentiary Regulation.
17 Art. 226, Penitentiary Regulation.
18 Art. 222, Penitentiary Regulation.
19 Art. 226, Penitentiary Regulation

visit them regularly, send them money, parcels and occasionally pay for their lawyers as well.

1.4 Overview of trends[20]

1.4.1 Sentencing Trends

On the basis of the data provided below the overall trends in sentencing can be described as follows. As it can be seen from Table 3, the number of final decisions (i.e. decisions against which no ordinary appeal is possible) ordering imprisonment has been slightly increasing in the past ten years. In the past few years this number has been around 32,000. In about 65% of the cases, the execution of the sentence is suspended. In case of almost all the sentences ordering less six months imprisonment the execution of the punishment will be suspended. There are no official data relating to short term sentences within the meaning of the project's conceptual framework. In Hungary, sentences of less than five years' imprisonment are regarded as short sentences. Most of the offences for which imprisonment is imposed are crimes against property (55%-60%), among which theft is the most frequent (50-66%). The following can be said concerning the social background of the persons sentenced to non-suspended imprisonment. The proportion of recidivists has constantly been around 80% in the past ten years. 95% of perpetrators sentenced to non-suspended imprisonment are adults. Approximately 80% have finished only the primary school, while less than 2% have university or college diplomas.

1.4.2 Characteristics Foreign Prison Population

Concerning the sentences of foreigners, from the comparison of Table 1 and Table 2 it can be established that in the past ten years the number of convicted foreigners has increased with 75%, while the number of non-suspended imprisonment sentences imposed on foreigners has not increased at all. The typical offences committed by foreigners are human trafficking, abuse of drugs and fraud.[21] Around 90% of foreigner convicts are male. Most of the foreign convicts sentenced to imprisonment come from Europe (90%). There are no official data collection with a view to the social background of foreigners.

20 Data in this section were provided by the Department of Informatics and Computer Application of the Chief Public Prosecutor's Office.

21 Data provided by the NHPS.

Table 1 Data concerning convicted foreigners

Year	*Number of convicted foreigners*	*Male*	*%*	*Female*	*%*
1996	2 192	2 000	91,2	192	8,8
1997	2 358	2 130	90,3	228	9,7
1998	2 772	2 477	89,4	295	10,6
1999	2 790	2 482	89,0	308	11,0
2000	2 967	2 611	88,0	356	12,0
2001	3 283	2 835	86,4	448	13,6
2002	3 261	2 878	88,3	383	11,7
2003	3 091	2 617	84,7	474	15,3
2004	3 515	3 071	87,4	444	12,6

Source: Department of Informatics and Computer Application of the Chief Public Prosecutor's Office.

Table 2 Number of foreigners sentenced to imprisonment

		out of which Eurpoean	
Year	*Number of foreigners sentenced to imprisonment*	*number*	*%*
1996	296	282	95,3
1997	546	497	91,0
1998	451	419	92,9
1999	485	437	90,1
2000	421	381	90,5
2001	418	376	90,0
2002	402	370	92,0
2003	336	296	88,1
2004	301	268	89,0

Source: Department of Informatics and Computer Application of the Chief Public Prosecutor's Office.

Table 3

Number of defendants sentenced to imprisonment		*out of which*				*out of not-suspended*			
		not-suspended		*suspended*					
Year		= n	%	= n	%	*6 month-3 years*	*3-15 years*	*15-20 years*	*Life sentence*
1996	25 180	9 976	39.6	15 204	60.4	5 673	1 062	5	21
1997	27 592	10 837	39.3	16 755	60.7	6 177	1 223	4	16
1998	30 939	11 710	37.8	19 229	62.2	6 559	1 264	2	9
1999	31 720	12 058	38.0	19 662	62.0	6 978	1 286	5	12
2000	32 373	12 203	37.7	20 170	62.3	7 572	1 498	3	13
2001	32 370	12 600	38.9	19 770	61.1	8 299	1 674	5	9
2002	32 444	12 262	37.8	20 182	62.2	7 711	1 594	6	10
2003	31 626	11 767	37.2	19 859	62.8	7 751	1 669	13	22
2004	30 839	10 608	34.4	20 231	65.6	6 948	1 480	9	22

Source: Department of Informatics and Computer Application of the Chief Public Prosecutor's Office.

1.5 Overview of national legislation

1.5.1 Penitentiary Legislation

The following list contains the most important statutes related to detention with their names as used in this study.

- Act IV of 1978 on the Penal Code – Penal Code
- Act XXXIV of 1994 on the Police – Police Act
- Act CVII of 1995 on the Penitentiary System – Penitentiary Act
- Act XLIII of 1996 on the Service Relationship of the Professional Members of Armed Organ – Armed Organs Act
- Act CXXXIX of 1997 on Asylum – Asylum Act
- Act CLIV of 1997 on Health Care – Health Care Act
- Act XIX of 1998 on the Criminal Procedure – CCP
- Act XXXIX of 2001 on the Entry and Stay of Foreigners – Alien Policing Act
- Decree 19/1995 (XII. 13.) of the Minister of Interior on the Order of Police Jails – Police Jail Regulation
- Decree 6/1996 (III. 6.) of the Minister of Justice on the Implementation of the Rules of
- Imprisonment and Pre-trial Detention – Penitentiary Regulation
- Decree 11/1996 of the Minister of Justice (X. 15.) on the Disciplinary Responsibility of Detainees in Penitentiary Institutions – Disciplinary Decree
- Decree 30/1997 (X. 11.) of the Ministry of Social Welfare – Juvenile Reformatory Regulation
- Decree 5/1998 (VII. 12.) of the Minister of Justice on Health Care Provision for Inmates – Penitentiary Medical Regulation

- Joint Decree 27/2001 of the Minister of Interior and the Minister of Justice (XI. 29.) on the Implementation of Detention Ordered in the Alien Policing Procedure – Alien Policing Detention Decree
- Government Decree 170/2001 (IX. 26.) on the Implementation of the Alien Policing Act (Alien Policing Decree)
- Decree 17/2003 of the Minister of Justice (VI. 24.) on the Activities of the Probation Service (Probation Service Decree)
- Decree 36/2003 of the Minister of Justice (X. 3.) on the Implementation of Forensic Compulsory Treatment, Temporary Forensic Compulsory Treatment and the Tasks and Operation of the Forensic Observation and Psychiatric Institution – IMEI Regulation
- Law Decree 11 of 1979 on the Implementation of Sanctions and Measures – Penitentiary Code.

1.5.2 Penitentiary Legislation & Foreigners

Apart from the statutes pertaining to the alien policing procedure and the different forms of detention related thereto, only the Penitentiary Regulation contains provisions specific to the detention of foreigners. These rules will be discussed below. The reason for the lack of special regulation in the statutes is that with regard to most aspects of detention foreign detainees are not perceived to be different from Hungarian ones: the rights and obligations of foreign detainees are more or less the same as those of Hungarian nationals, while their special needs are acknowledged only to a restricted extent. Foreigners may be subject to any kind of sanction set out in Hungarian laws, while there is one type of sanction that may be applied only in relation to foreigners, namely expulsion. There is however, one particular type of detention that is applied significantly more frequently against foreigners than against nationals, and that is pre-trial detention. The reason for this is that in the case of a foreign suspect or defendant who does not have a permanent – or even temporary – address registered in Hungary, the court tends to accept that there are well-founded grounds to presume that his/her presence throughout the procedure may not be secured in any other way, mostly because the court would not know where to send the summoning orders for the different procedural acts.

2 TREATMENT OF FOREIGN PRISONERS

2.1 General

There are no significant differences in the treatment of foreigners compared to national prisoners. The most important factor that can lead to the social exclusion of foreigners in a penitentiary institution is the lack of knowledge of the Hungarian language. Experience shows that in most cases "newcomers" can survive with the help of detainees who speak their language and have been detained long enough to obtain a relatively good command of Hungarian. However, language can be a really serious barrier for those pre-trial detainees who are detained in places of detention run by the police, where not so many people are held at the same time. In these cases it is highly unlikely that any other detainee in the same facility speaks a language the foreigner understands. All the problems that foreigners have to face in a penitentiary institution are in a certain way connected to the linguistic barriers. The rights and obligations of national and foreign prisoners are basically the same but in practice there are certain differences as to how they can exercise their – formally equal – rights. Therefore the most important rules applying to the detention of all prisoners will be described and the actual differences if any will be pointed out.

2.2 Living conditions and facilities

The number of people to be placed in a cell shall be defined in a way that each inmate have six cubic meters of air space and – in the case of adult male inmates – three square meters of moving space. Minors and women shall be provided with three-and-a-half square meters of moving space. When calculating the moving space, the space covered by equipment and furniture shall not be taken into account.[22] (The required moving space is four square-meters, the required air space is ten cubic meters for pre-trial detainees.)[23] In the cell there must be a washbasin with running water and a separated toilet with proper ventilation. The prison governor regulates when and how cell doors are to be kept open. In the course of detention, the following categories shall be separated from each other: a) women from men; b) pre-trial detainees form convicts; c) accomplices form each other based on the decision of the prosecutor or the court (depending on the phase of the procedure); d) healthy inmates from ill inmates, those suffering from infectious diseases from those with non-infectious diseases, HIV-positives from all other detainees; e) adults from juveniles; f) smokers from non-smokers.[24]

2.3 Reception and admission

There are certain important differences concerning the reception procedure if the detainee is a foreigner. As it was outlined above, the penitentiary institution has an obligation to immediately notify the competent embassy or consulate upon the admission of a foreign inmate. The institution may only refrain from this if the inmate requests so in writing.[25]

Foreigners have a legally prescribed right to receive upon arrival information on the internal rules of the penitentiary institution in a language they can understand. There are information leaflets prepared by NGO's and the NHPS for that purpose. If there are no leaflets translated into a language the foreigner understands, an interpreter shall explain the rules pertaining to detention and the foreigner signs a declaration that he/she has been informed about his/her rights and obligation.[26] Despite the legal provisions, practice shows that written information in foreign languages can rarely be found in

22 Art. 137, Penitentiary Regulation.
23 Art. 239, Penitentiary Regulation.
24 Art. 39, Penitentiary Regulation.
25 Art. 222, Penitentiary Regulation.
26 Art. 2 and 24, Penitentiary Regulation.

Hungarian places of detention.[27] The foreigner shall also be informed if an international treaty makes it possible that the execution of his/her imprisonment be transferred.[28]

In its report upon its 2005 visit, the European Committee for the Prevention of Torture and Inhuman or Degrading Treatment or Punishment (CPT), also noted this problem.[29] The report declares that that "at most police establishments visited, the delegation did note the presence of the [...] information sheets; however, they were not always available in foreign languages. [...] The CPT welcomes the Hungarian authorities' efforts to improve the provision of written information to persons in police custody. The Committee invites the Hungarian authorities to take further steps to ensure that the information sheet is available in all police establishments in an appropriate range of languages and is systematically given to detained persons."[30] With regard to the general rules, in the beginning of the criminal procedure, the detaining authority (usually the police) has to inform a family member or another person selected by the suspect about his/her whereabouts, therefore the penitentiary is not obliged to notify anyone about the admission. But the detainee is entitled to call his/her family. Due to the absence of general provisions on telephone contacts, the rules of telephoning are specified in the internal rules (house rules) of each penitentiary institution. If a detainee has no money, he/she cannot cover the cost of the call. Hence, it can easily happen that notwithstanding the right to make a phone call the detainee cannot use the phone.

2.4 Work - Education – Training – Sports - Recreation

One of the most sensitive issues concerning the social exclusion of foreigners in detention is their participation in work and education. In theory all the prisoners have the right to request to be given paid work unless there are reasons (e.g. illness, medical examination, other serious reasons) preventing it.[31] (Taking part in basic maintenance tasks, such as cleaning the prison is not considered to be work in this sense, thus one is not entitled to payment for it).[32] Working is one of the most important – if not the most important – activities during detention. The salary detainees receive for work performed in detention enables them to buy essential supplies[33] and save some money for the time of the release, which may have a crucial importance in the case of foreigners, who usually have to cope with the situation without the support of relatives. Furthermore, working is also of key significance from the point of view of mitigating the detrimental psychological effects of detention. Finally, when deciding upon conditional release courts always take into consideration as a relevant factor whether the detainee has been working or not. In spite

27 See for example the mission report of the International Helsinki Federation for Human Rights (IHF) on the IHF's visit to Hungary: http://www.ihf-hr.org/documents/doc_summary.php?sec_id=3&d_id=4218

28 Art. 222, Penitentiary Regulation.

29 Report to the Hungarian Government on the visit to Hungary carried out by the European Committee for the Prevention of Torture and Inhuman or Degrading Treatment or Punishment (CPT) from 30 March to 8 April 2005 hereinafter: 2005 CPT Report), see at: http://www.cpt.coe.int/documents/hun/2006-20-inf-eng.htm

30 2005 CPT Report, point 25.

31 Art. 36, Penitentiary Code.

32 Art. 102, Penitentiary Regulation.

33 The most essential hygienic articles are provided by the penitentiary administration in terms of the law.

of what is set forth above, our experience is that most of the foreigners are not provided with work in prisons due to the very simple reason that they do not speak Hungarian. Obviously, there are certain kinds of work where speaking Hungarian is not essential, but when prison administration can offer work for only part of the detainees it is natural that those who are the most likely to do their job with the least problems will be selected for such positions.. (The rate of employment among convicted detainees has constantly been around 60 percent.)[34] Another aspect of the issue is that prison work is often preceded by a training period, and the persons providing training only speak Hungarian. Finally, as a result of the general lack of workplaces, many of the foreigners do not have the opportunity to work, consequently they do not earn a salary, cannot access additional articles besides the food and hygienic supplies provided by the penitentiary (unless such articles are sent to them in parcels by relatives or the consulate), and they have less chance to be conditionally released.

Penitentiary institutes provide elementary level education, and – upon a request by the detainee – can also permit participation in secondary and college education, or vocational training. As a rule, the prison service will bear the costs related to participation in elementary education or vocational training.[35] There is no information about education or vocational trainings organized in foreign languages. Therefore many of the foreigners are not in the position to take part in educational activities offered by the prison administration.

Detainees – and therefore foreigners as well - are entitled to do some sports activities. They may use all the facilities provided for this purpose (table tennis, body building room, football etc.) in line with the internal rules. Foreigners are also entitled to recreational activities, e.g. they can use the library. However, in some penitentiaries there are no books in foreign languages. In certain institutions there are not enough Hungarian books either, while in most police jails there are not any books at all. For pre-trial detainees the law does not guarantee the right to participate in education at all.

2.5 Food – Religion – Personal hygiene – Medical care

In theory, foreign prisoners are entitled to practice their religion. The law declares the right to choose, express and practice their religion.[36] This includes the right to take part in communal gatherings (this right is revoked when a person is under solitary confinement, security isolation and detention in special security cell), keeping contact with the cleric without supervision, buying and keeping religious books and items, opining regarding his/her child's religious education, being informed about religious events.[37]

Rights related to religion may be practiced as set forth in the house rules. It is also prescribed that the practice of religious rights may not breach the order and security of the institution (e.g. accomplices must be separated even if they wanted to pray together). It is the duty of the penitentiary to provide adequate place for practicing religion but it is the church that has to provide the sacral necessities. In practice this means that in some

---

34 See: Double Standard: Prison Conditions in Hungary. Hungarian Helsinki Committee, Budapest, 2002. p. 143.

35 Art. 73-74, Penitentiary Regulation.

36 Art. 36 and 118, Penitentiary Code.

37 Art. 93-99, Penitentiary Regulation.

of the institutions there are rooms appointed for this purpose but due to lack of financial resources there are not enough rooms for all the religions. In certain prisons there is a catholic chapel as well.

There is a difference between the situation of adherents of the four so-called historical denominations and of followers of other religions. The penitentiary system has institutionalized relations with the Catholic, the Lutheran, the Calvinist and the Jewish denominations (based on Decree 13/2000 of the Minister of Justice). Priests and pastors of these religions visit penitentiaries on a regular basis. If an inmate needs another religious representative, then he/she needs to submit a request, and the representative's visit has to be permitted by the penitentiary's warden. The above Decree however claims that based on the needs of the inmates, all registered churches (their number in Hungary is over one hundred) may perform religious activities in the prisons. Muslim detainees claim to sometimes face problems in this respect. The HHC has received complaints that in certain cases the imam was not permitted to enter the penitentiary but this does not appear to be a general problem.

Concerning food and accommodating special religious/dietary needs or requirements the same can be stated as concerning practicing religion. The Penitentiary Regulation provides that the dietary needs based on religious belief shall be taken into consideration. However the Regulation provides at the same time that the existence of this obligation depends upon the possibilities of the given institution.[38] Therefore if in a certain institution there are very few foreign detainees with special dietary needs and it would be too expensive to provide them with proper food then the institution concerned is not obliged to do that. According HHC's experience, in the vast majority of the cases such dietary needs are accommodated, but HHC has heard about shortcomings in this respect as well.

The law does not allow deviation from the general dress code, therefore religious dress requirements cannot be met. Remand prisoners are entitled to wear their own clothes, which in theory should mean that at least in this case religious clothing is allowed, but there is no information about practice in this regard and related complaints have not been heard either. The same goes for personal hygiene requirements, so it is up to the warden's "goodwill" to ensure such possibility within the frame of the house rules.

2.6 Consular and legal help

As a general rule, contacts are regulated in accordance with the International Convention on Consular Relations, and bi-lateral treaties. A foreigner in pre-trial detention has the right to keep contact with the representative of his/her diplomatic mission in writing or verbally (by phone or visits) without restriction and supervision.[39] With regard to convicted inmates, only written correspondence is expressly exempted from supervision. [40] Upon admission to an institution, the respective mission is to be noticed, unless the detainee explicitly asks to refrain from this (in writing). [41] The assistance that may be provided by consular authorities includes: personal visits, sending parcels (the frequency

38 Art.147, Penitentiary Regulation.
39 Art. 244, Penitentiary Regulation.
40 Art. 225, Penitentiary Regulation.
41 Art. 22, Penitentiary Regulation.

is not limited, visits may occur out of the timeframe set out by the house rules, based on prior agreement) or sending money, taking over the costs (duty, postal, other) of receiving packages from abroad, requesting a report on the situation of the detainee. (The detainee's requests to the mission for visits, packages and money are to be forwarded without delay.)[42] No proper information is available to judge whether the assistance provided is adequate or not, but it may be pointed out that it is also up to the given consulate's willingness to be active in this respect, and some countries' missions seem to neglect these tasks.

Defendants whose mother tongue is not Hungarian or do not speak the language of the procedure (which of course includes foreigners in pre-trial detention) are entitled to receive legal assistance from an ex officio appointed lawyer. There are general problems with the work of appointed lawyers (no substantive legal help, failure to keep contact with the client),[43] which is frequently aggravated by the fact that the given appointed lawyer does not speak the language of the client. While interpretation is provided by the authorities during procedural acts (such as interrogations), and on these occasions the authorities usually leave some time for the counsel and the defendant to communicate with the help of the interpreter, consultation with the detained foreigner between procedural acts (e.g. before a court hearing) is impossible for most ex officio counsels, as the fee of the interpreter (which is by the way usually significantly higher than the fee for the ex officio appointed lawyer) should be advanced by the lawyer and can only be reclaimed later in the procedure. If the detainee cannot retain a lawyer of his/her own it is very likely that he/she cannot afford to pay for the interpreter, and it cannot be expected form the lawyer to advance the interpreter's fee either. For all these reasons in most cases the indigent foreigner detainees do not have the possibility to consult their lawyer.

2.7 Contact with the outside world

Basically the general provisions apply for convicted prisoners and pre-trial detainees as well. (For pre-trial detainees, any form of contact with any person – apart from the lawyer or an employee of the consulate – requires prior authorization by the prosecutor or – in the trial stage – the court.) Written correspondence is not limited, for foreigners one letter per month may be sent to a relative at the cost of the institution, provided that the foreigner lacks the necessary financial means (otherwise it is borne by the detainee).[44] At least one occasion per month must be provided for visits, the minimal length is 30 minutes, two adults and two minors may be present at a time.[45] Further details are stipulated in the house rules, so the institution may decide at its own discretion about the scheduling. The internal rules of penitentiaries usually provide that in case of a visitor coming form abroad the time allowed for the visit is two hours. A phone may be used in accordance with the house rules (no minimum or maximum length or frequency is prescribed by the law), at the detainee's cost.[46]

---

42 Art.226, Penitentiary Regulation.

43 See: András Kádár: *Presumption of Guilt*, Hugarian Helsinki Committee, Budapest 2004 pp. 21-39.

44 Art. 225, Penitentiary Regulation.

45 Art. 89, Penitentiary Regulation.

46 Art. 92, Penitentiary Regulation.

Institutions are rarely in the position to keep newspapers available at all, so there is no chance for foreign-language newspapers, but it is possible to receive them in packages. Usually there are different channels on television, but there is no information if foreign-language channels are available or not. Other visitors allowed: representatives of monitoring bodies of international organizations, churches, clerics, civil organizations. (Prison cleric missions, churches, civil organizations and foundations may conclude cooperation agreements with one or more institutions, in order to perform various tasks.)

2.8 Re-integration activities - Prison leave

In this respect the general provisions apply to foreigners. Detainees (sentenced to maximum- or medium-security imprisonment) may be placed into a so-called 'transitory group' within the institution two years prior to release (after a minimum of five years served in prison), where some restraints are relaxed: e.g. leave may be permitted for not more than 24 hours, or – as a reward – for not more than 15 days, but this institution is far from being called semi-freedom. [47] From six months prior to release, it is possible to ask for information, or a personal hearing from the probation officer regarding re-integration (employment, housing, education, social welfare, family issues, etc.), and the probation officer can provide assistance in these issues. [48] As a general rule, leaves are provided (and seen) as rewards. Short-term leave may be granted for a maximum of five, ten or fifteen days per year in the maximum-, medium-, and low-security regimes respectively. Short-term leave (for 24 hours) may also be granted as a reward.[49] The provisions for conditional release are as follows. The earliest date is set out by the Penal Code[50] (depending on the crime committed, and the severity of the regime to which the individual is sentenced to), unless the criminal court excludes the possibility of such a measure in its verdict (based on certain legal criteria). Upon the earliest date, the penitentiary judge decides on the conditional release, on the basis of the penitentiary institutions opinion.

2.9 Release – Expulsion

Special procedures depend on whether the detainee will be expelled from the country or not. If expelled by the criminal court after his/her releasethe foreigner is transferred to the alien policing authority which executes the expulsion. In the vast majority of cases foreigners convicted by the criminal court will be expelled. The criminal court may impose expulsion as an additional penalty to imprisonment. (The alien policing authority also has a right to order expulsion for a number of reasons, for instance if a foreigner breaches the provisions of immigration law.)[51] The expulsion may be ordered with terminal effect (in case of certain serious criminal acts, such as trafficking in person, or kidnapping), or for a definite period between one and ten years (the time of the prison sentence is not taken into account when these years are calculated). No recognized refugee may be expelled, while immigrated foreigners may only be expelled if a sentence

---

47 Art. 29, Penitentential Code.

48 Art. 196, Penitentiary Regulation.

49 Art. 41 and 41/A, Penitentiary Code.

50 Art. 47, Criminal Code.

51 Art. 61, Criminal Code.

of more than five years may be imposed through the Penal Code, while in case of minors, foreigners having a family, or having a legal status in Hungary this penalty may only be imposed, if the sentence is imprisonment of ten years or more.[52] The alien policing authority reviews if the principle of non-refoulement should be applied (the detainee may request review by the penitentiary judge during the imprisonment as well). Otherwise, the expulsion order can be challenged in the original criminal procedure only. In case of terminal expulsion, exemption may be requested from the criminal court after ten years. The regulation on expulsion has just recently been amended to the form described above, therefore, its overall assessment is not possible yet.

2.10 Aftercare – Probation

In terms of the Penitentiary Code, the penitentiary institution is obliged to get information about where the prisoner wishes to settle after his/her release, and tries to assist him/her in arranging issues related to accommodation and work after release. In doing so, the penitentiary institution may approach the competent probation officer. The probation officer may visit the detainee in the penitentiary institution, may advise him/her and may attempt to assist the detainee in finding a job and/or accommodation. If necessary the probation officer shall assist the prisoner in re-establishing family contacts.[53] In terms of the Probation Service Decree, the probation officer shall also provide these services if a former prisoner requests so after his/her release. There are no specific provisions pertaining to the aftercare of foreigners: the regulation makes no difference between nationals and foreigners in this regard, so – theoretically – these services should be available for foreign prisoners as well. However, according to information provided by the Probation Service of the Justice Office (operating under the Ministry of Justice), foreigners are very rare among the clients of the service.

2.11 Staff

There is no special training for staff on dealing with foreign prisoners. The prison service is trying to solve language barriers by placing together with foreign prisoners detainees who speak both Hungarian and the language spoken by the particular foreigner.

2.12 Projects

There is no information on specific projects concerning foreign prisoners.

3 ADMINISTRATIVE DETENTION OF FOREIGN PRISONERS

3.1 Institutions

Alien policing jails are the institutions most frequently used for the execution of administrative detention. In those cases when the criminal court ordered the

52 Art. 61 (2) – (7), Criminal Code.
53 Art. 114/A, Penitentiary Code.

imprisonment and the expulsion of the foreigner he/she might temporarily be placed in a penitentiary after the person concerned served his/her sentence.. The number of such placements is extremely low; there were six foreigners placed in penitentiary while in alien policing custody in April 2006.

3.2 Responsible Ministry and legislation

Alien policing jails are under the scope of the Ministry of Interior (and are directly managed by the Border Guards). The main law regulating the forms of administrative detention is the Alien Policing Act, while the implementation of detention is regulated by Alien Policing Detention Decree. The rules were modeled after the rules pertaining to police jails. Article 1 (2) of the Alien Policing Act provides that in alien policing cases, the following authorities are entitled to take measures:
- the Office for Immigration and Nationality (OIN)
- the regional office of the OIN
- the Alien Policing Authority of the Border Guards
- Ministry of Foreign Affairs and Consulates authorized to issue visas

3.3 Capacity of institutions

Altogether there are eight alien policing jails in Hungary. Their official capacities are the following:

Györ	50
Nagykanizsa	56
Kiskunhalas	90
Orosháza	25
Nyírbátor	169
Balassagyarmat	10
Budapest	20
Szombathely	220

3.4 Length of stay

The Alien Policing Act provides a variety of long-duration detention measures aimed at foreigners intercepted by the Border Guards, police or Alien Policing Authority in illegal crossing of borders or illegal stay. These are the following:
a) detention for refusal[54]: in order to implement the readmission agreements;
b) alien policing detention[55];
c) detention in preparation for expulsion[56]: applicable during an alien policing procedure aiming at the identification of the foreigner or the clarification of his/her legal residence.

54 Art. 47, Alien Policing Act.
55 Art. 46, Alien Policing Act.
56 Art. 48, Alien Policing Act.

Type a) may be ordered by the Border Guards, while type b) and c) are ordered by the OIN. The administrative authorities may order the detention for five days. The court is entitled to extend the detention type a) and c) for up to 30 days, and type b) for up to 12 months. The different forms of the detention must be summed up, but their total length may not exceed 12 months. Data regarding the average length of stay in such forms of detention was not available.

3.5 Decisions procedure

Detention for refusal can be ordered by the Border Guard. Alien policing detention and detention in preparation for expulsion are ordered by the OIN. Alien policing detention can be ordered only after the OIN decides on the expulsion of the foreigner. During the procedure, the foreigner must be heard by a judge and an interpreter must be provided by the authorities.

The general procedure can be summarized as follows: Article 36 (1) of the Alien Policing Act provides that the alien policing agency of the Border Guard may refuse the entry of the foreigner who crossed or attempted to cross the state border illegally if he/she has been arrested within 30 days from crossing the border and if because of the illegal crossing a readmission agreement is applicable (measure of refusal). Furthermore, Article 47 (1) of the Alien Policing Act makes it possible to place the foreigner in detention whose 'refusal' can be implemented within 30 days from the date of the arrest in order to ensure the implementation of the refusal measure (detention for refusal).

Therefore, in the case of intercepted foreigners, an alien policing procedure is initiated in order to refuse their entry, their 'detention for refusal' is ordered and they are transferred to detention facilities operated by the Border Guard. Alien policing expulsion may be ordered against the foreigner who has violated or attempted to violate the rules of entry and exit (Article 32 (2), Alien Policing Act). However, Article 40 (1) of the Act provides that prior to passing the decision ordering alien policing expulsion, it shall be examined whether the principle of non-refoulement applies[57]. Moreover, Article 39 (2) of the Alien Policing Act excludes the expulsion of unaccompanied minors if the unification with his/her family or appropriate state/other institutional care is not guaranteed for him/her in the state of origin or another admitting state. In practice, if 30 days 'detention for refusal' have elapsed and expulsion was not executed, the Alien Policing Department of the OIN can take a decision on expulsion which then provides the legal basis for further confinement of the foreigner. This type of detention is practically identical with the detention for refusal and is generally implemented in the same detention facility, in the very same cell. Detention pending expulsion is only prohibited by law in the case of unaccompanied minors while asylum seekers with special needs can be detained.

The lengthy detention of asylum seeker asylum seekers in alien policing jails is a particular problem. The question whether an asylum seeker asylum seeker who enters the country (formally) illegally will be detained for a year in an alien policing jail or he/she will be placed in an open reception centre (operated by the OIN) depends on accidental circumstances and on arbitrary decisions of the authorities. If the asylum seeker asylum seeker manages to file an asylum application with the OIN before he/she is caught by the Border Guards, he/she will become an officially recognized asylum seeker who has the

57 Art. 43, Alien Policing Act.

right to legally reside in Hungary until his/her application is adjudicated. If however the asylum seeker (who arrived to Hungary "illegally") is apprehended by the Border Guards before that happens, an alien policing procedure will be initiated against him/her before he/she could possibly submit the asylum application. He/she will be expelled from the country, and although the execution of the expulsion will be suspended as soon as he/she submits an asylum application, the pending expulsion will serve as the basis of the alien policing detention.

Another particular problem to be pointed out is the lack of medical care of foreigners detained in alien police jails. Article 78 (1) of the Alien Policing Decree provides that foreigners placed in an alien police jail are entitled to all necessary medical care free of charge if needed. In practice, in case of medical problems which cannot be dealt with in the jail, they are transferred to a local hospital and are permanently guarded by border guard officers. This places an undue burden on the Border Guard as they have to employ four or five officers to guard a single foreigner and also on the hospital that does not wish to see officers with guns in their wards. In case of mental problems, the patients will be returned after some days of medication to the alien police jail where they usually refuse to take the prescribed medicine and are not under the supervision of a trained psychiatrist; consequently, their mental state deteriorates. As a result foreigners held in alien police jails who did not commit any crime are in this respect in a worse situation than convicted detainees.

In its 2005 report, the CPT pointed out two further problems. The delegation called attention to the fact "that access to a lawyer was not provided in the early stages of deprivation of liberty, i.e. before foreign nationals were transferred to a Border Guard holding facility", and recommended "that the Hungarian authorities take measures to ensure that immigration detainees have an effective right of access to a lawyer/legal representative from the very outset of their deprivation of liberty (i.e. from the moment when the persons concerned are obliged to remain with a law enforcement agency)".[58]

The delegation also noted "that foreign detainees were not systematically provided with written information about their rights in a language they understood, in particular at Border Guard stations at points of entry", and recommended "that steps be taken to ensure that foreign nationals detained under the aliens' legislation and asylum seekers are systematically issued at the very outset of their deprivation of liberty with a form setting out in a straightforward manner their rights and the procedure applicable to them; the form should be available in an appropriate range of languages".[59]

3.6 Appeal

It is not allowed to lodge an administrative appeal against the decision imposing detention.[60] However, it is possible to file an application to the court within five days to review the lawfulness of the imposition of the detention order pending expulsion.

Built-in review exists with regard to detention for refusal and detention in preparation of expulsion. The rules are as follows. The detention may be ordered by alien policing

58 2005 CPT Report, point 28.

59 Ibid.

60 Art. 49 (1), Alien Policing Act.

authorities for five days. After five days, the local court may extend the detention until the individual leaves the country.[61] In most cases an extension is given for 30 days.

After six months, the judicial review is shifted from local courts to county courts. The maximum duration of detention is 12 months[62]. Furthermore, Article 53 (1) of the Alien Policing Act provides that the combined period of the alien policing detention, detention for refusal and detention in preparation for expulsion applied against the foreigner shall not exceed 12 months. Detention shall be terminated immediately when the reason for ordering it has ceased. In principle, the court shall consider the legality of the detention. Detention is frequently prolonged to the maximum duration of 12 months. Some courts do not review adequately the lawfulness of the expulsion or whether it is enforceable, while others conduct a thorough assessment.

3.7 Irregular stay

Illegal/irregular stay 'eo ipso' does not constitute a crime. Article 22 (1) of the Government Decree 218/1999. (XII. 28) on Petty Offences provides that those who enter Hungary illegally may be fined for up to HUF 100,000. Article 22 (2) provides that those who break the law regulating travel documents may be fined for up to HUF 50,000. The Penal Code provides that those foreigners who have been expelled from the country or are banned from entering and staying in the country, but nevertheless stay or enter without a permission, do commit a crime and may be punished with up to one-year imprisonment. In practice the typical sentence is suspended imprisonment and expulsion but pending procedure foreigners are frequently taken into pre-trial detention.

3.8 Numbers

Data on numbers of detained irregular foreigners was not available.

3.9 Expulsion

Data on the percentage that will be expelled after administrative detention was not available.

3.10 Not-expelled prisoners

Article 56 (1) b) of the Alien Policing Act provides that – when the maximum period of detention (12 months) has expired but the reason of ordering the detention still exists and when the expulsion or readmission may not be ordered due to an obligation incumbent upon Hungary on the basis of international treaty – the regional alien policing authority may order the foreigner to stay in a designated place, restricting personal freedom. The mandatory place of stay may be designated in a community shelter when the foreigner is unable to support himself/herself, i.e., does not have appropriate accommodation and financial income. It can also be the private estate of a person who had invited him/her under the obligation to support him/her. The operative part of the resolution shall

---

61 Art. 47(4) and Article 48(3), Alien Policing Act.

62 Art. 46, Alien Policing Act.

determine the place of mandatory stay. The costs incurred in relation to staying at a community shelter are borne by the foreigner. If 18 months have passed since ordering mandatory stay at a community shelter but the circumstances due to which it has been ordered continue existing for reasons beyond the control of the foreigner, another place of stay is designated for the foreigner. In certain cases the authorities, upon the request of the foreigner, permit him/her to continue staying at the community shelter for humanitarian reasons.

3.11 Detention irregulars under criminal law

According to Article 54 (2) of the Alien Policing Act, in the course of implementing detention in a penitentiary institution, the detained foreigner shall be separated from those who are in custody, or in preliminary arrest as well from convicts. In practice, foreigners are placed only in alien policing jails. Only those foreigners are accommodated in the Nagyfa Penitentiary Institution who have committed a crime and the court ordered their expulsion. In this institution expelled foreigners are placed separately from Hungarian citizens.

3.12 Minors

Minors shall not be put in detention. Article 52 of the Alien Policing Decree provides that in alien policing procedures, the alien policing authority examines whether the application of rules determined by the Act and the decree pertaining to unaccompanied minors apply to the minor foreigner staying unlawfully in the country. In the course of this examination, it is examined whether the foreigner is a minor and if yes, whether there is any person obliged by virtue of legal rule to be guardian of the foreign minor. If the alien policing authority had ordered detention of the foreigner and it is revealed in the course of the procedure that the rules pertaining to unaccompanied minors are applicable, detention is terminated and a designated place of stay is ordered for the unaccompanied minor.

4 NATIONALS ABROAD[63]

4.1 Numbers and composition group

The Ministry of Foreign Affairs is informed about a couple of hundreds of cases of Hungarian nationals detained abroad per year, including all forms of detention (from short term custody to prison sentences). In 2005, close to 800 Hungarian nationals were incarcreated for shorter or longer periods of time.

---

63 Information in this section was provided by László Takács, Head of Department of Consular Affairs at the Ministry of Foreign Affairs.

4.2 Detention countries

The countries where on average most Hungarian nationals are detained are Austria, Germany and Italy.

4.3 Reasons for detention & sentencing

According to information provided by the Ministry of Foreign Affairs, minor traffic offences and offences related to breaching the rules of staying and working in the particular foreign country constitute the majority of offences for which Hungarian citizens are detained abroad. According to the Ministry's estimation, between 50 and 75 percent of the offences are of this nature. Minor offences against property also constitute a relatively significant portion of the offences committed by Hungarian nationals in foreign countries.

4.4 Involved organisations – tasks and activities

Most tasks related to Hungarian nationals detained abroad (visits, packages, and so on) are performed by the 98 official foreign representations of the Republic of Hungary. In countries where no such representations function (and also in areas which are geographically difficult to access for official Hungarian consular authorities), these tasks are fulfilled by honorary consuls (their number is about 200).

The Ministry of Foreign Affairs also tries to establish contacts with civilian organizations in order to make sure that detained Hungarians do not remain without any contacts. On an occasional basis, the Ministry approaches Hungarian organizations or Hungarian citizens in the particular foreign country, and asks them to pay visits to Hungarian detainees. This is done on a voluntary basis, without any payment.

4.5 Release and reception home country

No institution has been established with the purpose of providing assistance after release and in connection with reception in Hungary.

4.6 Aftercare

No institution has been established with the purpose of providing aftercare for Hungarians previously detaineed abroad.

4.7 Public opinion and media

The issue of Hungarians in foreign prisons is usually not in the focus of public debates and media coverages. One exception was the story of four young Hungarian men, who were imprisoned in Ecuador for acting as drug couriers. The young men were arrested one by one between December 2004 and the April 2005. The public opinion took notice of their stories after an article was published about them and the horrible conditions in South American prisons in August 2005. For a while, the issue was in the center of attention, but after late 2005, the discussions died away.

5 EVALUATION AND RECOMMENDATIONS

On the basis of the above description it can be concluded that the following are the main reasons for the social exclusion of foreign prisoners:

- Most foreigners cannot participate in work activities, education and vocational training. The ultimate reason for that is the existence of language barriers. The solution for this problem is unclear as due to budgetary constraints the government cannot allocate financial sources for this purpose.
- It is not an unconditional obligation of the penitentiary to provide meals that meet the religious requirements of foreign (or national) detainees. The solution could be to impose unconditional obligation upon the penitentiaries to respect the religious requirements in all aspects.
- Foreigners with special dressing requirements due to religious belief are not allowed to wear clothes other than the prison uniform. The solution might be the same as for the previous shortcoming.
- The actual willingness of consulates to help foreign prisoners is not always satisfactory. In case of prisoners coming from those countries the lack of any external support might result in extreme separation from the outside world.
- Indigent foreign detainees frequently do not receive adequate legal assistance as they cannot pay for the interpreter's fee and the government does not advance that cost. The government should advance a lump sum in each case for covering the cost of interpreters.
- The medical treatment of foreigners detained in alien police jails and suffering from long lasting somatic or mental illness cannot be dealt with. A solution to this anomaly could be terminating the alien policing detention in case of a seriously ill detainee and to place him/her, depending on his/her health condition, either in a civilian hospital or in a reception centre for asylum seekers where appropriate medical care is accessible and available.
- The law does not exclude the possibility of placing someone in alien policing detention who has applied for asylum. Detention rules are often arbitrarily applied and detaining asylum seekers is still the rule rather than the exception. This breaches international law and sometimes national law standards. Asylum seekers should not be detained except when they refuse cooperation with the asylum authority or severely violate the order of a reception centre.
- Alien policing detention should not be treated as a form of punishment. It is a measure used to keep people available for the execution of the expulsion (expulsion) order, therefore the rules pertaining to foreigners in such detention should be much less severe than the ones concerning criminal suspects or convicts.
- The maximum duration of alien policing detention should be further reduced to six months.

Chapter 13

Ireland

Mary Moore

1 INTRODUCTION[1]

1.1 Overview of penalties and measures

There are insufficient sentencing statistics available in Ireland to explore if there has been a bias in sentencing at Court towards custody.[2] However the relatively high use of custody, especially outside of Dublin can be seen from Court Services Report.[3] In Dublin, Probation supervision was generally used more frequently than immediate imprisonment, in Limerick immediate imprisonment was more common than Probation Supervision and Community Service combined. A high use of suspended prison sentences and low use of Community service characterized both areas[4]. O'Donnell notes another trend as the decline in the number of admissions[5] to prison[6] under sentence. There were 6866 in 1994, and 5160 in 2001. The Court Service Report[7] shows a fall of 10% in the number of prison sentences imposed by the District Court 2001-2002 while the average daily population of prisoners is now relatively stable

The length of sentences imposed and the time spent in custody on sentence appears to be increasing. The average length of time for a life sentence prisoner to serve prior to consideration for release on license has increased to 13 years between 1996 and 2001 from less than eight years in 1978 to 1980. In 2003 and since the Minister for Justice, Equality and Law Reform has made a number of statements making it clear that prisoners serving life sentences will expect to serve very substantial sentences.[8] The Minister has indicated that temporary release in the community should be considered only after 15 years of a life sentence except in the most extraordinary circumstances.

1.2 Overview of the Prison System

1.2.1 Organizational Structure

The Irish Prison Service is under the aegis of the Department of Justice, Equality and Law Reform. The financial allocation for the Irish Prison Service in 2004 was €305.8 million.[9] The Irish Prison Service comprises fourteen prisons of which eleven are medium

---

1 This report was compiled with assistance from the multi-disciplinary team in Mountjoy Prison, comprising the Governors, Chief Officers, Librarian, Chaplain, Psychologist and Head Teacher; the Chaplaincy Service and the Managers of the Visitors' Centres in Mountjoy and Cloverhill Prisons; the Irish Commission for Prisoners Overseas, particularly Grainne Prior; and the Irish Prison Service. Special thanks to Gerry McNally, APPO and my colleagues in the Probation Service who advised me on various aspects of their work in this area. I am also grateful to Eileen Farrell, PO whose dissertation on working with foreign nationals detained in Irish prisons was an invaluable starting point.

2 O'Donnell, 'Imprisonment and Penal Policy in Ireland', *Howard Journal of Criminal Justice,* 2004, 43 (3), pp. 253-256.

3 Court Services, *Court Services Report*, Dublin 2003, pp. 105 - 108.

4 O'Donnell, ibidem, p. 258.

5 The term 'admission to prison' is used instead of 'committal to prison' throughout this document.

6 O'Donnell, ibidem, p.258.

7 Court Services, *Court Services Report*, Dublin 2003, p.100.

8 Dáil Éireann 25 February 2003, Seanad Éireann, 3 April 2003.

9 Department of Justice, Equality and Law Reform, *Irish Prison Service Annual Report*, 2004, p. 5.

security, with one high security and two open prisons.

The prisons mentioned below are all closed medium security prisons. Portlaoise is a high security prison and Loughan House and Shelton Abbey are open prisons. The information is taken from the Irish Prison Service Annual Report Daily Average Number of Prisoners (2004: 16)

Table 1 Daily Average Number of Prisoners 2004

	Institution	*Average Number in Custody*
Dublin	Arbour Hill Prison	138
	Cloverhill Remand Prison	392
	Dochas Centre Mountjoy	84
	Mountjoy Prison	485
	St Patrick's Institution	198
	Training Unit	87
	Wheatfield Prison	374
Outside Dublin	Castlerea Prison	210
	Cork Prison	274
	Limerick Prison	260
	Loughan House(open centre)	72
	The Midlands Prison	439
	Portlaoise Prison	123
	Shelton Abbey (open centre)	49

The average cost of keeping a prisoner for one year was €83, 800.00 in 2003.[10] According to the report of the Prison Service Cost Review Group (1997:19) in 1996 it cost €69,327.70 to keep one person in prison for a year in Ireland in comparison to €50,027.68 in the Netherlands, €40,250.70 in England and Wales and €32,251.35 in Canada. On 21 March 2006 the Minister for Justice, Equality and Law Reform responded to a parliamentary question on the cost of keeping an offender in prison. His response is included below:[11]

Minister for Justice, Equality and Law Reform (Mr. McDowell): The key performance indicator identifying the cost and efficiency for the prison service is the cost of keeping an offender in prison. This has fallen over the last three years from €84,750 in 2002 to €83,800 in 2004 as set out below. The reduction in cost is due to the strict budget management, and in particular overtime management. In this regard, I am pleased to inform the Deputy that I have reversed the unacceptable trend of spiralling overtime costs that has been a feature of our prisons operations for many years. As a result of my determination to tackle this unsustainable dependence on overtime to run our prisons there was a reduction in the overtime bill of some €13.4 million in 2004 compared to 2003.

10 Ibidem, p. 7.

11 Parliamentary question, Dáil Debates, Vol 688 [10855/06], 21 March 2006.

Table 2 Cost of keeping an offender in prison.

Prison/Place of Detention	*2002*	*2003*	*2004*
Arbour Hill	71,550	73,600	70,400
Castlerea	72,100	75,250	70,000
Cork	71,050	72,350	75,000
Cloverhill	72,400	83,300	76,100
Curragh	72,400	70,100	Prison closed
Fort Mitchell	100,100	96,050	Prison closed
Dóchas	Included in Mountjoy	Included in Mountjoy	82,800
Limerick	86,450	90,200	73,000
Loughan House	62,850	67,700	63,900
Midlands	72,850	77,300	75,900
Mountjoy	95,900	97,900	91,800
Portlaoise	206,700	232,100	225,200
Shanganagh Castle	169,450	Prison closed	Prison closed
Shelton Abbey	84,850	80,100	82,000
St Patrick's	85,550	82,300	79,800
Training Unit	63,600	71,800	72,300
Wheatfield	72,350	75,800	71,300
Overall	84,750	87,950	83,800

In 2005 the Irish Prison Service staff establishment comprised 2925.5 posts with 17 positions at Governor Level 1, 11, 111, 12 positions at Deputy Governor Level and 19 positions at Assistant Governor Level.[12]

Inspections: Inspection bodies include the Inspector of Prisons and Places of Detention, Mr. Justice Dermot Kinlan, appointed on a statutory basis with effect from April 2002. One of the terms of reference of this post is to inspect and report on prisons and other places of detention managed on behalf of the Department of Justice, Equality and Law Reform by the Irish Prison Service. The Inspector submits a written report at the end of each year. The first Annual Report of the Inspector of Prisons and Places of Detention was published on 2 July 2003. One of the recommendations in this report was asylum seekers should not be held in prison while awaiting a decision regarding Irish citizenship- those applicants should be detained elsewhere.[13]

Visiting Committees visit prisons on a regular basis and report on various aspects of prison life e.g. the prison buildings, the management of the prison, conditions and treatment of prisoners, including food, health, medical care, education and preparation for release. Visiting Committees hears requests and complaints that persons in custody make to it. The members are free to visit every part of the prison. The committee reports on these matters at least once a year to the Minister for Justice, Equality and Law Reform. In the Mountjoy Prison Visiting Committees Annual Report attention was drawn to 'slopping

[12] Department of Justice, Equality and Law Reform, *Irish Prison Service Draft Annual Report,* 2005.

[13] Department of Justice, Equality and Law Reform, *Irish Prison Service Annual Report*, 2003, p. 113.

out' in the prison and in the interests of health and safety and welfare to both staff and prisoners the Report urges the Minister for Justice to address this situation without delay [14] The Irish Prison Services has plans for the development of new prison complexes in Dublin and Cork to replace older institutions and to meet best standards in prison accommodation.

Ireland ratified the Council of Europe Convention for the Prevention of Torture and Inhuman or Degrading Treatment or Punishment in 1988. Under this Convention, the Committee for the Prevention of Torture (CPT) has a right to visit and report on places of detention. Ireland's first visit from the Committee was in 1993 and there have been two further visits in 1998 and 2002. The CPT has written a report after each visit and areas of concern have been highlighted. An inspection visit by the CPT to Ireland is planned during 2006 as part of the CPT's published programme.

The CPT's report on its 2002 visit was published on 18 September 2003 in conjunction with the government's response. In the CPT's opinion prison is not a suitable place to hold persons who are subject to an expulsion order and who have not been convicted of a criminal offence. In those cases where it is necessary to deprive a person of his/her liberty for an extended period then specially designated detention centres would be more suitable.[15]

1.2.2 Foreign Prisoners

The increase in the numbers of foreign nationals in the general population in Ireland has been dramatic in the last ten years and particularly since the enlargement of the EU in 2004 with the inclusion of ten new States. The Statistical Yearbook of Ireland (2005) indicates that foreign nationals made up 5.8% of the population in 2004. For the first time, the census on 23 April 2006 will be available in 11 foreign languages (Arabic, Czech, Chinese, French, Latvian, Lithuanian, Polish, Portuguese, Romanian, Russian and Spanish. Additional information in the above languages and also Estonian, Slovak, Turkish and Yoruba is available on the Central Statistics office website).[16]

An overview of the statistics for 2004 show that 8820 persons were sent to prison, 5064 of those admitted under sentence. 946 foreign nationals were detained under immigration laws, a reduction of nearly 50% on the 2003 figure.[17] A total of 1804 persons (20.4%) sent to prison in 2004 indicated that they were foreign nationals. This compares with 25.6% in 2003 and reflects the reduction in the number of persons detained on immigration matters. According to the Annual Report of the Irish Prison Service the reduction reflected the sizable reduction in the number of asylum applications received in the state that year.[18] 90% of foreign national prisoners are detained on administrative detention in the Pre–Trial Cloverhill Prison[19] and in the Dochas Centre (Mountjoy Women's Prison). Sentenced foreign national prisoners are scattered among the other prisons. There are currently 226 foreign national prisoners serving sentences for a range of of-

14 Mountjoy Prison Visiting Committee, *Annual Report*, 2004, p. 1.
15 *CPT Report*, 2003, par 69.
16 *Irish Times*, 30 March 2006.
17 Department of Justice, Equality and Law Reform, *Irish Prison Service Annual Report*, 2004, p. 7.
18 Ibidem, pp. 10-11.
19 The term 'Pre-trial' will be used instead of 'Remand' throughout this document.

fences coming from 44 different countries. This figure includes 109 non-EU nationals.[20] Up to 2003 a breakdown of figures for non-national prisoners was not deemed necessary, as nearly all prisoners were Irish. To illustrate this O'Donnell refers to a survey of prisoners carried out in 1996. Only three of the 108 male prisoners interviewed at that time had current addresses outside of Ireland.[21]

In response to a Parliamentary Question on 11 October 2005 the Minister for Justice, Equality and Law Reform states the number of foreign nationals serving a prison sentence and their States of origin. Out of the total number of sentenced persons of 2520 on that date, there were 172 foreign nationals. The number of non- EU nationals totalled 86 or 3.4% of the sentenced population. The number of non-Irish EU nationals amounted to 91 and corresponded to 3.6% of those serving sentences. A total of 93% of sentenced prisoners were of Irish nationality. The highest number of non-Irish prisoners was British (64) that can be explained by close geographical and economic ties. In descending order there were 17 South Africans, 14 Chinese, eight Lithuanian, seven Romanian, seven Nigerian and five Polish.[22]

Under the Transfer of Sentenced Prisoners Act 1995 & 1997 seven prisoners transferred into the State (five from the UK, one from Panama and one from the United States) and four prisoners transferred out of the State in 2004 (all to the UK). In total, one hundred and seven prisoners have now transferred here from abroad and sixty prisoners here transferred out since the Act came into operation on 1 November 1995.[23]

1.3 Overview involvement Consulates, Embassies, Ministries home country, Probation service home country, NGO's etc

Based on feedback from Probation Officers in prisons countrywide it appears that there is generally little contact with Probation Services outside of Ireland. Contact is usually in relation to repatriation applications with the United Kingdom. In these instances contact is maintained through phone calls and letters/reports. In Ireland admission procedures are called committal procedures. For the purpose of this report the term admission is being used rather than committal. At admission prisoners should be informed that they might request the governor to inform a consular representative of the country of which the prisoner is a citizen of his/her detention. At the moment there is no obligation to do this in writing. Prisoners have access to free telephone calls to nominated persons whether that is a solicitor or consular representative or family member. Consular representative is notified promptly if a prisoner dies in custody.

The experience of the Probation Officers in the prison is that many foreign nationals have few visitors and receive few visits. Prisons around the country facilitate visits by charitable and religious denominations for foreign national prisoners but it would appear to be done on an ad hoc basis. Prison officers, chaplains, Probation staff have identified isolation and lack of any contact with others as a major issue. The following are an ex-

---

20 Parliamentary question. *Dail Debates*, No.448, 3 May 2006.

21 P. O'Mahoney, 'Mountjoy Prisoners: A Sociological and Criminological Profile,' Dublin 1997, pp. 39, Stationary Office.

22 Parliamentary question. *Dáil Debates*, Vol. 607, No. 2, 11 October 2005.

23 Department of Justice, Equality and Law Reform, *Annual Report* by the Minister for Justice to the Government on the operation of The Transfer of Sentenced Persons Act, 1995 & 1997 for the period 1 January 2004 - 31 December 2004, 2005.

ample of the types of organization or non-governmental bodies that visit the prison:

- Befrienders Organization visits the Dochas Centre (Mountjoy Women's Prison).
- Individual religious (Catholic nuns and priests/ representatives of other religious denominations) visit particular prisoners sometimes over long periods of time.
- Open *heart* House (This project challenges the isolation of HIV through peer support & provides a range of services and facilities. The centre caters for cultural diversity and the outreach worker visits the prison to maintain the contact established with individuals in the community that includes foreign national prisoners.).
- The Guild of St Philip of Neri (a branch of the St Vincent de Paul which is the longest established charitable organization visiting prisoners in Ireland). A French speaker sometimes accompanies the members of the St Vincent de Paul in order to include visits to foreign national prisoners that are of benefit in particular to the West and North African prisoners who they visit.
- Doras Luimni (Limerick) is an organization specifically for asylum applications and foreign nationals who have difficulties about issues of expulsion who the prison may contact if a prisoner needs assistance.
- Integrating Ireland is an independent network of community and voluntary groups who work to promote the full integration in Irish Society of asylum seekers, refugees and immigrants. It has not been possible to get a comprehensive list of those organizations that visit prisoners but some do intermittently including SARI (Sport Against Racism visit the young people who were involved with them originally in the community while in custody) Many are awaiting decisions on expulsion orders and who sometimes end up in custody prior to being removed from the country.
- The Dun Laoghaire Refugee Project and the Irish Refugee Council Dublin also visit on an intermittent basis.

1.4 Overview of trends

1.4.1 Sentencing Trends

The average daily population in Irish Prisons has continued to rise over the past ten years while in recent years the numbers of persons committed under sentence has fallen. [24]O'Donnell refers to the falling number of prison sentences imposed by the District Court between 2001-2002. He also refers to the increasing number of foreign prisoners entering the Irish Criminal Justice System. While the average daily population of prisoners in the Republic of Ireland has grown significantly since the mid 1990s, recorded crime statistics have fallen. O Donnell attributes these trends to a number of factors including the 'politicalisation of the debate about crime, build up of long term prisoners, an expansion of the remand population and a reduction of the use of early release to ease overcrowding'.[25]

1.4.2 Characteristics Foreign Prison Population

Prison accommodation in the Republic of Ireland is used to hold a proportion of failed

---

[24] O'Donnell, ibidem, p. 259.

[25] ibidem, p. 253.

asylum seekers, pending expulsion.[26] O'Donnell argues that it is also inevitable that the prison population will change as minority groups appear before the Courts on criminal charges. He reports that in 2002, in eight out of the 59 homicides that took place, the victim was a foreign national (four Chinese, one Welsh, one Lithuanian, one Latvian, and one Portuguese).[27] Ireland has changed from being a homogeneous society with high unemployment in the 1980s to a more culturally diverse country with low unemployment and a thriving Celtic Tiger economy that has attracted many foreigners to its shores.

Garret FitzGerald noted that in the 1970s Ireland was the European country with the highest net emigration rate while in the last decade it has experienced net immigration.[28]. It is not unexpected then that those persons entering the prison system will reflect this change and will come from a variety of different national and ethnic backgrounds. However as trends in other countries show minority and marginalized groups can be over represented in the prison population. According to O'Donnell[29] it is not clear to what extent 'the sudden change in the complexion of admissions to Irish prisons reflects targeting by the police, differentiated patterns of offending or sentencing, or the changing composition of the resident population'. As Tonry [30] suggests, 'members of minority groups are over represented among crime victims, arrestees, pre-trial detainees, convicted offenders, and prisoners in every Western country.'[31]

Statistics from the Irish Prison Service Annual Report on the composition of the prison population in 2004 reflect what is common in prison populations elsewhere:
- Many more men (89%) than women (11%);
- more than two thirds of men and three quarters of women are between 21 -40 years;
- nearly half the population came from addresses in Dublin;
- of the admissions to prison three fifths were serving six month sentence or less;
- Four fifths of admissions under sentences of one year.

Reports on the profile of prisoners suggest that there is a disproportionately higher level of mental illness among people admitted to Irish prisons than in the general population that is similar to trends in other countries.[32] While there has not been any study of the particular mental health needs of foreign nationals in Irish prisons the National Health Service UK identified the following factors in the UK as increasing the likelihood of mental disorders particularly depression developing; isolation, worry about the fate of families, reduction in hope due to long sentences and concern about what will happen on release. Poor literacy has also been identified as an important issue [33] and deprivation and

26 The word 'expulsion' is used instead of ' deportation' throughout this document.

27 O'Donnell, ibidem, p. 262.

28 *Irish Times,* 1 April 2006.

29 O'Donnell, ibidem, p. 263.

30 M. Tonry, (ed.) 'Ethnicity, Crime and Immigration: Comparative and cross national perspectives', *Crime and Justice, A Review of Research*, Vol. 21. Chicago, University of Chicago Press, 1997, p. viii.

31 O'Donnell, ibidem, p. 265.

32 Department of Justice, Equality and Law Reform, 'Mental Illness in Irish Prisoners: Psychiatric Morbidity in Sentenced, Remanded and Newly Committed Prisoners'. H.G. Kennedy, S. Monks, K. Curtin, B. Wright, S. Linehan, D. Duffy,, C. Teljeur, and A. Kelly, National Forensic Mental Health Service, 2005, p. 89.

33 Irish Prison Service, M. Morgan – M. Kett 'The Prison Adult Literacy Survey: Results and implications', Dublin 2003.

disadvantage can lead to problems whatever a person's nationality.[34]

1.5 Overview of national legislation

The main legislative provisions are to be found in a number of Acts of the Oireachtas and in secondary legislation including:
- Irish Nationality and Citizenship Act 1935. (defines Irish citizenship)
- The Aliens Act 1935 [an alien or non national as defined by this act]
- The Criminal Justice Act 1960
- The Prisons Act 1970 (primary piece of legislation relating to prisons)
- The Transfer of Sentenced Persons Act 1995 &1997(prisoner repatriation)
- The Refugee Act 1996 (Places and Conditions of Detention) Regulations 2000
- The Immigration Act 1999 (Expulsion) Regulations 2005
- The Equal Status Act 2000
- The Criminal Justice (Theft and Fraud Offences) Act 2001 (sections 26 and 29 relate to offences which include false passports or forgeries of official documents)
- The Illegal Immigrants (Trafficking) Act 2000
- The Immigration Act 2003 (Removal Places of detention) Regulations 2005.
- The Immigration Act 2004.
- Prison Rules 1947
- The United Nations Convention of Human Rights [ratified by Ireland in 1956]
- The Geneva Convention [signed by Ireland in 1951]
- United Nations International Convention on the Elimination of All Forms of Racial Discrimination [adopted and ratified by Ireland 2001]
- European Convention for the Prevention of Torture and Inhumane or Degrading Treatment or Punishment Strasbourg, 26.XI.1987
- Convention determining the State responsible for examining applications for Asylum lodged in one of the Member States of the European Communities. Dublin Convention EC Official Journal C 254, 19 August 1997.
- Council of Europe Convention for the Protection of Human Rights and Fundamental Freedoms as amended by Protocol No. 11,Rome, 4.XI.1950

The Irish Citizen Child Scheme was introduced in 2005 and a new Immigration and Residence Bill is to be introduced in 2006.

---

[34] O'Mahony Mountjoy Prisoners: A Sociological and Criminological Profile, Dublin 1997, Stationary Office.

2 TREATMENT OF FOREIGN PRISONERS

2.1 General

Emigration has always been a feature of Irish life. Immigration is a recent phenomenon. Economic necessity forced many Irish people to travel across the Irish Sea to Britain and across the Atlantic to America. Irish expulsion to Australia was initially as a form of punishment for crimes committed in Ireland in the 19th century. Emigration to Australia has since been a choice destination. As a country we are used to saying goodbye to people. While we are renowned for being a welcoming people this was in the context of tourism. Our ability to assimilate and integrate other nationalities on a permanent basis has not been tested up until the 1990s. There is a view that as a country Ireland was unprepared for the demands posed by large-scale immigration.

Ireland has attracted an influx of foreign nationals drawn to it by the prosperity of the Irish economy. The National Action Plan against Racism[35] says that the 2002 Census of Population provides the most comprehensive breakdown of national diversity in Ireland to date and identifies five main regions of origin for foreign nationals living in Ireland. These are UK and other EU nationals (3.4% of the total population), Asian (0.5%), African (0.5%) non-EU European nationals (0.5%) and the United States (0.3%). With 9% of the workforce and 10% of population foreign born according to Central Statistics Office we have reached levels of immigration that other European countries took decades to achieve. [36]There have been 750,000 newcomers from 211 countries since 2000.

Ireland in the 21st century has low unemployment. Industries have been sourcing workers from other countries to keep the Irish economy booming. Recent debates concerning foreign nationals taking Irish jobs have featured in the national media. Media views have challenged this and at a recent seminar in Dublin in March 2006 it was stated that there was no evidence of displacement of Irish workers since the accession of the ten new states in 2004. However there was concern raised about the lack of integration measures e.g. in schools and about the exploitation of migrant workers.[37]

A small proportion of the foreign national population in Ireland are asylum seekers fleeing from countries where war and torture are the norm. There was a noticeable increase in the numbers of applicants seeking asylum during the 1990s that has been attributed, in some quarters, to the limited immigration legislation in operation up to 2003. The number of applications rose from 39 in 1992 to 7724 in 1999.[38] The figures increased to 11,630 in 2002 and decreased to 4304 in 2005.[39] The drop in numbers seeking asylum in Ireland was, at least in part as a result of a change in legislation.

The Irish response to asylum seekers is well documented in a report 'Beyond the Pale' on asylum seeking children and social exclusion in Ireland.[40] This report considers the implications of direct provision (hostel accommodation plus €15 per week per adult) that

---

35 National Action Plan Against Racism, 2005, p.50.

36 *Irish Times,* 10 March 2006.

37 *Irish Times,* 10 March 2006.

38 S. Mullally, *Manifestly Unjust: A Report on the Fairness and Sustainability of Accelerated Procedures for Asylum Determinations*, Irish Refugee Council, 2000, p.15.

39 *Sunday Tribune,* 26 March 2006.

40 B. Fanning, A.Veale, D.O'Connor, *Beyond the Pale: Asylum-seeking children and Social Exclusion in Ireland,* Irish Refugee Council Dublin 2001.

was introduced in 2000 that meant that asylum seekers were not entitled to full rates of supplementary assistance.
Some foreign nationals come into contact with the criminal justice system and the next section focuses on conditions for foreign nationals in a prison setting.

2.2 Living conditions and facilities

Living conditions and facilities for foreign nationals in Irish Prisons are in general, the same as for Irish prisoners and tend to vary depending on whether the prison is old or new, but there tends not to be any separation. Cork prison is the main committal prison for the Munster area and it houses approx 265 prisoners. There is no separate area for pre-trial prisoners. Few foreign national administrative detainees awaiting removal are held in this prison.

In Cloverhill Pre-Trial Prison (Dublin) a separate wing is used to house non-Irish nationals. Staff in this prison says that in the early days there had been limited knowledge and experience in working with other nationalities and assumptions were occasionally made about who might get on with whom. In recent times there is an increasing awareness of the sensitivities of different cultures. The facilities on this wing are the same as on other wings of the prison with the exception that there are three beds to a cell rather than two. In the report prepared by Kelly[41] on administrative detention this was remarked on and while it was suggested that the burden of overcrowding fell on the foreign prisoners the Irish Prison Service has indicated that any overcrowding was and is borne equally among all prisoners irrespective of origin. In the Dochas Centre, (Mountjoy Women's Prison) there is no separation policy. In practice most foreign nationals are in the two drug free houses which have both a mixture of Irish and non-Irish foreign nationals. On the 27 January 2006 there were nine Irish women and nine foreign national women in each of the two drug free houses.

2.3 Reception and admission

The reception procedures for foreign prisoners are the same as for national prisoners. When a prisoner arrives at a prison there are a number of procedures that are gone through which are common to all prisons. On being committed to prison each prisoner on reception sees a medical officer, medication is arranged if necessary and personal details are taken. Admissions are required to see the Governor, this usually happens the following morning when an interview is conducted.

In Mountjoy Prison, there is a questionnaire for new admissions that has been translated into fourteen different languages. In practice the questionnaire is not always useful: a prisoner might be able to write down the answers on this form in his/her language but the person issuing the questionnaire would not understand the replies. As there is no on call interpreter service; the prison management occasionally requests other prisoners to translate where necessary. After the admissions interview with the Governor it is decided where each prisoner will be assigned in the prison. This decision can be based on factors

---

41 M. Kelly, *Immigration – Related Detention in Ireland.* A research report for the Irish Refugee Council, Irish Penal Reform Trust and Immigrant Council of Ireland. Human Rights Consultants, Dublin 2005.

such as a person's previous history, whether they are first time offenders, whether they have health or mental health problems, whether they are drug users and what their behaviour has been like during previous sentences.

The Department of Justice, Equality and Law Reform and the Irish Prison Service are committed to updating the current Prisons Rules published in 1947. A new information booklet to be issued will be based on the New Prison Rules that are due to be approved by the Minister for Justice, Equality and Law Reform. It is intended that the booklet will be available in a number of languages for the benefit of foreign prisoners. In the meantime prisons provide locally prepared information booklets in English to prisoners on regimes and services.[42]

Foreign prisoners are advised on admission about their entitlements to communicate with a representative of their diplomatic mission and asked if they wish to avail of this. Prisoners are also entitled to call a family member at this stage. Special consideration is given in the Cloverhill Pre-Trial Prison to prisoners being able to contact their families at appropriate times for the families. Clocks with the different international time zones are placed in the main circle area of the prison to facilitate prisoners contacting family at the right time. Such clocks are not available elsewhere but assistance is given to foreign nationals to contact family as required.

In Mountjoy Prison efforts are being made to create a five to ten minute video programme for television in the reception area. This will show how the prison system works and what services are available to prisoners. It is intended that it will be available in different languages. In Cork Prison notices about Prison services are put in strategic locations in the prison in different languages by the Education Department.

2.4 Work-Education-Training-Sports-Recreation

There are no separate provisions for foreign prisoners with regard to work or education. The majority of foreign nationals are either on remand where there is no obligation to engage in education, work or training or are short sentence prisoners who often do not engage in these activities. Many foreign nationals serving longer sentences in Mountjoy Prison work in the kitchen areas (this is hard work but would be considered a good job with privileges not enjoyed by other prisoners e.g. longer time unlocked from cell, access to preferred food). Others participate in training and working in the computer area.

The Education Service Computer Class that accommodates six pupils is always full and at least half the participants are non-nationals. The Art class takes place twice a week and it too is well attended by non-nationals. There are currently two non- national students studying for their Leaving Certificate English. There is an ESOL (English for Speakers of other languages) Course on offer twice a week and it is very well attended. At time of writing (April 2006) there were five to six Moldavian, two Lithuanian, one Algerian and two Chinese prisoners attending these classes. The teachers have commented on the enthusiasm of foreign nationals for education that is evidenced by the fact that they arrive first each morning. Some staff have expressed a concern that this group could be the subject of harassment as they avail of the services that Irish prisoners may find it hard to commit to and might resent others obtaining.

Senior prison staff in both Mountjoy Male and Female Prison commented that for-

42 Department of Justice, Equality and Law Reform, *Irish Prison Service Annual Report*, 2004, p. 82.

eign women serving long sentences were keen to avail of education. They consistently attend educational classes and avail of work opportunities which allows them to send money home to families.

2.5 Food-Religion- Personal hygiene-Medical Care

There are at present 20 full time and three part time chaplains working in the Irish Prison Service. The Chaplaincy provides spiritual and pastoral care to the prison community.[43] The Chaplaincy caters for everyone and they can also bring in representatives from different religions. The prison chaplains have recommended that the inappropriate use of prisons being used as detention centres for expulsion should cease and that a less severe but secure environment be provided where access to the latest information regarding their legal status and entitlements.[44]

Until recently the vast majority of prisoners have been Roman Catholics. In Mountjoy Prison there is Mass every Sunday at 9.30 am which takes place in the Church and a Protestant Service led by the Minister for the Church of Ireland which takes place in a room on D Wing. Many of the non-Catholic prisoners attend this service. The chaplains in Mountjoy also facilitate other denominations coming into the prison at the request of prisoners. The Greek Orthodox Church representative visited a number of times and left information for prisoners with the chaplains. These visits are facilitated in the professional box visiting area where the representative can meet with the prisoner on a one to one basis. Visits by spiritual advisors perhaps for cultural reasons appear to be infrequent to Muslim prisoners.

A Medical Officer sees all prisoners as soon as possible after admission. The medical officer is a doctor appointed to the prison who attends daily and as required. A person in custody may be examined by a Psychiatrist as a result of a Court Order, a Court Recommendation or on the referral of the Prison Doctor. Other disciplines in the prison make referrals on behalf of a prisoner to the psychiatric services. If a prisoner requires in-patient psychiatric care arrangements are made for the prisoner to be transferred to the Central Mental Hospital in Dundrum.

A recent report on mental illness in Irish prisons confirmed that specialist psychiatric care is provided in all the main prisons on an outpatient sessional basis, increasingly delivered by modern multi-disciplinary 'in-reach' teams, at least in the prisons within reach of Dublin. [45]The findings of this report indicate that a higher proportion of people in the Irish Prison system than in the community are diagnosed with severe mental illnesses. This level exceeds international averages for men on remand.[46]

---

43 *National Prison Chaplains Annual report,* 2003, p. 1.

44 Ibidem, p. 5.

45 Department of Justice, Equality and Law Reform, H.G. Kennedy, S. Monks, K. Curtin,B. Wright, S. Linehan, D. Duffy, C. Teljeur and M. Kelly, *Mental Illness in Irish Prisoners: Psychiatric Morbidity in Sentenced, Remanded and Newly Committed Prisoners,* 2005, p. 106.

46 Ibidem, p. 2.

2.6 Consular and legal help

The draft Prison Rules to be approved by the Minister for Justice, Equality and Law Reform include the following provisions regarding consular access:

17.
1. a foreign national shall be provided with the means to contact a consul and, in addition, an asylum applicant shall be provided with the means to contact:
- The United Nations High Commissioner for Refugees or the Representative in Ireland of the High Commissioner, and
- subject to such limitation as to numbers as the governor may reasonably impose, national or international authorities and organizations whose principal object is to serve the interests of refugees or stateless person or to protect the civil and human rights of such persons.

2. A person to whom paragraph (1) applies shall be informed in particular of his or her entitlements under Rule 40 (Visit by legal adviser or relating to court appearance).

41.
1. A foreign national shall be entitled to receive a visit from his or her consul at any reasonable time or where he or she is a stateless person the consul of a state of his or her choosing who is willing to visit him or her.
2. An asylum applicant shall be entitled to receive a visit at any reasonable time from-
- such national or international authorities or organizations, as may be designated by the Minister, whose principal object is to serve the interests of the refugee or stateless person, and
- a consul of a state of his or her own choosing[47]

2.7 Contact with Outside World

Foreign prisoners have the same visiting entitlements as national prisoners. The prison rules provide one visit per week of 30 minutes for sentenced prisoners. One additional special visit per week can be requested at the discretion of the Governor. Pre-trial (remand) prisoners are permitted one short visit each day. In both the Male and Female Mountjoy Prisons in Dublin there is flexibility about visits for foreign nationals. Family members who have travelled from abroad to see their family member are granted at the discretion of the Governor, visits on the days that they are in the country during both morning and afternoon (for example if a family visit for a long weekend then they would be able to visit Friday morning and afternoon, Saturday morning and afternoon and Monday morning and afternoon).

Special arrangements at the discretion of the Governor can also be made for a prisoner for one of the visits to be in a less clinical visiting facility (family members may stay for lunch in the Dochas Centre if desired) but this is dependant on availability of prison staff because such visits require one prison officer to supervise one prisoner. The prisoner needs to request extra visits if his /her family is coming. In Mountjoy Male Prison the visiting system requires that prisoners put six named visitors on their visitors list. If this has

[47] This can be referenced to the 2005 publications prisons page at www.justice.ie.

not been done a visitor may not be allowed to see a prisoner. If the prisoner has not requested visits the family may not be allowed to visit. In practice prisoners with limited English may be at greater risk of confusion arising around visitor arrangements though prison managements do seek to actively remedy such visiting problems where they do occur.

Each prisoner is granted a six-minute phone call every day for no charge. The number of letters a prisoner can send out of prison is two per week and the number of letters in, is unlimited. All letters may be censored except to legal advisors and any legal documentation. Television in the cell is available in virtually all prisons - programmes are in English.

Visitor Centre: The Visitors Centre at Mountjoy Prison is a well-staffed, comfortable and pleasant environment for families who come to visit with children. There are similar centres at Cloverhill Prison and at the Midlands Prison. The Visitors Centre provides tea and coffee facilities in a hospitable atmosphere with a child care area for children. The Centre also links up with the prison on behalf of prisoners and their families in certain instances. The Visitor Centres have noticed the increase in the foreign nationals' families using the centres.

2.8 Re-integration activities – Prison leave

The Probation Service in the prisons work towards the re-integration of prisoners back into their communities. The Probation Officer will seek to address the factors that resulted in a person coming to prison in the first place and attempt to help to put in place measures which would help to reduce recidivism and support resettlement in the community in partnership with relevant statutory and voluntary services.

2.9 Release – Expulsion

There is no provision in Irish Law for the automatic expulsion of a foreign national who has committed a criminal offence. For the year 2005 to April 2006 seven non-EU nationals convicted of offences, and who served a prison sentence for same, had been issued with Expulsion Orders. Of those, four had been deported and a further four had applied to return voluntarily to their countries of origin. [48]

Arrangements for foreign national prisoners released in Ireland are as for Irish prisoners. The Irish Economic and Social Forum Report on Re-Integration of Prisoners[49] found that release from prison 'can be a very traumatic experience' particularly for those who have been in prison for a long time, have unmet needs about accommodation, training or employment, dependence on drugs or alcohol or family difficulties. The report recommends pre and post release strategies for positive sentence management. At present the Irish Prison Service is developing an integrated sentence management system that seeks to provide a seamless transition from custody back into the community with the support of services in prisons and in the community.

---

48 Parliamentary question. *Dail Debates*. No. 190, 4 May 2006.

49 National Economic and Social Forum Report No 22, Re-*Integration of Prisoners*, 2002 p. 83.

2.10 Aftercare – Probation

Apart from those being repatriated, there is very little contact with probation services in other countries in relation to foreign nationals. Probation staffs in prisons report that their experience is that foreign nationals can be socially quite isolated. At times they do not seem to have much information about their legal rights and they are often anxious as to what is going to happen to them on their release from prison. On occasion they are distrustful of authorities and do not readily disclose links or family contacts in their reported country of origin. Many fear being expelled from the country.

There is no statutory aftercare for persons completing a sentence except for prisoners who are granted temporary release with a condition of supervision by the Probation Service by the Minister for Justice Equality and Law Reform, those convicted of offences under the Sexual Offenders Act 2001 or those who may have a period of post release supervision imposed by the Circuit or other Court. (The Judge imposes a prison sentence to be followed by a condition of supervision by the Probation Service for a specified period with particular conditions).

Many of those subject to Court directed post release supervision in the Dublin area are referred to the Bridge project, an intensive community based probation supervision initiative which is one example of a re-integration initiative which is staffed largely by the Probation Service and the City of Dublin Vocational Education Committee. To date there have been no foreign nationals subject to the Bridge programme.

The Linkage Programme is a re-integration initiative that is supported and funded by the Probation Service. Training and Employment Officers prepare, plan and implement training/or employment placements for offenders referred to them by the Probation Service. There were a total of 272 referrals from prisons and places of detention in 2004 but there is no breakdown as yet of referrals by nationality.

2.11 Staff

It is evident that there are increasing numbers of foreign nationals in our prisons that reflects the changes in Irish Society in the last ten years. A National Action Plan Against Racism was published in 2005 '*Planning for Diversity*- the National Action Plan Against Racism'. Mainstreaming an intercultural strategy within the prison service' is one of the objectives in this plan.[50] The Irish Prison Service initiated independent research on racial and cultural awareness in Irish prisons that was published in 2003. Training and information on human rights is provided to all prison staff at induction. The Irish Prison Service is currently reviewing its internal procedures for staff training and processing of prisoner complaints.[51]

In England and Wales the HM Inspectorate of Prisons report ' *Parallel Worlds*' found that there was no shared understanding of race issues within prisons and that the variety of viewpoints of prison management, staff (white staff and visible minority staff) and prisoners highlights the difference in perceptions. The existence of Race Relations Liaison Officers (RRLO), a Race Relations Management Team and a Prisoner Diversity Repre-

---

50 Department of Justice, Equality and Law Reform, *Planning for Diversity - the National Action Plan Against Racism*, 2005 par. 7.1, p. 34.

51 Department of Justice, Equality and Law Reform, Irish *Prison Service Annual Report*, 2003, p. 87.

sentative has resulted in good practice in those prisons in England and Wales. However prison surveys regularly found that black and minority ethnic prisoners 'have worse perceptions of their treatment than white prisoners across many key areas of prison life'.[52] The report highlights the key areas that need to be developed and concludes that leadership and training are 'critical elements in breaking down the different perceptions and experiences.'[53] This is an area currently undergoing particular development in the Irish Prison Service.

2.12 Projects

Below are just three examples of projects that reflect the range of initiatives taking place:

Special Projects outside of the prison setting. The Irish Commission for Prisoners Overseas (ICPO) requested the Council for Research and Development, a commission of the Irish Bishops Conference, to undertake an evaluation of their family support service for families of prisoners serving sentences overseas. The main findings of this evaluation highlighted the financial difficulties of families who had to finance a visit to support their relative or to meet the cost of basic prison supplies such as clothing, food, stamps and phone cards. The lack of clear information and legal support services emerged as a significant problem for families struggling with a foreign legal and prison system. Families were particularly concerned about the lack of any statutory or formal post release support for their relatives on release from prison. This interesting project focuses attention on those who have emigrated from Ireland. While emigration has decreased in the past decade the CSO figures in 2005 show 16,600 people had emigrated with 50% of those in the 15-24 age group. The experience of the Irish Commission for Prisoners Overseas is that many of those who emigrate are vulnerable and more likely than most to end up in need of services.[54] Similar issues arise for non-Irish prisoners in custody in Ireland. One of the main recommendations of the Report was that the Department of Foreign Affairs should provide an allowance to Irish citizens in prison overseas and that a visitation allowance be provided to all families of prisoners overseas, in order to ease the financial burden of imprisonment on families. Other recommendations included the suggestion that fact sheets on the prison and legal system in different countries should be prepared to support families by providing them with practical advice and information.[55] The overall aim of the research was "to evaluate the needs of families of Irish prisoners overseas, in relation to the service provided by the ICPO and support services in general".[56] The findings of this evaluation are helpful when we turn our attention to the families of foreign national prisoners in custody in Ireland. It is clear that many of the same issues would arise for them.

2.12.1 Special projects within the prison

In 2002 the Probation Service at Mountjoy Prison, in collaboration with the Education

---

52 HM Inspectorate of Prisons, Parallel *Worlds - A Thematic Review of Race Relations in Prisons,* 2005, p.1.

53 Ibidem, p.3.

54 Submission by Irish Commission for Prisoners Overseas (ICPO) to Joint Committee on Foreign Affairs Sub-Committee on Human Rights, 16 June 2005.

55 Separated Families: Reviewing the needs of Families of Irish Prisoners Overseas, 2005, pp. 26 - 27.

56 Ibidem, p. 1.

Unit, recognized the special circumstances of the increasing number on foreign prisoners and successfully introduced an inter agency programme to address the specific needs of and provide information and support to foreign prisoners.[57] A Probation Officer at Mountjoy Prison completed a dissertation on the subject of working with foreign prisoners detained in Irish Prisons.[58] In conjunction with the team of Probation Officers working in Mountjoy Prison she helped to identify the main issues arising in relation to working with foreign prisoners. Concerns were also raised about prisoners repatriated from England to Ireland and their misunderstandings about the Irish Criminal Justice System. Some prisoners coming back to Ireland to complete their sentence encounter difficulty adjusting because of structural and operational differences in the two prison systems. The Probation Service in Mountjoy Prison identified significant issues such as the absence of information and advice about what was available in the prison and on statutory rights and entitlements of foreign national prisoners. In response it was decided to consult with the prisoners themselves and to see what the needs were and how they might be addressed. The Prison Governors supported the International Group Mountjoy and there was an input from all the disciplines within the prison. (Prison staff, governor and chief officer, librarian, chaplain, and psychologist). The group ran from Easter to Summer (2002) one morning a week for 10-12 sessions and it took place in the school. There were 10-12 participants with nine different nationalities including French, Belgian, Chinese, Russian, Lithuanian, Scottish, Nigerian, Libyan, and Algerian. A number of the referrals came from D wing where there were a number of Lithuanians whose needs had to be addressed. However other referrals came from all areas of prison. This initiative proved very useful.

Making a Difference. The inter agency programme developed a picture of the specific needs and requirements of the group. While all prisoners may experience stress and fear in a prison setting this group of international prisoners expressed a strong sense of isolation through lack of communication. While there were televisions, for many these were of limited use as their English was poor and all the channels were in English. The group identified in particular feelings of anxiety related to isolation. Some of the suggestions and specific requests made by the group were acted upon by Prison Staff. These included:

- *Newspapers:* Librarians spoke to prisoners and on their request ordered Chinese and French newspapers once a week. Since then, depending on where the foreign national prisoners are from, newspapers are bought on an ad hoc basis by both the library and the school.
- *Learning English:* Linked to school and provided dictionaries in the relevant language to those in the group. This service has developed and notices about English Classes have been translated into 14 different languages.
- *Visits*: Prison Governors approved flexibility for visits for foreign nationals. However the prisoner must go to the Governor in advance of the visit and apply for special visiting arrangements.
- Letters (prison regulations allow two letters a week out of the prison). The prisoners requested more flexibility with this, as some wanted to write as often as they wished as many of the group received no visits. The Governors facilitated this request for the for-

57 Department of Justice, Equality and Law Reform, *Irish Prison Service Annual Report*, 2004, p. 84.

58 E. Farrell Working with Non-Nationals detained in Irish Prisons. Unpublished dissertation. University College Dublin 2003.

eign national prisoners in this group.
- *Food:* The home economics teacher in school encouraged making dishes of ethnic nature in class.

In some cases the foreign nationals did not want their family to know that they were in prison. They refused any help with getting in touch with their consular representatives, as they did not want to increase the likelihood of family finding out where they were. One of the teachers involved in the multi-national group provided an illustration of this when she related the story of two Chinese prisoners who were having photographs taken in the group. They requested that the photos be taken in front of a blackboard to suggest to their families that they were indeed studying as their families believed them to be.

***Special Projects within the Prison Setting*.**

The Annual Report of the Inspector of Prisons and Places of Detention 2002-2003 identified the existence of racism in the prison system.[59] The Irish Prison Service had already, at that time, initiated independent research on racial and cultural awareness in Irish prisons having recognized the changing profile and ethnic diversity in the community and prison populations. The 'Evaluation of Research and Training Project for Intercultural Awareness' was conducted in Wheatfield prison in 2002 was published in February 2003. The purpose of the project was to determine the nature of intercultural awareness, communication and racial equality within a prison in Dublin with a view to subsequently informing policy.[60] The Irish Prison Service continues to review its internal procedures for staff training and processing of prisoner complaints.[61]At local level prisons have responded to these new demands. Two handbooks were published in 2003 one for staff and one for prisoners entitled 'Inappropriate Behaviour'. These were produced by the Irish Prison Service for Cloverhill Pre-Trial Prison as a policy statement on racism, harassment and bullying. There has been anti-racism training for both staff and prisoners on this and it is currently being considered for the main committal prison in Dublin.

3 ADMINISTRATIVE DETENTION OF FOREIGN PRISONERS

Foreign prisoners in Ireland who are held in custody not because of a criminal offence but because they have no permanent or temporary resident permit for Ireland are considered in this part of the report. The treatment of foreign nationals held under administrative detention in Ireland will be considered in this part and comparisons made with the treatment of foreign prisoners imprisoned under Criminal law in Ireland which were dealt with in the above section. This type of detention is based on migration or administrative law not criminal law. Detention for immigration purposes is referred to as administrative detention in this paper. A recent research report 'Immigration –Related Detention in Ireland' is the first of its kind in this area of law and is referred to throughout this section. This independent report recommends that the practice of holding immigration detainees in prisons in Ireland be brought to an end as prisons are identified in

59 *First Annual Report of the Inspector of Prisons and Places of Detention* 2002-2003, pp. 65-66.

60 Fitzpatrick Associates, *Evaluation of Research and Training Project for Intercultural Awareness*. Wheatfield prison, Dublin 2003, p.1.

61 Department of Justice, Equality and Law Reform, *Irish Prison Service Annual Report*, 2003, p. 87.

the report as inappropriate places in which to hold immigration detainees.[62] The report defines the term 'prisoner' as including all four categories of immigration related detainees namely (1) persons refused permission to land, (2) those detained during the asylum process, (3) people detained pending expulsion and (4) those remanded in custody for immigration-related reasons (awaiting trial).[63]

The European Committee for the Prevention of Torture (CPT) in the report on its visit to Ireland in May 2002 made clear that "a prison is by definition not a suitable place in which to detain someone who is neither convicted nor suspected of a criminal offence. In those cases where it is deemed necessary to deprive persons of their liberty for an extended period under Aliens legislation, they should be accommodated in centres specifically designed for that purpose, offering material conditions and a regime appropriate to their legal situation and staffed by suitably qualified personnel".[64]

3.1 Institution

Ireland uses existing prisons to place this group of people whereas some European countries have created special detention centres

3.2 Ministry responsible and legislation

The Department of Justice, Equality and Law Reform is responsible for the administrative detention of foreign prisoners in Ireland with the overall responsibility lying with the Minister for Justice, Equality and Law Reform. The laws that apply to this group are complex and the growing body of legislation in recent years is evidence of the legal complexity of the issues involved.

3.3 Capacity institutions

The Committee for the prevention of Torture (CPT) 2002 recommended that the holding of administrative detainees in prisons should be reviewed. Nearly all administrative detainees are housed in two prisons in Dublin where they have access to the same facilities as other prisoners.

3.4 Length of stay

Under section 5(6)(a) of the Immigration Act 1999, the period of detention may not exceed eight weeks in total. Most persons, however, are detained for periods less than eight weeks because the sole purpose of detention is to ensure that the person will co-operate in making arrangements, such as securing travel documents. The Supreme Court has considered the constitutionality of certain amendments of the Immigration Act 1999. The Supreme Court judgement of 28 August 2000 held, with regard to detention on foot of

---

62 M. Kelly, ibidem, p. 2.

63 Ibidem, p. 48.

64 Report to the Government of Ireland on the visit to Ireland carried out by the European Committee for the Prevention of Torture and Inhuman or Degrading Treatment or Punishment (CPT) from 20 to 28 May 2002, CPT 2003, 36, par. 69.

an expulsion order, that "in all circumstances the safeguards which do in fact exist and which will be further outlined in this judgement are perfectly adequate to meet the requirements of the constitution".

3.5 Decisions procedure

The Department of Justice, Equality and Law Reform is responsible for the administrative detention of foreign prisoners in Ireland.

3.6 Appeal Procedure

The safeguards to which the Supreme Court judgement cited above referred include the right to challenge, by judicial review, the validity of the expulsion order. The court also held that the extended grounds for detention would not contravene Article 5 of the European Convention on Human Rights and Fundamental Freedom. (Parliamentary Question 43, Dáil Éireann 27 April 2006) Administrative detention can be appealed through the District Court and to the High Court on a *habeas corpus*, judicial review or other legal application.

3.7 Irregular stay

Under the Immigration Act 2004, illegal /irregular stay in Ireland is a criminal offence on two grounds and the maximum penalty is 12 months imprisonment. (Section 4 (2) Immigration Act 2004 and Section 6 (1) Immigration Act 2004.[65]) In addition persons can be detained pre-trial for immigration related reasons under the Criminal Justice (Theft and Fraud Offences) Act 2001. Sections 26 and 29 relate to offences that include false passports or forgeries of official documents. These criminal offences are punishable by fines or imprisonment of 5-10 years.[66]

3.8 Numbers

The number of people detained for immigration related reasons in 2004 was 946, which was a significant reduction form 1852 the previous year.[67] However those held under the Immigration Act (1999) in 2004 were imprisoned for longer: 619 persons were imprisoned for over 51 days in comparison to 367 for the same period in 2003. While the numbers of those detained fell the length of time for those held in prison increased.[68] These figures do not reflect the total number of people detained for immigration–related reasons during this time as persons refused permission to land in Ireland are another category. Few would be taken to prison before being returned to their point of origin.[69]

---

65 Ibidem, p. 19.

66 Ibidem, p. 45.

67 Department of Justice, Equality and Law Reform, Irish *Prison Service Annual Report* 2004, p. 11.

68 M. Kelly, ibidem, pp.15-16.

69 Ibidem, p. 16.

3.9 Expulsion

No up to date figures available. There is no preparation for release/expulsion for administrative detainees apart from the work of the chaplaincy in this area. It appears that when persons detained under administrative law are being deported neither the person himself or herself or their families are informed in advance of their expulsion from the country. As this can often happen at any given time it is less likely that families will know or be informed. On occasion 10-15 foreign nationals can be brought up to the prison for expulsion at any one time. The authorities arrange transport arrangements, usually flights.

3.10 Not expelled prisoners

No information

3.11 Detention irregulars under criminal law

Administrative prisoners are detained with prisoners who are detained under criminal law.

3.12 Minors

No up to date figures available.

3.13 Reception and Admission

Admission procedures are the same for administrative detainees as for sentenced prisoners and detainees. Information booklets are given to all prisoners on admission to Cloverhill Prison but only in English at the moment. While admission interview questions have been translated into nine languages in both of the above prisons, staffs say that they can be less than helpful for instance if one is trying to find out if a woman is unwell. Kelly has suggested in his report that immigration related detainees bear the burden of the overcrowding in the prison system in both of these institutions. The Irish Prison Service has indicated that overcrowding, where it occurs bears equally on Irish and non-Irish prisoners and detainees. It is only in Cloverhill (Pre-Trial) Prison that there have been instances of three foreign prisoners or administrative detainees to a cell. Female immigration detainees at the Dochas Centre, Mountjoy Prison will often be detained in one of two houses the first of which should accommodate two but occasionally has more women. Female immigration detainees will often be held in one of two houses that have a fairly stable population of drug free, sentenced and long-term prisoners.[70]

In October 2005, new procedures were put in place that removed responsibility from prison management to either inform the prisoner about making an application for asylum or to process asylum applications. This applies for persons detained under the Immigration Act for refusal of leave to land. Instead the Governor should inform the detainee that she/he could make contact with the Garda National Immigration Bureau (GNIB) who

70 Ibidem, p. 50.

on receipt of a faxed copy of a form of notification from the prison will visit within 24 hours. In the event that a detainee indicates that s/he wishes to apply for asylum, the Immigration Officer will conduct an initial interview with the detainee and will forward the process from there.

3.14 Work-Education-Training –Sport-Recreation

There is no work, training, or educational services at present in Cloverhill Pre-Trial Prison where most administrative detainees are housed. Inmates are out of their cells for six and a half hours each day. There are plans for the development of work and training facilities. The building has been completed and is due to open in the near future. The daily routine is the same as for all other pre-trial prisoners where the use of the recreational yard is available in the morning and use of indoor recreational facilities (including snooker and table tennis) is available in the afternoon. At the Dochas Centre (Mountjoy prison) women are unlocked from the cells for around 12 hours per day (7am -7pm) during which time they are free to avail of the various activities and facilities. The prison library in Cloverhill has a multicultural collection of books, talking books and a limited selection of music CDs, in the following languages: Russian, Arabic, Chinese, Serbian, Romanian, Polish, Portuguese, French, Spanish, Albanian and Croatian. In addiction some foreign language and cultural interest magazines are held e.g. *Jeune Afrique Intelligent, New African, Argumenty y Fakty* (Russian newspaper) and *African Geographic.*

3.15 Food-Religion-Personal Hygiene-Medical care

The Prison Service has responded well in relation to food, to the diversity of nationalities and special dietary requirements are provided for in both these institutions (No complaints received in the study mentioned above which considered this issue among others.) All religions are facilitated through the chaplaincy in both institutions. Consideration is given in Cloverhill (Pre-Trial) Prison to the special needs of Muslim prisoners and efforts are made to allow them to do their customary religious rituals. Special food is ordered in, prepared by a Muslim cook and ordered from recognized Muslin traders. Advice was sought by the prison authorities from the Muslim Community about these issues. In the Dochas Centre, Mountjoy Prison, the female prison, all dietary requirements are taken into account and the chef prepares what is requested. Consideration is also given to clothing and the type of material used. For instance Muslim prisoners will not wear the white nylon shirts as the material is like silk and offends the men.

The mental health needs of immigration detainees are well illustrated in CVS Consultants and Migrant and Refugee Communities Forum.[71] The NHS (National Health Service) have done studies of refuge communities in England and Wales which show a high prevalence of mental health problems on two levels, problems of adjustment and those experiencing problems of post traumatic stress relating to incident in country of origin. Isolation, fear about the future and bereavement and loss of station in new country all feature as identifiable factors in a person's mental health. There are few studies done on the mental health of immigration or asylum seeking detainees.

---

[71] CVS Consultants and Migrant and Refugee Communities Forum, A *Shattered World: The Mental Health Needs of Refugees and Newly Arrived Communities,* 1999.

3.16 Contact with the Outside World

Immigration detainees at both Cloverhill Prison and the Dochas Centre Women's Prison are granted the same visiting entitlements as pre-trial prisoners, one 15-minute visit every day, Monday-Saturday and free telephone calls of up to six minutes every day. In the recent report by Kelly [72] it was recommended that time spent speaking to a solicitor by telephone should not be counted as part of time for telephone calls. There is a television in every cell but stations are only in the English language.

Visitor Centre: The Visitors Centre attached to Cloverhill Prison has many foreign national visitors. Communication difficulties and the need for leaflets and literature in other languages have been identified as issues to be addressed. Another area of difficulty is families unwilling to talk about their home lives. They are sometimes suspicious of staff at the centre as they are not sure whether they are prison or police personnel or independent. Visitors may not be aware that this is a confidential service and may be reluctant to ask for information or advice.

3.17 Re-integration activities- Prison leave

There is no prison leave or local settlement programme for this category of administrative detainee.

3.18 After-care- Probation

Probation personnel in the pre-trial prison have limited engagement with administrative detainees. In other prisons there is some limited involvement.

3.19 Staff

Training in cultural awareness and diversity is ongoing for all services working in prisons. As mentioned before, training and information on human rights and diversity is provided to all prison staff at induction and further initiatives are being developed and implemented on an ongoing basis.

4 IRISH NATIONALS DETAINED ABROAD

4.1 Numbers and composition group

There are reported to be approximately 700 Irish Prisoners in England and Wales of whom approximately 50 are women according to the ICPO.

---

72 M. Kelly, ibidem, p. 54.

Table 3 Number of Prisoners in contact with Irish Commission for Prisoners Overseas (ICPO) on 28 March 2006. (ICPO database)

MALE	*FEMALE*	*TOTAL*
497	26	523

AGE	*NO OF PRISONERS*
Under twenty	3
Between 20 and 35	170
Between 35 and 50	62
Over 50	136

4.2 Detention Countries.

The main countries of detention for those in contact are England and Wales followed by the USA. 448 are detained in the UK (England and Wales, not including Northern Ireland), 29 in USA, and 14 in Spain, 7 in France and smaller numbers in other countries. The Irish Commission for Prisoners Overseas says many prisoners may not know of their organisation or choose not to have contact with them. Some people do not put themselves down as Irish in the UK prisons. The official figures are probably an underestimate. Only very recently have the number of Jamaican prisoners and Nigerian prisoners overtaken the Irish prisoners in the UK prison population. The ICPO does not have contact with all prisoners but their newsletter is distributed widely.

Table 4: The main reasons for detention where known of Irish Prisoners Overseas. (ICPO database)

REASON FOR DETENTION	*NUMBER*
Homicide	36
Robbery	19
Assaults	11
Sexual offences	9
Drugs	5
Larcenies	5

TERMS OF SENTENCE	
1-3 years	18
4-6 years	91
7-10 years	82
11-15 years	53
over 15 years	34
life	72

4.3 Involved organisations – tasks and activities

The organisations involved with Irish prisoners overseas are the Department of Foreign Affairs, Department of Justice, Equality and Law Reform, local Irish Embassies, Irish Commission for Prisoners Overseas (ICPO), HM Prison Service in the UK, Probation Service UK, Chaplains in the UK prisons.

4.4 Release and reception home country

There is no single organisation responsible for ex prisoner emigrants returning to Ireland. The Probation Service provides a voluntary advice and referral service to prisoners returning to Ireland who contact the Service and call into any Service office. Where the ICPO have prior information and they do in many cases they send on information such as the 'What Now' information booklet published for people leaving prisons by the Department of Social Welfare and Family Affairs in advance of their return and the names of services in the prisoners' home area.

4.5 Aftercare

If the person is homeless they are referred to the Homeless Persons Service Unit of the Health Service Executive. The Homeless Persons Service Unit also provides information and support to those people who may be coming home from prison overseas to families. In some cases the ICPO arrange for ex prisoners to be met at Dublin airport and brought to their accommodation.

4.6 Public opinion and media

With some notable exceptions, the return of Irish prisoners is not and has not been a major issue for the media and general public.

5 EVALUATION AND RECOMMENDATIONS

In order to redress the social exclusion of foreign prisoners it is necessary to look at a variety of solutions.

- *Legal Rights and Entitlements.* There is a lack of easily accessible information in the language of users about legal rights and entitlements. Information booklets, prison rules, handouts on how to apply for a telephone card need to be provided in a variety of languages, text and recorded. [73] Translation, translators and accessible information are needed. The report on Immigration –related detention in Ireland recommends that all newly admitted detainees be provided with an information booklet including details about prison life and about the legal rights and entitlements of immigration detainees. There is an urgent need for translation of basic information to be undertaken.
- *Isolation.* Isolation and lack of communication is a matter of particular concern and

[73] M. Kelly, ibidem.

importance for non-national prisoners. Few visits or no visits, no contact with the outside, lack of reading material in own language all contribute to a sense of isolation. The absence of family contact and significant others can contribute to anxiety and depression. There is a need to develop community based support links, personal and emotional and cultural understanding, access to information and communication for foreign prisoners in recognition of their particular circumstances and needs. This might be done through a non-Government community based initiative.

- *Staffing*. Recruitment of staff from minority groups is important resource in addressing minority and cultural issues. This has been actively pursued and initiated in the Garda Siochana. The Irish Prison Service and other criminal justice agencies would also benefit from this approach. In addition to supporting engagement with the community it is also an important signal of inclusion and recognition.
- Training on cultural diversity needs to be further developed as a core part of basic and ongoing training and practice development. Such training is currently underway in the Irish Prison Service. Farrell (2002) advocates more resources and training in working with minority groups. She also advises that we should look at Britain as a country with a rich experience with ethnic and cultural minorities for models of improving practice and learning from that experience.
- The development, implementation and monitoring of clearly stated and managed diversity policies, practices and structures in all areas of the criminal justice system would underpin and support the current commitments. For example, the UK (England and Wales) has a race relations policy statement, race relations committees, a language line and embassy training days all of which would be welcome here. In the report Parallel Worlds[74], leadership and training are considered critical to breaking down different perceptions and experiences. It stresses that the training needs to be specific to race awareness and that it needs to be mandatory.
- A standard protocol and practice guidelines for the management of prisoners who are not Irish citizens that recognizes their status as non-Irish citizens and addresses their special needs should be developed and implemented. See [See Corrections Department NZ accessed 20-10-05]
- *Communication with Consular Services and Other Agencies*. Improved co-ordination and co-operation between Consulates, Embassies, and Ministries, Probation Services and Non Government Organisations is an important and achievable priority that would enhance current services, alleviate distress and improve information and communication channels. There is also a need for more information for families and one point of contact.
- There is a need for further development of documented anti-discriminatory and anti-oppressive practices for services and service providers in the community and in places of detention.

[74] HM Inspectorate of Prisons, Parallel Worlds - A Thematic Review of Race Relations in Prisons, 2005.

Chapter 14

Italy

Paola Balbo

1 INTRODUCTION

1.1 Overview of penalites and measures

In Italy, prisons and the wings inside are organised in maximum, medium and low security regimes according to the seriousness of the crimes committed. Kind of sentence, length of it and way of serving are decided by court again according to the offence, the possible length of sanction provided by law and the dangerousness of the person. When law admits it (because the minimum fixed by law has been served and the convict – both foreign and national, EU or non-EU – has adhered to behaviour-requirements), the tribunale di sorveglianza decides on the admission to the requested measure. Alternative measures can be affidamento in prova (similar to probation), affidamento in prova for drug addicts, home detention, semi-liberty and conditional release. Foreign prisoners account for nearly 40% of the total prison population. They come from a wide array of countries, and each region of Italy and each individual penitentiary institution within each region may have different provisions and opportunities for work and re-integration, according to national directives and local conditions. Thus, it is very difficult to determine one valid state of affairs for the entire national territory of Italy.

1.2 Overview of the Prison System

The institutions of the Italian Prison System can be categorized as follows:
- 162 pre-trial detention institutions: Case mandamentali (local prisons) and Case circondariali (district prisons);
- 37 institutions for serving sentences: Case di reclusione (anche presso case di custodia circondariali) (confinement/reclusion prisons, even at district prisons) and Case di arresto (anche presso case di custodia mandamentali o circondariali) (arrest prisons, even at local or district prisons);
- eight institutions for serving safety measures: Colonie agricole (agricultural camps), Case di lavoro (camp of work), Ospedali psichiatrici giudiziari (judicial psychiatric hospitals);
- Observation centres.

The following table shows the national prison population according to gender and type of institution on 30 June 2006 according to the National Department of Prisons:

37 reclusion prisons

	women	*men*	*total*
Convicts	210	8,256	8,466
Accused	49	744	793
Totals	259	9,000	9,259

162 district prisons

	women	*men*	*total*
Convicts	1,481	28,141	29,622
Accused	1,098	19,882	20,980
Totals	2,579	48,023	50,602

Eight institutions for the execution of safety measures

	women	*men*	*total*
Convicts	80	1,276	1,356
Accused	5	42	47
Totals	85	1,318	1,403

Total

Sum	2,923	58,341	61,264
of which foreigners	1,342	18,879	20,221

2 TREATMENT OF FOREIGN PRISONERS

2.1 Generale

According to the Italian Penitentiary Law of 25 July 1975, n. 354, there are no differences between Italian and foreign prisoners and detainees, neither concerning their stay in prison nor in the serving of sentences in general and in the possibilities of re-insertion. The availability of work and training as well as the forms and contents thereof depend on what each Region of Italy and each prison administration has organised in each geographic area. The basic principle is stated in Article 1 of the Penitentiary Law: "Penitentiary treatment must suit to humanity and must guarantee the respect of dignity of the individual. Treatment is marked by an absolute impartiality, without discriminations because of nationality, race, economic and social conditions, political and religious opinions"[1].

The principle of non-discrimination has been interpreted in the sense that the more foreigners enter prisons to serve a sentence or pre-trial detention, the more the prison directors feel the necessity to reorganise aspects of common life such as religion, food, and the organisation of cells and wings in order to respect those cultural differences the change of which cannot be demanded.

2.2 Living conditions and facilities

Convicts and detainees are assigned to institutions and prison wings with regard to the possibility of common re-educative treatment and to the opportunity of avoiding mutual prejudicial influences (Article 14, law n. 354/1975) and, of course, to the crimes committed.

1 P. BALBO (2005), *Diritto penitenziario internazionale comparato. Esecuzione penale in carcere e in area esterna, Laurus Robuffo*, Roma.

2.3 Reception and admission

If treatment within penitentiary institutions and procedures of admission to measures that are alternatives to prison should be the same for all prisoners regardless of any possible discriminatory characteristics, practice shows us that this is in fact not always the case.

It is true that admission to affidamento in prova (similar to probation with supervision), to home detention, to semi-liberty or just to licences is applicable to every convict who fulfils the legally prescribed requisites. However, it is just as accurate that the court of surveillance cannot in fact apply such alternative measures if there are no reference points, centres or structures outside of prison where a foreigner can stay and be under supervision as required by law.

It is the same reason for which judges and courts prefer to pass a prison sentence even when an alternative measure should be indicated better by law because of the length of the sentence. However, some more recent decisions pronounced by the Court of Cassazione go in the other direction. In 2005 it was confirmed that imprisoned foreign citizens without a visa or regular residential permission also have the right to benefit from measures that are alternatives to prison, in the respect of the principle of equal dignity to Italian citizens. This is due to the aim of re-education and social re-integration that the punishment has (and has to have), in accordance with this principle and to the principle of non-discrimination between Italian citizens and foreigners, regardless of whether they have entered the country regularly or illegally (Cass. Sez. I crim., sent. 8 May 2005, n. 22161, rel. Silvestri). Before, the Court of Cassazione has had the opportunity to clear that a petition for *affidamento in prova* of a foreign prisoner who has to be expelled can not be declared inadmissible *de plano* and this because this measure simply defers but does not stop his/her serving sentence. In fact, should he/she return to Italy again, serving of the sentence must recommence (Cass. Pen., sez. I, 24 Oct. 1995, n. 4752, Padilla Chaves).

2.4 Work – education – training – sports – recreation

Article 35 of the same DPR n. 230/2000 prescribes that linguistic and cultural differences of foreign citizens serving custodial sentences have to be taken into account. Moreover, improvements need to be made in providing cultural mediators, even through agreements with local public administrations or voluntary organisations.

Working opportunities have to be improved inside prisons as well as possibilities to participate in training courses. Convicts as well as persons under safety measures are obliged to work, which is performed in agricultural houses or in working houses.

2.5 Food – religion – personal hygiene – medical care

Inmates and detainees are free to profess their religion, learn it and practice it.

Regarding health assistance, foreign prisoners and foreign interned persons, stateless persons and persons without fixed residence are provided with health assistance from the public health service of the region/locality in which the prison is located (Article 18 sec. 2, Regulation, Decreto del Presidente della Repubblica (D.P.R.) 30 June 2000, n. 230).

Prisoners and detainees have the right and the freedom to profess their religion and to be assisted by ministers of their faith[2].

2.6 Consular and legal help

In 1987 it was reminded to governors of prisons and their staff that they are to advise each foreign prisoner or detainee immediately after his/her entry into a prison establishment that he/she has the right to communicate with Consular Representation of his/her State, as well as to receive visits from their representatives, as guaranteed by the Convention of Vienna[3].

2.7 Contact with the outside world

According to Article 18 of Law n. 354 of 1975 prisoners and detainees are permitted to communicate (35 r.e.) and have correspondence with (36, 37 r.e.) their relatives and others. Meetings and face to face conversations are conducted in appropriate cells within the view of penitentiary officers, however in a form that does not enable auditory monitoring (71 r.e.). Special treatment and opportunities are reserved to conversations with relatives.

Phone correspondence with relatives and with third persons in particular cases may be allowed as long as it is in line with conditions and provisions that are indicated by regulations. This is regulated by administrative dispositions of the Department of Prisons.[4] These state that because of the need to listen in to all telephone conversations in order to understand and be aware of their content, conversations in foreign languages that no prison officers understand can lawfully and properly be denied. The Central Direction of the Department of Prisons is conscious of this situation and has ordered prison governors to find and provide reliable interpreters who will simultaneously translate phone conversations in order to make the calls comprehensible for the officers in charge of monitoring them. Officers are authorised to interrupt telephone conversations if they suspect or can circumstantially prove the planning of illicit activities or activities that may be a threat to the order and safety of the establishment.

This also means that other questions such as for instance communication with families and consular representations are partly regulated by the Procedural Criminal Code and partly by the Immigration Law, as stated before.

2.7.1 Foreign prisoners detained under criminal law and who will remain in the country of detention after release

According to Italian law, not all foreign prisoners are forced to return to their country because of the kind and/or length of their sentence. This means first of all that foreigners have the right to be admitted to measures that are alternatives to prison, and to cultural,

---

[2] Art. 26 law n. 354 of 1975; DPR n. 230/2000 artt. 58 and 116.
Circolare D.A.P. 6 May 1997, n. 535554. *Assistenza religiosa ai detenuti ed internati ex art. 5 DPR 431/76*, referred to the possibility of professing the Muslim faith.

[3] Circolare D.A.P. 12 June 1987. *Art. 36 Convenzione di Vienna. Comunicazioni relative ai detenuti stranieri.*

[4] Circolare D.A.P. 26 Oct. 1988, n. 3254/5704, *Corrispondenza telefonica dei detenuti ed internati. Conversazioni telefoniche in lingua straniera.*
Circolare D.A.P. 3 Jan. 1990, n. 698564.1/3. *Conversazioni telefoniche in lingua straniera.*

training or working opportunities inside and outside the institutions. Treatment during the sentence is to be individualised based on each individual inmate, but with opportunities offered to everyone without discriminations. The cases in which expulsion for sentenced foreigners can be applied regardless of whether they are regular or irregular before their sentence - are clearly defined by law.

A further element introduced in 2003 is the opportunity for foreign prisoners to obtain the conditional suspension of serving the final part of a sentence to detention (so called *indultino*), unless they are in one of the situations indicated in Article 13, sec. 2 of the Immigration Law, D. lgs. 25 July 1998, n. 286 on illegal entry. It is obvious that the conditional suspension of a sentence is not admissible for foreign prisoners as well as for Italian inmates in such well defined cases as:

- when the sentence is the result of conviction for offences against individuals such as slavery, prostitution of women and children, pornography and similar, trafficking of human beings, harassment and sexual abuse of children, sexual abuses by a group[5];
- when a person has been declared habitually or professionally criminal, or as having a tendency or inclination towards criminal behaviour (Articles. 102, 105 and 108 CP);
- towards those put under a regime of particular control (Article 14-bis L. 26 July 1975, n. 354), apart from cases indicated by art. 14ter or the same law which prescribe the way to appeal the particular regime adopted according to art. 14 bis.
- when the convict has been admitted to measures that are alternatives to prison;
- when the interested person has renounced.

A sentence can be conditionally suspended when at least half of a sentence has already been served, and the remaining period is no longer than two years.

The conditional suspension of a sentence (in the sense of serving sentence) can be decided and applied just once, having taken into consideration the punishment as prescribed by art. 663 cpp. The part of the sanction on which the measure of anticipated liberty has been granted has to be subtracted from the length of sentence upon which conditional suspension is applied (Article 54 L. 26 July 1975, n. 354). Upon request of the individual in question or of his/her legal defence, the magistrate of surveillance provides an order about the suspension (Article 69-bis, sec. 1, 3 and 4, L. 26 July 1975, n. 354). As well as in all other cases, including those in which expulsion is imposed as an alternative or substitutive measure, the magistrate of surveillance can request all the documents and information he needs from the competent authorities.

Within five years of its adoption without having committed any offence, the sentence is extinguished.

2.7.2 Foreign prisoners detained under criminal law who will be expelled to their home country or a third country

The Department of Prisons has adopted administrative dispositions in order to be able to respect national rules referring to the expulsion of foreign prisoners.

---

5 It. Criminal Code, book II, Title XII, head III, sec. I, and art. 609-bis, 609-quarter and 609-octies. Art.4-bis L. 26 July 1975, n. 375 and successive modifications.
Immigration law has introduced more severe sanctions against those citizens or foreigners sentenced for offences such as illegal immigration, prostitution and traffic of human beings and adopted in those cases the maximum security regime inside prison prescribed by art . 4 bis of penitentiary law.

If general rules concerning expulsion derive from Immigration law, in 1993 the problem of the costs of expelling a person and which administration should cover the arising expenses were brought into consideration. The Ministry of Justice has formulated the opinion that if deportation and – in particular – accompanying irregular migrants to the border are a responsibility of the bailiffs and thus represent part of the jurisdictional decision of expulsion, as a consequences the costs have to be covered by judicial administration. However, if we divide the procedure of expulsion into two separate parts, the first one represented by accompanying the foreigner to the border which is specifically executed by bailiffs, and the second part represented by sending foreigners back to their state of origin by the police – the costs have to be divided between the Ministry of Justice and the Ministry of Interior[6].

The situation is different for prisoners who have to be extradited from Italy or are sent to Italy from other countries.[7]. In 1996 the penitentiary police were given the responsibility to transfer prisoners who have to be extradited from the penal institution to the border (so called *estradandi*) and from the border to prisons (so called *estradati*). In particular, in the case of extradition abroad, there are three hypotheses of procedures. According to the first one, when the *estradandi* inmate is in one of the seven regions mentioned by authority, he/she is taken from the prison he/she is in to the one the competent bureau of the Ministry has indicated, and the transfer is a duty of penitentiary officers. This duty is also assigned to them when the temporary institution to which the person is taken is in one of the regions, and in this case the penitentiary police have to take the inmates to the border, too. In the second case, if the institution for temporary permanence is in one of the regions where the competence for the transfer lies with the Carabinieri or the State Police, penitentiary officers take the inmates from the prison they are in to the institution of temporary permanence and from there to the border. The third case is given by the regions where the service of transfer is not yet a duty of the penitentiary police, in which cases the responsibility lies with the Carabinieri and the State Police.

In cases of extradition from abroad, inmates are handed over to penitentiary officers by the foreign judicial authority in one of the regions where the penitentiary is competent for the transfer of inmates from the border to the prison to which he/she has been assigned. Otherwise, the extradited inmate is handed over to the police who have been charged to do this.

Direction of the Department of Prisons gave in the past dispositions in order to send foreign prisoners who had been released and who returned to their country the money gained during their serving sentence[8]. In particular, it was ordered that before their release foreign prisoners who are entitled to an amount that is in fact not payable at the moment of their removal can leave an address to which the sums will be sent, or to consent to the payment being sent to the consular representation of their state of origin, which is then in turn responsible for seeing to it that the inmate receives his/her money.

---

6 Circolare M.G.G. AFF. CIV. 9 Sept. 1993, prot. n. 5/36/U/-1588. *Legge 12 agosto 1993, n. 296. Spese per l'espulsione dei detenuti stranieri.*
Circolare M.G.G. AFF. CIV. 15 Nov. 1993, n. U 1905-S/36. *Legge 12 agosto 1993, n. 296. Spese per l'espulsione dei detenuti stranieri.*

7 Circolare D.A.P. 21 MAy 1996, n. 3428/5878. *Detenuti estradandi e/o estradati. Estradizioni per l'estero ed estradizioni dall'estero. Competenze e modalità di esecuzione delle tradizioni.*

8 Circolare D.A.P. 20 July 1999, n. 552569/13. *Corresponsione di somme pertinenti a detenuti stranieri.*

3. ADMINISTRATIVE DETENTION OF FOREIGN PRISONERS

3.1 Institution and capacity

In 1999 regulations were adopted that referred to Centres of Temporary Permanence and Assistance[9]. First of all, the chief constable communicates to foreigners kept in a centre of temporary permanence not only the order referring to his/her delay, but also the one referring to his/her expulsion. In the same order he/she has to be informed of the right to defence and that the defence council can either be a lawyer of his/her own choice or who is chosen and appointed by the court. Also, a foreigner has to be advised of the fact that he/she can request free legal aid that is covered by the State. When he/she is admitted to a centre of temporary permanence, a foreigner has to be advised of the rules that he/she has to respect. One of the most important rules is the prohibition to leave the institution without permission, because in that case he/she will be kept back by public officers. The length of his/her detention must be limited to the time necessary to execute the expulsion or repelling, and must cease if the judge of peace does not confirm the measure of expulsion.

According to regulations, the following ought to be safeguarded inside centres of temporary permanence and assistance: freedom of conversation inside and with visitors from outside; conversations with lawyers and ministries of faith; freedom of correspondence, even phone conversations; fundamental rights of the person; basic health service.

Judges must authorise foreigners kept in one of the centres to go to hospitals while advising consular representations in the meanwhile, in order to prepare the documents valid for returning home. It is always the judge who authorises a person who is being detained in a centre of temporary permanence to go away from the centre for the time necessary to visit a relative or a cohabitee who is in serious danger of life or for other exceptional reasons.

3.2 Decision Procedure

3.2.1 Judicial expulsion

Expulsion has been adopted towards non European foreigners in the cases described by Article 235 and 312 c.p. and on the basis of Article 686 of procedural criminal code, as briefly indicated below.

Expulsion from the national territory of Italy is decided by the judge in a number of cases:

- Foreigner sentenced to at least ten years of detention.

---

[9] DPR 29 Jan. 1999. *Regolamento di attuazione del testo unico delle disposizioni concernenti la disciplina dell'immigrazione e norme sulla condizione dello straniero*, artt. 19 a 23.
Direttiva generale del Ministro dell'interno 30 agosto 2000 in materia di Centri di Permanenza temporanea ed Assistenza ai sensi dell'art. 22, comma 1, DPR 31 agosto 1999, n. 394, in *Gli stranieri, Rassegna di studi, giurisprudenza e legislazione*, n. 3, settembre-dicembre 2000, p. 360.
O. DI MAURO, *I centri di permanenza temporanea per immigrati. Aspetti legali e funzionali*, in www.dexl.tsd.unifi.it/l'altrodiritto/migranti.

- Foreign convicts sentenced for one of the offences on traffic, abuse or possession of drugs (Article 3, 74, 79, 82 and 86 DPR 9 Oct. 1990, n. 309). In this case it is an obligatory measure.
- Foreign convicts sentenced for one of the other offences indicated in the same DPR 9 Oct. 1990, n. 309 and in this case it is a facultative measure.
- Expulsion as a safety measure (Article 15 of D.lgs 25 July 1989, n. 286).
- In all cases in which a foreigner is sentenced for one of the offences against the personality of the state (title I, artt. 241 – 313 cp).

It is also prescribed that every time the foreigner violates the order of expulsion that has been decided by the judge, the sanctions established for cases of misdemeanours to the order of an administrative authority as prescribed in the law on public safety are applied (Article 235 cp).

3.2.2 Expulsion as safety measure

According to Article 200 C.P., safety measures can be applied to a foreigner but their application does not prevent a person from being expelling in the cases indicated by Article 235 cp.

Here we can also include the dispositions of Article 15 of D. lgs. n. 286 of 1998 regarding expulsion as a safety measure. Article 15 states that, out of the cases indicated by the Criminal Code, a judge can issue the expulsion of a foreigner who has been sentenced for some of the offences described in Articles 380 and 382 of the Procedural Criminal Code, provided that he/she is socially dangerous.

With regards to the procedure of expulsion it is said that the chief constable is immediately advised of the ruling of pre-trial detention or of the final sentence of conviction to detention against an alien[10], and the same communication is sent to the respective consular authority in order to initiate the procedure of identifying the subject and to permit the execution of expulsion immediately at the end of preventive custody or detention.

3.2.3 Administrative expulsion

This definition includes all the possible forms of expulsion that can be adopted by the Minister of the Interior, by prefect or by the chief constable. Article 13 of the Immigration Law (Decreto legislativo n. 286/1998) introduces a first possibility that applies when there are public order or state safety reasons. In this case the Ministry of the Interior can decide on the expulsion of an alien even if he or she is not resident in the territory of Italy, advising the Prime Minister and the Minister for Foreign Affairs.

Administrative expulsion is decided by the prefect when the alien:

- has entered the national territory of Italy by means of dodging border controls and he/she has been repelled in concordance with Article 10;
- has remained in Italy without having acquired a visa in the time fixed by law, unless delay depends on circumstances beyond the alien's control, or when visa has been revoked or cancelled, or it has expired for more than 60 days without a request of renewal;

[10] In this context 'alien' specifically refers to those foreigners who come from States outside of the European Union and to those it is referred to Italian Immigration Law.

- belongs to one of the categories indicated in Article 1 of law 27 Dec. 1956, n. 1423, as substituted with Article 2 of law 3 Aug. 1988, n. 327; or in Article 1 of the law 31 May 1965, n. 575, as substituted with Article 13 of the law 13 Sept. 1982, n. 646.

3.2.4 Expulsion as a substitutive or alternative measure to prison

A further possibility of expulsion is applied after conviction (Article 16 of D. lgs n. 286/1998). If a judge passes a sentence for an unpremeditated offence, applies the sanction asked ex art 444 Procedural Criminal Code towards a foreigner in one of the situations described in Article 13, section 2, the sentence is for a maximum of two years in prison and conditions for conditional suspension of the sentence (Article 163 It. C.P) are not present nor the forbidding causes stated in Article 14, section 1 of the Immigration Law, he can substitute the same sanction with the expulsion for a period of at least five years. In these cases, as well as any other administrative expulsion to which the Constitutional Court has assimilated this one, expulsion is executed by the chief constable, even if the sentence is not definitive and the procedure is the same as that of administrative expulsion (Article 13 of D. lgs. n. 286/1998).

Expulsion can not be applied when a person is convicted of one or more of the crimes indicated in Article 407, sec. 2, litt. a) of the Procedural Criminal Code, or for those indicated in this law and punished with an edictal sanction of more than two years.

If a foreigner who has been expelled because of a sentence that was passed for an unpremeditated offence or as a means of serving sentence ex Article 444 CPP enters the country again illegally before the time fixed by law has passed, the substitutive measure is revoked by the competent judge.

The expulsion is ordered against an identified or imprisoned alien who is in one of the situations described in Article 13, sec. 2, and who has to serve a measure privative of liberty, even if less than two years of the sentence remain. It can not be ordered in cases of convictions for one of the crimes of Article 407, sec. 2, litt. a) of the Procedural Criminal Code, or for one of the offences indicated by immigration law.

Responsibility for ordering the expulsion of a convict lies with the magistrate of surveillance, who decides with a justified decree once he/she has received information about the identity and nationality of the foreigner from the bureaux of police. The decree of expulsion is communicated to the alien who can lodge an appeal within 10 days to the tribunal of surveillance. The court then decides within 20 days.

3.2.5 Procedures to execute administrative or judicial expulsion

In any case, expulsion is ordered with a justified decree which is immediately executable, even if submitted to burden or appeal from the concerned individual. When an alien is submitted to a criminal proceeding and he/she is not in preventive custody, the chief constable, before the expulsion can be carried out, has to request authorisation to do so from the judicial authority. Authorisation can only be denied if there are binding trial needs connected to an assessment of the responsibility of persons who have participated in the crime or who are accused in proceedings for connected offences, as well as regarding the issues of the victims. In such a situation the execution of the measure is deferred until the judicial authority confirms that procedural needs have ceased to exist. Once authorisation has been granted, the chief constable executes the expulsion according to the manner provided for by Immigration law. Authorisation is considered granted if the judicial authority does not reach a decision within fifteen days after the request had been filed. While waiting for authorisation, the chief constable can adopt the measure of keeping the person in a centre for temporary permanence.

The judge authorizes an expulsion when he/she confirms the issue unless one of the causes such as arrest in flagrance or stop occurs, and preventive custody in prison has been adopted ex art. 391, sec. 5, CPP, or if one of the reasons apply for which authorisation can be denied because the person corresponds to one of the categories according to which removal is required. Also, the same procedure is adopted towards foreigners who have been subjected to a criminal proceeding, after the measure of preventive custody has been revoked or declared extinguished for some reason.

The judge, with the same measure of revocation or extinction, decides about the issue of authorisation to expulsion. The measure is immediately communicated to the chief constable.

In the cases in which the judge has the proof that expulsion has been issued, if the measure has not been pronounced yet, he/she enters a so-called non-suit ("way not to proceed"; non luogo a procedure). The things indicated in section two of Article 240 Criminal Code are always confiscated. In such a case the dispositions referring to prohibition of entry after expulsion are applicable as are the sanctions in cases of violations of this order.

If an expelled foreigner (illegally) returns to the territory of Italy before the fixed time period (10 years as general rule; five years if after release; or depending on whether the sentence indicates a period of less than ten years) has passed, or – if the time is longer than that – before the end of the prescribed term for the most serious offence for which there has been proceedings against him/her, Article 345 of the Procedural Criminal Code applies. In accordance with Article 307 of the Procedural Criminal Code, if the alien had been released because the time limit for pre-trial detention had passed, preventive custody can be imposed.

Expulsion is always executed by the chief constable in the form of accompanying the individual to the border by the police, except if the foreigner has been staying in Italy because his permit of stay has expired and a renewal thereof has not been requested. In that case the expulsion order also contains an injunction to leave Italy within fifteen days. The chief constable issues the immediate transportation of the alien to the border just in cases in which the prefect points out that there is a real danger of the foreigner escaping from the execution of the measure.

In the two hypotheses mentioned above, the chief constable communicates to the judge of peace immediately and, however, within 48 hours from its adoption the measure with which it has been decided to accompany the foreigner to the border. Execution of the measure of removal from the territory is deferred until the decision confirming it has been reached. The confirmation-hearing is held in the Council Chamber and the presence of a lawyer, announced in good time, is necessary. Furthermore, the concerned party must also be informed in good time and be present at the hearing.

3.3 Appeal procedure

According to Prisons' Regulations[11] in each prison there is a list of the lawyers of the district, which has to be displayed in a fashion so that it is visible for all prisoners and detainees to see. In order to guarantee a person's freedom of choice, prison operators are strictly not allowed to directly or indirectly influence choices of legal defence counsel.

Generally speaking, however, the right to defence in cases of expulsion or repelling is not as well safeguarded as it ought to be. There has been an evolution since 2002. Immigration law has been amended also because of the sentences of the Italian Constitutional Court, and there is no doubt that knowledge of the rights and right to an interpreter and/or translator are not fully achieved.

A person can file an appeal against an expulsion order only to the judge of peace of the locality where the order was passed, within 60 days. The competence to decide on appeals against administrative expulsion mainly lies in the hands of judges of peace. Their decisions are made within 20 days of the date on which the appeal was lodged by the directly interested person. Regarding the procedure of appeal, it has to be said that this kind of appeal can be subscribed even personally, and it can also be presented through the Italian diplomatic or consular delegation in the State of destination. Subscription of the appeal from the interested person is authenticated by the officials of diplomatic or consular delegations who certify authenticity and take care of its forwarding to the judicial authority. A foreigner is entitled to legal assistance from a lawyer by trust with a special proxy issued in front of the consular authority. Furthermore, he/she can also be granted legal defence that is paid for by the state and, in case of absence of a defence counsel, he/she is assisted by a lawyer who is chosen by the judge among those enrolled in the table of Article 29 of dispositions on application, coordination and temporary of the Procedural Criminal Code, decreto legislativo 28 July 1989, n. 271, as well as by an interpreter if necessary.

The issue of expulsion has to be confirmed by the judge within 48 hours, and this confirmation has to be justified. Before reaching a decision, he/she has to check whether terms and time-limits have been accorded with, that the requirements of the mentioned article are present and that the person has been heard, so long as he/she was present on the day of the decision. While he/she is waiting for the definition of the proceeding for confirming the measure, the foreigner who is to be expelled is detained in one of the centres of temporary permanence and assistance. There is also the possibility that the measure of expulsion is defined before the concerned person is transferred to a centre. Once confirmation has been achieved, the measure of accompanying the foreigner to the border becomes executive. If the measure is not confirmed or if the time limit for reaching the decision elapses, the measure of chief constable loses every effect. The decree of confirmation can be appealed to the Court of Cassazione. However, this appeal does not defer the execution of removal from Italy. The term of 48 hours within which the judge of peace has to confirm the measure starts from the moment of its communication to the chancery.

---

[11] DPR 30 June 2000, n. 230, art. 24.

Due to the short amount of time that judges of peace have to make a decision on whether or not to expel a foreigner[12], the police headquarters provide them with the necessary support and the availability of a proper area in order to facilitate the decision.

Nowadays, one very important change is given by Article 3 of *Decreto legge* 27 July 2005, n. 144 converted, with modifications, in the law 30 July 2005, n. 155 concerning new dispositions about the expulsion of aliens for reasons of preventing terrorism. For terror-suspects, the appeal procedure of Article 13 sec 5-bis of the Immigration Law – that had previously been declared unconstitutional and was consequentially abrogated by the Constitutional Court in sentence n.222 of 2004[13] because it was a violation of the right to defence – has been reintroduced. In fact, in Article 3 that is under examination here it is established that against the decree of section 1 an appeal can be lodged with the administrative tribunal that is competent for the territory. However, a jurisdictional appeal can never suspend the execution of the measure.

Article 3 introduces a new possibility of expulsion apart from the administrative one indicated in Articles 9, section 5, and 13, sec. 1, of the decreto legislativo n. 286 of 1998. The Minister of the Interior or the prefect can dispose the expulsion of a) an alien belonging to one of the categories of Article 16 of law 22 May 1975, n. 152, or b) a foreigner in regard of whom there are founded reasons to suppose his/her stay in Italy can in some way facilitate (even international) terrorist activities. Persons suspected of terrorist activities are expelled immediately, except if they are in prison, in which case the rules for the execution of expulsion of a foreigner under a criminal proceeding are adopted (sec. 3, Article 13 decreto lgs. 25 July 1998, n. 286), and those referring to suspension of executing deportation in cases of appeal (of sec. 5-bis of the same Article 13). The prefect can also omit, suspend or revoke the measure of expulsion ex Article 13, sec. 2, of D. lgs. n. 286 of 1998 when there are the conditions to concede permission of entry as described in the decree on the fight against terrorism, or when it is necessary to do so to obtain information for the prevention of terrorist activities, or to continue investigations of informative

---

12 Decreto legislative (D. lgs.) n. 286/1998, as indicated in sections 4 and 5, and in art. 14, section 1.

13 Constitutional Court sentence n. 222 of 2004 (abstract): "The order regulated by art. 13, sec. 5-bis, contravenes principles affirmed by this Court in the sentence mentioned above: the order of accompanying to the border is executed before the confirmation from judicial authority. The foreigner is sent off in a coercive way from the national territory without a judge having pronounced himself on the restrictive order of his/her personal freedom. It is so frustrate the safeguard indicated in the third sec. of art. 13 Const. and that is the loss of effects of the order in hypothesis of denial or lacking confirming from a judicial authority within the successive 48 hours. And with freedom it is violated the right to defence the foreigner has in its unsuppressible nucleus. The censured disposition does not make provision for, indeed, the alien has to be heard by a judge, with the help of a lawyer. It in not under discussion the discretion of the legislator in shaping a proceeding scheme characterized by swiftness and articulated on the sequence police's order – judge ratification.. However, whatever the scheme chosen is, in it the principles of jurisdictional defence have to be realised; the actual control on the order *de libertate* can not be eliminated, nor can it be bereave the party concerned of any defensive safeguard.

Censures proposed by remitting parties cannot finally be over resorting to the thesis of the so-called "double line" of defence for the alien: ratification only 'papery' of the order of accompanying to the border and successive appeal against the decree of expulsion with proper defensive safeguards. It should be in fact eluded the prescriptive significance of art. 13 Const., as appeal on the decree of expulsion (art. 13, sec. 8) does not guarantee immediately and directly the good of personal freedom on which accompanying to the border engraves".

activities directed to single out or to capture the perpetrators of terrorist-motivated offences.

The execution of measures of expulsion in cases of terror suspects can not be suspended during jurisdictional proceedings in application of Article 21 of law 6 Dec. 1971, n. 1037 and successive modifications or of Article 3 of royal decree 17 Aug. 1907, n. 42. An exception to the procedure of appeal after expulsion is contemplated in just one case. In cases of appeals against expulsion orders as described in sec. 4 of the cited article and of appeals as defined in Article 13, sec. 11, of decreto legislative 25 July 1998, n. 286, some information could be covered by State secret. In that case, if a decision depends on knowledge of acts for which there is the secret of investigation or of State, the proceeding is deferred until the moment the act or its main contents can not be communicated to the administrative tribunal. If suspension goes on for a period longer than two years, the administrative tribunal can fix a term within which administration is forced to produce new elements to decide or to revoke the appealed measure. After the term mentioned above has elapsed, the administrative tribunal decides on the basis of what it has.

3.4 Procedures to communicate the order of expulsion and consequences of its violation

The decree of expulsion and the consequent measures indicated in section 1 of Article 14, such as every other act referring to entry, stay and expulsion, are communicated to the concerned person with the indication of the ways in which he/she can lodge an appeal. Furthermore, they are translated in a language he/she understands or, if this is not possible, into French, English or Spanish. Decrees of expulsion as fixed by Immigration Law can be appealed against at the administrative tribunal of Lazio, in Rome.

Except in cases concerning asylum seekers, pregnant women and persons under the age of 18 (Article 19, D. lgs. n. 286/1998), expelled foreigners are returned to the country of which they are citizens or – if this is not possible – to the country from which they crossed the border into Italy.

Expelled persons can not return to Italy without a special authorisation from the Minister of the Interior. Should a foreigner nonetheless violate this prohibition of entry, he/she can be sentenced to between one and four years of imprisonment, and is then expelled again immediately after being accompanied to the border.

In case of expulsion disposed by judge, the transgressor of the prohibition of re-entering the country is sentenced to prison for between one and four years. Foreigners who are accused of the offence of section 13, who are expelled, and who then return to Italy can be imprisoned for a term between one and five years..

In case of unauthorised re-entry (sections 13 and 13-bis, D. lgs. n. 286/1998), the arrest of the offender even out of the cases of flagrancy is obligatory and decision is taken during a proceeding with direct rite.

Unless stated otherwise in the ruling, in general the prohibition of returning to Italy after having been expelled lasts for ten years. Orders can indicate a shorter period, however no shorter than five years, but the person's behaviour while he or she was in Italy has to be taken into account. The described dispositions are not applicable to foreigners who can objectively show that they entered the national territory before the date on which the law n. 40 came into force (6 March 1998). In such cases the chief constable can adopt the same measures indicated in cases of expulsion of persons who have to be identified or for whom means of transportation have to be found.

3.5 Minors

Decreto legislativo of 25 July 1998, n. 286 (Articles 13, 15, 16, 19, 31, 33) specifies that minors below 18 years old can not be expelled, unless their expulsion depends on their right to stay with their parents or tutor should they be expelled. In case an issue of expulsion has been decided against a minor foreigner, the same procedures as those adopted for adults apply. The rules are those referred to illegal entry and to judicial, administrative or as alternative to detention measures. The Tribunal for Minors is responsible for decisions on whether the chief constable can expel a minor foreigner from the country.

In case of illegal entry and of the consequent administrative expulsion, the eventual presence of minors in centres of temporary permanence seems out of real control. Formally, Italy ratified the International Convention on the Rights of children but in practice the situation is quite far from one that safeguards the rights of children[14].

3 NATIONALS DETAINED ABROAD

The matter of Italian nationals detained abroad is briefly concentrated in the numbers given by the Italian Minister for Foreign Affairs[15] in terms of what forms of assistance Consulates and Embassies can provide.

The arrest of nationals abroad, according to declarations from the Minister for Foreign Affairs, can cause very complicated situations. Sometimes a very unusual discrepancy between the committed offence and the resulting sanction can be registered. In this context, there is an example concerning two Italians who were sentenced in the Maldives. They received life sentences for the unlawful possession of light drugs. In such cases it is possible to adopt extraordinary interventions in order to provide help and to effect the liberation of a prisoner. If a national is arrested in a foreign country, the Consulate can:

- visit the detainee, if it has been formally requested;
- provide assitance in finding a lawyer;
- assist in maintaining contacts with the relatives in Italy;
- provide – when it is necessary and admitted by local disposals – health assistance, food, books and newspapers;
- intervene with the aim of transferring a prisoner to Italy, if the national has been detained in one of the countries which signed the Strasbourg Agreement on the transfer of prisoners, or bilateral agreements ad hoc;
- intervene, in particular cases, to support a request of pardon based on humanitarian reasons.

Consulates can not:

- participate in trial as for the national;

---

14 We remand to Amnesty International report on detention of minors in Italy, published by Association Antogone, http://www.associazioneantigone.it/cpta/cpt.htm

15 http://www.esteri.it/ita/5_32.asp#9

- cover the legal costs of detained persons;
- effect better treatment in the prison where the national is detained.

The official statistics of 2002, 2003 and 2004 about the distribution of Italian nationals detained abroad with a distinction between sentenced prisoners, persons awaiting their trial and the country in which they are detained are published in the MAE (cp. 2).

Table 2.41 – Italian prisoners abroad according to their judicial situation and geographic area (year 2004)

Geogrpahic Area	*2003*			*2004*		
	Awaiting Trial	*Convicts*	*Total*	*Awaiting trial or extradition*	*Convicts*	*Total*
Europe	843	1.829	2.672	1.042	1.757	2.799
American continent	72	323	395	100	321	421
Mediterranian and Medio Oriente	2	10	12	8	10	18
Africa Sub-Sahara	5	1	6	10	2	12
Asia and Oceania	21	64	85	15	14	29
Total	943	2.227	3.170	1.175	2.104	3.279

Source: DGIT

Table 2.41.1 – Italian Prisoners abroad according to their judicial situation and country of detention (year 2004)

Country	*Prisoners*		
	Awaiting trial or extradition	*Convicts*	*Total*
Albania	3	2	5
Austria	-	37	37
Belgium	123	150	273
Bulgaria	1	-	1
Croatia	3	1	4
France	103	205	308
Germany	520	830	1.350
Greece	3	5	8
Ireland	-	2	2
Luxemburg	7	8	15
Malta	1	4	5
Norway	1	-	1
Netherlands	30	30	60
Poland	3	1	4
Portugal	19	18	37
United Kingdom	59	83	142
Czech Republic	1	4	5
Former Rep. Yugosl. Macedonia	-	3	3
Romania	5	5	10
Serbia & Montenegro	1	2	3

Country	*Prisoners*		
	Awaiting trial or extradition	*Convicts*	*Total*
Slovakia	5	-	5
Slovenia	1	3	4
Spain	111	141	252
Sweden	-	1	1
Switzerland	41	215	256
Hungary	1	7	8
Total	1.042	1.757	2.799

Source: DGIT

Table 2.21.2 – Italians detained abroad according to judicial situation and country of detention – American Continent (year 2004)

Country	*Prisoners*		
	Awaiting Trial or extradition	*Convicts*	*Total*
Argentina	19	8	27
Bolivia	-	2	2
Brazil	15	23	38
Canada	-	7	7
Chile	-	1	1
Columbia	9	7	16
Costa Rica	7	8	15
Cuba	2	5	7
Ecuador	7	5	12
Mexico	-	2	2
Panama	1	2	3
Paraguay	2	-	2
Peru	5	9	14
Dominican Republic	1	3	4
United States	25	199	224
Venezuela	7	40	47
Total	100	321	421

Source: DGIT

Table 2.41.3 – Italian detained abroad according to their judicial condition and country of detention – Mediteranian and Middle Eastern Countries (year 2004)

Country	*Prisoners*		
	Awaiting trial or extradition	*Convicts*	*Total*
Algeria	-	3	3
Egypt	-	1	1
United Arad Emirates	1	-	1
Jordan	1	-	1
Marokka	4	6	10
Tunisia	1	-	1
Yemen	1	-	1
Total	8	10	18

Source: DGIT

Table 2.41.4 – Italians detained abroad according to judicial situation and country of detention – Sub-saharian Africa (year 2004)

Country	*Prisoners*		
	Awaiting trial or extra-dition	*Convicts*	*Total*
Cameroon	2	-	2
Cape Verde	1	-	1
Ivory Coast	4	-	4
Eritrea	1	-	1
Kenya	2	1	3
Mauritius	-	1	1
Total	10	2	12

Source: DGIT

Table 2.41.5 – Italians detained abroad according to judicial condition and country of detention – Asia and Oceania (year 2004)

Country	*Prisoners*		
	Awaiting trial or extradition	*Convicts*	*Total*
Afghanistan	-	-	-
Australia	3	2	5
Cambodia	-	1	1
Japan	-	3	3
India	5	3	8
Indonesia	-	1	1
Myanmar	-	1	1
Thailand	7	3	10
Total	15	14	29

Source: DGIT[16]

5 EVALUATION

When focussing on foreign prisoners, central thought has to be aimed at the fact that there are three potential elements that can be correlated or at least be put in connection with each other: conditions of detention; the legal position of convicts or accused persons; the status of foreigners. Each of these three elements represents a component of the sentence or of detention conditions taking into consideration that they influence the decision on the kind of sentence to be served or the regime of detention also according to the seriousness of the crime committed and to the risk of evasion and/or absconding of the persons (i.e. pre-trial detention instead of home detention, bail instead of freedom under supervision, detention in the regime indicated by the court with regard to the offence instead of admission to alternative measures to prison).

Recent Italian legislations[17] represent an example of how European framework decisions and disposals may be applied, but in a sense that sometimes reduce the defence of human rights, or at least the possibility of a true and complete defence thereof. Each country has to be very careful and, moreover, to work with the aim of improving the system of serving sentence towards a more adequate regime that is able to respect a multiracial and multicultural prison population, and that is trained in a way to avoid macroscopic mistakes[18].

16 http://www.esteri.it/ita/6_40_222.asp

17 I refer mainly to: 1) law 22 aprile 2005, n. 69 – Disposizioni per conformare il diritto interno alla decisione quadro 2002/584/GAI del Consiglio, del 13 giugno 2002, relative al mandato d'arresto europeo e alle procedure di consegna tra Stati membri; 2) Decreto legge 27 luglio 2005, n. 144 convertito con legge 31 luglio 2005, n. 155 (on terrorism).

18 I mention here an episode that occurred on January 2006 during a proceeding at a Tribunal of surveillance in Italy. A black man in prison serving his sentence appealed against the order of expulsion against him according to art. 16 of D. lgs. n. 286/1998. He denied the legitimacy of his expulsion and the Court had difficulties in determining his citizenship, because the prison was not able to provide any documentary support in order to clarify this. In the end the black man said that he was from the Netherlands and that he was a Dutch citizen. The prison staff had not asked and, even

Under the profile of serving sentences it is more and more desirable to transfer prisoners to their state of origin. However, preliminary to this there is the need of basic conditions: a homogeneous minimum level of execution, first of all inside prison, and then outside of the institutions; stopping treatment that is inhuman or in any way harmful of dignity[19]; prohibition of torture; improvements in the provision of interpreters and translators.

The right to translation is guaranteed by law, but it is violated in practice. By law alternative measures have to be admitted but the lack of opportunities outside quite often makes this impossible. Improving true bilateral agreements has to be considered. The execution of sentences in the country of origin is rarely admitted because:

- there is very shallow knowledge of penitentiary systems;
- very few agreements have been signed between EU Member States in order to make it admissible,
- there is a misunderstanding of what the alternative measures are and what they aim to achieve, and of the role that judging and administrative States have to play.

---

more seriously, nobody had even thought of the possibility of him being a European Union citizen. The colour of his skin and language difficulties could be adduced as inadmissible reasons.

19 Just to mention an example, the prohibition of private and intimate relations within partners that some States still hold on to is absolutely useless with regard to what the sanction represents, and increases violence inside prisons as well as cases of sexual abuse.
See P. BALBO, *Sesso e carcere*, in '*Sessualità Diritto e Processo*', (a c. di) G. Gulotta e S. Pezzati (2002) Giuffrè ed., Milano, p. 86 sgg

STATISTICS FROM MINISTRY OF JUSTICE DEPARTMENT OF PRISONS
(situation on 31 December 2005)[20]

CITIZENSHIP

Foreign detainees according to their nationality *On 31 Dec 2005*

Country	WOMEN	MEN	SUM
Afghanistan	1	1	2
Albania	64	2907	2971
Algeria	8	1300	1308
Andorra		1	1
Angola	1	6	7
Argentina	8	47	55
Atol NaurNAURU		2	2
Australia	1	6	7
Austria	2	14	16
Bangladesh	1	34	35
Belgium	5	25	30
Benin	1	6	7
Bielorussia		9	9
Bolivia	20	39	59
Bosnia-Herzegovina	25	109	134
Brazil	58	126	184
Bulgaria	12	92	104
Burkina Faso	1	3	4
Burundi	1	12	13
Cameroon	4	14	18
Canada	1		1
Chad		1	1
Chile	17	142	159
Cina Popolare	25	254	279
Columbia	43	155	198
Congo		14	14
Costa Rica	1	5	6
Croatia	39	181	220
Cyprus		1	1
Czech Republic		4	4
Czech Republic	4	20	24
Dominican Republic	55	127	182
Ecuador	17	122	139

20 All statistics can be consulted on website of Italian Ministry of Justice: http://www.giustizia.it/statistiche/statistiche_dap/det/detg00_organigramma.htm

Foreign detainees according to their nationality *On 31 Dec 2005*

Country	WOMEN	MEN	SUM
Egypt	1	197	198
El Salvador	1	5	6
Eritrea	1	14	15
Estonia		2	2
Etheopia	1	14	15
Finland	1		1
Formosa	1		1
France	10	148	158
Gabon		26	26
Gambia	1	72	73
Georgia		3	3
Germany	14	98	112
Ghana	11	129	140
Great Britain	5	25	30
Greece	2	44	46
Guatemala	2	9	11
Guinea		9	9
Guinea Bissao		3	3
Guinea Equatoriale		1	1
Honduras	1	3	4
Hungary	3	48	51
India		68	68
Iran		21	21
Iraq		115	115
Ireland		1	1
Isola Di Cuba	5	6	11
Isola Di Dominica	3	3	6
Isole Bahama		2	2
Isole Del Capo Verde	1	6	7
Isole Maldive		1	1
Israel	2	35	37
Ivory Coast	3	53	56
Jamaica		7	7
Japan		2	2
Jordan		10	10
Kazakhstan	1		1
Kenya		4	4
Kirgyszstan		1	1
Kuwait		1	1
Laos		2	2
Lettonia	1	2	3

Foreign detainees according to their nationality *On 31 Dec 2005*

Country	WOMEN	MEN	SUM
Libano		42	42
Liberia		64	64
Libya		44	44
Lithuania	2	59	61
Macao		1	1
Macedonia	6	125	131
Madagascar		2	2
Malaysia		8	8
Mali		14	14
Malta		2	2
Marocco	38	4170	4208
Mauritania		17	17
Mauritius		4	4
Mexico	2	19	21
Moldavia	27	263	290
Mongolia	4	2	6
Mozambique	1	2	3
Netherlands	14	54	68
Nicaragua		1	1
Niger		5	5
Nigeria	204	568	772
North Yemen		2	2
Norway		1	1
Pakistan		60	60
Palestine		154	154
Panama	1		1
Paraguay	4	5	9
Peru	21	145	166
Phillipines	10	40	50
Poland	20	177	197
Portugal	1	22	23
Romania	185	1602	1787
Russian Federation	15	53	68
Rwanda		14	14
Senegal	2	264	266
Sierra Leone	2	41	43
Singapore		3	3
Slovakia	4	12	16
Slovenia	2	56	58
Somalia	3	21	24
South Africa	2	8	10

Foreign detainees according to their nationality			*On 31 Dec 2005*
Country	**WOMEN**	**MEN**	**SUM**
Spain	12	115	127
Sri Lanka	1	48	49
Sudan	1	32	33
Surinam		1	1
Sweden		3	3
Switzerland	2	21	23
Syria		19	19
Tanzania	1	30	31
Thailand		1	1
Togo	1	14	15
Trinidad and Tobago		1	1
Tunisia	19	2057	2076
Turkey	3	81	84
Uganda	2	3	5
Ukraine	23	129	152
United States	4	5	9
Unknown Nationality	3	20	23
Uruguay	5	28	33
Venezuela	29	88	117
Vietnam		2	2
Yugoslavia	140	719	859
Zaire		2	2
Total	**1.302**	**18.534**	**19.836**

JUDICIAL CONDITION

Situation on 31 December 2005

DETAINED POPULATION ACCORDING TO REGION OF DETENTION AND LEGAL POSITION

	Legal position					
Region of detention	Awaiting first judgement	Appellant	Clai-mant	Final	Interned	**Total**
Abruzzo	218	224	104	1.284	63	1.893
Basilicata	50	40	19	337	-	446
Calabria	440	247	92	1567	1	2.347
Campania	1.877	807	377	3.912	337	7.310
Emilia Romagna	838	521	262	1.976	255	3.852
Friuli Venezia Giulia	159	72	41	558	-	830
Lazio	1.133	757	234	3.768	3	5.895
Liguria	307	155	117	880	1	1.460

Lombardia	1.835	1.141	379	5.113	185	8.653
Marche	192	85	49	624	1	951
Molise	43	23	13	332	-	411
Piemonte	848	571	227	3.077	4	4.727
Puglia	905	260	191	2.480	2	3.838
Sardegna	214	201	124	1.427	23	1.989
Sicilia	1.375	708	289	3.862	178	6.412
Toscana	836	421	100	2.565	129	4.051
Trentino Alto Adige	83	53	6	280	-	422
Umbria	177	94	35	717	-	1.023
Valle D'aosta	36	33	18	193	-	280
Veneto	638	269	99	1.724	3	2.733
National Total	12.204	6.682	2.776	36.676	1.185	59.523

Situation on 31 December 2005

FEMALE DETAINED POPULATION ACCORDING TO REGION OF DETENTION AND LEGAL POSITION

	Legal Position					
Region of detention	Awaiting 1st judgement	Appel-lant	Clai mant	Final	Inter -ned	**Total**
Abruzzo	16	3	2	7	-	28
Basilicata	-	-	-	22	-	22
Calabria	12	4	-	22	-	38
Campania	66	46	7	157	-	276
Emilia Romagna	46	20	11	84	-	161
Friuli Venezia Giulia	8	3	-	14	-	25
Lazio	97	47	37	287	-	468
Liguria	12	11	3	39	-	65
Lombardia	128	89	28	299	63	607
Marche	11	3	1	11	-	26
Molise	4	3	-	8	-	15
Piemonte	57	26	4	104	1	192
Puglia	47	16	12	129	-	204
Sardegna	18	8	4	22	-	52
Sicilia	39	8	9	77	-	133
Toscana	54	27	3	109	4	197
Trentino Alto Adige	5	3	1	15	-	24
Umbria	10	5	1	41	-	57

Valle D'aosta	-	-	-	-	-	-
Veneto	43	28	10	131	2	214
National Total	673	350	133	1.578	70	2.804

SEX

Situation to 31 Dec. 2005

DETAINED POPULATION ACCORDING TO REGION OF DETENTION AND SEX

Region Of Detention	Male	Male %	Female	Female %	Total
Abruzzo	1.865	98,5	28	1,5	1.893
Basilicata	424	95,1	22	4,9	446
Calabria	2.309	98,4	38	1,6	2.347
Campania	7.034	96,2	276	3,8	7.310
Emilia Romagna	3.691	95,8	161	4,2	3.852
Friuli Venezia Giulia	805	97,0	25	3,0	830
Lazio	5.427	92,1	468	7,9	5.895
Liguria	1.395	95,5	65	4,5	1.460
Lombardia	8.046	93,0	607	7,0	8.653
Marche	925	97,3	26	2,7	951
Molise	396	96,4	15	3,6	411
Piemonte	4.535	95,9	192	4,1	4.727
Puglia	3.634	94,7	204	5,3	3.838
Sardegna	1.937	97,4	52	2,6	1.989
Sicilia	6.279	97,9	133	2,1	6.412
Toscana	3.854	95,1	197	4,9	4.051
Trentino Alto Adige	398	94,3	24	5,7	422
Umbria	966	94,4	57	5,6	1.023
Valle D'aosta	280	100,0	0	0,0	280
Veneto	2.519	92,2	214	7,8	2.733
National Total	56.719	95,3	2.804	4,7	59.523

ENTER PRISON FROM LIBERTY

Year 2005

	Total of entries			of which foreign		
Region Of Detention	WOMEN	MEN	TOTAL	WOMEN	MEN	TOTAL
Abruzzo	241	1438	1.679	86	397	483
Basilicata	33	574	607	14	108	122
Calabria	109	2170	2.279	37	344	381
Campania	866	9065	9.931	291	1356	1.647
Emilia Romagna	520	5344	5.864	332	3248	3.580
Friuli V. Giulia	204	1681	1.885	112	971	1.083
Lazio	973	7547	8.520	611	3742	4.353
Liguria	249	2438	2.687	121	1317	1.438
Lombardia	1469	12828	14.297	998	7947	8.945
Marche	192	1549	1.741	140	871	1.011
Molise	39	369	408	9	66	75
Piemonte	1544	7918	9.462	1292	4804	6.096
Puglia	468	6997	7.465	207	1207	1.414
Sardegna	123	1653	1.776	46	160	206
Sicilia	289	6671	6.960	78	1041	1.119
Toscana	553	4991	5.544	294	2802	3.096
Trentino Alto Adige	117	1259	1.376	61	749	810
Umbria	98	1120	1.218	51	616	667
V.Aosta	16	160	176	6	71	77
Veneto	827	5185	6.012	618	3385	4.003
National Total	8.930	80.957	89.887	5.404	35.202	40.606

SEMI-LIBERTY

Situation on 30 June 2005

Region Of Detention	Italians	Foreigners	Total
Abruzzo	16	2	18
Basilicata	15	0	15
Calabria	64	1	65
Campania	203	2	205
Emilia Romagna	110	22	132
Friuli Venezia Giulia	51	3	54
Lazio	104	11	115
Liguria	97	19	116
Lombardia	169	12	181
Marche	14	2	16
Molise	4	0	4
Piemonte	84	14	98
Puglia	215	3	218
Sardegna	43	1	44
Sicilia	132	4	136
Toscana	143	29	172
Trentino Alto Adige	17	8	25
Umbria	12	9	21
Valle D'aosta	1	0	1
Veneto	101	33	134
National Total	1.595	175	1.770

AGE

Figures as recorded on 31 December 2005

PRISON POPOLATION ACCORDING TO THE COUNTY (REGIONE) OF DETENTION AND AGE

Region Of Detention	Age groups										
	18 to 20	21 to 24	25 to 29	30 to 34	35 to 39	40 to 44	45 to 49	50 to 59	60 to 69	> 70	??	Total
Abruzzo	34	136	270	384	325	256	216	219	49	4	-	1.893
Basilicata	9	23	77	67	89	73	38	54	12	3	1	446
Calabria	31	137	370	466	413	334	265	263	54	13	1	2.347
Campania	125	531	1.202	1.379	1.288	1.006	718	779	205	77	-	7.310
Emilia Romagna	129	379	676	722	630	487	346	350	107	18	8	3.852
Friuli Venezia Giulia	18	74	138	150	146	109	76	78	37	3	1	830
Lazio	132	439	789	1048	1048	864	611	707	215	40	2	5.895
Liguria	47	162	199	287	258	186	137	137	40	6	1	1.460
Lombardia	244	718	1.371	1.532	1.505	1.141	821	974	286	52	9	8.653
Marche	14	74	138	174	191	134	90	104	27	4	1	951
Molise	1	21	51	92	81	66	46	42	8	3	-	411
Piemonte	125	348	780	964	859	596	418	465	132	16	24	4.727
Puglia	63	383	703	795	680	456	329	321	85	20	3	3.838
Sardegna	29	140	317	407	391	275	183	175	56	16	-	1.989
Sicilia	135	546	1.046	1.207	1.090	884	589	658	216	40	1	6.412
Toscana	118	351	633	686	730	559	393	422	135	18	6	4.051
Trentino Alto Adige	17	56	68	78	72	59	30	31	11	-	-	422
Umbria	13	76	143	183	190	144	109	115	41	8	1	1.023
Valle D'aosta	14	38	48	53	42	43	14	21	6	-	1	280
Veneto	72	288	463	531	478	345	242	239	64	9	2	2.733
National Total	1.370	4.920	9.482	11.205	10.506	8.017	5.671	6.154	1.786	350	62	59.523

Situation to 31 Dec. 2005

FEMALE DETAINED POPOLATION ACCORDING TO THE COUNTY (REGIONE) OF DETENTION AND AGE

	Age groups											
Region Of Detention	18 to 20	21 to 24	25 to 29	30 to 34	35 to 39	40 to 44	45 to 49	50 to 59	60 to 69	> 70	??	Total
Abruzzo	1	3	4	6	3	5	3	2	1	-	-	28
Basilicata	3	1	3	3	2	2	5	2	1	-	-	22
Calabria	1	3	8	3	8	3	5	6	1	-	-	38
Campania	5	21	33	37	47	49	38	32	11	3	-	276
Emilia Romagna	6	16	29	25	39	22	12	8	4	-	-	161
Friuli Venezia Giulia	-	3	3	3	4	4	4	3	1	-	-	25
Lazio	23	52	56	73	72	63	56	59	11	3	-	468
Liguria	-	8	10	15	12	8	4	7	-	1	-	65
Lombardia	21	46	83	101	97	92	68	74	24	1	-	607
Marche	1	3	3	4	8	5	1	1	-	-	-	26
Molise	-	-	3	5	2	1	2	2	-	-	-	15
Piemonte	10	19	42	36	37	26	9	7	5	-	1	192
Puglia	2	20	32	33	34	27	28	20	4	3	1	204
Sardegna	-	3	7	17	10	5	6	4	-	-	-	52
Sicilia	1	7	16	25	25	19	17	17	4	2	-	133
Toscana	5	24	29	37	38	27	14	15	7	-	1	197
Trentino Alto Adige	2	4	4	3	6	4	-	1	-	-	-	24
Umbria	1	3	9	12	9	11	4	3	3	2	-	57
Valle D'aosta	-	-	-	-	-	-	-	-	-	-	-	-
Veneto	8	21	49	34	35	27	19	17	3	1	-	214
National Total	90	257	423	472	488	400	295	280	80	16	3	2.804

LENGTH OF SENTENCES

Situation on 31 December 2005

FINAL CONVICTS ACCORDING TO REGION OF DETENTION AND LENGTH OF SENTENCE

	Length of sentence													
Region Of Detention	Up to 1 year	1 to 2 years	2 to 3	3 to 4	4 to 5	5 to 6	6 to 7	7 to 8	8 to 9	9 to 10	10 to 20	> 20	Life sentence	Total
Abruzzo	102	119	117	162	105	75	53	53	56	37	211	110	84	1.284
Basilicat	20	35	25	41	36	21	23	12	14	8	65	28	9	337
Calabria	89	130	161	185	162	113	95	68	72	73	280	88	51	1.567
Campania	274	385	560	568	436	317	232	181	134	92	382	218	133	3.912
Emilia Romagna	174	191	168	274	202	150	89	66	74	49	331	130	78	1.976
Friuli Venezia Giulia	94	101	93	85	61	27	15	10	8	5	38	9	12	558
Lazio	314	365	411	564	377	284	236	167	118	94	480	228	130	3.768
Liguria	132	120	125	166	95	54	37	25	18	19	65	19	5	880
Lombar Dia	561	483	523	608	512	336	249	233	191	158	793	329	137	5.113
Marche	47	52	45	69	62	43	37	26	23	14	92	67	47	624
Molise	22	31	34	38	33	18	18	11	15	14	59	27	12	332
Piemonte	267	312	351	409	318	245	155	132	118	79	402	170	119	3.077
Puglia	225	277	317	400	252	206	146	115	94	62	270	88	28	2.480
Sardegna	150	197	181	220	122	102	63	45	27	30	177	77	36	1.427
Sicilia	347	400	486	506	377	327	207	175	151	97	504	209	76	3.862
Toscana	222	221	189	267	197	133	105	105	89	67	517	321	132	2.565
Trentino Alto Adige	65	67	48	51	14	17	2	2	-	3	8	3	-	280
Umbria	51	38	55	67	54	41	34	24	14	16	118	97	108	717
Valle D'aosta	26	25	37	36	14	20	8	6	4	2	10	3	2	193
Veneto	174	209	233	254	166	115	86	68	48	39	224	83	25	1.724
National Total	3.356	3.758	4.159	4.970	3.595	2.644	1.890	1.524	1.268	958	5.026	2.304	1224	36.676

FEMALE FINAL CONVICTS ACCORDING TO REGION OF DETENTION AND LENGTH OF SENTENCE

Region Of Detention	Length of sentence													
	Up to 1 year	1 to 2	2 to 3	3 to 4	4 to 5	5 to 6	6 to 7	7 to 8	8 to 9	9 to 10	10 to 20	> 20	Life entence	Total
Abruzzo	3	2	-	1	-	-	-	1	-	-	-	-	-	7
Basilicata	4	2	-	3	5	1	2	-	-	1	3	1	-	22
Calabria	-	3	3	5	4	2	-	1	1	-	3	-	-	22
Campania	13	11	23	37	20	14	6	9	6	3	13	1	1	157
Emilia Romagna	8	11	7	20	11	8	4	3	-	2	9	1	-	84
Friuli Venezia Giulia	3	2	5	1	2	-	1	-	-	-	-	-	-	14
Lazio	24	24	26	63	24	29	24	16	5	6	27	8	11	287
Liguria	6	1	5	9	6	2	3	-	3	2	2	-	-	39
Lombardia	32	31	23	34	38	25	12	14	12	13	42	15	8	299
Marche	3	2	2	2	1	-	1	-	-	-	-	-	-	11
Molise	3	1	2	1	-	-	-	-	-	1	-	-	-	8
Piemonte	14	12	15	22	10	6	2	4	6	3	7	3	-	104
Puglia	9	8	20	20	17	9	8	6	8	4	13	3	4	129
Sardegna	2	2	3	5	3	-	-	-	-	1	5	1	-	22
Sicilia	5	5	5	17	6	10	7	5	-	2	12	2	1	77
Toscana	15	8	11	23	13	10	5	7	6	-	8	2	1	109
Trentino Alto Adige	7	2	3	2	-	-	-	-	-	-	1	-	-	15
Umbria	1	1	3	3	2	5	6	2	-	1	14	2	1	41
Valle D'aosta	-	-	-	-	-	-	-	-	-	-	-	-	-	-
Veneto	14	14	17	25	15	11	7	3	3	4	16	2	-	131
National Total	166	142	173	293	177	132	88	71	50	43	175	41	27	1.578

OFFENCES

Data for 31 December 2005	Italian				Foreigners					
Kind of offences	*Women*	*Men*	*Sum*	*%*	*Women*	*Men*	*Sum*	*%*	*Total*	*%*
ASSOCIAZ. DI STAMPO MAFIOSO (art. 416bis c.p.) (Mafia association)	45	5.514	5.559	3,1	8	117	125	0,3	5.684	2,5
LEGGE DROGA Drugs)	853	20.413	21.266	12,0	689	10.974	11.663	24,2	32.929	14,6
LEGGE ARMI (Firearms and explosives)	407	33.368	33.775	19,1	41	2.096	2.137	4,4	35.912	16,0
ORDINE PUBBLICO (Public order)	47	2.664	2.711	1,5	69	665	734	1,5	3.445	1,5
CONTRO IL PATRIMONIO (Against estate)	1.391	53.790	55.181	31,2	877	12.112	12.989	27,0	68.170	30,3
PROSTITUZIONE (Prostitution)	29	297	326	0,2	168	910	1.078	2,2	1.404	0,6
CONTRO LA PUBBLICA AMMINISTRAZIONE (Against public administration)	153	5.290	5.443	3,1	42	2.489	2.531	5,3	7.974	3,5
INCOLUMITA' PUBBLICA (Public safety)	32	1.858	1.890	1,1	7	167	174	0,4	2.064	0,9
FEDE PUBBLICA (Social belief)	290	6.625	6.915	3,9	224	2.920	3.144	6,5	10.059	4,5
MORALITA ' PUBBLICA (Public morality)	6	209	215	0,1		60	60	0,1	275	0,1
CONTRO LA FAMIGLIA (Against family)	40	1.076	1.116	0,6	11	144	155	0,3	1.271	0,6
CONTRO LA PERSONA (Against person)	710	24.031	24.741	14,0	350	8.130	8.480	17,6	33.221	14,8
CONTRO LA PERSONALITA' DELLO STATO (Against the personality of the State)	126	391	517	0,3	1	57	58	0,1	575	0,3
CONTRO AMM.NE DELLA GIUSTIZIA (Against admninistration of justice)	244	6.233	6.477	3,7	58	610	668	1,4	7.145	3,2

ECONOMIA PUBBLICA (Public economy)	8	610	618	0,3		6	6	0,0	624	0,3
LIBRO TERZO DELLE CONTRAVVENZIONI (Infringement)	86	4.691	4.777	2,7	28	626	654	1,4	5.431	2,4
LEGGE STRANIERI (Law on aliens)	4	201	205	0,1	216	3.002	3.218	6,7	3.423	1,5
CONTRO IL SENTIM. RELIGIOSO E LA PIETA' DEI DEF. (Against religious feelings and pity for the dead)	27	1.171	1.198	0,7	5	46	51	0,1	1.249	0,6
ALTRI REATI (Other offences)	62	3.968	4.030	2,3	10	211	221	0,5	4.251	1,9
TOTAL OFFENCES	4.560	172.400	176.960	100,0	2.804	45.342	48.146	100,0	225.106	100,0

Fonte: D.A.P - Ufficio per lo Sviluppo e la Gestione del Sistema Informativo Automatizzato – SEZIONE STATISTICA

Note: In case of more and of different categories offences ascribed to a person, he/she will be counted more times, one for each crime. So, general result is higher than the number of persons.

Chapter 15

Latvia

Leine Zeibote

1 INTRODUCTION

1.1 Overview of penalties and measures

Deprivation of liberty as a measure or penalty is foreseen in criminal laws, administrative laws and immigration laws. The table below describes different measures according to which a person can be kept in custody in Latvia.

Measure or penalty	*Responsible for execution*	*Place of execution*	*Application*
Detention before charges in Criminal Procedure	State Police; Ministry of Interior	Cells in Police Units, Isolation units	- Short term detention, not more than 8 hours - Decision of investigator in criminal case - Law on Short Term Detention Order[1]
Administrative Arrest	State Police Ministry of Interior	Cells in Police Units, Isolators	- 1- 15 days - Administrative sentence under Administrative Offence Code - Imposed according to decision of judge
Detention as a security measure in criminal procedure: - pre trial -during trial of first instance -during appeal process	Prison Administration Ministry of Justice	Investigation prisons, Investigation units in prisons	- According to decision of investigation judge or judge - The total amount of time spent in detention cannot be longer than deprivation of liberty term provided in the sanction of Criminal Law - For criminal violations the term of detention before first instance judgment cannot exceed 3 months, for less serious crimes – 9 months, for serious crime – 12 months, for especially serious crime – 24 months.[2]
Deprivation of liberty – criminal sentence	Prison Administration; Ministry of Justice	Open, semi-open, closed prisons, correctional institution for juveniles	- Imposed by decision of judge according to decision of judge - Term of deprivation of liberty from 6 months to 20 years

1 Aizturēšanas kārtība likums (Law on Short-term Detention Order), adopted 12 October 2005.
2 Kriminālprocesa likums (Code of Criminal Procedure), Section 277.

Measure or penalty	*Responsible for execution*	*Place of execution*	*Application*
Detention of Illegal immigrants and asylum seekers before identification	State Border Guard; Ministry of interior	Cells in Police Units, Isolation units Detention centre for illegal immigrants	- Detention according to immigration Law - 10 days according to decision of State Border Guard up to 20 months according to decision of court
Detention as a compulsory medical measure	Ministry of Health	Closed units in Psycho-neurological hospitals	- According to decision of court in criminal matters - Term is not set in Criminal Law

Each year, according to sanctions of state, more than 40 000 persons are deprived of their liberty. There are around 100 closed institutions in Latvia, among them – 15 prisons, 28 Police Detentions / Isolation units, nine psycho-neurological hospitals, 30 social care centres and a centre for illegal immigrants and other institutions.[3]

Types of Criminal offences and Criminal Sentences

According to the Criminal Law, criminal offences are divided into criminal violations and crimes. Crimes are sub-divided as follows: less serious crimes, serious crimes and very serious crimes:

- a criminal violation: deprivation of liberty for a term not exceeding two years;
- a less serious crime: deprivation of liberty for a term exceeding two years but not exceeding five years;
- a serious crime: deprivation of liberty for a term exceeding five years but not exceeding ten years;
- an especially serious crime: deprivation of liberty for a term exceeding ten years, life imprisonment or the death penalty.

Article 36 of the Criminal Law sets the forms of sentences. One of the following basic sentences may be adjudged against a person who has committed a criminal offence:

- the death penalty;
- deprivation of liberty;
- custodial arrest;
- community service;
- fine.

In addition to a basic sentence, the following additional sentences may be adjudged:

- confiscation of property;

3 Latvian Centre for Human Rights and Etnic Studies, *Handbook for Monitoring Closed Institutions*, Riga 2003.

- expulsion from the Republic of Latvia;
- fine;
- limitation of rights;
- police supervision.

The death penalty – death by shooting – may be adjudged only for murder in especially aggravated circumstances. The death penalty may only be applied where a crime has been committed in times of war.

Deprivation of liberty can be determined for a term of not less than six months and not exceeding fifteen years; for especially serious crimes for a term not exceeding twenty years. In cases specifically provided for in this Law, deprivation of liberty may be determined for life (life sentence). Deprivation of liberty can be imposed in closed custody, semi-closed custody, open custody, as well as in the correctional facility for juveniles. When ruling in a case, the adjudging court determines in which type of correctional facility it will impose the deprivation of liberty.

Custodial arrest shall be determined for a term of not less than three days and not exceeding six months. Custodial arrest in practice is applied only to soldiers since there are no places of execution for this sentence. Soldiers serve their sentence in the guardhouse. Custodial arrest may not be applied to pregnant women and mothers caring for an infant under the age of one.

Figure 1 Persons sentenced in 2004: 13 222

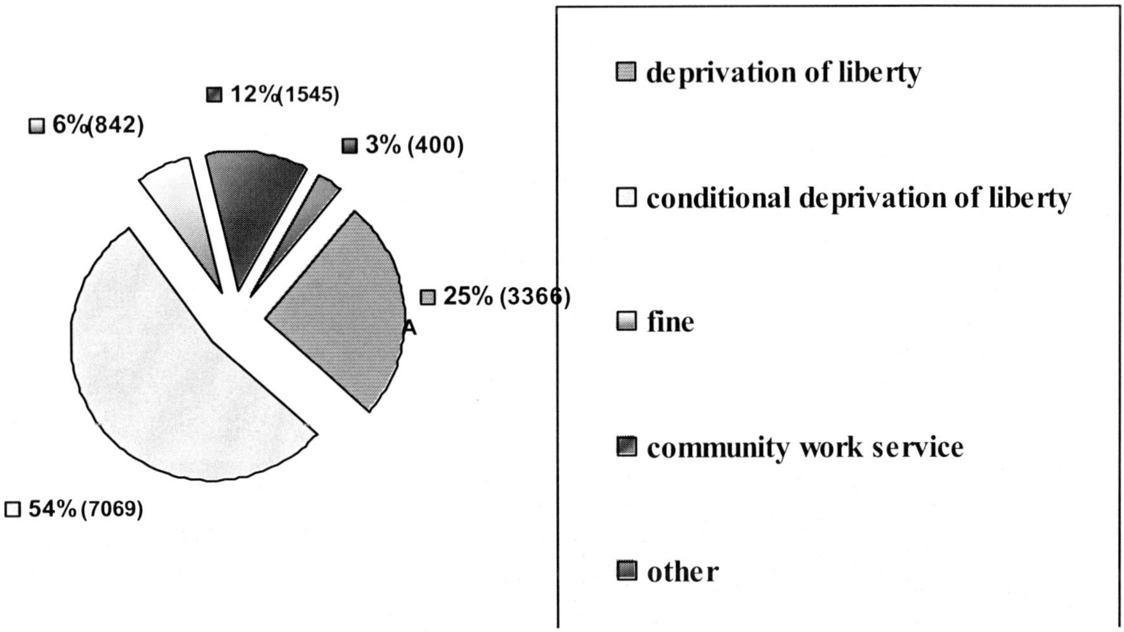

1.2 Overview of Prison System

a) There are 15 prisons and one juvenile correctional institution under the Prison Administration. There can be a mixture of different regimes within individual prisons. Overall, there are five open, eight semi-closed and eight closed departments. According to data from the Prison Administration, the Latvian prison system has an overall capacity of 9,166 places, of which 6,537 are filled. The majority of these places are in closed and semi-closed departments (4,073 and 1,273 respectively), while the open wings had a capacity of 255. The remaining places are in pre-trial-detention wings (3,052 for adults, 209 for juveniles), hospitals (200 places) and juvenile prisons (134). In the administration of prisons in 2000 the responsibility was shifted from the Ministry of the Interior to the Ministry of Justice. The number of employees on in the Latvian Prison Administration and prisons 1 January 2006 was 3,126. The ratio of prison staff to prisoners was 1 to 5[4]. On the same date there were 171 vacant posts (or 5,5%). Fluidity of employees in 2005 reached 15%. Prison staff is under Specialised Civil Service, similar to police staff. 23,7 % of staff have a university degree, 73.6 % have a secondary school degree, and 2,7% have not finished secondary school. There is a training centre for prison staff which organizes all in-service training for prison personnel under the Prison Administration. The Centre runs the professional education courses "Prison inspector" and "Prison guard". 404 persons attended this training in 2005.

Supervision of prisons regarding violations of human rights is performed by the State Human Rights Office. Representatives of this institution regularly visited prisons during 2005, reviewed complaints of prisoners and consulted prison staff. A Draft Law from the Ombudsman is pending in Saeima. In 2005 the budget of the Prison Administration was 21 953 673 Lats. The financing of the prison system has been insufficient in recent years and this has had an effect on all fields of operation of the prison system. The daily expenses per prisoner were 7,55 Lats. In 2005, the Prison Administration received 5,044 complaints from prisoners, of which 2,148 concerned the imprisonment regime and unsatisfactory prison conditions.[5] During 2005 a concept paper on the development of the prison estate and a concept on prisoners' health care were accepted by the cabinet of ministers.

4 Concept of Development of the Prison System, accepted by the Cabinet 2 May 2005, Order No 280.

5 2005 Prison Administration Annual Report, available in Latvian on www.ievp.gov.lv

Table 1 Composition of Prisoners[6]

	01.01.2002	*01.01.2003*	*01.01.2004*	*01.01.2005*	*01.01.2006*
Total number of prisoners	8,426	8,215	8,169	7,632	6,949
a) Number of sentenced persons	4,750	4,639	4,900	4,970	4,750
Citizens of Latvia	3,054 *64%*	3,121 *67%*	3,319 *68%*	3,408 *69%*	3,229 *68%*
Non-citizens and permanent residents	1,172 *25%*	1,114 *24%*	1,358 *28%*	1,374 *28%*	1,425 *30%*
Citizens of other countries	39 *0.8%*	40 *0.9%*	39 *0.8%*	41 *0.8%*	29 *0.6%*
Without any citizenship	485 *10%*	364 *8%*	184 *4%*	147 *3%*	67 *1.4%*
b) Number of persons in pre-trial detention	3676	3576	3269	2662	2199
% of persons in pre-trial detention of all prisoners	*44%*	*43%*	*40%*	*34.8%*	*31.6%*

b) Foreigners can be detained in all institutions described in the first part of this report (see table on page 1 and 2). So far the issue of foreign prisoners has not become a live issue in Latvia. The number of foreigners in the prison system is small and the detention of non-Russian speaking foreigners is a very rare occasion for prison staff. On 1 February 2006 there were only three non-Russian speaking foreigners in Latvian prisons. Most of the time foreigners are successfully integrated in the prison population since the majority of the prison population is Russian speaking.

Table 2 Nationalities of sentenced foreigners in prisons on 1 February 2006

Russia	Lithuania	Belarus	Ukraine	Estonia	Armenia	Moldova	Azerbaijan	Uzbekistan	Sweden	Finland	USA
24	12	6	4	3	3	3	2	1	1	1	1

There is no special training for prison staff and there are no special rules for the detention of foreigners. Data of foreigners in pre-trial detention is not collected and analysed, and thus not available. The issue of persons without any legal status and documents has been challenging for the Prison administration during the past years. Many prisoners were not registered in the Register of Inhabitants and did not receive a personal code in the nineties. This situation has been improved - in 2005 there were only 67 persons without citizenship compared to 485 in 2002.

6 Data from the Prison Administration.

1.3 Overview of involvement of Consulates, Embassies, Ministries home country, Probation service home country, NGO`s etc.

Consulates and embassies assist foreign prisoners in the communication with institutions in their home country. Mostly consulates are involved in helping to obtain the legal status in the home country and the necessary documentation. There have been some cases when embassies delivered interpreter services to nationals of their country. The Prosecutor General Office is involved in the transfer of sentenced persons to their home countries. The number of transferred sentenced persons is 42. The State Human Rights office is an independent state institution and its competence is to review complaints on violations of human rights. Employees of the centre regularly visit places of detention, prisons and detention centres for illegal immigrants. In 2005 the office received about 500 complaints from prisoners. There are no data about the number of complaints from foreign prisoners, but employees of the office referred to two complaints concerning language barriers. One of them related to problems in communicating with the prison doctor. The Latvian Centre for Human Rights and Ethnic Studies (LCHRES) is the NGO that is most active in the field of human rights and ethnic relations. The centre's activities include monitoring, research and policy analysis, advocacy, human rights education and training, organization of seminars and the provision of legal consultations to victims of human rights violations. LCHRES experts regularly monitor prisons and detention centres for illegal immigrants. In 2004 LCHRES printed the leaflet "Information for immigration detainees" in Latvian, Russian, English, French, Spanish and Arabic. The leaflet is available in Olaine Detention Centre for Illegal Immigrants.

1.4 Overview of trends

62,173 criminal offences were registered in the territory of Latvia during the year 2004, an increase of 19,1% compared to 2003. In the past five years the crime level has not changed. Around 60% of the registered criminal offences are thefts.[7]

Table 3

year	*1990*	*1991*	*1992*	*1993*	*1994*	*1995*	*1996*	*1997*
Sentenced persons	7,159	7,372	9,097	11,280	10,877	9,797	10,428	12,772
Sentenced to deprivation of liberty	N/d	N/d	N/d	4,162	3,225	2,839	2,195	3,238
% of deprivation of liberty among all sentenced persons	36.6	35.2	36.1	36.9	29.6	29.0	21.1	25.4
year	*1998*	*1999*	*2000*	*2001*	*2002*	*2003*	*2004*	*2005**
Sentenced persons	12,952	12,862	12,689	12,679	12,615	13,586	13,222	11,240
Sentenced to deprivation of liberty	2,930	2,865	3,305	2,886	3,551	3,260	3,366	2,680
% of deprivation of liberty among all sentenced persons	22.6	22.2	26.0	22.7	28.1	24.0	25.5	23,8

*Data on sentenced persons in 2005 is not available at the time of preparation of this report.

7 State Police Report on Crime and Operation of Police in 2004, available onlineat www.vp.gov.lv

In 2004 there was a decrease in the overall number of prisoners and the share of adult pre-trial detainees. At the same time the incarceration rate remained high – 326 prisoners per 100,000 inhabitants. The average length of imprisonment increased to 4,5 years in 2005.[8] The number of serious crimes in Latvia has grown which has in turn resulted in an increased in the number of prisoners in closed prisons.[9] Analyses of sentencing trends show that the number of persons sentenced to less than one year has been relatively stable. The number of persons sentenced to five to ten years is growing (from 281 in 2002 to 566 in 2004). The total number of inhabitants in Latvia on 1 January 2006 were 2 290 765, of which 1 834 282 (80 %) were citizens, 418 432 (18.3%) were non –citizens, 37 843(1.7%) were foreigners, and 198 were persons without any citizenship.[10] "Non-citizen" is a special status granted to former citizens of the Soviet Union and their children that have entered Latvia to live after 17 June 1940. These persons have the right to attain citizenship through a naturalization procedure. On 1 January 2006, 0,6% of the total prison population were foreigners, while a further 1,4% were persons without any citizenship. The latter category can include persons belonging to Latvia or to another foreign country. In comparison, foreigners have rather long sentences and most of them have been sentenced for violent crimes.

Figure 2 Length of sentence of foreign prisoners on 1 February 2006

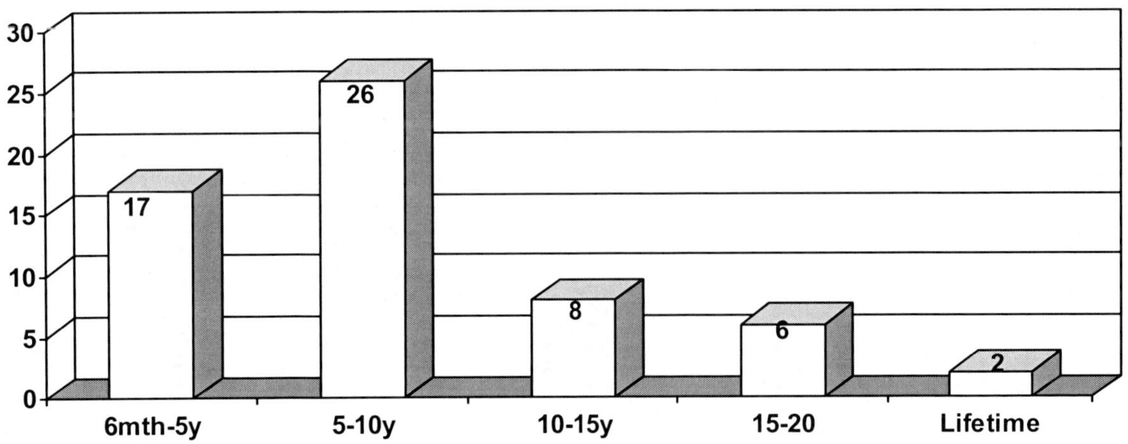

8 Latvian Centre for Human Rights and Ethnic Studies (LCHRES), *Human Rights in Latvia in 2004*, Riga 2005.
9 Concept of Development of Prison System, accepted by the Cabinet 2 May 2005, Order No 280
10 Data from the Board of Citizenship and Migration Affairs, www.pmlp.gov.lv

1.5.2 Criminal Procedure Law sets the principle of equal treatment for all persons regardless of their race, nationality, citizenship, social status, religion, gender, education, language and other possible characteristics.[13] Foreign prisoners have the same legal position and the same rights and obligations as national prisoners. Chapters 69 and 70 of the Code of Criminal Procedure provide procedures for the transfer of sentenced persons abroad and for receiving sentenced persons from foreign countries. Latvia recognizes the principle of reciprocity; therefore transfers are also possible in cases where there is no mutual agreement between countries. Latvia has ratified the Convention of the Council of Europe on the Transfer of Sentenced Persons – adopted on 21 March 1983 – and has concluded bilateral agreements with several countries (Russia, Estonia, Lithuania, Ukraine, Belarus, Kyrgyz Republic, Poland, Moldova, and Uzbekistan) on judicial cooperation in civil and criminal matters. The central authority for the organization of transfers is the Prosecutor's General Office. Since 2000 Latvia has received 26 sentenced persons from abroad. In 2005 Latvia received two persons from Lithuania, one from Russia, Germany, Austria, and Estonia. Since the year 2000, Latvia has transferred 42 persons to foreign countries. In 2005 Latvia transferred five persons to Lithuania, three to Estonia, one to Belarus, one to Azerbaijan and one to Sweden.[14]

2 TREATMENT OF PRISONERS

2.1 General remarks

The treatment of prisoners in Latvia has been the focus of attention of human rights experts. The first periodic visit to Latvia by the CPT took place in 1999, the second in 2002. The committee expressed its concerns regarding the treatment of prisoners in Latvia, as well as the lack of progress in numerous fields. Overcrowding, inter-prisoner violence, material conditions in prisons, and the regime for prisoners serving life sentences were areas mentioned by the CPT in its report to the Latvian government in 2003. In 2004, there was another visit to Latvia, but the corresponding report had not been published at the time of writing. The stagnation of the prison system is obvious and it is recognized by the Prison administration and the Ministry of Justice. A permanent lack of funding has resulted in numerous problems such as a lack of rehabilitation possibilities and poor material conditions for prisoners and prison staff. The Ministry of Justice has elaborated several concept papers that are aimed at resolving the situation concerning poor conditions of the prison's estate (including hospitals), as well the employment and education of prisoners. To examine the situation of foreign prisoners I have visited Jelgava Prison and have interviewed several representatives of the Prison Administration, representatives of the State Human Right Office and the State Probation Service. According to the existing legislation there is no difference in the treatment of foreign prisoners. Laws do not contain special rules on living conditions, reception and admission, work, education, training, food, religion or any other aspect described in this report. However, the lack of special regulations sometimes generate unequal opportunities for

13 Criminal Procedure Law, Section 8.

14 Data from Prosecutor`s General Office www.lrp.gov.lv

In practice prisoners receive extracts from "Regulations on the Internal Order in Prisons". These extracts are also available in Latvian and Russian, and are on the walls in the living areas of the prison. The full text is available from the head of the unit upon request of the prisoner. Translations in other languages are not provided by the state. In Riga Central prison embassies made translations of the rules for the inmates.[16] According to the Law on the Detention Order, detained persons must be informed about their rights and obligations in a language that he/she without any delay, as well as of the authorities to which he/she can submit complaints. If necessary an interpreter will be invited.

2.4 Work – Education – Training – Sport – Recreation

Work and education in prisons is one of the main problems faced by the Latvian Prison administration. In 2005 only 1,286 of all sentenced persons with the capacity to work were actually employed (17.6 % of all sentenced persons). The majority of employed prisoners (63.04%) were employed in prison maintenance activities such as kitchens, warehouse workers, janitors, stokers, hair-dressers, bathhouse attendants, cobblers and motor engineers. Only 29% of the employed prisoners worked in production such as wood-processing, tailoring, metal work and agriculture.[17] Access to work for foreign prisoners is the same as for national prisoners, according to the relevant law. It is not possible to evaluate whether foreigners have less possibilities to be employed as the overall rate of employment in prisons is very low. Prison staff have acknowledged that nationality does not have an impact on the employment of prisoners but some authorities mentioned that the language barrier may be an obstacle in employing foreigners. This does not apply to Russian speaking prisoners.

In 2004 nine out of 15 prisons offered some education, but only eight percent of the prisoners took part in general educational programs, and less that five percent participated in accredited vocational training programs. The majority of detainees who were involved in the educational activities were juveniles.[18] 171 adult prisoners were involved in programs of general education in 2004, and it should also be mentioned that adult remand prisoners are not involved in educational activities. 364 prisoners were involved in professional education programs in 2004.[19] Possibilities and opportunities to be involved in educational activities are low for both national and foreign prisoners. There are also equal opportunities to be involved in sporting activities and recreation for national and foreign prisoners. They can use gym, and play basketball or other outdoor games. In the lowest level of regime the activities are limited as the regime provides only one hour of walking per day. In the medium and highest level of regime there is more time for activities. Libraries are equipped with literature in the Latvian and Russian languages. Russian speaking foreigners therefore have better access to literature than other foreigners, who are dependent on the help of relatives and consulates.

---

16 Data from the administration of Riga Central Prison.

17 Data from the Prison Administration.

18 Latvian Centre for Human Rights and Ethnic Studies (LCHRES), *Human Rights in Latvia in 2004*, Riga 2005.

19 Pētījums „Ieslodzīto un no ieslodzījuma atbrīvoto personu izglītības, nodarbinātības un sociālās rehabilitācijas pakalpojumu pieejamība". P.93.

2.5 Food – Religion - Personal hygiene - Medical care

Legal rules concerning religion, food, personal hygiene or medical care are applicable to both national as foreign prisoners. Religious activities for sentenced persons and persons on remand are organized by the chaplain service and can be performed by the representatives of nine religious confessions (Lutheran, Roman Catholic, Russian Orthodox, Baptist, Old Believer, Methodist, Judaist, Seventh-day Adventist, and Pentecostal). Prisoners in the highest and medium regime level can freely access the special room for religious activities, but for those in the lowest regime meetings with religious representatives are available in cells. For example, in Jelgava prison there are services in Latvian and Russian every morning. If a prisoner wants to meet a religious representative of his/her confession, the chaplain communicates with the representative of the confession and organizes a meeting for the prisoner. The chaplain plays a major role in the organization of the social life in prison, for example by providing English language courses, musical concerts and lectures. When asked about possibilities to meet prisoners' dietary requirements, the prison authorities informed that there are no possibilities to offer special diets. However, prisoners can use products bought in the prison store. The list of products available for purchase is limited by the regulations of the Cabinet of Ministers. There are limited possibilities to carry different religious accessories (e.g. scented oils) as these articles are not on the list of items permitted to be carried in prison. According to the internal rules of order in prisons, sentenced persons shall wear shortly-cut hair, beards and moustaches. Exceptions apply only to persons who have scars on their face or head and have permission from the chief of medical service.[20] The use of baths or showers and changes of underwear and bedclothes shall be guaranteed at least once a week. Sentenced women have access to washrooms every day. Remand prisoners and sentenced persons have the right to wear personal clothes. These items can be sent by relatives or other persons. Equal medical care is guaranteed to foreign and national prisoners. However, overall evaluation of the heath care services in Latvian prisons by the CPT in 2002 pointed out serious shortcomings, most prominently the fact that the buildings and equipment were vastly out of date. A new prison hospital is currently under construction as is expected to be taken into operation in 2007..

2.6 Consular and legal help

Foreigners can correspond and meet with representatives of diplomatic and consular missions. Expenses of such correspondence are covered by the state and letters are not subject to censorship. Furthermore, meetings with representatives from their home country are not deducted from the total number of visits to which inmates are entitled (see 2.7 below). In some prisons regular consultation hours with consular representatives are organized. Prison authorities pointed out that consulates are mainly involved in helping foreign prisoners attain legal status and documentation. There are cases in which they help to establish contacts with state authorities in the foreigner's home country. There is a different level of involvement of embassies – some are more active than others. For example, the Finnish embassy helped with translations as their national could not understand the language and the prison did not have the resources to provide this service. Legal aid during

[20] Rules of Internal Order in Prisons, section 24.

criminal proceedings is guaranteed by the Code of Criminal Procedure. If the person cannot afford an advocate, the state ensures participation of an advocate in the procedure and fully or partly covers the expenses. If a person does not master the state language, he has the right to use the services of an interpreter free of charge.[21] According to the State Ensured Legal Aid Law, the categories of persons entitled to receive legal aid funded by the state are Latvian citizens, Latvian non-citizens, stateless persons, EU nationals legally residing in Latvia, third country nationals legally residing in Latvia, asylum seekers, refugees, and persons under subsidiary protection.[22]

2.7 Contacts with the outside world

Prisoners and remand prisoners can communicate with persons via mail, phone calls and meetings. Communication of remand prisoners can be restricted only according to a decision of an investigation judge[23]. Correspondence of a sentenced person is subject to censorship, and postal mails and parcels are subject to check-ups. In 2004 amendments to the Sentence Enforcement Code provided that correspondence of sentenced persons with UN bodies, parliament, prosecutors` offices, courts, sworn advocates, the National Human Rights Office, and, in the case of a foreign prisoner, the relevant diplomatic or consular mission, may not be subjected to censorship and, with the exception of a sworn advocate, the postal expenses are to be borne by the prison authorities. Remand prisoners also have unlimited possibilities to contact diplomatic authorities and their correspondence with diplomatic authorities, human rights bodies, prosecutors` offices and courts may not me subjected to censorship.[24] Prisoners in closed prisons have the right to three to six long term visits and four to six short term visits (each up to two hours) per year depending on the regime in which they are being detained. Additionally they have the right to one to three phone calls per month. The duration of long term visits varies from six to 24 hours.[25] Prisoners in semi-closed prisons are entitled to more meetings – up to eight long term meetings of 48 hours and eight short term meetings. Likewise they can make up to four telephone calls per month depending on their regime. Short meetings are allowed with relatives or other persons in the presence of a prison representative. Persons eligible to make long-term visits to prisoners are immediate relatives such as parents, children, brothers and sisters, grandparents, grandchildren, as well as spouses. Should a convict have no immediate relatives or should they not visit him/her, long-term visits from other relatives or other persons may be allowed, dependent on a decision by the respective prison administration. Short term and long term meetings can be organized at equal time intervals. For example, if there are six short term visits per year, they can be held every two months. There are no special exceptions for foreign prisoners or national prisoners with families abroad concerning the organization of visits. Short as well as long meetings may be substituted by telephone calls at the cost of the convict or the person to whom the call is made. This possibility is frequently used by foreigners as visits from relatives are rare. Remand prisoners have the right to one short term meeting per month and at least one five minutes phone call per week.

21 Code of Criminal Procedure, Section 11.

22 English text of State Ensured Legal Aid Law is available at http:// www.ttc..lv

23 Code of Criminal Procedure, section 12.

24 Apcietinājumā turēšanas likums (Law on detention Order), Section 23.

25 Sentence Execution Act. Art. 50.

Telephone calls, including long-distance calls and postal expenses shall be covered by prisoners themselves and prisons have no means to cover these expenses for prisoners who have no access to work. Prisoners in semi-closed prisons in the highest regime have the right to short term leave in the case of death or serious illness of a close relative. In these cases, the involved prisoners receive a temporary identification document. Practically they can attend a funeral in Latvia (yet not abroad) since this temporary card is not a valid travel document. Prisoners have the right to use their personal television set or a TV from the prison. Latvian and Russian channels are available in all prisons, while some institutions have cable TV with programs in English. According to data from the prison administration all prisoners who do not master Russian have access to TV channels in English.

2.8 Re-integration activities

Reintegration work in prisons in Latvia is connected with the arrangement of necessary documents. Many prisoners do not have passports or personal codes. Six months prior to their release, a probation officer meets with the prisoners and finds out about his societal needs like work, a place of residence, family, etc. The person is informed about the services provided by probation service and receives assistance from a probation officer in setting-up a plan for living and possibilities to stay in a half-way house. If a person wants he/she can conclude a voluntary agreement and access assistance of probation regardless of his/her citizenship. The State Probation Service began supervising released offenders in society since 2006. On 1 April 2006 there were five foreign nationals under supervision, one of whom was on parole. All of them had lived in Latvia for a long time and had families there.

Both in theory and in practice equal assistance is granted to both national and foreign prisoners. There are better opportunities for the communication with foreign prisoners (English speaking) since many of the probation officers master the English language. Parole is granted to persons regardless their citizenship. Applications of sentenced prisoners are reviewed by the administrative commission of the prison (representatives from prison, probation, prosecutors office) and then by the judge. In interviews representatives of the commissions mentioned cases in which foreigners had been granted parole. Usually, foreigners are expelled after release according to the judgment of a court or a decision by the Board of Citizenship and Migration Affairs. An example in a research paper of the Latvian Police Academy on parole[26] describes a case where a judge had not granted a person parole because his belonging to a certain country could not be legally established.

2.9 Release –Expulsion

Expulsion from Latvia is either a criminal penalty or an administrative measure under Immigration Law. A citizen of another state or a person who has a permanent residence permit of another state may be expelled from the Republic of Latvia if a court finds that, considering the circumstances of the matter and the personality of the offender, it is not permissible for him or her to remain in the Republic of Latvia. Expulsion from Latvia is

[26] Latvijas Policijas akadēmija (Latvian Police academy), *'Nosacīta pirmstermiņa atbrīvošana no kriminālsoda"*, Rīga 2004, p. 22.

adjudged as an additional penalty and execution thereof takes place only after the basic penalty has been served. Temporary and permanent residence permits and expulsion orders under Immigration Law are issued by the Office of Citizenship and Migration Affairs. A temporary residence permit is cancelled if a foreigner by judgment of a court has been found guilty of committing such a criminal offence in or outside the Republic of Latvia for which the law provides a sentence of imprisonment for a time not less than two years. A permanent residence permit is cancelled if a court finds a foreigner guilty of having committed a serious or especially serious crime in the Republic of Latvia. If a foreigner is married to a Latvian citizen or non-citizen a permit can only be voided in cases when it is needed for the safety of the state and society. If an alien does not have a lawful basis to reside in the Republic of Latvia after having served a sentence for criminal offences committed in the Republic of Latvia, the Head of the Office shall make a decision regarding the forcible expulsion of the irregular migrant.[27] According to data from Prison Administration on 1 February 2006 there were 35 persons on the expulsion list. 15 from them did not have personal documents (passports) in their prison files.

2.10 Aftercare-Probation

In the case in which foreign offenders stay in the country after their release they are allowed to make use of aftercare facilities and support from the probation service. There are no special provisions for foreign offenders. Ex-offenders can stay in one of eight half-way houses financed by the Probation Service. The Probation Service covers six months of stay in the program, and in some cases this support can be prolonged to nine months. So far there have been no foreign nationals in the half-way houses, but there have been a few in voluntary aftercare. Further aftercare provisions include assistance in developing a plan to resolve problems, participation in programmes to combat substance abuse and anger management courses, which are free of charge.

2.11 Staff

The staff of the prison service does not receive special training to deal with foreigners. Since there have been few non-Russian speaking foreigners in Latvian prisons, training concerning foreigners has not been organized. However, language training is necessary now because only few staff members master the English language.

2.12 Projects

According to information from the Prison Administration there are no special projects for foreign prisoners organized by the Prison Service or NGOs.

3 ADMINISTRATIVE DETENTION OF FOREIGN PRISONERS

The first Immigration Law in Latvia dates from 1992. The issue of asylum seekers did not become a live topic until the independence of Latvia. The first law on asylum seekers and

[27] Immigration Law, Section 48.

refugees was enacted in 1998. Prior to this, persons who came to Latvia were detained in the detention centre "Olaine". In the mid-nineties there was quite an active movement of refugees that passed Latvia on their way to Scandinavia. In the literature we can find a description of a group of 120 asylum seekers who were kept in "Olaine" for one year. They were eventually granted refugee status in Scandinavia. In that time the state was not materially prepared to receive asylum seekers, so the help from other countries (Sweden, USA) and the UNHCR[28] played an important role. The reception centre for asylum seekers "Mucenieki" was opened in 1999. According to the data from the Office of Citizenship Affairs and Migration 68 asylum seekers have been accommodated there since the opening of the centre. Conditions are good and persons have the right to move freely outside the centres. In 2005 seven persons were accommodated here. Since 1998 Latvia reviewed 161 applications from asylum seekers:

- eight persons have received a refugee status (five men, one woman and two juveniles) from 1998 to 2001. One of these persons became a Latvian citizen through naturalization in 2004.
- nine persons received alternative status from 2002 to 2005 (three from Belarus and six from Russia). Five lost it in 2004 as they returned to their countries of origin.

Until 2002 all questions related to immigrants and asylum seekers (detention, interviewing, identification and housing) were the responsibility of the Immigration Police of the State Police. The Office of Citizenship and Migration Affairs was responsible for decision making on the status of a person. Since reorganization in 2002 the responsibilities have been with the State Border Guard and the Office of Citizenship and Migration Affairs. According to Section 51 of the Immigration Law the State Border Guard has the right to detain a foreigner who has illegally crossed the state border of the Republic of Latvia or otherwise violated the procedures prescribed by regulatory enactments for the entry and residence of irregular migrants into the Republic of Latvia. In the cases referred to in Section 51 of the Immigration Law the State Police officials have the right to detain an irregular for three hours until handing her/him over to the State Border Guard. An official of the State Border Guard has the right to detain a foreigner for a period not exceeding ten days. Such an official also has the right to detain a foreigner for more than ten days, however only pursuant to the decision of a judge of the District Court. Based on an application from the State Border Guard, a judge then decides whether to detain the foreigner for up to two months or to refuse his/her detention.. The State Border Guard may apply repeatedly for an extension of the term of detention, but the total period may not exceed 20 months. The decision may be revoked by the judge himself pursuant to a protest of the prosecutor. Furthermore, the chairperson of the Regional Court can also revoke such a judgement. In this case, no objection from the prosecutor is necessary.

The actual period of detention of illegal foreign nationals was rather long before 2003 and there was no time limit for detention pending their removal from Latvia. This problem was noted by the CPT after its visit to Latvia in 2002.[29] The situation has improved since the adoption of the Immigration Law in 2003 that set the maximum limit of 20

---

[28] European Community initiative EQUAL project: Soli pa solim (Step by Step), research paper, *"Latvijas iedzīvotāju, valts amatpersonu un NVO attieksme prēt patvēruma meklētājiem (Attitude of inhabitants, state authorities and NGO`s towards asylum seekers")*, 2005.

[29] Report of CPT from visit to Latvia in 2002, Section 43.

months. Amendments to the Immigration Law in 2005 have resulted in a shortening of the intervals in which a foreigner's administrative detention should be reviewed by a judge. According to data from the State Border Guard, 307 foreigners have been detained under Article 51 of the Immigration Law. Forcible expulsion has been applied to 190 foreigners.

Illegal foreigners are detained in detention premises at border posts and police short term detention isolators. These detention places are used for detention that does not exceed ten days. Foreigners detained for periods longer than ten days are placed in detention centre "Olaine". The majority of persons detained are persons who have illegally crossed Latvia's border and who have otherwise violated the formal legal procedure of entry or stay of foreigners in the country. This category includes persons who have entered Latvia legally in the past and who have long established links with the country including a fixed residence and a family, but who have for various reasons failed to apply for or renew the necessary documents. Some of them were persons who had requested asylum but whose identity had not been confirmed yet, or whose asylum request had been rejected and were waiting expulsion.[30] In those cases in which it has been impossible to establish a detainee's link with any country or impossible to expel him/her or to give any legal status to stay in Latvia, the Board of Citizenship and Migration Affairs issues a departure document.

Detention Centre "Olaine"

Detention Centre Olaine is an institution under the State Border Guard, with a capacity of 80 places. There are plans to extend the premises of the centre so that it can accommodate 200 persons. The staff of the centre consists of 30 persons. On any given day the detention centre accommodates around 10 -20 persons. In 2005, 153 people were accommodated in the detention centre, of which 22 were staying in the centre on 13 January 2006.[31] In 2004 the detention centre accommodated 146 persons, while in 2003 174 persons were admitted to the institution. The figure for 2002 was 214.. The average length of stay in the centre is three weeks up to two months. There were several cases in which the length of stay was over a year due to difficulties with providing documentation or the course of appeal procedures.

One of them is the case of six asylum seekers from Somalia. Experts of the State Human Rights Office and Latvian Centre for Human Rights and Ethnic Studies have regularly visited Olaine Detention Centre and expressed their opinion during interviews that the psychological atmosphere in the centre is relaxed and that the staff has a good relationship with the detainees. Similar observations were made by the CPT in 2002 (atsauce uz zi□ojuma 46.punktu)[32] The State Human Rights Office has not received complaints concerning conditions in the centre in the past years. However, the Centre for Human Rights and Ethnic Studies has received several complaints concerning the detention regime. Main concerns of Latvian human rights experts are laid down in the Report on the Situation of Fundamental Rights in Latvia in 2005.[33] Experts expressed the opinion that

30 Latvian Centre for Human Rights and Ethnic Studies (LCHRES), *Human Rights in Latvia in 2004*, Riga 2005.

31 Data from the State Border Guard.

32 Report of CPT from its visit to Latvia in 2002, Section 43.

33 http://cridho.cpdr.ucl.ac.be/DownloadRep/rapports2005/NationalReport/CFRLatvia2005.pdf

in some areas the rules concerning detention of illegal immigrants are more restricting than those applied to persons kept in custody for criminal offences.

The detention regime in the detention centre "Olaine" is governed by the order issued by the State Border Guard and they have not been made public. Regulations include such fundamental rights as meetings with relatives and other persons and the rights to education. These regulations are not available on a public data base of legal acts as they are internal regulations of the State Border Guard. Amendments to laws are being prepared to change the situation. Similar regulations concerning prisoners sentenced under Criminal Law are included in the Sentence Execution Act and "Regulations of the internal order in prisons" issued by the Cabinet of Ministers. Regulations concerning daily norms of food and means of personal hygiene are contained in the Regulations of the Cabinet of Ministers No 339 of 6 August 2002, and these regulations are applicable to all categories of detained persons (criminal and administrative). The possibility to carry out activities of work and education in the centre is limited. The only place where detained foreigners can spend time outside the premises irrespective of the season is a small asphalt backyard.[34]

Amendments to the Asylum law provide that the minor children of an asylum seeker or minor asylum seekers can be ensured that the acquisition of education is in conformity with the laws in force. The Cabinet of Ministers shall determine the procedures according to which education shall be ensured. Such an obligation does not exist in the case of illegal immigrants.

In the beginning of 2005 the project for renovation of detention centres was approved by the Cabinet of Ministers (Data from the State Border Guard), but financing has not yet been allocated. Renovation will ensure better conditions for living, more space for activities and meetings.

Language issues have not been a major problem for communication on a daily basis as the majority of detainees and staff of the centres speaks Russian or English. Problems arise if persons do not communicate in these languages. In the case with the asylum seekers from Somalia only one of them could speak some English and there is no interpreter of the Somali language in Latvia. However, language barriers can impact the execution of the legal rights of detained foreigners, for example their right to appeal. The law provides the obligation to explain a decision in an understandable language but does not provide the obligation to issue written translation, therefore preparation of an appeal in due time can be difficult. According to the Immigration Law illegal immigrants have the right to receive assistance from a lawyer but this right is limited if persons do not have financial means as there is no state guaranteed legal aid for illegal immigrants. According to the Law on State provided legal aid, the categories of persons entitled to receive legal aid funded by the state are Latvian citizens, Latvian non-citizens, stateless persons, EU nationals legally residing in Latvia, third country nationals legally residing in Latvia, asylum seekers, refugees and persons under subsidiary protection. Asylum seekers can receive legal aid for appeal procedures within the process of granting asylum.

There is a room for religious activities in the centre, but there is no religious representative. Since the majority of persons stay in the centre for a short term, there is no practical need to employ a chaplain. The staff of the centre will organize a meeting with a religious representative if one would ask. To improve the capacity of the staff, the State

[34] *Ibidem.*

Border Guard is involved in an exchange project of staff to foreign countries and improvement of English language skills of personnel of Olaine detention centre.

4 NATIONALS DETAINED ABROAD

Information on Latvian nationals sentenced abroad is kept by the information centre under the Ministry of Interior. It was not possible to gather information during the preparation of this report. Information is stored on statistical cards and it is processed manually. So far statistics on Latvian nationals detained abroad has not been gathered. According to the 1959 Council of Europe Convention on Mutual Assistance in Criminal Matters, states will exchange information on nationals sentenced abroad. The central authority is the Ministry of Justice. Data available from the Ministry of Justice of Latvia shows that Latvia has received information from the following countries: Portugal, Norway, Sweden, France, Germany, Lithuania, Italy, Finland, and Denmark.

5 EVALUATION AND RECOMMENDATIONS

This report gives an incomplete overview of the questions regarding foreign prisoners in Latvia. There are several reasons for that:

- data for some categories of foreigners has not been collected (persons in pre-trial detention, number of foreigners among sentenced persons);
- data is collected but is not summarized (data about Latvian nationals detained abroad);
- within this given time period deeper research of legislation and practice was not possible.

More accurate data collection would be desirable to attain a better understanding of the situation of sentenced foreigners in Latvia. However, some conclusions and recommendations can be made. The Latvian prison administration is working successfully with Russian-speaking foreigners but is not materially prepared to receive non-Russian speaking foreign prisoners. Only a limited share of prison staff can communicate in foreign languages other than Russian. Translation of all the main legal acts concerning detention must be done in Russian and English and should be available for prisoners. Language training of prison staff would improve their skills in communicating with foreign inmates. That would also provide the opportunity to conduct educational visits abroad and learn from the experience of other countries. More flexible visiting rules would foster the socialization of foreign prisoners. Financial assistance for foreigners who do not have financial means and cannot be granted work in prison would be desirable to cover long-distance phone calls and postal expenses.

Generally the situation of treatment of illegal immigrants does not differ from the situation of prisoners under criminal law. There are some exceptions. For example, rules of internal order in prisons were adopted by the Cabinet of Ministers, but in the detention centre for illegal immigrants the rules are set by an internal order of the State Border Guard. Adopting the new regulations of the Cabinet of Ministers on the order of detention of illegal immigrants would generate a better legal situation for illegal immigrants.